GROWING WITHOUT SCHOOLING

GWS Back Issues, Volume One
Issues 1–12
August, 1977–December, 1979

Published by Holt Associates Inc.
2380 Massachusetts Ave. Suite 104
Cambridge, MA 02140
(617) 864 - 3100

First printing, 1997
Second printing with new material added, pp. 259 - 261, 1999

Printed in Saline, MI by McNaughton and Gunn

ISBN 0-913677-10-8

Contents

Foreword

I can still remember how it felt to read these issues of GWS for the first time. I first wrote to John Holt in 1978, after reading his books and agreeing with them but still finding myself stuck in high school. He wrote back and told me, among other things, "What you almost certainly don't know is that we are publishing a little magazine now. ... One way to keep in touch with what I am thinking is to subscribe to the newsletter, as I write a great many of my thoughts into it as they occur to me." He enclosed an issue, and I eagerly devoured its plain, four-column, small-print pages.

GWS was full of treasure, that was clear right away. First of all, it was, as John had said, a place where he wrote his latest thoughts on just about anything, so reading those early issues was a way of seeing a mind at work. Some of the pieces from those pages—"On Social Change," "Serious Teaching," "Finding True Work"—are classic Holt, essential reading for anyone who wants to understand his thinking during that period. And because these and other writings later made their way into the book *Teach Your Own*, truly interested readers can enjoy comparing early drafts with later ones.

Second, GWS was a place where a community was being built. I could see that people responded to each other's letters, reached out and helped one another. They made information and experience available to one another instead of hoarding it for themselves, and this was exciting to me.

Third, in the world of GWS, writers were, foremost, people who had something to say. You didn't get published in GWS because of who you were or how much you had written elsewhere (in fact, many of the early letters were printed anonymously). You got in because you had something to contribute to the ongoing conversation, and even if you weren't going to be read by millions, you knew that the people who read what you wrote would really pay attention to it. When John excerpted from one of my letters, I was as proud as I've ever been at publication.

As I write this, I've edited half as many GWS issues as are in existence (56 of the 112 issues published). It's been a long time since I've gotten an issue without knowing exactly what would be in it. But I've never forgotten the excitement of receiving GWS as a general reader. Because I was so devoted a reader of GWS before I became its editor, I always regarded it as a living entity that already had a strong personality of its own. In these early issues, what you see is that quirky, vibrant personality in the making.

— Susannah Sheffer

Introduction

Courage. That is the quality that strikes me most from these first twelve issues of Growing Without Schooling. The courage of John Holt to publicly change his mind and help create alternatives *to* school after spending much of his life advocating for school reform and alternative schools, and the courage of parents to follow their convictions that their children can be taught and allowed to learn in family and communal settings outside of school. Teaching and learning in this way is completely different from the prepackaged, curricularized experiences that fill school programs, and Holt recognized this as a strength of unschooling, as opposed to simply duplicating school in one's home. His creation of the word "unschooling" to describe taking children out of school and allowing them to learn in one's home and community was deliberate; "homeschooling" had too many connotations for Holt that simply meant turning one's home into a miniature school. However, the choice of words—unschooler or homeschooler—didn't seem all that important to the early readers of GWS; as you can tell from these issues, they were far more concerned with the political, legal, and educational issues surrounding their ability to live and learn with their children. In issue three Holt wrote:

> In its short life to date, GWS has already changed its character somewhat. It is turning out to be less about teaching than I thought it would be, and more about law, less about what your children can do once you get them out of school, and more about what you may have to do to get them out. I rather regret this. I am much more interested in helping children to explore the world and to find out and do interesting and worthwhile things in it, than I am in arguing about and fighting with schools. But it begins to look as if, like Moses in Egypt, we may have to find ways to make things a bit hot for the school Pharaohs, if only so that they will let our people go.

Holt recognized early on that not all unschoolers cared for his ideas about children and learning, and some were more than eager to duplicate school in their homes; this did not bother Holt. He wrote in GWS #2:

> Some feel that the school curriculum is dull, fragmented, devoid of context, in George Dennison's words, that it destroys "the continuum of experience." Others may feel that the school curriculum is fine, but that they don't do a very good job of teaching it.
>
> What is important is not that all readers of GWS should agree on these questions, but that

we should respect our differences while we work for what we agree on, our right and the right of all people to take their children out of schools, and help, plan, or direct their learning in the ways they think best.

> In all these matters, we at GWS have our own opinions, and will express them. This is not going to try or pretend to be an unbiased publication. We will be very biased. But we will try to be as useful as possible to all our readers, whether or not we agree with them on all details. And on the issue about which we are all agreed we will print as wide a range of ideas and opinions as our readers send us.

The inclusiveness of Holt's vision for unschooling, and his determination to help but not command people to achieve it, is important. Many of the people writing in these early issues feared the schools would break up their families (which some schools, acting through the courts, did), put the parents in jail (which some schools, acting through the courts, did), and attempt to abolish homeschooling totally (which some schools, acting through the courts, did); as a result, you will meet many of these early pioneers in GWS simply as initials: "D," "L", etc. This fear, as noted, was not unfounded; indeed, when I started work at GWS in 1981 we still had a file called "The Brown Paper Wrapper Folder" for subscribers who wanted their issues sent with no identifying marks since they feared the postal workers would report them as truants or worse just for subscribing to GWS! Now that homeschooling is legal in all fifty states and many foreign countries, this fear may seem more like paranoia; I trust that by reading these issues you will sense the climate and history of the times.

These first twelve issues are a blueprint for how ordinary people, *without* the help of legal institutions like the ACLU, without government or corporate funding, and without the support of their local schools, can understand and use the law to reclaim their right to live and learn with their children. The readers engage Holt in a dialog about strategy and tactics for unschooling—sometimes disagreeing with Holt, and sometimes Holt disagreeing with them—and the points they raise about how to create social change that allows unschooling are as relevant today as they were twenty years ago. But GWS is, as Holt notes above, not just about the practical legal matters involved in getting children out of school. It is also about the myriad of ways that people, especially young people, learn and grow into competent, mature adults.

Holt's criticisms of schools serve several purposes in these pages. By deflating and debunking the claims schools make about how they, and only they, can help young people learn, Holt, a former celebrity school teacher, helped give confidence and support to parents who, for any number of reasons, felt they had to compare their children's learning to that done in schools. Such criticisms of schooling also help build the case against compulsory education, not just compulsory attendance, because Holt saw how schools will not only try to prevent "uncertified" people from helping children learn, but also claim their professional status makes them the only ones who can "mold children's minds," something ordinary people dare not do since they might somehow botch up the molding. Holt, expanding on this insight which he gained from his work with Ivan Illich, builds the case against compulsory pedagogic manipulation of children in hundreds of ways from the first issue of GWS. This is a theme that can be traced through every issue we've published in the past 20 years, and it is more important now than ever as educators continue to view children as machines in need of proper inputs, rather than as individuals living and learning in a variety of contexts and faced with a number of choices. "It is not what we teach children but how we treat them that determines what type of people they will become," Holt once told me. This is why unschooling is as much about social change as it is about school reform: unschooling is about creating or reclaiming places and events for adults and children of all ages to live and learn together. Certainly there may be places and times when one wants to learn in traditional school settings; unschooling isn't about denying access to school to anyone, but rather, about being able to choose to learn in a school when one needs, or wants, to do so. "But children learning this way will choose to play all day and never do any serious learning," some will argue. The response to that criticism is spread throughout the pages of GWS, and crystallized in these first twelve issues.

These pages are filled with many ideas for helping children learn, ideas for teaching, and support for allowing children to learn things on their own—"Useful Resources," "Sensible Phonics," and "Learning Exchanges" are some of the many headlines that demonstrate these aspects of GWS—but, most importantly, these ideas come not from college textbooks and curriculum theory, but from the real lives of people working with children in their homes and communities. Further, the success of the variety of methods employed by unschoolers in these early issues is striking: there are stories about unschooled kids getting good jobs or entering and attending competitive colleges well before Grant Colfax made a media splash in the eighties by being the first homeschooled boy admitted to Harvard. Unschooling—or homeschooling if, as one person writes in these pages, that term "unnerves" you—is proving to be an important event in the history of schooling; rather than a passing fad; homeschooling is still growing and shows no signs of diminishing in popularity despite the millions spent on advertising, awards, and events to promote the importance of going to school and the comparatively minuscule amount of money spent to promote homeschooling. This first volume of our back issues is a fascinating record of history in the making, an inspiring documentation of what "ordinary" people are capable of doing, and a tribute to the people who had the courage to dare to do something different with their own lives.

— Patrick Farenga, Publisher

Some textual notes:

To preserve the historical document as much as possible, we have not attempted to update any addresses, phone numbers, or prices.

While we retain some stories about subscriptions and other office business to show how Holt conceived and developed his work, we often cut information about these "housekeeping" topics, especially those on postage and subscription rates. We also cut the Directory of Families, which appeared as the last article in each issue since GWS #2 and is still an important feature of GWS today. Our current Directory of homeschooling families is available from us; write us if you want to get one.

We also added the publication date of each issue, which Holt deliberately kept off the early issues, since, as you will read, he viewed GWS as an ongoing reference work whose material won't go out of date. Postal regulations, and the complaints of some readers, eventually made GWS put its publication date inside each issue; in recent years we have adopted the standard practice of putting the date on the cover.

Other than these points, the text of each issue is reproduced exactly as it appeared in 1977–1979, complete with the many abbreviations Holt used to speed his writing and make more space. One change we did want to make to these early issues is to make them easier to read. The original small type and cramped 4-column layout led some of the first subscribers to complain about how hard GWS was to read, but Holt was proud of the huge amount of information he was able cram into his pages, and he was well aware of the value he was providing in doing so. He was loath even to increase the size of the type: in GWS #11 he wrote, "…we are [now] doing the main body of the text in a Pica-sized typeface—10 characters per inch. This loses us a few words per page, which I regret. If you find the new type easier to read, it's worth it." We hope you find our current effort to make these first 12 issues of GWS easier to read worth it.

Acknowledgments

GWS has always relied on its readers to provide its content; this volume also relied on GWS readers to type its content. The issues in this volume were typed for us by the following volunteers:

Patty Allen
Suzanne Carter
Mary Pat Crevatas
Kathleen Gerety
Grant Gibbs
Helen Harrison
Marie Hopper
Isabelle Nidever
Regina Tricamo
Nicholas Wyborski

I created the index for this volume, but it could not have been done without all the previous indexes done by Rachael Solem, Madalene Murphy, Patti Pitcher, Peggy Roberts, and, especially, Laurie, Ken, and Alex Huffman, who compiled and completed the index for issues 1–90 that we sold for several years.

Special thanks must also be given to:

Peg Durkee and Donna Richoux, whose early support and labor enabled John Holt to get these first 12 issues printed and distributed; Sue Miller, who coordinated all the volunteer typists and helped me in the early stages of creating this volume; Aaron Falbel for his masterful copy editing, kind support, and understanding of GWS; Susannah Sheffer for her thoughtful ideas about this volume, her commitment to GWS as its editor and as a writer—her first contribution appears in GWS #9 (you'll have to guess which story it is).

As all the people who read and support GWS can attest, it is a labor of love. For my wife Day and I, it has become a mutual labor of love. We were married in 1983 and have worked together at GWS since 1987. I could not have completed this project, nor many others over the years, without Day's help and love, both in and out of work.

—Patrick Farenga

GWS Back Issues, Volume One
Issues 1–12
August, 1977–December, 1979

GROWING WITHOUT SCHOOLING

Issue No. 1

August, 1977

This is the first issue of a newsletter about ways in which people, young and old, can learn and do things, acquire skills, and find interesting and useful work, without having to go through the process of schooling. In part, it will be about people who, during some of their growing up, did not go to school, what they did instead, and how they made a place for themselves in the world. Mostly, it will be about people who want to take or keep their children out of school, and about what they might do instead, what problems come up, and how they cope with these. We hope, also, that children who are, right now, growing without schooling will let us know how they feel about this. If they do, we will not identify them as children, except as they do in their own writing.

GROWING WITHOUT SCHOOLING, or GWS as we will call it from now on, will be in part an exchange. Much of what is in it, we hope, will come from its readers. In its pages people can talk about certain common ideas, needs, concerns, plans, and experiences. In time it may lead to many informal and personal networks of mutual help and support.

GWS will come out whenever we have enough material to make an interesting issue. This may at first be only three or four times a year. Later, as more people read it and send in material, it may come out as often as six times a year.

GWS will not be much concerned with schools, even alternative or free schools, except as they may enable people to keep their children out of school by 1) Calling their own home a school, or 2) enrolling their children, as some have already, in schools near or far which then approve a home study program. We will, however, be looking for ways in which people who want or need them can get school tickets—credits, certificates, degrees, diplomas, etc.—without having to spend time in school. And we will be very interested, as the schools and schools of education do not seem to be, in the act and art of teaching, that is, all the ways in which people, of all ages, in or out of school, can more effectively share information, ideas, and skills.

SUBSCRIPTIONS

GWS will be supported entirely by subscriptions, not by advertising, foundations, universities, or government grants, all of which are unreliable. We will do our best to print as much useful material as possible at the lowest possible cost. But we think it best that those who use a service should pay the cost of it. We also want those who work on GWS to be paid a decent wage, if only for the sake of staying power. People who work for nothing or for token wages soon grow tired of this and quit. We want this newsletter to come out as long as people feel a need for it. This can only happen if those who put it out do not have to do so at great personal sacrifice.

This first issue is four pages. All following issues will be eight pages, perhaps in time more than that. Subscriptions are $10 for six issues. A Times Two or 2X subscription (we mail two copies of each issue) will be $12 for six issues; a 3X subscription will be $14 for six issues, and so on, $2 more for each additional issue. Thus, two or more people or families can take out multiple subscriptions and split the cost. In this way, two people can get GWS for $6 a year each; four for $4 a year each; eight for $3 a year each, and so on. Or, people or bookstores, can take out multiple subscriptions and resell individual subscriptions or copies. Also, people may buy in quantity copies of any issue.

All subscriptions to GWS will begin with Issue #1 unless you tell us otherwise, i.e., please begin my subscription with Issue #2, or #3, or whatever.

Someday, if we get enough subscriptions, we may be able to lower the subscription price. This will not be for a while; even at its present price, GWS will probably not be self-supporting until we have around 2,000 subscribers. And as we said, we think GWS must be self-supporting. Charity is fickle, and we mean to be around for a while.

ON SOCIAL CHANGE

In starting this newsletter, we are putting into practice a nickel and dime theory about social change, which is that important and lasting social change always comes slowly, and only when people change their lives, not just their political beliefs or parties. It is a process that takes place over a period of time. At one moment in history, with respect to a certain matter, 99% of a society think and act one way; 1% think and act very differently. Some time later, that 1% minority becomes 2%, then 5%, then 10, 20, 30, until someday it becomes the dominant majority, and the social change has taken place. Some may ask, "When did this social change take place?" or "When did it begin?" There is no answer to these questions, except perhaps to say that any social change begins the first time one person thinks of it.

I have come to understand, finally, and even to accept, that in almost everything I believe and care about I am a member of a minority in my own country, in most cases a very small minority. This is certainly true of all my ideas about children and education. We who do not believe in compulsory schooling, who believe that children want to learn about the world, are good at it, and can be trusted to do it without much adult coercion or interference, are surely not more than 1% of the population and perhaps much less than that. And we are not likely to become the effective majority for many years, probably not in my lifetime, perhaps not in the lifetime of any reader of GWS.

This does not trouble me any more, as long as those minorities of which I am a member go on growing. My work is to help them grow. If we can describe the effective majority of our society, with respect to children or schools or any other question, as moving in direction X and ourselves, the small minority, as moving in direction Y, what I want to do is to find ways to help people who want to move in direction Y, to move in that direction, rather than run after the great X-bound army shouting at them, "Hey you guys, stop, turn around, you ought to be heading in direction Y!" In areas they feel are important, people do not change their ideas, much less their lives, because someone comes along with a bunch of arguments to show that they are mistaken, and even wicked, to think or do as they do. Once in a while, we may have to argue with the X-bound majority, to try to stop them from doing a great and immediate wrong. But most of the time, as a way of making real and deep changes in society, this kind of shouting and arguing seems to me a waste of time.

WHY KEEP THEM OUT?

Jud Jerome (Downhill Farm, Hancock, MD 21750) has written us a long letter, which we will print in this and the next issue. (I hope many other readers will follow his good example.) His youngest child, Topher, after a year of kindergarten, did not go to school again until he was 10. Then he went for a few months to a small "free School" on another commune. After a while, his parents took him out. Of this, Jud writes:

...In regard to Topher, though, I should add that though we were glad he was happy and enjoying himself [in school], we were also sad as we watched him deteriorate from a person into a kid under peer influence in school. It was much like what we saw happening when he was in kindergarten. There are certain kinds of childishness which it seems most people accept as being natural, something children have to go through, something which is, indeed, a shame to deny them. Silliness, self-indulgence, random rebelliousness, secretiveness, cruelty to other children, addiction to toys, possessions, junk, spending money, purchased entertainment, exploitation of adults to pay attention, take them places, amuse them, do things with them—all these things seem to be quite unnecessary, not "normal" at all [note: except in the sense of being common], and just as disgusting in children as they are in adults. And while they develop as a result of peer influence, I believe this is only and specifically because children are thrown together in schools and develop those means, as prisoners develop means of passing

dull time and tormenting authorities to cope with an oppressive situation. The richer the families children come from, the worse these traits seem to be. Two years of school and Topher would probably have regressed two years in emotional development. I am not sure of that, of course, and it was not because of that fear that we pulled him out, but we saw enough of what happened to him in a school situation not to regret pulling him out.

I have snatched this paragraph out of the middle of Jud's letter because it seems to me to answer so perfectly a question many ask me when they first think of taking their kids out of school: "But won't they miss the social life?" To this I say that if I had no other reason for wanting to keep kids out of school (and I have many), the social life would be reason enough. In all the schools I have taught in, visited, or know anything about, the social life of children is mean-spirited, competitive, exclusive, status-seeking, full of talk about who went to who's birthday party and who got what Christmas presents and who got how many Valentine cards and who is talking to so-and-so and who is not. Even in the first grade, classes soon divide up into leaders, energetic and (often deservedly) popular kids, their bands of followers, and other outsiders who are pointedly excluded from these groups.

And I remember my sister saying of one of her children, then five, that she never knew her to do anything really mean or silly until she went to school—a nice school, by the way, in a nice small town.

USEFUL RESOURCES

N.A.L.S.A.S (National Association for the Legal Support of Alternative Schools, P.O. Box 2823, Santa Fe, NM 87501). This small organization, under the leadership of Ed Nagel, has done much important research into compulsory attendance laws, the right of people to start and run their own school, and the right of people to enroll their children in distant alternative schools which then approve and supervise a home study program. People from at least two other states have enrolled their children in the Santa Fe Community School (where Ed Nagel teaches) in this way, and in at least one case, and I think more, local courts have upheld their right to do this. N.A.L.S.A.S. needs and deserves support.

The Last ? Resort, newsletter of the Committee to End Violence Against the Next Generation (or EVAN-G), 977 Keeler Ave., Berkeley, CA 94708. Members receive the newsletter, a very complete survey of court cases, newspaper stories and editorials, and other events in this field. The newsletter is scary reading; large numbers of children are still being brutally beaten, often for the most trivial offenses, or no offenses at all. One boy, who had sprained his ankle and had a note from a doctor saying that he should not exercise on it, was severely paddled and in fact injured by a coach (the coaches and Physical Education teachers seem to be among the worst offenders) who told him to high jump during a Phys. Ed. class. The school sadists are in most cases upheld by the courts, most recently by the Supreme Court. Most Americans like the idea of beating up on kids, and are ready to seize on almost anything as an excuse to do so.

SEE (Selective Educational Equipment, Inc., 3 Bridge St., Newton, MA 02195). These folks produce and/or distribute some very good school materials, many of which could be used at home. I will comment later in detail about some of the materials available. For the time being I urge you to get their catalogue. They have very good stuff for measuring things.

Outlook, a quarterly ($6/yr.,$10/2 yrs.) pub. by Mountain View Center for Environmental Education, Univ. of Colorado, 1511 University Ave., Boulder, Colo. 80309. The only serious (but not stuffy) publication about *teaching* (as opposed to classroom management, tricks to keep the kids busy, etc.) that I know of in this country. Since the editor, Tony Kallet, is a musician, it is likely to have very good stuff about music.

Home Study Institute, Takoma Park, Washington, D.C. 20012. This well established, respectable, and very extensive correspondence school seems to be run by, or somehow connected to, the Seventh Day Adventists. They offer accredited elementary, high school, and other programs. At first glance, these seem to be very conventional, use standard school texts, etc. This has this advantage, that most schools will accept the credits or certificates of the Institute as being as good as their own.

Their course of study for all elementary and secondary grades includes some kind of bible or religious study each year, presumably from the Seventh Day Adventist point of view. Whether people of other religious faiths, or none at all, can waive this particular requirement, I have yet to find out.

On page 15 of their catalog is this interesting statement:

School attendance laws vary from state to state. Parents are advised to counsel with the Educational Secretary of the local Seventh-Day Adventist conference regarding compulsory attendance laws and teacher qualification requirements in the area where they live. We will be glad to give assistance if the need arises. In New York, in the case of Foster, 330 N.Y.s 2d8, Family Court of City of New York, Kings County, Feb. 16, 1972, the Court stated: "It is settled law that a parent need not avail himself of formal education facilities for a child in order to satisfy the requirements of the law, it being sufficient that a systematic course of study be undertaken at home and that the parent render qualified quality instruction.

This suggests that the Adventists have had a good deal of experience in bucking compulsory attendance laws, and (judging from the size of their catalog) that

considerable numbers of children are using their courses instead of attending schools. In short, these folks may already know a great deal that we need to find out. We at GWS will look further into this and tell you what we find out.

School Violence and Vandalism—a report of the Subcommittee to Investigate Juvenile Delinquency (Sen. Birch Bayh, Chmn,) of the Committee on the Judiciary of the United States Senate. For sale by Supt. of Documents, U.S. Govt. Printing Office, Wash. D.C. 20402; $4.95.

This is a two-volume report, the first stating the problem, the second proposing ways (most of them rather foolish) for dealing with it. You may be able to get Vol 1. free from Sen. Bayh's office; if not, it is worth $4.95 as an official statement of what life in most schools is really like.

Children's Rights Report, published by the Juvenile Rights Project of the American Civil Liberties Union Foundation. 11 issues, $15/yr. Vol.1, No.8, May 1977, discusses the Supreme Court ruling on corporal punishment in the schools. Well worth reading.

ACCESS TO THE WORLD

The following is part of an article that came out in the *New Schools Exchange Newsletter*, and later, in the magazine *Green Revolution*.

[In this alternative school] there is more than a little talk about the curriculum, so carefully planned, guided, and enriched. So here in free and alternative schools we are still doing what conventional schools have always done. We take children out of and away from the great richness and variety of the world, and in its place we give them school subjects, the curriculum. Perhaps we may jazz it up with chicken bones, Cuisenaire rods, and all sorts of goodies from EDC. But the fact remains that instead of giving them access to more and more people, places, tools, and experiences, we are cutting the world up into little pieces and giving it to the children according to this or that theory about what they need or can stand. I say instead that what they need is *access* to more and more of the real world; plenty of time and space to think over their experiences, and to use fantasy and play to make meaning out of them; advice, road maps, guide books, to make it easier for them to get where they want to go (not where we think they ought to go), and to find out what they want to find out. Finding ways to do all this is not a small matter. The modern world is dangerous, confusing, not meant for children, not generally kind or welcoming to them. We have a great deal to learn about how to make the world more accessible to them, and how to give them more freedom and competence in exploring it. It is not a small subject. But it is a very different thing indeed from designing nice little curricula.

————————————

A small footnote. To people who are thinking of

starting new schools, perhaps because there seems no other way that the law will let them teach their own children, my strong advice is, keep that school as small as possible, the absolute minimum that the law will allow and still call it a school. The problems of schools, the difficulties of running them, the troubles they get into with the authorities, seem to increase, roughly, with the square or maybe the cube of the size of the student body. Four or five kids can go anywhere with an adult; a dozen gets to be a problem; two dozen is a big problem; and forty or fifty you have to get a permit from City Hall. Keep it small, keep it cheap; there is no other way to go.

MORE FROM JUD JEROME

"The next daughter down the line was twelve when we moved to the commune. She finished that year of school on "independent study," living at the farm, turning in work to teachers back at the city. But when Fall came she did not want to enroll. To avoid the law we enrolled her in a "free" school in Spokane, Wash., run by a friend, who carried her on the rolls, though she has not yet, to date, seen that city or that school. She spent most of the first year here at the farm, pitching in as an adult, learning from experience as we were all learning. While she was still thirteen we went to help another commune, in northern Vermont, with sugaring, and she loved that place—which was very primitive and used horse-drawn equipment—so asked to stay. This was an agreeable arrangement on all sides—and she has lived there now for over five years, except for one, when she was sixteen. That year she and her mate (ten years her senior) went to Iceland (Vermont was not rugged enough for them) to winter, working in a fish cannery. The next Spring they traveled, camping, to Scandinavia, hiked the Alps, then flew home—coming back with $3000 more than they left with after a year abroad. Last year she wanted to apply for a government vocational program, for which she needed a high school diploma, so went to an adult education class for a few months, and took the test, passing in the top percentile (and being offered scholarships to various colleges). She "graduated" earlier than her classmates who stayed in school. I think her case illustrates especially dramatically the waste of time in schools. She is by no means a studious type, would never think of herself as an intellectual, has always been more interested in milking cows and hoeing vegetables and driving teams of horses than in books, and in her years between thirteen and eighteen moved comfortably into womanhood and acquired a vast number of skills, had a vast range of experiences in the adult world, yet managed to qualify exceptionally by academic standards. By comparison, her classmates who stayed in school are in many cases stunted in mind, emotionally disturbed, without significant goals or directions or sound values in their lives—in large part (in my judgment) specifically because of their schooling."

THE OTHER WORLD

The house magazine of a leading hotel chain contained the following advertisement, for itself:

When you stay at———you're in among them... a never-ending parade of famous faces. The pace-setters work and play at———. The people who shape events and places. The elevator door opens and *she's* there beside you, the fabled face known in millions of homes throughout the world. Or suddenly the mood tenses, people rush forward to see or touch him as he pauses briefly, surrounded by his entourage, and then he's gone. What he did today, while *you* were staying at the———
———, reported (sic) in the world press tonight.

ON COUNTING

Many years ago I knew a child of about four whose older brothers and sisters were "teaching her to count." One day I heard her say, "One, two, three, four, five, seven, six, eight..." at which point the older kids said indignantly, "No! No! Seven comes *after* six!"

"Comes after." It seemed to me that from such words children could get a very strange idea of numbers, that they were a procession of little creatures, like dwarves, the first named One, the second named Two, the third named Three, and so on. Later on these dwarves would seem to do mysterious and meaningless dances, about which people would say things like "Two and two make four, " etc. It seemed likely that any child with such an idea of numbers would soon get into trouble, and this did indeed happen with this four-year old. Later, I asked some adults who had always been hopeless with arithmetic what they thought of this idea of mine, and many of them laughed and said this was indeed how they had always felt about numbers, and why they could never make any sense of them.

It seems to me most important that a child *not* be taught to count number names in the absence of real objects. The *Sesame Street* approach (like many other things on that program) is dead wrong. When little children first meet numbers they should *always* meet them as adjectives, not nouns. Not "three" or "seven" all by itself, but "three spoons" or "seven matches" or "five pennies" or whatever. Time enough later, probably much later, for children to intuit slowly that the noun "five" is that quality which all groups of five objects have in common.

Nor is it a good idea for children always to meet numbers in the counting order. We might at one moment show a child of two one object, but the next thing we show might be five of some other object, or eight, or whatever. Numbers exist in nature in quite random ways, and a child should be ready to accept numbers where he finds them.

It would also be helpful to have children see, and in time learn to recognize all the numbers smaller than ten by the kinds of patterns they make. Thus, a child being shown three small objects might at one time see them in a row, at another, in a triangle. Four objects could be shown in a square, or in a row of three with the extra one on top. The patterns for five could be a regular pentagon, or a square with a fifth dot on top, or perhaps a square with the extra dot in the center. And so on. Such patterns could be put on cards, perhaps with the number symbol or digit on the other side. I'm not at all suggesting that children should be forced or even asked to memorize these cards. But if children had such cards to look at and play with—they all love regular playing cards—they might in time come to know all these patterns, and would thus have ways other than counting to identify small numbers. In this connection a set of dominoes might be a useful toy, and many young children would enjoy playing with them, even if they were doing no more than matching patterns.

It also seems to me important, when we adults count things for children, that we *not* do what most of us do now, that is, move from one object to the next saying as we go, "One, two, three,....." The child sees us touching these objects, which otherwise look the same, and saying a different word for each one, and may well decide that "one, two, three,....." are the names of the objects, dwarf style. We would do better, as we count each item, to move it to the side, saying as we move the first, "Now we have one over here," then as we move the second, "Now we have two over here," and then in turn, "Now we have three," "now we have four," "now we have five," and so on. Thus at each point the child can see clearly that the number name refers not to a particular object but to the size of the group of objects that we have set to one side.

In time we could introduce the idea of ordinal numbers, which show the place of an item in an array, rather than the size of a group of items. Thus, given a row of small objects, we might touch them in turn, saying as we go something like, "This is the first one, this is the second one, this is the third one, and the fourth one, and the fifth, and the sixth... etc." No need to talk at first about the words "cardinal" and "ordinal." If we simply do our counting in a way that reflects the nature of these ideas, the child will soon intuit the difference. Later, when he fully grasps the idea that one set of number names refers to the quantity or size of something, while another set refers to the place of something, he may be interested in hearing the words "cardinal" and "ordinal." If not, no matter.

When we count a group of small objects, we do not always have to count by ones, and can just as well count by twos or threes. The child will see from this that there are many ways of counting and that he can pick the one that seems most handy. He will also get a running start on learning some simple products.

A few children, of course, grasp these notions of cardinal and ordinal in spite of our very confused and confusing ways of presenting them. But most do not, and I suspect many children would move more confi-

dently into the world of numbers if we introduced them as I have suggested here.

A SCHOOL STORY

In his wonderful book *How to Survive in Your Native Land* (Bantam paperback available from GWS) James Herndon writes:

In September of 1967 I looked through the cumulative folders we were going to have in our class for the coming year, that is to say, the next Monday. I read what I already knew—the first grader with the testable high IQ, the remarked bright student, leader, reads at third-grade-level, headed for the big time; and the fourth grader with low-average capability, IQ 89, lazy kid, must-be-pushed-to-achieve, reads-at-second-grade-level, discipline problem, parents cooperative.

The first grader and the fourth grader are the same kid.

———————————

I read this once to a group of school administrators. I asked them if they had kids like that, and if so how many, in their schools or school systems. None of them knew. I asked if any of them had ever checked through their files to see whether they had some kids like that. None of them had.

WE NEED TO KNOW

We would like to print, in later issues from time to time, or perhaps someday in a separate directory, the names and addresses of our subscribers, so that people may get in touch with each other directly, or perhaps arrange to meet if they happen to go through each others' home towns. Please let us know whether we may put your name and address in such a directory. Also, if you write us something, please let us know if we may print your name, or name and address, with your letter.

We also need to know, for as many states as possible, what the laws about compulsory school attendance, about acceptable alternatives to it, such as tutoring and home study, and about people starting their own schools, actually say. One group of people who probably know are the Seventh-Day Adventists (see in this issue under USEFUL RESOURCES). I would also suggest writing to your state representative and/or senator, not your state department of education. The department of education is itself a part of the school bureaucracy, and is very likely to give you a version of the laws which is tilted in favor of the schools, or to conceal from you any parts of the law that might help you escape the schools. Your legislator probably has no such interest. He is probably not a radical critic of the schools, but he is also most certainly concerned that they spend so much money and are always asking for more, and also, that for what they spend, they don't seem to get much results. More on this in the next section.

We also need to know (see again USEFUL RE-SOURCES) any decisions that the courts may have made in your state to interpret school and school attendance laws. These will vary from place to place. Many people write or tell me about this or that court decision which told some parents that they could not teach their children at home, but almost no one knows of court decisions which went the other way.

We also need to build up a list of people with teacher's certificates who can and will act as tutors (real or paper) for children who are learning at home. People have written me that the schools in their area will not let them tutor their children at home because they do not have certificates for that state. (By the way, I think it very unlikely that the law contains any such specific requirement; this is more likely to be the schools' interpretation of the law.) I have suggested that they try to find someone with such a certificate who would be willing to say that they were the child's tutor. How much tutoring they would actually do, they and the parent could decide.

All this information we will have to get from you, the readers.

LETTER TO A LEGISLATOR

Dear Legislator,

I am a parent of school age children, and am seriously thinking about teaching them at home. I fear, with good reason (here you might cite the Bayh report—see USEFUL RESOURCES), that in schools they will be exposed to and tempted by all kinds of drugs, sex, and violence, and many kinds of peculiar ideas. I also fear that they may not learn anything, may indeed pick up from their peer group a contempt for learning, and in any case, that because of the large classes, they will not be able to get the kind of individual attention and help that I can give them at home.

I would therefore like to have the full text of all the laws in this state relating to school attendance, to alternative possibilities such as tutoring at home, and to the possibility of parents making their own home a school. I have written to you instead of the State Department of Education because I fear that, since their interest is in keeping my child in the schools, they may give me a somewhat biased version of the laws.

I would also like to know anything you may be able to tell me about court decisions in this state interpreting these laws. Thank you very much in advance for your attention and help.

———————————

Please don't use this as a form letter. I offer it only to suggest an approach that would be likely to appeal to most legislators, of whatever party or beliefs.

Please let us know, if you send any such letter, what response you get, and if you get any.

WHAT TO SAY TO NEIGHBORS

One mother, who was keeping her child out of school, said to me one day that people—neighbors, relatives, people she knew—kept asking where her child was in school, and that she didn't know what to say to them. I suggested that it wasn't their business and that she didn't have to tell them anything. Later she said that she had tried that, but that it had not done any good—they kept insisting that she tell them. This seems to be one of those things that people feel they have to know about other people.

After thinking about it a while I suggested that when people asked where her child was going to school, she say something like this, "Well, he's in a special program." If people then asked what kind of program, she could say, "It's very new, and somewhat experimental, and they don't want me to talk about it."

All of which, by the way, is perfectly true.

She tried it out on a few people and said it worked fine. Maybe it will work for others.

SIX HOURS A DAY

When they first think of taking their child out of school, people often say to me, "How am I going to teach him six hours a day?"

I say, *"Who's teaching him six hours a day?"*

As a kid, I went to the "best" schools, some public, most private. I was a good student, the kind that teachers *like* to talk to. And it was a rare day in my schooling that I got *fifteen minutes* of teaching, that is, of concerned and thoughtful adult talk about something that *I* found interesting, puzzling, or important. Over the whole of my schooling, the average was probably closer to fifteen minutes a week. For most kids in most schools, it is a lot less than that. Many poor, nonwhite, or unusual kids, in their entire schooling, never get any teaching at all. When teachers speak to them, it is only to command, correct, warn, threaten or blame.

Anyway, your kids don't need, don't want, and *couldn't stand* six hours of your teaching a day, even if you wanted to do that much. To help them find out about the world doesn't take that much adult input. Most of what they need, you have been giving them since they were born. As I have said, they need *access*. They need a chance, sometimes, for honest, serious, unhurried talk; or sometimes, for joking, play, and foolishness; or sometimes, for tenderness, sympathy, and comfort. They need, much of the time, to share your life, or at least, not to feel shut out of it, in short, to go some of the places you go, see and do some of the things that interest you, get to know some of your friends, find out what you did when you were little and before they were born. They need to have their questions answered, or at least heard and attended to—if you don't know, say "I don't know." They need to get to know more and more adults whose main work in life is not taking care of kids. They need *some* friends their own age, but not dozens of them; two or three, at most half a dozen, is as many real friends as any child can have at one time. Perhaps above all, they need a lot of privacy, solitude, calm, times when there's nothing to do.

Schools do not provide any of these, and no matter how or how much we changed them, never could provide most of them. But the average parent, family, circle of friends, neighborhood, and community can and do provide all of these things, perhaps not as well as they once did or might again, but well enough. People do not need a Ph.D. or some kind of Certificate to help their children find their way into the world.

A SCHOOL STORY

The following are excerpts from a news story in *The Real Paper* (Boston, Mass.) of 3/17/76, headed "Doping Springfield School Children."

Dr. Leo Sullivan of Boston prescribed 15 milligrams of Ritalin daily to another ten-year-old boy. On a certificate filed with the Department of Public Health he listed this diagnosis: "immaturity." Under tests administered he wrote "none" and under alternative treatment he wrote "none."

Over 60 percent of all the children certified last year apparently never received alternative therapy before drugs were administered and an equal number never received anything more than a physical exam for diagnostic purposes.

———————

Despite a nine-month investigation by the attorney general's office, and another by the Department of Public Health, no abuses were officially found in the Springfield schools.

Neither investigative agency did more than make a few phone calls. DPH did nothing at all except send the Springfield press a release saying that no abuses were evident.

During the past week, however, *The Real Paper* has obtained sworn affidavits describing numerous cases of abuse.

In one instance, the mother of a first grade child reports that her son was one of five children placed on drugs by Dr. Ploof after a teacher referral. When the teacher found little behavioral change with Dexedrine, Dr. Ploof prescribed Ritalin. A pharmacist refused to fill the prescription because of the child's age, and the mother got worried. She refused to place her child on any more drugs.

She was told that if the child were not kept on drugs he would not be allowed in school. According to the affidavit, the mother agreed to place her child back on drugs, but secretly substituted one-a-day vitamins for Ritalin. During a public hearing on the controversy, the teacher defended drug therapy, saying this child had improved considerably since taking drugs. The teacher was shocked when the mother announced her trick.

In another affidavit, the mother of an eight-year-old girl says that her daughter was placed on Ritalin by Dr. Ploof after a teacher referral and a 20-minute evaluation by the doctor. The drug had little effect, so without any reevaluation Dr. Ploof raised the dosage two times over the phone.

That child eventually left the Springfield school system and did very well in a private school.

In the most disturbing story of them all, Dr. Ploof prescribed Ritalin for an epileptic first-grade boy. Ritalin is dangerous to epileptics. Had it not been for a rediagnosis by a second physician, the child might have suffered effects ranging from convulsions to death. The father is considering a suit against both Dr. Ploof and the school system.

I said that this story was typical, and it is, as Schrag—Divoky's *The Myth of the Hyperactive Child* makes plain. This kind of thing goes on in school systems all over the country. Everywhere I go to lecture to education students, they tell me that in the schools where they do their practice teaching many children are on drugs, and they describe many of these drugged children as being "like vegetables."

There are Dr. Ploof's everywhere. They are never brought to account. It would seem wise to be extremely skeptical of any kind of psychological or neurological diagnosis made by any doctor, psychologist, or other expert or professional connected in any way with the schools, and to have any such diagnoses checked by outside and independent persons (if you can find such).

It is instructive to read what the *Physician's Desk Reference* has to say about Ritalin. And it may be worth noting that in Sweden (so I have been told) Ritalin is felt to be so powerful, dangerous, and little understood that doctors may not even prescribe it.

This matter, and many others equally sinister and important, including the keeping of secret, detailed, misleading, and damaging reports on schoolchildren, are dealt with carefully and at length in *The Myth of the Hyperactive Child* (Dell paperback available from GWS). I strongly recommend it.

THE SELF-RESPECTING CHILD

This is the title of a book by Alison Stallibrass, published in England by Thames & Hudson, Ltd., London. It is the best book I have seen about the ways in which very young children explore the world and use, test, and develop their powers. Since no American publisher was willing to print an American edition, GWS is selling the British edition.

One of the interesting and surprising things Ms.

Stallibrass says is that, even for four and five year olds, bicycles are much safer than tricycles. She has found that children that young are perfectly able to ride real bikes, which have this great advantage over trikes, that they can't run away with the child on a hill.

There are many delightful photos. One, which perfectly expresses the spirit of the book, is of a sixteen-month-old child standing at the top of a jungle gym, to which she has climbed by herself, holding on with one hand and with the other waving away an anxious adult who has come running up to "help." A wonderful book.

HELPLESS

In the last year or so, a number of people have talked or written to me about their children. They tell a familiar story. The child, who had always been alert, curious, bright, eager, was now fearful, bored, withdrawn, etc. All these people had tried to get the schools to make changes, without results. Many of them had tried to find alternative schools; either they could find none, or could not afford them, or felt they were not really different from or better than the public schools. All of them said to me, early in our talk or correspondence, "I just don't know what to do, I feel so helpless." I say, "Take them out of school altogether." They say, "The law won't let me." I say, "There are ways." They say, "I don't know how to teach my own children." I say, "Yes you do, or at least, you know as much as anyone else." Sometimes they do take their children out of school, sometimes not. But even if they don't, it changes everything to know that if they want to, they can. They say, "I don't feel so helpless anymore."

GWS is to help people to feel less helpless.

A STUDYING TRICK

Here's a good trick for people who have to learn a list of disconnected facts—name and dates in History, formulas in Chemistry, Physics, or Math, capital cities, etc. Get some 3 x 5 cards. On one side of each card put half of your piece of information, on the other side put the other. Thus, on one side, "Columbus discovered America," on the other, "1492." Or, on one side, "Salt," on the other, "Sodium Chloride" or NaCl. Then use the cards to test yourself. Shuffle them up, put aside those you know, work on those you don't. You'll find that just deciding what to put on the card in the first place will do most of the work of memorizing it.

THEY REALLY SAID IT

A number of parents, in different parts of the country, have sued the schools because after spending years in them their kids had not learned anything. A judge on the West Coast recently threw out one such suit, saying in his ruling, in plain black and white for the world to see, that the schools had no legal *obligation* to teach anyone anything.

I foolishly mislaid the news clipping about this. If anyone can send us the details of this case and ruling, I will be grateful.

GROWING WITHOUT SCHOOLING

Issue No. 2

November, 1977

Quite a few people have written us about the first issue of GWS. They like it, say it makes them feel less alone, isolated, helpless. One said it was like a beacon. We hope many others feel this way.

Some liked its plain looks. One or two thought we should jazz it up a bit, to look more like other magazines. (We have no plans to do this.)

We see that we didn't make it clear enough that if two or more people take out a joint subscription to GWS, all copies of each issue will be sent to one of them, who must then mail or deliver the other copies to the other subscribers. Sending all copies to one address is what makes it possible for us to sell joint subscriptions for less. The record joint subscription so far, by the way, is a 14X sub. from a group in Seattle, who by this means are getting GWS for about $2.55 each.

A single subscription is $10 for six issues; a 2X sub, $12; a 3X sub, $14: and so on up. If you don't say otherwise, all subs begin with Issue No. 1.

You may buy extra copies of Issue #1 for 50 cents each, or 25 cents each for orders of 10 or more. Extra copies of all later issues will be $2 each, two for $3, $1 each for orders of five or more. Please send checks (U.S.$) made out to GROWING WITHOUT SCHOOLING.

SERIOUS TEACHING

My first teaching job was to tutor an otherwise interesting and bright teenager whose school skills were at about second or third grade level. Top specialists had pronounced him "brain-damaged." In spite of the label, he wanted to read, write, and figure like everyone else, and wanted me to help him.

Not having studied "education," I had never heard of "brain damage," didn't know enough to know that it was just a fancy way of saying, "We don't know what the trouble is." But it was clear to me that brain damage or no, it was my task and my responsibility to find out what was keeping him from learning and to figure out something to do about it. Working with him, I found out that he had a very precise, thorough, and logical mind, and had to understand a thing thoroughly before he could move on to the next. He asked hard questions; to find answers to some of them took me many years. But if I did not solve his problems, perhaps my belief that they *could* be solved was enough. Some years later, while in the Army, he wrote me, and told me what books he was reading—serious, adult books. He had clearly solved his problem himself.

In short, I was what I call a *serious* teacher—I would not accept fancy excuses and alibis as a substitute for doing the work I had chosen and had been hired to do—help children learn things. If they were not learning, as many were not, I couldn't blame it on them, but had to keep trying until I found something that worked. As *How Children Fail* makes clear, this often took a long time, and I failed as much as I succeeded. Another book about serious teaching is James Herndon's *The Way It Spozed to Be*, a very funny, truthful, and in the end sad story about his first year's painful struggles—finally successful, for which he was fired—to help students that the rest of this school had long since given up on.

The reason that schools are no good at their work is above all that they are not serious. "Good" schools and "bad," private and public, with only a few exceptions they have always run under this rule—when learning happens, the school takes the credit; when it doesn't, the students get the blame. In the old days the schools said the kids were stupid, bad, lazy, or crazy. Now they say they have mysterious diseases like "minimal brain dysfunction" or "learning disabilities." Under whatever name, these remain what they always were— excuses for the school and teachers not being able to do their job.

LIFE IN SCHOOLS

(From a letter from Raleigh, N.C., which by the way is supposed to be one of the enlightened areas of that state.)

"Only today I had a luncheon with a good friend whose 9th grade son has on his permanent record (thanks to one of his teachers this year) these 'crimes': suspension from school for three days because of breaking into lunch line, going up a flight of stairs used by the teachers but not permitted to students and saying 'dang' back to a teacher for saying something to him, and a comparable list of 4 other unbelievable offenses.

A 5th grade boy and son of good friends was spanked in front of the class when he was out sick for the day. He was used as an example to the class so that the class would not be tempted to do the same thing, i.e. think of being out sick.

A 2nd grader took more money to school than her teacher thought she should have. She argued with the mother, who said that the money was actually that of the child. She was accused of stealing and spanked. Two months later on April 1st, the same teacher told her class to put on their coats and hats as they were going outside to play. After they were dressed, she told them "April Fool!" Nothing could be done about her treatment of the children; it was all legal. ..."

Defenders of the schools might say that such incidents are the exception rather than the rule. It would be easier to believe this if unjust and cruel teachers ever got into trouble for acts like these. I have not yet heard of this happening.

READING GUIDES

In *Freedom and Beyond*, and again in *Instead of Education*, I proposed a reading program which for little or no money might help children, above all poor children (or adults), to read better. I proposed that we have what we might call "Reading Guides." Anyone who could read could volunteer—college students, younger children, housewives, older or retired people, or anyone of any age who in daily life might come in contact with children or other nonreaders. The guides would wear some identifying armband, hat, button, etc. so that anyone wanting information could easily spot them. Seeing a guide wearing a sign, you could ask him either or both of these questions: 1) You could show him a written word and say, "What does this say?" 2) You could say, "How do you write such and such a word?" That's all the guide would have to do.

A school, a church, a group of parents, a block committee, a branch library, or students themselves (in or out of school) could run such a program. It would cost little or nothing. There would be no need to test or screen the guides; there is no reason why they should have to know every word they might be asked.

So far, no one I know of has tried to start such a program. This is not surprising; most people now believe, after all, that only "official" programs run by "professionals" can get anything done. Every year these programs cost more and fail worse. We can only hope that when ordinary people get enough fed up with these incompetent experts, they will begin to act for themselves.

ANGRY ASPS

ASPS are what I call people who constantly Attack Schools but Protect (or promote) Schooling. In one breath they say, "Schools are terrible to, and for, poor kids." In the next they say, "Schools are the only way that poor kids can escape being poor." The logic is hard to follow. Schools have made it far harder for poor kids to escape from poverty than it used to be. There are hundreds or thousands of jobs, that people used to do perfectly well without college or even high school diplomas, that people now have to have diplomas to get. And how the schools, which have always despised, ignored, insulted, and oppressed poor kids, are suddenly going to protect and help them, the ASPS never

make clear.

One ASP wrote me a furious letter about GWS, saying "How is a welfare mother with five kids going to teach them how to read?" The answer is, teach them herself. If she can't read, but one of her children can, that child can teach the other children, *and her*. If none of them can read, they can get a relative or friend, or neighbor, or neighbor's child, to teach them.

Reading, and teaching reading, are not a mystery. The schools, in teaching the poor (and the rich, too) that no one can teach a child anything except a "trained" teacher, have done them (and all of us) a great and crippling injury and wrong. A number of poor countries have had mass literacy programs, often called Each One Teach One, in which as fast as people learn to read they begin to teach others. They found that anyone who can read, even if only fifty or a hundred words, and even if he only learned them very recently, can teach those words to anyone else who wants to learn them. Every now and then, in this country, a school, often a city school for poor kids, lets older children, fifth or sixth graders, teach first graders to read. Most of them do a better job than the regular teachers. Quite often, older children who themselves are not very good readers turn out to be the best teachers of all. There is a clear lesson here, but the schools don't seem able to learn it, mostly because they don't want to.

People who make careers out of helping others—sometimes at some sacrifice, often not—usually don't like to hear that those others might get along fine, might even get along better, without their help. We should keep this in mind in dealing with attacks from ASPS.

And this may be the place to note that "trained" teachers are not trained in teaching, but in classroom management, i.e., in controlling, manipulating, measuring and classifying large numbers of children. These may be useful skills for schools, or people working in schools. But they have nothing whatever to do with *teaching*—helping others to learn things.

READING, CHICAGO STYLE

(From a recent *Chicago Tribune*)

"It has been ten years in the making, but Chicago school officials now believe they have in place a complete sweeping program to teach children to read—a program that may be the pacesetter for the nation... it is built upon the concept developed by Benjamin Bloom, distinguished University of Chicago professor of education, that children should master—bit by bit—elements of reading. .... For some years, a Board of Education reading expert, Bernard Gallegos, has been putting together a package of the reading skills children need to learn in elementary school. At one point, Gallegos' list topped 500 elements. It has since been reduced to 273 over grades 1 through 8. The first skill a child needs to master, is to repeat two– and three–syllable words. The second is to point out objects by going from left to right. ... some other skills the child should acquire: knows long vowel sounds (Ed. note—there is nothing 'long' about them, the word is inaccurate and needlessly confusing) places accent marks on accented syllables (Ed. note—I was reading at near-college level before I began to do that), and identifies rhyming patterns. This is the final skill. (No. 273)"

———————

This might be quite funny if it were not so horrifying. 500 skills! What could they be? When I taught myself to read, I didn't learn 500 skills, or even 273; I looked at printed words, on signs and in books, and puzzled them out; each one I learned made it easier for me to figure out the next. And how did the 500 get cut down to 273?

ASPS would do well to take a look at Bernie's first skill: to repeat two- and three-syllable words. In practice, this is going to mean the children, black, Hispanic, Asian, or from other non-WASP groups, are going to have to pronounce these words the way the teacher *wants* them pronounced. Until they do, they will not be allowed to go on to the next step, or into the next grade. So step No.1 in the Chicago schools is going to be to talk like white people, and until you can do that, you won't be allowed to do anything else.

This, in spite of the fact that many people in the West Indies or Africa, or for that matter Great Britain, can read fluently, though they speak an English that few Chicago teachers would understand.

The schools were never intelligent; as I pointed out in *Instead of Education*, they have never even tried to find out how many children teach themselves to read, or in what ways; nor have they tried to find out what skillful readers did to become skillful (they read books that were "too hard" for them); nor have they learned anything from the experience of people like Dennison, Fader, Herndon, Kohl, who taught kids to read that the schools said could not be taught.

But now the schools are beginning to make stupidity into a system, even a kind of pseudo-science like alchemy, or phrenology, the old "science" of reading people's characters from the shapes of their heads. Like all pseudo-sciences, the pseudo-science of "education" has all the trappings of real science, including mysterious big words, plenty of measurement, plenty of numbers. But this is as far from reality, and its precision is just as spurious, as medieval arguments about how many angels could stand on the head of a pin (326.734 angels). The alchemists tried to measure what did not exist; the educators say something even stupider, that nothing exists except what they can measure.

Not long ago, a teacher in Baltimore, who being *serious* had found a way to make good readers out of children who had never read before was fired, because when the school board adopted some new reading program and ordered all teachers to use it, she sensibly

and responsibly refused to scrap her reading program that worked. This will happen in Chicago; most of what few good reading teachers they have will quit or be fired. The children will be so busy trying to learn how to pass 273 reading tests that they will have no time to read, and what's worse, no desire. Indeed some children who *can* read will probably be held back because they can't pass some of the 273 tests. Then, ten years or so from now, we will hear about some great *new* plan.

LIFE AT HOME

A mother of four children, the wife of a career officer in the U.S. Armed Forces (both of them "church-going Catholics"), who for obvious reasons prefers that we not (yet) give her name, has written us a splendid letter, saying, in part:

"Always, always must we parents and anyone else who undertakes a revolutionary change which seriously affects the lives of others remind ourselves that we do so for selfish reasons. My husband and I began to get cold feet ("sounds like an epidemic," our daughter said) two or three days before school started this year; what urged me to continue with our plans was the thought that I would be very unhappy if I didn't give it a try. It was certainly not that we didn't consider what was best for the children; we believed (and believe) they would be better off growing up at home than in a classroom. But keeping them home was mostly *my* decision, *my* experiment, *my* act of faith. What I hope is that the children not only will flower more truly in their home environment, but also will be enriched by growing up with parents who are attempting to live their beliefs. I hope that they will learn the true meaning of action, that a wrong seen is a wrong to be righted; a better way seen, one to be taken.

We did not give C (12), M (9), S (7) and K (5) a choice between school and school-at-home. As the excitement in the neighborhood mounted during the week before school started, the boys were disturbed about our decision. But we felt that they had been so completely indoctrinated by our society's trust in schooling that they would never decide "in our favor" if we gave them a choice. If after two or three years of this experiment they are still determined, we will discuss it. Living as we do, in the heart of school-going, career-pursuing, achievement-oriented culture, we had to operate this way. We justify it by the fact that we are their parents and, we think, of all the people on earth, wisest when it comes to their upbringing. We monitor their socialization as we do their TV and sugar consumption. And yes, they're doing fine. They're generally contented. Only S complains about staying home, and that less often each month. They occupy themselves continually and, though I don't get out much, we get on each other's nerves very little, even when it's been raining for days.

You'll notice I didn't say back there, "We monitor

their education." That's because the whole subject is an embarrassment. We are *in charge* of their education (thank you, state), but if the local superintendent came to take a look, he wouldn't think we were doing such a slam-bang job of it. We are using the Calvert Home Instruction courses—because we said we would. But we are not using them the way they were intended to be used. For one thing, they are highly structured, so well organized that any dummy who can read could use them with his child. If they were followed faithfully, there would be no time left for teaching, that is, being there when a child needs help in learning something. I've been in a quandary several times and I've tried to teach a child something he either already knew or wasn't ready for. All in the name of following the curriculum and staying on schedule. And my heart really isn't in it. I think, for instance, doing a scheduled lesson on the Industrial Revolution, which right now is utterly boring, when you've spent hours over the last few weeks watching and discussing the Rome of "I, Claudius," is stupid. You scribble some hasty answers to questions about the Industrial Revolution and you forget all about it.

But I am getting smart and here is basically what we do about "education." At the beginning of each month the children each make and decorate a folder out of 12" by 18" sheets of construction paper. We fill the folders with paperwork, including the tests which Calvert provides; we never send these in to Calvert since we are not using the Advisory Teaching Service. This "proves" that we are keeping up in (almost) every subject. There is not nearly so much paperwork done as Calvert demands, but every paper is perfect. When the children make mistakes, they erase and correct them immediately. I make no traditional teacher's marks on their papers such as X's, checks, happy faces, etc.; but I dispense National Wildlife stickers freely. (I hope that I am teaching them that mistakes, in work and in life, are not irrevocable; and though I don't know if it means anything, I like the idea of keeping reminders of myself off their work.)"

(Ed. note—I interrupt only to say that I think it means a great deal, and can't imagine a more humane or sensitive way of putting it)

"Many of the drawings that they all do spontaneously at the dining room table are put into the folder in case anyone wonders if we are having 'art.' If on a school day we go somewhere "educational;" we paste a souvenir of the trip on a piece of colored paper and include it. The two older children each keep a list of pages done in separate workbooks and include these in their folders. So we actually look pretty good, even if we aren't. And the filled folders at month's end, which we ritually arrange and staple, seem to give the children a sense of accomplishment.

What I would really like to do is put all the Calvert courses out in the rain. (The children keep them in their original cartons.) For one thing I am really too busy for all that nonsense, between housework, normal family activities, and a couple of my own interests, and for another I think it is an empty ritual. During the week after *No More Schools* (Ed. note—a weekend conference) I kept notes on academically related activities which the children did spontaneously. Here are the notes for one day:

C taught M and me to play "Go Fish" and "Concentration;" she asked if "Concentration" helped in life.

C and I played gin rummy.

S worked on crossword puzzles.

S read *Put Me in the Zoo* silently twice, then aloud to K.

K built with blocks.

(When asked, C, M, and S each helped with chores.)

C tested her memory of names of states (45/50) and their capitals (35/50); invented charades to describe 3 countries.

M showed S placement of U.S. and England on map (which hangs on wall).

C read *Rocky* and we discussed possible jealousy of Stallone's wife.

I played "War" with K and used phrases "greater than" and "less than."

S read aloud phrases on back of Ivory Snow box.

S went out to play in his knight's costume (homemade: result of reading about knights).

I read *Little Toot* to M and K; M asked ques. about vocabulary.

S and I discussed bees (when the queen flies out of the hive; how bees aid in pollination) after he got stung by one.

M counted his money.

Also from that week:

M cut open avocado seed and we discussed seed coat, embryo, seed leaves and true leaves...

K built aircraft carrier with blocks.

S made reconstituted juice, reading label to determine amount of water to add.

C suggested own math project, figuring cost to carpet upstairs rooms.

(I took C to Self-Sufficiency Seminar at community college.)

S used tape measure to measure several objects around house. He reported lengths and widths in both centimeters and inches.

C read *The Metric Book of Amusing Things to Do*, and did an exercise with curves and straight lines.

S and K read *The Question and Answer Book of the Human Body*.

C took her and S's temperature.

C continued with her project to average a book a day for a month for the Mental Health Readathon. The most serious books included *David Copperfield* and *Treasure Island*.

We went to the library.

We toured the replica of the Santa Maria in the harbor.

What is important to remember about these activities is that because they were self-initiated they were meaningful; that is, because they fit in with an ongoing and/or current interest, what was learned is not likely to be forgotten. This deepened my curiosity about what the children would teach themselves if they were freed from imposed school work entirely. Hopefully, next year I can move toward satisfying this curiosity. (Ed. note—They will be stationed in another country)

...I began this mental evolution, this change in my attitude toward schooling, after reading Ivan Illich and your *Escape From Childhood*. I was ready for the conversion that took place, in what must have been a very deep part of my soul; it was "Of course, why didn't I think of that?" when I learned that children could grow up at home. And so I, and then soon, we, began to change the way we were bringing up our children. We had been conscientious parents, but we had (and have) a lot to learn. We are learning to listen, to stop what we are doing to pay attention when it is needed, to answer questions simply, to sit around and just talk sometimes.

More learning comes out of just plain talk than can be imagined. (Ed. note—this was my point about the Ny Lilleskole in *Instead of Education*) I hung M.C. Escher's "Verbum" on the dining room wall and several conversations that started with "How did he draw that?" occurred, and careened wildly through design, artist's materials, optical illusions, evolution, and the Gospel of St. John. With C, I can see the encrusted layers of school-rigidity falling away; several times a lesson with her has dissolved into a conversation about her real worth as a loving, responsible human being versus the graded, classified, surely stupid person she sometimes felt herself to be in school.

GOOD BOOKS CHEAP

A good place to buy, at low cost, the kind of books that many or most children would find interesting (partly because they are not children's books, but about the grown-up world) is Publishers Central Bureau; Dept. 516, One Champion Ave., Avenel, N.J. 07131. It is what they call a remainder house. When publishers find they have printed more copies of a book than they think they can sell, the sell the extra copies at very low cost to remainder houses, who sell them, usually by mail, at much lower than the original cost. I strong recommend that you write for one of their catalogues.

Here, from a recent one, are some of the sample titles that might interest many children: *The Baseball Encyclopedia* ($9.98); *The Anatomy of Costume* ($7.98), *A History of Clothing; The Encyclopedia of the Horse* (10.98), a sure bet for many girls; *The World of Clowns* (9.98); *Lost Cities* (2.98); *The Vikings* (2.98); *Frank Leslie's Illustrated History of the Civil War* (12.98); *Ripley's Giant Book of Believe It or Not* (6.95), a sure-fire success (like the *Guiness Book of Records*, which Pub. Clear. does not sell): *Prehistoric Man* (5.98); *The Time of the Buffalo* (3.98); *National Football League—The First Fifty Years* (3.98), a sure winner for many boys; *Railways Then and Now* (7.98); *The Horse, Through 50 Centuries of Civilization* (15.96), probably well worth the price; *Gold and Silver in the West* (5.98); *Timber: Toil and Trouble in the Big Woods* (3.98); *History of Aviation* (17.95); *Hitler's Luftwaffe* (9.98); *The Adventures of Sail, 1520–1914* (17.95); a number of books by Beatrice Potter (*Peter Rabbit*, etc.) and many others.

Worth looking into.

RECYCLING TOYS

(From *Briarpatch Review*, 330 Ellis St., S.F. Cal. 94102)

".....Knowing that children lose interest and outgrow toys that are in still good condition and that quality toys are too expensive, we created Toy Go Round—an alternative way of disposing of toys. The toy's original owners can share them with younger children and at the same time support new interests with money returned from their resale.

We each had "like new" toys in the basement, attic, or closet because they were too good to give away or throw out. ... Both of us wanted to use our talents and skills, have fun, create our own job and provide a service for others.

We began in Sept. 1976 selling outgrown toys belonging to our children and friends—returning 50% to the toy's owners. In ten months Toy Go Round had grown to over 250 individual accounts. People bring in outgrown toys, books, and games on consignment and receive 50% share upon their sale. Checks are available the first of each month for all items sold the previous month. ...

Children with their own accounts often return to make a purchase and to see what they have sold and what toys with *their* code number remain on the shelves for someone else to buy and enjoy.

We have done much research on prices and pricing, quality and availability. If a toy comes in "like new," we check to see what a reasonably priced store is selling the new one for, then we automatically discount it 30%. We have many catalogs and price lists to use as guides. ...We estimate our prices on toys to be sold by their condition and play value. For example, a cobbler's bench might be nicked and dented and appear "well-loved" but if the pegs and hammer are intact, it still has good play value.

...We scrub, repair, improvise many a tail, ear or wheel, make missing pieces to wooden puzzles with a jigsaw and try to give others advice with their problem or sick toys.

When games arrive with missing pieces, we code them, set them aside to wait for another to arrive. Then we combine pieces, and both accounts receive credit.

We match up toys to make complete sets. Some of our toys have returned a second and third round.

Toy Go Round assists in fund-raising for schools and playgroups. They collect and bring in toys in the group's name and receive the 50% upon their sale. They are also able to buy toys and supplies from us economically.

Our bulletin board, one whole wall, is overflowing with wanteds, for sales, playgroups, schools and community activities for children.

…We have assembled an arts and crafts corner. Collage materials, homemade play dough, paint, etc. are available at all times. We have wood scraps, large-headed pounding nails and scrap craft paper of varied size, color and texture. Burlap and yarn for stitchery and wire bundles for creating sculptures are popular items. Recycled computer paper and cards are sold by the bundle for 10¢ and 5¢.

Toy Go Round welcomes handcrafted toys and games giving 75% to the maker. Personalized birthday banners are made upon request.

…You are always welcome to stop by for a visit. You'll find us at 1715-B Solano Ave., Berkeley, Cal,— Tues.,Thurs., Sat., 12:00–5:30."

Andora Freeman, Joy Ernst

People who want to work with or in some way make themselves useful to children, and don't want to work in schools, may find some good ideas here. In *Instead of Education* (available from GWS), I suggested toy libraries, but on the whole I like the toy recycling store even better.

Though I haven't asked them, I would guess that Toy Go Round might well accept toys sent by mail.

Briarpatch Review is a quarterly, $5/yr., about small, self-supporting businesses. Many readers of GWS might find it useful, esp. those on the West Coast.

BEFORE YOU WERE THREE

This is the title of a new and much needed book, by Robie Harris and Elizabeth Levy, with 100+ superb photos by Henry Gordillo (pub. by Delacorte Press). It is a book for young children about what they (and other children) were like when they were even younger. It seems a perfect book to read aloud to 3-6 year olds, or for slightly older children to read themselves. It will surely spark hundreds of questions, conversations, rememberings, about being a baby or toddler, and about growing up. It would help children to understand themselves better, and other children, and younger brothers and sisters, too. I can't recommend it too highly.

If enough GWS readers are interested in this book, we could add it to the list of books we sell, so that if people couldn't find it in local bookstores they could get it from us. Let us know if you have trouble finding it locally. But do look for it. It could be immensely valuable.

LIFE AT HOME (cont.)

"In *Blackberry Winter*, Margaret Mead (who did not attend school regularly until she was eleven) said that children used to be brought up by means of stories. I thought I'd like to try that with my own children but didn't know how to start until Sean began to ask questions last summer about the origins of man and the universe. He would ask me, "How did God make Adam and Eve?" or "How did God make the earth?" Knowing nothing, I knew everything, and I began to enjoy answering his questions, which I did with stories. One evening as his father was tucking him into bed he said, "You know, Daddy, every day I ask Mommy how you make things—and she always knows the answer!" Sure enough, the next morning as soon as he awoke he sat up and asked me, "How do you make stones?" My knowledge of geology is scant, but I managed to bring the earth from big hunks of rock through earthquakes, thundering ocean waves, etc. to little stones, which by the way are made of minerals like gold, copper and calcium. He nodded his head, satisfied, and laid back on his pillow.

When K asked me where he came from, I followed the advice of A.C. Harwood (who was writing on Rudolf Steiner's philosophy of education) to tell the child a truly spiritual story of his origin and not to get bogged down in biological details. He loved hearing about what went through God's mind as He decided where to send a little blond baby. I included some biological details, too, but we had already discussed them several times (on his level, of course). He was delighted.

…I must include one more thing. C and M have joined the junior swim team at—, which has, in the absence of school, become a focus for their lives. Four or five times a week they practice rigorously and attend meets on some weekends. They love it and we are happy about it for several reasons. The physical benefits now and in adulthood, when their bodies will crave the exercise they are giving them now, are great. They meet children with a common interest. They have chosen to join the team, it is not compulsory P.E. They are engaged in competition in a real sense; no amount of apple-polishing or cheating can get them to the other end of the pool any faster. But most of all, it is an example of the best kind of learning (life) activity; they go to an expert (the swimming coach) to learn a specific skill (swimming) and they do it while they learn it (they participate in meets no matter what their times)."

May I underline, among all the good things in this letter, J's words, "knowing nothing, I knew everything." We don't have to know everything, or even very much, to give useful answers to children's questions. A child asking a question does not want to know everything; he wants to take a step or two further into the world in a given direction. It is all right even to make a wild guess, and then to say, "That's what I think, but if you like we can look it up in a book and see what it says." This gives the idea that when you don't know something you *can* always go look it up somewhere.

I think with sorrow and horror of an article I read in which two college-graduate parents said that they were looking for a school for their four-year-old because "we were not competent to teach him ourselves." The schools work hard to make them, and everyone, think this way. But it is not true.

UNSCHOOLING AND THE LAW

GWS will say "unschooling" when we mean taking children out of school, and "deschooling" when we mean changing the laws to make schools non-compulsory and to take away from them their power to grade, rank, and label people i.e. to make lasting, official, public judgments about them.

I have seen, in detail, the compulsory school laws of a few states. The experience of people so far makes clear that whatever the laws say, if the local superintendent and/or school board are willing to let you take your children out of school, you may do so; if they are not willing, you will probably have to fight for the right to do so in court (unless, of course, you decide simply to try to escape the schools' notice). The wording of the law in your particular state may have much to do with the grounds on which you make your fight.

In his letter elsewhere in this issue, Jud Jerome urges that in as many places as possible we test the constitutionality of compulsory school attendance (hereafter CSA) laws, in other words, claim that such laws violate one or more of the constitutionally guaranteed rights of parents and/or children. Ed Nagel at N.A.L.S.A.S. (see GWS #1) agrees with him. I don't for reasons I will explain, but I do agree that the issue is well worth exploring. We should try to find out from experts in constitutional law, and also to decide for ourselves, on what grounds we might make such a claim. If you have ideas about this, please write us. You might ask your local branches of the American Civil Liberties Union or Emergency Civil Liberties Committee what they think. So far, most branches of the ACLU have not been willing to consider CSA as a civil liberties issue, or to take any interest in it.

The most obvious claim we might make is that CSA deprives children of liberty without due process of law, and without the overriding excuse of national emergency which in time of war justifies the draft. We might also claim that CSA violates the rights of parents to control the instruction of their own children, though such a right is not stated or even clearly implied in the Constitution.

I don't think there is a chance in a million that the U.S. courts would sustain such claims. In the first place, in the recent case of the Amish (*Yoder vs. Wisconsin*), the Supreme Court said that while they

would grant the Amish the right not to send their children to high school, they did so only because the Amish were an established religious group who had long proved the depth and strength of their religious convictions. The court then said explicitly that they would not grant this same exemption to other people on "philosophical grounds." In other words, if you are a member of a religious group (preferably conservative in its views and way of life, like the Amish) which *for a long time* and even at some risk has insisted on keeping its children out of school, the Court may sustain you. Otherwise, no.

In the second place, the even more recent decision of the Supreme Court, allowing the use of "corporal punishment" in schools, shows that this court, like most citizens, takes a very light view of the liberty and dignity of children. A court which holds that the schools may beat children, often very brutally, and often for the most frivolous of reasons, is surely not going to rule that children do not have to go to school at all.

In the third place, even when the judges are not elected but appointed for life, courts are political bodies, sensitive to public opinion, and as such are extremely unlikely, by calling CSA unconstitutional, to pass a law that 95% or more of the people would strongly oppose. Such court decisions invite meddling with the Constitution itself—witness the Constitutional Convention resolutions right now circulating among our state legislatures. Even if the Supreme Court thought CSA a bad idea, which it clearly does not, it would almost certainly not rule against it unless it felt a fairly weighty body of public opinion behind it, perhaps not a majority but at least a powerful and influential minority. We can hope this may be so twenty years from now, but it is not so today.

Some will say we should try anyway; it would at least be educational. Perhaps it would. But it would divert time, energy, and money better spent elsewhere. It would give us more public visibility than we are ready to have, or than it would be wise to have. And it is very possible, if the courts did make a positive decision in favor of CSA, that we might be worse off than before, since such a decision might close off loopholes through which many of us now escape. Finally, since the courts generally don't like to reverse previous decisions, we would probably be better off having the Supreme Court say nothing until there is a fairly good chance they will say Yes.

These are my opinions/guesses. If you have ideas about this, please write us.

Nor do I think that local or state courts will rule that schools in general, or the local schools, are so unkind, threatening, competitive, violent, or even incompetent, that any parents who want can take their children out of them. It would be wiser to ask them to decide each case, as it comes up, on its own merits. *The broader the decision, the more likely it is to go against us.* What I think we may be able to get many courts to say, in particular cases, is that the track record of schools is not so good that they can claim (as they do) that nobody but themselves is competent to teach children. In some cases the courts may also agree with us that because they are so concerned to hold onto their students/customers the schools can hardly even be considered disinterested or fair judges of the teaching competence of others. This is important; the schools are going to go into court with the claim that since they are the certified experts in education, they and only they are fit to judge whether or not the parents are competent to teach their own children.

FROM "D"

The writer of this letter has been writing me very interesting and valuable letters for a year or more about unschooling. For the time being, he thinks it better not to have his name and address attached to what he is writing. He says, in part:

".....Here is the information I want to share with you (on issues raised in GWS), which I'll take up in the order in which they appeared.

1. HOME STUDY INSTITUTE is the correspondence school of the Seventh Day Adventists Department of Education (which maintains, primarily, a worldwide system of parochial day schools, like the Catholics and Lutherans, and also colleges.)

Waiving the Bible/religious study: we ordered the complete second grade course for A, omitting (and thus, not having to pay for) all the "Bible" materials. This is fine with HSI—the "Bible" stuff is *not* required, as HSI does not want to discriminate in any way against those of other faiths (it's open to anyone, regardless of belief, or lack of it). Dynamite service, incidentally; all materials arrived via UPS in less than a week!

Re the "conventional" aspect: this has been the case with the Calvert school stuff... it has been *no* drawback whatsoever with our 1st-grader. He *loves* the stuff— really! And of course, the parents can modify freely.

Re the experience of the Adventists: HSI told me that their "assistance" would be limited to giving testimony (i.e. they can't afford defense costs, or anything). You should keep in mind when considering the considerable number of children enrolled in HSI— and by the way, HSI feels that Calvert, which advertises in the *National Geographic* each month, has a larger elementary enrollment—that the great majority of students are children of missionaries, etc. so that HSI's experience in "bucking compulsory attendance laws" may not be that great. (Ed. note—a good point. Still, I would think that testimony from HSI to the effect that many children had used their programs at home with good results might be very valuable to unschoolers)

Let me add here that the Adventists are, I've found, *not* a reliable source of information regarding possible loopholes in the state laws (as you suggest in the "We Need to Know" section). After receiving a very encouraging, confident letter from HSI's Director of Studies

saying, in effect, "Go ahead and do it," I wrote to our state Adventist Superintendent of Schools who deflated the whole idea by replying that home study is not allowed in Ohio! This was blatantly wrong, as I had already discovered a provision for home-study in Ohio law (and had it verified by an attorney)—so the man plainly did not know (although he thought he did) the state laws.

(D points out that the Bayh report is still being sent out free from his office.)

2. WE NEED TO KNOW—I've learned a lot about "legal research" just from doing it, and I want to share what I know:

First, let me hasten to point out that *everything* you folks want to know about the various state laws, court cases, etc. is contained in the study put out by the Mass. Center for Public Interest Laws. (Ed. note—title and address at end of this letter) The only thing this book *doesn't* give you is the exact text of each of the state laws. It does, however, refer you to the specific title, section, etc., so that you could easily get this information for yourself.

I would suggest that it's more educational and satisfying to go to the local library and look up the laws for yourself than to ask your state legislator (who will have to do just that, as he certainly will not be familiar with them...). Any large public library, like the main library of a large city system, or the public library in the county seat, will have volumes of all the laws of one's home state. Once you find the "Education" or "Schools" section, there is usually a subsection entitled "School Attendance." After each of the specific laws, court cases relating to that law are listed and commented on, but while you're in the law books, you'll want to look at the index at the back—which is usually quite extensive—for cross-references to subjects like "home study," "private school," "tutoring," etc. which will lead you to other laws dealing with these.

Often the education laws are also bound in a separate volume as well (e.g. Baldwin's *Ohio School Law*) which contains a "text" section setting forth all of the laws in a more readily understood, almost narrative form, which, however, ...you'd want to cross-check with the statutes themselves. Finally, while you're in the local library, you might want to look at a commentary on the state's laws, called (state name) *Jurisprudence*, which will give you a concise overview of the statutes and related court cases.

(Ed. note—the names of these volumes may vary from state to state, but people in the library will help you find what you are looking for)

The Final Report: Legal Implications of Compulsory Education, National Institute of Education, Project #NEG-00-3-0061, by Wm. Aikman and Lawrence Kotin, (Sponsored by HEW) Avail. from Mass. Center for Public Interest Law, 2 Park St. Boston MA 02116, $10.75.

You may also be able to get this report, perhaps free, from the National Institute of Education, HEW, 1200 19th, N.W., Washington D.C. 20008.

LOOKING UP THE LAW

I took D's good advice, and did what I had been saying for some time that people ought to do—get information for themselves, instead of depending on some expert. Went to the main Boston Library, asked at the information desk where I could find state laws, was sent to a reference room, asked again there. They told me to look up in a law index the numbers of the particular laws I was interested in, then come back and fill out a slip for the books themselves. The law books used to be on open shelves, but people (law students, perhaps?) were stealing them, so now they are all on reserve. I picked the index that seemed easiest to use, made up my list of statutes, took them to the desk, and soon had the law books. I found the Massachusetts education laws scary reading, much more tightly drawn, threatening, and punitive than I had expected. One would suppose that they dealt with dangerous criminals rather than children. Of course, they were written around the turn of the century, and so, written *by* rich Yankees and aimed *at* the children of poor (probably mostly Irish) immigrants. I had hoped to find that the School Boards and Superintendents had been given the task of running schools, but that the task of enforcing school attendance laws had been left to other agencies, perhaps the police. Not so; in this matter, the schools *are* the police. They can demand information about children, and people have to answer. If they refuse, or give wrong answers, they can be fined. Nothing in the wording of these laws encourages the idea that the state looks kindly on children and wants to help them. On the contrary, the impression is that the state considers unattended children a danger, and wants them all safely locked up.

The trouble with reading laws is that one cannot tell, from the books, which laws are actively enforced and which are what they call a Dead Letter, laws long ignored because it is easier to ignore than repeal them. Our state codes are full of such laws. Many of the older states still have on the books laws on sexual conduct that, if strictly enforced, would put most of the population in jail—to name one example, laws in one state saying that a man may not kiss his wife on Sunday.

At least one Massachusetts law on education is such a Dead Letter. It provides, again under the threat of penalties, that the Superintendent of each school district shall take an annual school census i.e. find out what children live in every household in the district and where they go to school. Perhaps some districts still take such a census, but no one has asked me any such question in the twenty years I have lived in Boston. Is the same information available somewhere else? I can't imagine where.

At any rate, D is right. Whatever in practice the laws may mean, ordinary people can at least find out what they *say*, and they should find out.

However, I still think it is useful and probably important for people to write their state legislators on this subject. The lawmakers ought to know that some citizens are concerned about this. We in turn need to know which if any lawmakers are sympathetic to unschooling, and which strongly oppose it. We need to begin to make legislative allies. For in the long or maybe not so long run, unschooling will be a political matter.

DO WE NEED LAWYERS?

Several people have written recently to say they want to take their children out of school, and feel they need a lawyer. We have been trained to think of ourselves as incompetent, dependent on experts and professionals, in more and more areas, so it is natural that when we have to deal with the law we should think, "I need a lawyer." But it may not be so; a lawyer may be no help, even a hindrance. Recently the owner of the building in which I had rented an apartment for nineteen years decided to make it into a condominium. I planned to buy my apartment, but knowing nothing of condominium law, I hired a lawyer to represent me. He got into a tangle with the lawyer of the building owner, and only when the building owner and I by-passed our lawyers and began to deal with each other directly could we get our business done.

A newly published book has some words on this that may be useful: *Disabling Professions*, five essays by Ivan Illich, Irving Zola, John McKnight, Jonathan Caplan, and Harley Shaiken. (Pub. in Great Britain by Marion Boyars Publishers; 18 Brewer St., London, W1R 4AS. U.S. distribution—22 South Broadway, Salem NH 03079. Pub. in Canada by Burns and MacEachern Ltd., Suite 3, 62 Railside Rd., Don Mills, Ontario M3A 1A6) In his article "Lawyers and Litigants; A Cult Revised," Jonathan Caplan, a British lawyer, says, in part:

"Do we need a lawyer? In any system of criminal justice the answer is unqualifiably that we do. But in relation to every other issue—that is to say, every noncriminal matter—the role of the lawyer should be open to question."

(Ed. note—how would Mr. Caplan classify unschoolers? Clearly when he talks about criminal law, he has something very different in mind—robbery, assault, murder. The schools will of course accuse unschoolers of breaking the law, yet I think we would be closer to the truth, and wiser, to consider unschooling as part of civil rather than criminal law)

"The second half of the twentieth century is the age when experts were revered and when expert advice became an expensive commodity. For the professions this was a Klondike since all professional advice passes as expert. But legal advice is not invariably expert. ...To seek legal advice may, therefore, cover a multitude of situations none of which necessarily arise from the need to consult a lawyer at all. Frequently legal advice is simply common sense or experience of the kind of which most rational people are capable, yet we choose to pay lawyers for the reassurance of involving some intelligent third party in our personal affairs. In such a way we consult lawyers as a lovesick teenager would consult an agony columnist. To gain an ally at a time of doubt or distress. To have an audience with someone who is dispassionate...

In the majority of legal consultations, all that a lawyer does is to elicit the facts and then to restate the client's position in terms of legal rights and duties so as to highlight the strengths and weaknesses of the case. Like a soothsayer of the law, a lawyer predicts a court's reaction to a given situation. His experience and judgment may often be invaluable (Ed. note—in the matter of unschooling, most lawyers have no experience whatever, and hence no basis for judgment), but much more often this mere stating of the odds is unnecessary (Ed. note—in our case, irrelevant, since we are determined to unschool whatever the odds and are only concerned to find a way) and people could help themselves equally well if only they were educated and encouraged to do so.

The truth is that, nine times out of ten, cases are decided not on a point of law but solely on their facts and the merits. Judges rationalize their conclusion of what is just in the circumstances before them; they do not deduce it from rules and legal precedent... The late Lord Reid, a distinguished member of the appellate committee of the House of Lords, used to advise extra-judicially not to waste time arguing law but to establish a case on it merits as quickly as possible. *It is precisely the facts and the merits which are best known to the litigant himself* (Ed. note—especially in unschooling cases), and a large part of the cost of all legal consultations is accounted for by the time it takes to explain them to a lawyer so that he can repeat them at a later stage. Yet facts can, in the course of such retelling, lose their force or cogency and litigants in many cases might do better in presenting their cause themselves and in establishing the merits...

Legal systems give no confidence to litigants to go it alone. They call for dependence on lawyers. The complexity of pretrial procedure, the ritualized style of pleadings, the public arena of the court—all contribute to make the pursuit of even the most simple claim a professional venture.

...Left alone, people are unsure of their rights and even more unsure of how to press for them... There is a grave risk, therefore, that a litigant representing himself will not be able to get into the best position for negotiation before trial (Ed. note—irrelevant in unschooling cases) or to maneuver to his best advantage at trial. (Ed. note—Again, probably largely irrelevant) In this curious way, it may be that our legal systems have made representation the prerequisite to complete justice.

Where does all this leave us? Perhaps we need lawyers to advise us on procedural matters, what sort of motions to put before the court, delaying tactics, etc.

But we are not likely to find many lawyers who know, or even are willing to find out, as much about the law on CSA and unschooling as we can find out for ourselves. The ideal, of course, will be to assemble—GWS may help in this—a body of lawyers who are as strongly committed to unschooling as we are. This will not be easy—most lawyers are more likely to be on the side of their fellow professionals, the educators.

On one point Mr. Caplan's words are both reassuring and important. Legal trickery is not going to determine whether we win or lose. Years ago the *Saturday Evening Post* used to run stories about an old Yankee lawyer named Ephraim Tutt, who won all his cases (in which justice was clearly on his side) by digging up some obscure point of law that his opponent had never heard of. This made most people (including me) feel more than ever that the law was a mystery, full of dirty tricks. Mr. Caplan is saying that even without the legal trickery the judge would have ruled for Mr. Tutt and his clients, solely on the merits of their case. It is up to us to learn how to make the strongest case for ourselves. But we are as likely to be able to do this as anyone else.

LEADERSHIP

Unschoolers are leaders, though many of them may not think of themselves this way. Leaders are not, as we are often led to think, people who go along with huge crowds following them. Leaders are people who go their own way without caring, or even looking to see, whether *anyone* is following them. "Leadership qualities" are not the qualities that enable people to attract followers, but those that enable them to do without them. They include, at the very least, courage, endurance, patience, humor, flexibility, resourcefulness, stubbornness, a keen sense of reality, and the ability to keep a cool and clear head even when things are going badly.

True leaders, in short, do not make people into followers, but into other leaders.

"D" (cont.)

"For the court cases themselves, you have to go to a law library—which are maintained by local bar associations and often 'bar' admittance to the public. (Ed. note—some lawyers may have this material in their offices, and might let you read it. Or a friendly lawyer might arrange for you to get into the local law library) If this is the case, go to the nearest law *school* library and make yourself at home. You can either register at the desk as a nonstudent, or just walk around pretending you're a student. You can look up (with a bit of assistance at first) any case cited in your state laws (or elsewhere for that matter) and read and copy (for a fee) the entire text of the decision. You can get the texts of the big pro-home study decisions (*People v. Levisen*, Ill. and *State v. Masse*, N.J.), just for your edification.

Another thing the law school library has is complete sets of state law volumes for each state. ...Let me relate how I used these just last week. A man in Mass. wrote me that he'd asked a lawyer if there were any loopholes in Mass. Law regarding home study. The lawyer... found one, which this man is now using. (Ed. note—I am not sure, but will ask D., what this loophole is) The man did not quote the law to me, and I was anxious to see how closely it paralleled our own state's loophole. So, I got the volume of Mass. law relating to "Schools" or "Education"... opened to the section of "School Attendance," and there in the very first law was the short phrase that constituted the home study loophole; this took less than 5 mins. I then skimmed the cases cited throughout the section (after each of the laws) and found one described as relating to home study (*Commonwealth v. Renfrew*). I read the entire decision in this case, which cited and thus led me to several other important Mass. cases (as well as some from other states). I was done in less than half an hour, and had a great time.

(Ed. note—I have to repeat what I say in the section "Unschooling and the Law," that no matter what the law says, if the local school board decides to take you to court it will be the judge and not the wording of the law that determines whether you can teach your child at home. As Chief Justice Holmes said many years ago, "The Constitution is what the Judges say it is." In any state (i.e. all states except Miss.) which has CSA, the law will not say that parents may teach their children at home whether the local authorities like it or not. The law gives local school authorities full power and discretion in this matter. Some school boards will say, as they already have, "Sure, teach your kids at home, just let us know what you're doing." Most, I predict, will not, and many of these professional helpers of children will pursue their escaping helpees with great determination and vindictiveness)

"...But, since our original inquiry, a landmark court case here in Ohio—*State v. Whisner* (351 N.E. 2d 750)—has greatly diminished the legitimacy of these "standards" as they relate to private schools. Rev. Whisner's church had a school which did not meet the "standards," and some of the language of this decision is worth quoting as it pertains to the rights of parents:

'...it has long been recognized that the right of a parent to guide the education of his or her children is indeed a fundamental right guaranteed by the Due Process Clause of the Fourteenth Amendment.

In the opinion of a majority of this court, a general education of high quality can be achieved by means other than the comprehensive regimentation of all academic centers in this state. In the words of Thoreau, "If a man does not keep pace with his companions, perhaps it is because he hears a different drummer. Let him step to the music which he hears, however measured or far away."'

Pretty far out, huh? Quoting Thoreau and all. This is the only Ohio court decision interpreting school attendance laws that's worth noting—and its significance is that *perhaps* parents could call their home a private school and get away with it (without meeting the absurd "standards").

I have at hand the complete citations for the two major successful home study cases:

1. *People v. Levisen*, 404 Ill. 574, 90 N.E. 2d 213 (S. Ct. Ill. 1950);

2. *State v. Massa*, 95 N.J. Super, 382, 231A 2d 252 (Morris County Ct., L. Div. 1967).

There are others, where the courts decided in favor of the parents (and home study):

3. *People v. Turner*, 98 N.Y.S. 2d 886 (New York, 1950);

4. *Wright v. State*, 209 P.179 Oklahoma, 1922);

5. *State v. Peterman*, 70 N.E. 550 (Indiana, 1904);

6. *Commonwealth v. Roberts*, 34 N.E. 402 (Mass. 1893);

Finally, a recent Vermont case similar to Whisner:

7. *State v. LaBarge*, 357 A. 2d 121 (1976).

That's about all I know, John. Hope it's of some help.

———————————

I should say it is. Much thanks to D, who has set us all a good example. Don't be put off by those letters and numbers in the citations. They all mean something perfectly simple, and the law books themselves will tell us what they mean.

Let me repeat Mr. Caplan's advice—judges are not going to rule for us just because we can show them favorable citations from judges in other states. But such citations will give our cases more weight. It will probably be a very good idea to cite them when we first write school authorities about unschooling our children. It will show them that we know something about law and will not be a pushover in court. Some of them, at least, may decide that it will be easier to let us do what we want than to go to the expense and trouble of taking us to court, in a case which they may well lose.

FROM JUD JEROME

"When the oldest three of our five children were in the early grades, Marty and I told them very clearly that we never wanted them to go to school a single day thinking that we were making them go or that they were going for our benefit. If they chose to go, that was their business. If it developed that someone had to go to jail over their nonattendance, that would be a family matter we would have to discuss at the time, but they shouldn't assume that going to school was the best answer, even then. We made a point of signing their

21

grade cards without looking at them, never pushed, never went to school functions. In spite of this general lack of encouragement, they performed better than average by school standards—probably because they came from a stimulating home filled with people who were intellectually engaged. But when the oldest was fifteen we moved from Ohio to Maryland, and she was resistant to attending the new high school, which was big, impersonal, populated by youngsters who had segregated themselves into mobs of snobs and greasers (Ed. note—a fairly standard social pattern in most high schools)—by their own denomination, and Michelle didn't see that she fit into either group... the day she was 16 she got her driver's license, moved into an apartment with another young woman in the city, got a job—all with our approval. There was never any hostility or tension with the family; she simply thought it was better for her development to be self-sufficient. In the next two years she worked at various jobs, joined a communal group ... and finally decided that she wanted to go to a community college. She took and easily passed the high school equivalency test to qualify her to do this. She is still in college, earning scholarships to support herself, with very clear vocational goals which enable her to put up with the collegiate nonsense ...

The second daughter also quit at 16, the earliest legal age to do so, in order to live with a man in California. After an interlude she enrolled in school there, as she really wanted the diploma for vocational reasons, and didn't trust herself to pass the high school equivalency. For a year she was in and out of schools and new living situations. We had, meanwhile, moved to a communal farm, and for a while she lived here with us and attended the nearby small-town high school, where she was miserable. The students—and even the teachers—continually teased her, for being "different" (i.e. for not having grown up in that town), for living in a commune, above all for being "bookish," or having intellectual interests. Often she would call home in tears, asking us to pick her up and bring her home. Finally she quit and moved back to the town where she had started high school, shared an apartment with her older sister, and finished her class—not in the least delayed by her year's absence. She, too, is now in college and doing well (by their standards).

TO PARENT

"I'm not going to try to talk you into taking your children out of school. If they insist on going, let them go. But let's keep the facts straight. It is possible to do interesting and useful work in the world, even be "successful," without a college degree. It is hard, but then it is hard to do those things even *with* a college degree. Most of the people now getting college degrees are going to be doing work that is not very interesting, and that people used to do without college degrees.

Also people can get into graduate school without going to college. One friend of mine got into a leading American theological seminary, another into the leading Canadian law school, with only a year of undergraduate college. The former is the minister of a big church, the latter perhaps the outstanding student in her class. Other people I know or know of have gone to college without going to high school. In short, even if you get off the school road, you can get back on whenever you want, and you will probably be ahead of the people who stayed on it all along.

If kids want to go to college so they can enjoy the social life, go to football games, join sororities/fraternities, etc. OK, if their parents can afford it. But let's not kid ourselves that anyone learns anything very important in those places. As far as securing their future goes, they might be a lot better off to get an external degree and put in the bank the money they would have spent on college tuition."

JUD (cont.)

"Our fourth daughter is aphasic and a special case. When she reached school age we began putting her in various special education classes, but by the time she was six the teachers were begging us to take her out. They said she needed a residential school—and we agreed, since her adjustment at home and in the neighborhood were no better than that in school. We found a residential school which was, in fact, a religious commune, based on the teaching of Rudolf Steiner (Camphill). Jenny was immediately happy there, and it was evident to us and to the staff at the school that this was an excellent home for her. In my view it is not the schooling so much as the total environment of the village-like commune which is the primary educational force in her life. Since the law requires that the state provide free education appropriate to such special needs, and since we would never be able to afford keeping her there on our own (though the costs are very low compared with those at conventional residential schools), she is there on state funds. Interestingly, our most serious battles with the educational system have not been to keep the other children out, but to keep support for Jenny at Camphill. Since the staff at that school are European trained, they do not have the credentials required by law for state approval. No one in the Department of Education denies that the school is excellent in every respect and perhaps the only available placement for Jenny which meets her particular needs, but we continue to have a battle with the officials to continue receiving support for her. (Ed. note—It seems more and more clear that an important function of compulsory education laws is to provide jobs for teachers, specialists, teachers of teachers, administrators, etc.)

Our fifth child is a son, Topher, who was five when we moved to the commune. He had had a few months of kindergarten—which he loved—but we could already see the effects of acculturation on him—e.g.

increasing possessiveness, preoccupation with money and spending, giggling attitudes toward sex and nudity, sassy, silly, rebellious patterns he was picking up from the other children. We were eager to get him out of school and keep him out. We investigated the laws in PA., where our commune is located, and found that one could not qualify for home instruction unless there were evidence of physical, emotional, or mental disability—and if one so qualified, the system would send instructors into the home (which we wanted no more than we wanted him to go to school). So we applied for a license as a private school with one student. We had plenty of people with credentials on the farm, plenty of educational materials, and we were amused and confident as we filled out the elaborate forms asking whether the boys and girls had separate bathroom facilities (we have a two-holer, one marked *men* and the other *women*), and so on. ...We ... complied with the most absurd inquiries. ...Nothing happened. For nearly six years now, nothing has happened. Our application, with its $25 fee, apparently is sitting in the back of the file of the Head Honcho of Private Schools in Harrisburg. ... Each fall—at least for the first three years or so—the local Superintendent would send us a letter demanding that we report where our school-age children were enrolled, and we would reply that he was enrolled in our private school and tell the Superintendent that if he had any questions he should consult the State Department of Private Schools .... Recently he has stopped asking.

In all those years we have not had other school-age children than Topher living at the farm. At times he grew very lonely, and at times visiting relatives and friends would strongly imply to us that we should do something about his schooling. We explained that he had "lessons," but we were very lackadaisical about them. That is, we had a wide variety of books and educational materials available, and when he asked for us to work with him, we did so, and occasionally we would take the initiative in encouraging him to work on reading, mathematics, or some other academic study. We were intrigued by the things he chose to study: for example, he often chose the most conventional kind of workbooks, the sort one finds at low cost in toy stores, and one of the books which helped him most in learning to read was a very old-fashioned Dick-and-Jane teacher's edition, complete with vocabulary lists and inane questions and exercises for lazy teachers in the back. I am not sure whether Topher chose these materials from the wide array of things available to him because he found them to be actually on his level or whether they fit his conception of what school was and thought that somehow he was creating the equivalent of school if he used them. Mostly, though, he learned simply by following adults around, helping, asking questions, becoming involved. By age eight, he was baking bread and cakes, repairing machines, wiring lamps and rooms, and had considerable knowledge of automobiles, calculators, tape recorders and videotape equipment, and usual farm tasks such as gardening,

animal care, forest and wildlife, rocks (he has always had a strong interest in geology and electronics), weather, and machines of all kinds. He helped us at many tasks in our small factory, manufacturing planters from oak logs. But he had little opportunity to play with other children except when they visited the farm or we happened to be on a trip where children were. It was for the company of children, especially, that we thought perhaps he needed some experience in school.

So this past winter we moved temporarily to another commune, a hundred miles away, which had a small "alternative" school (26 students). Topher attended four months (middle of his tenth year), and at the end of the school year he passed at grade level or above all the standardized tests the teacher had to give to satisfy state requirements. He loved the school—but then, he loves most things he does. He was very frustrated by the noise his little class of six students made, at their lack of focus on "school" matters such as reading, writing, arithmetic, social studies, art, science. The teacher (whom he also loved), in desperate efforts to keep their attention, took the class often on "field trips"—to museums, a power plant, a circus, a park, a polling place (when she had to vote), and Topher complained that his whole life has been a field trip, and he wished they would just stay in school and study. He is not actually a very studious child—for example, doesn't read much on his own. But it somehow seemed a waste of time for him to have this rare experience in school wasted in play. He would have gotten over that had he gone another year.

But his parents couldn't take it. It was too disruptive for the family living away from home—and we anticipated that it might be a couple of years before Topher was willing to live there without his parents. At first that seemed worthwhile—a sacrifice we might make. But for many personal reasons aside from those having to do with Topher and school, we decided that we had to find another alternative. (Ed. note—the rest of this part of Jud's letter was reprinted in GWS# 1, under the heading "Why Take Them Out?")

Luckily (I think) the "alternative" we have hit upon came in the form of three more children, girls, moving to the farm. This fall there will be at least four and perhaps five children here between the ages of 6 and 13. So, as we put it to them, we will have "school" here. We have agreed to rotate adults who will give the children about two hours a day (and so far as we know that means 7 days a week, all year long) of attention to "academic" matters. Already this summer the pressure has come from the children to get underway, to have "school." It seems like a game to them, and we have agreed to play. But if we are going to give them hunks of our time, we expect in return that they will give hunks of theirs to chores and farm work. Privately we think they are likely to learn more in the latter activities than in those they regard as "school." Already, though, other families are considering moving here, and I am wondering what our situation will be when there are eight or ten or a dozen children on the farm. In the interest of consolidating the chore of overlooking child activity, we might find ourselves creating a "school" in spite of ourselves. Furthermore, as we have more children, the State is quite likely to develop more interest in what we are doing. I believe this is a financial matter: the appropriation for the local schools is probably based on a head-count, and in this poor and sparse county the Superintendent is not likely to let too many warm bodies go unnoticed as he has let Topher go.

I think it may be urgent that the GWS network get behind some kind of local action to test the constitutionality in state after state and at the federal level, of compulsory education laws. There is only a limited amount we can do for one another exchanging ideas and experiences: most of us going through this have had similar experiences, and though there is some satisfaction in hearing that we are not alone, that doesn't really help much. Banding together—e.g. joining in neighborhoods or communal groups—is not much of an answer either, for unless the laws change, the more we are concentrated, the more motivated will the authorities be to do something about us, and the more children we have in one place the more the dynamics will force us back into schooling patterns. But I think we are likely to need legal help at our farm as early as this fall—1977—and certainly in the future. I hope we can begin accumulating a directory of lawyers who are sympathetic and have some special knowledge of school law. (Ed. note—I suspect there may be a very few of these, but we certainly should know about them)

Write me—Downhill Farm, Hancock, MD 21750 (717-294-3345)—if you want to know more about anything I have said here or see some way we may be of help to one another."

For my views on the constitutional question, see the section "Unschooling and the Courts" in this issue of GWS.

NEWS FROM IOWA

Two families in a small town in Iowa, trying to unschool their children, have met rigid and angry opposition from the schools. One parent's request to teach her child at home has been turned down by both local and state school boards. The other family's appeal to the state board has not yet been heard, though the state Attorney General has ruled that in this matter the state board has no power. (Could the Governor have said, "Don't get me into that can of worms!")

In her appeal to the state board, one parent made (among others) these points:

"Iowa law provides for alternative education to that provided by public schools (a) if teacher is competent and (b) equivalent education will be provided. Specific provisions (229.0 and 229.4) authorize that such alternative education may be in the form of private instruction.

A. (The mother/tutor of the child in question) is (a) a certified teacher in the State of Iowa (b) otherwise qualified by experience and training as a specialist in education—formerly in charge of coordinating Head Start programs for six counties in Southern Minnesota. (c) has taken special courses of study, including a Montessori Diploma from London, England, and a degree in alternative education.

B. Education records of (the child) indicate her to have been evaluated as a superior student by the (local) school system as well as the open school (Wilson) which she attended in Mankato, Minn., and the school she attended in London, England. Much of this can be attributed to home instruction and environment.

C. In denying permission the (local) school board did not contest competence of teacher."

In spite of state law, and the overwhelming evidence of competence, the local Superintendent turned down the parent's request. Before her appeal could be heard by the state board, he requested and obtained a warrant against mother and child under the truancy statute. Pending the state hearing, mother and child went to live with relatives in another state. The child is now back home, enrolled in a local Catholic school. The mother has not yet, as far as I know, asked that school to allow and support a course of partial or complete home study.

(Though they are appealing on slightly different grounds, the other family expects the state board to turn them down as well. They plan to appeal to the courts; we have discussed by mail and phone what might be the best ground for this appeal.)

Both local and state boards, in ruling against the parent, said that her proposed program was not "equivalent," though neither said in what respects it was not so, or how it could or should be changed to make it so. I have suggested that the strongest appeal these families could make would be to say that the local and state boards, in acting as they have, have in effect nullified state law. Clearly the legislature meant to allow alternative methods of instruction, including individual tutoring. Clearly, by "equivalent" they did not mean identical; parents and/or tutors can obviously not do in a home everything done by a large school, and even if they could, why would they want to? The legislature clearly meant to allow people to do things *different* from what was being done in school: "equivalent" refers to results (i.e. that the child know how to read and write , be able to go to college, etc.) rather than specific methods.

The legislature did give local school boards the right to approve or turn down proposed alternative programs, but not the right to turn down all of them. The school boards must, then, stand ready to approve programs that meet certain requirements. These requirements must be public, explicit, and reasonable. The legislature cannot have intended that people would have to guess in advance what the school boards would approve. Nor can people be required to do the impossible, like provide their children a full-sized basketball court or machine shop.

I further suggested, and this seems to me a good idea even for people whose children (with the schools' consent) have been unschooled, that all *or any part of* the school's activities and programs should be available to all the children of the community, whether or not they are full-time students at the school. Nothing in the law or in reason says that if a child is not in school *all* of the time he has no right to be there *any* of the time. If school boards want to say that things which can only be done in school are an essential part of any "equivalent" program, then they have to let *all* children in the community, even those being tutored at home, into the school to do those things. Otherwise, they impose impossible requirements, and so, in effect, nullify the law. This argument, if upheld, would dispose of the schools' claim that home programs, by definition, cannot be equivalent because the child does not have the "social life" of the school.

This seems to me a kind of model for legal action in states whose laws specifically allow for alternative methods of instruction, whether or not they name home tutoring as one of them. In states (if there are such) where the law does not specifically allow for any instruction other than in state-approved schools, our best bet is probably to say that it should, that to impose a uniform theory and method of instruction on all the parents of the state is not a proper intent of the legislature, if that was in fact their intent. On this issue we might find other grounds for support in the state constitution, or in other laws relating to parents and children. If not, we might have to go into the Federal courts. But for reasons set forth elsewhere, I think we should avoid this if we can.

Meanwhile, as a happy city-dweller, may I observe that our "impersonal" big cities may be better places for unschooling than our friendly, kindly small towns.

MIXED ALLIES

Those who read GWS, and want to take or keep their children out of schools, may have very different, in some cases opposed reasons for doing this.

Some may feel that the schools are too strict; others that they are not strict enough.

Some may feel that the schools spend too much time on what they call the Basics; others that they don't spend enough.

Some may feel that the schools teach a dog-eat-dog competitiveness; others that they teach a mealy-mouth Socialism.

Some may feel that the schools teach too much religion; others that they don't teach enough, but teach instead a shallow atheistic humanism. I think the schools degrade both science and religion, and do not encourage either strong faith or strong critical thought.

Some feel that the school curriculum is dull, fragmented, devoid of context, in George Dennison's words, that it destroys "the continuum of experience." Others may feel that the school curriculum is fine, but that they don't do a very good job of teaching it.

What is important is not that all readers of GWS should agree on these questions, but that we should respect our differences while we work for what we agree on, our right and the right of all people to take their children out of schools, and help, plan, or direct their learning in the ways they think best.

In all these matters, we at GWS have our own opinions, and will express them. This is not going to try or pretend to be an unbiased publication. We will be very biased. But we will try to be as useful as possible to *all* our readers, whether or not we agree with them on all details. And on the issue about which we are all agreed we will print as wide a range of ideas and opinions as our readers send us.

WRITING IN SCHOOL

(From the Aug. 1977 issue of the monthly magazine *Mother Jones*)

Pumping Polysyllabism

"Two Chicago English professors have found that a good way to improve your grade on a term paper is to use what they call 'verbose, bombastic' language.

Professors Joseph Williams and Rosemary Hake say they took a well written paper and changed the language a bit. They kept the ideas and concepts the same, but wrote two different versions—one in simplified, straightforward language and another in verbose language, loaded with pedantic terms.

They then submitted the two papers to nine high school teachers; they were surprised to find that all nine gave the verbose papers nearly perfect scores but downgraded the straightforward essays as too simple and shallow.

The professors then submitted the same two papers to 90 more teachers and came up with similar results. Three out of four high school teachers and two out of three college professors gave higher marks to pompous writing."

Reason to wonder what these same college professors mean when they tell us, as they do all the time, that today's students "can't write."

JUST ENOUGH TEACHING

Not long ago, an extremely intelligent and capable friend (Ed. note—now a brilliant student at law school), not at all daunted by most forms of learning, and a lover of music, told me that she wished she could read music, but that ever since she had studied music in school, the task had seemed hopelessly mysterious, terrifying, and impossible. I asked if she could think of any special part of it that seemed harder than the rest. She made a large gesture and said "All of it. I just don't understand *anything* about what those little dots mean on the page." I asked if it was the rhythm or the pitch that seemed most mysterious. After some thought, she said the pitch. I then said (there was a piano handy), "If you like, I think I can show you in a few minutes how to find on that piano any given note." She agreed. Within half an hour she was very slowly playing, by herself, a piece out of a beginning piano instruction book.

Five things made it possible for me to help her to find out how to do this. 1) It was her idea, her interest; she wanted to do it. 2) I was at all times ready to stop if she wanted to. She knew that I would not, in my enthusiasm, push her into the confusion, panic, and shame into which eager or determined teachers so often push their students. 3) I accepted as legitimate and serious both her anxiety and her confusion. Even in the privacy of my own mind, I did not dismiss any of her fears or questions as silly. 4) I was ready to let *her* ask all the questions, to wait for her questions, and to let her use my answers as she wished. *I did not test her understanding.* I let *her* decide whether she understood or not, and if not, what question to use next. 5) I was not going to *use* her to prove what a gifted teacher I was. (Ed. note—I might once have done so) If she wants to explore written music further, that's fine. If she wants to ask me for more help, that's fine too— though even better if she can do it without my help. But if, having proved to herself that she can figure out what notes mean, she doesn't want to do more of it— well, that's fine too.

Editor—John Holt
Managing Editor—Peg Durkee

GROWING WITHOUT SCHOOLING

Issue No. 3

March, 1978

In its short life to date, GWS has already changed its character somewhat. It is turning out to be less about teaching than I thought it would be, and more about law, less about what your children can do once you get them out of school, and more about what you may have to do to get them out. I rather regret this. I am much more interested in helping children to explore the world and to find out and do interesting and worthwhile things in it, than I am in arguing about and fighting with schools. But it begins to look as if, like Moses in Egypt, we may have to find ways to make things a bit hot for the school Pharaohs, if only so that they will let our people go.

The dozen or so letters and phone calls I have had about this during recent months don't add up to much of a sample, perhaps not even a representative one. They suggest, though, that many people who ask their local schools to approve some kind of home study program are going to meet, not sympathy and support, not even intelligent questions, but threats—"We'll take you to court! We'll put you in jail! We'll take your kids away from you!"

So it may not be a good idea just to walk in cold into the Superintendent's office and say, "I want to teach my kids at home." It may be better to do some groundwork first. What kinds, GWS will discuss. If I had children, and wanted to teach them at home, I think I would ask someone from out of town, perhaps even out of state, to write the local School Board saying, in effect, " I am now teaching my children at home, am thinking of moving to your area, and am looking for a school district in which I can go on doing this. What requirements and conditions would I have to meet in order to be able to do this in your community?"

To put the question this way puts the School Board in bit of a spot. If they say, "It doesn't make any difference what you do, you can't teach your children at home under any conditions," they may be violating state law. In any case, such a statement will not look very good if the matter ever goes to court. If they say, "You must meet such and such conditions," and you later meet them, it will be harder for them to say no. If they begin asking prying or hostile questions, or do not answer at all—well, there is your answer. Whatever you decide to do next, you will not have revealed yourself to them.

Meanwhile, I hope that readers of GWS who have unschooled their children with the approval of the local schools will tell us how they did this. It may help us approach schools in other communities

NEW RECORD

We now have about 405 subscribers. A number of magazines have mentioned us, which has been helpful. *New Age* (Feb. 78) and *Radcliffe Quarterly* (Mar. 78) have run good stories about us. We plan to run short classified ads in a number of publications, to see whether this will bring in new subscribers and supporters. In the long run, what will best help GWS grow will be people who like it telling other people about it.

About half of our subscribers have individual subscriptions, the rest group subscriptions. In GWS #2 we said that the record group sub, 14X, came from a group of teachers in Seattle. The record has now moved to Milwaukee, where people at the Multicultural High School have taken out a 15X sub.

This school, by the way, sounds like a very interesting place, and may make Milwaukee a good city for unschoolers with high-school aged children. The local school system tolerates and even supports Multicultural as a handy place to put kids whom the regular schools don't know how to deal with. But the result is that it keeps the truant officers off the backs of many young people while they are doing useful work, earning some needed money, or studying and learning about the world in ways that make some sense to them.

AN IRONY

The Boston Globe of 2/28/78, in a story about school attendance, says, "On a typical day, about 70% of the school system's 65,000 youngsters attend classes." They say nothing about the missing 30%. Who are they? Why do they stay away? What do the schools do about them?

The answers are, probably, that most of them are poor; that they stay away because they hate school and can see, even if they haven't got anything much else to do with their time, that the school is wasting it; and that the schools do almost nothing to get them back.

There is irony here. As I said in an earlier GWS, compulsory school attendance laws were invented by rich people and aimed at poor kids. These rich people said in effect, "We educated people are perfectly capable of teaching our own children, but the poor don't give a damn about their kids and wouldn't know enough to teach them anything even if they wanted to. So, unless we lock up those kids in school all day long they are just going to run around the streets, cause trouble, get in bad habits, become drunks and criminals. We've got to put them in school to make them into good, obedient, hard-working factory hands."

The irony is that if you are in fact the kind of kid that compulsory attendance laws were first aimed at, you can skip school all year long and nobody will pay any attention. The streets are full of the kinds of kids that schools were designed to keep off the streets. But if you are one of those now rare people who really care about the growth of your children and are willing to take the responsibility for helping that growth, and you try to take them out of schools where they are not growing but shrinking, the schools are likely to begin shouting about courts and jails. Strange.

MORE FROM "D"

I asked D (see GWS #2) about the 'loophole' he referred to in Mass. law. He replied, in part:

"*Mass. General Laws Annotated*, Vol. 9 (Chapters 69-78), (West Pub. Co., 1969), Chapter 76—"School Attendance," section 1 of which states that 'attendance shall not be required of a child ... who is being otherwise instructed in a manner approved in advance by the superintendent or the school committee' (p. 429 of the edition specified above). The 'otherwise' in the context of the full section means 'other than in an approved school.' ... At the end of section 2 ('duties of parents; penalty') of this chapter (p. 434), however, the case of *Comm. v. Renfrew* (1955) 126 N.E. 2d 109, 332 Mass. 492, is cited, warning that *prior* approval, (which the Renfrews failed to obtain) is crucial—and without it parents are liable to be prosecuted ... as for those letters and numbers in the citation, this is what they mean: *volume* 126, in the *Northeastern Reporter* (N.E.), *Second Series* (2d), *page* 109; the same case is also cited in volume 332 of the Massachusetts state reporter, on page 492. (Ed. note—other states and regions will have comparable volumes and abbreviations) ...

Stephen Arons wrote an excellent article last year ... reprinted as a pamphlet ($1.00) by the Center for Independent Education (Box 2256, Wichita KS 67201), "The Separation of School and State: Pierce Reconsidered", in which he argues "that the Constitution protects the right of parents to pass their values along to their children." He emphasizes the First Amendment as preserving "individual consciousness from government coercion." ...

Another excellent pamphlet from C.I.E. (also $1.00) is *Litigation in Education: In Defense of Freedom,* By William B. Ball who was counsel for the defense in *Wisconsin v. Yoder* and in Ohio's *Whisner* case. ...

A year or so ago, the Committee on Academic Freedom of the American Civil Liberties Union began to study the matter of compulsory schooling; its chairman is David Cohen (ACLU, 22 E. 40, NY NY 10016).

About using lawyers, I know of several cases where a *letter* to school authorities from a lawyer convinced them at the outset of the strength of the parents' position and thus avoided prosecution, another where a lawyer was able to arrange a pretrial conference with the D.A. who then disposed of the case with a writ of *nolle prosequi,* and another where a lawyer was able to

get a case tried before the most sympathetic judge (who was an old ACLU lawyer, and ruled in favor of the parents); indeed, the latter particularly is the real value of getting a local lawyer—he knows the local courts and judges, and can really do some effective maneuvering for position."

Again, many thanks to D for more good research. If others of you send information to GWS, please try to be as complete as D about your sources, so we (or others) can look up the same material. And isn't it good to know that all those mysterious letters and numbers, that we have been seeing for years after law citations, in fact mean something quite simple and sensible.

I have read the Arons and Ball pamphlets and recommend both of them, but even more the Ball. If Arons is talking about what he thinks the courts *should do,* I and most of us will agree with him. If he is talking about what they are likely to do, he seems to me too much of an optimist. Ball seems more tough-minded.

I agree very strongly about the use of lawyers for maneuvering purposes. Even there, though, the more we can learn about how our courts run, who the local judges are, and so on, the better off we will be. One thing we might do well to find out is whether the *procedures* of a given court (in which we might someday find ourselves) are written down, and if so where. It would be useful reading. The more we know, and can show we know, about the law, the less likely the schools are to want to tangle with us.

FROM ALEX

Alex Marton; 11460 N.W. 30th Place; Sunrise, FL 33323, has written us a most interesting letter, saying in part:

"I really enjoyed issue #2 of GWS. I particularly got turned on by some of the legal questions covered in the letter from "D". I took his advice and went to the nearest law library, which happens to be at the Court House. By the way, the Court House Law Library is open to the public, at least, in my case, and you don't have to pretend being a student or anything because nobody really cares.

Anyone who is really interested in the general background of what the courts have said in relation to various claims by parents who were tried for failure to comply with their state's compulsory attendance laws can get an excellent overview in 65 ALR 3d 1222. Incidentally, this numbering system also is very simple: ALR stands for *American Law Reports*, 65 means volume 65, 3d means this is the third set of books (there as also ALR 1st and ALR 2d), and 1222 is the page number where the report starts.

For the record, I would like to raise issue with the somewhat optimistic view "D" seemed to convey with regard to some of the court cases favorable to Home Study. In point of fact, only *People v. Levisen* and *State v. Massa* are true home study cases. *People v. Turner* was actually decided *against* the parents, the court's position being that a 'private school' within the meaning of the compulsory attendance law was a formal or established type of institution; the court also pointed out that the state could not be burdened with the expense and difficulty of supervising 'schools' taking the form of parents instructing their own children at home."

———————————

I interrupt to note that this was exactly the point that one court made when it threw out the suit that some parents had brought against a school system because their child had graduated without knowing anything. The court said, in effect, if we let these parents get damages from the school, tens of thousands of other people will also sue, and this will cost the state too much money. One might say that justice, rather than the state's finances, ought to be the concern of the courts. It does not always work that way. The courts have an interest in keeping the machinery of government running, more or less smoothly, and they are not likely to make decisions which might threaten to bring the machinery to a stop.

———————————

"*State v. Peterman* had to do with a case where the child was taught in the home of a retired schoolteacher. The court held this situation to constitute a private school within the meaning of ... the compulsory education law. Not exactly relevant to home study, but at least a step in the right direction, although not much because the teacher was in fact certified by the state.

Wright v. State appears to be, in its language, philosophically more sympathetic to the parents' right to choose as they see fit. It suggests that if the moral training afforded by the public and private schools in a district should not comport with the reasonable requirements of the parents, and the parents are well able themselves to give or to obtain for their children instruction in the subjects in which the state can require instruction, and actually do so, the state cannot compel attendance at either a public or private school. Even here, the court recognizes the state's right to require instruction in specific subjects. How does the state insure that its standards are being met? (Ed. note—they are obviously not being met in most schools)

That was one of the points in *State v. Whisner*, where Rev. Whisner's religious school did not obtain state "approval" (actually never applied for it) because it felt that compliance with the school board's minimum standards would violate their free exercise of religion. It is interesting to note that the Ohio Supreme Court, which finally decided the case in favor of the school on rather abstruse interpretations of the "free exercise" clause, nevertheless ended by admonishing both parties on their overly litigious course in

search of a resolution, and suggested that Whisner himself might have saved himself much cost and embarrassment had he attempted to deal with the School Board by availing himself of the judicial review of the administrative proceedings guaranteed by such and such and so on. In other words, the court would have preferred Whisner and the parents to go through the morass of dealing with the bureaucracy because basically the court subscribes to the idea that the educational establishment has jurisdiction. It only ruled in favor of Whisner's school because it saw a threat to the free exercise of religion."

———————————

I interrupt again to point out that as a general rule, and in all kinds of cases, the courts do not want to hear cases unless the parties have "exhausted all available remedies." In other words, don't come up to our rung of the judicial ladder unless and until you have dealt with all the people on the lower rungs. There is a sensible reason for this. If everyone tried to bypass lower courts and go directly to the Supreme Court, the Supreme Court would have as many cases as all the lower courts put together—cases would come in a hundred times faster than the Court could decide them.

I am quite sure that this is one reason why the Supreme Court decided as it did in the matter of corporal punishment. There may well have been a majority of judges who felt that in the case before them the beating inflicted by the school was indeed excessive. But someone, at the very least chief Justice Burger—and it is worth noting that Chief Justice Warren before him was greatly concerned about the overloading of the federal courts—must have said, "Look, if we rule that this punishment was cruel and unusual and so prohibited by the Constitution, ten thousand people every year are going to come into the federal courts asking them to rule that *their* children's punishments were also excessive."

———————————

"Religion was also the prime element in *State v. LaBarge*, specifically an "unapproved" religious school. In all these "private school" cases where the school is a "religious" school, courts have interpreted the statutes rather strictly, and have relied quite heavily on arguments relating to First Amendment considerations. Again, there is not much here to comfort the parent who is not motivated by religious imperatives in his desire to withdraw from the established system.

Even in *State v. Massa*, where the mother taught her daughter at home, the favorable decision is guided by the fact that the New Jersey statute required attendance at a public school or ... to receive *equivalent* instruction elsewhere than at school. The parents were lucky and the court, in its summary, opined that defendant's daughter had received education equivalent to that available in the country's public school, and that there was no indication of bad faith or improper motive on defendant's part. *But* it also said that ... had the wording of the statute been something other than "equivalent" education, the whole case might have gone differently. In the end result, there is little sympathy to be found anywhere for the principled parent who simply does not want to have official education shoved down his throat.

The most encouraging note seems to come from *People v. Levisen*, the Illinois decision where the court said that (1) school is a place where instruction is imparted; its existence is not dependent on the number of persons being taught; and (2) the object of the compulsory education law is that all children be educated, not that they be educated in any particular manner or place. This is good news, although, to take things in context, the case is somewhat vitiated by the fact that the parents were Seventh Day Adventists and the withdrawal from school was somewhat religious in nature. I believe that the quotes from the court rulings sound like ringing calls to freedom when taken in isolation, but the true meaning of the decisions can only be evaluated by looking at the whole picture.

I can say one thing about what I learned in a couple of days at the library reading up on these cases, as well as on the many that went against the parents, and the commentaries appended to them. Courts have interpreted their state laws very close to the letter; decisions favorable to parents were on the second or third appeal; the precise grounds on which most of these decisions were made do not point in a direction that would make a principled parent feel optimistic about a future lawsuit involving him and his children. As a matter of fact, the experience of reading through these volumes gives me pause regarding the kind of society we live in, and the liberties we take for granted..."

Many thanks to Alex Marton for his good research and letter. I think we should heed his warnings. In most places, unschooling children will not be easy. The more we understand that it will be hard, and why, the better our chances of doing it anyway.

FRIENDLY LAWYERS

D also sent the names of some lawyers "who are sympathetic and know about unschooling."

William B. Ball (*very* sympathetic); Ball & Skelly; 127 State St.; Harrisburg, PA 17101.
Robert P. Baker; On The Square; Sarcoxie, MO 64862.
Helen Baker; 2555 Kemper; Shaker Heights, OH 44120.
David C. Gibbs; Gibbs, Craze, & Thompson; 6929 W. 130th St.; Cleveland, OH 44130.

To which I would add the name of a lawyer I met recently in Boston:

Steven S. Tokarski; Fletcher School of Law and Diplomacy; Tufts University; Medford, MA 02155

May I suggest that (except in cases of great urgency, where something must be done right away) people who want to get in touch with these lawyers write them a letter, and *not* call them on the phone. Writing takes more time for the writer, but saves it for the reader; a lawyer can read in a few minutes what we might spend half an hour trying to explain, Also, the law works by the written word, and it will be good for us to try to get our thoughts down clearly and simply on paper.

These lawyers are much more likely to stay friendly if they are not besieged by phone calls from unschoolers.

By the way, if some of our readers are lawyers, or know lawyers, who would like to be added to this list, please let us know.

NEWS ITEM

From a Cleveland, Ohio paper, Dec. 8, 1977.

"... Juvenile Court Judge Angelo Gagliardo in September found Tom and Martha Lippitt guilty of civil neglect charges for not enrolling their daughters Amy, 7 and Alice, 8, in state-approved schools. The charges were brought by the South Euclid-Lyndhurst School Board.

The husband spent a week in jail for not complying with the judge's order that the children be enrolled in a properly chartered public or private school.

Mrs. Lippitt and another woman operated a three-pupil unchartered school until Mrs. Lippitt and her children disappeared when Judge Gagliardo threatened to jail both parents and place their children in county custody.

Her husband, who is an insurance man and John Birch Society member, last night called public schools a cesspool. ...

Mrs. Lippitt said she will continue to teach her children herself, as she did while staying in six different locations with them while away. She is a former teacher."

Mrs. Lippitt has appealed the civil neglect charge—the news story does not say to what court. The judge has stayed a bench warrant for her arrest until the appeal is decided. I have asked my informant to send me any later news stories on this case. Perhaps some GWS readers who live in Ohio might look further into this.

Note carefully the words about the judge staying

the bench warrant for her arrest. In GWS #2 we told about a woman in Iowa who was denied permission to teach her own child. Since then I have read about a man in Greenwich, Conn., who was in fact arrested—police came to his house and took him off to jail, because he had been keeping a child out of school. In both these cases, and any like them that may come up, it would seem wise to ask the judge, as was done in Cleveland, to stay the arrest warrant until the case has made its way through the courts to some final decision. After all, according to the principles on which our legal system is based, we are entitled to be presumed innocent of any crime, including keeping a child out of school, until the courts have declared us guilty. This may mean that while the issue is being decided, which may take some time, we can keep the child at home.

MONEY

A friend writes "The kids don't get allowances. I don't even like the word in that context. If adults 'allow' children to have money than who 'allows' adults to have it? Each week $5 goes to each kid and it is called a share. The family receives about $75 a week from rental of income property and $20 of it is the kids' share to do with as they wish. A sort of guaranteed income. It's either a lot of money or a little depending on how you look at it. All real needs are provided by the adults as a gift. We have the connection and money-earning skills (Ed. note—and the legal right) to earn what is needed. We even have enough extra energy to provide a lot of the wants but some of them the kids have to get on their own. We provide honey—you buy your own sugar. We provide wheat and oats, you buy your own Cocoa Pops and Twinkies. Exceptions are numerous because we all like that junk but the point is still made—I buy my junk, you buy yours. If you are smarter than me you will buy less than I do.

On rare moments of weakness I get heavy and play God. S got sore at someone one day and smashed a glass in the middle of the road to demonstrate his feelings. I considered it a transgression on all our freedoms so I ordered him to clean it up. He did a sloppy job of it, maintaining his position. I asked him if he had cleaned it all up. He said he did. I asked him if he would pay $.10 apiece for any he had left. He said, "Sure." We all went to work and he paid. If he had said, "No, and you have no right to require me to pay," I would probably have backed down and found some other way to lean on him. The use and abuse of power is always a question only half answered. We try to keep the question fresh."

———————————

A nice way to put it. It *is* a tough question. One could say that the political history of the human race is one long struggle to find a decent and workable answer to it.

On money, a friend told me that when her daugh-

ter was about five she gave her an allowance of $.10 a week. The child had a couple of younger friends in the neighborhood, about 4 and 3, with whom she played, and it turned out after a while that she was giving *them* an allowance of a penny or two a week.

No two ways about it, little people want to do what big people do.

On the whole, I tend to think that children, particularly from the age of about eight on, should be given less money than many of them are now, but should instead be given a chance to earn much more than they do now. How much each family can afford or will want to give or pay a child they will of course have to decide, but it seems to me better if most of this is earned.

My reason is this. Thoreau, in his essay *Life Without Principle* (as fine as his essay on *Civil Disobedience*), said something about like this: "The cost of a thing may generally be reckoned, broadly speaking, as the amount of *life* that must be exchanged for it". A very important truth (under any kind of economic system), and important for even quite young children to learn. Children who ask themselves, "Is (or *was*) that toy, doll, game, etc. worth the time I will have to work (or did work) to earn the money to pay for it?" are asking a useful question. To use a phrase now much in fashion, they are "clarifying their values" (or at least some of them) in the only way values can be clarified—by making choices which cost something.

LEGWORK

A father called me the other day. For many good reasons he is thinking of suing his local school. Looking for a good lawyer to represent him, he asked advice from a nationally famous expert on Constitutional law. This lawyer recommended a lawyer friend. When the father interviewed that lawyer, he was surprised and discouraged to find that he planned to turn most of the work of the case over to a young assistant, who though he knew little or nothing about the law in this area, would charge him $50 for every hour he spent on the case. The father mentioned a book that he thought had an important bearing on the case; the lawyer had never even heard of it. Later the father said to me, "I'm not going to pay him $50 an hour to read that book. I can't afford to educate him at that price."

Quite right. He can't afford to, and he shouldn't. People who make $100 or more can afford to pay other people $50 an hour to do leg work and research for them. People who make $5 or $10 an hour have to do that leg work and research themselves and use the $50 per hour person to do *only* those things they can't do for themselves. Take this book the father thinks the lawyer should know about. The smart thing for the father to do is to go through the book, copy the pages he thinks are of the greatest importance, make a digest of the rest, and have the lawyer read that. It will take the lawyer a few minutes and cost the father a few bucks.

For a while at least, we are not likely to find many lawyers, anywhere in the country, who know as much about the law on unschooling as we know *or can readily find out*. This is not an issue about which lawyers, above all experienced and famous lawyers, have concerned themselves. We cannot count on them to work out good strategies and write good briefs for us—at least, not at a price that most of us can afford. We are going to have to do most of the research, decide what legal action we want to take, what courts (federal, state, or local) we want to go into, what kind of decision we want from them, put together all our necessary supporting evidence, statutes, citations, etc. and then show these to some lawyers, ask them what they think, and if they think we have a good case, ask them to polish it up and see if they can steer it through the courts.

EXPERTS

In the preceding piece I said that the parents had good reasons for wanting to sue the schools. When their child was six, he went to school. Soon after, on the basis of a *twenty minute* examination by a school psychologist, he was labeled "hyperactive" and put in a special class. Looking into it, the parents found out that most of the children in that class were seriously retarded. They took their child out of school altogether and, still wanting to obey the law, asked the school to send them a tutor. The tutor arrived and within a few minutes, in the presence of the parents, asked the child, "How long have you been emotionally disturbed?" The parents told the tutor they would not be needing his services, and the child has not been back to school since.

The story reminds me that I was traveling on a plane not long ago. As we got up to leave, I saw that in the row ahead a pleasant and intelligent looking young woman was reading a book called, as I remember, *Structure of Behavioral Disorders in Children*. She had another book with much the same kind of title. I assumed that she was studying to be a teacher, "Special Ed" teacher, or school psychologist, and reflected gloomily that she will probably do far more harm in her work than was ever done by an old fashioned teacher with a hickory switch, or even some of our present-day paddle freaks.

RIGHT AND LEFT

Schools get very upset and anxious about right and left. If a child writes a letter backwards, or reads off some letters in wrong order, or does anything else to suggest he is confused about right and left, adults begin to talk excitedly about "mixed dominance" and "perceptual handicaps" and "learning disabilities." The child is quickly labeled as "having a serious problem."

Specialists (if the school can afford them) are called in and told to take over.

A child once asked me a question that not only completely surprised me, but also suggested that when children are confused about right and left, the reason may be something wrong, not in them, but in *us*, the adults, and the way we talk about right and left. In short, the child's confusion *makes sense*, and if we only understood that, we might easily straighten it out.

I was in an early elementary classroom, working on something with some children in a corner of the room. I needed something in my desk, and asked a child if he would get it for me. He said OK, and asked where it was. I said, "In the top right hand drawer." There was a pause, Then he said, "Whose right hand, mine or the desk's?"

For a second, I was baffled. What on earth could he mean? Then I saw, and understood. When he looked at the desk, it was as if he saw a living creature, looking at him. So I said, "Your right hand." Off he went, brought back what I had asked for, and that was that.

Later, I thought that many young children must be animists, and see objects as if they were living creatures. I wondered how many of them might have had that same question in their minds, without ever getting round to asking it. And if they didn't ask it, how did they ever learn the answer? I decided after a while that one way or another they learned it from experience. They went to the desk, looked in *its* right hand drawer, found nothing, looked in *their* right hand drawer, found what they wanted, and so learned which was meant. Like the infant I described in *How Children Learn*, who at the dinner table asked people to pass her the salt, pepper, butter, etc. so that by seeing what was passed she could find out what those words meant.

But some children might not interpret the desk experience in that way. They might assume that the adult had made a mistake about the drawer. Or they might think that they themselves had made a mistake about which was right and which was left. The kind of children who *worried about mistakes* (because their parents or teachers worried) might be particularly ready to blame themselves for any confusion.

Only recently, as I began to think about writing this piece, did I realize that our adult rules about right and left are even more confused than I had thought. Thus, when we ask a child to get something out of our right hand coat pocket, we mean the *coat's* right hand, not the child's. When we talk about the right headlight of a car, we mean the car's right hand. The right hand (or starboard) side of a boat is always *its* right hand. But the right hand entrance to a house is *our* right hand, not the house's. In short, we adults talk sometimes as if things were people, and sometimes as if they were not, and there's no rhyme of reason at all in the way we do this. Why should a car or boat or train have its own right side, but not a house?

In the theatre, of course, the confusion about whose right or left is meant, the audience's or the actors', was so great the they invented the words "stage right" or "stage left" to mean the right or left of the actors as they looked at the audience.

Under photos of groups of people, we see, "Reading from left to right, Jones, Smith, etc." A child, being shown such photos, might hear someone say; "That's me over on the right." Our right? Or the right of the group? So the people on the right are really on the left, and vice versa. Some children might see this as more of the world's delightful nonsense. But other children might think in panic and terror. "Why don't they make up their minds which way they want it? How do they ever expect me to get it straight?"

We might well ask, how do any of us ever get it straight. Most of us get it straight the way we learn the grammar of our language, which is so subtle and complicated that (I am told) no one has yet been able to teach it to a computer. Children learn very early that the words "I, you, she, etc." refer to different people depending on who is saying them. Not an easy thing to figure out, when you come to think about it. Yet no one ever explains that to them. Nor do they say to themselves, somewhere in their growing up, "*I* refers to the person who is talking, *you* to the person talked to, *we* to both of them together, and *he, she,* or *they* to the people talked about." They just use the words that way, and it works.

In the same way, children don't think to themselves, "Cars, coats, boats, trains, planes, all have their own right hands, but photos, books, desks, houses do not." They just learn from experience which is which, and don't worry much about the contradictions, just as most French children don't worry about why a house should be feminine and a building masculine, or a coat masculine and a shirt feminine.

In short, most children master the confusion of right and left because they never become aware of it, any more than I did until just a few days ago. Others may become aware of the confusion but are not troubled by it and don't feel any need to set it right or make any sense of it—it's just the way things are. But some children, like the boy I wrote about in "Serious Teaching" (GWS #2), are philosophers. They examine everything. They like things to make sense, and if they don't, to find out why not. And still others are threatened and terrified by confusion and paradox, above all, by seeing people act as if something made sense when it obviously doesn't. At some deep level of their being, they wonder, "Am I the one who's crazy?"

I suspect that most of the children who have persistent trouble with right and left in school or in life are of this latter kind. After a few right-left mistakes, which they make only because they have not yet learned our crazy right-left rules, they begin to think, "I must be stupid, I never can figure out right and left." Soon they go into a blind panic every time the words come up. They work out complicated strategies of bluff and avoidance. When people ask about right and left, they learn to get other clues. ("You mean the one over there by the window?", etc.). In general, they assume (which they were all too ready to assume in the first place) that there is something wrong with them.

If this is true, or to the extent it is, what might we do about it? One thing we should not do, which the schools are very likely to do if they ever buy this theory of mine, is to set out to "teach" the rules of right and left, as they now "teach" the rules of phonics, or colors or shapes or sounds, as if no one ever learned anything unless it was taught. I can just see workbooks with lists of things that have their own right hands, and things that do not, and daily tests for the children, etc.

Most children have always figured out right and left without much teaching, other than being told when very little, "This is your right hand, this is your left foot, etc." Let them go on learning it that way. But if a child seems to be confused or anxious about this, then we can begin to make the rules more explicit. We can say, "I mean *your* right hand, not the desk's," or "I mean the *coat's* right hand, not yours, perhaps adding, "I know that sounds a little crazy, but that's just the way we do it, don't worry about it, you'll get used to it."

EAST AND WEST

Thinking about right and left brought back an old memory. Years ago a teacher of geography told me of a most interesting and surprising discovery. Teachers who teach young children about maps and directions find out that some pick it up quickly. But others, when shown a map and asked to point East, act like the children I described in *How Children Fail*—wave their hands in all directions while carefully reading the teacher's face for cues, watch their smart classmates, bluff, fake, wait it out, and so on. Most teachers let it go at that. Good students, bad students, you get all kinds.

But somewhere a serious teacher, unwilling to accept failure and blame it on the students, noticed something. A few children, shown a map and asked to point East, almost always pointed wrong, *but always in the same direction.* In time, people looked into it further. They found that a certain small percentage of people, some of them children, some adults, had a very strong sense of direction. It was as if they had a compass in their minds, or as if under their feet the ground was everywhere marked with direction lines. Whether their compass and direction lines were correctly labeled, whether the East they pointed was in fact true East, I don't know. But they always pointed the same way.

My mother had that kind of sense of direction. Driving without a map on strange, winding, suburban roads, when the rest of us had long since lost our bearings, she always knew about where we were, which way we were headed, and which way we needed to go to get where we wanted. An inborn gift? Perhaps, though some have probably learned it, like old sailors. At any rate, for children with such a gift, the question, "Which way is East?" can only mean, "Which way is *true* East, or *World-East?*" If we understood this, we could make the distinction (which we ought to make anyway) between *world-East* and *map-East.* Once children understood the relation between maps and the territory being mapped, which we could help them see by making maps of their room, the house, the yard, the block or neighborhood, the town, etc., we could then ask questions like, "If you were here (showing a point on the map) and began to walk East, show me on the map where you'd be going." Or we could walk first, and then see on the map where we had walked. After doing this a few times, a child would be able to show map-East, map-North, etc.

I talked to a teacher friend (Math) about this. He laughed and said that when he was a kid he thought for quite a few years that North, world-North, was straight up, and world-South straight down, since all the maps he had seen in school were on the walls. In time, he figured it out for himself—*by* himself.

Recently these thoughts about East and West have led to a new thought. Suppose there were some people who thought that Right and Left, like East and West, referred to something *in the world itself,* in short, that Right meant world-Right and Left meant world-Left. How could they ever figure out, from our talk about Right and Left, which was which? One minute world-Right would seem to be here, the next minute there. We can hardly imagine their confusion and terror. Most of them would soon decide that they were just too stupid to figure out what seemed so easy for everyone else. Small wonder they would fool psychologists. They would talk and act just as if something was indeed wrong inside their skulls or skins. Yet they (or we) could clear up all that confusion if they (or we) just thought to ask a couple of the right questions.

What to do? Above all, keep calm. If a child shows some confusion about right and left, don't panic, give him plenty of time to figure it out for himself. Some things we could do might help. When we first tell the child which is our Right hand and which our Left, it would probably be a good idea for both to be facing the same way, the child standing in front of us or on our lap. At some point, facing the same way, we might each hold a toy in our right hand, and show that when we are facing the same way, the right hands are on the same side, but that when we turn to face each other, the right hands are on the opposite side. Probably not a good idea to talk very much about this, or try to explain it, or in any way make too big a production of it. Just show it casually now and then, as another interesting fact about the world.

Beyond that, we should not assume, because children know that this is the right hand and this the left, that they understand all about right-hand drawers and coat pockets and headlights, in short, all our crazy rules about right and left. For some time, when we talk about such other things, we should point out which side we mean. If the child seems unduly puzzled or anxious about all this, then we can make the right-left rules more explicit.

In my mind's eye I can see a little right-left reminder—a little rug, or piece of heavy cloth, or wood, or even cardboard, with an outline of the child's two bare feet, side by side, the right foot marked R, the left

L. When the child stands on it, with his feet pointed the same way, he can tell which is which.

If any of you ever had as children, or have now, these (or other) confusions about right and left, I will be grateful if you will write me about them. Or, if you try out some of these ideas with your own children, let me know how they work out. Above all, let me know if you have some right-left ideas of you own.

TEACHING MACHINE

When the Santa Fe Community School was just starting, a young inventor, who hoped to market one of the "teaching machines" then much in fashion, lent one of his models to the school. It was a big metal box, that sat on top of a table. Through a window in the front of the box, one could see printed cards. Beside the window were five numbered buttons. On the card one might read something like this: "An apple is a 1) machine 2) dog 3) fruit 4) fish 5) musical instrument." If one pushed button #3, a little green light went on above the buttons, and a new card appeared behind the window. If one pushed any of the other buttons, a red light went on. In short, like most "teaching machines," it was a rather fancy way of giving multiple choice tests.

On the day the inventor brought the box to school, the children, aged 5 through 8, gathered around the machine to see how it worked. The inventor showed them how to use it, and for a while the children took turns pushing the buttons and answering the questions on the cards. This only lasted a short while. Then the children began to say, "Open the box!" Someone opened up the front panel, showing the cards, mounted on a revolving drum, and beside each card, on the drum, five little holes, and a metal plug to stick into the hole matching the "right answer" on the card. The children considered this a minute, and then all fell to work—*making cards.* After a while they all had some cards to load into the machine. Bargains were struck: "I'll play using your cards if you'll play using mine." One child would load up the machine with his cards, and put the answer buttons in the right places, then another child would come and take the test, then they would trade places. This went on for perhaps a day or so, all very serious.

Then, so the friend told me who was teaching there at the time and saw all this, the game began to change. There was much loud laughter around the machine. The teachers went to see what was going on. What they saw was this. A child would load the machine, as before, and another child would take the test. Up would come a card saying something like, " A dog is a 1) train 2) car 3) airplane 4) animal 5) fish." The child taking the test would press button #4, the "right answer," *and the red light would go on.* The cardmaker would shriek with laughter. The child being tested would push the buttons, one by one, until he or she hit the right one and the drum turned up the next card. Then, same story again, another right answer rewarded with the red light, more shrieks of laughter. When one child had run through all his rigged cards, the other would have a turn, and would do exactly the same thing. This happy game went on for a day or two. Then the children, having done everything with the machine that could be done with it, grew bored with it, turned away from it, and never touched it again. After a month or so the school asked the inventor to come take his machine back.

This little incident tells us more about the true nature of children (and all humans) and the way they learn about the world (if we let them) than fifty years worth of Pavlovian behaviorist or Skinnerian operant conditioning experiments. Sure, "Psychologist and Pigeon (or Rat. etc.)" is a good game, for a while at least. But everyone wants to play Psychologist; nobody wants to play Pigeon. We humans are not by nature like sheep or pigeons, passive, unquestioning, docile. Like these children, what we want is to find out how the machine works, and then *to work it*. We want to find out why things happen, so that we can make them happen. Maybe we want this too much; in the long run (or not so long) it may be our undoing. But that is the kind of creature we are. Any theory of learning or teaching which begins by assuming that we are some worm-like or rat-like or pigeon-like creature is nonsense and can only lead to endless frustration and failure.

LEARNING MUSIC

The Oct. 5, 1977 issue of *Manas* quotes, from the book *Piano: Guided Sight Reading*, by Leonard Deutch, this interesting fragment:

"The famous Hungarian and Slovak gypsies have a century-old musical tradition. This colorful folk has brought forth numerous excellent instrumentalists, notably violinists. They learn to play much as an infant learns to walk—without teaching methods, lessons, or drills. No written music is used. *The youngster is merely given a small fiddle and allowed* (Ed. italics) *to join the gypsy band.* He gets no explanations or corrections. He causes no disturbance, for his timid efforts are scarcely audible. He listens; he tries to play simultaneously what he hears, and gradually succeeds in finding the right notes and producing a good tone. (Ed. note—I do quite a bit of this playing by ear in my cello practicing) Within a few years he has developed into a full fledged member of the band with complete command of his instrument.

Are these gypsy children particularly gifted? No, almost any child could accomplish what they do. *The band acts as teacher talking to the pupil in the direct language of music.* (Ed. italics) The novice, by joining the band, is immediately placed in the most helpful musical atmosphere and psychological situation; thus, from the beginning, he finds the right approach to musical activity."

NEWS FROM CA.

"... we have moved to .... This was an effort on our part to take G (10) and D (9) out of isolation and into the world where there are other answers to people to relate to other than public school. In some ways it appears (we have been here such a short time) to be successful. The children are not going to school this year and as a family we enjoy the quietness of the school hours for family things. Then when school is out there are 12 children here in our townhouse complex of the ages for G and D to have a variety of friends. They appear to be a compatible group. It is just that we find these children tend to bring home with them a lot of the actions and attitudes that they learn at school and thus the interaction among the children is very similar to a school situation. However, at home G and D are free to walk away from it, and also we are hoping that we might be a positive influence that will help these children to see there are other ways.

So far we haven't been hassled about the children not being in school. The landlord and all the other families in the complex know they aren't. They don't understand but don't seem to have any desire to cause us trouble. One child asked G if she didn't go to school. When G said No the girl replied, "What do you do? Just stay home and be dumb?" G and D have learned to play it cool and just drop the subject. The Librarian asked G the other day to take part in a project and asked her when she gets out of school so they could plan the time for the project. G told her two o'clock. I asked her why she just didn't tell her she wasn't in school and G said, "I just wasn't in the mood to hassle all the questions that follow." (Ed. note— smart G! This is not a matter about which, unless I knew them very well, I would trust most public officials)

...While it is true that our children were enrolled in public school last year they attended only a short time. We took an extended trip from the end of Sept. to the first of Dec. The children went back to school when it reopened in Jan. Then the snows came and closed the schools for 19 days in Jan. and Feb. The last of Feb. we took another trip and were gone until the second week in April, at which time the children went back to school but only a few days a week (whenever they chose to go). ... G did happen to be there for the achievement tests though and that proved something interesting too. G had been turned off Math through a bad experience in the fourth grade and we told her to just tune it out until she felt she wanted to try again so all through last year she just didn't do it. (Ed. note—the smartest thing to do.) If she was given a page of multiplication to do she added them, as she likes to add. But because she was absent for one day of the tests she had to make them up and thus got to see her folder and how she had done on the tests she had taken earlier. She scored above grade level even in Math. She says she is just a good guesser as she didn't know at all what she was doing. But this story just confirms what you and we already knew about achievement tests!"

This sounds like an unusually relaxed school system. More and more schools are threatening to fail children, *no matter how much they may actually know*, if they miss more than a few days of school. This widespread and growing (and inexcusable) practice of using grades for disciplinary purposes or to compel attendance is something GWS will have much more to say about.

AND N.J.

Nancy Plent (see Directory) writes, in part:

"Enclosed is some information on New Jersey school laws for your files. [*A Digest of Laws and State Board of Education Regulations Regarding Private School in New Jersey*—from State of New Jersey, Department of Education; 225 West State St.; Trenton 08625] Pages 2 and 9 have the information unschoolers want. (Ed. note—will quote these sections at end of this letter) As you can see by the digest, New Jersey makes it easy to start a private school, and they leave you alone once started.

Please be sure my name and address are in the next directory. I have a N.J. teacher's certificate and plan to file the affidavit which makes me a private school. I may be able to help someone else with these two items.

I've long planned to teach my son, Eric, now 6, at home. Before GWS, I was waking at night in a cold sweat just thinking about the conflicts involved. I was going to do it anyway, but on my gloomy days it feels good knowing that someone else out there agrees with me. I have no such support here and would really welcome mail from other N.J. people, or anyone for that matter.

A couple of things I've learned that may help others. One of my first steps was to call the ACLU. They promised to research the laws for home education if I gave them my reasons in writing. They also referred me to an Education Law Center. I don't know (Ed. note—I don't either) whether this kind of office is unique to N.J., but it seems to me that other states might have similar offices tucked away somewhere. A few phone calls might locate it.

The lawyer I talked to there was very encouraging and had no inclination to defend public education to me. He told me about the Massa decision and that I might have to prove equivalent instruction, the key words in N.J. He recommended having a well-organized curriculum to show, and set hours of study. (I'll be able to "show" this, but I don't live well organized with set anything.) His final advice was to confront the local principal with my plans as a matter of "professional courtesy." He explained—if someone sees you out during school hours and reports you, the principal will feel foolish and annoyed that he isn't on top of things in his district and will come down on you harder.

I know you disagree with this (Ed. note—not always), and D felt it was wrong. This is a small town I live in, however, (pop. 1200). As you have pointed out, it isn't as easy in a small town. Besides, I was raised in the best American tradition (Ed. note—not unique to us) of guilt and fear. If I tried to hide out during school hours, every phone call and ring on the doorbell would start my heart pounding furiously. No, for cowards like myself it's best to put the whole thing out in the open and have several alternative plans ready in case you lose.

So far, the local school doesn't seem to know what to do about me. Since I was courteous and matter of fact with them, I'm getting back the same treatment. (Ed. note—it doesn't always work that way, but it's still a good way to begin) The board lawyer asked for an outline of my educational plans after I called the Massa decision to their attention. I'm waiting for their reply to my reply. I'm sure I'll stop promoting the direct approach if they decide to take me to court. The idea is far from appealing. ...

After sending to Calvert and Home Study Institute, I got to wondering how hard it would be to start a correspondence school. The state sends out a thick pamphlet on instructions and procedures. It is *much* harder to do than to start an actual school, but not impossible. I feel that it might be helpful at a later time to have an approved correspondence school in each state. (Ed. note—I agree) The danger here of course is that the authorities feel so comfortable with duly approved stuff that they might eventually disallow a parent's curriculum. ...

This past October I placed an ad in *Mother Earth News,* looking for parents doing home education. I thought I'd start a newsletter or *something* just for contact. (Thanks for doing it first!) It was my last desperate attempt to find an alternative to starting a school. ...

The first answer to my ad was from D, and he told me about GWS. After months of this very alone feeling, you can see why I walked around with a silly grin for days after getting my first copy. ...

About lawyers. I agree we are better off not to have ourselves interpreted and thereby watered down by them. I'm keeping mine informed just in case, but I find that the very act of having to explain my position to others has strengthened me. Being deeply involved, parents become more informed than a lawyer takes time to be. Chances are also good that in a short time any parent can be better informed than the local school board on school laws and alternatives, which certainly can't hurt.

One private school in N.J. was started by two couples who refused to send their children to public school. I have the name of the lawyer who convinced the school board not to take them to court. One of these mornings I'll write to ask about her availability for similar cases, and will pass along her name if she is interested.

I hope more stories about the lives of unschooled people (I think that term is beginning to unnerve me!) will reach GWS. (Ed. note—I see her point. Why don't we just use the word "unschoolers" to refer to people who are trying to get their children or themselves out of school or did so at some time in the past?) We all want to believe that our children will lead happy, even exciting lives as a result of what we do, but most of us have to operate on faith. Actors' children or child actors get to stay out of school and we can all see that they have some elusive advantage over most of us. But most of us don't personally know any actors' children or *any* children who have lived very long without schooling. No matter how firm our commitment we all need reassurance.

My only success story for unschooling: I had a boy in my first third grade class who always handed in a cartoon for a book report, drew cartoon figures all day instead of doing his school work, spelled his entire 20 word list wrong (words like CAT and PLAY) but defiantly added "Mississippi" and "hippopotamus" at the bottom, spelled correctly, and questioned the necessity for every assignment. Enough to unglue any new teacher, especially when his mother vigorously defended him. Eventually she took him and her other four children out of state and just avoided the authorities. Last year this same boy (now 24) had a book published on cartoonist Max Fleischer. News of him and the rest of his offbeat, creative, busy family always cheers me and renews my faith in what I'm doing.

That's all I have for now. I'll be happy to hear from anyone in N.J. who contacts you."

———

Thanks for a fine letter. The digest of N.J. laws on education says on p. 9 that people must cause children between 6 and 16 to attend school "or to receive equivalent instruction elsewhere than at school." On page 2 it says, "The state Department of Education is not charged with approval of private elementary schools nor private day kindergartens. Such schools which may include all, part, or some combination of grades from kindergarten through eight, do not need a license to operate."

At least, they don't need a state license. They may require some kind of local approval, and they will probably have to conform to various Fire, Health, and Safety codes, which in some states, at least, are so drawn as to make it virtually impossible to call a home a school.

As for that third-grader, about the only thing that a really bright child *can* do in most classrooms, to keep from being driven crazy with boredom, is to raise Cain one way or another.

And it may not be long before some group of professionals, trying to create still another monopoly for themselves, will be able to lobby through the N.J. legislature some sort of law requiring elementary schools to have a license from the state—all this in the name of "raising standards." Perhaps not. Anyway, let's make use of all such opportunities we can find.

A BABY

A mother writes about her 19 month old baby:

"The lumpkin is booming. *Understands* English—even tries to hang up his coat if you ask him to. If anyone (or two, I mean) are kissing he stands there smacking his lips till he gets kissed too. Learned how to pull his chair up to the counter to get 6 doz. cookies at once. Sets up a course in the bedroom, over and under things, and goes over and over it. Loves to dance—last night with bouzouki music on the radio he put his arms up in the air and danced with such seeming accuracy a Greek sort of dance that I decided he must have been a Greek mountain man with an affinity for dancing in the past."

(A month or so later) "He is really into talking, but not making much sense to us yet. He sounds so sure of himself, has so much variety and inflection, that I think he's pretty sure of what he's saying. He does have several real words which he uses quite clearly, got 'snow' and 'truck' (Ed. note—important words for this mountain family) the other day. I am sort of keeping track of them in the order they come in, and may eventually teach him to read those words in that order, seeing as how they must be awfully important for him. Still no word for me, or for B [his father] either for that matter. Probably because we're ever present."

CAPABLE CHILDREN

A friend, S, writes:

"I am making lists with the kids. We each have a list of what we do during the day and cross off as we do them. In the grocery store we each have a list of the stuff we need to get, each person having certain things to get. I got my typewriter fixed and the kids take turns typing on it. If they both want to do it, we use a timer so each person can do it a certain number of minutes. ... M is making the sauce for lasagna and F is waiting for the water to boil to put in the noodles. (Ed. note—M is 6, F is 4).

M has learned his letters since he was 1 or 2 but hasn't learned words because, I can see now, I was trying to sound them out. We found a box of cardboard letters at the thrift shop. He spelled out a sentence in a book that he got from the library, and we picked out the letters from the pile and made the words on the rug. That was fun.

When M was less than 2, one of his favorite snack foods was peas. F was going to sleep in my arms and I didn't want to get up and make him any, so he got a pan out, put water in it, got a chair and got a package of peas out of the freezer, opened it (Ed. note—I would have thought that would be the hardest part), put them in the pan, and turned the fire on. From the time they were about 1 1/2 or 2 they have used knives (which had not been sharpened for a while) to cut vegetables and stood on chairs by the stove to cook French fries themselves. A couple of weeks ago they climbed up the ladder and helped D (their father) paint our mobile home roof white. (I'm too scared to climb up the ladder!) The thing is, any child could do the same if their parents let them. ... their children might get hurt ... but I don't think the risk is much greater, if at all, than the risk we'll get hurt doing the same things. Kids don't want to get hurt any more than we do. They welcome suggestions that will prevent them from getting hurt (such as putting French fries in with a slotted spoon instead of dropping them in with their fingers)."

I suspect children get hurt most often when doing things they are not supposed to do, in a spirit of defiance and excitement, rather than when doing something sensible and natural that they do often and like to do right.

The head of a big adventure playground in London once told me that when parents could come right into the playground, the children often hurt themselves, doing things to impress, scare, or defy their parents, but that once the parents were told that they had to wait for the children outside the playground (in a spot with chairs, benches, etc.) the accidents stopped.

S continues: " I don't feel I teach them enough, they seem to be turned off by my trying to teach them, but they seem to be learning some words or asking me about them by reading labels on food, names on letters, signs, and stuff like that. They are very interested , especially M, in numbers from looking at the calendar, playing SORRY (a board game), counting stuff, and most importantly, using money.

An interesting thing here: games that would seem to us to be innately competitive, they don't play that way. When we play "Slap the Jack," whoever's pile is getting low gets to "Slap the Jack" so he can get more cards. Or when we play SORRY, they make sure it's OK with the other person if they're going to send him back to Start, or we decide who has the most men out of his Start so his can get sent back. And when someone gets a man home we all clap and yell, "Yay! Yay!"

I've read this part many times, and every time I am touched by the thought of this game of SORRY, with everyone cheering when anyone's man gets home. It won't take much of school to knock that spirit out of those children.

George Dennison wrote eloquently about this in *The Lives of Children.* Even the toughest New York street kids, thrown out of public schools for their violence, understood that, as much as they loved and needed to win, what was most important of all was to have a good game and keep the game going. It's only when they come under the control of nutty adults that children learn to think, in the words of Vince Lombardi, that "winning isn't everything, it's the only thing."

ABE'S BABY

Manas is a weekly magazine, very much worth reading, hard to describe in a few words, other than to say that in plain, strong, nonacademic English it talks about old-fashioned important ideas like Truth, Meaning, Purpose.

The Jan. 4, 1978 issue had a quote from *The Farther Reaches of Human Nature,* by the famous (now dead) psychologist A.H. Maslow.

"Our first baby changed me as a psychologist. It made the behaviorism I had been so enthusiastic about look so foolish that I could not stomach it any more. It was impossible. Having a second baby, and learning how profoundly different people are even before birth, made it impossible for me to think in terms of the kind of learning psychology in which one can teach anybody anything. Or the John B. Watson theory of 'Give me two babies and I will make one into this and one into the other.' It is as if he never had any children. We know only too well that a parent cannot make his children into anything. Children make themselves into something."

He's right. Spending some time around a baby is about the best cure for behaviorism I know.

M AND THE STOVE

I asked S how M learned to cook so young. She replied:

"The stove. What could have become my first battle with M. He learned to turn the burners on. I said no, dangerous. Effect, naturally: *fun, interesting,* do it all the time. So I slapped his hand, slightly, grabbed him up, me in tears, was he? I don't even remember, holding him on the couch, what to do, what to do. Slowly it dawned on me. There wasn't a damned thing dangerous about him turning them on. I was always with him, could keep the stove cleared, his hand was way below the flames. What was I afraid of? *If people knew,* of course. So I let him turn them on, watched, kept my mouth shut. He turned them all on, went over to the table, stood on a chair, and watched them, turned them all off, back on the chair and looked at them (he was so far below the flame he couldn't see them by the stove, his hand just reached the knobs). How old? Less than 16 mos. Did this for a while, then a couple of times the next day, *and that was all,* he never 'played' with them again except to turn one on when he saw me getting a pan out to cook something in. Or after F was born to turn them on for himself, when he wanted to cook something. No, one other time when he was much older and his friend was over he thought it was funny to turn them on and see how afraid his friend became.

Why did he not respond to my 'no! dangerous!' Because there was no real fear in my voice. Children *will* respond to you when you say something's dangerous if you really are afraid they are going to get hurt *at that minute.* I read somewhere that you have to teach children to do what you say because if you don't they could be out in the street and a car coming and they wouldn't get out of the road when you yelled at them to. That's not the point at all. They're responding mostly to the fear in your voice in that situation, not to the fact that you're telling them to do something.

People are always worrying too much about the future, extrapolating out of the present, with children. They think, if I let them turn the burners on now, they'll always want to turn them on. ..."

I would add three comments to this (to me) sensible (but probably controversial) letter. First, the main reason M no longer needs or wants to play with the stove is that *he can cook on it.* It isn't a toy any more, but a serious tool, that he and the grown-ups use every day. Before they can drive, little kids love to sit at the wheel of a parked car turning the wheel this way and that. But who ever saw a kid doing that, *who could actually drive?* It would be baby stuff. And it would be baby stuff for M to play with the stove on which he (and his younger sister) regularly cook food that the whole family eats.

Secondly, the reason that M responds quickly to strong fear or other negative emotion in his mother's voice is that he doesn't often hear this kind of emotion. Children who constantly hear in the voices of adults the tones of fear, disgust, anger, threat, soon take that tone of voice to be normal, routine, and turn it off altogether. They think, "oh, that's just the way they always talk." Then when we really want them to pay attention to that car (or maybe dope peddler) coming down the street, they no longer hear us at all.

Finally, the panicky feeling that if I let children do some little thing now, even something that isn't bad, they will do some terrible thing later, is what makes so many schools and teachers (and parents) so obsessive and panicky about "discipline"—and is the reason they have so many discipline problems. As EVAN-G (see GWS #1) points out time and again, most of the children who get "corporal punishment" in school i.e. are brutally beaten, often with heavy paddles, are far too small to present any physical threat to teachers or school, and are beaten for trivial offenses that more often than not have nothing to do with discipline i.e. for being late, being sick, getting homework in late, doing badly on a test, forgetting to bring money for

something, or sneakers to gym class, and so on. By constantly asserting their coercive and punitive authority, the schools slowly destroy their moral authority, until for many kids the best reason of all for doing anything is that the school doesn't want them to do it.

A GIRL SKATING

This was the title of a short story, by Laurie Colwin, in *The New Yorker.* Ms. Colwin and *The New Yorker* have given permission to quote this excerpt:

" ... I did not want to be taught to skate. I wanted that mastery all to myself. The things you teach yourself in childhood are precious, and you have endless patience for them. My parents knew that I skated, but they knew that I did not want to be encouraged or given fancy sweaters for Christmas. I did not want them to witness my achievement, or comment on it, or document it. I did not want praise for effort."

CHORAL READING

Years ago, a psychologist friend of mine, "Dr. Robert Kay (Ed. note—I've lost touch with him, if anyone knows his address, or if he reads this, please write) told me about a very interesting way of teaching reading called Choral Reading. It was basically like the old "Sing Along With Mitch" TV show. The teacher would put on the board, in letters large enough for all the children to see, whatever they were going to read. Then she/he would move a pointer along under the words, and at the same time the children would read the words. The children who knew a word would read it; those who were not sure, would perhaps read softly; those who didn't know at all would learn from those who were reading. No one was pointed out or shamed, everyone did as much as he/she could, everyone got better.

For a few years, before the place became rich and stylish, my parents lived in Puerto Vallarta, Mexico. Now and then they used to visit a small elementary school not far from where they lived. The teacher taught reading through singing. The school was poor—now it is probably five times as rich, and has all the latest reading materials, and five times as many reading problems. The teacher wrote the words to a song on the board—perhaps a song that all the children knew, perhaps a new song that she taught them—and as she pointed at the words, the children sang them, and so doing, learned to read.

Any number of parents have told me this story: they read aloud to a small child, a favorite story over and over again. One day they find that as they read the child is reading with them, or can read without them. The child has learned to read simply by seeing words and hearing them at the same time. Though he probably couldn't answer questions about it, *he has learned a great deal about Phonics.* Nobody taught him to read, and he wasn't particularly trying to learn. He wasn't listening to the story *so that* he would be able to read later, but because it was a good story and he liked sitting on a comfortable grown-up lap and hearing it read to him.

LET'S READ

This is the title of a book, by Leonard Bloomfield and Clarence Barnhart (Wayne State Univ. Press; Detroit, Mich.), which could help many children *teach themselves to* read. This was not the authors' idea—they meant parents to use the book to teach their children to read. I think this is not useful or necessary and will in most cases be harmful. Learning to read is easy and most children will do it quicker and better and with more pleasure if they can do it themselves, untaught, untested, and helped only when and if they ask for help.

The first 59 pages are introductions and instructions. I urge that you ignore them. Much of them are a kind of running argument with the Look-Say people, who when the book was first published were in control of school reading and reading texts i.e. *Dick and Jane.* Bloomfield and Barnhart talk sensible about what was wrong with Look-Say and even say a few sensible things about what ought to be done instead. Thus, they do understand that since we *talk* in syllables, not single letter sounds, i.e. say "cat" and not "cuh-a-tuh" we should learn to read that way. But like most teachers they believed that children learn only what they are taught, and also that they learn best when they are taught one little thing at a time, getting each one down cold before going on to the next. They also have the child looking at picture stories to make sure he can read from left to right. Not necessary at all. In fact, much better *not* to talk about left and right in connection with reading—just show children with a finger which way it goes.

The authors also say that the child should learn all the letters of the alphabet, capitals and lower case, *before* starting to read. Again, not necessary at all. There is no connection between knowing the names of the letters in a language and being able to read, i.e. turn written words into spoken words, in that language. I can read (in that sense) in three languages in which I do not know any letter names at all. Knowing the names and order of letters is useful, but a separate task, which children can and will pick up easily as they go along. But we ought not to let this task clutter up the exciting adventure of figuring out what written words say.

On page 60 begins the good and useful part of the book. At the top of the page are all the one-syllable English words that end in *-an:* can Dan fan man Nan pan ran tan an ban van. Then come a number of short sentences using these words. On page 61 the *-at* words: bat cat fat hat mat Nat pat rat sat at tat bat, with sentences using both *-an* and *-at* words. Next page has *-ad* words, and the next pages, in order, words ending in -

-ap, -ag, -am, -ab, -al, then *-ig, -in, -id,* and so on. We could of course figure out those words for ourselves, but it is handy to have them all printed out, in big print. Each page has sentences using the new words of that page, plus all the words that went before. They don't make very interesting stories, but as the authors rightly point out, at this stage children find it exciting enough just to figure out what the words say. Later, when they have more words to work with, the stories get a little better. But by the time a child works her/his way to page 100 (or even much sooner) she/he will know enough about how the reading game works to start puzzling out real books, magazines, signs, cereal boxes, etc.

I see it as a book for a child to browse through. When my niece was about four, I gave the book to my sister, thinking she might use it to teach her. As I have written elsewhere, neither she, nor later, her younger brother, would stand for being taught—they just refused to go along. But the book was left in sight where the little girl could get at it, and she was encouraged to think of it as hers. Pages 60-65 are covered with little brown marks which I take to be her fingerprints. She must have spent quite a few months looking at those pages, thinking about them, before she figured out the system and went on to look at other books. I wasn't there when she was teaching herself to read, and as she did most of the work in private, often with her door shut, asking very few questions of anyone, no one knows exactly what she did.

I would guess that many little children would like to browse in *Let's Read* in much the same way. It is big, grown-up, official looking, obviously not a "children's" book. There are only four pages of line drawings in it; all else is print. But much of the print is large enough to be easy for little children to see, and of words small enough to be easy for them to figure out. If I had a young child, I would give her/him this book (along with others), and let her/him decide how she/he wanted to use it—if at all. If the child asked me to read it aloud, I would, perhaps moving my finger under the words as I read them. Though on second thought I suspect that some children would take this to be teaching and make me stop doing it. If the child asked questions about this word or that, I would answer. Otherwise, I would leave child and book alone. Some, or many, like my nephew, will not choose to use it at all. But those who do may find it a helpful tool. If you get it and use it, tell us what happens.

GNOMES

This book (text by Wil Huygen, illustrations by Rien Poortvliet, U.S. publisher Harry N. Abrams, Inc., NYC) is one of the most unusual, interesting, beautiful and wholly delightful books I have ever seen, for children, or for any one of any age with a love of nature and a taste for fantasy. Anyone who likes the Tolkien books will surely love it.

It purports to be a scientific study of Gnomes, their geographical range, habitat, physiology (there is a lovely illustration of a gnome skeleton), customs, diseases—everything that anthropologists might write about any strange culture. As such, it makes a little bit of fun of science and scientific studies, but such gentle and good-natured fun that I can't imagine that any scientist would mind.

Having once decided to write their book as a scientific report, the authors (as in all good fantasy) play it straight; they do not burlesque scientific reports, nor invite the reader to join them in making fun of what they have written. Their tone is absolutely serious, and they ask the reader to suspend disbelief and take their report seriously. In other words, they write as if (they might well ask me, "Why do you say '*as if* '?") gnomes really existed. They are, to be sure, less "objective" than most social scientists claim to be. They like and admire gnomes and clearly hope that the reader will too.

What makes the book, and not just for children, are the illustrations. The jacket says that Poortvliet is Holland's most popular illustrator, and one can well believe it. On every one of the 200+ pages of the book are the most beautiful water color illustrations. They convey very strongly the authors' love of nature and of animals, but they are not Disney-ish, preachy, or sentimental. The animals are animals, not people disguised as animals, not looked down on as "Man's dumb friends," but wild, strange, dignified creatures. The gnomes live among them as the first among equals, helping them out of traps, curing and healing their diseases and injuries, and receiving different kinds of help from them in return. The Gnomes, in short, are the kind of stewards of the earth that we have not yet learned to be.

I have given the book to a few friends of various ages, and all love it. It costs $15, and considering the number and beauty of the illustrations, is an incredible bargain. I have already read it through about four times myself, and expect to read it many times more. I can't imagine a book that I would more enjoy reading to or exploring with children. Do try it.

COUSTEAU SOCIETY

The Society (Box 2002, NYC 10017) has for years been exploring the oceans and ocean bottoms and learning about the creatures who live there. More recently, it has begun to struggle to save this ocean life from growing pollution. The society publishes an interesting magazine about its work, and also a calendar and posters which have some of the most beautiful color photos and printing I have ever seen. Children will like these. They like to know, and need to know, too, that the earth is still full of many strange, wonderful, and beautiful things, and also people doing exciting, demanding, difficult, and interesting work. The

people on the CALYPSO, the Society's research ship, are all sailors, explorers, divers, and scientists—a fine mixture, and proof that there is still work worth doing.

THE FLYER

With this issue of GWS we enclose a flyer, which we have make up for mass distribution, or for posting. One way to help GWS find more readers might be to get some of these flyers from us, and send them to friends, hand them out at meetings (if you think that useful and appropriate), put them on literature tables or on bulletin boards, or wherever you think people might see them. Most towns where there are many students or young people are likely to have many such b-boards, particularly where young people buy stuff or hang out, such as natural and organic food stores, bookstores, record stores, craft centers, etc.

If you should decide to use some of these flyers, may we suggest that you get some pressure-adhesive labels from a stationery or office supply store, put GROWING WITHOUT SCHOOLING and *your own address* on them, and stick the labels over the GWS return address on the flyer. Then people who want a sample issue of GWS, or who want to subscribe, will tell *you.* (You can get extra copies of GWS #1 from us—see above.)

This will have at least two advantages. You will know right away what other people in your community are interested in unschooling, and if people do want to subscribe, you can get them together in a joint subscription, and so save them some money.

Of course, it may not be a good idea to put your name on these flyers, or even to hand them out at all in your home town, if you have unschooled your children without the OK of the local schools.

Editor—John Holt
Managing Editor—Peg Durkee

GROWING WITHOUT SCHOOLING

Issue No. 4

May, 1978

As we go to press, we have close to 500 subscriptions. In recent weeks many more inquiries and orders for single copies, have come in because of articles or other material about GWS in *Radcliffe Quarterly, Mothering,* and above all, the Canadian magazine *Natural Life,* which has brought us many new subscribers from Canada.

As in the U.S., it seems to be easy to unschool one's children in some parts of Canada, hard in others. People are doing it in some of the Maritime or Plains provinces, also in Quebec. Others, in Ontario, have run into the usual troubles—police, arrests, etc. We plan to write about all this in more detail. Please send any news you have.

RADCLIFFE STATEMENT

The *Radcliffe Quarterly* invited me to write a short piece for their March 1978 issue. I wrote about GWS, saying, in part:

"The idea of 'education' seems to me to have embedded in it a number of ideas, all of them new-fangled, mistaken, and harmful. These include:

1) Learning is an activity separate from the rest of life, done best when one is not doing anything else, and best of all in places where nothing else is done.

2) Important learning is, must be, and can only be the result and product of teaching. What we learn for ourselves, from the experience of our daily lives, can only be trivial or untrue.

3) Teaching is best done, and most often can only be done, by specialists who do no other work.

4) Children cannot be trusted to learn about the world around them. They must be made to learn, told what to learn, and shown how.

5) Education is a people improving process; the more of it we have had done to us, the better we are.

6) People are raw material, bad in their original state, but almost infinitely processable and improvable.

7) People have no rights to refuse any processing or treatment that their betters believe will improve them.

.... Aside from being deeply rooted in the harmful ideas about education just listed, [schools] treat their students with what Charles Silberman, no sentimental child-worshipper, once called 'appalling incivility.' Beyond that, they are appallingly *incompetent* at their work, even as they define it, having always found it easier to blame all their failures on their students. Because the schools adamantly refuse to take the responsibility for the results of their teaching, they cannot even begin to learn how to do it. How much simpler to call students 'learning disabled' than to figure out why they are having trouble learning what the teacher is trying to teach. Worse than that, the informal, haphazard, and fumbling incompetence of the schools in their earlier years, which at least left some room for the work of a few serious, responsible, and competent teachers, is now being organized into a system, a pseudo-science, which leaves no room at all. To be a truly responsible and competent teacher at any level of the system, up to and including graduate school, carries the grave risk of not getting tenure or being fired. In the country of the incompetent, the competent are not kings but pariahs."

BATTING PRACTICE

The eight-year-old I talk about in "Rub-On Letters" lives in a little house on a small side street, really more an alley. Cars seldom come through, so kids can play there safely. In one part of the street there are high board fences on both sides, which makes it a good place for small ball games. My friend and her friends often play their own version of baseball here. For a bat they use a thin stick about three feet long. The ball is a playground ball about six inches in diameter. The rules fit the space perfectly; with that stick, no one can hit that ball over those fences.

The day I arrived, after dinner, she asked me if I would pitch some batting practice. I said "Sure," and we had about forty-five minutes worth in the alley. Next morning after breakfast she asked again, and we had about an hour more. Some of the time she very kindly pitched to me—I was amazed to find how hard it was to move that squishy ball with that skinny stick.

The point of the story is that in all this I did something of which I am quite proud, that I don't think I could or would have done even five years ago. In our almost two hours of play I did not offer *one word* of coaching or advice. The words were more than once on the tip of my tongue, once when she tried batting one-handed (she did better than I thought), once when she tried batting cross-handed (she gave it up on her own), now and then when she seemed to be getting careless, not watching the ball, etc. But I always choked the words back, saying to myself, "She didn't ask your for coaching or advice, she asked you to pitch batting practice. So shut up and pitch." Which I did.

Nor did I give any praise. Sometimes (quite often, as it happened) when she hit a real line drive. I let out a small exclamation of surprise or even alarm, if it came right at me. Otherwise, we did our work in silence, under the California sun. I remember it all with pleasure, and not least of all the silence. I hope I can be as quiet next time.

TO THE ACLU

I have recently written to Mr. Aryeh Neier, Director of the American Civil Liberties Union, more or less as follows:

"Dear Mr. Neier—Thanks very much for your kind invitation to take part in your National Convocation on Free Speech on June 13. ...

I think that compulsory school attendance laws, in and of themselves, constitute a very serious infringement of the civil liberties of children and their parents. This would be true, I feel, no matter what schools were like, how they were organized, or how they treated children, in short, even if they were far more humane and effective than they actually are.

Beyond that, there are a number of practices, by now very common in schools all over the country, which in and of themselves seriously violate the civil liberties of children, including:

1) Keeping permanent records of children's school performance. I would consider this inexcusable even if there were nothing in the records but academic grades, It is nobody's proper business that some child got a C in Social Studies when she or he was eight years old.

2) Keeping school records secret from children and/or their parents, a practice that continues even where the law expressly forbids it.

3) Making these records available, without the permission of the children or their parents, to employers, the police, the military, or to other branches of the government.

4) Filling these records, as experience has shown they are filled, with many kinds of malicious and derogatory information and misinformation. This may include, not just unconfirmed teachers' 'reports' of children's misbehavior, but also all kinds of pseudo-psychological opinions, judgments, and diagnoses about the children and even their families. For examples, see *The Myth of the Hyperactive Child*, by Schrag and Divoky (Pantheon).

5) Compulsory psychological testing of children, and including the results of these tests in children's records.

6) Labeling children as having such imaginary diseases as 'minimal brain dysfunction,' 'hyperactivity,' 'specific learning disabilities,' etc.

7) Compulsory dosing of children with very powerful and dangerous psycho-active drugs, such as Ritalin.

8) Using 'corporal punishment' in school, which in practice usually means the brutal beating of young children for very minor or imagined offenses.

9) Lowering students' academic grades, solely for disciplinary and/or attendance reasons. Not only is this practice widespread, but school administrators openly boast of it, though in fact what it amounts to is the deliberate falsification of an official record.

10) In all of these matters, and indeed in any conflict between the child and the school denying anything that could fairly be called 'due process.'

As long as such outrages go on, I can't get very excited about such issues as the controlling of violence and sex on TV, the rating of motion pictures, the censorship of student publications, or the banning of textbooks and library books on various grounds. People who argue strongly about such things, while accepting without protest the practices I here complain about, seem to me to be straining at gnats while swallowing camels. ...

To return once more to the matter of compulsory school attendance in its barest form, I think you will agree that if the government told you that on 180 days of the year, for six or more hours a day, you had to be at a particular place, and there do whatever people told you to do, you would feel that this was a gross violation of your civil liberties. The State justifies doing this to children as a matter of public policy, saying that this is the only way to get them educated. Even if it were true that children were learning important things in schools, and even if it were true that they could not learn them anywhere else (neither of which I believe), I would still insist that since in other (and often more difficult) cases the ACLU does not allow the needs of public policy as an excuse for violating the basic liberties of citizens, it ought not to in this case."

TESTING IN THE SCHOOLS

Peter Perchemlides, B-2 No. Village Apts., Amherst MA 01002, is fighting in court against the local schools for the right to teach his child at home. Not long ago I wrote him, in part:

"Since the schools are demanding the right to judge your program, I think you have the right, as a citizen, taxpayer, and the parent of the child whose education they wish to control, to judge theirs. More specifically, I would like to suggest that under the Massachusetts Freedom of Information Act you demand, and if necessary go to court to get, answers to a number of questions about your local school system, including the following:

1) At the various grade levels, how many hours of school time are allotted each week to *uninterrupted* reading—that is uninterrupted by questions, corrections, or demands from teachers? In short, how much of just plain reading are students allowed to do at school?

2) At the various grade levels, how much time each

week are the students allowed in the school library? What restrictions are there on the use of the library itself, or on the borrowing of library books?

3) In addition to those in the school library, are there books (other than textbooks or workbooks) in the classroom? How many, and how chosen?

4) At the various grade levels, how many children are reading below grade level (both national, and state)?

5) At the various grades, how many children are reading at least two years ahead of grade level? Since grade-level simply represents the national or state median, a serious parent would hardly consider it an acceptable standard for any child much more than eight years old.

6) Of the children reading below grade level two years ago, how many (among those still in the local schools) are now reading at grade level or better? In other words, how effective are the schools at *improving* the reading of students who are having trouble?

7) At each grade level, how many children have been designated as having 'learning disabilities?'

8) Of the children so designated two years ago, how many are now judged to be cured or freed of them? In other words, how successful are the schools in dealing with and overcoming these problems?

9) Same questions for 'emotionally disturbed.'

10) Same questions for 'hyperactive' or 'hyperkinetic.'

11) On the basis of what tests, of what duration, and administered, scored, and judged by whom, are these judgments about 'learning disabilities,' etc. made?

12) To what degree are school records, including these judgments, and results of other school-given psychological tests, available to the scrutiny of parents?

13) To what degree is it possible for parents who disagree with any such judgments to challenge them or seek independent confirmation of them, so as to be able to clear their children's records of possible incorrect and/or derogatory information?

14) At various grade levels, what percentage of children are being medicated with psychoactive or behavior modifying drugs, such as Ritalin? What medical examination do the schools give, and how often, and by what doctors, to check for possible harmful side effects of such drugs?

15) What is the policy of the schools about altering students' grades for reasons of discipline or attendance? What percentage of students in the system have had their grades so lowered?

16) Where grades have been so lowered for such reasons, what provisions have been made for students and their parents to restore the correct academic grade to the student's record?

You might consider some kind of community-wide publicity about this case. I imagine some kind of public statement, perhaps a letter to the editor of a local paper, perhaps an ad, saying more or less, 'There is much talk these days about the family being the most important influence on a child's life. We agree with this, and therefore want to undertake the primary responsibility for the education of our child. The superintendent of schools of this district, Mr......... is trying to prosecute us as criminals because we want to do this, and is threatening to put us in jail and to deprive us of the custody of our child. To this end he seems willing to spend quite a bit of the taxpayers' money, which might better be spent in improving the quality of the local school.' And so on. You might ask those citizens who feel you should have the right to teach your own child to make this view known not only to you but to the Superintendent and the local School Board."

———————————

These seem to me questions which people, whether unschoolers or not, might do well to ask in almost any school district. The schools' answers, or their refusal to answer, might in some instances make up a valuable part of a court case against the schools. Not all states will have Freedom of Information laws; you will have to check to find out. In states which do not, you might say something like this: since the courts have said, in two different jurisdictions, that people may not collect damages from schools because their children did not learn anything there, they have in effect established the rule of *caveat emptor*—let the buyer beware. This being so, the courts can hardly deny the buyer the right to ask questions about the product—schooling for his children—which in this case he is being compelled by law to buy. In some cases, at least, this argument may be enough to persuade a reluctant school system to answer your questions, or if not, to persuade a judge to tell them that they must.

FROM FLORIDA

A mother writes: "I got the information back I sent for from the [Florida] Dept. of Ed. on the rules for setting up a private school. There are hardly any! Here is stuff from page 1:

'References to non-public (private) schools are noticeably absent in the Florida Statutes and in the Fla. Administrative Code. The only direct or inferred references to these schools which are made are limited to registering annually with the Dept. of Ed., compulsory attendance, sanitation, voluntary participation in certain programs, incorporation, and distribution of student records. Aside from general business considerations the majority of their operations are not regulated in any manner.

Under the current statutes and regulations there are no laws governing at least those educational aspects of non-public schools listed below:

(a) length of school day

(b) length of school year

(c) certification, educational attainment, or

specialized training of teachers or administrators.

(d) content and comprehensiveness of the curriculum

(e) graduation requirements

(f) content, retention, transfer, and release of student records....’

[The mother goes on] But anyway, it’s unbelievable. All you do is fill out what looks to be a one-page form every year. I just can’t believe it’s so easy. (Ed. note—according to another mother who has been doing it for some years now, it is just as easy as it looks)... I wonder if other states are like that. (Ed. note—N.J. seems to be, and I have been told that starting your own school is very easy in Cal., Texas, and Oregon, though I have not yet seen the regulations for these states) Maybe I should write and find out.”

BEATING THE SYSTEM

In Jan–Feb ’78 issue of the British Magazine *Resurgence,* John West has an article, “How I Beat The System,” which I think holds some useful lessons for unschoolers. In 1954 he was completing his basic Army training, in Virginia, hiding from the Army his desire to become a writer, and wishing he could get sent to Europe. An Army-wise friend tells him how. He writes in part:

“The military hierarchy is modeled upon Kafka’s *Great Wall of China.* Yet, within this fabulous complexity, the destinations, and therefore destinies, of one and all at Ft. Belvoir are in the hands of one top sergeant; one old, bored, hung-over top sergeant buried in Administration HQ. ... The trick is to go see him three weeks prior to the end of training. But there is no legitimate way to work this. No one cares that I want to go to Europe. ... I wait for the appointed time, go AWOL for the afternoon, and head for the labyrinth where administration is being administered—the familiar knot of anxiety in the pit of my gut. It’s not being AWOL that terrifies me. It’s the prospect of having to bluff my way through the hierarchy to get to Sgt. Ffuffuff. I’ve been advised to think up a good excuse. I can think of none. Then, at the last minute my Muse responds. To the dreaming Pfc. at Reception I say, ‘I’ve been sent to see Sgt. Ffuffuff.’

And I’ve hit upon the magic word, the military ‘open Sesame!’ I’ve been ‘sent’, therefore am following an order, therefore I *must* get to see Sgt. F. ...Even Captains and Colonels will drop what they’re doing to point the way. I could get to see the President this way! I’ve been ‘sent!’

A variation of the same gambit works on Sgt. F. ‘Sgt. F,’ I announce, ‘I have permission to see you.’ Permission! It’s the other magic word. Someone in charge, an officer, has set his imprimatur upon my quest. It’s not Sgt. F’s to reason why. I don’t even know a phony excuse. I just tell him I want to get to Europe, and

mumble vaguely about carrying on with my studies when my service is up.

He rubs the sleep out of his eyes, rearranges empty coffee cups and overflowing ashtrays , extracts the document...Next to my name, on the otherwise virgin paper, he pencils in, ‘Europe if possible.’ and that is all there is to it.”

Only four soldiers were sent to Europe. West was one of them. The moral is plain. It pays to know how big systems work.

FROM L

L writes about his son, saying, in part:

“My wife and I did not begin with the notion that our son would not go to school. We named him Neil, after A.S., true, but assumed he would find an alternative school at age five. What we did begin with was ... a conviction that we would help him in any way possible to realize his potential. ... Since this meant that we were *available* (Ed. italics)—without ever being intrusive—he quickly began to *use* us regularly, hourly, for learning, and we found that by the time he was two we literally couldn’t stop him from spending his day in learning. He read very well by two, and by three and four moved into continuous lessons in nature, history, science, and so on. ... Here is an example: at three, in Central Park, he was looking at the pretty trees, and I mentioned that they could be distinguished from each other by type, this was an oak and that a beech, and others were like them. “Let’s make a map of all the trees in Central Park!” he said, having seen a map before. Well, normally this would have been shunted off, but since I really had been practicing what I preached we did indeed spend every day for the rest of that summer and several days a month in following summers making maps of all the trees in Central Park (almost all of it). I didn’t know much about trees, but we got a book to identify them, and one could find us every afternoon in the park, me trudging behind my son while he shouts, “One more hill daddy, it’s another Schwedler Norway Maple.”

By the time he was 5, he was so used to getting up in the morning with the ecstatic prospect of learning all day long that I hated to disabuse him of the notion that learning was natural by sending him to school. Still I took him to a few and asked him to make his own decision and of course he said he thought it would be like going to jail which he also thought he preferred not to try. Since he was not registered anywhere, no one knew of his existence so I didn’t have to test the New York State law which says only if home learning was “equivalent” to schooling could he legally be kept at home. (Legal research showed constant harassment of N.Y. parents who tried to prove equivalence, like saying home tutors could only be those who had N.Y.State teachers' licenses—I found anyone with a teacher's license to be useless as a tutor to a self-regulated child, so to this day the state still doesn't know he exists.)

During his early years my wife and I and a couple of friends taught him all he wanted to know, and if we didn't know it, which usually was the case, it was even better for we all learned together. Example: at 7 he saw the periodic table of elements, wanted to learn atoms and chemistry and physics. I had forgotten how to balance an equation, but went out and bought a college textbook on the subject, a history of discovery of the elements, and some model atoms, and in the next month we went off into a tangent of learning in which somehow we both learned college level science. He has never returned to the subject, but to this day *retains every bit of it because it came at a moment in development and fantasy that was meaningful to him."*

I have italicized those words because they seem to answer, I would hope for all time, the question I have so often been asked by defenders of compulsory learning and compulsory schooling: "How can a child know what he needs to learn?" I have always said, but never with an example as eloquent and persuasive as this, that though the child may not know what he may need to know in ten years, he knows, and much better than anyone else, *what he wants and needs to know next,* in short, what his mind is ready and hungry for. If we help him, or just allow him, to learn that, he will remember it, use it, build on it. If we try to make him learn something else, that *we* think is more important, the odds are good that he won't learn it, or will learn very little of it, that he will soon forget most of what he learned, and what is worst of all, will soon lose most of his appetite for learning anything.

Some might say that in helping him make that map of the trees in Central Park, L was acting as a teacher to his son. I would say that he was not so much a teacher as an energetic, enthusiastic, resourceful friend and partner. This is what children really like best. Popular children are the ones who are always thinking up interesting and exciting things to do—and they are even more popular if, when someone *else* suggests a good project, they willingly throw themselves into that. A child will say of another child, "Aw, he's no fun, he never wants to *do* anything." L is clearly not like that.

Some might read into L's letter the idea that learning means learning something out of a book, or having other people teach you things. I'm not sure whether L thinks that or not, I know I *don't* think it. Most of what I know I was not *taught,* in school or anywhere else, and most of that I did not learn from books—though I love books, read a great many of them, and get a lot from them. I learn a great deal, and more every day, by seeing, hearing and *doing* things, and thinking about what I see, hear, and do.

TO A DEAN

A good friend of mine is the Dean of the Dept. Of Education of a major university—I hope soon to be able to say which one. He wrote me, not long ago, saying that he thought that home study should be one of the legal choices offered to parents. I wrote back, saying , in part:

"I'm glad you feel as you do about home study. May I pursue the matter just a little bit further. You say that your main concern is 'to make certain that the child... is given the best chances for learning and developing.' I have to say first of all that nobody 'makes certain' that this is true of children going to schools. On the contrary, no amount of demonstrated brutality or incompetence on the part of the schools will enable children to get out of them. But beyond that, I wonder whether there really is any way to 'make certain.' If we say to people, in effect, 'You can teach your children at home, as long as you can give some sort of absolute guarantee that this will be best for the child,' the result will be that nobody will be able to do it. I think we have to say that people ought to be judged capable of teaching their own children unless someone can show beyond reasonable doubt, that they are not capable. The burden of proof ought to be on the state to show that people cannot teach their own children, rather than the other way round.

Later you speak of 'certain sensible and sensitive gate-keepers' to see that things work out OK. Here the problem gets very difficult. Plenty of judges and legislators would probably agree that many parents are indeed capable of teaching their own children, and even of doing this better than the schools. But they would surely insist that some are not capable. Who is to decide which is which? The trouble with giving this power to the schools is that it is a little like telling me that I can own any car I want, or even do without a car, as long as I have the approval of the local General Motors Dealer. The schools are by now a 120+ billion dollar a year business, based almost entirely on forced consumption, and they are not likely to make decisions which will let some of their unwilling customers escape.

In GWS #2, I describe a case in point. A mother in Iowa, certified to teach in that state, and with a great deal of teaching experience, was denied permission to teach her child at home by the local school superintendent (by all reports, a long way from anything you or I would consider a sensitive gate-keeper), a decision later upheld by both local and state school boards. In all this, no one challenged or questioned her competence as a teacher or asserted that her child would get an inferior education. She had in fact been teaching the child at home, and the child was by the school's own admission a superior student. All the local superintendent could say in defense of his decision was that if he allowed this woman to teach her child at home it would set a precedent.

It is a serious problem. If we say to people, 'You can

teach your own kids at home if the local schools approve,' we are effectively saying to the vast majority that, no matter what their qualifications or their plans, they cannot do it at all. But if we do not give school boards this power to decide who may teach and who may not, to whom will we give it? How will we judge?

I think of a boy I know, now twelve, who never went to school until he was eleven. When he first went, largely so that he could meet other children in a new town, he was given school tests, and tested at *12th grade* in reading! But he didn't even start reading until 8! Now, after not much more than a year of school, he has recently won a city-wide competition (in a large city) for elocution in Spanish, a language he never studied until the last year or so. Yet obviously, if people had given him standardized tests at age 7, they would have said on the basis of these that his home education was deficient and that he should be returned to school.

In other words, the question is not only *who* decides who can teach their children at home, but *on what basis.* If we say, for example, that children can study at home as long as they do as well on all school tests as students—or good students—in school, we change very little. The whole point of many of the people who dislike school is that they want to get away from its rigid timetables and dividing of the world into little water-tight compartments. All my experience leads me to believe that, aside from any of the other bad things it does, the school's way of structuring and ordering knowledge is *in itself* a massive obstacle to growth and learning.

I hope we can find a way out of this dilemma which will be acceptable on the one hand to people like myself, and on the other hand to professional educators as humane and enlightened as I believe you are."

FROM A TEACHER

A reader who has been doing some substitute teaching in a private elementary school, writes:

"I found myself ... in 3rd grade for four days. The two teachers team teach and so I had to team teach. Both are old-fashioned dedicated types who push math and reading workbooks. I almost went wild. I couldn't figure out the questions and answers (I refused to use the teacher's answer book) and the kids were frustrated and in pain sitting still. By the second day I could see these kids never had time to think let alone read as a pleasure—just word-grabbing, mind-reading work-books. In their room were paperbacks, *Charlotte's Web* and many more goodies not yet touched, because apparently the kids 'can't read well enough yet.' I went to the ... principal and said I couldn't continue unless the reading time while I was there became silent reading. She agreed to it but was not very happy about me, I could easily sense. I told the kids new rules, 'If you don't know a word and are really bothered by it,

signal and I'll come whisper in your ear. No sounding it out, no vowels, no syllables, no questions, just the word.' Very few asked after the first few minutes. But they asked for silent reading twice a day."

Jim Herndon makes much the same kind of report in his book *How to Survive in Your Native Land.* When he and one or two other teachers stopped asking the children questions about their reading, stopped grading them, stopped tracking them, *and just let them read,* they all read better, even the ones who had been very poor readers. But even that school could not think of anything so sensible and simple as 'a reading program,' and refused to learn anything from it.

Children reading for their own pleasure rarely stop to ask about words. They want to get on with the story. If the word is important, they can usually make a good guess about what it is. "He drew an arrow from his quiver." Easy to see that a quiver is some sort of gadget to put arrows in. More complicated words they figure out by meeting them in many different contexts.

People learn to read well, and get big vocabularies, from *books,* not workbooks and dictionaries. As a kid I read years ahead of my age, but I never looked up words in dictionaries, didn't even *have* a dictionary. In my lifetime I don't believe I have looked up even as many as fifty words—and neither have most good readers.

MOTIVE

Whenever I hear school people say, "The students aren't motivated, how do I motivate them?" I think of the story about the American anthropologist (I think it was Margaret Mead) and the Balinese.

This took place in the 1920's, when very few Westerners had ever been to Bali. The anthropologist was talking to some Balinese, trying to learn about this strange and very different culture. At some point she asked about their art. The Balinese were puzzled by this question. They did not know what she meant by art. So she talked for a while about art and artists in Western cultures. The Balinese considered this for a while. Then one of them spoke, "Here in Bali we have no art," he said. *"We do everything as well as we can."*

It is a sad story. In the cultures of the West, by now *the* world culture, there are so few people who do everything as well as they can that they seem very special (even peculiar), and we have to invent special names for them, special places for them to work, special uses for what they make.

The point of this story is that very little children are like the Balinese. Just about everything they do, they do as well as they can. Except when tired or hungry, or in the grip of passion, pain, or fear, they are moved to act—or "motivated," as the schools say— almost entirely by curiosity, desire for mastery and competence, and pride in work well done. But the schools do not recognize or honor such motives, cannot even imagine that they exist. In their place they put Greed and Fear. (To which the Peer Group, in its time, adds Envy.)

So when school people talk about motivation and not being able to motivate the kids, they are really saying, "What'll we do? They won't jump for our carrots any more, and they no longer fear our sticks." I don't know what to do about their problem. All I say is that it was a problem that didn't need to happen, and happened only because they made it happen.

But what about people who have taken their children out of school, children who have been numbed and crippled in spirit by years of "reinforcement," petty rewards and penalties, gold stars, M-and-M's, grades, Dean's Lists. How can unschoolers revive in their children those earlier, deeper, richer sources of human action? I don't know. I suspect the best thing to do is be patient and wait. After all, if we do not constantly re-injure our bodies, in time they usually heal themselves—if we don't pick our scabs they grow back into healthy skin. We have to act on the principle or faith that the same is true of the human spirit. In short, if we give children (or adults, for that matter) enough time, free or as free as possible from destructive outside pressures, the chances are good that they will once again find within themselves their reasons for doing things.

ON SAYING "NO"

Not long ago I visited a friend who had a beautiful, lively, affectionate year-old husky pup. The dog, with no identifying tags, had just dropped in one day, and my friend had not been able to find his owner. But the pup was happy in his new home, and showed no desire to leave. He had only one fault. He loved to be petted, and if you had been petting him, and stopped, or if he had just come up to you, he would put his paw up on your leg, let it fall, put it up again, and so over and over until you did *something*. This dirtied clothes, scratched skin, and hurt. His new boss had tried now and then to break him of this habit, by scolding him, pushing him away, or whatever, but it hadn't done much good. He was too busy with his work to spend much time on it, and hadn't really made up his mind (or understood) that the dog was his for keeps. One day I thought that as long as I was visiting, had some time, and was fond of the pup, I would take a shot at breaking him of this habit.

So, every time he came up to me I would pat him for a while and then stop and wait, my hand poised to block his paw when it came up. When he raised it, I would catch it, a few inches off the floor, and lower it gently, "No, no, keep the paw on the floor." Then I would pat him, say what a nice dog he was, and after a while stop again. Soon the paw would come up once more, and I would catch it and go over the whole thing once again, Sometimes I would do this with him sitting,

sometimes with him standing. After a few repeats I would back away from him; then, as he came toward me, I would say in a gentle but warning voice, "Now, keep those paws down," or "Now remember, four on the floor." I would have my hand ready to catch the paw when it rose, which at first it always did. But before long he began to get the idea, and quite often the tone of my voice, the sound of my words, and perhaps the position of my body and hand, would be enough to remind him, and he would keep the paw down. I was only there a few days, and won't claim that I broke him of the habit altogether. But he was much better about it, and usually only one warning and paw-catch would be enough to remind him.

The point is that even a little dog is smart enough to know that "no" does not have to be just a *signal*, an explosion of angry noise. It can be a *word*, conveying an idea. It does not have to say, "You're a bad dog, but we're going to scare or beat the badness out of you." It can say instead, "You're a good dog, but that isn't what we do around here, so please don't do it any more." Even a little dog can understand that, and act on it.

And if the dog, why not a child? There is no reason why, except in rare times of great stress or danger, we cannot say "No" to children in just as kind and gentle a tone of voice as we say "Yes" to them. "No" and "Yes" are both *words*. Both convey ideas which even tiny children are smart enough to grasp. One says, "We don't do it that way," the other says, "We do." And most of the time, that is what they want to find out. Most of the time, except when overcome by fatigue, or curiosity, or excitement, or passion, they want to do right, do as we do, fit in, take part.

Not long after my visit with friend and dog, I visited two other friends, and their smart and altogether delightful fifteen-month-old boy. Around dinner time, in the little kitchen-dining room, I took out my cello and began to play,. The baby was fascinated, as I hoped he would be. He stopped what he was doing and came crawling across the floor toward the cello at top speed. His parents looked a bit nervous, but I said, "Don't worry, I'll defend the cello, I won't let him hurt it." He came to the cello, pulled himself up to a standing position, and began to touch and pluck at the strings, below the bridge. At the same time, keeping the bow (which he might have been able to damage) well out of his reach, I plucked the cello strings above the bridge, and made nice sounds. Now and then I could see that he was being overcome with a wave of excitement, and that he wanted to bang on the cello, as little babies do. But when his hands began to make these impulsive gestures, I would catch them, like the paw of the pup, and slow them down, saying softly, "Gently, gently, easy, easy, be nice to the cello." When his motions grew smaller and calmer I would take my hands away. For a while he would caress the wood and pluck at the strings. Then he would begin to get excited again. But as soon as he did I would catch and slow down his hands again, saying as before, "Gently, gently, nice and easy." After a while he would crawl away, while I talked a bit with his parents. Then I would play some more, and he would come crawling over for more looking and touching. I might have to say, "Gently, gently," once or twice, but hardly more than that. Most of the time this tiny boy, still just a baby, was as gentle and careful with the cello as I was. And all this in only one evening, the first time he had ever seen such a strange and fascinating object.

A SINGLE PARENT

Ann McConnell; 386 Prospect St., New Haven, Conn. 06511, writes, in part:

"I am writing you in response to your note in the most recent issue of the *Radcliffe Quarterly*. ... As a feminist single mother I cannot help but wonder what exactly the implications are supposed to be for the real lives of my child and myself. The lives of mothers and children are not determined separately; for better or worse, our fates are bound up together. The fact is I do not know how I would survive if my daughter were not in school.

Here is my situation: I am deeply in debt, on account of having been in law school for the past three years. I decided to go to law school, as it happens, in response to the pressures of trying to support myself and child through do-good jobs and welfare. My daughter is now 6 years old and attending first grade in the local public school. She is unhappy there, although the school is known as a "good" one, and regularly comes home outraged at all the indignities she is subjected to e.g. she is not allowed to go to the bathroom when she wants to, *or talk during lunch,* or draw on the reverse side of her school papers when she is forced to wait.

The italics above are mine. I interrupt to say that I hear quite often about schools, often "good" schools like this one, where children, even very young ones, are not allowed to talk at lunch. Is this the great "social life" the schools like to talk about? Convicted criminals in maximum security prisons are allowed to talk at lunch. Why not first graders?

I have some friends who are working in schools, or in schools of education, and who like to think of themselves as "educational reformers" or "humanistic educators." I feel like saying to them, "Here is a modest goal for you to work toward. Try to change the schools just enough so that children will be allowed to talk at lunch. Until you can do at least that much, I don't want to hear any more talk about all you are doing for educational reform."

Ann McConnell continues:

"She also does not seem to be learning to read or

do arithmetic at anything that seems to me to be a reasonable rate. And although it is clear to me that she has an extraordinarily logical and creative mind, she has begun to develop a sense that in her teacher's eyes she is actually 'dumb.' She begs me not to make her go to school. I am sympathetic—but the only alternative is to let her come to law school with me, and she dislikes that too (not without reason). Next year I have a job as Visiting Assistant Professor at the University of Miami Law School, which will, unfortunately, mean I am busier than ever. (Ironically one of the courses I plan to teach will be 'The Rights of Parents and Children.') Money will be a problem ... So I certainly doubt that I will be in a position to hire any sort of mother/teacher surrogate. We also do not know any circle of friends who might take up the slack. (Sometimes I know such arrangements do work out, but one plainly cannot count on this.) What, then, can I realistically do to provide my daughter with an acceptable environment in which to live and learn? I frankly do not know.

It seems to me that although the details of my problems are unique, its general structure is almost universal. A scarcity of time and money, a need to cope. The trouble is not that I or other concerned parents are insufficiently 'radical' in outlook. I was in fact quite prepared to drop out as long as it seemed to me that that was the most authentic means of handling human existence. But my practical and human need to live in a 'public' social and economic world proved inescapable. I recognized, moreover, that my daughter's need was not to have a mother dedicated to creating an immediate 'ideal' world for her: she too has to ultimately live in the world I inhabit. This seems as though it would lead to a pat solution, but it doesn't; for it is never clear at what point one begins to rationalize the outrageous. Instead, I like so many friends find myself in a perpetual quandary.

The one thing I am certain of in thinking about my daughter now is that a 'solution' to her problems will have to take mine into account too. I don't know whether I am saying all this to you in the hope that you will have anything immediately helpful to say, but since in the past you have had much to say that was useful, maybe if you recast your thinking about the lives of children as thinking about the lives of mothers-and-children, you would come up with something. I hope so anyway."

A REPLY

"Dear Ann,

Thanks very much for your good letter. I understand your problem, at least a little, because for most of the eight years or so I've known her, a good friend of mine has been in the same spot. For a number of these years she worked to support herself and her child. Then she studied to get a Master's Degree in Education, and is now in her second year at law school. During all that time it would have been very difficult for her not to have had her child in school—though of course, like you, she had to make other arrangements when school was not in session.

However, I think I know her well enough to say that if at any time during those years her child had been really unhappy at school, or had been asking her not to make her go to school, or even if she had felt that school was doing the child real harm (as it does to most children), she would have made other arrangements, however difficult that might have been. As it was, because the child's father could and did pay for private schooling, she was able to send her to a quite nice elementary school, where the child was quite happy, and could learn about the world in her own way. One result of this is that (though her teachers were always worrying about her reading) she now reads four or five years ahead of most children her age. Her last two years of (public) school have not been very interesting, but she has at least been free of most of the anxieties and pressures that torment other children, and by now has ways of finding out about the world on her own. She is also good at sports, and liked by the other children, which helps.

I gather that your own situation is more difficult, in that you are not able to afford anything other than public school. If this is in fact so, it seems that your only choices right now are either to take the child with you wherever you go, or to leave her in school. May I suggest that even now, and certainly in the very near future, you may have other choices.

To take first the matter of custodial care, I would agree, or at least would not dispute, that a six year old needs some sort of babysitter. But I would say most emphatically that this is not true of a ten, or even an eight-year-old. In other words, I think (because people have done it) that if you began to train and educate your child toward independence and self-reliance, in two years or so (perhaps less) she would be perfectly able to spend large amounts of time at home by herself. By that time she would know who and how to call for various emergencies, how to provide for her own needs (getting meals, etc.), and how to occupy herself happily and constructively with any one of a number of activities.

Of course, she may not want to do this. But, were she my child and I in your shoes, it is a choice I would want to offer her. In other words, I would say to her that for some time to come she was going to have one of three choices or perhaps only two—1) To go with you wherever you go, staying out of other people's way and occupying herself as best she can 2) To go to public school, which will certainly be as bad as (or even worse than) the one she is in now 3) To stay at home, for much of the day and maybe all day, by herself. Then I would say, 'If you want to take the third choice, you are going to have to get ready, practice, learn a number of things, like how to cook and take care of food, how to look up numbers in the phone book, how to talk to strange adults over the phone, and how to find interesting things to do all by yourself for many hours at a stretch. Do you want to do all this? It's OK if you don't, but then the only other possibility is school, and the chances are we won't be able to find a school you like any better than the one you are in now.'

You can give her plenty of time to think about this, talk it over, and so on. But she will have to decide. If she decides to go for independence and self-reliance, you can start working on that right away. If this possibility interests you, perhaps in later letters we can talk more about how to do that.

I have put the choices rather extremely, go to school or stay home all day by yourself, to prepare the child for the worst possible case. In reality, the choices may often not be quite that extreme. Thus, starting at whatever time of day school lets out, you will probably be able to make arrangements for the child to visit other children, or have some of them visit her. Or there may be other places she may be able to go to, one example being the children's room at the Public Library. After school lets out the child is no longer an outlaw and it will be safe, as far as truancy is concerned, to be seen in public places. If you are living in a large city, and she has learned to become self-reliant, which will mean among other things being able to use maps, find her way, and use whatever public transportation may be available, there may be a number of interesting places where she can go by herself.

Also, you may be able to find and afford people to be with the child not for the whole day but for a few hours, and perhaps in that time to take her to some places she might not be able to go by herself. In short, once we get past the idea that there has to be an adult with her every minute of the day, the problem becomes more manageable. And you may even be able to find some people to do this without pay, perhaps on some sort of barter arrangement. I'm not sure what kind of skills you have to swap, but I suspect you have quite a few of them.

The other question is, can you, and without spending a ton of money, make your home, probably a small apartment, into a place in which your daughter *could* spend many happy, interesting, and fruitful hours by herself? You not only can, but you can make it into an environment far more varied and productive than anything she is likely to find at school. GWS will in part be about ways to do this. And are children in fact *capable* of spending long hours happily and productively without constant adult supervision and attention? Yes they are—after all, and not so long ago, large numbers of them used to do it all the time. You will have to respond generously to her need and requests for attention and friendship when you come home. But you will surely want to do that anyway. And it will be helpful if, as far as she wants to and you are able to, you let her share in your daytime life—something that will get easier as she gets older. My friend's daughter, at age ten, went a number of times to law school classes, and often found them quite interesting.

I hope some of these ideas may be of some use to you, and I would like very much to know, if you can find the time to tell me, how you feel abut what I have suggested here."

ADDITION

In GWS #1 there was a short piece on Counting, about ways in which parents could introduce numbers to little children, so as to avoid the panic and confusion they cause in so many people. Here I would like to take these ideas a bit further.

Sometime during first grade most children will be told, and asked to write down and to memorize, that 2+3=5. This may be called "a number fact," or "an addition fact," or both. They will be given a list of such facts to memorize and repeat on demand. Their books and teachers will "explain" and illustrate this fact in different ways, such as showing a picture of two baby chicks, then one of three baby chicks, then one of five baby chicks—or some other "cute" thing that little children are supposed to like.

Another number fact that the children will be told is that 3+2=5. They will almost always hear it as a separate fact, not connected with the fact 2+3=5. Some children will wonder why the two number facts come out the same. Once in a great while, one of them will ask why. If the teacher is old (and fortunate) enough never to have much training in the New Math, she/he may answer something simple and sensible like, "They just do, that's all." If the teacher has had some of the New Math, the answer may be something like, "Because addition is commutative." This is just putting a big mystery in place of a little one. If the child understood what "commutative" meant, he/she might say, "I can *see* that it's commutative; what I want to know is, *why* is it?" But children don't say things like that, they just slump back in their seats thinking, "One more thing that makes no sense."

Meanwhile, they go about the dull rote work of committing all those unrelated facts to memory. To spur them on, there are plenty of tests, questions asked before the whole class, lots of opportunities for mistakes, humiliation, shame—the usual scene. After a year or so of this, a few children are good at parroting back those number facts, while most don't know them and never will—they have already joined the giant Army of people who "can't do Math."

In second grade the children will be told two new "number facts" or "subtraction facts." One is that 5-2=3, the other that 5-3=2. Again, they will hear these as

separate facts, not connected with each other or with the addition facts they met in first grade. Again, their teachers and textbooks will give various explanations of what subtraction "means." In one "good" school I taught in, there was a near civil war about this. One group of teachers wanted to say that 5-3=2 means or can mean, "What do we have to add to 3 in order to get 5?" This is how people count change in stores—they begin with the amount of your purchase, then add change and bills to it to equal the amount of money you gave to them. A perfectly sensible method. But the other faction in this school, including the head of the Lower School Math department, denounced this as "additive subtraction," and told the elementary teachers that they must not use *or allow the children to use* this way of thinking about subtraction, that they had to think only in terms of "taking away." For all I know, the school may still be doing this.

At any rate, there are the children, struggling in the face of growing anxiety (theirs and their teachers') to memorize all these disconnected and meaningless facts, as if they were learning the words to a song in a language they did not know. Small wonder most of them never learn them. (In five fifth grade classes I taught, in "good" schools, less than half of the children could add and subtract reliably, even small numbers without using their fingers, or making little dots on paper, etc.

None of this is necessary. The truth is that 2+3=5, 3+2=5, 5-2=3, and 5-3=2, are not four facts but four different ways of looking at *one* fact. Furthermore, that fact is not a fact of arithmetic, to be taken on faith and memorized like nonsense syllables. It is a fact of nature, which children can discover for themselves, and rediscover or verify for themselves as many times as they need or want to.

The fact is this:

If you have before you a group of objects—coins, stones, etc., which looks like the group on the left, then you can make them into two groups that look like the ones on right. Or—this is what the two-way arrow means—if you have two groups that look like the ones on the right, you can make them into a group that looks like the one on the left.

This is not a fact of Arithmetic, but a fact *of nature*. It did not become true only when human beings invented Arithmetic. It has nothing to do with human beings. It is true all over the universe. One doesn't have to know any Arithmetic to discover or verify it. An infant playing with blocks or a dog pawing at sticks might do that operation, though probably neither of them would notice that they had done it; for them, the difference between ***** and *** ** would be a difference that didn't make any difference. Arithmetic began (and begins) when human beings began to notice and think about this and other numerical facts of nature.

Early in human history people began to invent special names to talk about that property of a group of objects that had to do only with how many of them there were. Thus, a group of five kittens, a group of five shoes, and a group of five apples have in common only that there are the same number in each group, so that for each kitten there would be one shoe or one apple, with none left over. And it is a property of the number 5 that it can be separated into the two smaller numbers 2 and 3. It is another property of 5 that it can be separated into 4 and 1. And it is still another property of 5 that these are the *only* two ways in which it can be separated into two smaller numbers. If we start with 7, we can get 6 and 1, or 5 and 2, or 4 and 3; with 10 we can get 9 and 1, 8 and 2, 7 and 3, 6 and 4 or 5 and 5. Every number can be split into two smaller numbers in only a certain number of ways—the bigger the number, the more the ways. (There is a regular rule about this, a simple one, which you might enjoy finding yourself.)

Once we get it clear in our minds that

$$***** = *** **$$

is a fact of nature, we can see that 3+2=5, 2+3=5, 5-2=3 5-3=2, whether we put these in symbols or in words, ("plus," "added to," "take away," etc.) *are simply four different ways of looking at and talking about that original fact.*

What good is this? The good is that instead of having dozens of things to memorize, we have only four, and those all sensible. Once a child can turn ***** = *** ** into 3+2=5 or any of the other three forms, it can look at any other number, find out how it may be split into two parts, and then write down all the ways of talking about that.

Thus a child might take ********, find out by experiment that it could be split (among other ways) into ****** and **, and then write down 6+2=8, 2+6=8, 8-2=6, and 8-6=2—and then do the same with 7 and 1, or 5 and 3, or 4 and 4. In short, all the number facts that children must now *be given,* and then memorize, they could discover and write down for themselves. The advantage of this is that our minds are much more powerful when discovering than when memorizing, not least of all because discovering is more fun. Another advantage is that so much of Arithmetic (and by extension all Mathematics) that now seems mysterious and full of coincidences or contradictions, would be seen to be perfectly sensible.

One last point. On one of the times when I talked about this to some teachers, one man said that his school was already teaching Addition this way. It turned out that what he meant was that in their textbooks, for every "number fact" i.e. 4+3=7, there was an illustration of four baby chicks, three baby chicks, and seven baby chicks (or whatever). But this completely missed the point I was trying to make, and am making here. ** *** = ***** is *not* "an illustration" of the fact 2+3=5. ** *** = ***** *is* the fact, and 2+3=5 only one of a number of ways of talking about it and putting it into symbols.

ANN REPLIES

Ann McConnell wrote back, in part:

"My daughter and I have come to a solution ourselves. I agree with you entirely that she deserves to participate in any decision about whether or not she goes to school. Even at age 6 she is almost (but not quite) capable of taking care of herself during the day at least. So the possibility of letting her stay at home by herself does not seem ridiculous to me. I already sometimes leave her for an hour or two alone. She takes messages on the phone, makes peanut butter and jelly sandwiches, and puts on phonograph records. Still, I don't think she could be happy spending the majority of her time in a solitary state, simply because she happens to be a very sociable person. That in fact is the basis of one of her primary objections to school: *the teachers there place too many barriers to interpersonal interaction.* (Ed. italics—in short, they prevent social life)

One idea I have had though about helping her to read in a non-school setting is to hire a nine-year-old I know who is a good reader to help her. (Ed. note—a wonderful idea, which I hope other readers will try out) . The nine-year-old is the son of a good friend of mine and he is currently in trouble at the same school my daughter goes to because he has been choosing to read *A Tale of Two Cities* under his desk instead of working on his workbook. The age difference strikes me as about right: C doesn't have to feel inferior due to the fact that A can read so much better than she, because he is obviously three years older. A seems to like the idea too. (His seriousness is being treated as a positive advantage, for a change). I'll see how this goes, but it is occurring to me that maybe I have hit upon a large part of the solution to my problem.

Next year we will be moving to Miami. I will certainly have a lot more (money) than I have now. I will try to find some sort of reasonable private school for C to go to. (Though I shall certainly be discussing with her the possibility of staying home from school entirely.) There are several things that Miami offers a child that New Haven does not: a children's theater group, the chance to learn Spanish, and easy access to swimming. All of these opportunities interest C greatly. So the importance of school may not be so great there. I hope so anyway."

———————

So do I. It will be interesting, next year, to hear how things go.

The workbook. The schools no longer surprise me, but they still amaze me. I think of a boy I knew who went off to a "good" boarding school. Until that time he had been interested only in Science. That was his path into the world. Literature, books, reading, unless closely connected with Science, did not interest him at all. The school "exposed" him to Dickens. He loved Dickens so much he started off on a project of reading *all* of Dickens's books—quite a project for a thirteen- or fourteen-year-old. Was the school pleased? No. They wrote scolding letters to the boy's mother about his never having his English assignments done, even threatened to fail him in English.

RUB-ON LETTERS

The GROWING WITHOUT SCHOOLING at the head of each issue, and the titles for each section, have been made with a gadget called RUB-ON Letters and Numbers (E.Z. LETTER QUIK STIK, P.O. Box 829, Westminster, Md. 21157). The letters are inked onto the back of a heavy piece of clear plastic. You put the plastic, ink side down, on a piece of paper, then rub on the top of the plastic, over the letter, with something pointed (but not so sharp as to pierce or cut the plastic) like the tip of the cap of a ball point pen. This forces the ink onto the paper. When you can tell from the look of the plastic (the letter looks more gray than black) that you have rubbed all the ink off, you lift up the plastic, and there the letter is, sharp and black on the paper, just as if it had been printed.

I took along a set as a present to an eight-year-old I was visiting. When I arrived, she and a friend were there. I gave her the present, and showed her how it worked. When I finally lifted up the plastic and showed the nice sharp black letter on the page, she and her friend said with one voice, "Neat-o!" They instantly fell to work, and soon had made signs for their names, my cello, and a number of other things.

I think it might be a very good way to make letters and/or words or signs for a small child just at the point of figuring out how to read. The letters look so *official*, not something made in the home, but part of the big world outside. They grab the eye more than letters made with a felt-tipped pen. They might be useful for older children too, learning to write letters, or perhaps having trouble with spelling.

You can get these at good stationery or office supply stores, or if not there, from the maker.

TEACHERS' "SKILLS"

Someone doing "educational research" recently sent me a long list of questions to answer about what "skills" teachers did or did not need. The first big question asked how important it was for teachers to have "communication skills." The first one listed was the ability to listen attentively and sympathetically. I thought, "So far, so good." But then the question went on to add something like, "i.e. as in Rogerian listening." I thought, "Aw, bleep!"

Right there, in a nutshell, is what is wrong with this research, and why research and researchers like this will never make teaching better, and will almost surely make it worse. Carl Rogers has said some very sensible and important things. *But he did not invent listening!* Good listening is not a trick. People have been listening to

other people, often sympathetically and attentively, for hundreds of thousands of years. Human societies could never have endured, or even existed, if they had not. We are listening animals as much as talking animals. When "educators" try to make this universal and natural human act into a *technique*—above all, a technique which only specially trained people are supposed to have—they kill it stone dead.

Anyone who says to himself, "I am going to listen attentively and sympathetically to John, here, *so that I can get him to do something I want,*" is no longer capable of listening, least of all sympathetically. He is looking for weaknesses, openings, ways to get at me. Some of the most insufferable people I have ever met and spent time with have been people who pride themselves on being experts in "communications skills." That was exactly what was wrong with them. They did not make me feel that they were talking or listening to me, but that they were practicing their communications skills on me, which is not at all the same thing.

For years, teachers have been taught in their training to smile at children—little ones, at least—and give them lots of praise. And for just that many years children have known (see *How Children Fail*) that the least real and honest things about their teachers have been their smiles and their praises.

CALCULATORS

About ten years ago the smallest and cheapest scientific calculators were about the size of a large office typewriter and cost about $350. I used to tell teachers that in twenty-five years pocket-sized calculators costing less than $50 would do all of the work now done in elementary and secondary math. Well, it only took ten years, and some calculators costing only $20 will do everything in elementary and secondary math and much more besides. The other day I bought for $20 a calculator, Texas Instruments Model SR 40 (other companies make similar machines) which does all the operations of Arithmetic, plus Negative Numbers, the Trigonometric Functions, Logarithms, Roots, Exponents, and more. It can answer, in a flash, many more questions than I know how to ask it.

With one key the machine will do multiplication tables, of any number, small or large. Or, we can begin with a certain number, and then count backwards by 1's, 2's, 5's, or whatever, so that we can do tables backwards as well as forwards. All kinds of games and contests can be made out of this.

Even if I were getting a calculator for a very young child—and I would get one for any child—I would get one of these scientific calculators rather than one which just adds, subtracts, multiplies, and divides. Seeing keys marked *sin, cos, tan, ctn, log,* etc. many children will sooner or later begin to wonder what these symbols mean. Here will be a chance to take a look at some parts of Math that the schools, chained to their timetables, will not talk about for years.

The other day I showed my calculator to a friend, the head of a private elementary school, who has always been interested in Math and Science. He was very excited by it. But when I suggested having some of these in his classrooms, his face fell. "We couldn't do that," he said. "They are too desirable. The children would steal them to take home." Perhaps so. They ought to be in the homes in the first place.

In an airplane magazine I just read that, in spite of fierce opposition from many teachers and parents ("a plain old pencil was good enough for me"), more and more schools are using calculators in their classrooms. But they all say (according to the article) that the children can be shown how to use the calculators only *after* they have learned to do arithmetic with the old paper and pencil—which for many children, as I learned as an arithmetic teacher, means never. No one seems to have thought that children might use the calculators to learn pencil arithmetic, that having played multiplication table games with the calculators, they might find one day to their surprise that they knew most or all of the tables, or that having learned to add with the calculators they would then want to learn to add without them.

But because schools are dumb about calculators does not mean that unschoolers have to be. Get a calculator for your own children. Let it be a tool for them to use for their own pleasure, a way of reaching out into the world of Mathematics. If some of them are not interested, that's all right too—they can find other ways of exploring the world, even the world of Math. As for those who like to explore it this way, let them explore it as far as they can. For not much more money, one can get programmable calculators, which lead into the world of computers and computer programing, a world so far closed to me, but important in these times, and very interesting to many young people.

POLITICS OF SCHOOLING

When rich and poor live in a country, the rich naturally want to make sure—or as sure as they can—that their children will not be poor. To be able to do this is one of the many fringe benefits of being rich. They have many ways to do this. One is to make knowledge, and so, access to interesting and well paid work, expensive, scarce, hard to get. This is part of what schools do.

Today, most people in the fast-growing field of solar energy do not have solar degrees. Much of the work, and of the most important work, is being done by backyard inventors, hobbyists, amateurs. The colleges and universities are only just beginning to give degrees in solar energy. Ten years from now many (but still not all) of the people in the field will have these degrees. When there are enough of them, they, or the colleges and universities which gave their degrees, will probably begin to try to get laws passed saying that you can't work in solar energy *unless* you have such a degree.

They will, in short, turn one more field of human action into a "profession," i.e. a legal monopoly, which only those can do who have had a lot of expensive schooling.

This, of course, has already happened in the law. Abraham Lincoln (like many others) did not learn law by going to law school, but by reading law books. People used to speak, not of "studying law," but of *reading* the law. In those days poor boys (hardly ever girls) could become lawyers by reading the law, and then working in law offices, doing lowly jobs at first, but learning more and getting more responsibility as they learned, probably in the long run setting up their own law offices. No doubt even then the sons of the rich had an advantage. But the poor at least had a way in. Not any more. In many or most states, you can't practice law or even take the bar exam unless you have been to law school—and there are ten or twenty times as many people trying to get in as there are places for them. This is what the Bakke uproar is about; if people could become lawyers by reading the law on their own, that argument would probably have never come up.

Beyond this, the "good" jobs in law go, almost without exception, to the graduates of "good" law schools, who with few exceptions are graduates of "good" i.e. in most cases expensive colleges. A few poor kids make it through this obstacle course, just enough to fool people into thinking that it is a fair race.

Much the same is true of the other "professions." Almost everything that you now have to have an advanced degree to do, was once—often not so long ago—done by people without such degrees. Where did they learn what they knew? Like Abe Lincoln, by reading books, by using their eyes and ears, by asking questions, by working.

A man is now urging publicly that all teachers, including nursery school and kindergarten teachers, should be required by law to have a Doctor's degree in Education. (Which means that they will have learned how to treat children like rats or pigeons, and if they don't respond, to call them "sick.") Who is this man? None other than the President of Teachers College of Columbia University. Not hard to figure that one out. One more legal monopoly. Some of these "educators" may soon be urging that without such degrees no one should be allowed to teach anybody *anything*.

Schools like to say they create and spread knowledge. No; people do that. What schools try to do is corner the market on knowledge, so that they can sell it at a fancy price. That's why they want us to think that only what is learned in school is worth anything. But we don't have to believe it.

AN IMPORTANT DECISION

From a recent *Boston Globe:*

"The Supreme Court ruled yesterday that federal judges may play only a limited role in government decision-making on nuclear-power safety.

The justices served notice on lower courts to leave nuclear power regulation to the regulatory agencies established by Congress and the states. Unless judges find 'substantial procedural or substantive reasons' they should not intervene, the high courts said.

The court, *without dissent* (Ed. italics), overturned a federal appeals court ruling which held that the Nuclear Regulatory Commission had failed to consider adequately the dangers of nuclear waste in approving licenses to two power companies for nuclear reactors in Vernon, VT and Michigan.

In an opinion by Justice William H. Rehnquist, the justices rebuked the appeals court ... 'Nuclear energy may some day be a cheap, safe source of power or it may not,' Rehnquist wrote. 'But Congress has made a choice to at least try nuclear energy, establishing a reasonable review process in which courts are to play only a limited role.'

' ... Time may prove wrong the decision to develop nuclear energy, but it is Congress or the states within their appropriate agencies which must eventually make that judgment.'

The justices said the courts should set aside regulatory agency decisions only for substantial reasons specified by laws passed by Congress—and 'not because the court is unhappy with the result reached.'

The Supreme Court's decision comes when critics of nuclear power are turning increasingly to the courts to block or delay, nuclear projects. The justices' ruling seemed likely to limit use of the courts as a means of opposing nuclear power. ..."

———————

I quote this decision for what it tells us about the way in which this present Court thinks, and will probably continue to think. The Supreme Court fears, and with some reason, that people will begin to think of the Federal Courts, and the Courts to think of themselves, as a kind of super-legislature, where laws may be passed that neither Congress nor the state legislatures would consider passing. Pushed far enough, this would change our structure of government from one with three branches—Executive, Legislative, and Judicial—to one with only two, Executive and Judicial, with the Legislative playing a very inferior role.

I personally think that nuclear power is neither necessary nor safe. Nor do I much admire the present Supreme Court. None the less, I think that in the long run the position they are taking is a wise one. For courts to overturn policies approved by legislatures merely because they disagree with them seems to me a very bad idea for many reasons, not least of all because it gives the supporters of these policies nowhere, politically speaking, to go. If a majority of the people, through their legislators, approve a certain policy, and the courts throw it out, there is nothing for that majority to do but start talking about Constitutional Amendments—a very risky business.

We should remember, too, that it was not very long ago, during the time of the Great Depression and the New Deal, that a conservative or right-wing Supreme Court, the famous Nine Old Men, were throwing out important economic legislation that Congress and a large majority of the people favored. In the long run, there is no reason to believe that judges will be more liberal, enlightened, or humane than legislators. Moreover, if legislators don't vote the way we want, we always have a chance to vote in some new ones. But if Federal judges don't vote the way we want, there is almost nothing we can do—we are stuck with them for life.

In any case, it seems clear that this Supreme Court will not make laws about compulsory school attendance, or the right of people to teach their own children, which the state legislatures have not made. There is, I think, a good chance that if, in a state whose laws say that parents may teach their children at home, a local school board effectively makes that impossible, the Supreme Court may someday rule that the board has no right to do that. But the Court will almost certainly not rule that any states who have not yet passed laws allowing for home instruction ought to and must do so. It may hold school boards to whatever laws exist, but it will not make new laws. Which means in turn that in the long run if not the short, unschoolers are going to have to think about making friends and getting support in their various state legislatures.

A POSTER

How ideas are born: I have been thinking about the best words for a classified ad, to use in various papers and magazines, the fewer words the better. For a while I considered, "Are schools making your kids stupid?" Not quite right—why put a fact in the form of a question? One day these words came to me: "Don't *let* school make your kids stupid." Better—not just a statement but a call to act.

The other day in Harvard Square, I saw a vacant store on whose windows people had put dozens of posters and announcements. I tried to imagine the GWS flyer up there (see GWS #3), and it occurred to me that it might be lost among all the others. What we need, I thought, is something that will catch the eye, even from across the street. Suddenly I thought of the classified ad. How would it do for a poster? OK, but something more was needed. What else are we saying that we want people to hear? Early one morning the other words came to me. In my mind's eye I now see:

**Your Kids Were Born
S M A R T
Don't Let School Make Them
S T U P I D**

I see the letters of SMART in bold, sharp-edged type face, slanting forward, maybe a little star over each letter. Behind the S, some very fine lines, to give the idea of rapid forward motion. I see the letters of STUPID drawn freehand, shapeless, fat, lumpy, leaning backwards, little curly lines around it to suggest something settling down in a cloud of dust. I even see them in color, SMART in some mixture of red, white and blue, STUPID in dark brown. Then at the bottom of the poster, "Read GROWING WITHOUT SCHOOLING—for sample issue, send 50 cents to, etc."

By next issue we hope to have a version in black and white to show you. Meanwhile, we'd be glad to hear any design suggestions or possible variations that you might come up with. I am excited by this idea, think it may help us find new friends.

NEWSSTAND SALES

People have asked us what kind of special arrangements we have for newsstands, bookstores, health food stores, etc. who might want to sell GWS by the individual copy. We have no special arrangement. What they can do is take out a group subscription and then resell individual copies at whatever they think is a sensible price. With a 4X sub, a store could get GWS at about 66 cents per copy, and then sell them for $1 each. With an 8X sub, they could get copies at 50 cents each, and perhaps sell them for 75 cents. As they order more, the unit price will come down.

Unlike most magazines, GWS will not refund money for unsold copies. Too expensive and complicated. Someday we may be able to make special deals with newsstands and stores, but not now and probably not for some time to come.

SECRECY

Some of the people who have written us wonderful letters—J and D in GWS #3, and others—have for various and good reasons chosen to keep their names and addresses a secret. The problem, though, was how other people could write to them. Here is how. If you would like to write to, for example, D (or the writer of "Money" in GWS #3), address your letter to D—GWS #2 (or "Money"—GWS #3), c/o GROWING WITHOUT SCHOOLING, 308 Boylston, etc. Put "Please Forward" on the envelope. When we get it, we will put D's (or "Money" 's) address on it and send it on.

If later D (or whoever) wants to write directly to the other person, say Smith, and reveal his name and address, he can do that. If not, D can write a letter to Smith, put it in a stamped envelope addressed to Smith,

and put *that* envelope in an envelope addressed to us at GWS. When we open our envelope and find the letter to Smith, we will put it in the mail. (Of course, if people write *us* letters without putting down their address, which happens now and then, we are helpless—and frustrated)

Some may feel that all this secrecy is exaggerated and foolish. I agree that it is unfortunate, but in these times I don't think it is at all foolish.

Editor—John Holt
Managing Editor—Peg Durkee

GROWING WITHOUT SCHOOLING

Issue No. 5

July, 1978

A mother writes to Peg Durkee:

"You probably don't remember, but one afternoon some months ago I called and asked for your help in removing our son from the public schools. My plea was answered on the spot with several suggestions on how we might gather information on which to base our decision.

I'll skip over all the soul-searching, the agonizing over alternatives, and get to the heart of the matter— "J" has been set free! He is enrolled at the Santa Fe Community School but is actually learning at home. As soon as the decision was made he seemed to be released from some terrible burden, he immediately began taking charge of his own life and learning, and began to approach everything with the zest and enthusiasm formerly reserved for his own nature study, sports and building projects. For example, he always hated math, and the necessity of doing math homework caused the most unhappy and miserable hours in our household. Now he has set himself the task of getting math and is proceeding to do so with none of the emotional overtones formerly present.

We owe you a great big 'THANK YOU.' If you had not responded in such a helpful way, the idea might have died right there. It's not an easy task for a poor working-class family to attempt this kind of thing—in fact it's a bit terrifying. Yet, I feel strongly that working-class kids are most hurt by public schools and most in need of being set free. (Admittedly not too many parents I know would agree with this right now.) Anyway, we need all the help we can get, and we appreciate your willingness to give it."

A LEARNING EXCHANGER

From the Member's Feedback section of the newsletter for the Learning Exchange, P.O. Box 920, Evanston, ILL 60204, this letter from Derrick White, a Learning Exchange member from the South Shore neighborhood of Chicago:

"I am a pack rat.

In actuality, that's not so unusual. America is full of them. As a nation, we collect everything from rare coins and stamps to beer cans. However, I collect an unusual commodity: information. Unused, unobtrusive information.

You may ask, what do I do with the information I collect? My favorite thing is to come home and reach back into the recesses of my imagination and record whatever it is I pull out. In other words, I am a writer— at least I fancy myself as one.

One of the organizations that has helped me perpetuate this pastime is The Learning Exchange. When I first heard about it two years ago, I was writing a script for an amateur movie, another hobby of mine. Through The Learning Exchange, I found another movie maker who was extremely helpful in the project.

I owe an immeasurable debt to The Learning Exchange for the amount of aid, information and advice I've received. When I wrote a play that included a sequence about magic, I found two magicians through The Learning Exchange who were very helpful in giving me information that enabled me to write it. Later, I wrote a screenplay that included a fencing battle. Through The Learning Exchange, I discovered two fencing champions and became so interested in the sport that I soon will be starting lessons in the Spanish style of fencing.

What's my real success in actually selling some of my works? Fair. I have a teleplay currently searching for a buyer. And I have finished a novel that a publisher is interested in. But whether or not they actually are sold, it really doesn't make any difference. I'm 17, not even out of high school yet. So, what if immortality holds off for a while? I've still got two, three more good years left. Pack rats are known for their patience."

THE CHILD FINDERS

A reader from Anne Arundel county in Maryland has sent us a pamphlet put out by the local schools, which I reproduce in full.

(Cover page)
"We're looking for children with special needs." [Then, a drawing of a cute little girl—the children in these kinds of pamphlets are always cute—looking up impishly and seductively, supposedly at her adult helper.] Please help us find them."

(Next page)
"CHILD FIND [in large letters] is the name which has been given to the all-out effort to locate children who will be in need of Special Programs in the Anne Arundel County Public Schools. [Picture of more cute children.]

Please join the search. The sooner we can find the children, the sooner we can plan an adequate program. To learn more, read the detailed information inside. Then contact us."

(Next page)
"The purpose of CHILD FIND is to locate and identify children ages birth through 20 who may be in

need of special services, and to solicit the help of parents, friends, agencies, medical personnel and others in this effort. Upon receiving a referral on a child, the Anne Arundel County public school system will assess the needs the child appears to have. We hope through this procedure to be able to identify all pupils who will be in need of special services, so that we may make adequate provisions for their coming to school. After reading some of the guideposts, below, you may find you wish to refer a child to us. You may do so by completing and mailing the form which is part of this brochure, or by calling 224-7689 and relaying the information by telephone. Please help us identify the children who need extra help.

Anne Arundel County Public Schools.

We want to know if you have a child, or know of a child who...

Has trouble seeing or hearing

Appears to be learning much more slowly than other children

Is listless, tired , or overactive

Is not understood by people outside the family

Does not understand simple stories as told or read

Has ear aches or running ears

Talks in an unusually loud voice

Turns the same ear towards a sound he/she wishes to hear

Frequently rubs eyes or complains that eyes hurt

Sometimes or always crosses one or both eyes

Every child can learn. Education can be broken down into the smallest units, so special children can understand, learn, and develop a sense of self worth and go on to become self-sufficient adults. (Ed. note—this phrase, which appears in one form or another in much of the propaganda of the compulsory helpers, is code for 'If you don't pay to have them fixed up now, you'll have to pay to keep them on welfare later.') These are the goals for each child. Your criteria when determining whether a child may need special help should not be limited to those listed above. Any condition which gives you cause for concern can be a basis for referral. We will evaluate the child's need once the referral comes in."

(Next page)
[blanks for the following questions:]
1. Child's name. 2. Date of Birth 3. Parent's or Legal Guardian(s)' Name 4. Child's Age/Grade 5. Address 6. Phone No. 7. Person Referring 8. Relationship to Child 9. Phone No. 10. Is the parent or legal guardian aware of this referral? (Ed. note—this is code for 'Do you wish your name to be kept secret?') 11. What type of special help do you think the child might need? 12. What things have you noticed that caused your concern? 13. Is the child now receiving help for your area of concern? If so, where?

[Then another picture of children, which I will describe later. On the back of this page is the return address: Anne Arundel County Public Schools, Divisions of Special Education, 2644 Riva Road, Annapolis, MD 21401. This whole back page, folded, becomes a postage-paid return envelope. The schools want to make it as easy as possible to turn in your neighbor's children. No waiting around while you look for an envelope or stamp.]

At a conference not long ago I described this pamphlet to a man from North Carolina. He said that there were many such programs in his state. I asked him, as I now ask GWS readers, to send any and all information you can find about such programs, including copies of pamphlets similar to the one described here.

Some of the things the schools are asking people to look for are innocent and sensible enough, signs of bad vision or deafness. Nothing wrong with wanting children with bad vision to have glasses, or deaf children to have hearing aids. But there are surely ways of doing this without setting up this elaborate spy system, this mini-CIA. The school system must have spent much money to distribute this pamphlet. Why not spend the same money to say to the general public and to parents, "Here are some signs of bad vision or hearing. If you notice them in your children, have their eyes and/or ears examined. If you need the names and addresses of doctors who can do this, or need some help in paying for such examinations, let us know, and we will be glad to give such information or help." Something like this could be put in many public places.

What this pamphlet says, in addition to what it seems to say, is, "Parents can't be trusted to look after the needs of their children. Only we trained professionals know enough, and care enough, to do that." A great deal of what professional educators say and write carries this same message—it is one of the things that student teachers are trained to believe. We alone know. We alone care.

It might be very much to the point, in any school district having such a turn-in-a-kid program, to ask, publicly, some of the questions for schools that I proposed in GWS #4. How successful have the schools been in meeting the special needs of children who have already been identified?

Worth noting here that a recent issue of *Today's Education*, the official magazine of the National Education Association, which goes to all members of the Association i.e. probably three quarters or more of the teachers in the U.S., had a special issue on Learning

Disabilities, in which they said, among many other absurdities, that while the experts did not know the cause of 'learning disabilities' they did know that they *could not be cured*, but only "compensated for." In plain English, what this means is that if your child is having trouble learning to read, he must have a reading learning disability, which in turn means that he will *always* have trouble with reading. The only remedy they offer is to tell him that it is not his fault, and to try to think of good substitutes for reading. Such is the wisdom of the schools. GWS will have much more to say about "learning disabilities" in later issues.

Meanwhile, as I say, we can and should make very strongly, to the general public, the point that schools that do not know how to solve the learning problems of the children they already know about, have no call and no right to demand that people start turning in each other's children. I would not grant them that right even if they did know how to solve all of children's learning problems. But a great many people who might not agree with me on the broad issue of the rights of citizens vs. compulsory helpers can probably be persuaded to agree on the narrower issue, that schools should not claim they can solve problems unless in fact they can solve them.

I said I would describe the picture at the back of the pamphlet. It is of eight children, four girls and four boys, in a classroom. They are young, eight at the oldest. All are cute, except perhaps one—a fat boy, with glasses. Even he is fairly cute. Seven of the eight are looking at the teacher, all of them smiling. The other is a boy in the front desk, reading, head resting on one hand. ("That Billy! Always has his nose in a book!") Of the seven looking at the teacher, one is a girl, standing by her desk, holding a book out of which she is reciting something. Of the other six, five have their hands raised, and the other one, a girl in the front row desk, looks as if she knew. In other words, a teacher's dream of a class—little children, all cute, all smiling, all knowing the answer. Two-legged talking puppy dogs. Just what so many people wish children were.

The cover of the issue of *Today's Education* which deals with "learning disabilities" is also of a cute, smiling, faintly wistful, little boy. I stress this point because the sentimentality of schools about children is only the reverse side, and indeed a root cause, of their habitual hostility and cruelty to them. They don't see them as people but as pets, to be patted as long as they obey, but quickly scolded or beaten if they do not.

WHAT THEY'RE SELLING

The May, 1978 issue of *Mother Jones*, 607 Market St,. San Francisco CA 94105, printed, under the heading "The New Pepsi Generation," the following story:

"The Pepsi-Cola Company is sponsoring what it calls a 'learn and earn project' in hundreds of U.S. schools—a project encouraging kids to sell the company's soft drinks at school functions in return for class credit.

The project is sponsored jointly by a group called the Distributive Education Clubs of America, or DECA. Participating students sell Pepsi-Cola at pep rallies, basketball games and other school functions. Then, each spring, the students write up their Pepsi-selling success story for a chance at national prizes—shares of stock in Pepsi-Cola.

According to literature the company sends to teachers, the project helps 'strengthen students' broad understanding of business.' Pepsi doesn't mention however, that it also helps strengthen the company's sales figures.

Another company reportedly involved in the education game is Savannah Sugar Refining Corporation. Savannah puts out a booklet for students that might make a dentist weep. The booklet, called *Sugar Through the Ages*, includes statements such as 'Scientists have found that generous amounts of sugar are a valuable part of well-balanced diet for growing children.'"

FAN LETTER

An old friend, Dave Armington, writes, in part:

"A note to say how delighted we are with GWS. ... I told [a friend] about GWS, in case he hadn't heard already, reminded him not to miss the easily visible logo for the "Pinch Penny Press" (what a super name!), and told him (by way of high praise) that GWS is the only stapled-together, squinty-eye-print, no illustrations, read-me-if-you-dare tract that I have ever been willing to read, have enjoyed reading, and want to go on reading when the next issue arrives, which it will sooner or later depending on how much other people feel like writing to him, and in either case it will be a surprise when it arrives, which is another good reason for subscribing because why should anyone send out a paper if he doesn't have anything to say? And I would have mentioned already (but didn't because I didn't have time) a sneaky feature on the back page called 'Directory' which is where the editor will put your name if you want him to put it there, for no special reason except I suppose that some people just like to see their names in print and here's a chance to get some free publicity so why not take it, something like the guy who put an ad in the paper which said, 'this is absolutely your last chance to send $1.00 to Box so-and-so, Chicago' (or wherever), and retired on the proceeds ..."

Well many thanks for kind words. We like the name Pinch Penny Press, too. We started using it before we began to publish GWS, but were only printing a lot of inexpensive reprints. The logo was designed by Peg Durkee's cousin Jim Hayes, who is a painter and man of many talents. I think Dave is the first person to mention either name or logo.

As we said in GWS #4, we will probably be coming out about every other month. But we don't promise this. If, as may well happen, I get very involved in writing another book, I may well skip a month or two here and there.

As for the Directory, it has another purpose. I really hope that now and then people listed in the Directory will write to each other—as some already have. If they live not too far apart, or other circumstances bring them within reach of each other, they may meet, become friends. Or their children may become friends, visit back and forth. In *Escape From Childhood* (av. fr. GWS) I said that even in a society where many adults despise, fear, and even hate children, there might slowly build up a mini-society, a network of people who liked, trusted, and respected children, and that these people might create a community (extending all over their country or countries) in which their children could grow up, move about freely, and have access to much of the world. GWS and the Directory may in time help to do this.

Other possible uses. People in the Directory might actually swap toys, equipment, etc. Or, several families might join forces to buy for their children something that by themselves they could not afford, like an electric portable typewriter, with each family having it for a certain part of the year. This might be better even where money was not a problem, as kids tend to get bored with something when it is around the house all the time, and might be more interested in it if it showed up every once in a while. I can imagine doing something like this with a good telescope, or an electronics construction kit, or even books.

Dave also asked what we will do when the Directory gets so big that it crowds everything else out of the magazine. Well, we are already only printing the full Directory in every third issue. When it gets beyond a certain size, we will shrink the Directory type even smaller. (No complaints, please, think of the phone book.)

And if you like GWS, please tell your friends. They don't necessarily have to be unschoolers (Dave isn't), might want to read the magazine just because it (or part of it) is interesting. In the long run, word of mouth is probably what will bring us most of our readers.

TIME OF OUR OWN

A mother writes in part:

"When we met you last fall, we had just begun our first year of keeping the children out of school, and I promised to write when we were a little further into it. Now I would like to share some thoughts and observations.

The decision to keep the kids, 5 and 7, out of school this year was somewhat forced down our throats.

There were no other options. But when we started swallowing, we found it slid down rather easily, and when we returned from our summer in the mountains, we found the first issue of GWS waiting in our mailbox. We knew we were on the right track.

We entered the year with no preconceptions or plan of action. I just figured life would go on, and so it has. We go to bed each night and wake up each morning, the day passes and the necessary work gets done. I know that I live in a healthy environment and that I continue to grow as a person, and I trust that is so for my children, as well, though I haven't been 'monitoring' their 'progress,' nor can I point to any tangible proof of 'achievement.'

About ten days a month I go to the city to work in a print shop. It is my habit, generally, to wake up early and spend an hour or two quietly planning my day according to what needs doing and what I feel like doing. But on my 'work' days I find it very difficult to 'get into' that kind of contemplation. Such a large chunk of the day is already planned for me. If I go to work several consecutive days, by the fourth or fifth day I feel very removed from the core of myself, and find it much easier to contemplate doing what at other times would seem irresponsible to me. I seem to have less energy for recycling, conserving fuel, paying good attention to my husband and children, etc. When I abdicate the responsibility for structuring my own time, a certain moral strength seems to be lost as well. Who can guess at the degree of personal alienation we as a society cause our children by structuring so much of their time for them? I am beginning to think the greatest harm is not in the 'what' or the 'how' of this structuring, but in the very fact that five days out of seven, nine months out of twelve, six hours out of the center of those days, we remove from children the responsibility for their time. Perhaps it is not even the length of the time that is crucial, but simply the fact of the interruption. I know from my own experience that even a small interruption—a dental appointment, say, or a meeting or lecture I have to give—can halt the flow of my own creative energies for a length of time much greater than the interruption itself. Once I change from active to passive participant in structuring my time, a certain numbing takes place so that it is much easier to stay passive, 'killing time' until the next prescribed activity, like fixing dinner or whatever. I have noticed that the only periods of real 'boredom,' when the children complain of having nothing to do, are on days when a chunk of time has been planned *for* them. There is certainly nothing wrong with planning things to do together, but I have grown wary of too much planning *for*, and of removing it from its natural niche in the unique pattern of a particular day to an artificial projection into the future of anonymous days: 'every Tuesday we will ...'

I have never known how to 'stimulate' the children. I know that as a parent I should be raising my children in a 'stimulating' environment, so that they will not be 'dulled' or 'bored,' but what is more stimulating: a roomful of toys and tools, and gadgets, bright colors and shiny enameled fixtures, or a sparsely furnished hand-hewn cabin deep in the woods, with a few toys carefully chosen or crafted, rich with meaning, time, and care, and intimate with the elements of the earth? The only world I can show them, with any integrity, is my world.

Perhaps that is why field trips were such a disappointment for us. We started off in the fall doing 'something special,' *i.e.* 'educational field trip,' once a week. After about a month we all forgot about taking these trips. They were fun, certainly interesting, but I think we were all sickened by the phoniness. Everyone knew the only reason we all trooped into the city to the aquarium was because Mom thought it would be a 'good experience.' Of much more continuing interest and, probably, greater educational significance in the truest sense, are the weekly trips into town to do the errands—to the bank (where we all have accounts and are free to deposit and withdraw as we please), the post office, grocery store, laundromat, recycling center (source of income for kids outside of parents), drugstore and the comic book racks—and the evenings at the library and swimming pool. Those things are *real*, things I would do even if no one joined me, that just happen to be important activities for all of us.

When I am trying to 'stimulate their interest' in something, the very artificiality of the endeavor (and rudeness, really—I have no business even trying) builds a barrier between us. But when I am sharing something I really love with them because I also really love them, all barriers are down, and we are communicating intimately. When they also love what I love—a song, a poem, the salmon returning to the creek to spawn—the joy is exquisite: we share a truth. But our differences are also a truth. Common thread and fiber we share, but not the whole piece.

And so I do my work each day, work which is full of meaning for me, and offer to teach it to them: cooking, sewing, splitting wood, hauling water, keeping house, writing, reading, singing, sailing on the lake, digging in the garden. Sometimes they are interested, sometimes not. But if I were to try to 'stimulate' them, sugarcoating various tasks, making games of various skills, preaching, teaching *me* to them, they would not have the time—great, empty spaces of time—in which to search deep within themselves for what is most true about them.

And neither, then, would I.

Who can explain the chemistry of creativity? I can sit at a desk in a well-lit room, with paper and type-writer in front of me, a subject clear in my head, yet the results of my efforts are merely mediocre. But when I am in a spot of my own choosing, a spot in which strands of fantasy, imagery, memory, and emotion, and perhaps some other deeper, indefinable essence converge, I am able to produce an immensely satisfying piece of work. Sometimes when I am writing I appear to be wandering aimlessly throughout the woods, or sitting idly on the bridge, dangling feet and tossing pebbles into the slowly moving water. But all the while my mind is working, trembling with the tension of an unarticulated thought, until I find the linear expression for that formless entity. Knowing these things about myself, how can I guess at the workings of my children's minds? And not knowing, how can I presume to interfere, to lock them into sterile rooms, to lure them away from 'idle' moments?

I have no idea if the year at home has been 'good' or 'bad' for the children. I know of no 'standardized' test to measure the strength of one's spirit or the integrity of a self, yet these would be the only measure that would interest me. I did discover myself to have a learning disability—in thirty years I still have not learned that one's friends cannot be trusted, and therefore I was surprised, though I'm told I shouldn't have been, when a 'friend' in whom we had confided turned us in to the school district. I don't have the time or energy to devote to locking horns with some 'attendance officer' right now, so we are opting, instead, for a lower profile, forcing us to give up, at least for now, the easy openness with which we are most comfortable in relating to others."

FROM OREGON

"The 'school' I was talking then of trying to organize never materialized, mainly because there wasn't anybody who wanted to organize it. Which makes me all the more sure that schools are artificial to life anyway and that there are other ways we can figure out to do exciting things with our kids. So I spent the rest of the year on my land, building on my house and weaving and sewing dolls for the Christmas fairs. After the turn of the year, I turned to what I hoped would be more lucrative for the time I put into it, as money was becoming more and more necessary, and I joined a tree-planting crew with the Hoedads, a tree-planting cooperative working out of Eugene. The crew I am on is officially called Sprouts and is a 'school crew'— that is, it is made up of parents, and a few non-parents who are interested in kids, who wanted to plant trees and still be with their kids. So we have a cooperative 'school' worked out where we take turns planting and keeping the kids. So far we have been perfectly free with each other to do whatever we want to do with the kids, so some kid days turn out to be super fun; others fall flat. I myself put a low emphasis on reading and math on a group basis; I would rather spend my time in the woods with the kids. But I find that any theories of teaching and learning that I may have or have had are constantly being challenged just by who the kids are and what they are teaching me.

I have a beautiful and deep friendship with one of the kids, an eight-year-old girl. One day she and I were building a dam on the creek in order to create a pool to submerge in after taking a sweat in the newly built sweat lodge. She said to me, 'Isn't it amazing how much I am teaching you?' That made me laugh; all this time I had been spending with her I had been patting myself on the back for what *I* had been teaching *her!* But I had also been aware of all that she was teaching me—only, it wasn't anything else she thought she was teaching me, but something intangible about teaching and learning and children and living."

NOBODY SEES BACKWARDS

A few years ago a national magazine (I think *Time*) ran a full page ad for some outfit with a name like American Society for Learning Disabilities. At the top of the ad, in large letters, were the words, "SEE HOW JOHNNY READS." Then a photo, of an open children's book printed in very large print, large enough so that people reading the ad could read the book. The story was of The Three Little Pigs. But many of the letters in the story had been shifted and turned around in odd ways. Some were upside down or backwards. Sometimes two adjacent letters in a word had been put in reverse order. Sometimes a word was spelled backwards. Then, beneath the photo, again in large letters, the words, "THINK HOW JOHNNY FEELS." Then some text about all the children suffering from "learning disabilities" and all the things the Society was doing to cure or help them.

The message was plain. We were being asked to believe that large numbers of children in the U.S., when they looked at a book, saw something like the photo in the ad, and so, could not read it. Also, that the Society could and would do something about this—it was not clear just what—if we gave it enough support.

I looked once more at the children's book in the photo. I found that I could read it without much trouble. Of course, I had two advantages over the supposed "learning disabled" child who was looking at this book. I could already read, and I already knew the story. I read it a bit more slowly than I ordinarily would; now and then I had to puzzle out a word, one letter at a time. But it was not hard to do.

This was by no means the first time I had heard the theory that certain children have trouble learning to read because something inside their skins or skulls, a kind of Maxwell's Demon of the nervous system (look up this Demon in an elementary Physics text, or perhaps encyclopedia or dictionary of science, if you are puzzled and curious), every so often flipped letters upside down or backwards, or changed their order. I had never believed the theory. It failed the first two tests of any scientific theory 1) that it be plausible on its face 2) that it be the most obvious or likely explanation of the facts. This theory seemed (and still seems) totally implausible, for many reasons. And there were and still are much simpler and more likely explanations of the facts (more on this later).

What facts did this theory set out to account for? Only this, that certain children, usually just learning to read and write, when asked to write down certain letters or words, wrote some letters backwards, or reversed the order for two or more letters in a word, or spelled entire words backwards—though note that most children who spell backwards do not at the same time reverse all the individual letters.

I never spent much time thinking about how to prove that this theory was wrong. I was busy with other work. For a while I taught in a school right next door to what was then supposed to be one of the best schools for "learning disabilities" (hereafter l.d.) children in New England. I began to note that in that particular learning hospital no one was ever cured. Kids went in not knowing how to read, and came out years later still not knowing. Nobody seemed in the least upset by this. Apparently this school was felt to be "the best" because it had better answers than anyone else to the questions, "Once you have decided that certain children *can't* learn to read, what do you do with them all day in a place which is supposed to be a school?" Later, when I was working full time lecturing to groups about educational reform, I had other contacts with l.d. believers and experts. The more I saw of them, the less I believed in them. But I was still too busy to spend much time arguing with them or even thinking about them.

Then one morning in Boston, as I was walking across the Public Garden toward my office, my subconscious mind asked me a question. First it said, "The l.d. people say that these children draw the P backwards because when they look at the correct P they *see* it backwards. Let's put all this in a diagram."

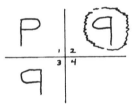

In space #1 is the correct P which the child is asked to draw or copy. In space #3 is the backward P which he draws, because (we are told) this is the way he sees it. In space #2 is what the child supposedly sees when he looks at the P in space #1. (The wavy line represents perception)"

Then came the $64 question.

"Now, what does the child see when he looks at the backwards P in space #3, that he has drawn?"

I think I stopped walking. I may have said aloud, "Well, I'll be damned!" For obviously, if his mind reverses all the shapes he looks at, the child, when he looks at the backwards P in space #3, *will see a correct P.* So our diagram would wind up looking like this:

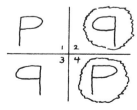

This imaginary child, if he did what the l.d.

experts say he does, would look at #1, see #2, draw #3, *and looking at that, see #4.* What he had drawn would not look *to him* like what he was trying to copy. He would think, "I've made a mistake," and draw his P the other way round. That is, he would if his drawing was, as the l.d. experts claim, an accurate copy of what he was perceiving. Even if his mind reversed every shape it saw, *a backwards P would still look backwards to him!* To put it still more broadly and fundamentally, we cannot tell by looking at the shapes people draw whether they perceive shapes backwards or not, *since they would draw the same shapes in either case!*

So the "perceptual handicap," "he-draws-backwards-because-he-sees-backwards" theory goes down the drain. It does not explain what it was invented *to* explain. Nor does it explain anything else—this event, the child drawing the letters backwards, is all the evidence that supports it. Why then does this obviously false theory persist? Because, for many reasons, it is very convenient to many people—to parents, to teachers, to schools, to l.d. experts and the industry that has grown up around them, and sometimes even to the children. The theory may not help anyone learn to read, but it keeps a lot of people busy, makes a lot of people richer, and makes almost everyone feel better. Theories that do all that are not easy to get rid of.

The first time I gave this proof of mine, that the sees-backwards-draws-backwards (hereafter SBDB) theory is false, was to a meeting of psychologists and others in New Jersey. I invited them to draw themselves, on a handy scrap of paper, the diagram reproduced above. By the time I told them what to put in space #3, a few people, perhaps half a dozen, began to laugh, with the delighted surprise that truly smart people feel when they meet a completely new idea. They smiled at me, I at them; they had already got the point. When I said to the others, "Draw in space #4 what the child sees when he looks at space #3," I could see from their faces that they were getting the point. Some laughed, some shook their heads wonderingly, as if to say, perhaps, "Why didn't I see that, it's so obvious." Quite a few people's mouths literally fell open.

But I must add that this was not a meeting of l.d. specialists. They had no vested interest in the SBDB theory. When I went through this same demonstration before 1000+ people at a l.d. conference in Montreal, they did not seem to respond at all. They sensed, quite rightly, that I was setting some kind of trap for them, and were putting all their mental energies into not falling into it. As far as I could tell, few even drew the diagram. But more about this group later.

But then, why *does* the child draw the P backwards? If he is not reproducing the shape that he perceives, what is he doing?

The answer is plain to anyone who has watched little children when they first start making letters. Slowly, hesitantly, uncertainly, and clumsily, they try to turn what they see into a set of instructions, a "program," for their hand, and then try to make the hand carry out the instructions. This is what we all do. We

are not walking copying machines. When we try to draw a chair, we do not "copy" it. We look at it a while, and then we look at the paper and "tell" our hand to draw, say, a vertical line of a certain height. Then we look at the chair again, then back at the paper, then "tell" our hand to go halfway up the vertical line and from that point draw a horizontal line of a certain length or a line slanted at a certain angle. Then we look back at the chair for more instructions. If, like trained artists, we are good at turning what we see into instructions for our hand, we will produce a good likeness of the chair. If, like most of us, we are not good at it, we will not.

In this way, the child looks at the P. He sees there is a line in it that goes up and down. He looks at the paper and tells his hand, "Draw an up and down line," then draws it. He looks back at the P, sees that at the top of the up and down line there is another line that goes out to the side. He looks at his paper, tells his hand to go to the top of the up and down line and then draw a line out to the side. This done, he looks back at the P, sees that the line going out to the side curves down and around after a while and then goes back in until it hits the up and down line again. He tells his hand to do that. It may take him two or three tries to get all the way around the curve. Sometimes he will have trouble remembering which way the curve has to go round. But eventually he gets his line back up to the up and down line.

At this point, most children will compare the two P's, the one they looked at and the one they made. Many of them, if they drew their P backwards, may see right away that it is backwards, doesn't look quite the same, is pointing the wrong way—however they may express this in their minds. Other children may be vaguely aware that the shapes are not pointing the same way, but will see this as a difference *that doesn't make any difference,* just as for my bank the differences between one of my signatures and another are differences that don't make any difference.

But I suspect that most children who often reverse letters do not in fact *compare* shapes. I suspect that, like so many of the children I have known and taught, they are anxious, rule-bound, always in a panicky search for certainty. What they do is turn the P they are looking at into a set of instructions, and memorize the instructions, and then compare the P they have drawn *against the instructions.* "Yes, there's the line going up and down, and there's the line going out sideways from the top, and there it is curving down and around and coming back into the up and down line again. I followed all the instructions, obeyed all the rules, so it must be right." Or perhaps they try to compare shapes, but are too anxious to see them clearly. Or perhaps by the time they have shifted their eye from the P they were looking at to the P on their own paper, they have forgotten the original P, or dare not trust the memory of it that they have. This feeling of suddenly not being able to trust one's own memory is common enough. Now and then I find myself looking up a phone number two or three times in a row, because each time I start to dial the number I have the panicky thought, "Did I really remember it right?" I can usually only break out of this foolish cycle by saying to myself, "Right or wrong, dial it anyway." It usually turns out to be right. But I can understand how a certain kind of self-distrusting person (by no means rare) might go through this process a great many times.

It is possible, too, that a child, making up a set of instructions for his hand, might try to use the ideas of Right and Left, but might also have some of the confusions I talked about in GWS #4, so that "right" when he was looking at the P might mean the opposite of "right" when he was drawing it. The fact remains that whatever may be children's reasons for drawing letters backwards, there is no reason whatever to believe that seeing them backwards is one of them.

TEACHER STORY

A student teacher writes:

"Reading has never been my best subject. When I was little, and even now, I never read for fun or enjoyment. When I was in the fourth grade we had got into our reading groups and I was called on to read. As I read I came across a word that I couldn't pronounce and the class laughed. I was so embarrassed that I ran out of the room. Well, from that point on whenever we were going to get into our reading groups I would pretend to be sick and leave the room. After about two weeks of this game the teacher and my mother had a conference. The teacher realized what I was doing and why. They both talked to me about the situation, but I never felt the same."

We can only wonder how many people have been made, and are being made to feel this way, every day. The same student teacher goes on:

"I worked in a child care center last quarter for a class I was taking ... a class of three, four, and five year olds. I thought then and I think now that it's very hard for a teacher to teach different age groups. It's hard to know what level to gear your unit. I do agree with you, though, about it helping the children. The three year olds were reading better than some of the five year olds. The older children were reading to the younger children and this was motivating the older ones as well as the younger ones. The younger children wanted to be able to read like their peers, and the older children felt they were important. So, you see, *I agree that this situation helps the children, but my question is, what does the teacher do about planning her lesson? Who or what age level should it be geared to?*" (Ed. italics)

This is a sad story, again, probably repeated tens of thousands of times every year. It makes me think of one of those Walt Disney nature films—but run backwards,

the butterfly turning into the caterpillar. This young, smart, observant, perhaps even potentially gifted teacher is being turned, *by her training*, into an incompetent. She *sees* the children teaching and learning from each other, *sees* that it works, that they learn better. But her head has been stuffed so full of nonsense about "methods," "lesson plans," and "gearing her unit," that she cannot make use of what she has been told by her own experience. She has been made immune to experience, even her own. Unless good luck – hers and ours – takes her out of the classroom, she is well on her way toward inflicting on bored and resisting children forty years' worth of units and lesson plans.

READING READINESS

A while ago I wrote a letter to the *New Schools Exchange Newsletter,* which they printed, as did (later) the magazine *Green Revolution,* I wrote, in part:

"Our professional experts on the 'teaching' of reading have said a great many foolish things, but none more foolish than the notion that the way to get children 'ready to read' is to show them a lot of books full of nothing but pictures and ask them a lot of silly questions about them. This is standard practice almost everywhere, as far as I know.

The proper analogy can be found, as is so often true, with children learning to speak, that extraordinary intellectual feat we all accomplished before the adults got it into their heads that they could 'teach' us. Children get ready to speak by hearing speech all around them. The important thing about that speech is that the adults, for the most part, are *not* talking in order to give the children a model. They are talking to each other because they have things to say. So the first thing the baby intuits, figures out, about the speech of adults, is that it is *serious.* Adults talk to make things happen. They talk, and things *do* happen. The baby thinks, feels, this is a pretty serious activity, well worth doing.

When I was a kid, I taught myself to read, as many children do. Nobody taught me, and as far as I can remember, nobody helped me very much or read aloud to me. When we were a little older, a grandmother read aloud to my sister and me, but by then we were already skillful readers. She read the *Dr. Doolittle* books by Hugh Lofting, and to sit on the sofa, one on each side, was a very happy scene, all the more so because she read these stories with the greatest seriousness, without a touch of sentimentality or condescension, no 'cute' inflections in her voice.

One of the things that made me want to read was that in those days (long, long ago) children's books had very few pictures in them. There were a few illustrations here and there—magnificent ones, many of them painted by Andrew Wyeth's father, N.C. Wyeth. Pirates, knights, Scottish highland chiefs—great pictures. But there weren't enough of them in any one book to give me any idea of what the stories were about, so I realized that to find out what those pictures meant I was going to have to read the book. Which I soon learned to do.

What children need to get ready for reading is exposure to a lot of *print*. Not pictures, but print. They need to bathe their eyes in print, as when smaller they bathed their ears in talk. After a while, as they look at more and more print, these meaningless forms, curves, and squiggles begin to steady down, take shape, become recognizable, so that the children, without yet knowing what letters or words are, begin to see, as I once did myself, after looking at a page of print in an Indian type face, that *this* letter appears *here,* and again *here,* and that group of letters appears *there,* and again *there.* When they've learned to see the letters and words, they are ready to ask themselves questions about what they mean and what they say. But not before, just as, when I am learning a foreign language, there is no use telling me that such and such a word means such and such a thing until my ears have become sharp enough to pick it out from other people's talk.

All of which leads to a concrete suggestion. I propose that schools, or people not sending their children to any school, or anyone who wants to make it easier for children to *discover* how to read, use as one of their 'reading readiness materials' the large print edition of the *N.Y. Times.* The print is large enough for children to see and recognize. The paper is clearly a part of the adult world, and therefore attractive. It is serious. It has real information in it. It can be put up on walls, etc., but is not so precious that one has to worry about its being torn, defaced, etc. A year's subscription brings enough printed material so that it could be shared out among many schools, families, etc. In low income communities, it might actually be put on the walls of buildings or the windows of stores, for children (and others) to look at. In some cases it might be defaced or torn down. But not, perhaps, if everyone knew what it was up there for.

Beyond this, I would suggest that we put into the visual environment of young children, both in school and out, and not just in the pre-reading years but for a while thereafter, all kinds of written stuff from the adult world. Thus, among other things, timetables, roadmaps, ticket stubs, copies of letters, political posters, bills, various kinds of official forms, copies of bank statements, copies of instruction manuals from various machines, copies of contracts, warranties, all those little throw-aways that we find in banks, etc. In short, lots of stuff from the adult world out there where all those people are doing all those mysterious and interesting things. Oh, and old telephone books, above all, classified telephone books. Talk about social studies; a look at the Yellow Pages tells us more than any textbook about what people do, and what there is *to* do.

Note, too, that all this stuff is free, so there is no problem in its not being available to low income kids."

I have sent copies of the large print *Times* to some families I know. What they did with them, if anything, I don't know. One family said that the children liked the paper, used it in many different ways, and that one child became very interested in the crossword puzzles, which I had not expected. But then, one can never guess what children may be interested in.

ON CLASS BIAS

A mother and teacher recently wrote me a letter, to which I replied, in part:

"You say, 'the only people who can hope to get their kids out of the schools safely are upper or middle class whites.' Not so, or at least not necessarily so. Some of the people who right now have their children out of school are not middle class at all. Only a week or so ago I talked with a woman who some years ago ran a paid tutoring service in San Francisco for parents whose children were not in school. She told me that about *70%* of her clients were working class families. I do not yet know whether these people had taken their children out of school with the school's consent, or whether they had simply hidden their children from the school. I did ask her why these parents had taken their children out. She said that in almost every case the schools were not helping these children learn and were saying that they were incapable of learning. Some families simply refused to accept this and began teaching or having their children taught at home. I will find out more about this, and will write about it in GWS.

You also say, 'If the children are young, it means in most cases that their mothers must stay home instead of working.' Well, that depends on what you mean by young. Another mother wrote about this. In my reply I said that six-year-old children probably needed an adult with them for most of the day, but that ten-year-olds and probably eight-year-olds did not, at least not if they had been trained and prepared for independence and self-reliance, which seems to me perfectly possible. Since all this is coming out in GWS #4, I won't repeat it here.

Later you say, 'working class, and especially Black, parents who take their children out of school are likely to be hounded by the authorities to the fullest possible extent.' Well, again, this depends, for one thing, on whether the *authorities* know that the children are out of school. Is this an easy thing to conceal from the authorities? In large cities, I would say that it was. As we all know, very high percentages of the children enrolled in big city public schools are truant every day. *The Boston Globe* reported not long ago that, on an average day, only about 70% of the children enrolled in the schools here are actually in school. If it is that easy for kids just to hang out in the streets, it ought to be even easier for them to be at home doing something interesting and worthwhile. You are absolutely 100% right when you say that if push comes to shove and the parents get into a really open dispute with the authorities, poor people, especially nonwhite, are going to have a much harder time of it than middle class whites. No argument about that at all. What I am saying is that most of the time it should be possible to avoid such disputes.

Later you say, 'poor kids need a high school diploma more than middle class kids do—they have a much harder time getting a job without it,' True. But kids can get high school diplomas without going to a high school, for example, by taking high school correspondence courses. Also, people can stay out of schools for quite a number of years, and then go back in. No one has to decide to leave schools forever. They can step off the school track whenever they want, and get back on it when they want—in all probability, ahead of the people who stayed on it.

You say, 'A related problem is that working class parents have less confidence in being able to teach their own kids (because if you're so smart why ain't you rich), and therefore in fact *are* less able to teach their kids.' True enough. But this is almost equally true of college graduates. It really is. In any socioeconomic group, the number of people who think that they are capable of teaching their children and doing a better job than the schools is *extremely* small. We have to begin with them, show what's possible, and hope that other people will make the effort. In every case, it takes a kind of leap of faith.

On the matter of 'overthrowing the social structure,' see my little article "On Social Change" in GWS #1. The word 'overthrow" simply does not describe any series of events that I can possibly imagine, certainly not in this country. I not only would not agree that it is impossible to get profound social change by small gradual steps, but would insist that that is the only way.

You speak later of building 'anything more than a small group of white dropouts,' Quite the reverse. I am interested in helping young people to find ways to live active, responsible lives in society, to find work worth doing.

You say, and I agree 100%, 'we should help each other teach our kids, teach each other's kids; arrange our lives so that larger numbers of people than just nuclear families share the responsibility of deschooling (may I say unschooling) and educating children. I am thinking, for example, of neighborhood discussion groups about what the schools do to children and why. What experiences have people had with the schools, and what do these experiences show? Parents can give each other advice about how to fight in various situations, and help each other construct alternatives. I do not at all mean that we should water down what we say in order to be more acceptable to more people. I think we should be absolutely straight forward with as many people as we can who are oppressed by schools, and I think we will find many people who agree and have a lot of experience and ideas to offer.' And I agree with your next observation, 'also I think this kind of support would help kids and parents who are not yet ready to pull out of school to at least see their school experience in a psychologically healthy way. It would help them to direct their anger at the schools rather than turn it inward and blame themselves as the schools want them to.' Absolutely; in fact I first made that point in the early part of my book *What Do I Do Monday?*

You later speak of 'a decision, which, if we make it, (my husband and I), may get us into a lot of trouble.' I believe very strongly in avoiding any and all such troubles if you possibly can. I see no point in direct confrontations with the authorities if you can avoid them, certainly not until we are a good deal stronger than we are now. I am not interested in heroic defeats. I think we ought to think of ourselves, if we have to use a military metaphor, like pilots who have parachuted down behind enemy lines in time of war. The thing to do is to be as inconspicuous as possible.

P.S. You speak of being 'worried' about 'overdoing the bookishness.' I think we have to lock horns with this issue. There was a time, fifty and more years ago, when poor and working class people in this country were not afraid of books on serious subjects. To people who asked me about helping their children, I would say something like this, 'You have to get over the idea that books are for rich people, and not for you. Your children will not think of books as an interesting and useful way to find out about the world unless you yourself do.' So I would have no hesitation in asking people to read this or that, whatever it might be. Most of my books are written in very simple language; if there are things which people don't understand, they can ask you, or me. That is part of the process of getting smart, not being afraid to ask questions when one doesn't understand something."

NO COMMENT

From a story in the *New York Times*, May 7, 1978:

"The minimum competency movement has built on earlier trends such as the 'back to basics' movement, and the cumulative changes in the approach to the teaching of reading were evident here in the millions of dollars of new instructional materials on exhibit [at a conference of more than 10,000 teachers, reading specialists, and others at the annual meeting of the International Reading Association] in Houston's convention center."

FROM A MOTHER

"My daughter, 6, has attended schools on and off for a few years and *always* learns more in the 'off' times!

After several months in public school her formerly perfect numbers are often backwards. Because of a teacher's remark to her in kindergarten, 'If you're such a good reader, why are you poor in Math?'!!!

After months of 'cooling it' about Math and lots of manipulative counting 'games,' she's enjoying Math again—but still thinks she's *bad* in Math.

I can see 'socialization' creeping into her ways and I want her out of school!

As a 'welfare mother', I get additional hassles about schooling for my kids. As a former English teacher, I may be able to arrange some 'home study' deal, but am afraid to ask the authorities for info which could lead to my entrapment. They are already questioning my child's tardy and attendance record, so I'm trying to keep as low a profile as I can."

(A few months later.)

"I got in touch with a free, open school which I had heard good reports about—the X School. They agreed to take my daughter on their enrollment as a 'correspondence, home-study' student. When I asked if they wanted us to send her workbook sheets to them for supervision and checking, the teacher said, 'Is she addicted to workbooks?' (Ed. note—many children are) We'll get her through withdrawal with some ditto sheets, until she gets creative again.' I loved it!

Since mine is the first such arrangement they have made, I want to wait a while before spreading the news—until we see how well it works.

One day I decided to take L out of school (after several weeks of one-or-two days per week attendance due to various 'complaints'—headache, bellyache, sore throat) I walked into the 'open' classroom, with its Science Corner, its Library nook, its Life Science (animals) areas, etc. and felt a wave of uncertainty. 'Can I provide as rich and diverse an environment? Will she resent being taken away from her peers?' Then I noticed that I have *never* seen anyone working—independently or in a group—in any of these nifty study areas! Then I noticed that 5 little boys (excluded from the 'group singing') were writing 'I Must Behave In Class' ten times on pieces of paper.

That did it!

I told the teachers and principal that we would soon be moving and that L would be enrolled at the X School. Transfer papers were rapidly issued and we walked out—free!

L went through a few days of sadness about leaving 'her' school, but soon began doing math games, drawing great pictures, reading a biography of Thomas Jefferson and a book on Astronomy (she's 6!).

We lie low in the morning and then if she's asked why she's not in school, she says she's 'connected to' the X school. Soon we'll drive there (about 1 hr.) and meet the teachers and set up whatever needs doing to keep the authorities off us.

If I'm accepted at the University, we'll be moving there and I'll 'neglect' to enroll her anywhere, continuing her X School thing. Another option possible is to make my home a 'field school' of the X School and me their 'delegated teacher.' (Ed. note—this is a new idea to me. Sounds like something we ought to try in some other places)

I feel great about the decision and L seems so much less tense and hyped-up. The secret, I think, is to not ask anyone for permission—then no one has to say no.

Guess what! She's not writing any numbers or letters backwards any more!

You were right—the Calif. State law is *very* lenient regarding private schools and very vague about what constitutes one. Thank you again for your wonderful encouragement and excellent newsletter."

ACCESS TO D.C.

"We are a family of three, mother, father, and daughter Susan, age 8 years this May, who have been home tutoring each other for 2 years. After we had watched our beautiful daughter's life, liberty, and creativity systematically destroyed by ... kindergarten teachers, Susan decided she wanted to stay at home the next year. The last chapter of *Instead of Education* gave us strength, especially the last paragraph. For us, schools are foreign lands that are difficult to imagine. Our life is free and our work and learning are directed at goals that we hold dear to our own needs, not the goals of society. We have taken control over our lives, we have attained power to run our own affairs. Susan takes care and responsibility for herself, she stands on her own two strong legs, she speaks clearly, thinks clearly and answers only to her conscience. She is happy, talkative, interesting and interested and can choose for her life any damn thing she pleases.

We live in Washington, D.C. on Capitol Hill about two miles from the museums of the Smithsonian Institution. Susan and her mother walk there almost every day, observing, playing, meeting people, going to movies, listening to music, and riding the merry-go-round. They see a fantastic variety of nature movies. They know art and history museums exhibit by exhibit. Susan can drag you through the history of the universe, through natural history, on up to the latest Mars landing. They eat lunch near the water fountain, see the latest sculpture, take pictures of their favorite spots, marvel at the beautiful spring and fall days. They attend mime shows, tape record jazz concerts, ride the double decker bus to their favorite 'explore gallery' where things can be played and jumped in. Tuition is very cheap, we all have fun, and we all learn a great deal.

Susan lives in a world of marvelous *abundance;* her resources are unlimited. She has not been 'socialized' by school to think that education is a supply of scarce knowledge to be competed for by hungry, controlled children. She doesn't play dumb 'Schlemiel' ... Our home and neighborhood are like a garden full of fresh fruit to be picked at arms length by all who want to.

She likes to paint, draw, color, cut out and paste. She compares her work to that in the museum. We give our comments and ideas when requested.

We have hobbies in astronomy and camping. Her father is a pediatrician who enjoys working with her in constructing electronic gear. She has excellent soldering techniques and has soldered many connections in our home brew electric computer now used in his office.

Her mother works with Susan on home art projects and nature studies. They cook together, shop together and are much envied by her father.

In D.C. home tutoring is allowed by law. Biannual reports are required by a B.A. or equivalent home tutor (parent or friend). Fifteen hours per week of instruction.

We are interested in contacting other people in the D.C. area who home tutor their own children and who are interested in their own continued learning about the world. We are interested in people who want to help children take power over their own lives and future.

Sincerely,
Robert and Sharon and Susan Dickey"

From a later letter:

"Susan has always had small, very well-coordinated hands and began working with circuit boards at the age of five, wiring and soldering transistors and resistors. The inner workings of televisions, radios, stereos, and other electronic devices seem to mystify not only children but most adults, and this activity has served to de-mystify Susan along with bolstering her confidence in her ability to do something of significant value and to be able to do it with a man on an adult to adult level.

Since our tutoring at home is completely legal with the District of Columbia government, I openly admit to most people that Susan doesn't go to school and that she's tutored by us at home. I am so independently secure in my thinking and am having such a positively rewarding experience from home tutoring that I can only view the feedback I get from other people as amusing. It's amazing that grown adults with education and experience in the world will admire and envy what we are doing, yet they view themselves as completely unqualified for home-tutoring their own children... Our experience with Susan has only been positive and rewarding and to see her in action, to view her productivity, and to speak with her gives testimony enough for the positive."

FROM JULIA

One of our readers (J in GWS #2) wrote to another (D in GWS #2), saying in part:

"Last spring and summer as we put together our plans to take the kids out of school, we decided that our best excuse (as far as the school system was concerned) was that we were going to be transferred in the middle of the school year, possibly to England. We said this in writing twice: once in our initial letter in May, 1977, and once in a long essay I wrote in August to explain our reasons, philosophy and capabilities. After several phone calls, letters, and a visit by us to the superintendent, he finally relented and sent us his letter of approval. We could hardly believe that in his letter, which we always thought and still do think is the only important document in this whole mess, he said not a word about tests for our children or other educational requirements (except that we were to use the Calvert course, as we had planned). The letter also said that if we did not receive final orders for duty outside the country the children were to be re-enrolled in public school. ...

...But this is what the superintendent forgot—that we can write and type letters even better than he can. A total of seven letters have passed between his office and us since March 3; his four, terse and authoritative; our three, long, impassioned and detailed. One of ours was three single-spaced typewritten pages, with four Xeroxed enclosures, and we sent all of this, all seven pages, not only to him but to all the other people (school system lawyer, head of Department of Pupil Services, and two school principals) he was sending carbon copies to.

...One of the people I contacted for support was a Board of Education member; I asked her if there was some way we could appeal to the Board of Education. She called me right away and assured me there was a long red tape procedure that would have to be followed before our case could leave the school system and be given to the Juvenile Court. A pupil personnel worker would have to contact us, forms would have to be filled (slowly, she suggested), and a decision would have to be made. If we didn't like the decision, we could appeal to the Board of Education. She urged me to check out the grievance procedure in the Board of Education policy manual, which I did (there is a copy in the Public Library). I asked her if she thought the superintendent might try to cut the red tape in our case in order to make an example of us, and she didn't see why he should since no publicity has attended our case.

So what it all comes down to is partly what you've been giving an admirable example of in GWS (Ed. note—she is referring to D here), *knowing* the laws and regulations that apply; but it also helps if you can think like a bureaucrat. In Maryland, if your children aren't in school, the worst that can happen is a $50/day fine. No one is precipitously arrested; children are not separated from parents. (Ed. note—these things have happened in Ohio, Connecticut, and perhaps other states) So at least you're physically safe while you waste your time and theirs writing letters. Apparently very few people end up being fined."

In a letter to GWS, J goes on, saying in part:

"…The following is taken from a newspaper article on truancy in Anne Arundel County: 'Out of 3,000 cases referred to the pupil personnel department last year, Miller (head of the department) said, 300 went to juvenile services for hearings. Miller indicated that it is difficult to enforce the attendance law, citing 25 requests for formal hearings last year that were denied by the courts. Under the law parents could be fined up to $50, but Miller implied the law has been difficult to enforce. In the last 15 years, he said, there have been no more than six or seven cases where a district court judge fined parents.'

My husband talked with this Mr. Miller on the phone once this spring; the conversation was cordial, like two old antagonists meeting again. He said he was following the superintendent's orders in calling to tell us we would have to put the children back in school. When my husband said that we wouldn't and once again explained why and then asked what was the next step, Miller said he didn't know; he would have to go back to the Superintendent to find out what to do. Except for a letter confirming the telephone conversation, we never heard from them again.

Regarding *The Final Report: Legal Implications of Compulsory Education* by William Aikman and Lawrence Kotin of the Mass. Center for Public Interest Law (see GWS #3), it is not easy to find a copy of it. I had my local library conduct a search for it through the state library system, without success. Last summer I wrote to the Mass. Center for Public Interest Law and never received an answer. Recently I wrote to the National Institute of Education and received from them a 'Directory of ERIC Microfiche Collections (Arranged by Geographic Location)" and a form for ordering the Aikman-Kotin report. The report is not available except in microfiche and it costs 83 cents plus postage, which would be 85 cents. (Ed. note—she wrote 85 cents—could she mean 98 cents?) Write to ERIC Document Reproduction Service, P.O. Box 190, Arlington, VA 22210. Order ED number 130387 and specify microfiche. Most public libraries probably have microfiche readers. Or call the nearest university, community college or state or local department of education, ask if they have an ERIC microfiche collection and if you may search through it for this report. Many of these places (according to the Directory) have facilities for reading and reproducing pages from ERIC documents.

Please use our names in GWS and put us in the directory; we'd be glad to hear from anyone now or after we move in July. Our new address will be:

Dennis and Julia McCahill
Staff / CINCUSNAVEUR
Box 69
FPO New York 09510

P.S. This spring there is a series of six lectures being held at the public library all about how the judicial system of Maryland works. It is being presented by the Committee on Public Awareness of the Judiciary of the Maryland State Bar Association. I think any unschooler who thinks he may have to face court proceedings would do well to find out whether his own State Bar Association offers a similar service. They may be quite willing to answer requests for information. In any case, it is comforting just to have some idea how the courts work."

Thanks for another very helpful letter. Let me second the advice about dealing with bureaucrats. Bury them in paper. Send copies not only to people in the bureaucracy, but newspaper editors, political people, anyone you think might be interested. If the b'crats send you forms to fill in, fill them in slowly—and I would suggest, a little bit incorrectly. Some of you may know *The Good Soldier Schweik*, for me one of the great comic novels, about an ordinary Czech who frustrated, not to say maddened his Austro-Hungarian rulers and bosses by pretending to want to cooperate with them, all the while making as many and as serious mistakes as he dared. (An American version might be Step 'n' Fetchit.) B'crats like to explain. Pretend to listen very intently—but then misunderstand. This stratagem may not be for everyone, but if it appeals to you, go as far with it as you can.

Even if you don't want the particular report Julia is talking about, it might be a good idea to look into the ERIC facilities in your area anyway. It may be a way of getting hold of important books that have gone out of print. I will be talking about one such book in the next GWS.

TO A READER

P.S. As you can see from the enclosed Radcliffe Statement, I don't believe in the idea of "education" either. I think the idea of education is a deeper one than the idea of schooling, and on the whole a much worse one. I don't want to be understood as saying that I think that education is a wonderful thing but schooling a bad way to achieve it. I don't like the notion of *doing things* to people to make them better, whether or not we do these things in places called schools.

You say that the need to pass on human knowledge is a "social problem." That's like saying that the need to get oxygen in the bloodstream is a physical problem, which we "solve" by breathing. You and I don't breathe to "solve" the problem of getting oxygen in our bloodstream, we breathe because it's natural. A healthy society transmits knowledge without thinking about it, as it lives and does its work. When it begins to think about the "problem" of transmitting knowledge, it's already a sign that something is seriously wrong.

To describe learning as "an organic part of a wholistic, human-scale community" seems at first reasonable enough. But there is still something seriously wrong with it. In such a community, nobody would even think about "learning." Life would be what it always has been—work, play, ceremony, politics (large-scale or small), family, friends, sex, birth, sickness, old age, death. Merely to talk about 'learning" is somehow to separate it from all of these.

It's like the old story about the man with the long beard. He had an enemy, who thought for years about how to do the bearded man in. Finally he said one day to the bearded man, "When you go to bed at night do you put your beard under the covers, or outside the covers?" The bearded man had never thought of it before. That night when he went to bed the question came back into his mind. He put the beard outside the covers, but that didn't feel right, and he couldn't sleep. He put it underneath the covers, but that didn't feel right either, and he still couldn't get to sleep. He tried it half in, half out, tossed and turned all night trying to figure out what to do with his beard, and soon died of insomnia. I think it is often a very dangerous business to raise unconscious processes up into the level of consciousness, to turn natural acts into "skills" which can only be learned by being taught.

Later you say "All this requires 'teachers' of tremendous humility and sensitivity to their potential power in a school situation." Who are these 'teachers,' who have nothing else to do? A healthy community wouldn't have anybody in it who did nothing else but "teach." All human beings are teachers. Teaching, like learning, is an integral part of all human life, and when we make of it a special and separate kind of activity, we instantly and inevitably corrupt it.

I think "free education" is a contradiction in terms.

FROM A FATHER

Mike Murphee writes from Florida, saying, in part:

"My wife and I wanted to say that while we enjoy GWS, all the talk about lawyers and going to jail only makes us paranoid. We are low profile people and don't believe in confrontations. Our little girl just turned 7 and would normally be in first grade, but we never registered her and haven't had any problems about this.

Right now, we live in a married housing section of a university, which is a fairly liberal area. Our friends know that we don't send our daughter to school, though we haven't publicized this. They just shrug their shoulders and don't worry about it. When we move from here in June we will continue our low profile and don't expect trouble. We're also not going to look for trouble by telling the schools we don't want to send our

children there. If anyone asks why our daughter doesn't go to school we'll probably just tell them that she has a private tutor and change the subject.

My wife and I both wonder about all the talk about home study courses. We're not interested in *teaching* our children (we also have a boy who is 16 months old). The idea of sitting down for a half hour a day and going over a workbook with my daughter is very unappealing. We are interested in her learning, but we thought that was done by providing access to the world, conversations, doing things and just being involved in living.

It seems to me that some people are still hung up about having their children be winners (as is discussed in *Instead of Education*). I'm not a very ambitious person myself and if my children do not become lawyers, doctors, or molecular biochemists that's fine with me.

My wife and I do not want to send our children to school, because we wish to see a saner society develop and we feel this is a step in the right direction. It is the same reason we subscribe to *Mother Earth News* and are looking around for a farm to buy. We feel that GWS can help promote a saner society. This is what we would like to see in GWS, the affirmation of a way of life where everyone cheers when the SORRY man reaches home. (Ed. note—see 'Capable Children' in GWS #3)

Nancy Plent mentioned in GWS #3 that she would like to hear about people who didn't go to school. While talking together on a show on PBS, Rudolf Serkin and Isaac Stern (Ed. note—a very famous classical pianist and violinist, for those who don't follow that music) *both* revealed they never went to school. Neither seems any the worse for it.

I just remembered a story about some Navajo children in a reservation school. Whenever a group of them were sent to the board to do an arithmetic problem, they would all finish at the same time. The fast ones would wait for the slower ones to figure it out so as not to embarrass them. (Ed. note—the schools combat this with all their strength) This is something we should all strive for. The continual ranking of children that schools do is one of their worst activities. (Ed. note—but one of the their real purposes, one of the things which the general public *insists* on) If you don't want to send your kids to school, then you shouldn't worry about their progress or compare them with other children (favorably or unfavorably).

My wife feels that you got a little carried away with the right-left discussion. The point to be made is that it is possible to grow up and live a happy and productive life without having a clear understanding of right and left. It is basically an academic distinction. It just doesn't seem good to make such a big thing out of it. If your conclusion is to have faith in the kids and basically let them work it out for themselves, why go into such detail?

Your idea about the rug with right and left footprints on it is a good idea, but it sounds like something they would have in a progressive school. (Excuse me for the cheap shot.) It goes back to what I said about *teaching* children. I don't want to spend my time thinking of cute, non-threatening ways to teach them academic ideas. While some things like the rug might occasionally be helpful it is very easy to get carried away. Just give them the fiddle and let them join in the playing."

———————————

There certainly is a tendency for teachers who are good at thinking of clever ways to teach things to get carried away with it. I recognize it in myself. More comment on Mike's good letter in the next section.

A REPLY

"I'm sorry all that talk about lawyers, etc. makes you anxious, but this is a part of the political world within which we unschoolers have to work. People are in cold fact threatened with jail, or in some cases even sent to jail. One of the things GWS wants to do is to prepare people as well as possible for what may happen if they begin to take their children out of school. I agree with you that simply not telling the schools about children is one way, and a good way to proceed. But it is not everyone's way. As Nancy Plent rightly points out, if you live in a small town you are just not going to be able to keep your kids out of school without the school finding out about it. Other unschoolers, also living in small towns, and planning to live there for a long time, want to live as regular members of the community and not a kind of outsider or outlaw, and therefore feel that it is important that their unschooling be out in the open. People will disagree on such matters of tactics; GWS aims to be as useful as possible to all of them.

As you will have seen in GWS #4, it seems to be very easy for people in Florida to call their own home a school. In other states this is very difficult.

I agree entirely with what you say about teaching your children. Other readers of GWS may not agree. What I am trying to say is that if you are going to get into teaching your children, there are ways of doing it that are much better than others. Also, as in the case of "J," (GWS #2) using some approved home study program may be an unavoidable part of the deal that some people have to make with their local schools.

I'm sure you are right about some people being hung up on wanting their children to be winners, though they might speak in terms of a 'happy, productive, etc. life.' Others might say that, while they don't particularly care whether their children become prominent in society or not, they are eager not to close off any such possibilities, should they prove to be what the child wants. Such people would say, 'If my child decides some day that s/he wants to be a doctor or a lawyer, I don't want to have made that impossible by unschooling her/him.' That seems to me fair enough.

I had and have a number of reasons for putting in the article about Right and Left. For one thing, some of the people who read GWS, and I hope as time goes on more and more of them, are teachers, educators, teachers of teachers, educational psychologists, etc. I want them, as well as any parents whose children may be having trouble with right and left, to consider very seriously that the difficulty may lie in the world and not in the child. There is nothing more guaranteed to get children stuck with one of those fancy sounding school labels than showing some confusion about right and left. Some people, now or in the future, who read GWS, may have children who have had such labels stuck on them, and may themselves believe that those labels are valid. I want to persuade them that they are not.

Also, there is the legal question. I don't think we are going to persuade the courts for a very long time to come to allow people to escape from compulsory schooling merely by showing that most schools are cruel, inhumane, everything you yourself believe them to be. But we may be able to get our children out of school if we can show that in important matters the schools are simply incompetent, don't know how to do their work, and that these diagnoses that they are constantly slapping on children have no basis in fact. The stupidity of schools, in connection with this matter of right and left, is or may be part of the legal case which we will someday build against them. As far as the little right-left reminder goes, if it doesn't appeal to you, skip it. GWS is not a Manual about 'How to Teach Your Child At Home.' It is a collection of suggestions for people to use if they think they may be useful. If you don't care whether your children know the difference between right and left, that's fine, I think I would agree with you. But some people do or may care. I want to speak to their needs as well.

I want to return again to the point of the piece entitled 'Mixed Allies,' in #2. A lot of very different people, with very different ideas about children and the way to bring them up, are going to be reading GWS, and for very different reasons. I don't want the newsletter to be only useful to a very small group of people who agree with me—or you, or anyone else—about everything. I agree with you about helping to promote a saner society. Since I think that schooling is one of the important things that makes the present society un-sane or downright insane, I think unschooling is an important part of that process. But I don't think there is any reason at all why all unschoolers, or all readers of GWS, should agree with me on what constitutes a saner society or the best ways to get there.

We have thought about dating each issue of GWS, but don't plan to do it. For many reasons, we think it is helpful both to the readers and to us if all subscriptions start with Issue #1. We are not, after all, printing stock market quotations or baseball scores or other news that goes quickly out of date. Most of what we print in GWS will be as useful in five or ten years as on the day we print it, and we don't want to have to reprint things for the sake of people who may come in later. In short, we don't make the distinction you make between 'current' and 'back' issues. All issues are equally current. But, feel free to put your own date on any issues as they arrive. I can't imagine that we will ever print anything more important than, say, the articles in GWS #1 about Jud's girl staying out of school, or about counting, or the little study tip, or ....etc. I want everyone who reads GWS to read those pieces. In that sense, the word 'newsletter' may be a little bit misleading. What we really are, I guess, is a reference book published a piece at a time."

THE THERAPEUTIC STATE

I recently wrote Erwin Knoll, Editor of *The Progressive* (Madison, Wisc.), saying in part:

"The term 'Therapeutic State' was coined by Dr. Thomas Szasz, as far as I know. I define it thus. In the Therapeutic State (hereafter TS), if A, usually some sort of 'professional' or 'expert,' wants to do something to B that he thinks would be good for B, and can persuade enough other people, C, D, E, F etc. that it will be good for B, he doesn't have to persuade B. In fact he doesn't even have to ask B. The TS is built on the idea of Compulsory Help. The TS's official helpers have the power to say to anyone, 'You need our help, whether you admit it or not, and we are going to help you whether you want it or not.' In the TS, no one has a right to refuse what the professional helpers have decided he needs.

The TS invented the greatest anti-libertarian device of the last 300 years. It is to call unwanted behavior, not 'crime,' but 'sickness,' and the means to prevent and control that behavior, not 'punishment' but 'treatment.' With this little invention, the Constitution, the Bill of Rights, and all of the legal and political defenses which people have struggled to create against tyranny over hundreds of years, disappear in a puff of smoke. All the professional helpers have to do is certify that someone is 'sick,' and they can do anything they want to him that they think will make him 'well.'

You are surely familiar with the fundamental legal principle of the 'Assumption of Innocence,' which holds that people must be judged innocent of crime or wrong until they have been proven guilty beyond a reasonable doubt. There is no comparable Assumption of Health. The professional helper does not have to prove to me, or to a jury of my peers, that I am 'sick' and in need of 'treatment.' All he has to do is assert it.

It is a great deal more than a strange coincidence that in Russia today opponents of the regime are classed as 'mentally ill' and sent to 'mental hospitals' where they are 'treated' until the state judges that they are 'sane' enough to be let out. Our psychiatrists, etc., get very indignant about this—when it happens in Russia. But in this country, when something more than a million children, and perhaps much more than that, are forcibly dosed with extremely dangerous psycho-active drugs, like Ritalin, to 'cure' them of imaginary diseases like 'hyperactivity,' etc., hardly anyone complains.

In the pre-Therapeutic State, it was relatively hard to use the law to control people's behavior. First, one had to get laws passed saying that certain acts were illegal. Secondly, these laws had to survive tests in the courts. Thirdly, some government agent had to formally accuse a citizen of committing the illegal act. Fourthly, in a process which was in itself difficult and time-consuming, the government had to prove that the accused person had actually carried out the illegal act. Even with all we know about the difference in justice for rich and poor, this system put a heavy burden on people who wanted to tell other people what to do and what not to do. But in the TS, all these cumbersome steps can be avoided, by the means I describe. Just call the unwanted behavior 'sick,' and the proper experts can do anything they want in order to 'treat' it.

Quite a good deal has been written about the abuses of the mental illness system, about the trivial reasons for which people can be put in mental hospitals and kept there for very long periods of time, and about the terrible things that can be done to them. I won't add to this. But I do want to point out that compulsory schooling is another example of the TS, in which children are forcibly 'treated' for the 'crime' of ignorance. In order to prevent this 'crime,' society says, with the support of virtually everyone, that we can take children for as many days a year as we want, compel them to be at certain places, usually within certain rooms and even certain seats, where for the most part they are not allowed to move or even to talk, and there can do to them anything we want, including what in any other context in society would be called torture. Small wonder that after twelve or more years under such a regime most young people don't take very seriously the idea of rights or civil liberties, their own or anyone else's and do not protest when the government or the police or the professional helpers make still further inroads into them.

These ideas may come as something of a shock and may even seem absurd. For reasons I have never really understood, the political left and civil-libertarians have always had a very soft spot in their heart for compulsory schools. I don't fool myself that this will be easy to change. But I hope what I've written here may perhaps induce you to think about it in a slightly new way.

I urge most strongly that you read and give serious thought to the Schrag-Divoky book *The Myth of the Hyperactive Child*, which goes into many of these matters in greater detail. (Available from GWS, $2 + 30 cents postage.) And in general, I would ask all libertarians and all those on the political left, 'How can we expect to treat children like slaves for the first eighteen to twenty-one years of their life, and suppose that they will then magically turn into free and independent citizens?'"

A SPEECH DEFECT

A parents writes that his son who is not in school, and is in other ways a very happy, active, growing child, has a speech defect (involving mostly vowels) that makes it hard for others to understand him. The parent has not taken the child to any local professional speech therapist, fearing that such therapists might want to consult with the child's school teachers, and finding that he had none, might report him to the school authorities. But he is also afraid that if he does not take the child to a therapist, and later on the schools do track him down, the fact of his not having sought "professional help" will be used against him by the schools and/or courts. He asked what I thought about this. I replied in part:

"I think I agree that if the schools catch you they will in fact be looking for any nail to hang you on. There is a very real possibility that they might try to use your 'failure' to 'seek professional help' for speech difficulties as some kind of further evidence of unfitness. After all, in more than one place the schools are trying to hang a 'neglect and abuse' charge on parents for merely failing to send children to school.

Therefore, I think it would indeed be prudent to 'cover yourself' by consulting with a 'professional,' providing this does not entail the even greater risk that the 'professional' would turn you into the schools. It might be wise to look up some of the literature on speech therapy, and write some letters to distant speech therapists, who would presumably have no interest in turning you in to your local school authorities. In other words, if one day you could show a court a whole lot of correspondence you had had with speech therapists in different parts of the country, to seek out the most effective therapies, I think it would probably be enough to free you of any charge of neglect. And if the speech therapists are like any other kind of therapists, they are so full of disagreements about the best way to treat various kinds of defects that you could say quite honestly and convincingly that you had sought opinions from a great many different sources in order to get some kind of consensus of opinion.

In this correspondence you might also say to these distant experts that since you live in a fairly isolated rural area and were not close to experienced speech therapists, you were eager to find out all you could about ways of working on it that you could practice in your own home. It is perfectly possible that absolutely none of the people you corresponded with might give you any encouragement on this, but would all say, "Don't try to do it yourself, seek out professional help.' But if you could get a couple of these distant experts to say that the techniques were in fact perfectly simple and that they could be carried out by you in your own home, this would be still further protection.

I agree with you that the problem is urgent, and I think you would be wise to make a strong effort to convince your child of this. I assume here, as always, that children are intelligent and responsible human beings, who want to understand how the world around them works. Were I in your shoes, I wouldn't hesitate to say to A that even if he wasn't worried about his speech defects, I was *very* worried, for all the reasons you have mentioned. I would add that I thought there was a real chance that someone hearing him talk this way might report him to various authorities, school and otherwise. I would go on to say that if this happened, those same authorities might very well use this speech defect, and the fact of your not having gone to a professional, as a reason to try to take A away from you altogether. There are solid reasons for you to be afraid of this situation, and I think you have every right to convey to him as strongly as you can the strength and depth of, and reasons for, your fear. I would say, 'This may not seem like an important problem to you, but it does to me, and I insist that we solve it and solve it quickly, or we may all be in very serious trouble.' This is one of the places where I would intervene quite forcibly to protect the child from a danger that he could not understand, just as I would not let him drink or eat everything he found in the medicine cabinet. In short, here is a position in which I would not hesitate to impose a good deal of adult authority.

There's no reason why this should take a long time. Children are good linguists, as you know. They very quickly pick up foreign languages. Once A is convinced that something really has to be done about this, you should get his speech straightened out, using the tape recorder, in a matter of months, or maybe even weeks. After all, learning to repronounce old words is in no way different from learning to pronounce new ones, and he is picking them up all the time. The thing is to make him aware that he is saying things differently from you (and by extension other people) and that this is a bad situation which has to be changed quickly."

RESEARCH

We can tell a good deal about how smart a particular group of experts is—or is not—by the kinds of research they do—or do not do.

In World War I we first began to see evidence that prolonged anxiety, stress, and fear can have great and destructive effects on the human nervous system. The trenches were a kind of satanic laboratory of stress. More soldiers than ever before lived for much longer times than ever before in cold and wet, under the constant threat of death, often under continuous heavy bombardment. Under these conditions many men suffered a condition or disorder to which doctors gave the name "shellshock." Some went stone deaf; some went totally blind; some became paralyzed, shook all over, lost all control of their muscles and limbs. The authorities first suspected faking, but it was soon clear that the affected soldiers were not faking. The only cure for these ailments, which in many cases looked like "physical" disorders, was to take these men out of stress, away from the front. After some time in a safe and calm place, they regained (in varying degrees) their sight, hearing, use and control of their limbs. Some—I don't know how many—may even have gone back to the front.

In World War II this happened again. Many of the British troops who spent days on the beaches at Dunkirk, totally exposed to continuous bombardment from both guns and planes, broke under this stress in exactly the same way. The doctors of World War II called their condition "psychoneurosis." The cure was basically the same—to remove the afflicted men from the scene of stress and danger. There was some argument about how they should then be treated. One military psychiatrist (perhaps one of many) claimed that soldiers would recover more quickly form psychoneurosis if they were kept under strict military discipline and made to feel that their duty was to get back into action as quickly as possible. Others—I believe the majority—disagreed.

The point is that we had very strong evidence that stress can cause what seem to be gross physical disabilities. I myself began to see, not only among the children I taught, but in myself as I struggled for the first time to learn a musical instrument, that anxiety could make it much harder for the children, or myself, to think, to remember, or even to see. In *How Children Fail,* which came out in 1964 and has by now been read by a good many millions of people in the education business, I described how one day, under pressure, I totally lost (for a short time) the ability to see meaningfully. Later, in *The Lives of Children,* George Dennison described, in the most painful and almost clinical detail, the effects of stress and fear on one of his pupils.

So it was reasonable to suppose, when educators began to claim that some children might be having trouble learning this or that because they had "perceptual handicaps," that they might look for possible connections between such inferred "handicaps" and children's fears and anxieties. So far, as far as I have been able to learn, very few of them seem to have done so.

Not long ago I was one of many speakers at a large conference of specialists in "learning disabilities." Before more than a thousand people I reviewed the evidence for a connection between anxiety and stress and perceptual or other learning disorders. I spoke of the medical experience of two World Wars, and of my own experience as a teacher and as a beginning learner of music. Then I asked for a show of hands response to this question: "How many of you have heard of—only heard of, not done—any research on possible connections between perceptual handicaps in children and their anxiety, however measured? How many have heard of any research to find whether and to what degree lowering measurable anxiety in children might lessen the incidence of perceptual handicaps?"

In that roomful of over a thousand experts in this field, only *two people* raised their hands. What the others may have known, I do not know. But only two raised

their hands.

I asked them what they knew. One told me of research I had long known about, done by a very original and controversial educator who, at least until very recently, had no degrees in Psychology and no standing whatever in the educational "establishment." He had found high correlations between perceptual handicaps and children's anxieties, and that lowering the anxieties did indeed greatly lower the incidence of such handicaps.

The other man who raised his hand did not speak. But later, he wrote to me a letter. He is, and has been for some time, a Professor of Education at a leading university in the very city in which this conference was held. He too had suspected the kind of connection I talked about, had worked out a way of teaching reading that he thought might lessen this anxiety, had used this method to teach a group of students officially labeled "perceptually handicapped," and had found that after quite a short time in his class, in the opinion of their regular teachers, his students were much less handicapped than they had been before. This, I would add, in spite of the fact that his classroom was nowhere as stress-free as others I have known, seen, and written about, or as he himself might have made it if he had had more time, had not been under pressure to show some fairly quick results.

There were other questions I have asked at other places and times, but did not think to ask there. When I first heard that boys were supposed to be four or five times as likely to have "perceptual handicaps" or "learning disabilities" as girls, I asked, in a letter published in a national magazine, whether any research had been done to look for possible connections between this four or five to one ratio and the sex of the teacher. I have yet to hear of any. And it would surely be interesting to see what connections there might be between the incidence of "perceptual handicaps" in children and measurable anxiety *of their teachers.* But again, as far as I know, no such research has been done.

We will have much more to say, in future issues of GWS, about this whole matter of "learning disabilities."

SKINNER'S GUN

A friend of mine, when still a student at Harvard, told me one day that he and a few friends had just had a very interesting conversation on the library steps with Prof. B.F. Skinner, famous for 'inventing' behavior modification and operant conditioning.

But first of all, he did not 'invent' behavior modification. The idea of using bribes and threats, rewards and punishments, to get people to do what we want, is very old, and is not made new by calling these rewards and punishments "positive and negative reinforcements."

On the other hand, operant conditioning is a new invention, or at least a very new twist on an old one. It is a way of getting other people (or dogs, rats, pigeons, etc.) to do what you want, *without ever showing or telling them what you want.* Very briefly, it works like this. If you have, say, an animal moving about at random, and if you give it a jolt of pain every time it moves, however slightly, in the opposite direction, after a while that animal will move almost directly in direction A, as far as it can. If you are watching human beings, and reward them every time they change their behavior, even in the slightest degree, in the direction of something you want them to do, after a while they will be doing that something you want, without your ever having told them to do it, and, what is even more important (and sinister), without their ever even having decided to do it. This is part of what Skinner means when he says, as he does all the time, that the human experience of willing and choosing is an illusion—all that has happened (he claims) is that without being aware of it we have been getting some kinds of reinforcements—rewards or punishments—from the outside. Control those rewards and punishments, he says, and you control human behavior.

Oddly and ironically enough, this is exactly how, as I will describe in a later GWS, the behavior of schools as institutions is controlled.

Anyway, on this particular day, Skinner (so my friend said) told the students that if he could just find a way to gain total control of human behavior, he would feel that he had not lived in vain. In other writing he makes clear why he wants this control. He wants to use it, and thinks he could use it, to make some sort of "ideal" society, without war, poverty, cruelty, or any one of the thousand other ills. This dream, ambition, delusion, is kindly enough. But it makes clear that Skinner (like most of his true believers and followers) is an exceptionally foolish man.

Now, believing in an absurd and mistaken theory about how humans think and feel does not of itself make Skinner foolish. The history of Science, after all, is a catalog of mistakes, a list or *wrong* answers, not right ones. But some very bright people have had very good reasons for believing (at least for a while) in some of those wrong answers. Even wanting to have control over all human behavior, though a rather grandiose ambition, does not of itself make Skinner foolish. What stamps him as foolish is thinking that if he *could* find a way to control all human behavior, *he* would be the one who would then be allowed to control it.

I have often imagined myself saying to him, "Fred, suppose you could invent what for metaphorical purposes we might call a Behavior Gun, a device such that, if you aimed it at someone and pressed the trigger, Z-z-zAAAPP, that someone would thereafter do exactly what you wanted. What makes you think that *you* would be allowed to point and shoot the gun? How long do you think it would be before large strong hands would gently (or perhaps not so gently) pry your nice new Behavior Gun our of your hands, while a voice said, 'Excuse us, Professor, we'll just take that gun, thank you very much, if you don't mind.' Has the thought never occurred to you that someone, someday, might point and shoot that Behavior Gun at *you?*"

In a recent magazine article Skinner asks sadly why we don't use what we already know about controlling human behavior. Oh, but Professor, we do! The trouble is that the "we" who are doing this controlling—military and political leaders, big businesses, advertising men and propagandists, the bosses of the mass media, tend to be people that Skinner (and I) do not much like or agree with. They do not seem to be particularly interested in using their power over human behavior to make a better world—though they probably have high-sounding words to justify whatever they want and do. They are (of all things!) mostly concerned to keep what power they have, and if possible to get even more. And any little tricks that Skinner and his equally woolly-minded behavior-modifying colleagues can think of to control human behavior, these people will be delighted to take over. Go, Professor, go!

What we (and he) would do better to think about is how to help people gain better control over their own behavior, and to resist better all those other people—leaders, bosses, and experts of all kinds—who are trying to control it. This is one part of what GWS is about.

Let me now answer a question that no one has yet asked, but that some surely will. Why bother to condemn Skinner in GWS? What have his ideas, good or bad, to do with taking children out of school?

Just this. Everywhere the schools say (often in a court, to which they have brought some unschooling parents), "We are the only people who know anything about teaching children. Unless you do it our way, you're doing it the wrong way." But their ways of teaching are heavily influenced by Skinner's theories. Many schools, and more every year, admit, no, *boast* that they are using behavior modification techniques in their teaching. So anything we can do to show that behavior modification and operant conditioning are the inventions of an essentially shallow and second-rate thinker may someday help people to persuade some court to let them teach their children at home.

SCHOOL STORY

In *The Way It Spozed to Be,* (copyright Simon & Schuster, repr. with permission) Jim Herndon tells about his first year of teaching, in a ghetto junior high school. Around November, the school mixed up his records, and told him that he would have to stop teaching until they could straighten them out. So, until after Christmas he worked at the Post Office, while a substitute teacher took his place. When he went back to his classes, the students had much to say about the substitute, Mrs. A.:

"Mrs. A was a better teacher than I, she was a real teacher, I wasn't no real teacher, she really made them work, not just have them old discussions every day; no, man, they were learning spelling and sentences and all they was spozed to. Moreover she was strict and didn't allow fooling around—all in all they felt they'd been getting somewhere. I looked in my grade book, up to now pretty empty of marks, and saw, sure enough, a whole string of grades after each name mostly, however, F's and zeroes. Many of them had nothing but zeroes, which I took to mean they had been busy not-doing this important work. I pointed this out to the class, but it didn't matter. They had been back on familiar ground; strict teacher, no fooling around, no smart-off, no discussions about how bad school was, and plenty of work. That was, after all, what school was and they were in favor of it.

7H was in a similar temper. They too had tales of plenty of real work, strict discipline, no talking, no gum, reading aloud every day, everybody—and then they came out with a long list of all of them who had been sent to the office for talking or chewing gum or refusing to read or laughing or getting mad at the teacher. Mrs. A gave them work on the board every day, they screamed, and she made them keep a notebook with all this work in it and they were spozed to bring it every day to work in and get graded on it. That was what real teachers did, they told me. I asked to see some of the notebooks; naturally no one had one. What about that? I asked. No use. She made us keep them notebooks, they all shouted. The fact that no one had kept or was keeping them notebooks didn't enter into it."

No, it didn't, and it still doesn't. What people want schools to do is make children learn things. Whether they actually learn them, or remember, or make use of them, is not important.

(*The Way It Spozed to Be* avail. from Holt Assoc., $1.25 + .30 postage.)

A LEGAL STRATEGY

Nat Hentoff writes a regular column for the *Village Voice*, 80 University Place, New York, NY 10003, in which he often attacks (among many other injustices and wrongs) so-called "corporal punishment." Not long ago I wrote to him, saying in part:

"Just read your column about the kid being beaten in school with an oar. Thinking about it, I had an idea for a completely new legal strategy in this matter. Since the Supreme Court (not surprisingly) has decided as it has on the Constitutional question, that road is closed, at least until we get some new justices (pray to Heaven we do!) or can think of another approach. Maybe I wrote this before, but I am absolutely convinced that the Supreme Court is not going to make any decision which will have as one of its results that the Federal courts are flooded with suits on these questions.

The legal strategy I'm thinking about is to sue the schools for negligence. I can imagine a parent saying, more or less, 'When I send an undamaged and healthy

kid to school in the morning, which I am compelled by law to do, I expect to get a healthy and undamaged kid back in the afternoon. It is a part of the school's responsibility to see that this happens, in so far as it is within their power to do so. Naturally, if the kid is running downstairs and slips and hurts himself, or injures himself playing baseball, or something like that, this is beyond the school's reasonable control. But when a kid comes home seriously injured because a teacher hit him with an oar for chewing gum, I say the school has been negligent. Questions of discipline have nothing to do with it. It is not my responsibility to solve the school's discipline or gum chewing problems. All I insist is that they find ways to solve them which do not injure my child. If they cannot or will not do that, I claim they have been negligent, and demand that they pay me damages.'

I suspect that some lower courts might sustain such an argument, and that if they did, the upper courts would not overturn them, precisely *because* they don't want to raise the Constitutional issue. In short, what worked against us might be made to work for us."

THE J-BOMB

By the time this issue arrives, readers will probably have read more than enough about the Jarvis amendment, or Proposition 13, in California. What it does is limit property taxes to 1% of the 1975-76 market value of homes, thus reducing current property taxes on the average from $12 billion to $5 billion a year. California may be able to make up for some of this lost revenue out of a large state surplus, and may also pass some new state taxes, though these now require a two-thirds majority in the legislature. We can expect this so-called "taxpayers revolt" to be followed in many other states, most of which do not have a large state surplus and many of which will not want or be able to pass additional taxes.

As a result, most schools and school systems in such states will have less, often much less, money to work with. Some, like the schools in Cleveland and 13 other cities in Ohio, where voters turned down emergency tax levies, may be thrown into severe crisis, may not even be able to stay open for as long as state law requires. What this may lead to, whether it will put an end to those taxpayers' revolts, no one can tell.

Meanwhile, we unschoolers and deschoolers (for the difference, see GWS #2), may have some new opportunities.

1) One thing we may be able to do is get a number of state legislatures to lower, or even do away with altogether, the minimum age at which people may take the state High School Equivalency exam. This lower age limit varies from state to state; in many it is 19, 20, or even 21. Clearly, the purpose of the law is to keep young people in school, even though they may have long since learned what the school says it is trying to teach them. School people are quite open about this;

when a bill to lower this minimum age was before a committee of the Mass. legislature, many educators said to the committee, in effect, "If we let kids take this exam earlier, we'll have a lot of them running around on the streets." The legislators promptly killed the bill. With Jarvis in mind, they may be much more ready to hear us when we say, "Why spend good (and scarce) tax money to keep young people in school when they have learned what the school is trying to teach them? Why not let them out, to get further schooling or to do useful work?" For less money than schools cost, we could find ways to do this. In other words, paying $15 to $20+ thousand a year to people to babysit teenagers may be a luxury that most states and communities can no longer afford.

2) We may also be able to get at least some state legislatures to state much more explicitly that, subject only to broad and reasonable requirements, parents ought to have the right to teach their children at home. We may even be able to get them to see that the requirement (in many states) that parents must have a teacher's certificate in order to do this is in fact nothing but a way of protecting teachers' jobs, and that tax-payer-voters may not like having their tax money used for this.

3) In general, we may be able to interest both legislatures and school systems in less rigid and expensive ways of sharing information and skill, that make more use of what ordinary, non-professional people know and can do—like the Learning Exchange of Evanston, Ill. and many other communities.

4) People whose local school system will not let them take their children out of school and teach them at home may be able to get the general public to put pressure on the schools, by saying something like, "With taxes as high as they are, and the schools hard pressed for money, how is it that Superintendent X is willing to spend so much time and money to prevent us from teaching our own children, when by doing so, we would be taking some of the load off the school system?"

I think we would be wise to pursue and exploit these opportunities as far as we can. Let us know about any steps you take in this direction.

IN A BOAT

The following letter, from Janet Howell, 1081 Kingsway, Alliance, Ohio 49601, may make some people say, perhaps angrily, "How many people can take their families on a cruise?" Not many. But a boat is a small place, and many things that can be done on a boat could be done just as well in a camper, or small mobile home, or even in a small city apartment. She writes, in part:

"...Are you planning an extended cruise with your family? What will you do about your children's education? How does education take place with young people on a boat? Is formal schooling necessary? If not, does education just happen? Are there ways parents can foster learning? Are there ways we can create a learning environment? (Ed. note—the world is a learning environment. So is a boat) Is there any special equipment needed?

Naturally, your arrangements with your own school district are of primary importance if the children do not want to miss a year of school. For high school young people, the state usually requires a certain number of credits for graduation. If your teenager does not want to lose any school time, he may have to avail himself of correspondence school courses. If this is his choice, the University of Nebraska offers not only a wide variety of subjects, but competent and caring instructors who make the courses as personal as the written word can be. (Ed. note—I forgot to ask Janet, but interested readers may if they want to, whether the family was living in Nebraska when they took these courses, or whether the University will send them to people in other states.) ... Our school system was extremely adaptable, allowing my husband and me to construct and supervise all learning experiences for our 11 year old as we saw fit.

Looking back and reflecting on a year's cruising with our 16 and 11 year old boys, I would rate our overall learning experience as 9 1/2 on a scale of 0 to 10. Some of the areas of learning we experienced growth in were mathematics, science, history, geography, English, boat maintenance, people, problem solving, family living, and spiritual awakening. ...

...We had some science books on the earth, the ocean, and the atmosphere. Keith, 11, became the teacher and *mother became the pupil*. (Ed. italics) ... mother was assigned her first test shortly after the switch. These were the instructions: 1) Study work text for unit test. 2) Test will start immediately after lunch. 3) No studying during lunch—that's family time. 4) Test is a 'closed book' one. 5) Good luck on your test.

We discovered that almost all cruising families have a library on board, and one of our favorite things to do when we met other families was to exchange books. We had many books on board ... some we particularly enjoyed sharing and discussing after we had all read them were *The Hunchback of Notre Dame* by Victor Hugo, *The Camerons* by Robert Crichton, *Wind From the Carolinas* by Irving Stone, and *Stars in the Water* by George Condon. We read the latter aloud as we crossed the New York Barge Canal, most of which duplicates the old Erie Canal.

Another project Keith initiated and developed was a new brochure for the Charlestown Landing restoration. We had visited this historic spot, and Keith had later observed that he thought their brochure needed updating and could be made more interesting to children. With minimal suggestion and direction, he wrote to the Charlestown Landing Foundation. They replied in a very personal letter that they were updating their brochure, and any suggestions he had would be considered. Keith proceeded to spend many hours designing a brochure, including the language and the art work. He eventually was presented with several of the new brochures containing some of his ideas, a year's family pass to the exhibit, and a Charlestown Landing patch to wear proudly on his jacket. Keith wrote several other letters to individual and company persons as part of his learning experience, and each one replied personally to his inquiries. We believe that he may have learned from this that people do pay attention to what others think, and that as an adult he may continue writing letters to the editors, to his Congressmen, and to his President.

Paul, the 16-year-old, was working independently on a correspondence course of advance math. He ... his younger brother and his father ... worked together on navigation problems. They sharpened their knowledge and teaching by trying to teach me. The boys spent many hours studying about, and then applying their knowledge, in boat design. This involved much mathematics and much debating and sharing. ... Most significantly, we learned how to live together."

————————————

I learned many years ago that one of the best ways, maybe the best way, to study for a test is to *make up a test.* Pretend you are the teacher, and make up a test, as much as possible, in form, like the ones the "real" teacher gives. Make up True-False questions, identifying questions, completion questions, short essays—everything you usually find on a test. Make the test as hard you can, and longer than the one you will have to take. Give it to a friend (mother or otherwise). If you have friends taking the same course, test them and have them test you. It really works.

Parents who are trying to help children who are stuck in school can do so, among other ways, by having the children make up tests in each course, which they, the parents, will take. The last part is important. Making up a test won't be much fun for most children unless someone else is actually going to take it.

A good way of learning or understanding something is to teach it or try to explain it to someone else— a volunteer, of course, someone who really wants to learn it. I studied Accounting one year in college, and was able to go through the motions enough to get as good a grade as I wanted to get. But I understood nothing at all of what Accounting was really about, how it worked, what it was for—until, years later, I tutored a boy on it, who was going to study Hotel Management in college and wanted to get a little jump on it. Then it all fell into place—for me, at least.

CHILDREN OF FILM

Some years ago a good friend of mine, Peggy Hughes, then living in Denmark, decided she wanted to make a 16mm. sound film about the Ny Lille Skole (New Little School), a small school in which she was working, which I describe in *Instead of Education* (from

Holt Associates, Inc. at $3.10 + .30 postage, paperback, $3.50 + .30 postage, hardcover) and mention elsewhere in this issue. She had done a small amount of black and white photography, but had never even owned a movie camera, let alone made a film with sound.

In time, working almost entirely alone, with occasional advice from the more experienced, she produced a film, about 45 minutes long, called "We Have To Call It School." I am not unbiased about the film; she and I are old friends, I loved the school and the people in it, and for some of the footage I was her sound man. But I think it is perhaps the most vivid, touching, and true film portrait of children that I have ever seen. Readers of GWS, and indeed anyone who likes, enjoys, and respects children will surely be charmed and delighted by it and may learn much from it.

Why should unschoolers want to see a film about school? The answer is in the title. Early in the film is a shot of the children arriving at school in the morning. Over this we hear the voice of one of the teachers, Erik, saying, "We have to call it school. The law in Denmark says that children have to go to school, and if we didn't call this school, they couldn't come here." But it is not a school in any way that we understand those words. It is a meeting, living, and doing place for six or seven adults and about eighty children, aged about six through fourteen. It is more like a club than anything I can compare it to. The children come there—when they feel like it, most of the time during the winter, not so often when spring and the sun arrive—and, sometimes with the adults, sometimes by themselves, do and talk about many things that interest them. In the process, they learn a lot about themselves, each other, and the world.

I think the film is important for unschoolers for many reasons, among them this one. What we need in our communities is not so much schools as a variety of protected, safe, interesting *spaces* where children can gather, meet and make friends, and do things together. Such spaces might include children's libraries (or sections of libraries), children's museums (a wonderful one in Boston), children's theaters (children making the drama as well as watching it), children's (or children's and adults') art or craft centers, zoos (also a wonderful one in Boston), adventure playgrounds, and so on. One such space was the Peckham Center for families which existed in London in the 1930's, and which I also describe in *Instead of Education* . (People are now working to get a new version of Peckham going in a small city in Scotland.) And another such space would be the Ny Lille Skole. It's not a matter of copying it exactly, but of catching the spirit of it.

You can rent or buy the film from Holt Association, Inc. To rent it costs $100 per day of use plus postage (allow two weeks for delivery); to buy it costs $350 per print. You may use it in two ways. One is simply to rent it, show it, and then discuss it, or draw what conclusions from it you will. The other is to have Mrs. Hughes come with the film (if her schedule allows), show it, and then discuss it and answer questions about it. We know from experience that people who see the film have a great many questions about the school. Mrs. Hughes' fee is $200 per day, plus expenses.

We hope some of you may be able to see it.

Editor—John Holt
Managing Editor—Peg Durkee

GROWING WITHOUT SCHOOLING

Issue No. 6

September, 1978

The label or address on your GWS (or envelope) will have on it a symbol like l 06, 3 12, etc. The *second* numeral is the number of the *last* issue of your subscription. If you like GWS, as we hope you do, please renew. You may renew for one year, two, or three. The latter will save you money and help us. Many thanks.

A reader from Florida, who is teaching her two children at home, writes, "As far as neighbors or strangers are concerned—everyone has thought it great that K and L are home and that we're working and learning together."

A new subscriber writes that she saw GWS (or something about GWS) on the bulletin board of the children's section of her public library. Other readers might see whether their library would post GWS on one or more of their bulletin boards. Or, subscribers might take out an extra sub for their library—though it might be a good idea to show GWS to the librarian first, and ask if they would like to have a sub.

The group subscription record has moved to Temple, ME, where readers have taken out a 16x sub.

Donnelly/Colt, Box 271, New Vernon, NJ 07976, sells a number of bumper stickers and buttons, mostly on antinuclear themes. But the button I like best (50¢, 15¢ ea. for 20 or more) just says "Question Authority."

When ordering books from us, please make checks out to Holt Associates, Inc. This will save us the work of transferring the money from the GWS account. Postage on all orders, 30¢ for first book, 15¢ each additional book.

NEWS ITEM

A friend sent a clipping from the New York *Daily News*, May 28, 1978. It may be worth noting that the *News* is a popular tabloid, generally more Right than Left in politics and aimed at the "man on the street." The story, in full:

SCHOOL'S OUT FOR FAMILY

Grand Rapids, Minn. (AP)—An Itasca County *jury* has found a Deer River couple innocent of violating the state's mandatory school attendance law in refusing to send their two children to public schools.

The jury agreed Friday with Joseph Palmer's argument that his wife, Ann, was capable of teaching the children, aged 8 and 10, at home.

In their two-day trial, the couple maintained that public schools were a corrupting influence on children and said the education provided by Mrs. Palmer, who has had one year of college, was adequate. *Palmer is a custodian in the Deer River school system.* (Ed. note—italics mine)

EQUIVALENT

Friends of ours live in a rich suburb with a "good" public school system. Last winter one of their boys broke his leg and had to wear a huge cast, which made it impractical to send him to school. The family (not unschoolers) told the school they wanted to be sure the boy kept up with his class. The school said, no problem, we'll send around a tutor, which they did, every week—*for an hour and a half.* It was enough.

EINSTEIN SAID

"It is, in fact, nothing short of a miracle that the modern methods of instruction have not yet entirely strangled the holy curiosity of inquiry; for this delicate little plant, aside from stimulation, stands mainly in need of freedom; without this it goes to wrack and ruin without fail. It is a very grave mistake to think that the enjoyment of seeing and searching can be promoted by means of coercion and a sense of duty. To the contrary, I believe that it would be possible to rob even a healthy beast of prey of its voraciousness, if it were possible, with the aid of a whip, to force the beast to devour continuously, even when not hungry, especially if the food, handed out under such coercion, were to be selected accordingly."

FROM A PARENT

A parent (from MO) writes, in part:

"...I have found your newsletter increasingly interesting and valuable. As I wrote to you about a year ago, I will not be sending my children to school (the oldest, now five, would normally be entering kindergarten this September). He has been reading now for about a year. I would not have believed anyone who told me a child could make the kind of progress D has made. He is interested in Space Travel and Astronomy and *we have made available to him all literature on the subject we could find.* (Ed. italics) He gobbles it up at incredible speed and begs for more. He reads books about the planets and can discuss intelligently the effects of gravity on the various planets and moons (e.g. that the moon has no air because it has insufficient gravity to hold the air, and that on Jupiter he would be squashed flat). Needless to say we are delighted, and more convinced than ever that this is the way to go."

Tx for good letter. D and others who share these

interests might want to read (if they are still in print) a number of science fiction novels by Hal Clement (one title I remember is *A Mission of Gravity*), all of them about what happens when living creatures from one kind of planet try to explore a very different kind of planet. In one, a group of aliens from a planet much hotter than Earth land here, and the story is about how they try to deal with our (to them) incredible cold. Worth looking up.

Before long, of course, it will be possible to show D (and other children like him) how they can look up and find for themselves literature on whatever interests them, and ask others the questions their parents can't answer.

THE CHILD TAKERS

From the Juvenile Rights section of the 1977 report of the ACLU:

"In the past year, the ACLU's Juvenile Rights Projects secured a major victory in its struggle to prevent the state from arbitrarily and unnecessarily separating children from their parents. The U.S. Court of Appeals for the Eighth Circuit upheld a lower court decision forbidding the state of Iowa from using its parental termination statute to sever the relationship between Charles and Darlene Alsager and four of their children.

The appeals court ruled that the state cannot 'terminate' parents without proving that they are harming their children in substantial and serious ways. For the first time a court recognized that there must be a more compelling reason for separating families than the state's assertion that it is 'in the best interests of the child.'

Relying on the *Alsager* decision, the ACLU then challenged a Virginia statute which authorized the temporary separation of children from their families in 'emergency' situations. The case, *Ives v Jones*, was successfully settled, and as a consequence the Virginia law was changed. No longer may children be witheld even temporarily from their parents unless clear and substantial danger to the child is shown. Moreover, parents whose children have been taken under a so-called emergency are entitled to an immediate hearing at which they may have counsel and other due process rights.

The *Alsager* decision also prompted a federal court in Albama to rule that the state's neglect statute was unconstitutional because of vagueness and amorphous definitions of 'child neglect'..."

————————————

Of all the threats that schools make to unschoolers, the most terrifying is the threat to take their children away. The decisions cited in the ACLU report suggest that, in some states at least, the courts may not allow the schools to carry out that threat. But of course this

depends on whether these courts would rule that unschooling children was harming them "in substantial and serious ways," or constituting a "clear and substantial danger" to them. In the politically so-called "conservative" states cited, the courts might so decide; what they are refusing to allow is the state taking children away from parents on what might be called psychological grounds i.e. because (as in the Alsager case) the parents had low I.Q.s.

I suspect that for some time to come we will not be able to get the ACLU or other civil liberties organizations to oppose compulsory schooling on Constitutional grounds. But we might be able to get these organizations and/or their state and local branches to say that unschooling children ought not to be grounds for the state to take them away from their parents. This in itself would be an important step. Let's look further into this. Do tell us what you find out.

GOOD NEWS FROM VT.

Catherine Lowther, R.D. 2, Hardwick, Vt. 05843, wrote us, in part:

"I am sorry to hear that so many people are having such a hard time taking their kids out of school. I thought you might like to balance the scales a little with a positive story.

I never sent my kids to school. They are 9 and 7 and I have always taught them at home. I have been approved by the State every year, the local authorities have been friendly, supportive, and even enthusiastic. The local school board has bought all our books and materials, to be returned to them when we are finished with them.

I noticed in GWS #4 you said that the burden to prove that a program is not equivalent to public school should rest with the state. In Vt. it does. [State Supreme Court decision.]

I also know three other families in Vt. who have taken their kids out of school without harassment."

————————————

Along with the letter, C.L. sent a copy of Vermont state law. Title 16, V.S.A., Section 1121(b) as amended Mar. 30, 1967, reads as follows:

"*Attendance by children of school age required*
a) A person having the control of a child between the ages of seven and sixteen years shall cause such child to attend a public school continually for the full number of days for which such school is held, unless such child is mentally or physically unable to attend; or is otherwise being furnished with equivalent education...

b) The determination of equivalency referred to in subsection (a) of this section shall be made by the State Department of Education and certified to the school directors." (Ed. note—I take it that school directors are the local school board)

Subject to this law, the state Board of Education approved a process for looking over and approving alternatives to public schooling. Within the State Dept. of Education there is a Committee on Equivalent Education which reviews private schools and also views private schools and also home instruction plans. The State says that home instruction plans shall be built around the Calvert Home Study Plan for the elementary years, and approved correspondence courses for secondary.

I asked C.L. whether the state watched her very closely to be sure that she was using the Calvert materials. She wrote back saying, in part:

"Thank you for writing and sending GWS #5. I've liked every issue better than the one before it. Especially appreciated your 'The Therapeutic State' and 'To A Reader.'

You may use my name and address and any part of my letters you wish. I will be glad to answer questions from you or anyone so long as they send postage—our income is quite beneath the imagination of most in this culture...

... The State prefers to have people use the Calvert course because it is, of course, tidier for them, but they cannot enforce this. ...In our case, we chose to use Calvert for the first two years after our daughter turned seven (legal school age here) because we didn't feel qualified to take on teaching her without experience or guidance. However, we found it becoming very limiting by third grade. It was like inviting public school standards into one's home. Greta was memorizing names and dates to pass tests and get grades and was getting more and more miserable under the absurdity of it. So for last year, fourth grade for her, first for our son, I devised my own curriculums which I submitted to the State on their application form and they approved it. I arranged that the local elementary school would review the children's work quarterly during the school year to comply with the State's request for a 'reliable means of showing evidence of learning.' The Town funded us $200 (my estimate of our costs) for materials. Public money for this is contingent upon State approval and will not be given for anything connected with religious purposes.

For the coming year, I have again written my own plan. Based on our record of having accomplished more than public school classes (according to the principal who reviewed our work), I am asking to report directly to someone in the State and that we show our papers only once at the end of the year. It is unnecessary and inconvenient both for me and the teachers who have to look over our work to spend any more time on it than that.

No officials have ever been to our home. I have voluntarily gone to the State twice and to the local superintendent often for information, and a variety of other reasons. I like to be out front and get along and feel that the people in authority may also be benefited by an open, cooperative attitude. Example lays the groundwork for trust. Everyone I have met has been friendly and respectful of our rights.

As for what I actually do with my kids, I seem to be more inclined to books than most of the people I've read or heard about (who may, quite understandably, be overreacting to compulsory and oppressive academics). We feel that facility with the symbols of communication is an invaluable tool without which the children would be handicapped in the world as it is today. We have done approximately a grade level's work in English and Math every year. Other than that, we pursue our own concerns. Both kids are fascinated by Science experiments and demonstrations, enjoy Geography, Anthropology, History, Art, and practical skills. We have a serious discussion of principles and values almost every day and we do go out to museums, concerts, hikes, etc. every Saturday.

One of the hardest parts of setting up our own curriculum has been seeing beyond the mold that growing up in this society put me in as far as determining what is important for my kids to know. They have helped me a lot with that. Their inspiration adds a lot of life to our plans and participating in choosing their path automatically fosters enthusiasm while following it."

Thanks for very good and encouraging letter. I have seen enough of Vermont to say that it is a very beautiful state. The winters are long and hard, but if they don't mind (or even like) that, unschoolers might find it a very good state to move to.

DOCTOR

When I go to conferences, meetings, colleges, etc. to give lectures, the people who meet me always call me "Doctor." When I tell them I am not Dr., just Mr., they are very surprised. They can't believe that anyone (other than a politician, athlete, or TV or movie star) could write a book or give a speech, unless s/he was a Dr. Some of them even say, "Oh, I just assumed that you ..." and their voices trail off. (A few then say, "Congratulations!")

School has taught us to think that only people who have spent a lot of time in school can have anything worthwhile to say—except now and then, when the educated talk to the uneducated to find out what 'they' think, as an anthropologist might talk to a remote tribe. We read eagerly what a distinguished (and compassionate) psychiatrist reports of the words of a housemaid. But suppose the housemaid had written down her serious thoughts about the world, and taken them herself to a publisher, and said, "Will you publish this book?" She would have been shown the door.

In his essay, "Intellect", Emerson wrote, in part:

"Each mind has its own method. A true man never acquires after college rules. What you have aggregated in a natural manner surprises and delights when it is produced. For we cannot oversee each other's secret. And hence the differences between men in natural endowment are insignificant in comparison with their common wealth. Do you think the porter and the cook have no anecdotes, no experiences, no wonders for you? *Everybody knows as much as the savant.* (Ed. italics) The walls of rude minds are scrawled all over with the facts, with thoughts. They shall one day bring a lantern and read the inscriptions. ..."

Years ago, in a Penguin collection of modern poetry, I read two poems by Edwin Brock. They made such an impression on me that when I read, the other day, an ad for *Invisibility is the Art of Survival* (New Directions Books, 333 Sixth Ave., New York 10014), a book of poems by him, I ordered it. My old favorites were in there, and many others I loved just as much— direct, powerful, bleak, marvelous, poems. Reading the short foreword, I was surprised to find that when he had written many of these poems, Brock had been a London policeman. I was also surprised and disappointed by my surprise. Why not a policeman poet, or musician, or painter, or philosopher, or anything else? No reason at all; we have just got used to thinking it can't happen.

As a matter of fact, when he first met the editor who had published some of his poems, Brock himself was a bit apologetic about his work. If he were to be taken seriously as a poet, he asked, shouldn't he find some other kind of work? The editor (good for him) said no, not at all. But it is hard for most people, even policeman-poets, to shake old school-trained habits of thought.

NO COMMENT

The Boston Globe, June 12, 1978, ran a story that said in part:

AMHERST—The Registrar's office here at the University of Massachusetts is preparing to mail out 10,000 grades to students, the result of a decision by some faculty members, who have been protesting stalled contract negotiations with the administration, to release the unsubmitted grades to the registrar on Monday.

The executive board of the faculty union, the Massachusetts Society of Professors, voted Friday to release the withheld grades. According to John Bracey, union vice president and chairman of the Afro-American Studies Program, the administration "has made a 180 degree turn in attitude."

"We feel the withholding of grades was effective in hastening the return of the administration to the bargaining table earlier this month," said Bracey.

...The withheld grades had been turned into the faculty union office and placed in a safe deposit box in a local bank. ...

THE WORLD AT TWO

The mother of the now two-year-old boy described in "A Baby" (GWS #2), writes of his further adventures:

"...One thing he gets mad about is being left behind by anybody. However, we just went on a trip ... I was quite nervous about leaving J with friends as he had been doing his falling down pass out tantrums for our benefit all week whenever anyone went to town without him (in spite of having the other parent on hand). But he just waved Bye Bye and went in the house and had a really good four days. As B [his father] said obviously he would only bother to pull the tantrum bit for us. He was very calm and very full of new games and words when we got him back, and I know he made progress on all fronts as a result of being away from us and with other interesting people.

...Around the farm he usually stays on the road or a few beaten paths. But within those limits he goes quite far and stays away as long as an hour and a half, playing with the goats mainly (we have four babies and three moms right now). Once he went into the trees and I couldn't find him because he was sitting down out of sight and playing quietly. I had about a five minute panic realizing the size of the national forest, but I found him about 100' away.

A couple of weeks ago I took him camping with friends while B was away working. It was J's first outdoor trip. We had to walk half a mile to get to a little lake that was beyond the reach of people in cars and J walked it all the way with a look of pure wonder on his face at the new sights, forest, adventure. He carried a pack, which mother made for me when I was a child, that had his pampers, some potatoes, and a can of beer in it, and was super excited by that. He stayed out of the lake, sang to us at the camp fire in Spanish tones of lalalala, lay in the tent for about an hour with his hand holding his chin, admiring the lake. He was so super he turned everyone on and everyone helped take care of him and was glad to have him along.

Then two days later we were to go on a long trip down the river so we left him with some friends, but decided at the last minute our boats weren't sufficient to carry us and our gear on that rugged and remote a trip, so we picked up J and just went camping on the river, taking our boat and going on short hops along stretches of the river where the road was. Again he was super and loved being with grown-ups who ate with their fingers and mushed all their food up in one cup just like him. B wanted him to go in the boat so he put him in a life jacket then tied a rope between them. J hated that and had all kinds of misgivings as water sloshed into the boat and he got wet and cold, but he didn't complain. Amazingly he just sat there and looked pissed off for about two hours. I think he was so glad to be included that he bore with the misery.

Earlier on that trip I was bathing him in the river and while I turned away for at least one second he fell in face first and started to sink in about two feet of water. I hauled him out sputtering (Ed. note—those mountain rivers are cold) and managed once he was OK to take him right back in the water with a sort of limp 'wasn't that fun' which worked, because he didn't panic or do much more than be a little cautious. He's got floaties now that go on his arms for swimming and he's been in a pool half a dozen times since then. He absolutely loves it and doesn't mind whole waves washing into his mouth, though we stay very close."

Wonderful letter. (Lucky J!) But I should say that part of what his mother and I have been writing back and forth about is that at home this little boy is not always "super," but often just as stubborn, angry, and difficult as two-year-olds are supposed to be. The point of this letter is that when he feels himself in a serious grown-up occasion, treated more or less as an equal, he very often rises to the occasion. I have found this to be true of many children.

A FAMILY GAME

Julia McCahill (now in England) writes, in part:

"I'd like to tell you about the Monopoly game C and M and I played a little while ago. I bought the Monopoly game in the spring and the kids took to it right away. It was before we got busy with moving and I had some time to spend with them—one day we played all day, from breakfast until I had to stop to fix dinner—but they enjoyed it so much for a while they usually played it without me.

At first they played it in a rather free-form way; the times that I entered the game I insisted on knowing the rules. This was okay. They quickly learned that when they landed on Income Tax it was usually more advantageous to pay 10% than $200 and were willing to learn how to calculate it. There were other rules too that forced them to do more mental calculating than they had been doing on their own and they took them in their stride. I just realized today, however, that I had made one jump too many ahead of them. I had discovered last spring if when you buy a property you improve it immediately with three houses the first rent you get covers this initial investment. They understood this immediately too and used it often. In fact, C wiped me out with it when we played last night. But, whereas they used it only when they felt like it or when I strongly advised them to, I used it ruthlessly.

I wonder how many people were touched by the account in one issue of GWS (#3) of the mother and children who helped each other reach the goal in

"Sorry!" I certainly was. I've been looking inward at my own competitive streak ever since. And I think this is one of the startling things that happens to you when you resume responsibility for your children's environment. The very first reason I had for thinking of taking (at first) our daughter out of school was a concern with the values she was being exposed to in fifth grade. (Her teacher had asked her to complete another child's Iowa Achievement Test answer sheet with random marks just so it would be full.) Values! I didn't know how many values there were, or how seriously I would be questioning my own habits.

I should have taken my cue from C when, during one of our first Monopoly games, she would want to give away some of her money, even when nobody was going broke; but I said there was nothing in the rules to allow that and made her stop. Fortunately, she forgot that restriction during the hiatus caused by our moving and when we unpacked the game yesterday went back to her generous ways. She beat me anyway, with assets totaling over $5000, compared to my $1180. Today I reduced her and M to tatters—even though I didn't want to and I kept giving away money as C had done! It wasn't until we were finished that I realized I didn't have to buy all that property and charge all those high rents—at least not any faster than they were.

So there you are. There's an anecdote for you; you got it instead of my journal and I got what I always get when I write something down, a clearer understanding and a firmer memory of what has happened."

Tx for wonderful letter and most instructive story. I hope to persuade Julia to send GWS some pages from her journal. I can't think of anything that would be more interesting and valuable to me and many other readers. Makes no difference if it is in rough and unorganized form; if anything, so much the better. And I hope nobody else will hang back from telling us an interesting story because they don't feel they can get the form just right. Just write it down as it comes to you.

LIFE IN SCHOOL

A friend of mine, now in fifth grade, with whom I have been corresponding for a couple of years, wrote recently:

"I was wondering if you knew anything about group pressure. You see, I'm the only one in my class that doesn't have a pair of Levi's.

Also, kids in my class are getting 'Clothes Allowance'—that's when they get money when they want to buy clothes. And they can buy as much as they want.

I've asked my father but he says no. Do you know what I should do?

This group pressure does affect schooling, I bet. I couldn't concentrate on my work for the last few days."

Since her next letter to me was on a very different subject, I don't know how this problem worked itself out—if it did. If anything, the pressures will probably be stronger next year.

HER OWN MONEY

Our leading Canadian correspondent has just written us a letter (one of many good ones), saying in part:

"H and M have just bought themselves ponies with their own money. You'll be pleased to learn (Ed. note—indeed I am) that H (who is 10) wrote a cheque for hers.

I don't know what other banking practices are like, but at our credit union any child can have a full-fledged account (and *must* be a share-holder in the corporation in order to have an account). Living in the country, we mail-order shop quite a bit and H's cheques have never been questioned. But perhaps the people who receive them don't know her age! I don't suppose they would ever dream that they were accepting a cheque from a 10 yr. old. If they knew, I wonder whether they would refuse to accept it or ask for countersigning?

Since H has a fully-personal account, not an 'in trust' one, we as her parents are not even allowed to touch her money. We found out the hard way! We went to the credit union to take some money out of her account and they wouldn't let us. They pulled out her file card and showed us her signature saying that only she was able to handle the money in that account. She had signed it when she was 5! I remember distinctly 'letting' her sign it, thinking condescendingly how 'nice' the experience was for her. Little did I know I was providing her a degree of absolute financial independence.

M (8) doesn't write cheques cause he doesn't want to learn how to sign his name yet. I suppose that could be gotten around, but the hassle's not worth it. So we've told him his account will remain 'in trust' till he can sign his name."

I love this story. I am so glad to hear that someone is doing what I have long felt many parents ought to do. Cheers for Louise! And cheers for H, too, deciding at 5 that her money was to be *her* money.

I think Louise is quite right about M's account. I can't think of a better way for him to learn the meaning and importance of being able to sign his name. WHen he learns to do it, as he soon will, it will not be to get praise from parents or teacher or a good mark on a report card, but for his own very practical reason.

The first school I taught in had an institution called the Student Bank, run by the school business manager.

It was a kind of Petty Cash fund for students. Probably had something to do with the fear that if students had much cash around their rooms (it was a terrible boarding school) there might be problems of stealing.

At the beginning of the school year the parents of each student would make a "deposit" in the student's account in the Student Bank (the amount was just added to the parents' bill). When the student wanted some cash, or to buy books, supplies, etc. from the school, s/he would write out a fake "check" and give it to the business manager, who would then give the student the cash, supplies, athletic equipment, or whatever. The manager kept a separate account for each student, just like a real bank, and was also supposed to see that each student kept her/his "check-book" balanced. The idea was to give the (teenaged) students some practice in keeping track of their own money and in finding out how banks worked.

During the year I was business manager I had to run the Student Bank. It damn near drove me crazy. Here we were, a few hundred yards from town where there was a real bank. Why not have the students open up accounts in the real bank, write real checks, get real statements, instead of wasting a lot of my (or someone's) time running a pretend bank?

Obviously in some families the children have so little money that no nearby bank will let them have an account. Nothing to be done about that. But I feel quite strongly that any child who has enough money so that a local bank will give her/him an account, ought to have one. It is real, grown-up, interesting, part of the big world out there.

AN ADVENTURE

A family I know has been traveling around the country in a converted bus, staying for a while in towns that interest them or where they know people they like, then moving on. They write, in part:

"We are on our way to Y. For now we have used up X. The kids are doing things over. It's often a tough decision. When we stay somewhere for a while we accumulate one thing and lose another. Security sets in. You know what to expect from the environment and there are fewer surprises each day, but surprises are a turn-on if you don't get scared and they keep you sharp. I happen to believe that people stay good at problem solving by staying busy at problem solving. ... F is beginning to say, "I don't have anything to do." That's nonsense—unless what he is really saying is "I don't have anything new to do." Kids seem to know the difference. Adults forget as routine becomes master. We know where to find everything now so the joy of the hunt is gone. We know the people now so we don't have to negotiate new relationships.

We spent a couple of days finishing off some work commitments and packing the rig. F bought a bicycle with money he earned and I bought another one for the rest of us. I welded up some racks to attach to the boat to carry them. We are getting heavier.

We are looking forward to getting to the cooperative. It's been a while since the kids have been there. They only remember pounding on big chunks of clay a potter gave them. Oh, also putting pennies on the railroad tracks to be flattened.

We got there in the afternoon. Everybody yelled when we turned the corner and they saw it. ... A number of old friends are here and an equal number of new people. We are welcomed and people find places to park the boat and bus. The coop is a true school with artists and crafts-people doing their workplay and making a living. There are lots of hugs and hellos for the first few hours and D makes a point of saying how delighted she is to have some kids around. I think maybe too many places don't have any kids. The schools have them all and they don't even appreciate them. Maybe if more workplaces could have kids and more kids could have workplaces it would be a happier world.

K found the ducks first. L has three grown mallards and a little pond by her trailer—one is sitting on a bunch of eggs. Someone lived here a year ago and the sculptor and the blacksmith built her a vertical house out of steel pipe and giant wood spools. G and F surveyed the place from atop it. I saw that the height was sufficient to kill, had to squelch my desire to say, "Get down" and settled for "Be careful." Soon kids returned from the tracks with squished pennies. We had a brief lecture from me on relating to railroad tracks and trains. That led to a discussion about panic—how much space is there under a train, etc.

A friend had just become "owner for a week" of a grocery store because the owner needed a vacation. S decided he would capitalize on the opportunity and try to get a month's worth of "ownership" out of a week. He hired me to do several electrical and carpentry jobs while the boss was gone. An impression must be made. Many improvements. Checkwriting power—hire—fire—chief for a day! We had to be there early and work before the store opened. I shook the kids up at six, we unplugged, battened things down, and were off. The kids followed me into the store toting tools. S said they could play in the store and the idea of having a supermarket all to yourself carried quite a charge. Supermarkets almost always come fully equipped with people—most of whom are adults. Children who are there are seldom wanted or welcome. They are usually being admonished by mother for handling the sacks of candy placed carefully within their reach by knowing management.

Well, not the case this morning—the store was theirs. They roamed the aisles for a while contemplating the space. G pushed back and forth through the swinging doors to the back about thirty times. The forbidding sign 'EMPLOYEES ONLY' had lost its terrible power. He was now an employee. Perhaps he

was the manager. I didn't ask him.

F handed me tools for a while and C played shopper. She pushed a cart around putting things in it and then she put them all back. I was surprised to see her choose that activity because she has done so much of the real thing, but, as I recalled, she never had the kind of choice making power she had now. When we go to a supermarket for shopping about 90% of the shelves are passed by. Within half an hour everyone felt at home and C sat down with K at a table in the deli and started reading her a book they had brought from the bus.

S arrived in a panic! The fresh juice making operation in the back room was two hours behind because the shipment of containers hadn't come. A big selling item for the store was fresh made juices of several kinds and they were made from fresh produce early each morning. Panic—the crowds would hit and there would be no juice. Money would be lost, good will would slip. Being 'owner for a week' S had fewer learning sets than your average supermarket manager so he said, 'Who wants a job?' F and G were low on funds—'We do.' 'Wash your hands and come with me.' They went back to the little juice factory in the back room and S introduced the new help to the juice man.

I stopped by about half an hour later and saw an amazing operation. I have never seen F and G work so hard with such enthusiasm. F was filling bottles with carrot juice and G was wiping, labeling, and pricing. The juice man was pouring bushels of carrots into a big peeling machine and then on to a grinder and then to a two ton hydraulic press. Gallons and gallons of carrot juice were flowing and the boys' eyes were wide and their hands were a blur. Before today carrots existed either one every few inches in a row in the ground or in one pound plastic wrapped bundles. These machines ate carrots like a giant dinosaur. The pace was intense. The juice man had his routines down pat and the kids picked up the rhythm. It was a dance and you had to keep in step. Commands came in three word sentences and they were obeyed. No time for discussion or explanation—real work—a real product—a real classroom. Sacks of carrots became 85¢ bottles of juice in minutes. G said, 'I don't care if S pays us or not, this is fun.'

Three hours later I was done, the store was open and they were still having fun. Three large garbage cans of dry carrot pulp sat outside the juice room door. F's shirt and pants were orange and drenched. G was restamping a case of bottles he had marked 58¢ instead of 85¢. No hassle over the mistake—just stamp them again. After all, the juice man had to throw out a whole batch of carrots that got to the shredder before they were peeled. Mistakes are part of what people do. Unfortunately in schools full of desks, they are forbidden.

I was having my breakfast on the bus when they finished and they popped in, each carrying a fist full of three dollars. They had worked harder in that three hours than I had ever seen them work before and they were ecstatic. They had new knowledge, new dignity (they saved the day) and some negotiable legal tender. My prize was to have been there to see it."

Wonderful story! Reminds me of something that Peter Marin wrote many years ago, about the need of young people (and not so young, either) to feel "alive, useful, and needed."

GREENLEAF

This is the title of a new, unique, and beautiful book, by Constance Bernhardt (pub. by Trunk Press, Hancock, MD 21750, av. here, $5). It is the story of a child's growing up, written by an adult, but told as the child—Constance herself—might have told or written it, year by year. When she first told me about the book and asked me to read it, I had grave misgivings, feared that the book would be full of adult ideas put in a child's mouth, or perhaps sentimental and idealized notions about "innocent" children. But, as I wrote in the preface to the book, "As I read, my misgivings gave way to astonished delight. Page after page, the book rang absolutely true, true to all my adult experience of children, true to all I could remember of my own childhood. I read on, now pleased, but still fearing the inevitable misstep, particularly when the child grew older. The misstep never came. To the very end, she never struck what seemed to me a false note."

The book is written in chapters, The Year Four, The Year Five, and so on, up through Thirteen. Let me quote a few bits from the Year Four, to give some of the flavor of the book, and (I hope) to tempt you.

"...I like the willow tree. It is where I take my naps. It is very green under the willow tree.
It is like a castle.
I like to pull on the leaves.
I pull hard but can never pull them off.
I want to climb the willow tree.
If I run to the tree real fast
I can run up it,
but when I run to the tree
it gets bigger.
It is a very big willow tree.
I can't reach around it.
I try.
I think I can reach around it
if I try some more.
I have a sister and she is the one thing smaller than me.
Her name is Karen. There is no place bigger than my back yard.
I bake gravel pies.
Karen eats them.
Daddy calls her 'pie-face'
because her face is a big circle.
Karen has a big mouth and her eyes are big circles.

Daddy picks her up and calls her 'pie-face.'
She just looks at him because she knows her name
is   Karen
but she doesn't know who 'pie-face' is
and who Daddy is talking to.

Karen is dumb.
She doesn't want to make lines on paper.
She can't say my name right.
I tell her my name.
I get mad at her.
I am bigger.
so she is scared.
My name is Connie.
I make her say it slow.
It is hard for her.
I don't know why it is hard for her.
I don't know why it is hard for her.
I don't know why it is hard."

In the preface I also wrote, "One thing, among others, that struck me as extraordinarily true and right was this child's view of her (two years) younger sister. Little children are not sentimental about their younger brothers and sisters. They don't think they are cute. They may get on well with them, even be quite fond of them. But even in their affection there is much tough-minded exasperation. Why are they so silly? Why don't they straighten up and fly right?" In this line, here are two other quotes, the first from the Year Eleven, the second from the Year Twelve:

"In the morning Karen and Jill and Julie (sisters) and I
meet and go to school.
We walk to the corner to take the school bus.
I don't see Jill at school
but we ride home on the bus together.
Jill is quiet and Julie is friendly.
Julie talks a lot and is always joking.
She sometimes tells Jill what to do.
I think this is strange
because Jill is older and knows more.
I tell Karen what to do.
She could never tell me what to do."

I interrupt to say, what volumes are written in those words! Then, in the next chapter, these words, which how many billions of people must at one time or another have said to themselves about their younger brothers or sisters:

"Karen is in the fifth grade.
I think it's strange that she
always seems younger than I was
when I was her age."

It is tempting to go on. (I am sorry that these narrow columns break up to some extent the lines, and so the rhythm, of the book.) As I wrote in the preface, I can hardly imagine that anyone who has any deep liking or sympathy or respect for children will not enjoy and even love this book. I do, and more each time I read it. I hope you will try it.

TEACHING WITHOUT SCHOOL

A reader writes:

"Back in '70-'71 I was reading all the school reform literature but something kept bothering me. I didn't realize what it was until I read   (av. here) where James Herndon said something to the effect that the trouble with school reform is that no matter what you do the fact still remains that school is irrelevant to real life. So I quit thinking about school and began concentrating on real life. But something made me pick up *Instead of Education* in the library the other day and I was delighted to find that you had articulated, in a way I could not, my own feelings. I also want you to know that you helped me immensely in a personal crisis of self-confidence and self-respect resulting from my living according to my feelings and still trying to maintain good relationships with parents and others who feel that without degrees and other educational system prizes any learning and skills are worthless and wasted.

My husband, G, is a teacher (see 'From a Teacher', this issue), and it may be helpful for people you talk with to know that we, a family of four, survive quite well on earnings from his part time t-eaching. G teaches music (guitar, drums, banjo, vibraphone, and theory) privately in a studio in a music store in T——(pop. 5,000) and A——(area pop. 19,000). The unemployment rate around here is usually about 9%, but G has a waiting list. Our net income (most work expenses are car-related) is around $4000 a year—G could take on more students, but our view of the good life does not include working at *anything*, no matter how well-liked, more than part time. We live quite well on that income because we live very simply. We built our own home, a simple cabin, we provide much of our own food, and almost all our own entertainment. We are still paying for our land (15 acres) and our car (1975 Honda Civic).

Alternative life styles are important for those who do not take the usual educational paths; as long as you don't tie yourself to the system you can be free of it. I would like to point out that we lived in Boston (Mattapan) for two years, '70-'72, and managed to have a very simple, inexpensive and happy lifestyle there too. (Ed. note—Boston is perhaps the most expensive of all U.S. cities to live in.)

G wants me to mention that he never planned on being a teacher. He just was always into music from the age of seven on and he was lucky throughout his life to have t-eachers who, as it turned out, served as models for him. Berklee College of Music there in Boston was in many ways a s-chool, at least when G was going there (70-72) and in their non-degree program.

You might also be interested to know that in this very rural area there are a lot of attitudes very similar to yours though I don't know if the people who hold them would agree to that. Farmers will sometimes say about S-school learning, 'That kind of knowledge is OK too, I guess.' But what is really respected is do-ers, and whenever there is a problem or project there is much sharing of information and skills. You get a lot of comment like, 'Well, The Brains say you should do it this way, but the way so-and-so did it was ...' Many of G's students are the children of farmers.

By the way, our kids go to S-chool. They want to at this point—first and second grade—all their friends do—we'll see what happens in the future."

————————————

Tx for very interesting and encouraging letter.

I used to say to teachers (and probably scared many of them in doing so), "Suppose, instead of working for a school, you rented a little office and hung out a shingle saying TEACHER. What do you know, what can you teach, that is so interesting or valuable that people would come to you of their own free will and pay you to teach it to them?" Most of them, of course, had no answer. It is nice to hear about someone who is actually doing that, and not only "surviving," as the saying goes, but leading an interesting and satisfying life.

A CITY AS TEACHER

A good friend of mine in London, Leila Berg, has written many wonderful books for children and about them (one of them, *Look at Kids,* I hope to add to the list of books we sell here if the British publishers will let me). When I first told her about GWS, she wrote back, in part:

"I've always been very interested in education without schooling. As a child (Ed. note—she grew up in a poor family in a poor working-class district), I got my real education from the Manchester concerts (with their marvelous program notes), the gramophone record shops (where they were always so kind as to let this naive child spend two hours every time playing records, pretending she wanted to buy one and never doing so), the magnificent Manchester Reference Library which seemed to have every book published on open display, all the Manchester theatres where I sat up in the gods (Ed.—the highest balcony) for one and six, all the trade-show cinemas where I managed to scrounge free tickets ...

When J had just left school and hadn't yet managed to get into drama school, and I thought she might have a whole year off (and her schooling had been ghastly!) I fixed her up with a program of all kinds of fascinating things to go to, out of London's resources (including the London Youth Choir, an experience that had a creative effect on all her future). ..."

Though Britain, despite all we read in the papers, is a much richer country now than it was then, it would probably be much harder, and in many cases impossible, for a poor child to do in Manchester or any other big city what Leila did as a child. For one thing, as she herself has pointed out in her books, people are generally less kindly to children. Also, the prices of plays and concerts have gone way up.

But there are still a great many interesting things for a child to see and do in a city. One problem is that most poor children don't know about them. GWS will have more to say about this in later issues. A good book about this is Colin Ward's *A Child in the City* (see elsewhere this issue).

NEWS ITEM

A GWS friend and reader from CA has just sent us this clipping from the *San Francisco Chronicle* of 2/31/78:

WOMAN WHO STARTED HER OWN SCHOOL —
Yacolt, Wash.

For Trisha Smith, 11, and her sister, Sarah, 8, school is as close as the converted garage at their house. Their teacher is their mother, and that has the state upset.

In the fall of 1974, Patricia Smith decided she could not rely on the public school system to educate Trisha and took her out of the second grade.

'I found that the public schools were encroaching on my religious beliefs ... I believe in a supreme being ... And the religion I was teaching at home was being aborted in the classroom,' said the quiet-spoken woman.

Mrs. Smith, a Mormon, said, 'You know, you don't have to be a Bible thumper or a fanatic,' to want to mix religious training with education.

She said a major concern with public schools was that the theory of evolution was being taught as 'fact, not fiction.'

She began teaching her daughters at home, but was soon confronted with a lawsuit brought by the state.

Her school meets state law by holding classes five hours a day, five days a week, but with only two years of college, Mrs. Smith does not have the required teaching certification.

She received a suspended fine of $100 and was ordered to comply with state law.

Clark County prosecuting attorney Jim Carty said he would take action upon receipt of a complaint from the school board which he expects when school resumes this fall.

'I understand she has some jail time hanging over her from that previous action,' Carty said.

Mrs. Smith said her school is incorporated through the state of Washington and is associated with the National Parents League Inc. of Portland.

The head of National Parents League, Mary Royer, said it helps people like Mrs. Smith set up schools to educate their own children. She said the organization has worked with 275 schools in 28 states, including 20 to 22 in Washington.

Mrs. Smith said her children take the Stanford Achievement Tests at the end of each school year, and that Trisha showed a seventh-grade level of comprehension as she completed the fifth grade this past school year.

Gordon Ensign of the state Superintendent of Public Instruction's Office in Olympia said the Stanford test is generally recognized as an acceptable means of measuring student achievement.

While it is 'pure joy' to teach her daughters, Mrs. Smith said, she spends hours a day preparing for classes.

Trisha said some of her friends envy her not having to attend public school. 'They think I go to school in pajamas,' she said.

She sees friends after school and says she does not miss public school.

Trisha has another impression. 'I don't think the kids in public schools learn as much as we do.'"

I am going to write the National Parents League, to find out what I can about them. They may prove to be a very useful ally to unschoolers. Meanwhile, if any readers know something about them, I'd be grateful if they'd tell us.

FACTS AND THEORIES

The schools might save themselves much trouble if they would learn and understand the differences between facts, observations, reports, and theories, which they tend to roll into one big lump. A piece of meat in the store is a fact, and so is its weight. When the butcher weighs it on the scale, what he sees is an observation. How close his observation is to the fact depends on how accurate his scale is and how accurately he reads it. When he tells you, or writes on a sticker, that the piece of meat weighs a pound and a half, that is a report, which may or may not be accurate, depending on how honest and/or generous the butcher is. If you take the meat home and weigh it on your kitchen scale and get a different weight, you may invent a theory to account for the difference—your scale is off, the butcher's scale is off, he read the weight wrongly, he is a cheat.

In science, the only things we can call facts are objects and events *out there*. From the facts we get observations and reports, which are never 100% accurate or complete, and from these we make up theories. Einstein knew, and wrote, that scientific theories were not facts, but what he called "constructs," which is to say, inventions, stories, or as Mrs. Smith would have it, fiction. The point and virtue of a good scientific theory or story is that it seems to explain, connect, make sense of many or all of the observations or reports we have at hand. Someone said of Einstein that when an astronomical observation seemed to confirm his Theory of Relativity, someone congratulated him on having been proved right, to which he correctly replied, "A thousand experiments can never prove me right; a single experiment can prove me wrong."

Some scientific theories, or fictions, are quite testable, as in much of Chemistry. Others, as in Astronomy, where people try to "explain" events that took place millions of years ago, are not testable at all. Evolution is another such theory. It is a story that many people accept, mostly on faith, because it seems to make sense of the world for them. Others reject it for almost exactly the same reason. I have heard and read a number of 'scientific' criticisms of the theory of evolution, at least the shallow version taught in schools, that make a lot of sense to me. There are a great many questions it does not answer and observations it does not explain.

I only mention all this because the schools, in their legal attacks on unschoolers, are likely to present themselves as the defenders of reason and science against superstition, and we must not let them get away with that. Most of what they teach is not so much science as a kind of uncritical science-worship, in which scientific inventions are looked on as miracles, and very tenuous theories are called facts.

JOBS, CAREERS, WORK

The April 5, 1978 issue of *Manas* (see GWS #3) quoted, from a collection of Paul Goodman's writing titled *Nature Heals* (pub. by Free Life Editions, 1977), these words:

"Brought up in a world where they cannot see the relation between activity and achievement, adolescents believe that everything is done with mirrors, tests are passed by tricks, achievement is due to pull, goods are known by their packages, and a man is esteemed according to his front. The delinquents who cannot read and quit school, and thereby become still less able to take part in such regular activity as is available, show a lot of sense and life when they strike out directly for the *rewards* of activity—money, glamour, and notoriety. And it is curious and profoundly instructive how they regress, politically, to a feudal and band-and-chieftain law that is more comprehensible to them. The code of a street gang has many an article in common with the Code of Alfred the Great.

It is disheartening indeed to be with a group of young fellows who are in a sober mood and who simply do not know what they want to do with themselves in life. Doctor, lawyer, beggar-man, thief? Rich man, poor man, Indian chief?—they simply do not know an ambition and cannot fantasize one. But it is not true that they don't care; their 'so what?' is vulnerable, their eyes are terribly balked and imploring. (I say 'it is disheartening,' and I mean that the tears roll down my cheeks; and I who am an anarchist and a pacifist feel that they will be happier when they are all in the army.)"

Paul Goodman was writing here about poor boys. But, even in the more hopeful Sixties, it was just about as true of affluent kids. In those days I was quite often asked to speak to high school assemblies, mostly in rich suburbs of big cities. I almost always talked about the difference between jobs, careers, and work. A job, as I defined it, was something that you did for money, something that someone else told you to do and paid you to do. Probably not something you would have done otherwise, but you needed the money, so you did it.

A career was a kind of stepladder of jobs. If you did your first job for a while, did what you were told and didn't cause any trouble, whoever gave you that job might give you a new job. This job might be slightly more interesting, or at least not so hard-dirty-dangerous. You might not have to take orders from so many people, might even be able to give orders to a few. You might be able to make a few more choices, and would probably get more money. Then, if you did that job OK for a while, your boss might then give you a still better job, until you had gone up the job ladder as far as you were going to go. This adds up to a career.

By "work" I meant (and mean) something altogether different, what people used to call a "vocation" or "calling"—something which seemed so worth doing for its own sake that they would have gladly chosen to do it even if they didn't need money and the work didn't pay. I went on to say that to find our work, in this sense, is one of the most important and difficult tasks that we have in life, that unless we are very lucky we cannot expect to find it quickly, and indeed, that we may never find it once and for all, since work that is right for us at one stage of our life may not be right for us at the next (which has happened to me more than once). I added that the vital question "What do I really want to do? What do I think is most worth doing?" is not one that the schools will often urge us or help us to ask of ourselves; on the whole, they feel it is their business only to prepare us for employment—jobs or careers, high or low. So we are going to have to find out for ourselves what work needs to be done and is being done out there, and which of that work we most want to take part in.

As I said these things, I looked closely (as I always do) at the faces of my hearers, to try to get some sense of how they felt about what I was saying. What I saw, and what I usually heard in the question periods that followed, made me feel that most of those students were thinking, "This guy must have just stepped off the space ship from Mars." Work worth doing? Work that you would do even if you didn't need money, that you would do *for nothing*? For most of them it was not just impossible, but unimaginable. They did not know, hardly even knew *of*, any people who felt that way about their work. Work was something you did for external rewards—a little pay, if you were like most people, or wealth, power, fame if you were among the fortunate. I found myself thinking often about something else that Paul Goodman had written: "Ours is the first civilization in history that has imposed on the elite of its younger generation a morale fit for slaves." To which I would add something that Hannah Arendt once wrote about slaves in ancient Greece. Slaves could earn money, own property, even get rich (some did). What they could not do was work for anything *but themselves;* in other words, they could not fight, or vote, or hold office. They were only *allowed* to be what in our times most people *choose* to be—what economists call Economic Man, people who work only for their own personal gain.

Of course, in saying this about the young people I talked to, I am to some degree guessing (and therefore perhaps projecting). Of one thing I am certain. There was never, anywhere, a hopeful, positive, enthusiastic response to what I said. I cannot remember even one among all those students, the most favored young people of the (then, at least) most favored nation in the world, who said or later wrote to me. "Mr. Holt, here's what I am interested in and care about, how can I find a way to work at it?"

FINDING TRUE WORK

I was on a westbound U.S. submarine, a few days out of Pearl Harbor, when the news broke about the first atomic bomb. Since while in school I had heard about the splitting of the atom and the enormous amounts of energy that this released, I knew the bomb could not remain a secret, and that before long any country that wanted could find a way to make them. I decided for myself, and by myself (I don't remember how) that the only way to prevent the worldwide spread of nuclear weapons, and in the end, nuclear war, was to have some sort of world government. Having decided that, I did not quite know what to do about it. When we returned to the U.S. in October, to "mothball" our sub, I tried to find out what I could about any other people who might be talking or writing about, or working for, world government. By the middle of the following summer I decided that I had to find a way to do this work full time. I found there were three world government organizations, and went to them to ask for a job. Two had nothing. The third said they had nothing at the moment, but that in the fall the young man working in their mail room would be going back to college and that I could have his job for $35 a week. I said I would take it. In the fall I began work, making up and sending out packages of literature, stamping the mail, keeping the membership card files, running the Addressograph machine, and doing whatever odd jobs turned up. One day they told me that a young lawyer named Conrad Shadlen had just asked for someone to give a talk on world government to the Junior Chamber of Commerce in Bayonne, N.J. On that day all our other speakers were busy. Would I do it? I gulped and said I would. It was the first of about 600 speeches that I was to give for the organization. After a while I left the mail room and began to work as a "field organizer," traveling about, giving speeches and trying to start local chapters of the organization.

I did this work for six years, then (for many reasons) left the organization, spent much of the year living and traveling (it was then cheap) in Europe, and came home, not sure what I wanted to do next, but thinking that I might try to go into farming, since I was even then very interested in what we now call Ecology. My sister, who had been trying without success to persuade me to be a teacher, did persuade me to visit a small, co-ed boarding school, the Colorado Rocky Mountain School, that John and Anne Holden had just opened in Carbondale, Colo. My sister thought that since the school planned to do much of its own building and food raising, I might learn there, while working, many things I would need to know if I did go into farming. In a spirit of, "It can't hurt to take a look," I went to the school, two weeks after it had opened. I spent a day there, living the life of the school, going to some classes, talking to the students, helping some of them with their work, playing informal soccer with them.

I liked it. From my insides I got a message like the one I had received years before, when for the first time I went down into a submarine. It said, "Right now, this is the place for you." Next day, just before I left, I said to John Holden as we walked around the school, "You know, I like it here, and I'd like to stay and work here." He made what some people might have taken as a rather negative reply: "Well, we'd be glad to have you, but the trouble is, we haven't got any place to put you, and we haven't got anything for you to do." To this I made what many years later we were to call An Offer He Couldn't Refuse. I said, "Well, if you get some sort of roof over my head, I don't much care where you put me, and if you're feeding me I can probably live without money, for a while at least, and I'm pretty sure I can find something to do." He laughed and said, "If you're willing to come out here on that basis, come ahead." Two weeks or so later I was back. For a month or two I lived in a little building, once a granary, that they were turning into an infirmary. I slept on a cot, not far from the table saw, stepped over piles of sawdust to get to it, lived out of my suitcases. I found plenty to do. I began cooking breakfast for the school every day, tutoring individual students in Economics, Trigonometry, Reading, coaching soccer. When another teacher left to get married, I took over her room and her salary (about $1750). By the next year I was teaching regular classes in English and Math, and was the school business manager. A year later they hired a full-time business manager, but I then started teaching French. I taught at that school four years, worked very hard, had a good time, learned a great deal.

The point of these stories is that a great many of the people who are doing serious work in the world (as opposed to just making money) are very overworked and short of help. If a person, young or not so young, came to them and said, "I believe in the work you are doing and want to help you do it in any and every way I can, will do any kind of work you ask me to do or that I can find to do, for very little pay or even none at all," I suspect that many or most of them would say, "Sure, come right ahead." Working with them, the newcomer would gradually learn more and more about what they were doing, would find or be given more interesting and important things to do, might before long become so valuable that they would find a way to pay her/him. In any case, s/he would learn far more from working with them and being around them than s/he could have learned in any school or college. (see Jud Jerome's letter in GWS #1)

A SLOW START

I have a close friend whom I have known since he was in high school. His marks were good, his parents had money, so when he finished high school he went to a prestige college. Soon he had to choose a major. Since English had been his best and easiest school subject, and since he liked books, he chose English. A few years later he had his B.A. degree in English. It had cost him four years of his time and his parents about twenty thousand dollars of their money. With it, and fifteen or twenty cents, he could buy a cup of coffee almost anywhere. But not much else. What to do? Well, his marks were still good, he still had time, his parents still had money, so he went to a prestige graduate school to get a Ph.D. degree in (necessarily) English. Some years later—we had remained good friends all this time—when he had completed all the course requirements for a Ph.D., and was finishing up his thesis, I asked him, "When you finish up all of this stuff, what are you going to do?" The question seemed to surprise him. After a pause, he said, "I don't know, teach English in some college, I guess." I said, "Is that what you really want to do?" This question seemed to surprise him even more. After another pause, He said, "Well, no, not particularly. But what else *can* I do?"

I said nothing, only thought (and still think) that this didn't seem a very good way to spend seven or so years of one's life and $35,000 of one's parents' (or someone's) money. Soon he began to teach English at a small state university, in the Western mountain country he loved. The only problem, he soon found, was that the students in his classes were at college only to get the ticket. They were not in the least interested in any of the things he had learned and wanted to teach. All they wanted to know was, what do we have to do to pass the course. That they were so polite about it made it even harder—it would have been more interesting if they had argued furiously that his course was a complete waste of time.

For a while he tried to tell himself that he would put in his time, collect his paycheck, and concentrate on the farming, hunting, fishing, hiking, camping, and skiing that he really loved. It didn't work. He stuck it out for some years, every year hating his teaching, his department, and the university more and more. Finally he quit.

Now, after some difficult years, he is a carpenter and small builder and contractor doing careful and skilled work in a town where there is demand for it. He has found his work. But it still seems too bad that he had to spend seven or eight years getting ready to do, and eight years more doing, a job that meant nothing to him. The years and the money could have been better spent.

Even then, he was fortunate in having enough money in his family so that he could run the risk of leaving his job and looking for work worth doing. Most people can't do that. I think of a young woman (by no means unique), about to graduate from a School of Education, who, when I asked her what she had learned, said, "Well, I've learned two things, anyway—I've learned that I don't like children and I don't like teaching." When I asked why she went on with it, she said, "I have to, I've spent too much time and money learning to do this. I can't turn around and start learning to do something else."

To students who used to ask me whether they should go to, or stay in, or go back to college, I used to say, "Look, a college degree isn't a magic passkey that opens all the doors in town. It only opens a few, and before you spend a lot of time and money getting one of those keys, you'd be smart to find out what doors it opens, and what's on the other side of those doors, and whether you want to go through them." I also used to ask them, "What do you want to do? Suppose you had in your hand whatever college ticket you are thinking of getting, what would you like to do, *choose* to do, right now?" Most looked at me with blank faces. They would like to be some sort of -icians or -ologists. I would reply, "OK, suppose you were one, then what would you like to do?" This stopped them. They did not know any -icians or -ologists, and had no idea what they did or whether they themselves might want to do it. They saw these "careers" only as slots that school might enable them to slip into.

Every year the major academic disciplines—History, English, Modern Languages, Economics, etc.—have big conferences. Hundreds of people with brand new Ph.D. degrees go to these conferences, hoping to land one of the by now scarce jobs. They hold their tickets up in the air and say, in effect, "Please hire me, someone, anyone, I'll do anything you tell me to." There is a well known name for these gatherings. It is "slave markets."

REMEDIAL

In the July/Aug. 1971 issue of the magazine *Society* Norman and Margaret Silberberg wrote, "We have found seven longitudinal studies of remedial reading. Not one shows any long-term beneficial effect." They also quote from a speech that President Nixon gave in early 1970, after almost $1 billion had been spent yearly on reading programs under the Elementary and Secondary Education Act of 1965. He said, "Before-and-after tests suggest that only 19 percent of the children in such programs improve their reading significantly; 15 percent appear to fall behind more than expected, and more than two-thirds of the children remain unaffected—that is, they continue to fall behind."

Of course, in this matter President Nixon was not an impartial source of information. For political reasons of his own, he wanted to repeal the Education Act. But in this instance he was surely quoting material given him by education 'experts' in H.E.W. Meanwhile, if there has been any later evidence that remedial reading programs have become more successful, it has been a well-kept secret.

FROM ART HARRIS

Harper's Weekly, during its short life, published a letter from Art Harris in Arlington, Vt. He wrote, in part:

"Seven years ago, my wife and I came to the conclusion that the public schools our two boys were attending were damaging, rather than enhancing, the learning process for them, and we decided to do something about it. Our older son, a voracious reader then in the sixth grade, was bored in the classroom because almost everything that was taught he had already discovered on his own. For him school was a long review and an authoritarian prison which sapped his strength.

...Our attorney discovered a provision in the education laws of our state (Ed. note—then NY, as I recall) that provided for in-home schooling. True, the statute was undoubtedly drafted for the infirm, and perhaps, for child actors as well, but if we could provide an 'alternate' but 'equivalent' educational experience, we could conceivably comply with the law.

The board of education decided not to fight us, perhaps to avoid the possibility of our pointing out publicly the deficiencies of the schools. We were assigned an advisor from the school system, who, after a nervous six months, left us alone.

...We did not draw up a curriculum, a study plan, or an outline of courses. Such moves are the first step in *formalizing* the learning process, whereas we feel the best learning takes place informally. The narrow structuring of school courses has always appalled us. Who are these schools to decide that architecture, archaeology, anthropology, astrology, or astronomy, (to take only the As) don't belong in the elementary grades? We believe that all subjects fuse and interlock and the mere definition of a subject is the first step in taking away some of its mystique. For the joy of learning (remember that?) is in discovering—even in discovering subjects—and in satisfying one's curiosity.

More for appearances than anything else, we borrowed some of those dull textbooks and readers from our school-assigned advisor, stashed them away, and proceeded on our own—or rather, I should say, our two boys proceeded pretty much on their own, for all too often an adult gets between a learner and the material.

Perhaps I sound vague about this. There's a reason. We simply left our oldest boy alone. He read, sometimes eight to ten hours a day. He watched some TV, went to a fair number of movies. With no adults around to order him, to test him or spoonfeed him, he delved into metallurgy (his interest in cycling got him into this), nutrition (on his own he became a vegetarian), architecture. In fact, you name it, chances are he was into it—geology, Zen, meteorology, etc.

Yes, we bought a few books, but mostly he used the library. Nobody taught him the Dewey Decimal System; he learned it because he needed to find books. Sometimes a radio or TV host would discuss a book with an author on tour. More often than not the host had not read the book but (to the surprise of those who feel TV kills reading) our son often went to get it from the library, even if that meant paying 25 cents for a reservation.

Shortly after he turned 17, our oldest son took his high school equivalency test and scored well in all areas. He promptly got his high-school diploma. The very first college he applied to, Bard College in New York State (Ed. note—Barron's College guide rates it 'very competitive'), accepted him, and gave him a full scholarship. I had always said an admissions director would be enchanted with the idea of accepting a self-educated child. He began college this fall.

Our other boy developed in a way that gratified us. It took almost a year of not doing very much at all for him to shed the school-instilled idea that he was dumb (Ed. note—sometimes it takes much longer). I think our six-month trip to Mexico did much to dispel that notion, for of the four of us he learned the most Spanish. Nobody 'taught' him a word of the language— he just picked it up along with a lot of confidence in himself.

We put absolutely no pressure on him to read. True, we bought a few books on dyslexia and by using their suggestions helped to introduce him to simple printed words. And when others his age got interested in comic books, he really wanted to read. Only then did we make a big effort to help him. He still reads below what the schools call 'grade level,' but that doesn't bother us.

After being out of school for five years, he expressed a desire to go back to school last year—mostly because all his playmates were in school. So we let him. Almost immediately he became bored, occasionally sullen, and began once again to have feelings of inferiority. The school, locked into grades and classes and schedules, still has no provision for the special learning he requires.

I feel he's more adrift back in school than he ever was out of school. I also see signs of school learning that are anything but salutary, for the school had its ninth-grade smokers, trashers, punchers, sexists, extortionists, and stealers, as well as a handful of authoritarian types (passing as teachers) who tell him that he may not wear his jacket in class, that he cannot talk while walking to an assembly hall, that he can't do this or that. ...

———————

I asked Art Harris what sort of peer group pressure may have led his younger son to go back to school. He replied, In part:

"I don't know how to analyze the 'peer group pressure' which took C back to school. Certainly the kids didn't *like* school—it was more that they played with him all summer and sort of knew the inevitability of their returning to school in the fall, and urged him to come along as part of their gang. They talked about the woodworking shop and also soccer. Apparently these were to be enjoyed and the rest to be endured.

C had been out of school so long (and left at primary grade) that he had forgotten how bad it was. The first week back in school he had a jacket on in class and was commanded to remove it. He said he was cold. That made no difference. He was to remove it— the light 'baseball jacket' was for outside, not inside. I later told him he had a perfect right to wear the jacket in class—but by now he had already become subdued again. We noted immediately he was irritable afternoons—the return to school had affected his personality—for the worse. ...

So there was no ostracism—he was, in school and out, always popular, gregarious. I think after a while— although he wasn't teased—he felt slightly different with his at-home education, and while they didn't tease him, they put pressure on him to join them for their own gang/amusement/pleasure. The sports was used as a lure. ..."

To which I would only add, as I said before, why shouldn't a child, whose parents are paying taxes to support the local schools, be able to go to them *only* for woodworking and soccer, if that's what s/he wants? I'd like to see a legal test of this.

In another letter, writing of his first talks with the schools about taking his boys out, Art writes:

"...the very best thing I did was put aside a weekend and write a long (9 or 10 page, single spaced) explanation of what we intended to do, where we got our crazy ideas (Holt, Illich, Leonard, Kozol, Dennison, et al.), how we felt about education, what our qualifications were, etc. Made a dozen copies or so for school people—anyone who'd take one—truant officer, superintendent, head of grade schools, school psychologist—even had copies for the school's legal

chap. I believe this was the turning point—to put it in writing—showed we were serious, gave people chance to appraise us calmly by what we said. Half the time people don't listen—they resist and are thinking of how they'll reply. But when you catch them quietly by giving them some reading material, it often reaches them. I feel that weekend was well spent—they realized too how serious we were, and the books we'd read. I quoted from some of these books, your own included, JH."

———————

Agree this is a good idea, for many reasons. Doesn't *always* work, though, as some people have found out. But it is always worth doing.

NO COMMENT

The magazine *The Futurist*, issue of June 1977, quoted these words (with accompanying drawing) from the book *Future Facts: A Forecast of the World As We Will Know It Before the End of the Century*, by Stephen Rosen (pub. by Simon and Schuster, New York):

"Emergency alarm system developed originally for a racially troubled high school in California features a transmitter which people carry on their persons. When the clip is removed, a nearby receiver lights up, indicating that the emergency signal has been relayed to the master control panel. A map on the master control station pinpoints the location of the emergency, and help (Ed. note—probably in the form of police or armed security guards) can be on the way within 30 seconds. ....."

READING PROBLEMS

The reason the schools' efforts to deal with "reading problems" so seldom make them better and usually make them worse was put very clearly by George Dennison in *The Lives of Children*—so clearly, simply, and powerfully that I would have thought no one in the world could have failed to understand it.

He had been telling about his work, at the First Street School—a very small (23 students) private free school for mostly poor kids—with a twelve-year-old boy, José, who when he came to this country at age 7 could read Spanish, but after five years in public school could read neither Spanish nor English, nor do anything else that the schools had been trying to teach him to do.

With some pointed questions Dennison showed why José could only have seen the task of reading as uninteresting, unreal, humiliating, and terrifying. He then wrote:

"José's reading problem is José. Or to put it another way, there is no such thing as a reading problem. José hates books, schools, and teachers, and among a hundred other insufficiencies—*all of a piece*—he cannot read. Is this a reading problem?

A reading problem, in short, is not a fact of life, but a fact of school administration. It does not describe José, but describes the action performed by the school i.e. the action of ignoring everything about José except his response to printed letters."

Simple enough. But schools have never been, and are not now, willing or able to understand it. So their "problems" get worse.

ON READING

Years ago I visited some friends; their youngest child, whom I had not seen since she was a tiny baby, was about five. After sizing me up for a while from a distance, and deciding that I seemed to be OK, she made friends, and soon asked me if I would "help her read." Not quite knowing what she meant, I said I would. She got her book, Dr. Seuss's *Hop On Pop*, led me to a sofa, and when I was seated, climbed up, snuggled against me, and began slowly to read out loud. What she then did, and what she wanted me to do, I describe in the chapter on Reading in *How Children Learn*. The point I make here is that the first thing she had to do, before the work could begin, was to get in cozy physical contact with me.

In *The Lives of Children*, describing his work with twelv- year-old José, the tough street kid, Dennison makes the same point. He could only work with José at all when the two of them were alone in a locked room. The possibility that other children might see his ignorance and confusion would have been enough to stop José dead right at the start. Even alone with his good friend George, he could barely master his self-hatred and panic. Of these meetings Dennison writes:

"And so our base of operations was our own relationship, and since José early came to trust me, I was able to do something which, simple as it may sound, was of the utmost importance; I made the real, the deeper base of our relationship a matter of physical contact. I could put my arm around his shoulders, or hold his arm, or sit close to him so that our bodies touched. ... The importance of this contact to a child experiencing problems with reading can hardly be overestimated. ..."

I have to add here that the trusting had to come before the touching. To touch or hold a child who has not yet decided to trust you will only make that child far more nervous.

In any case, whether you are a "gifted" five-year-old or a terrified illiterate twelve-year-old, trying to read something new is a dangerous adventure. You may make mistakes, or fail, and so, feel disappointment, or shame, or anger, or disgust. Just in order to get started on this adventure, most people need as much comfort, reassurance, and security as they can find. Obviously, the typical classroom, with the other children ready to point out, correct, or even laugh at every mistake, and the teacher all too often (wittingly or unwittingly)

helping and urging them to do this, is the worst possible place for this.

At the Ny Lille Skole (New Little School) in Bagsvaerd, near Copenhagen, which I describe in *Instead of Education*, there is no formal reading program at all—no classes, no reading groups, no instruction, no testing, nothing. Children (like adults) read if and when, and what, and with whom, and as much as they want to. But each child knows—it is not announced, just one of those things you find out by being in the school—that anytime s/he wants, s/he can go to Rasmus Hansen, a tall, deep-voiced, slow speaking teacher (for many years the head teacher of the school), and say, "Will you read with me?" and he will say Yes. The child picks something to read, goes with Ramus to a little nook, not a locked room but a cozy and private place, sits down right beside him, and begins to read aloud. Rasmus does almost nothing. From time to time he says softly, "Ja, ja," meaning "That's right, keep going." Unless he suspects the child may be getting in a panic, he almost never points out or corrects a mistake, if asked for a word, he simply says what it is. After a while, usually about twenty minutes or so, the child stops, closes the book, gets up, and goes off to do something else.

Hardly anything one could call teaching. As it happens Rasmus was "trained" as a reading teacher. He told me that it had taken him many years to stop doing, first one thing and then another, all the many things he had been trained to do, and finally to learn that this tiny amount of moral support and help was all that children needed of him, and that anything more was no help at all.

THIRTY HOURS

I asked Rasmus how much of this "help" children seemed to need before they felt ready to explore reading on their own. He said that from his records of these reading sessions he had found that the most amount of time any children spent reading with him was about thirty hours, usually in sessions of twenty minutes to a half hour, spread out over a few months. But, he added, many children spent much less time than that with him, and many others never read with him at all. I should add that almost all of the children went from the Ny Lille Skole to the "gymnasium," a high school far more difficult and demanding than all but a few secondary schools in the U.S. However and whenever the children may have learned it, they were all good readers.

Thirty hours. I had met that figure before. Ten years earlier, I had served for a few weeks as consultant to a program to teach reading to adult illiterates in Cleveland, Ohio. Most of the students were from thirty to fifty years old; most were poor; about half were black, half white; most had moved to Cleveland either from Appalachia or the deep South. There were three sessions, each lasting three weeks. In each session, students went to classes for two hours a night, five nights a week i.e. thirty hours. To teach them, the teachers used Caleb Gattegno's *Words in Color*, a very ingenious (I now think, too ingenious) method. Used well, it can be very effective. But it makes great demands on teachers, that is, it can be used very badly. Few of the (volunteer) teachers in the program had previously used *Words in Color*; they themselves had been trained in an intensive course just before they began to teach the illiterates. I observed a good many, but by no means all of the teachers in one of the three sessions. Most of them used the method fairly well, one or two very well, a few very badly. The students and classes themselves varied; some classes were much more supportive, some students much more bold and vigorous than others. I don't know what if any follow-up studies of the program were ever made, or what the students did with their new-found skill. My strong impression at the end of my three weeks was that most of the students in the classes I had observed had learned enough about reading in their thirty hours so that they could go on exploring reading, and become as skillful *as they wanted to be*, on their own.

Some years later I first heard of Paulo Freire, who until the Army ran him out of the country had been teaching reading and writing to illiterate adult peasants in the poorest sections of northeastern Brazil. One might say that his method was a kind of politically radical, grown-up version of the method Sylvia Ashton Warner described in her books *Spinster* and *Teacher*. That is, he began by talking to these peasants about the conditions and problems of their lives (this is what the Army didn't like), and then showed them how to write and read the words that came up most in their talk. He too found that it took only about thirty hours of teaching before these wretchedly poor and previously demoralized peasants were able to go on exploring reading on their own.

Thirty hours. One school week. That is the true size of the task.

MULTIPLICATION, ETC.

This article continues the ideas in the articles on Counting in GWS #1 and on Addition in GWS #4 (which you might refer back to).

Just as they were given lists of unrelated "addition facts" and "subtraction facts" to memorize in first and second grades, so most children, when they reach third grade, will begin to meet "multiplication facts." One such fact would be that 2 x 3 = 6, another that 3 x 2 = 6. If children ask about this coincidence, they may well be told, as they were about addition, that "multiplication is commutative," which of course explains nothing, just tells them in fancier and more mysterious words what they already knew. They will almost certainly be given a list of "100 multiplication facts" to memorize (called "learning the times tables") and will be tested on these often. Still later, probably in fifth grade, they will begin

to meet fractions, and will be told that 1/2 x 6 (sometimes "one-half of six") = 3 and that 1/3 x 6 = 2. Still later, they may be told that 2 and 3 are factors of 6. So, somewhere between first or second and about seventh grades (depending on which standard arithmetic texts their teachers have been ordered to use) the children will have collected (complete with "explanations", illustrations of baby chicks, pies, etc.) these more or less unrelated facts connected with the number 6:

$$2 \times 3 = 6$$
$$3 \times 2 = 6$$
$$6 \div 2 = 3$$
$$6 \div 3 = 2$$
$$1/2 \times 6 = 3$$
$$1/3 \times 6 = 2$$
$$6 \times 1/2 = 3$$
$$6 \times 1/3 = 2$$
2 is one-third of 6
3 is one-half of 6
2 and 3 are factors of 6

But, as I said about "addition facts" in GWS #4, these are not separate "multiplication facts" or "division facts" or whatever. They are *one* fact, a fact not of arithmetic but of nature, a natural property of the number 6, which children can find for themselves and verify as often as they need or want to. The fact is that when you have this many objects:

* * * * * *

you can arrange them like this:

* * *
* * *

All those "facts" written out above are simple different ways of writing down and talking about this one fact. So anyone, having discovered this property or fact about 6, and having been told the different ways in which we write and talk about this fact, could look for and find similar facts about other numbers, and then use those same ways of writing them down.

People (young or old) who do this will find that there are some numbers (2,3,5,7, etc.) which they cannot arrange in more than one row and have the rows come out even. They might be interested in knowing that we call such numbers "prime" and all other numbers "composite." One of a number of properties of any and every whole number is that it is either prime or composite. Some people (young or old) might be interested in finding out for themselves what some of the prime numbers are, say, up to 200, or in learning that using modern computers people have been able to list all the primes up to some very large number (which I don't know, but which you could probably find out by writing Martin Gardner at *Scientific American* magazine in New York City). Or that no one has yet found a formula which they can prove will generate all the prime numbers.

I am not saying that what I have written above about properties of 6 and our ways of saying and writing them are things that every child should know, or that un-schoolers must be sure to tell their children. I suspect that what I have long said about reading, that more children would learn it, and learn it better, if it were illegal, is just as true of elementary arithmetic. And there are many people who are right now leading interesting, useful, satisfying lives who do not know any arithmetic at all. On the other hand, what I have said about numbers here seems to me interesting, and useful in many circumstances. Other things being anywhere equal, I would rather know it than not know it.

In any case, I do say that if we are going to show and/or tell children about multiplying, dividing, fractions, factors, and so on, we would do well to do it more or less as shown above, so that those different ideas of arithmetic are connected from the very beginning. And I think that at least some and perhaps many children might find it quite interesting to find out for themselves which numbers can be arranged in two rows, which in three, which in four, five, etc. and which can only be put in one row.

ABSTRACTIONS

This may be a good place to reprint something I wrote in *What Do I Do Monday?* (av. here) I had been writing about children using objects to find for themselves certain properties of numbers. I then added:

"To this sort of talk I have often heard the reply that numbers are abstract and must be taught abstractly. I have heard this used as a criticism of the Cuisenaire rods. People who say this do not understand either numbers or abstractions and abstractness, or the rods. Of course numbers are abstract, but like any and all other abstractions, they are an abstraction *of something.* People invented them to help them memorize and record certain properties of reality—numbers of animals, boundaries of an annually flooded field, observations of stars, moon, tides, etc. These numbers did not get their properties from people's imaginations, but from the things they were designed to represent. A map of the United States is an abstraction, but it looks the way it does, not because the map maker wanted it that way, but because of the way the United States looks. Of course, map makers can and must make certain choices, just as did the inventors of numbers. They can decide that what they want to show on their maps are contours, or climate, or temperature, or rainfall, or roads, or air routes, or the historical growth of the country. Having decided that, they can decide to color, say, the Louisiana Purchase blue, or red, or yellow—whatever looks nice to them. But once they have decided what they want to map, and how they will represent it, by colors, or lines, or shading, or whatever, reality then dictates what the map will look like.

So with numbers. The time may come when it is useful to consider numbers and the science of working with them without any reference to what they stand for just as it might be useful to study the general science of mapping without mapping any one place in particular. But it is *illogical, confusing, and absurd* to start there with young children. The only way they can become familiar with the idea of maps, symbol systems, abstractions of reality, is to move from known realities to the maps or symbols of them. Indeed, we all work this way. I know how contour maps are made—in that sense I understand them; but I cannot do what my brother-in-law, who among other things plans and lays out ski areas, can do. He can look at a contour map and instantly, in his mind's eye, feel the look and shape of the area. The reason he can do this while I can't is that he has walked over dozens of mountains and later looked at and studied and worked on the contour maps of areas where he was walking. No amount of explanations will enable any of us to turn an unfamiliar symbol system into the reality it stands for. We must go the other way first."

TEACHING

In my latest book, *Never Too Late,* which is about my own experience as a late beginner in music (Delacorte, Oct. '78—av. here), I write at one point:

"The trouble with most teachers of music or anything else is that they have in the back of their minds an idea more or less like this: 'Learning is and can only be the result of teaching. Anything important my students learn, they learn because I teach it to them.' ...

All my own work as teacher and learner has led me to believe quite the opposite, that teaching is a very strong medicine, which like all strong medicines can quickly and easily turn into a poison. At the right time (i.e. when the student has asked for it) and in very small doses, it can indeed help learning. But at the wrong times, or in too large doses, it will slow down learning or prevent it altogether."

All the argument I have ever seen or heard about teaching seems to me to have missed this central point. People argue about whether teaching is good or bad, as if it was clear that when learning is not happening, the cause must be that people are teaching badly, or not enough. It never occurs to them that the problem may be that people are teaching *too much,* and that whether the teaching is good or bad may have very little to do with it.

USEFUL RESOURCES

The *New Schools Exchange* (Pettigrew Ark. 72752) has published their latest (and very possibly, last) Directory. 120 pages long, it contains, among other things, a bibliography, a curriculum enrichment guide, a national directory of alternative and community schools, a list of full time adult education programs, a list of free universities, learning exchanges, etc. $5 per copy, 40% off on orders of 10 or more.

The Lifelong Learner, by Ronald Gross (Simon & Schuster, NY $8.95). Much information about independent learning. Some info seems to duplicate the NSE Directory i.e. the list of Free Universities, but in other respects they are different.

New Age Magazine, 32 Station St., Brookline Village MA 02146 (1.50 per copy) published in their Feb. '78 issue a list, complied by Nancy DuVergne Smith, of Alternatives in Higher Education, which means, ways of getting real degrees, real college and/or graduate school tickets, without actually going *to* those places. Best list of these I have seen, not duplicated in either of the two sources above. GWS may make a cheap reprint of it some day, and/or print it in the magazine. For the time being, order from *New Age*.

Green Revolution, R.D. 7, Box 388A, York, PA 17402 published in its Feb. '78 issue a Directory of Intentional Communities. Some readers of GWS have asked about these. I know of no better source of info on this subject. ($2)

The National Alternative Schools Program has published a Directory of Public Alternative Schools, including, among other things, a list (with brief descriptions) of over 1300 schools. "Alternative" has become an OK word in public education, so how "alternative" some of these schools are, and in what ways, people will have to find out for themselves. But it is a place to start looking, and there is a chance that some of these, like the Multicultural High School in Milwaukee, WI (GWS #3), might act as the legal shelter for a home study program. Order Directory from NASP, School of Education, Univ. of Mass., Amherst MA 01003 ($4.20, postage incl.) Make checks payable to Univ. of Mass.

WHY SCHOOL?

The Board of Public Education in Montana published in 1975 a pamphlet about educational goals. (I feel sure there are documents like this in many other states) At the top of the first page is a stylized picture of a child, a large plus sign, and a stylized picture of home, church, and school (with the school in front, home in the rear). Then this text:

IN MONTANA, A BASIC QUALITY EDUCATION HAS BEEN DEFINED AS "A PROCESS WHICH CAN ENABLE STUDENTS TO TRANSFORM THEIR POTENTIAL INTO ACTUALITY" (Definition adopted by the Board of Public Education in its 1975 *Report on Basic Quality Education*)

The EXPERIENCE of schooling, as one part of the educational process, should actively involve students in

communicating ideas, knowledge, thoughts, and feelings;
developing personal responsibility;
finding joy in learning;
reasoning critically and creatively;
being effective in a changing world;
assuming social responsibility;
learning who they are becoming; and
furthering their creative ability.
(Eight dimensions of basic quality education as adopted by Montana's Board of Public Education.)

[At the top of the second page, a big equals sign, then a stylized picture of child with arms and legs outflung, as if in joy, etc. Then this text:]

The OUTCOMES of the educational process should be students who have developed skills in reading, writing, speaking and listening (*communication*);
developed habits and skills necessary to maintain physical fitness and mental health (*fitness*);
learned the rights and responsibilities of citizenship (*citizenship*);
developed and applied skills which define and fulfill their learning needs throughout life (*lifelong learning*);
learned their career opportunities and capabilities (*careers*);
developed and applied standards for judging behavior (*character*);
acquired a positive attitude toward learning processes (*attitude*);
learned to live in harmony with and improve the environment (*environment*);
developed an understanding of their individual role and the roles of others as members of a family (*family*);
ability to recognize, define and seek solutions to problems (*thinking*);
ability to cope with change (*change*);
acquired knowledge and skills to purchase goods and services appropriate to their needs and resources (*consumerism*);
acquired attitudes and knowledge needed for participation in both mental and physical recreation activities (*recreation/leisure*).
(Montanans' Fifteen Goals for Education established through a survey as one part of the Montana Educational Assessment Program conducted by the Superintendent of Public Instruction.)

GOOD REASONS...

One might argue a long time (and people do) about whether the above listed goals or purposes are good ones, or are things that schools can do better than anyone else, or do well, or even do at all, or whether what the schools do to carry out these purposes makes sense, or works. Such arguments are a waste of time. For none of the items listed above are the real, serious, primary purposes of school. They are secondary purposes—at best, things the schools wish they could do, not things they have to do.

What makes these purposes secondary? Is it that in stating them the Montana Board of Education is not sincere? Not at all. They are as sincere as the day is long, probably spent weeks of wearying committee sessions in drawing up these purposes, which most teachers would no doubt strongly endorse. No, what makes these purposes secondary is not that school people don't believe in them, but that no one ever *gets in trouble for not doing them.*

When and where was a superintendent, or principal, or teacher ever fired because students were not good at communicating thoughts and feelings? Or because they hated learning? Or could not reason well enough even to avoid being taken in by ads and TV commercials, or the grossest appeals by politicians or journalists to their greed, fear, and envy? Or because they drank, smoked, never exercised, never walked if they could drive? Or never voted? Or thought it was OK to do anything you could get away with? Or did not know what the Bill of Rights was, could not understand it, and when compelled to read it, dimly thought it was some kind of Communist document (all of these views widely held by Americans, in and out of school)? Or went over their heads in debt buying things they did not need and could not afford? Or threw their bottles, cans, and garbage all over the landscape? Or spent thirty hours a week watching TV? Or ... etc., etc.?

No one has been fired, or is going to be fired, because huge numbers of people coming out of our schools think and do these things. Everyone who works in schools knows this. Therefore these purposes, however sincerely held, are not serious, not primary.

AND REAL ONES

How then do we find the real, serious, primary purposes of school? We find them by asking, *what do people get in trouble for doing (or not doing)?* When we apply this acid test to schools, we find that their primary purposes are three.

The first is to get kids out of the adults' hair—out of the house, off the streets, and out of the labor market.

The second is to grade, rank, and label them, so that later they may be funneled into this or that slot in society, and what is more important, will accept without protest, *as being all they deserve,* the slots (mostly not very good) they have been funneled into.

The third is to teach them about Reality, to prepare them for Real Life. For most of them this means boring, alienated work, empty of skill or serious purpose, and an equally alienated and passive leisure. In short, for a life of mass production and mass consumption, the factory and the TV set. Schools (as they always have) made children fit for the factory, not because they teach anything that will be useful (in or out of the factory) *but because they are like the factory.*

The modern bureaucracy—whether factory, office, store, hospital, government agency, school, or whatever—is a machine with people for parts. The work of schools is to turn children into the kind of people who can and will work as parts of a machine, and will scarcely even be able to imagine any other way they could work.

But, some might ask, where and when do people decide that schools are going to do these things? Does the Board of Education (of Montana, or any other state or city), having drawn up that fine list of secondary purposes, then hold another and secret meeting, at which they say, never mind that list, here is what we are *really* going to do? Do educators say to themselves, I know I am *supposed* to help kids be informed, critical, creative, etc. but what I am *really* going to do is teach them to do what they're told, believe without question whatever Authority tells them, and accept boredom and powerlessness as a natural, proper, and inevitable part of all life. No; there are no secret meetings, and educators (except for a few, many of whom are now busy organizing "traditional" schools) do not say such things to each other or to themselves. That is not what happens.

What happens is that schools and school people are taught to carry out their primary purposes in exactly the way that pigeons are taught to hit ping-pong balls down an alley with their wings. They are operant conditioned. Operant conditioning (see GWS #5) is a way of getting another creature (person, pigeon, rat, or whatever) to do what you want, without ever showing or telling what you want, and without that other creature even knowing what you want, or suspecting that you want anything. I often imagine, if pigeons could talk, that two of them might have this little conversation: A. "Why do you keep hitting that little ball with your wing?" B. "That's how I create food."

If you want to make a creature move North, the trick is to reward every Northerly move and punish every Southerly move, however slight. Before long that creature will move North as often and as far as it can. If you teach in schools, it doesn't take you long to find which way North is, i.e. to know that you will be in serious trouble if you don't keep the kids still and quiet, if you don't give a lot of tests and grades, or give mostly good grades, or if the children (up to and including college students) seem to like and trust you and to be having a lot of fun in your class. Before long there will be a reaction, from fellow-teachers (often from them first of all), from superiors, from parents, perhaps even from students themselves (She *made* us keep them notebooks!) Under this steady pressure, only a few teachers persist. After a while, most of them get tired of being isolated, looked on as freaks, made fun of. They quit—or they get fired.

Same for Superintendents. Scores of them, within the past ten years or so, have been fired, for trying to make their schools more interesting, attractive, exciting, and meaningful to their students. Many innovative administrators have said to me over the years that they take it as a simple matter of course that they will not last in any job for more than three or four years, which is as long as it takes (it often takes less) for the angry opposition to form that will throw them out. The teachers, principals, and superintendents who hold their jobs *do not innovate*—or only as much as is useful for public relations purposes. Traditional subjects, strict discipline (at least on paper and in theory—see *The Way It Spozed to Be*) plenty of homework, plenty of tests, plenty of grades (mostly low); that's what keeps your job or gets you a better one.

Sometimes the message comes directly. Some years ago a Professor of Education at a New Jersey college was asked to speak at a businessman's luncheon club in a nearby town. He talked about new kinds of teaching and learning in many primary schools in Great Britain and a few in this country. He was later told by the Superintendent of Schools in that town that within a few hours of the talk the head of one of the largest firms in town called up to say, "We don't want any of these new fangled ideas in our schools."

But usually the message does not need to be so quick or blunt. School people know which way North is, and where the food, and the electric shocks, come from.

SCHOOL STORY

From a *Boston Globe* story about the "reading crisis."

"...Others suffer from even more serious reading problems. A transitional aide at the X Middle School recalls that when he showed the book, *The Ocean World of Jacques Cousteau* to a student, the student asked what the title was.

'He got stuck on the word "ocean," the aide said, 'He was an eighth-grader and he couldn't even read.'"

A good example of school incompetence. Nothing in what the schools call "phonics" would help a student who did not know the word "ocean" to figure it out. The only word I can think of in which the letters " -cean" make the same sound as in "ocean" is "crustacean," hardly an everyday word. Two of the other main words in that title are French proper names. Maybe that student could read, maybe he couldn't. But no intelligent, thoughtful, and serious teacher would

make a judgment one way or the other on the basis of the student's response to this book title.

BOOKS AV. HERE

Acting Out, by Roland Betts, intro. by J. Holt ($8, cloth). From the introduction:

"This is a very funny, sad, unsparing, compassionate, and frightening account of the lives of people, both students and adults, in the public schools of one of our great cities ...a very accurate description of urban mass education and mass schooling in the United States—a failure and a disaster....

Where [the courts] have not [allowed parents to teach their children at home], it has usually been on the grounds that, however skillful the parents might be at teaching school subjects, and however high the test scores of their children might be, the parents could not... provide the necessary socializing, civilizing, democratizing experience of going to school with large numbers of other children. Having read Mr. Betts, I cannot but wonder, on what grounds could any reasonable judge *compel* children to attend the kind of schools here described. Indeed, I hope his book may be one piece of ammunition... for parents to use who are trying to get their children out of schools."

An important new book.

The Lives of Children, by George Dennison ($1.70, paper). In my review of it for *The New York Review of Books,* I wrote:

"...It is by far the most perceptive, moving, and important book on education that I have ever read.... It describes the lives of twenty-three poor children ...black, white, and Puerto Rican ... of the kind that our giant educational system conspicuously, totally, and hopelessly fails to reach or to help. [The First Street} school, spending no more money per pupil than the city's public schools, did not fail. The children got well, grew, learned..."

Then, I thought that schools were (or at least might become) serious about helping children. Their failure to read or heed this book was one of the things that convinced me that they were not serious, and could not be made so. A great and essential book (see GWS #5).

The Way It Spozed to Be and *How to Survive in Your Native Land,* by James Herndon ($1.25 and $2, paper). A serious and resourceful teacher, working in difficult situations, tries to learn, and does learn, how to do his job. Result—one school fires him, the next isolates and ignores him. Two perceptive, honest, revealing, and wonderfully comic books, worthy companions to Mark Twain. (see GWS #1 and #5)

The Self-Respecting Child, by Alison Stallibrass ($7, cloth). (see GWS #1)

The Myth of the Hyperactive Child, by Peter Schrag and Diane Divoky ($2, paper). A mistake corrected and/or a racket exposed. (see GWS #1 and #5)

Of my own seven books (the eighth, *Never Too Late,* will appear in October), perhaps the most immediately useful to unschoolers may be *What Do I Do Monday?* It suggests many specific ways in which children can explore the world (in writing, math, science, etc.) and learn and feel its wholeness and interconnectedness. These were written as classroom projects, but almost all of them could be done by children, or one child, in a family. Even for those who might not want to try any of these projects, the book will show how any interest or activity of a child can be encouraged, and can and will then lead to many other interests and activities ($2, cloth; $1.50, paper).

Instead of Education ($3.50, cloth; $3.10 paper) has a number of chapters about teaching, and about the proper relationship of teachers to learners, that might be very helpful to unschoolers.

Escape From Childhood ($7, cloth; $1.50 paper) is not about teaching or education, but about the great need of young people to be treated with seriousness, courtesy, and respect, to have contact with adults other than child specialists, and to feel they are a useful addition to the lives of the people around them.

Freedom and Beyond ($7, cloth; $1.50, paper) is about two things—should perhaps have been two separate books. The first half is about freedom—how people live, work, learn together in non-coercive relationships, some of the problems they run into, some ways of dealing with these. The second half of the book is about poverty—more specifically, about why schools and things done in schools can not cure poverty and usually only make it worse. Useful for dealing with the people who claim that compulsory schooling helps the poor, and indeed is their only hope.

How Children Fail ($1, paper). If your children are in school, and having trouble, this will probably tell you (and them) a lot about why. If they are at home, this may help you avoid some of the school's mistakes. It will also help you learn the signs in your children's behavior that will tell you that you are still making some of those mistakes, putting them under too much pressure of one kind or another.

How Children Learn ($1, paper). How little kids figure things out, before too much adult "teaching," in and out of school, makes them fearful, dependent, and stupid.

The Underachieving School ($1, paper). Useful chapters on reading, on why testing is useless and harmful, on important flaws in Piaget's experiments, and other myths of schools.

The Lives and Times of Archy and Mehitabel ($6, cloth). Nothing to do with education. A cockroach and a tough alley cat take a satirical look at life in the U.S.A. Written in the 20's and even truer and funnier today. A classic of comic verse.

A sample, just to tempt. In one poem, Archy tells of meeting Warty Bliggens, a toad who thinks that the entire universe was created just for him. When Archy asks how come, Warty Bliggens asks in return what the universe has done to deserve him. To this Archy comments (since he works the keys of a typewriter by diving on them, head first, he can't make capital letters):

> if i were a human being
> i would not laugh
> too complacently
> at poor warty bliggens
> for similar absurdities
> have only too often
> lodged in the crinkles
> of the human
> cerebrum

Editor—John Holt
Managing Editor—Peg Durkee

GROWING WITHOUT SCHOOLING

Issue No. 7

January, 1979

Many things have happened since you received GWS #6. Two unschooling families have won important rulings from state courts—more on this later. *Time* magazine, after talking at length with a number of unschooling families, ran a fine story about this in their Dec. 4 '78 issue. Soon after, I was invited to appear, with Linda and Bob Sessions and their children, on the Phil Donahue show in Chicago. In the four weeks since the first airing of the show (it goes out in different cities on different days), we received 2700 letters! Some of these sound only curious, but at least half sound really interested in our work. Needless to say, for the two of us to read and answer that much mail has been quite a task. And we expect another 1000 or so before we're through. If most of those who sound interested decide to subscribe, it should be a great boost to us.

The group subscription record has moved West again, this time to Lincoln, Neb., where readers have taken out a 22X subscription—and for 18 issues!

At the same time, the publishers of my newest book (*Never Too Late*—Delacorte) said that they were very interested in a possible book about unschooling. Much of the material for this would come from GWS, but I have already written 10-15,000 words of new material and have more still to write. All this action has delayed this issue of GWS. But barring other avalanches of mail, we should have #8 out fairly soon.

GOOD NEWS

Since we wrote the story "Help Wanted" in this issue, a Massachusetts Superior Court has handed down a ruling favorable to the Perchemlides family. It did not (as I did not think it would) say point blank to the School District, "Approve this family's program." What it said was, in effect, "Take another look at this program, and this time, be reasonable." The family will probably have to (and will be wise to) make a few small concessions to the schools, probably in the area of curriculum, though I have strongly urged that they not yield an inch in the crucial matter of testing and evaluation. But the effect of the ruling will almost certainly be that they will be able to teach their children at home.

The Judge's decision is long and intricate, and a very good lesson in how judges think. Since we are so late with this issue, I won't try to quote it or discuss it much here. (For $2, we will send you a copy of the complete ruling.) But he made one novel and (to us) extremely important and useful point, that the Constitution guarantees to citizens many implied rights, rights which it does not specifically name, and that the right of parents to control the education of their children is

one such implied right. He did not put this right under the First Amendment, but under the Ninth, saying that the right to educate one's children can be seen as a logical part of a general right to privacy, the right to control one's private affairs.

But he also said that the right of the states to oversee the education of the young was itself a constitutionally protected right, falling under the general heading of police powers. From this it follows that in this matter of education the rights of parents and the rights of states are competing rights, which must be balanced against each other. The schools, therefore, may not arbitrarily reject, as they did in this case, a proposed home teaching plan, without giving any reasons. They must give reasons, which must be compelling, and may not include such trivia as "the children will miss the social life," or "it will set a bad precedent."

This is the narrow line that we must try to (and I think can) persuade the courts to walk. Yes, the States may oversee the education of the young, and Yes, to that end they may establish schools and even make them compulsory, but at the same time, No, they may not establish a monopoly of schools or even of methods of schooling (this is the meaning of *Pierce* and other cases), and No, they may not say that for people to educate their own children is in and of itself a crime, or arbitrarily and without due process deny them the right to do so.

HELP NEEDED

Mr. and Mrs. Perchemlides (GWS #4), when they told the local school board that they wanted to take their child out of school, were told by them to submit a home teaching program. They did—twenty pages long, detailed and thorough. The school board (as often happens) called it "inadequate," without giving any reasons, or saying how they would have to change it to make it adequate.

In some states where the law makes home instruction a legal alternative, such action by school boards can, I believe, be attacked in court on two grounds: 1) It denies due process 2) It sets aside the stated will of the legislature. As I have said, I do not think we should try to get courts to rule that compulsory schooling, or things done in and by schools, are un-Constitutional. All such arguments lead to the Supreme Court, which if they hear such cases at all are for some time to come likely to rule against us.

Beyond that, I think we would be unwise to make it part of our legal strategy to ask local or state courts to overrule school boards by specifically approving home teaching programs which the boards have turned down. In the first place, the legislatures have specifically given that task to the school boards. In the second place, the courts may very well say that they are not competent to make such decisions. In the third place, they may fear (with good reason) that if in a few cases they do rule in favor of parents and against the local school board, they will soon be swamped with such cases. Finally, there is no reason to expect that in matters of education most judges will be any more tolerant or enlightened than most school boards.

But I do think we may be able to get many courts to say that if state law makes home instruction a legal option (and gives school boards the right to approve or disapprove such programs), these boards are legally obliged 1) to make public some explicit and reasonable standards which such programs must meet in order to be approved 2) to approve all programs which meet such standards, and 3) where they claim that a given program does not meet them, to state explicitly in what respects it does not and how it would have to be changed in order to do so.

This, legally, is where the Perchemlides family is at the moment. They are trying to convince the court that, in disapproving their program of home instruction, the local school board acted arbitrarily and unreasonably. To do that, they must persuade the court, not necessarily to overrule the school board by approving their program, but only to say that the program has enough intrinsic merit so that the board could not turn it down out of hand, without reasons. To help them, I have asked some Professors of Education I know to look at their program, and if they think it is good, or at least equivalent to what is done in most schools, to say so in writing. So far, four have agreed to do so, and I believe others will join them.

Which brings me at last to the point of this particular article. It would be very helpful if we had, from all parts of the country, a list of Professors of Education, and also, school administrators—Superintendents, Curriculum Supervisors, School Board Presidents or other officers and members—who would be willing from time to time to look over proposed home instruction programs of unschoolers, and if they think they are adequate and/or equivalent to what local schools provide, to put this in writing. Will you, readers of GWS, please help us make such a list, either by asking any Professors of Education, etc. you know if they would agree to be on such a list, or, if you are a Professor of Education, etc., by giving us your name. We would not publish these names in GWS (unless some people asked to have their names published). But we would send the list to unschoolers who asked for it, and they could get in touch with such Professors, etc. directly.

RULING FROM IOWA

In the case of The State of Iowa, plaintiff, vs. Robert Sessions and Linda Sessions, defendants, the following excerpts from the recent ruling of the District Court of Iowa in and for Winneshiek County may be of great interest to many GWS readers:

"The above cases, involving the filing of criminal charges and convictions thereon against Robert Sessions and Linda Sessions in Magistrate Court, now come before the Court upon appeals to District Court. The matters as criminal matters, as contemplated by statute, were heard *de novo* by the Court on appeal.... The Court, after reviewing the file, considering the evidence, statements of counsel, and the briefs and arguments submitted, now enters the following:

FINDINGS OF FACT

1. Robert Sessions and Linda Sessions were each charged under Section 299.1 in that each did unlawfully fail to have his or her 7-year-old son, Erik Sessions, attend a public school and/or obtain equivalent instruction elsewhere.
2. They were tried under that charge in Magistrate's Court. They were each found guilty and were each sentenced to pay a fine of $50 and costs were assessed against them... Appeal was thereafter filed....
6. The defendants requested the board of directors of the Decorah Community School District to approve their home teaching program. The board refused, and the matter was appealed to the State Department of Public Instruction, and a decision was rendered by the board... sustaining the position of the Decorah board and stating in substance (a) that the Sessions met the first test, that is, of an equivalent instruction program ...(b) The Sessions did not meet the second test, that is, the requirement of 'providing instruction by a certified teacher.'...
7. Thereafter, the Sessions filed a petition for declaratory ruling with the state board in which clarification and guidance or interpretation was asked in the following form: 'Precisely what must we do to comply with the "instruction by a certified teacher" clause of 299.1 of the 1977 Code of Iowa?'
On May 10, 1978, the board answered the query in letter form [stating in substance]... (c) '...the appropriate standard to be used to determine the amount of instruction required by a certified teacher is that portion of a normal day during which instruction occurs in the public school district of residence. ... strongly imply the necessity of teacher presence or close proximity throughout the instructional process.' ...This letter and information reached the defendants some time after their conviction.
8. Defendants assert the unconstitutionality of the charge in that: (a) the law is vague on standards of

public instruction. (b) It violates the 1st and 14th Amendments. (c) Denial of due process by the action of the Decorah Community School District Board...

The Court enters the following:

CONCLUSIONS OF LAW

3. Defendants further assert unconstitutionality by virtue of alleged violations of the 1st and 14th Amendments to the United States Constitution. Defendants in effect assert that their right to freedom of religion has been denied by denying the defendants their right to educate their child as they desire. The defendants cite the compelling case of *State of Wisconsin vs. Yoder*, 406 US 205, 32 Lawyers Ed. 2d 15, 92 Supreme Court 1526, and other citations in substantiation of their position. ...The Court feels that under the very concept of the *Wisconsin vs. Yoder* case cited by the defendants, that adequate showing has not been made to put the defendants' opposition on a religious plane. In the cited case the Court said in substance: ' ...a way of life, however virtuous and admirable, may not be interposed as a barrier to reasonable state regulation of education if it is based on purely secular considerations; to have the protection of the religious clauses of the 1st Amendment, *the claims must be rooted in religious belief.* ...' (Ed. italics) ...

This is not to say an individual or individuals must be a part of an organized religion to come under the concept of the cited case. But rather under the record in this case the defendants have not presented to the Court sufficient evidence to sustain their argument under the 1st Amendment....

6. Defendants urge the position that truancy violation, being a criminal charge, that the burden is on the plaintiff [sic] to prove all the elements of the crime beyond a reasonable doubt. This proposition is surely an accurate statement of the law. Applying this to the case before the Court, the burden would be on the State to show each of the following elements: (1) That the defendants failed to have their child attend school in a public school district; and (2) Failing to have the child attend public school, they did not cause said child to attend upon equivalent instruction by a certified teacher elsewhere.

The first element was proved. As to the second element, the State held that the parents did procure a program indicating an equivalent education. The query remaining then: Was the equivalent instruction provided by *a certified teacher elsewhere?*

...The Court's ruling in this case is not to be construed as the Court's passing upon the quality of education in the Decorah school system. ...The Court's function is essentially to determine whether or not the defendants have committed the crime alleged and are guilty thereof.

7. Finally the Court legally concludes that the burden is above set forth under the second element, 'failing to have child attend public school, did they cause said child to attend upon *equivalent instruction by*

a certified teacher elsewhere?' In this connection the Court must conclude that based upon the entire record, the State has failed to prove the alternate or second element, that is, that the schooling for Erik is not the equivalent by a certified teacher elsewhere [sic]. The Court concludes that there is a reasonable doubt as to the question of the certified teacher, and that as a consequence the defendants should be acquitted of the criminal charge.

In so ruling the Court *has considered of great significance the element of equivalency* (Ed. italics), the sincere effort on the part of the defendants to comply, the difficulties and long delay in their getting a response to their query on a certified teacher (in fact no response was received until after their conviction), *the inherent nature of the statutes contemplating a private tutorial situation as an alternate [sic] to public school attendance* (Ed. italics), and finally the conclusion that the legislature created a public school requirement with alternatives. *These alternatives may not be arbitrarily denied* (Ed. italics) but if the statute is to have a viable Constitutional aspect of validity, it must be a determinable, workable statute with the opportunity for a legitimate exception.

The Court can understand the concern over the propriety of 'opening the door' for many attempted exceptions (Ed. note—the State made much of this point in all its dealings with the Sessions). However, the Court feels that this is not a real threat under the statute and reasonably within the spirit of the statute. Exception as contemplated by the statute adds strength, not weakness, to the law.

8. Finally the Court merely concludes that the second and alternate element of the crime has not been proven beyond a reasonable doubt.

NOW, THEREFORE, IT IS THE JUDGMENT AND DECREE OF THE COURT:

1. The judgment and sentence of the Magistrate is reversed.

2. The defendants are hereby acquitted of the charges filed against them.

3. Costs are assessed to the plaintiff.

Frank D. Elwood, Judge
First Judicial District, Iowa

A LANDMARK CASE

This seems to me an extremely important decision, in some ways the most important decision on compulsory schooling that has yet appeared. To be sure, the court made its ruling on very narrow grounds. But that is why the ruling is so important. There is very little in it that most judges, *whatever might be their views on compulsory schooling,* would be likely to disagree with. It is, in short, a decision which we can expect many courts, at least in states where the law provides specifically for alternatives to schooling, to accept as a reasonable precedent.

What it boils down to is this. In all such cases 1) the burden of proof is on the schools 2) to show beyond reasonable doubt 3) that what the parents propose to do at home will be worse than what the schools are actually doing (not just talking about doing). There are very few school systems which will in fact be able to show this, either to a judge or a jury.

This gives us very good reason to believe that in most jurisdictions, in states whose laws provide for an alternative to schooling (unlike, say NH, which does not), any parents who prepare and present their case thoroughly and wisely can probably win a favorable ruling from a court.

It is worth noting, too, that Judge Elwood in Iowa held it very much against the State (i.e. the schools) that they did not cooperate with the Sessions in their efforts to find out precisely what the schools would accept as "equivalent." This means that when we ask schools what we must do to make our program equivalent, *they have to answer*. If we then do what they tell us we have to do, they are not likely to be able to show beyond a reasonable doubt that our program is *not* equivalent.

Not only will these arguments probably seem weighty to other courts, or juries, but they may well convince a good many school boards and their attorneys that bringing unschoolers to court will be far more trouble than it is worth. As a general rule, lawyers do not advise their clients to go to court unless they think they have an excellent chance to win.

Bob Sessions, writing about the decision in the *North Country Anvil* (a good publication, $7.50 for 6 issues, Box 37, Millville, MN 55957), says, "Judge Elwood …ruled in our favor on two counts: 1) he does not think the state proved our guilt beyond a reasonable doubt because they offered no good arguments that 'certified instruction' requires the identical number of hours of contact found in local schools, and 2) he believes that our providing an equivalent education to that to be got in schools satisfies *the intent of Iowa law* (Ed. italics). His decision does not specify how much certified instruction is adequate (Ed. note—thank goodness that question is left open) nor does he say that anyone with a program like ours should be exempted (Ed. note—but thanks to his ruling, most will be). The Iowa Department of Public Instruction still has review power regarding the adequacy of anyone's program, and all such programs must have 'significant' involvement of a certified instructor."

Later he says, "The county attorney has filed a motion for a re-hearing with the district judge, and he has said publicly that he is strongly predisposed to appeal to the Iowa Supreme Court. We have good reason to believe his motion for a re-hearing will be rejected, and we're also convinced that he will appeal.

To date we have spent about $3,000 on this case, $700 of which came in the form of mostly small donations from people like yourselves. Our reserves have been exhausted, and although working through the Supreme Court takes much time (a year to a year and a half), consequently allowing us to again save some money, it is also much more costly…. the only way we will be able to continue is through support from you."

I hope any GWS readers in a position to do so will give some of this support. (Rob't Sessions, Rt. 2, Decorah, IA 52101)

LEGAL STRATEGIES

A few general observations. Judges, in making their rulings, take into account a number of things—legal principle, legal precedent, the will of the legislature, and *the possible or probable social effect of their ruling*. Thus, parents who have sued the schools for damages because their children did not learn anything there have so far been turned down by the courts, on the grounds that this would lead to a rash of lawsuits that would bankrupt the schools. We may take it as certain that the courts will not in any foreseeable future make rulings which they think may lead to the speedy destruction of the public schools or the overturn of compulsory schooling. If we ask for such broad rulings, we will be turned down. But beyond that, either in asking for narrow rulings, or speaking of any we may be able to win, we must be careful not to make large public boasts and outcries to the effect that "this means the end of compulsory schooling." Judge Elwood's ruling may or may not be upheld by the Iowa Supreme Court. Almost certainly, it would not be if it had said that anyone with a program like the Sessions should be exempted from compulsory schooling, or that the Iowa Department of Public Instruction should not have the power to review such programs. The fact that the Sessions are willing to go to such trouble and expense to teach their children at home will be seen by the courts as part of the proof *they must have* that the Sessions will be serious and conscientious teachers. The courts may be ready to give the same permission to any others who can show that they too are willing to go to this amount of trouble. But they are probably not yet ready to give blanket permission to anyone just because they can put the right words down on a piece of paper.

In GWS #6, in a short piece entitled "Equivalent," we told about an injured boy, unable to go to school, to whom the schools sent a tutor—*for an hour and a half a week!* This was all he needed to keep up with his studies.

We didn't print that just to make one more joke against the schools. The Iowa case shows that this matter of equivalency is crucial. Any parents who are considering a court battle against the schools need to find out exactly what the schools are doing, including what they are doing about sick and/or injured children. How much home instruction by a certified instructor do the schools themselves provide? Are all tutors used by the schools in fact certified? Ask the schools, and the State Department of Public Instruction. But also, check up on their answers. People who work in large organizations may not know what is actually going on, and even when they do, may not always tell the truth about it.

In GWS #4, in the article "Testing the Schools," we suggested a number of questions that parents might ask schools. (We will add more questions soon.) We don't suggest these questions as a kind of school-baiting. They are serious, and have to do with the matter of equivalency.

Furthermore, when you ask these questions, or any others you may think of, put them in writing. Send copies to all members of the school board, to the school's attorneys, to all top administrators, curriculum planners, etc. If the school board has recently won, or is facing, a close election, send copies of these questions to their opponents.

The idea is not to spring these questions on the schools in the midst of a court battle. Ask the questions well in advance, and to as many people as possible. Give them plenty of time to answer. *For they have no answers!* In almost all schools, good or bad, the children who are behind grade level, in reading, math, or whatever, never catch up, but fall further behind. And the number of those who have fallen behind rises every year. At the high-powered boarding school I went to, C students did not become B and A students; they became D students. It's the same story everywhere.

FRACTIONS

Theo Giesy tells us a nice story:

"When Danile was 6 or 7, she was lying in my bed thinking about money and wondered how $1 would divide among 3 children. She thought about it awhile and said, 'You could break it into dimes and give each one 3, that leaves 1 dime, you break that into pennies and give each one 3, and I get the extra penny.' That was all her own, I made no comments or suggestions."

When I first taught fifth grade, before I had "taught" the children anything about fractions, or even mentioned the word, I used to ask them questions like this: "If you had three candy bars, and wanted to divide them evenly among five people, how would you do it?" Most of them could think of one or more ways to do this. But after they had "had" fractions, and had learned to think of this as a problem that you had to use fractions to solve, most of them couldn't do it. Instead of reality, and their own common sense and ingenuity, they now had "rules," which they could never keep straight or remember how to apply.

THE SOCIAL LIFE

Many people write that they would like to take their children out of school, but worry that this may hurt their social life, or social development. About this, a reader writes:

"…My mother tells me that after the first day in kindergarten I told her that I didn't need to go to school any more because I knew everything already. Great arrogance? Not really. I knew how to be quiet, how to listen to children's stories, and how to sing. I wanted to learn about the adult world but was restricted to a world which adults believe children wanted. My great pre-school enthusiasm died an early death. …

Shame was one of the first lessons that I learned. In the first grade I was told to color a picture of a mother and daughter working in a kitchen. It struck me that if I were to color the entire picture yellow, then it would be different from all the other pictures. When I handed it to the teacher I expected her to be pleased, if not genuinely excited. She, instead, glared at me for what seemed to be a long time and caused me to feel the deepest shame and self-contempt. …I was six years old.

Since spontaneity was dangerous—it conflicted with the teacher's view of how children should act—lying was a valuable survival technique …In first grade, the class was sent to the kindergarten room to do some work without supervision. I used this opportunity to take a plastic doll and stick the head into a plastic toilet in one of the furnished doll houses in the room. No one was sure who did it, but everyone thought it was amusing—except the teacher. She was red with anger (she was a nun, and working class Catholic schools in the early 1960's were not the most humane institutions) and I feared a severe beating. Suspicion was eventually focused on me and I lied with complete success, at least for me; another boy was blamed for the incident. I wish that I had said, 'Yes, I did it, so what.' But I was afraid…

Other incidents occurred to other people and were much more serious. I saw a boy of thirteen, seventh grade, try to explain why he did not have an assignment. His crime was that he spoke with indignation. Before he said three words the teacher stopped him and with a who-the-hell-do-you-think-you-are tone of voice called him to the desk and slapped him across the face with a rubber strap which was about 6 to 8 inches long and 1/4 inch thick. He cried; they always did when it was in the face. He never did get the chance to explain why he did not have the assignment. I'm not so sure that he didn't have it. It may have been that he could not find it quickly enough.

…This teacher, the principal, was a textbook authoritarian. Every violation of her largely unwritten rules would lead her to deliver the same angry statement: 'Don't challenge me.' She saw challenges in virtually everything even though we would never have challenged her. I'll just give you two of her biggest challenges.

Challenge number one involved misbehavior which the teacher present did not see, but the principal looking into the room did. The fifth, sixth, seventh, and eighth grades (it was a small school) were in this room to practice singing. She was furious, talked about challenges, and scolded the student vehemently. Then she proceeded to slap him halfway across the room. She gave him about eight or ten real haymaker slaps. I was standing only a few feet away at the time....One fact about this event showed how much in awe of authority we were: the victim of this violence did not raise his hands to protect his face. When it was over, all I could hear was the boy crying and my own heart beating.

Challenge number two involved the same boy. This time he urinated, or defecated, or both, in his pants. Perhaps he was ill or maybe he had a mental problem (Ed. note—Or perhaps he had merely been denied permission to go to the bathroom, which happens quite often in school). He didn't do this regularly. He was about twelve years old. Naturally, this called for punishment. He was forced to stand in front of each class in school while the teacher explained to the class his crime. When he came to our classroom the principal named him the school's stinker and told us why. But what I remember most clearly is the pained *smile* (Ed. italics—this is scary) on his face.

There were many incidents of fear and humiliation. Even though there were not many savage beatings, the point is that we lived in an environment where this could happen anytime. And we knew that. I had no clear idea that there was anything wrong with the school; I only had a vague feeling that things didn't have to be the way they were. I wasn't a noble child resisting tyrannical teachers. No, I loved the game of fear and humiliation and played like the masters.

'We can hardly wait to make someone pay for our humiliation, yield to us as we were once made to yield.' (*Freedom and Beyond*, p. 114)

I'm not sure when it started, but in the eighth grade a number of us would terrorize some of the timid boys in the school. We would push the victim around, ridicule him, pull his shirt out, spin him around, dust the chalk erasers on his clothes, mess up his hair, and chase him on the playground. It was easy to be friends with these boys when I was alone with them. But when there was a group of us the teasing would begin. *Since we were always in groups* (Ed. italics), the teasing of these boys, two in particular, was nearly unending. On the playground they had to avoid being seen. One of the boys would go home for lunch and not return until the last minute of recess. We did it without thought and it seemed to be only boyish pranks. It was sadism and I found it to be almost irresistible.

We then started to turn on the group members and practice our arts on the selected victim. I remember coming home with sore sides from laughing so hard at another's humiliation, but I felt empty and actually unhappy. The next day I would do it again. This only stopped when I became the victim. It was pure hell. Everyone you knew devoted all his time to your being

humiliated. Any one act was insignificant; slapping an unaware student in the back of the head was popular. But it happened all day long in a multitude of ways. Christmas vacation came and one of my prime torturers transferred to another school. Things cooled off for me, but not for the timid boys or the younger children in the school. We almost had serious violence with the male students several years younger than us.

I don't remember the beginning or the end of this sadistic behavior. I know that I didn't act this way before my last two years in grade school or since then.

I believe that I was lucky in not turning out to be an ignorant brutal person who delights in being such a person. My last two years in grade school show that I could have been. Fortunately, I had asthma and was able to stay home a great deal. While at home I would spend all day reading an encyclopedia for children. This gave me a love of learning which I never would have acquired at school. In my last two years in grade school I missed about sixty days of school, thirty each year. This allowed me to preserve what little sanity I had. In high school I started to read Erich Fromm, and in my second year I read *Summerhill.* By then it was clear to me what had been the source of my suffering. And my cruelty.

When I was at home and not in school because of illness (often I wasn't really sick), I was able to explore the world through reading. This could be done solely out of personal interest and at my desired pace. What a wonderful feeling to have an interest which one can freely nurture. *To act out of personal conviction was a feeling totally different from my feelings in school.* (Ed. italics) . . ."

Thanks for a most moving letter, and confession. It reminds me of a part of my own schooling. At one point I was in a public elementary school, in a class in which almost all the boys were bigger and older than I was; most of them from working class Italian or Polish families. One by one, the toughest ones first, then the others, more or less in order of toughness, they beat me up at recess. Which is to say, they punched me until they knocked me down and/or made me cry. Once a given boy had beaten me up, he didn't bother to do it again. There didn't seem to me to be much malice in it; it was as if this had to be done in order to find my proper place in the class. Finally everyone had beat me except a boy named Henry. One day the bigger boys hemmed us in and announced that Henry and I had to have a fight to find who was the biggest sissy in the sixth grade. Henry and I didn't want to fight, but they told us that if we didn't they would beat up on both of us. So for a while Henry and I circled around, swinging wildly at each other, the bigger boys laughing and urging us on. Nothing happened for some time, until one of my wild swings hit Henry's nose. It began to bleed, Henry began to cry, and so did I. But the bigger boys were satisfied; they declared that Henry was now the official biggest sissy in the class, and on the whole, they didn't pick on me much any more if they could find Henry. How he survived all this, I don't know.

I am also reminded of something a good deal more sinister, that I read in the program notes of the recording of Benjamin Britten's opera *Billy Budd*. At the time in which the opera is set, large ships used to go to sea with a number of cabin boys, perhaps twelve, thirteen years old. Now and then the crew—all this with the approval of the ship's officers—would use the cabin boys for some free entertainment. They would tie the left hands of each of the cabin boys to a mast, so that they were arranged round the mast like the spokes of a wheel. In the right hand of each cabin boy they would put a marlinspike. In effect a short wooden club. Then they would explain the rules of the "game." For every blow that a cabin boy was struck from behind, he could strike one blow—only one—at the boy ahead of him. If he was not struck, he could not strike. Then, to start things going, a crew member would strike one of the cabin boys. He would in turn strike the boy ahead of him, who would strike the boy ahead of him, and so on, blow after blow, round and round the mast, until they all, or all but one, lay senseless on the deck. The joy of the game, for the crew, lay not just in the sadism of it, but even more in knowing that any boy could stop the circle of blows, end the game, and save himself and his companions, just by refusing to do what was done to him. But apparently, this never happened, and the experienced and hardened older members of the crew knew that it was not going to happen.

The writer of the letter says, "to act out of personal conviction was a feeling totally different from my feelings in school." It is a very important part of the real and serious purposes of school to kill that feeling. The vast majority of the general public, and of the parents and teachers of most children in schools, feels that to act out of personal conviction is a luxury and an indulgence that they, and most other people, cannot afford. As one of the New York hardhats who violently assaulted a peaceful and legal anti-war demonstration later said to an interviewer, "I've got plenty of things I'd like to protest about, but I keep my mouth shut." And I have long since lost track of the number of schoolteachers and/or administrators who, defending coercion in schools, have said to me, "If I wasn't made to do things, I wouldn't do anything."

NO COMMENT

The Boston Globe of Sept. 1, 78 carried an AP story, saying in part:

BACK-TO-SCHOOL BOOSTS RETAILERS

NEW YORK—Many of the nation's leading retail chains reported record sales in August yesterday, sales they said were sparked by end-of-summer and back-to-school promotions.

GOOD NEWS FROM MO.

Albert Hobart, P. O. Box 112, Willow Springs, MO 65793, writes:

"For the past four years we have been teaching our nine-year-old son at home rather than sending him to school. It's been a pleasant and memorable experience for all of us. Our son is learning quickly and easily, and he seems to be a happy, good-natured, well-adjusted boy. The only thing we regret is that we haven't had more contact with other families whose children are learning at home.

Thus recently we decided to see what we could do to bring together a group of parents who are committed to helping their children learn without schooling. As we picture it, several 'unschooling' families would live in the same vicinity and get together from time to time for mutual support, good times, and the sharing of ideas. One of our most important goals would be to insure that our children have an ongoing opportunity to play and grow together and develop lasting friendships.

We've been interested in this idea for several years, but our home near Boston, Mass. never seemed like the appropriate setting. Our suburban neighbors were usually too involved with the school way of raising their children to even consider the kind of informal learning arrangement we had in mind. We soon discovered, moreover, that many parents who were teaching their own children shared our desire to live in a more rural environment where they could garden, raise farm animals, and, in general, live a more self-sufficient life.

As a result we decided to move to the Missouri Ozarks. I grew up in St. Louis, so I was already familiar with the area, but the main reason we chose to settle in the Show Me State was that it's legal in Missouri to teach your own children. We've met a number of families in this vicinity whose children are learning at home, and none of them have had any problems with the school authorities.

We particularly like the Ozarks because the people who live here have an admiration for self-reliance and a distrust of government interference in their private lives. Thus they seem more sympathetic towards home education than people we've met elsewhere.

(As a word of warning, however, I think I should repeat an excellent point made in GWS #2; regardless of what the law says, school authorities anywhere can make trouble for you if they want to. We think there are ways to avoid this difficulty, and we hope we've found an area where this sort of problem is least likely to occur. But should worse come to worst, we are prepared to work together with other parents to organize some kind of minimal private school. My wife is a certified teacher, and I've had some teaching experience.)

Another reason we like the Ozarks is that the cost of land is relatively low compared to other regions. Prices range from $300 to $400 an acre for a 40 acre plot, although the cost goes up for smaller parcels, high quality farmland, or places with creeks or springs. There's plenty of land available, so it should be easy for families to buy property within driving distance of each other.

The opportunities for employment in the Ozarks are probably similar to what they would be in most rural areas. There are certainly jobs available, but at comparatively lower salaries. On the other hand, it doesn't cost much to live here either. For instance, the property taxes on a 40 acre farm are usually less than $100 a year and sometimes less than $50.

If the ideas I've described sound appealing to you and you think your family might enjoy living in the Ozarks, please write. We'd be happy to give you more information."

(From a later letter) "Last week we held a pot-luck picnic at the campground where we've been staying. We think it was quite a success. 47 people attended, 21 adults and 26 children …many more than we expected. The parents discussed their various experiences and exchanged information, and everybody seemed to have a good time, especially the children. We're going to meet again in a few weeks, and we plan to invite more people. We don't know if it will turn into a regular get-together or not. We hope so. But we're certain that the parents who came feel more positive about what they're doing, and that some who were uncertain about home education are now committed to the idea.

Our son Robert continues to thrive. He met boys from three 'unschooling' families who live nearby. He really enjoys playing with these new friends, especially because he has so much in common with them. In fact, our son seems to enjoy everything about his life here in the Ozarks. He's so happy, so full of life and curiosity, that it's always a joy for us to be with him."

SCHOOL STORY

A recent UPI release from Providence, RI, says, in part:

"A 14-year-old boy who skipped high school and has been pulling straight A's at Rhode Island Junior College Thursday was allowed to stay in school while authorities test him to see if he is smart enough for college. (Ed. note—this is how the story is worded; I assume they mean that the decision to allow him to stay was made on Thursday.)

Jonathan Dellinger graduated from Cranston (RI) Junior High in June. The state said an education law prohibits the boy from leaving high school until he is 16.

But the boy enrolled in the college's continuing education program this fall and was getting A's in Spanish, introductory Chemistry, algebra, and funda-mentals of writing when the college forced him to withdraw Oct. 8.

Jonathan and his mother sued the college, con-tending his constitutional rights were violated when he was expelled because of his age.

Under the agreement announced in Superior Court Thursday by the State Education Department and the boy's lawyer, Jonathan will be allowed to take courses at the college for one semester.

In the meantime, he will undergo tests at the University of Rhode Island and lawyers for both sides will file written arguments within two weeks on whether the case (Ed. note—I assume this means his mother's suit) should be dismissed.

'I can't wait to get back to classes,' the youth said after the court settlement. 'All my friends are there. It's the first school I've gone to where I felt I really belonged.'

Jonathan's mother, Barbara McKinney, said the boy has an IQ of 155, 15 points above the theoretical 'genius' margin of 140.

Mrs. McKinney said the Cranston public school system 'virtually ignored my son's intelligence. He was always bored with his age group.' But she says she's 'content for the time being' with the state college….

Jonathan said he plans to apply to Brown Univer-sity next year.

After the agreement was reached, the boy's lawyer, Stephen J. Fortunato, Jr. moved to dismiss the case.

'We got what we wanted,' he said. 'Jonathan goes back to RIJC tomorrow and he'll be tested to see if he belongs in high school or college.'

But J. Peter Dougherty, a state lawyer representing the college, asked the court to continue hearing the case.

'The president of the college is getting calls from parents all over Rhode Island who say they have gifted high-school age children,' he said.

School people are unbelievable. They have some test which they say is a "good predictor of college success." That means, most of the people who have scored well on the test have later on got good grades in college, which suggests that any other kid who scores well on it will also get good grades in college. So now, with perfectly straight faces, they are going to give this test to this boy *who is already getting straight A's in college,* to find out whether he is smart enough to go to college!

It's like something out of *Alice in Wonderland.*

What is that junior college president so afraid of? Suppose there are many other young people in Rhode Island like Jonathan, perfectly capable of doing outstanding college work though only of high school age. Wouldn't that be a good thing? One would suppose that a sensible man, a man really interested in learning, would be delighted, would say, "By all means send them here, no use having them waste their time in high school."

Unless, of course, the real purpose of high school *is* to waste their time, *and to have them get used to having their time wasted.* Unless, in short, the purpose of school is not to speed them into useful life in adult society, *but to hold them out of it.*

The story suggests another way in which children who are good at school (know how to play the school game) might get out of one or more years of high school. Indeed, one reader of GWS has told me that during her high school years she was able to get out of going to high school by taking extension courses at the state university. It seems to me very likely that most courts would agree that a child who was taking college courses and getting good marks was getting an education "equivalent" to that provided by the local high school, and therefore need not attend that high school.

On the whole, I don't think it would be wise to make a constitutional issue out of this. Nothing in the U.S. Constitution says that people may not have various rights and privileges withheld because of age. Many such laws exist in every state—laws about drinking, driving, voting, etc. Not for a very long time to come are the Federal Courts going to overturn all such laws by declaring all age discrimination unconstitutional. But most state courts, as I said before, can probably be persuaded to rule, on one ground or another, that a child forbidden by the schools to do work that he has proved himself capable of doing is being denied some kind of educational opportunity guaranteed him by the laws of the state.

SENSIBLE PHONICS

Elsewhere in GWS I have said (and will probably say many times again) that most children, if there was interesting stuff around to read, would figure out for themselves how to read it even if we did not "teach" them anything, and only told them what words said if and when they asked us. To those who may disagree with this, and insist that some teaching is necessary or at least helpful, I would say that if we are going to try to "teach" children something about reading, we ought at least (unlike almost all schools and teachers) to do it in ways that will make their learning easier and not harder. That is, we should try to avoid telling them things that are inconsistent, self-contradictory, or just plain false.

Two small examples. In many first, second, etc. grade classrooms I used to see signs on the walls—and people tell me they are still up there—saying, "When two vowels go out walking, the first one does the talking." (Typical of the cutesy-wootsy way in which schools talk to young children.) What this means, of course, is that there are many vowel pairs—bAIt, bEAt, bOAt, etc.—in which the first of the two vowels makes the sound. OK to point that out to children, though the best way to do this would simply be to give ex-amples. But the trouble with the cute little sentence that the schools have cooked up to tell children this is that *it* contains two vowel pairs, *both of which violate this rule.* This might not bother some children, either because they already understand what the rule is telling them or (more likely) because they don't *think* about anything they hear in school. But some children do think about what they see and hear, and it is just such thoughtful and intelligent children who might very well be thrown for a loop by this dumb sentence on the wall.

Other example. Among the sounds which vowels make is one which is the same as the *name* of the vowel, as in bAke, bEEt, rOse, etc. The schools have tradition-ally called these sounds the "long" vowel sounds. By contrast, they give the name "short" to the vowel sounds in "bAck, bEt, bIt, etc. Now the fact is that there is nothing *longer* about the sound of A in bAke than its sound in bAck. We can say either word quickly or slowly, make either vowel sound as long or short as we wish. Again, calling one of these vowel sounds "long" and the other one "short," though it makes no sense—one might as well call one blue and the other green—might not bother the kind of children who (as I was) are ready to parrot back to the teacher whatever they hear, never mind what it means or whether it means any-thing. But it might be extremely confusing and even frightening to other kinds of children, including many of the most truly intelligent.

It might not even do any harm to call the sounds of bAck, bIt, pOt, etc. "short" vowels, as long as we made it clear that there was nothing really any shorter about those sounds, and that we just used this word because we had to use *some* word, and people had been using this one for quite a while, so we decided we'd stick to it. After all, that's why we call dogs "dogs"; there is no particular sense to it, it's just that we've been doing it that way for a long time. But to say to children things which make no sense, *as if they did make sense,* is stupid, and will surely cause some of them great and needless confusion.

I have to insist that these two small and perhaps not very damaging pieces of nonsense, and other and much larger and more damaging ones I will talk about in a second, were not invented and never would have been invented by parents teaching their own children. They were invented by people trying to turn a casual, natu-ral, everyday act into a "science" and a mystery.

Let's now take a broader look at the teaching of reading, more specifically, what most people call "phonics."

In "Reading, Chicago Style" (GWS #2), I pointed out that, according to a newspaper report, a Board of Education "reading expert" had made a list of 500 reading skills (later cut to 273, to be "taught" in grades 1 through 8) that children needed to learn in elemen-tary school. What those lists could be made up of I cannot imagine and do not want to know. In a word, they are nonsense.

The fact is that there are only *two* general ideas that one needs to grasp in order to be able to read a phonic language like English (or French, German, Italian, etc.—as opposed to, say, Chinese). 1) Written letters stand for spoken sounds. 2) The order of the letters on the page, from our left to our right, corresponds to the order in time of the spoken sounds.

It is not necessary for children to be able to say these rules in order to understand and be able to use them. Nor is it a good idea to try to teach them these rules by saying and then explaining them. The way to teach them—that is, if you insist on teaching them—is to demonstrate it through very simple and clear examples.

Aside from that, what children have to learn are, the connections between the 45 or so sounds that make up spoken English and the 380 or so letters or combinations of letters that represent these sounds in written English. This is not a large or hard task. But, as in everything else, the schools do a great deal to make it larger and harder.

The first mistake they make is to teach or try to teach the children the sounds of each individual letter. In the case of consonants, this amounts to telling the children what is not true. Of the consonants, there are only six or seven which can be *said* all by themselves—S (or the C in niCe), Z (or the S in riSe), M, N, V, F, J (or the G in George)—plus the pair SH. There are the borderline cases of L, R, W, and Y, but it seems wiser to let children meet these sounds in syllables and words. As for the rest, we cannot say the sounds that B, or D, or K, or P, or T, etc. make all by themselves. B does *not* say "buh," nor D "duh," etc. BIG does not say "buh-ig," nor RUB "ruh-buh." These letters don't make any sounds, except perhaps the faintest puff of air, except when they are combined with a vowel in a word or syllable. Therefore, it is misleading and absurd, as well as false, to try to teach them in isolation.

It is equally foolish and mistaken to try to teach the vowel sounds in isolation, in this case because each vowel makes a number of different sounds, depending on what consonants it is combined with. Since we can't tell what the letter A says except as we see it joined with consonants, then it makes sense to introduce the sounds of A (or any other vowel) *only* in the context of words or syllables.

All we have to do then is to expose children to the two basic ideas of phonics, that written letters stand for and "make" spoken sounds, and that the order of the written letters matches the order of the spoken sounds. The first we can do very easily by any kind of reading aloud, whether of words in books, or signs, or whatever. The second we can do by writing down, and saying as we write them, words which use the six or seven consonants that we can sound alone, and so can stretch out in time. Thus we could write SAM, saying the S as we write the S, the A as we write it, the M as we write it. Same with MAN, FAN, VAN, or MIS, or US, or IF. It is neither necessary nor a good idea to be too thorough about this. It is not a lesson to be completely learned and digested the first or second time. That is not how children learn things. They have to live with an idea or insight for a while, turn it around in some part of their minds, before they can, in a very real sense, discover it, say, "I see," take possession of the idea, make it their own—and unless they do this, the idea will never be more than surface, parrot learning, they will never really be able to make use of it.

Then, as children slowly take possession of these ideas about reading, we can introduce them to more words, and so more sounds, and the connections between the words and the sounds. In GWS #3 I mentioned a book *Let's Read,* which lists all the one-syllable words that can be made from different combinations of consonants and vowels. But it wouldn't take parents very long to make such lists for themselves—BAT, FAT, CAT, RAT, BIN, DIN, FIN, GIN, TIN, etc. There is no need for such lists to be complete, just long enough to expose the child to the idea that words that look mostly alike will probably sound mostly alike.

In any case, hardly any children will want to spend much time with what are so obviously teaching materials. They will want to get busy reading (and writing) real words, words in a context of life and meaning. No need to talk here about ways to do that—any people who read this are sure to have many ideas of their own. If we read and write, the children will want to; if we don't, they won't.

Let me say once again that I don't think even the very limited amount of teaching I have described here is really necessary or in most cases even helpful. All I say is, if you feel you must do some teaching, or if your child somehow expects and demands this of you (most won't), then try to avoid, in ways I have suggested here, the crippling mistakes of the schools.

A P.S. to the above. Another very common school mistake is to ask children to learn and memorize which letters are vowels and which are consonants. Schools usually do this by trying to teach the children some definition of "vowel" and "consonant." These definitions are almost always inconsistent and self-contradictory, such as "A vowel is a sound that you can say all by itself." As I have said, this is equally true of some of the consonants. I have thought about this from time to time, and have never been able to think of a definition of vowels and consonants which was clear, distinct, and allowed no exceptions.

In any case, this is a bad way to teach children anything. They think best (as I suspect we all do) when they can move from the particular to the general. Beyond that, there is no good reason why children learning to read should learn the words "vowel" and "consonant." Knowing or not knowing those words has nothing whatever to do with reading.

I have written elsewhere about playing a game with children in which they ask me to write a word, and I write it. Next time I do this, I may use one color pen to write consonants, and another to write vowels. Though I can imagine that some children, suspecting that I was trying to sneak in some teaching, might tell me not to do even that. If anyone tries this out, please let me know what happens.

A better variation of that game might go like this. We could write each letter on a separate card or piece of paper, vowels in one color, consonants in another. Then we could say to the child, "Put together any two, or three, or four (or more) of these cards, and I will tell you what they say." If a child gave us BSRX, we would do our best to make those sounds. The child would begin to notice after a while that the only combination of letters that make sounds that sounded like the words he heard around him were the ones that had both colors in them, and that these were very often in the form of consonant-color + vowel-color + consonant-color. If he ever asked, "What do you call this kind of letter, and what do you call this kind?" (I can't guess whether a child would be likely to do this), I would say, "We call these kinds of letters 'vowels' and these 'consonants.'" (If he asked why, I would tell him I didn't know.)

Mind you, I am not saying that any of these tricks or games are necessary, or even that they will help a child learn to read faster or better. But for people who for whatever reasons feel they want to do *something*, I suggest these as things that it might be fun (for both adult and child) to do, and, *as long as they are fun,* possibly useful, and probably not harmful.

TEACHING

The other day a memory popped up that I had completely forgotten. Some years ago I was reading aloud to a small child, as yet a non-reader, perhaps three or four years old. As I read aloud I had the bright idea that by moving a finger along under the words as I read them I might make more clear the connections between the written and the spoken words. A chance to get in a little subtle teaching. Without saying anything about it, and as casually as possible, I began to do this.

It didn't take the child very long to figure out that what had begun as a nice, friendly cozy sharing of a story had turned into something else, that her/his project had by some magic turned into *my* project. After a while, and without saying a word, s/he reached up a hand, took hold of my hand, and very gently moved it off the page and down by my side—where it belonged. I gave up "teaching" and went back to doing what I had been asked to do, which was to read the story.

MORE ON "NO"

The author of "Her Own Money" (GWS #6) writes, in part:

" ...You've made an excellent point about the difference between 'No' the angry signal and 'No' the meaningful word.... I think of some people who recently visited us—constantly slapping (lightly) their kids—No, No, bad boy, say 'please,' don't do that, etc.

About drove me crazy. And as you say, meaningless to the kids. I watched them totally tune out *everything* their parents did and said. Rightly so, too, for the kids weren't doing anything that I could see needed warning or reprimanding.

...there is a third kind of 'No," perhaps the most common of all, neither an angry explosion nor a meaningful word—the no, no, no that goes on all day with some parents. This constant hassling is simply a running, ineffective banter. The parents don't even *mean* it; there's no anger or even much reprimand in their voices. ...our cultural expectation is that kids are bad, always getting into trouble, and parents must be dictators controlling their kids (in the name of 'protection').

How to cope with these 3 kinds of 'No' is much more difficult, tho, than you make it sound.

You're saying, if we can become aware of how we use 'No' we can change our use of it. And I agree with you in two cases. First, as parents, we can simply SHUT UP! If we can sit back and listen to ourselves, we can hear how much negative harassment we throw at our kids. If a parent would seriously and objectively listen to what he says (thru his child's ears), he would be appalled and could probably with some effort change that kind of 'No.'

I think here of L (recently 3) who was pouring herself a glass of milk yesterday. She had gotten it from the fridge, opened it, poured from a fat 2-qt. carton a very small juice-glass of milk, had drunk it, then had gotten a paper towel and was wiping up the milk spilt on the table. There was more milk spilt than the towel could absorb so as she wiped now, the milk was being pushed off the table onto the floor.

I walked in at this point and started with the running 'No No' commentary in a whiny voice: 'Ooooh no L, you should have asked someone to pour you a glass of milk—no, don't wipe it up, it's going on the floor, now stop, don't do it, I'll do it, it's bad enough on the table—look, now you've got it on the floor—you're making more work for me.'

Happily at this point I was struck by a rare beam of sanity and it said to me, 'Oh, quit being such a bitch, L has just poured her first glass of milk all by herself and you're ruining the whole thing for her.'

And suddenly I looked and saw a very little girl trying very hard to grow up—trying to wipe up herself the mess she had made getting herself a drink of milk. And I said, 'L, I think Sparkle (dog) would like this extra milk.'

L stopped and looked at me. I had finally said something of meaning. All the negative harassment up till then she had been trying to ignore.

I said, 'If you get Sparkle's dish we can put the milk in it.'

She got it and we did.

AND immediately she began an animated chatter about how Sparkle would like this milk and how she had poured them both a drink of milk, etc. Until then, she had barely said one word. In fact, if I had pushed her far enough—'OK, L, get out of the kitchen while I clean up your mess'—she would have probably ended up crying (over spilt milk!).

But the happy ending here did not require too much effort on my part because I wasn't very emotionally involved. My mind could still be objective about the situation to the extent of being able to control and change it.

I think this is also why your suggestion would *work,* for teachers. On the whole, they are not emotionally involved with their students and could therefore make a successful intellectual effort to change their way of saying 'No' to children…. Parents are so emotionally interlocked (as well as emotionally open) with their kids that they are both trapped into destructive ways of relating to each other. The smallest trigger can set off the largest explosion …Children become scapegoats on whom their parents vent the worst of feelings (usually unconsciously). Of course, this also happens in school, or anyplace else. An adult in a bad mood will dump his frustrations on those under him in the pecking order, esp. on kids who are felt to be so much weaker. And then on it goes, kids pick on weaker kids, etc. It is within the nuclear family that this pecking order is at its worst. And that's why I disagree strongly with your theory that we can *easily* change the use of the word 'No' from an explosive signal to a gentle word. You say 'There is no reason why, except in rare times of great stress or danger …'

Aha! There's the problem. Yes, 'rare times of *danger.*' But certainly not 'rare times of great stress'— not when you're speaking of parents with their *own* children esp. when they are in their *own* home…. "

A very good point, in a very good letter. Actually, I said much the same thing in *Escape From Childhood,* that children, even if a great burden in every other way, are still useful to adults in that they give them someone below them in the pecking order, on whom they can take out all their frustrations.

As for teachers, they may not be emotionally linked with children in quite the same way parents are, but many of them are linked with them in another very powerful way i.e. they are afraid of them, afraid of losing their control over them, afraid the children will do things that will get them in trouble or even cost them their jobs. Such teachers treat students with (as Silberman said) "appalling incivility," harshly and rudely, as a matter of principle, the only way to keep their control over them. Many of them (see *The Way It Spozed to Be*) advise young teachers to do the same. "Get the upper hand right at the start, etc." As long as schools are jails i.e. compulsory, and work primarily on the basis of bribes and threats i.e. grades, get-into-college, etc. this is not very likely to change.

In writing my earlier piece on 'No' I guess I was really thinking about, and aiming at, those people who believe, as a matter of principle, that unless children hear the word 'No' with a lot of anger in it, they won't pay any attention to it.

STARTING A SCHOOL

To a parent who wrote about joining a few other parents in forming their own school, I said,

"Thanks for news of your school. One piece of heartfelt advice. People sending their kids to your school must be made to understand that if there is something they think those children *must* be taught or *must* learn, basics or whatever, it must be *their* responsibility to do that teaching, and to do it in their own home—or at any rate, away from the school. The school must be a place where people come together to do the things that interest and excite them most. Otherwise, you will be torn to pieces with arguments about whether the school should teach reading or arithmetic, or teach it one or four hours a week, or whatever. Believe me, I speak from the bitter experience of many people."

And this would be my very strong advice to any group of unschoolers who want to start a school as a way of escaping compulsory attendance laws, or giving their children a place to meet and be with other children, or for whatever reasons. OK to have rules which say, more or less, no fair hurting or bothering other people. Every human society has these, and children expect them and understand them. But the school must not try to *compel* learning, if for no other reason than this, that people will argue forever, and with increasing bitterness and anger, about what kinds of learning must be compelled.

PARENTS' RIGHTS

The Manchester, N.H. *Union Leader,* on Oct. 31, 1978, reported a decision of the NH State Supreme Court that may have great importance to unschoolers, not least of all because 1) NH is a politically "conservative" state 2) NH law does not mention home schooling as a legal alternative.

The story, reads, in part (I use quotes only as they appear in the story):

SUPREME COURT VACATES PARENTAL RIGHTS ORDER

…Noting that in an "ideal world, children would not be brought up in inadequate homes," the state Supreme Court yesterday declared that this "is not an ideal world, and to merely hold that inadequate parenting, *absent specific harm to the children* (Ed. note—italics mine), is sufficient to terminate parental rights in the best interest of the child is too vague a concept and places undue emphasis on the parental conduct rather than any harm to the child."

The high court thus vacated a 1977 order of the Merrimack County Probate Court which had terminated the parental rights of a 32-year-old father, identified only as "Robert H.," over his three minor children on the grounds of failure to correct the conditions leading to a finding of neglect.

"We outline the standard to be applied in such cases and remand," noted the Supreme Court. It said RSA chapter 170-C was enacted to provide for the involuntary termination of the parent-child relationship by a judicial process which will safeguard the rights and interests of all parties, and that a termination order must be based upon "clear and convincing evidence."

The high court determined that the government must "prove its case beyond a reasonable doubt before the permanent termination of liberty and natural rights of parents guaranteed under the N.H. Constitution, Part I, Article 2, can occur."

"We hold that absent a showing of *specific harm to the children* (Ed. italics), growing up in a so-called disadvantaged home is not a sufficient basis for coercive intervention. Robert H. may not be a model parent, but he is as entitled to help from the division [of welfare] as anyone else, and maybe more so," said the Supreme Court.

" …any termination petition under chapter 170-C must be proven beyond a reasonable doubt to meet the requirements of the N.H. Constitution," ordered the Supreme Court.

The high court noted that the father can neither read nor write, suffers serious heart problems, and because of limited job skills, is rarely steadily employed. The children are six, seven, and nine and "they are very much a family unit with strong sibling ties."

The legal point is obvious. If (as is the case) the courts will not allow welfare, etc. agencies to take children from such a parent, or even (as is also often the case) from parents who abuse their children up to the point of causing serious injury, they are not likely (if all the above is pointed out to them in a legal brief) to allow agencies to take children away from otherwise competent and loving parents simply because these parents refuse to send their children to school. As in the case cited above, the burden of proof will be on the state to show beyond reasonable doubt that in such cases the children are being specifically harmed by not being sent to school. This will be exceedingly difficult to prove, particularly if parents (having read GWS) go into court well prepared, and well armed with hard questions for the schools.

It might also be a good idea for unschoolers in all states to read their respective state constitutions, to see what these may have to say about the rights of parents with respect to their children and their children's education. Some of them, at least, like the constitution of N.H. (which I have not read), may be much more explicit about this than the U.S. Constitution. I have

said before and will say again that I think we would be very unwise to go into the Federal Courts with a broad Constitutional attack on compulsory schooling as such. This does not mean that we should not make the fullest possible use of anything we can find in state constitutions about parents' rights to influence or control the education of their children.

THE WORLD AT TWO (CONT.)

The mother of J (see GWS #6, "The World at Two"), writes:

"J is great. No naps now which means he is super go-power all day with a huge collapse about 7:30. He has his room all to himself now …and he really likes to hang out in there alone for an hour and a half most days, driving trucks around mostly. I've never seen a kid more into organizing things. He plays with dominoes and calls them either adobes, for building houses, or bales of hay, and has them stacked, lined up, or otherwise arranged in some perfect order; same with the trucks; he'll scream and yell, as per your theory of two year old behavior, if you snatch him up from a group of trucks and carry him off to lunch. But if you give him a couple of minutes to park them all in a straight line then he'll come willingly. Your theory (treat them like big people) works out over and over again; brush past him, leave him behind in the snow when you're hustling up to feed the goats and you get a black and blue screaming pass out tantrum. Treat them "Big" and things roll along. Only hangup is the occasional times you have to take advantage of your superior size and pull a power play. The trick is to learn to avoid the situations that once in a while make that a necessity, like not getting in a rush, and not letting them get so tired they break down completely—like letting dinner be late."

"As J gets nearer to, although still fairly far from, school age, I worry about trying to go it on our own; not at all about trying to teach him the basics but about what this little town is going to think because in a way it becomes a put down to them; we're not going to send *our* child to that crummy school; while they're more or less stuck with it. Already people say, 'When J goes to school, etc.' I just smile and shut up. Also J gets so desperate for kids I'm pretty sure he's going to want to go to that big building that always has a passel of children running around in front. Sometimes, just driving by houses where he suspects there might be kids, he says, 'I wanna see some kids, mommy.' Actually, we're working harder on it and he's getting to be around more but there are still long gaps."

I wrote back, suggesting, more or less, that when people talk about J going to school she say, "He's already going to school," and that when people ask where, she say, "Right at home." This in turn made me think of something so obvious that I can't imagine why I didn't think of it long ago. In GWS #1, I said that if unschoolers are asked by neighbors or other people where their children are going to school, they should reply that the children "are in a special program." I now think this is a mistake. Unschoolers should never say, or admit, that their children are not "going to school." They should insist that they are going to school. If people say, "Where?" they should say, "Right here in our own home."

My strong hunch is that this will satisfy a large number of otherwise critical people. In these days, most people believe in word magic. Not for them the wise advice of Justice Holmes: "Think things, not words." For them, the word is the thing, the label on the package is the contents. If the label says "New! Fresh! Pure!" it must be new, etc.

Many of these folks have in their minds, among other slogans and rules, the rule that children should "go to school." If we say that our children are "going to school," most of them will not get into complicated arguments about what is or is not a school," or whether our home is really a school, but will be satisfied that the rule is being obeyed. Some, of course, will not be satisfied, will say, "Why aren't they going to the same school as the other children?" But nothing we said or might say could satisfy these people. For them, school is the Army for kids, a bad experience that they do not want any child to escape.

In saying that our children who are learning at home are "in school," we are not just tricking people—though we may be doing that. We are also putting into their minds the important and very true idea that children (like everyone else) are always learning, no matter where they are or what they are doing, that the whole world is a learning place for them, that "school" does not have to mean only that big brick building with the cyclone fence and (usually) padlocked gates, but could mean any place at all. It will be much easier for such people, unless they are real Blue Meanies, to understand and accept later that some of the time—perhaps very little or none—our children may be in the red brick building, but that most of the time they will be "in school" somewhere else.

What I meant by "treat them like big people" was, of course, to treat them in the courteous and respectful way that we big people like to be treated. To snatch any child away from what s/he is doing, in order to do what we want done, is to say to that child, "Your interests and purposes are not serious and do not count." In the many years I have been watching children and adults together, in homes and in public places, I have seen many two-year-old "tantrums." Of those I have seen from the beginning (but who knows where anything "begins"?), except for a few that were brought on by exhaustion, almost all seemed to me to have been caused by a needless affront, often unintentional, to the child's dignity, that is, by someone treating the child as if what s/he was doing, or what s/he thought or

wanted, did not count. I have felt and still feel very strongly that most of these tantrums could have been avoided by taking a few extra seconds to show the child the kind of courtesy we would routinely show to another adult.

This mother's words show once again what nonsense it is to talk about children's "short attention span." In *How Children Learn* I wrote about an eighteen-month-old child trying to put together a ballpoint pen that she had taken apart. Though the task was much too hard for her small and unpracticed fingers, she worked steadily and patiently at it for at least forty-five minutes. When some of the schools in Great Britain began the unheard-of experiment of letting school children direct and control their own learning, they found that five and six-year-olds would often work on a single task for an entire morning or afternoon, and often for several days at a stretch. Most young children (at least when they are not dreaming, which is also important to them) pay a lot closer *attention* to the world around them than most adults. Their problem—at least it looks to us like a problem—is that almost everything in the world around them is interesting to them. Also, they see that world as all of a piece; it never occurs to them, as to us, that if they pay attention to *this* it means that they have *stopped* paying attention to *that*. They don't think in terms of paying attention to only one thing at a time.

What we really mean when we say that children have short attention spans is that they will not pay attention for very long to the things that *we* want them to pay attention to. A sensitive and concerned mother has just written me—I get many such letters—to say that she is worried because when she tries to teach her young child letters (or whatever) the child only pays attention for a couple of minutes. She fears there may be something wrong with the child. From the little she has told me, I doubt that there is anything wrong at all. The problem (if we have to think of it as a problem) is that most healthy and curious children *don't like to be taught*. The reason is not that they don't like to learn—they like nothing better. The reason is that they understand very well the unspoken (sometimes unconscious) assumption behind all *uninvited* teaching: "You are too stupid to understand why this is important, and/or too stupid to see it or find it or figure it out for yourself. Children refuse this kind of teaching as long as they can. If the time comes (as in school) when they can no longer find ways to refuse or escape it, they may soon decide that they are no longer capable of figuring things out, and can only learn when they are made to learn, told what to learn, and shown how. In short, they may soon become as stupid as the parents or teachers or schools believed they were all along. But they don't start out that way.

SCIENTISTS

Hanna Kirchner, writing in Poland about the work of Janusz Korczak, said, in part:

"He always stressed that by means of learning the everyday expressions from the obscure language of adults, the child tries to fathom the mystery of life. The child's fragmentary and incomplete knowledge of the world, welded together by imagination, creates a specific 'magic consciousness' which, as has been discovered in the twentieth century, exists among children and primitive people and may be associated with the origins of poetry."

She then gives this wonderful quote from Korczak's book *How to Love a Child:*

"[one child says], 'They say there is one moon and yet one can see it everywhere.'
'Listen, I'll stand behind the fence and you stay in the garden.' They lock the gate.
'Well, is there a moon in the garden?'
'Yes.'
'Here too.'
They change places and check once again. Now they are sure there must be two moons."

And yet they figure out, sooner or later, and *by themselves,* that there is only one moon. Forgive me for saying what must be obvious to so many GWS readers. Yet I know from experience that there will be many adults, including some who may one day, somewhere, read this piece, who will insist that children only learn there is one moon because adults tell them, and that if we didn't tell them they would never be able to figure it out.

A SELF-TEACHER

A mother writes from British Columbia:

"My daughter, T, for instance, who is eight, has been very interested in rocks, fossils and Indian artifacts for several years now. I don't know a great deal about these subjects, but we found some good books at second-hand stores, borrowed some from the library and were even given a pile of lapidary magazines about to be discarded. She has an enormous collection of specimens now (all collected herself), by no means all identified. We packed a box of fossils and pseudo-fossils (Ed. note—have no idea what a pseudo-fossil is) and took them to the Provincial Museum where some very friendly (and slightly bemused) curators did their best to identify them. She has found one artifact which we are pretty sure is the handle of a stone tool of some sort and we will take it to an expert for an opinion. We are also working on a plan for a water-wheel-powered

rock tumbler that she can polish stones in. The result has been a lot of learning and I doubt we've spent $10.00.

The children follow their interests where they lead and never refer to it as learning or school, and I don't either. T was interested in Indians and what foods they ate in the old days. Now she horrifies parents when she goes to town and feeds her friends roots from the licorice fern or peeled salmonberry shoots. But she knows much better than the parents, I suspect, what plants and berries shouldn't be eaten and why.

As far as reading goes, you say that it isn't difficult to learn to read and compared to some other things we learn I imagine you are right. Still I found it very confusing to explain to my daughter why the letter sounds changed like quicksilver from one word to the next. (Ed. note—but there's no *need* to "explain" it, and indeed, no *way* to explain it) That's why I was relieved to find the Open Court 1st grade reading program. I learned a lot of phonetics from it! You need two workbooks, reader 1:1:1 and 1:1:2, each $2.35, and either the Teacher's Guide for $12.66 or a phono. record of Millie's story for $6.64. The story introduces and ties together the phonetic sounds. The teacher's guide has other useful information besides the story but it's not absolutely necessary. With the books and record, a child could learn by himself.

We don't use any regular course material now. The books for elementary grades seem terribly superficial—a little bit about lots of things and not very much about anything. I find even young children like to learn about things in detail. T is up to grade level in most aspects of the three R's—definitely not spelling (taking after her mother, no doubt). (Ed. note—there were *no* spelling mistakes in this mother's letter) I would say that we haven't invested more than one hour a week in the last three years to maintain this level.

T spent a long time choosing a *Cricket* magazine to send you and I've got a feeling she wasn't looking for the best one. That's what makes the magazine worth $15, to us anyway. The stories are good and the binding is good, and the children save them carefully and read them again and again. Anyway she was glad to send it as long as it wasn't a favorite. I read her pieces out of your books sometimes and she's always interested. She and M, 5, thought the 62 item kindergarten check list (Ed. note—from *Instead of Education*) was very amusing. M said he didn't use bathroom habits—he likes the tub and the bath toys.

What I mean about explaining sounds is this—there's no more way of *explaining* why the letter *a* sounds one way in "cat," another way in "car," and still another in "call," than there is of explaining why we call a dog a "dog" and not a "blif" or "mub." We just do, that's all. Pressed, we might say to a child that our grandparents and their grandparents and their grandparents all said it this way for a long, long time back. Pressed still harder yet, we might say that some people

119

make it their work to try to figure out how people talked a long time ago, but that they have to do a lot of guessing, since of course the people aren't around any more to ask, and didn't leave any records like tapes or recordings.

I just read from cover to cover the issue of *Cricket* that T sent, and think it's wonderful! Stories, poems, articles, illustrations, puzzles—all seem to me just right. Cricket is a monthly ($15/yr., $27.50/2 yrs., $36/3 yrs., from Open Court Publishing Co., 1058 8th St., LaSalle, IL 61301), and a good bargain—there is more material in one issue than in many children's books.

As for phonics, you don't need all those materials. (See "Sensible Phonics" in this issue of GWS.)

N.Y. LAW

One of our readers from New York State sent us a letter, which she received from the office of the counsel of the State Education Department in Albany, and which may be of interest to other readers, both in NY and other states. It says, in full:

"Senator Javits has referred your letter of June 26, 1978 to this Department for response.

Pursuant to subdivision 1 of section 3204 of the Education Law, a student may satisfy the compulsory education law by attending upon instruction in "a public school or elsewhere." In cases such as *People v. Turner,* 277 App. Div. 317 and *In Re Meyer,* 203 Misc. 549 (to learn the meaning of those numbers, see 'More From D' in GWS #3, or ask any lawyer, law student, law librarian, or perhaps the librarian in the reference part of the Public Library), the courts have upheld a parent's right to instruct his children at home. It is necessary, however, that the local school officials review the proposed course of study to determine whether it is substantially equivalent to that offered in the public schools. I would, therefore, suggest that you contact your chief school officer and arrange to discuss your plan to instruct your child at home.

Enclosed is a Law Pamphlet 9 which describes the process by which the Board of Regents charters an educational corporation. If you wish to operate a school on a profit-making basis, you would follow the provisions of the Business Corporation Law. A further alternative is not to establish a corporation.

Sincerely,
(name)
Associate Attorney

cc: Senator Javits"

This letter suggests, first, that if you can get your U.S. Senator (or perhaps Representative) to write a letter about home schooling to the state educational authorities, they will respond fairly promptly (in this case, 2 1/2 months, which is probably quite good for state government), and secondly, that they will give you quite complete information. It might be worth finding out, sometime and somewhere, whether the kind of letter a state department of education sends out in response to a letter from a citizen is exactly the same as the letter they send in response to a letter from a U.S. Senator—and if there is a difference, what it is. If some readers make this political mini-experiment, do let us know what you find out.

What may be more important, the letter also suggests that, in New York State at least, the Board of Regents, the chief educational authorities of the state, have nothing to do with chartering profit-making schools. It would be interesting to find out how hard or easy it is, in NY or any other state, to set up a "profit-making" school. We might find out that this was a much easier way for parents to call their own home a school. Readers in NY and elsewhere may want to look into this—if so, again, let us know what you find out.

POLITICS OF KNOWLEDGE

Here are some interesting words about education from one of its earliest and strongest supporters. Sir Arthur Conan Doyle (of Sherlock Holmes fame), in the foreword of a book *Construction and Reconstruction of the Human Body,* by Eugen Sandow, published in London in 1907, wrote, in part:

"The strength of a nation is measured by the sum total of the strength of all the units that form it. It is a truism that anything which raises any portion of a man, his body, his character, his intelligence, increases to that extent the strength of the country to which he belongs. Therefore, since the State is so interested in these matters, it has every reason to examine into them and to regulate them. The truth is an obvious one, but it is only within our own lifetimes that it has been practically applied. 'Parents may do what they like with their children, a man may do what he likes with himself.' So ran the old heresy, which ignored the fact that the State must look after the health of its own component parts. Then came the Education Act of 1870. It was a great new departure. What it said was, *'No, your mind is not your own.* (Ed. italics) You may wish to keep it ignorant. But ignorant minds are a danger to the State. Therefore we must *force* you to keep yourself in better order.' That is as far as we have got yet in State ownership of the individual."

Most of those who first pushed through compulsory education thought this way. There were very few Jeffersons among them. But I want to look more closely at another part of Conan Doyle's thought. "You may wish to keep it ignorant." What did he mean by "ignorant"?

What he meant was almost certainly that this "you" might not want to learn the kinds of things that rich people knew in those days i.e. Greek, Latin, Ancient History (which they saw as a kind of morality play), Classical Literature, perhaps a little Mathematics. One of the many fringe benefits of being rich and powerful, in any society, is that you are able to say that some kinds of knowledge, i.e. the kind of things *you* know, are much more important than others, and therefore, that the people who have this knowledge i.e. you and your friends, are much more important and deserving than people who know other things. It is not hard to see why in any society powerful people, whether the rich or simply high government officials, should want to say that the kind of knowledge that most people pick up from everyday life and work is worth less than the kind that can only be picked up in special places.

AN "IGNORANT" MAN

Let's take a look at one of those "ignorant" men that Conan Doyle was worried about. In his book *Travels Through America*, first published in *Esquire* magazine, Feb. 76, Harrison Salisbury described his efforts to trace the Westward path of some of his ancestors. He describes one of them thus:

"…He [Hiram Salisbury] was a man of his time [1815] … I scan the journal for clues and reconstruct the post-Revolutionary American. I list his skills, one sheet of scratch paper after another. He knew every farm chore. He milked cows and attended the calves in birth. He physicked his horse. He plowed, he planted, he cultivated, hayed, picked apples, grafted fruit trees, cut wheat with a scythe, cradled oats, threshed grain with a flail on a clay floor. He chopped the corn and put down his vegetables for winter. He made cider and built cider mills. He made cheese and fashioned cheese tongs. He butchered the hogs and sheared the sheep. He churned butter and salted it. He made soap and candles, thatched barns and built smokehouses. He butchered oxen and constructed ox sledges. He fought forest fires and marked out the land. He repaired the crane at Smith's mill and forged a crane for his own fireplace to hang the kettle on. He collected iron in the countryside and smelted it. He tapped (mended) his children's shoes and his own. He built trundle beds, oxcarts, sleighs, wagons, wagon wheels and wheel spokes. He turned logs into boards and cut locust wood for picket fences. He made house frames, beams, mortised and pegged. With six men's help he raised the frames and built the houses. He made a neat cherry stand with a drawer for a cousin, fixed clocks and went fishing. He carved his own board measures (yardsticks) and sold them for a dollar apiece. He fitted window cases, mended locks, and fixed compasses. He hewed timber, surveyed the forest, wrote deeds and shaved shingles. He inspected the town records and audited the books of the Friendship Lodge, the oldest freshwater Masonic lodge in the country (still running). He chipped plows, constructed carding machines, carved gunstocks and built looms. He set gravestones and fashioned wagon hubs. He ran a bookstore and could make a fine coffin in half a day. He was a member of the state's General Assembly, overseer of the poor, appraiser of property and fellow of the town council. He made hoops by the thousand and also pewter faucets. For many years he collected the town taxes …

I have not listed all of Hiram's skills but enough. I do not think he was an unusual man. Put me in Hiram's world and I would not last long. Put Hiram down in our world. He might have a little trouble with a computer, but he'd get the hang of it faster than I could cradle a bushel of oats."

———————————

I tend to agree with Harrison Salisbury that Hiram, though perhaps not an unusual man in his time, would be a most unusual one in ours, far more knowing, skillful, intelligent, resourceful, adaptive, inventive, and competent than most people we could find today, in either city or country, and no matter how schooled.

But the real question I want to raise, and answer, is how Hiram learned all those skills. To be sure, he did not learn them in school. Nor did he learn them in workshops or any other school-like activity. Almost certainly, he learned how to do all those kinds of work, many of them highly skilled, by being around when other people were doing them. Nor were these other people doing the work in order to teach Hiram something. Nobody raised a barn just so that Hiram could see how barns were raised. They raised it because they needed the barn. Nor did they say to him, "Hiram, as long as I have to raise this barn, you may as well come around and learn how it is done." They said, "Hiram, I'm raising a barn and *I need your help.*" He was there to help, not to learn—but as he helped, he learned.

Almost a century later John Dewey was to talk about "learning by doing." The way for students to learn (for example) how pottery is made is not read about it in a book but to make pots. Well, OK, no doubt about its being better. But making pots just to learn how it is done still doesn't seem to me anywhere near as good as making pots (and learning from it) because *someone needs the pots.* The incentive to learn how to do good work, and to do it, is surely much greater when you know that the work has to be done, that it is going to be of real use to someone.

FINDING OUT

Since to so many people "learning" means what happens in school, or what is supposed to happen, I would rather use other words to describe what we humans do as a natural part of our living. "Finding out" seems to fit pretty well. Here, a reader talks about it:

"I am almost a caricature of the congenital unteachable. It may have been something I picked up from imitating my father, for I notice he shares the trait to this day. He is very quick to learn, but utterly resists being taught.

I began to see how much this unteachability pervaded my life when I began about a year ago to see how much of my childhood I could remember distinctly. Probably the extreme example was learning to play the piano. I am told that I started banging away on the family upright at about age four. One day my dad got tired of the noise and said something to the effect of 'If you're going to play, why don't you play *something*?' Well, I quit until my parents left the house, and when they came back that afternoon I was already picking out tunes. In a year I played 'Silent Night' at church Christmas ceremonies.

When we moved to a larger town, my parents resolved that I should go to a piano teacher. But I didn't want to practice scales, for I was already playing songs— and the teacher would not explain *why* I should practice. In three months she told my parents that I was the worst student she'd ever had and that I would never learn to play. This did leave me with a somewhat irrational (Ed. note—and very common) fear of the musical notation system (at least until I began to discover its logic myself) but to make a long story short I went on to become a good piano player and composer and have off and on supported myself in this way, playing all kinds of music. I still can't read notes (a common phenomenon among good musicians in their younger years, by the way) but now I *want* to learn so as to build a logical structure which could point the way to further improvement in my playing. A major goal in my life is to achieve the ability to spend large amounts of time working on this—in the meantime I'm working on fingerwork, doing things I only dreamed about a couple of years back. All absolutely self taught.

So much has been like this, I started drawing at about four, also holding the pencil the wrong way. People said that I would never be able to draw that way. After selling dozens of paintings and drawings, I still hold it that way—I don't like the other way, as it produces a more unsteady hand for me. When, at about twelve, I wanted to write books, my dad gave me an old Royal and left me alone. I learned to type at good speed with one right hand finger. When I get going I can type faster this way than some secretaries with their ten fingers. More recently, when I was typing the manuscript for my first 'real' book, I taught myself to use the index finger on my left hand, as a way to beat the boredom.

Then there was swimming lessons, which almost permanently made me hate swimming. A couple of years afterward, when I *wanted* to swim with my friends, I jumped in and swam as if I had always done so.

And there was writing. My father broke his usual hands-off stance to urge me to learn to write, when I was seventeen. I would not do so while being urged. In senior composition class I turned in pieces designed to meet the assignment, and no more—tortured pieces. When I had the chance to say something in a graduation address, the speech teacher (also the composition teacher) panned the address as 'terrible,' but it went over well. In that same last semester in high school, I poured my energies into writing (with a friend) an underground newspaper attacking compulsory education and poking fun at the pretenses of the school world. No one panned the writing here—they took it very seriously. And somehow the same year I won a statewide writing contest award.

I taught myself auto mechanics on my first car, after being told for years that I was low in mechanical ability. I became a good carpenter's apprentice in two months, building one and a half houses with just one carpenter working at the same time. I surprised them all (except my parents—who had been listening) when I switched from an undergraduate education in pre-law to master's work in engineering, putting to rest the old thing about how artsy-booksy types cannot cope with numbers.

How did I get through schools? Only one way—by taking the offensive. Way back around fifth grade, my parents supplied us kids with the *Golden Book Encyclopedia.* I lapped up each book as it came home from the supermarket. Not long after that I was tested for reading at school and was found to be reading five years ahead of my grade. What is more, the *Golden Book Encyclopedia* gave me two invaluable things which freed me from much of the meaningless work the schools had cut out for me. One, I acquired from the encyclopedia a working familiarity with many aspects of science, history, geography, and art—such that I still 'leaned on' this knowledge during exams as late as, say, tenth grade. Moreover, it taught me an understanding of how the world works, so that I could figure out what I did not actually know.

I recall what I did in fifth grade to free up more time to study airplanes, which I was then immersed in as a subject. The teacher wanted us to come up with five new words a week which we were supposed to define as a vocabulary lesson. (Ed. note—as if anyone ever learned words this way) Trouble was, words did not come to me at this steady pace. So, one day, I reached into the dictionary for two hundred-odd words and did a year's assignment in one bored stroke. Then I went back to gobbling up new and historical words as part of the new book I was writing on airplanes.

It was like this throughout college as well. In

undergraduate school I took political science and philosophy because I wanted to understand the mystery of government. The political science department wanted to talk about voting behavior studies and the philosophy department wanted to talk about mathematics, so I played the incorrigible in my second year and obtained an understanding which allowed me to graduate with a program in ethical philosophy and constitutional theory. The understanding was quite explicit: I offered a couple of professors the opportunity to 'supervise' the development of publishable work if they would only stay off my back with their extraneous demands. I wanted to get economics from this same school but found it so unintelligible that I was driven into home study, which has resulted in a good knowledge of (a different school of) economic theory.

When I went back to grad school I again entered on the explicit understanding that I would take some required courses and do some required research for the chance to be allowed hunks of free time to pursue an area that no one at the school even understood. It worked. So well, in fact, that I literally walked into a job working with the guy who my previous research had shown to be tops in the field.

And now I find some strange truths. With the top-notch people that make up our company, *what counts is the ability to teach oneself* (Ed. italics). As my employer puts it, 'Though we may seem to know a lot around here, we succeed because we start out by admitting our ignorance, and then setting out to overcome it.'

This points up one important idea noted in GWS #4: the 'need to know.' People often say of me that I 'know' a great deal about this or that; but often I have only average knowledge or less. In any given context, however, I can identify what I need to know next, and self reliance has taught me to immediately acquire the knowledge in ways which do not essentially differ from one case to the next. Thus it occurs to me that if people recognized knowledge as being important *only in relation to actual goals*—narrow or broad in scope—rather than being some kind of unquestionable goal in itself, they might better know how to go about acquiring it.

I know more than a few individuals who share my experience. Their existence assures me that a market exists for free schools offering not 'teachers' but *the resources necessary for self-teaching* (Ed. italics)…"

CREDENTIALS

The Washington Monthly recently reported:

"*The Washington Post* expressed outrage at the fact that lots of people were getting into law school with false credentials, passing the courses, and going into law practice… Gabrielle Ann Scott Elliott was one example. With only a tenth-grade education, she used false credentials to get into the University of South Carolina Law School, from which she graduated with above-average grades and then passed the South Carolina bar examination. Instead of being outraged by Ms. Elliott, shouldn't we be outraged by the phony system of credentials that deprives people of ability of the right to use their talent?"

ON LEARNING

The writer of the letter quoted in "Finding Out" later wrote again, saying in part:

"…I find that GWS has done for me exactly what I wanted it to do. I wanted it to open up some crevices in my thinking into which the stream of experience could deposit memories, insights, sayings, and other little gems."

(Ed. note—I have to interrupt just long enough to say that I have never heard anyone say better what one person's words (written or spoken) can, at best, do for another. We cannot give each other our experiences, but we can help each other to find new meanings from our own experiences. This is the true work of all serious writers and writing.)

"Until I read GWS it had not really dawned on me how possible it was for children to grow up by themselves without a great deal of aid/supervision. No matter that I had done this myself. Yes, I had already concluded that the ideal thing would be for children just to live—either alongside their parents or not, as they wished—and that this would be the best possible education. But as I now, through GWS, see many other people thinking the same thing and I visualize a world of such children, it dawns on me how very artificial it is to think in terms of schools at all, and how very accustomed we might become to having our institutions—all of them—open and accessible to children, instead of schools. I always thought the best school was a library, or perhaps a marketplace. I now think the single idea which symbolizes best this new education is the idea of a large number of adults all committed to being accessible to questions from children about their field of endeavor. It occurs to me that I have learned a great deal from merchants in this way, and in any auto-parts store they're prepared to educate in this fashion. (Ed. note—also hardware store, lumberyard, greenhouse, music store, etc.)

I think introspection is one of the great self-educational tools. One can be a scientist with one's own subconscious, testing and probing by means of imaginatively placing oneself in a certain position and then asking, 'How do I like (or dislike) that?' All you get, of course, is a reading of your feelings, but this leads to asking why one feels as one does, which in turn leads to identification of hidden experiences and implicit principles, which can then be questioned. I was fortunate that *for the larger part of my childhood, both parents worked and I was left large chunks of time to introspect.* (Ed. italics) I loved doing it and still do.

…Almost all the activities I have undertaken in life began with imitation. There was a time in adolescence when I even worried whether I had anything original to say or paint or play. But worrying did no good and I went ahead producing for my own gratification. Then later on I got a better perspective on the world and became aware that I was already pushing the limits in some things. How and when does imitation lead to originality? Why does some imitation always remain that? An interesting question.

I went through the first four or five grades being pretty much as cowed as everyone else when I could not understand phonics or the new math or any of the rest of it. For the longest time I could not remember multiplication or division and successfully hid it like virtually everyone else. But what overcame my fear was exasperation (and that names the feeling as well as the concept!); *I could not stand being bored* and this communal silence was certainly boring. I also began to get skeptical about schools after fifth grade and began to conceive of my ignorant questions as a way to find out if these were *real* teachers in front of me or not. I developed a kind of come-on in which I would raise my hand, openly apologize for my ignorance (Ed. note—a good move), and then ask questions no one else asked. As I got sharper I would start to probe the limits of the teacher; this was to relieve the boredom. It had the added advantage that it kept teachers unsure about my intent (which was unfortunately the best I could want from my high-school teachers) until *I* knew it. On the one hand I would ask a 'dumb' question and on the other I'd turn around with a tough one. If the teacher were relatively open-minded and good-hearted, the dumb question would be seen and welcomed as a sign of classroom comprehension, and the tough question would be seen and welcomed as an intellectual challenge. If the teacher were mean-spirited, the dumb question would be an opening to intimidate and the tough question would be dismissed casually. I entertained myself like this all through high school and learned a great deal. I won't say the 'method' was worked out in quite this Machiavellian way but this was its logic.

…When children are exhorted to show initiative they learn guilt about procrastination. Yet often people just want to think things out. Many people I know, who have a prodigal ability to do things, are creative procrastinators. That is, faced with large numbers of things to do, they delay doing things until they've had plenty of time to damn well feel like doing them. They delay until they've had time to plumb their subconscious on the subject, to look at all the alternatives, to question their assumptions, to fantasize about the subject, to sleep on it. Executives do this; why not children?"

One reason why not is that most children are not going to be executives, but people doing boring work. It is one of the chief tasks of schools (see GWS #6) to prepare them to do such work, and what's more, to do it as soon as someone else tells them to do it.

On imitation, the British composer Ralph Vaughan Williams once said or wrote that when he was very young, studying composition with Maurice Ravel, he said to Ravel one day that he was worried because everything he wrote sounded like imitation Ravel. Ravel said, in effect, "Don't worry about it, go right on imitating me, if you have anything original to say it will come out." Which it did—Vaughan William's later music sounds about as unlike Ravel's as one could imagine.

USEFUL BOOK

Mathematics—A Human Endeavor by Harold R. Jacobs (pub. by W. H. Freeman & Co., San Francisco CA), is about the best book on mathematics, for beginners, that I have seen. What Jacobs tries to do, and does very well, is give the beginner, or even the math-hater, an idea of what mathematical *thinking* is about, why human beings have found it so interesting, and how (to some extent) it has grown over the centuries. It is a delightful book, for people of almost any age. People who (like me) have done school math (and even gotten good grades) without ever having the slightest idea of what math is really all about, may find it interesting and exciting. People who have always feared and hated math may find there is no reason to fear and hate it. And I can't think of any book on math that would be more fun to read to and work on with even quite young children. I believe that it was written for high-school or even college students, but I would guess that quite young children would like it if they could work on it with an adult, perhaps to help them with some of the long words.

The book is laid out somewhat like a conventional text, in chapters, with questions and problems. But, unlike most texts, it begins by looking at the path of billiard balls on a table, and the ways in which we might think about that. From there it goes on to many other fascinating and unfamiliar topics. The mathematical illustrations are clear and well-chosen, and the book is sprinkled with pertinent and very funny cartoons from "Peanuts," "B.C.," and other sources. I can't recommend it too highly. My copy (cloth) says that there is also a paperback edition, but doesn't mention the price of either—but W. H. Freeman would tell you.

TEXTBOOKS

Jud Jerome (GWS #1, 2) writes:

"...I was teaching Topher algebra that day from a college text. I've got to tell you about this text. It is one of these programmed learning things, with a column of 'answers' you are supposed to cover up so that you are reading along and testing your comprehension all the while. Completely boring. Now the reason I am using it is that Topher has had all he can take without boring himself to death of fractions, decimals, all the 'arithmetic' processes. He is NOT an exceptional student, NOT especially interested in mathematics, but just a normal 11-year-old who hasn't had his brain dulled by school, and it doesn't take more than a few hours of attention over 11 years to learn how to add, subtract, multiply, divide, to get the basic ideas of fractions, and to learn that you can substitute letters or other symbols for numbers you don't know and go through the same processes. So far as I can figure out that's all there is to arithmetic and algebra (Ed. note—at least, school algebra) beyond practice, learning a few symbols, etc. at least up to quadratics and complicated exponents and roots.

Anyhow, this text. I wanted something to work on algebra with him, so asked Marty to pick up a college text. We are finding that, in general, though they are in themselves pretty terrible, *college texts are about at the level that 'elementary' students find the material interesting.* (Ed. italics) There is enough in the content to engage them so that they can concentrate on the processes. This is true even of literature. Sandy read and discussed a Hawthorne story recently with two 7-year-olds and an 11-year-old and found they had the important ideas even though they didn't know all the vocabulary. I could give many examples of how this works at various ages with various subjects, but, anyway, I wanted some college algebra book that didn't look too forbidding, and Marty came back with this two-volume programmed text on Algebra. Topher started and got bored working alone, and by working with him I could easily see why, as the text is endlessly repetitious, going over the same thing again and again with slightly different wording, apparently in the effort to drum it into heads of young people being cattle-prodded through junior colleges. It wasn't appropriate for Topher, *who still takes adults and learning seriously.* (Ed. italics) So by working with him I showed him how to skip ahead ten or twenty pages at a time, read a question, see if it was still obvious, and if it wasn't, go back a few questions to see where the necessary information was included. *In a couple of hours we were able to cover a hundred pages this way.* (Ed. italics)

But I got stumped when they started throwing around terms such as Commutative Law, Associative Law, Distributive Law. Now I remembered being embarrassed by those terms somewhere back in college math and I was ashamed that I had never learned what they meant. So I went through that part of the book with Topher with some care. And I still couldn't see why it mattered, or why such a fancy name had to be given to the obvious fact that it didn't matter what order you added things up in or multiplied things. I figured I must be missing some subtlety that was crucial to further study of mathematics. Then, in GWS, you disposed of the problem for me by pointing out that we are not, after all, studying mathematics, but Nature, truth—and the labels, which someone some time or other thought might be helpful, often obscured simple truths. You didn't say it exactly that way, but that's what I got out of it. The result was I felt liberated suddenly, and realized that I could help liberate Topher.

Except that there is the further problem that as I go at text after text with him telling him the book is foolish he begins to wonder whether the books are, indeed, foolish, or whether his father is arrogant and self-justifying. He doesn't say that he wonders, but I sense it. Eventually he is bound to wonder. For as I said, he takes adults, books, learning seriously, and it is probably very hard for him to believe that 'grown-ups' are deliberately deceiving and misleading and absurd to the degree that I imply they are.

Of course, part of the answer is that I was foolish to think that there is a college text suitable for him, and that if I spent the time I could think up better 'problems' and teach the subject better without texts, or if I were clever enough I could find examples in life which were more engaging and relevant than the problems in texts. But I am either not that clever or I won't take that much time, ...I would like something like workbooks, textbooks, to do some of this counseling and inventing for me. Eventually there may be such books. Some of our people may be writing them. Meanwhile, thanks for taking Commutative law, etc. off my back! ..."

Some interesting and important questions here. I'm not sure that we need to say that any particular textbook is misleading or foolish. If we are able, over and over again, to make clear to children (or others) what this or that textbook has made unclear, the children will soon draw their own conclusions about the worth of textbooks. If a child said to me, "This textbook isn't much good, is it?" I might agree that no, it wasn't. If s/he went on to say, "Well, why did you get it for me then?" I might say that none of the ones I looked at seemed to me any better. From this the child might conclude that textbooks were generally not much good, or perhaps, that there might be some better textbooks somewhere but that s/he was probably going to have to find them. Or, maybe, write them.

Many things in the world around me seem to me ugly, wasteful, foolish, cruel, destructive, and wicked. How much of this should I talk to children about? I tend to feel, not much. I prefer to let, or help, children explore as much of the world as they can, and then make up their own minds about it. If they ask me what I think about something, I will tell them. But if I have to criticize the world in their hearing, I prefer to do it in specifics, rather than give the idea that I think the world, *in general,* is a bad place. I don't think it is, and for all the bad that is in it, I would much rather be in it than out of it. I am in no hurry to leave. Even if I thought the world, and the people in it, was more bad than good, I don't think I would tell children so. Time enough for them to learn all that is bad. I would not have wanted to know, when I was young, all that I now know about what is wrong with the world. I'm not sure that I could have stood to know it. Time, and experience, and many friends and pleasures, have given me many assets to balance against that knowledge, things to put in the other side of the scales. Children don't have many of these. They need time to learn about some of the good things while they are learning (as they are bound to) about the bad.

TREE PLANTERS

The Nov. 8, 1978 issue of *Manas* (see GWS #3 and others) says in part:

"Five or six years ago a fifteen-year-old boy …learned that the trees in Southern California are dying (Ed.—because of smog) at the rate of about 50,000 a year…. He couldn't stand the idea of the forest fading away. What a picture—the mountains turned to wasteland, a moonscape without trees! …This youth—the Sierra Club has published a book about him, *Tree Boy,* by Shirley Nagel—went to work to replant the forests with smog-resistant seedlings. He organized help wherever he could find it—children, old men and women, handicapped people—and they all worked together to replant trees. He made friends with county, state, and national forest people—which requires a lot of doing for a lad in his teens—so that they took him seriously, valuing the help of his crews of earnest youngsters.

Today the Tree People go on planting trees, and telling about planting trees to school children, running education classes and workshops at their environmental center (some old fire department buildings with ten acres for growing things, and being reinhabited and rehabilitated by the Tree People). Now and then, the 'older' Tree People—hardly one of them yet twenty-five—go on speaking dates…. And they plant five to ten thousand trees a year, some in the cities, some in parks where a lot of people see them and see them being planted …Other people ask how do they do what they do. How do they fan this spark of theirs to a flame so that several thousand youngsters want to help plant trees every year? …"

A RECORD

The *Boston Globe* also reported that on opening day this fall (1978) attendance in the Boston public schools was at a record high. They didn't say whether it was a record for opening day or for any day. Nor did they say whether it was a record for the past five years, or ten, or twenty, or what. But it was a record, and they were mighty proud of it.

And what was this record? How many of the students signed up for school and supposed to be there on this opening day were actually there? You'll never guess.

74.5%.

Editor—John Holt
Managing Editor—Peg Durkee

GROWING WITHOUT SCHOOLING

Issue No. 8

March, 1979

In GWS #7 I said that we had received 2700 letters as a result of the TV show with Phil Donahue, and might get 1000 more. The total is now about 7500, and though the flood has slowed down a good deal, it has not stopped.

Of these letters, about half expressed some kind of sympathy and support, from mild to ecstatic. Perhaps 1000 or so said they definitely wanted to subscribe to GWS. (Had I guessed how much mail there would be, I would have tried to give the price on the air!). Another 1000 seemed strongly interested. As far as we can, I plan to follow up these people until they either subscribe or say, "Leave me alone!"

Only eight letters were critical and/or hostile, and none of them were what you could call hate mail. Of the eight, four or five did not so much defend the schools as criticize me for not trying to make them better.

Hundreds of the supporting letters (and about four of the critical) were from teachers or ex-teachers. Some of the latter had retired, many had quit in despair and disgust, or been fired. Many of those who are still teaching said things like, "I work in the schools, and I know what they're like, and I don't want that for my child."

Only one letter strongly defended the schools.

While doing the show, I said to Linda Sessions during a station/commercial break, and after we had heard some fairly hostile comment from the audience, that we were not there so much to convince the audience as to send out a signal. Later I read that about four and a half million families (mostly mothers, since it is a daytime show) regularly watch it. That's a lot of people. But there are a great many more still to be reached. We have much more signal sending left to do.

CBS "60 Minutes" wanted to do a show on the same subject, but was told by higher-ups that the number of unschoolers was not big enough to justify it. But another CBS TV show, called "Magazine," definitely plans to do a program on unschooling. At least one other big national show is looking into it.

The monthly magazine *Mother Jones* has a very good article on unschooling coming out. I have had long conversations about it with people from *The Ladies' Home Journal. Omni*, a new magazine of science and science fiction, has said they want to interview me. An interview with me, which I have not yet seen, has been published in the *Libertarian Review*. And all over the country the newspapers have been full of stories about unschoolers.

NEW RECORDS

The group subscription record has moved to a Southeastern state (for the time being, I can't say which one), where readers have taken out—hold onto your hats—a 74X subscription, for 12 issues! (Each reader will get GWS for about $1.32 per year, or $.23 per issue.)

The next largest group subscription is in Great Britain, where a group of people connected with the British unschooling movement called Education Otherwise have taken out a 40X subscription for 18 issues.

A GOOD INVENTION

From *The Amherst Record* (MA):

University of Massachusetts School of Education Dean Mario Fantini provided the idea of the 'portfolio approach' to evaluate the education of Richard and Keith Perchemlides, sons of Peter and Susan Perchemlides.

The portfolio approach is acceptable to Schools Supt. Donald Frizzle and to the family.

According to Fantini, video and cassette tapes, actual art works and photographs can be used to evaluate the children's learning instead of the weekly paper and pencil test. The portfolio becomes 'an archive of each child' he said.

In a telephone interview Thursday, Fantini said the Perchemlides asked his advice in developing an education program for their children. He said he spent 'countless hours' with the couple discussing their philosophy of education and their goals in educating their children at home.

Fantini, who specializes in different approaches to learning and teaching, approves the option of parents educating their children at home. But he said it is important to assess the benefits of this education to the child.

Fantini said 'it makes sense to have an outside evaluation by an individual or panel in a home education situation.' He said this third party review would be impartial and acceptable to school administrators."

FROM KY.

Mil Duncan (106 Lorraine Ct. Berea KY 40403) writes:

"...Bill and I have two sons, Graham 4 and Ian 3 [as of 10/78], who are full of curiosity and eagerness about the world. Since they were infants they have had books to hold and study and listen to—and lately their attention span for story or poem listening seems almost without limits. They love 'how things work' books and books that describe Indians' life styles and history. When we read books with more words than pictures (like *Wind in the Willows* or *Charlotte's Web* or A.A. Milne) they are still and attentive, and interrupt to comment on the story or to ask about words or expressions. They have the patience now to hear non-plot-like prose—to listen about the wind rustling in the trees and pouring over the characters' skin or fur—and to enjoy those descriptions as well...

In his *Autobiography* John Stuart Mill describes his unique education that his father provided him: (p. 21)

'There was one cardinal point, of which I have already given some indication, and which, more than anything else, was the cause of whatever good it effected. Most boys or youths who have had much knowledge drilled into them, have their mental capacities not strengthened, but overlaid by it. They are crammed with mere facts, and with the opinions or phrases of other people, and these are accepted as a substitute for the power to form opinions of their own... Mine, however, was not an education of cram. My father never permitted anything which I learnt to degenerate into a mere exercise of memory. He strove to make the understanding not only go along with every step of the teaching, but, if possible, precede it. Anything which could be found out by thinking I never was told, until I had exhausted my efforts to find it out for myself...'

Out of the blue last month Graham began to multiply. He said, "Mil, I know what 2 threes are,' and so forth... arranging with fingers or objects so that he can pose problems and solve them. Discovery fills every hour, doesn't it!"

UNSCHOOLERS

From the *Daily Review* (Hayward CA, May 1976):

GOING TO COLLEGE AT 16 IS NO PROBLEM FOR HIM

San Leandro—Though he is only 16, Mark Edwards has had no difficulty in adjusting to campus life in California State University, Hayward, where he is a full-time student this quarter...

[He] was able to enroll at Cal State... at the age of 16 because of the California High School Proficiency Examination for 16 and 17-year-olds given for the first time last Dec. 20.

The exam is designed for 16 and 17-year-olds who want to terminate their high school education before they become 18. Those who take the examination and pass it are awarded a Certificate of Proficiency which is the legal equivalent of a high school diploma and allows them to drop out of high school with parental permission.

Mark took the proficiency test Dec. 20 which was also his 16th birthday. He had no difficulty passing the test which he found to be 'simple' and 'trivial.' ...

Mark was accepted at Cal State on the basis of his scores on the Scholastic Aptitude Test and the American College Testing exam.

It was because of the proficiency examination that Mark was able to enroll in the California State College system.

Without [it], Mark's only alternatives would have been private colleges.

Mark is the son of Dr. and Mrs. Scott Edwards of San Leandro. His father is a professor of political science at Cal State and his mother is a junior high school teacher...

Midway through the eighth grade [Mark] decided to drop out of school, preferring to be tutored at home by his parents. ...being more advanced academically than his fellow students, he was often referred to as an 'egg head.'

He enrolled in Moreau High School in the ninth grade in 1974, but dropped out early in 1975 and completed his high school education at home. ...

At Cal State, Hayward, Mark is taking 17 units. He has already challenged one class, English 1001, written the test and received the credits. ...

———————————

Mr. and Mrs. Edwards sent me that clipping, and along with it one from the *San Francisco Examiner*, Jan. 10, 1979.

THIS FAMILY LEARNED ITS LESSON—KIDS STUDY AT HOME

...Five years ago [the Edwardses] decided to yank their children from the formal classroom atmosphere and have them attend class at home in San Leandro. ...

The Edwards children, aged 13 to 18, speak in glowing terms of their home-based schooling and claim it's given them poise and an insatiable appetite for learning that they wouldn't otherwise have had at their age. ...

The results are remarkable. Mark, the eldest at 18, is a junior at the University of California at Berkeley. Cliff is a sophomore at Chabot College, and 14-year-old Matthew is a freshman at Holy Name College in Oakland... The parents currently teach daughters Jennifer, 14, and Diane, 13. ...

The ongoing education, however, isn't as regimented as the usual day's schedule at a school. The father begins each day with a brisk morning jog, leading the children. Following that the daughters are given the day's assignment from their mother... One subject at a time—such as geography—is tackled for a few months... But if a daughter simply doesn't want to study one day, preferring instead to tend other chores, the studies are generally continued the next day. ...And the parents insist that relatively little time and money are spent for such an education..."

_____

With the clippings Mrs. Edwards sent this information:

"Mark and Cliff, 19 & 17, work almost a full week as well as attend classes. Mark works in a credit office and Cliff is a salesman for a radio store. They had no problems getting part-time work. Matt, 14, is a paid organist and pianist helping to defray his school expenses. ..."

A NEEDED LAW

The State of California has done something that I suggested in *Instead of Education*. (I don't mean to imply that they necessarily got the idea from me—though they may have.) In it I wrote:

"To further reduce the power of the schools and their tickets, we might also extend the idea of the high-school equivalency exam. In all states and territories, people who have never finished high school can, by passing an examination, get the equivalent of a high school diploma. Today, people may not take this exam until they reach a given age, varying from state to state between seventeen and twenty-one ...Clearly, the law does not mean to let any young person get out of school merely by showing that he has already learned what the school is supposed to teach him. But we might before long be able in many states to pass laws that one could take the equivalency exam at any age— or even laws that anyone who passed the exam no longer had to go to high school, and if below the school leaving age, must be admitted without cost to his choice of the state colleges. ...

This could be a great help to many poor or nonwhite children who would like to be doctors or lawyers or work in other professions. What keeps them out... now, as much as any other thing, is the extraordinary amount of time it takes to get the needed school credentials. ..."

A year or two ago someone introduced into the Massachusetts legislature a bill to lower the age at which students could take the high school equivalency exam. Public educators turned out in force to oppose it—as it turned out, successfully. But the political climate is changing, and today it might be possible in many states to persuade the legislatures to pass a law like the one in California.

SHERLOCK'S TRIUMPH

Merritt Clifton, editor/publisher of *Samisdat* (Box 231, Richford VT 05476), author of novels *24X12* and *A Baseball Fantasy*, writes:

"...consider Sir Conan Doyle's remarks quoted in GWS #7 in context with his own greatest literary accomplishment, the creation of Sherlock Holmes. Doyle advocates formal education; Holmes is self-educated. Doyle suggests learning is best accomplished in school, during childhood; Holmes experiments, toys & questions like an intelligent child on into adulthood, & conspicuously avoids any institutional connections. Doyle would lock children up; Holmes lets curious boys and girls play with his most precious equipment. Holmes's archenemy is the institutionally educated Professor Moriarty, who stands for everything Conan Doyle does—and Holmes triumphs, while Doyle died considering himself an abysmal failure. Doyle hated Holmes, as is well-known, and tried to kill him off in mid-career. Yet Holmes survived, as voice for the real, repressed man inside Conan Doyle. The outer Conan Doyle was afraid of his own true inner convictions. Fortunately, inner convictions overcame outer image. Sherlock Holmes, for instance, has taught more children to enjoy reading than all the institutional texts ever written. ..."

_____

Makes me want to read Holmes again, haven't since I was a kid, when I read all of him, and how I loved it.

ELECTRICITY

Theo Giesy writes:

"During the holidays while we had the tree up, Susie was wondering why all the bulbs go out on the series strings and only the burned out one goes off on parallel strings. (I still cling to and insist on using four series strings from my childhood) Darrin gave her a very nice explanation of the difference between series and parallel wiring. I have no idea where he picked it up. I asked him where he learned that. He said, where he learned everything. I asked what he meant by that. He said, from me. I know he only learned it from me in that I gave him time to learn what he was interested in."

ON "INFINITY"

A mother wrote me a wonderful letter, which has disappeared in my filing system (I was *sure* I knew where it was), talking partly about the problems she had with the letters B and D when she was little, and partly about her six-year-old's thinking and questions about numbers. One of his questions was, what was the number next to infinity. To this I wrote, in part:

"There is no number before 'infinity.' Kids talk about 'infinity' as if it were a number, but it isn't. The word 'infinite' means 'endless' or 'boundless.' You can't get to the end, or the edge, because there isn't one; no matter how far you go, you can keep on going. Not an easy idea, maybe, for a six-year-old, or even most adults, to grasp.

The family, or as mathematicians would say the 'class' of whole numbers, i.e., 1,2,3,4,5 ...has no biggest number. No matter how big a number we think of, we can always add some other number to it, or multiply it by another number. Mathematicians call this kind of class of numbers not 'infinite' but 'transfinite.'

There's a good chapter about transfinite numbers in a fascinating book which you may be able to get from a library, or perhaps from a university, called *Mathematics and the Imagination,* by Kastner and Newman. We learn that one transfinite class, such as the class of even numbers, is the same size as another transfinite class, the class of all whole numbers. It seems crazy at first, how can there be as many even numbers as there are numbers, since half the numbers are odd. Well, we can say that one class of things is the same size as another class of things if for every item in the first class we can match one and just one item in the second class. If for each right shoe we have one and only one left shoe, then we have just as many right shoes as left shoes, even if we don't know exactly how many we have. For every number in the class of whole numbers, 1,2,3,... we can make one and only one even number, by multiplying the first number times 2. 1 matches with 2, 2 matches with 4, 3 matches with 6, 4 with 8, 5 with 10, and so on no matter how far we go. So we can say those two classes are the same size.

There is a wonderful proof, what mathematicians call 'elegant' (and it is , too), that the class of fractions is the same size as the class of whole numbers. That really is hard to believe, since between any two whole numbers you can put as many fractions as you want. But there is a way to do that matching game again, so it must be true. There is another elegant proof that the class of decimals is larger than the class of whole numbers. But I won't say more about this now. Let me know if you can't find the book; I still have a copy and could make a copy of those pages.

The mathematician who did a lot of the early work on this was Georg Kantor. He showed that some transfinite numbers are bigger than others. Indeed, I think he found four or five different transfinite numbers, each bigger than the one before. The class of whole numbers was the smallest, the class of decimals the next smallest. Then a still larger one which represented (among other things) the class of all functions.

These are big ideas for a six-year-old (or anyone) to grapple with. Try them out, see what happens, don't be surprised or disappointed if he suddenly turns away from numbers and starts to look at something else. Meanwhile, see if you can encourage him to talk about 'infinite' instead of 'infinity.' There is no such *thing*, or mathematical idea, as 'infinity.' There is just the adjective 'infinite,' meaning, as I said before, without an end or an edge."

FROM NEWARK

Dean Schneider, 77 Custer Ave., Newark, NJ 07112, writes:

"...at a workshop the other day the speaker was talking about her experiences with unschooling in Newark. She, a member of a city poverty agency and former teacher, had a friend who actually never registered her child for school. When her child was six or seven and had not yet been to school, she started being hassled and threatened by the school authorities (I don't know how they became aware of the 'offense' in the first place). Despite her repeated defense that she was effectively teaching her child at home, the powers that be turned their screws. But rather than submit, the mother took her child and moved out of state. This was around 1974 or 1975.

After the meeting, I inquired as to other cases she knew about of parents, in Newark, taking their children out of schools altogether and teaching them at home. She said she had five or six friends who are thinking seriously about it. They are single parents (the number of mother-centered households in Newark runs about 50%) who had, themselves, gone through the Newark public schools and wanted nothing of the sort for their children. They were farsighted enough to plan their work lives and finances so they could take three or more years off, or at least juggle their time, to be at home to teach their children. Whether or not they too will encounter official resistance or pressure is unknown. In 1967, home study became legal in New Jersey under *State v. Massa*, 95 NJ Super, 382, 231 A 2nd 252 (1967). But this ruling, in itself, does not prevent legal or political maneuvering as has been seen in other states where home study is supposedly legal.

I have recently heard of other instances of parents unschooling their children in Newark and New York City. My next door neighbor seriously contemplated keeping her daughter at home last year, but then decided to enter her at the alternative school right up the street.

It appears that far from inhibiting attempts at unschooling, big city life is getting so rotten as to encourage it. When in one week one hears of half a dozen cases of actual or contemplated unschooling in a city with the dismal reputation of Newark, it becomes clearer that there is a willingness to pull out of public schools should conditions become desperate enough— even if this means arranging work lives to make it feasible, relying on friends or relatives, or training children for early independence and self-reliance (as you mention in GWS #4). This also appears to counter the claim that only middle class whites can afford to get their kids out of public schools. ...

...Even when children are in schools that parents find suspect, you hear of brothers and sisters, aunts and uncles, cousins and parents chipping in at night or on weekends trying to teach at home to reverse or mini- mize the damage wrought by the public schools. A student at my school last year, when asked, "How are you ever going to learn this stuff if you don't listen?" replied, "My uncle teaches me at home." Another former student in our third grade had very irregular attendance and this was considered a problem. Yet I tutored her during the summer and she picked things up very quickly, and is in fact ahead in her studies compared to other third graders (who have been more regular in attending school). From what she told me, it was evident that her mother made home instruction a regular part of daily life (after school). Another student told me today that she has a tutor come to her house from time to time....

In Newark, some parents have started their own schools while others have selected schools which are at least better, which can mean 'stronger academically,' more relaxed or more disciplined, happier or stricter. But in any case, creating or selecting their own school is an act by parents to acquire some say in their own lives and the lives of their children. And one way these alternative schools could support parents in unschool- ing is to offer to supervise or help develop home study programs for a small fee. This could be to provide just paper legitimacy or to actually work with parents to devise a plan of action. I know you mention this for parents using an alternative school outside their own state (*Instead of Education,* and *New Schools Exchange Newsletter* #131). This is a prospect I'm keeping my eye on in Newark.

Even a dismal city like Newark has a real world outside the school doors, and much to be learned from people in or out of schools. There's a good library system, a good museum with a number of workshops and programs, parks, zoos, airports, shipping ports, etc.—all things to learn from. Also, there is easy access to all New York City has to offer. ...Should unschooling happen more in Newark, there's a city out there to be used profitably. And if it can happen here, it can happen anywhere."

————————————————

At the moment, I know of only five schools in the country that are willing, so to speak, to provide cover for unschooling families. One is, of course, the Santa Fe Community School, which has already helped a number of families in this way. The others I will write about in GWS as soon as I have their permission to do so. Meanwhile, we need to know of more such schools. If any readers are part of a school which would be willing to do this—act as legal cover for unschooling families and/or help them with a home study pro- gram—please let me know. Thanks.

A SHELTER SCHOOL

No sooner had I written the above than I had a letter from Ed Nagel (P.O. Box 2823, Santa Fe, NM 87501—Tel. (505) 471-6928) on just this subject:

"...Re: home-study students enrolled at Santa Fe Community School, since 1974 – 75 we have enrolled about 100 students, from different states, of whom only 3 that I know of were ever challenged. One was Erik Sessions (still enrolled). Another was the child of a lady from Pa., on whose behalf Wm. Ball wrote a letter, obtaining a substantial delay of any action against her. Later she returned her child to prison. (Actually the child was never formally enrolled at SFCS during this period.) The third parent was fairly mobile; when her child's "attendance" was challenged in Pa., SFCS wrote a letter verifying her employment with the school as a supervisor of off-campus travel-study. This satisfied the local superintendent and ended any further queries.

There are others, occasionally, who attempt to obtain a legal "guarantee" from the local public school officials—asking the "boss" in effect if they can under- mine his operation—and, who, failing in this, become intimidated and soon retreat from their position. Or, they may *move* , literally, to another area/state where they may then proceed less conspicuously to provide an educational alternative, in some cases, at least, through SFCS.

As I write, it occurs to me that there may have been another challenge, but NONE of the parents whose children enrolled at SFCS have ever had to go to jail or paid a fine (the unenrolled child's parent from Pa. paid a fine, as I recall, *prior* to Ball's intervention), or lost a challenge throughout this five-year period.

Currently, there are between 40 and 50 students enrolled in home-study programs through SFCS, several within our own state. Of these, I would estimate about 1/3 have been enrolled for more than 2 years now. Of the many alternative schools doing this in other states which have been made known to me— roughly 30—only 3 have given me permission to put searching parents in touch with them, and then only under certain conditions; *everyone is paranoid.* No one wants to go to court; not the parents, not the schools; not the public officials who can manage to keep the news/noise down about the few 'unusual' arrange- ments they allow/tolerate within their district..."

Good news about SFSC. If I were planning to take children out of school, one of the first things I would do would be to enroll them at SFSC, or make such an arrangement with another school if I knew of one that would do it. I would do other things as well, but I would certainly do this.

As for school officials, several people have told me that they have had their children out of school, and that the schools, even though they had not formally approved this, were willing to let it go on, *as long as nobody complained.* But as soon as some nosy neighbor reported to the schools that such-and-such children were not in school, the schools had to make a big show of disapproval, start talking about law, courts, etc. What the officials are afraid of is that someone will say publicly, "How come you let those people get away with not sending their kids to school?"

What we need (among other things) is an answer for the schools to give to the nosy neighbors. Maybe if the schools can say, "That child is enrolled in a private school and we have nothing to say about him," it would solve their problem, and so, our problem.

ON "RELIGIOUS BELIEF"

A Canadian parent, writing about the Sessions case (GWS #7), discussed the part of the ruling that said that parents' claims to constitutional protection on religious grounds of their right to teach at home must be "rooted in religious belief." The court did not say what it would or would not consider "religious belief." About this, the parent went on to say:

"I see 'religion' as a concept that can be manipulated for unschoolers' benefit just as can the concepts of 'school,' 'teach,' 'educate,' etc. As you pointed out, unschoolers should say, 'Yes, our child goes to school,' and 'Yes, I am teaching my kids,' even if the method of teaching is simply allowing them to learn. ...

For 'religious belief,' what just about anybody could feel comfortable with is... the feeling that one's children are divine beings to be protected and nurtured to the best of the parents' ability. ...I'd say something like this: 'I believe that my children are Divine Beings and that it is my Divine Responsibility to educate my children according to God's Plan.' ....The trick is that 'God' and 'religion' can mean whatever one wants them to. 'God' doesn't have to be Judaeo-Christian; it can be Universal Energy, or Nature, or simply Love. ..."

I replied that this isn't what I meant at all. Such a statement might work in Canada (though I doubt it), but not in the U.S. What the framers of the Constitution wished to prevent, and what the Constitution itself forbade, has happened anyway. Judaeo-Christianity has to all intents and purposes become the official, state religion of the U.S. When the Constitution was amended to put the words "under God" into the Pledge of Allegiance, it was not just any God, anyone's personal definition of God, that people had in mind. It was the God of Christians and Jews.

Any people who are asking on religious grounds for the right to teach their own children will have a much better chance if they use the word "Christian." To defend home schooling on the grounds that children are some kind of Divine Beings would almost certainly be a disastrous mistake. In many parts of the U.S., people would consider that statement itself to be irreligious or blasphemous.

I would instead suggest that people say that what happens in schools offends their *Christian* beliefs about the way to teach and bring up children, as indeed I would think it *would* offend, and deeply, anyone who understood the word "Christian" to mean "based on the teachings of Christ." That is to say, on the New Testament as opposed to the Old, where those with a mind to have always been able to find excuses for greed, racism, hatred, violence, and cruelty.

It is of course possible that the courts might one day uphold the right of Moslem or Buddhist or Hindu parents to teach their children at home, on the grounds that both the daily life and the subject matter and values (both taught and untaught) of the average school classroom seriously violated their religious beliefs. I hope someone will make such a test case, and will follow it closely if they do. But as for such parents winning—I'll believe it only when I see it.

Meanwhile, if we can in good conscience apply the word "Christian" to our beliefs, it seems to me to make good sense to do so.

FROM QUEBEC

Helen Fox, 137 Chemin du Ruisseau, St. Clet, Quebec, writes:

"We are solving the school problem for our daughters (12, 8, & 3) in a combination of ways—home teaching before they are 6 so they read well and love math before they see a classroom. The French school, which in our little village here in Quebec is friendly, relaxed, even joyful (Ed. note—certainly not true of many or most schools in France), and for some reason much emphasis is put on sports (they tan in winter from skiing and skating every day) and "public" speaking. All we hope for them to learn at school... that we cannot teach them better at home... is French and a total immersion in a culture and life-style different from ours. They seem unaffected by geography books from 1947 (we read maps, go places & talk, after school) and the other idiocies that are so debilitating in the suburbs, and elsewhere.

They love school, & do well. I think they love the chance to live a completely different life than the one we live here, at home ... even a new personality is born in another language. I marvel at them, as I stumble along talking to their friends.

Interesting to note, though, that the older two much prefer reading in English (in which they've had no school training) than in French. They (esp. the older one) say it's because 'there's nothing good to read in French ... no action & adventure' but I imagine there's less action and adventure in the act of reading that was taught methodically.

These schools, by the way, are not great for French children. A *large* number repeat a grade, and many get disgusted in high school & quit to work on the farm (illegally). Class, in elementary school, is often a madhouse—but it's endured, even enjoyed, I suspect, by the teachers who, like most French Canadians I have met, really like kids & want to be with them."

In a later letter:

"French school ... is working so well that my 8-yr-old is reading a paperback called *'Preparez Votre Enfant a l'Ecole'* (Ed. note— *'Get Your Child Ready for School'*) in order to get ideas for her *own* school that she conducts for the neighborhood 3-6 yr. olds, in French. She also cooks dinner for 5 and writes short stories in English. ..."

It is now the law in Quebec that children from English-speaking families must go to French schools. (Quite a few were going even before that law was passed.) These children are taught to read, in French. Except perhaps in a few families, no one teaches them to read in English. But I have seen more than one report saying that where such tests have been made, these children have been found to read much better in English than in French.

LEARNING A LANGUAGE

Young children who come into contact with people who speak more than one language will learn to speak all of those languages, and usually without much trouble.

Older people, who have a lot of trouble, are amazed at this, and cook up a lot of fancy theories about the child having a special aptitude, or the child's brain being somehow different from the adult's, to explain why the child learns so much easier and faster.

The real explanation is simpler than this. The child, who speaks language A in his home, but who meets outside the home other people, especially other children, who speak language B, does not in any way set himself the task of "learning language B." In fact, he does not think of himself as speaking language A, or indeed any language. He just speaks, learns to understand what other people say, and to make them understand what he wants to say.

Now, all of a sudden, he meets some people whom he can't understand at all, and who can't understand him. What he wants and what he tries to do, is to understand those people, *right now*, and to make them understand him, *right now*. That is what he works at, and since he is smart, tireless, and ingenious, and not easily discouraged by difficulties, and since he gets instant feedback to tell him whether or not he is understanding or being understood, he very quickly gets good at it.

His parents think how wonderful it is that he is learning language B so quickly. But he is not trying to do that, would not understand what it meant "to learn a language," would not know how to do such a task even if people could explain to him what the task was. He is just trying to communicate with people.

I saw a most vivid example of this difference when, after my father had retired from business, he and my mother began to spend the winter half of each year in Mexico. My father, who had graduated from a "good" college (not a good student, but good enough to graduate), told himself sternly, and kept telling himself for six years and more, that he ought to "learn Spanish." My mother, who had not gone to college, and had been a very poor student—she had always been terribly nearsighted, but beyond that, probably bored to death—could not have cared less about "learning Spanish." What she wanted, like the little child, was to be able to talk to these people around her, who were very different from any people she had known, and who interested her very much. So, like a very young child—she always had a small child's keenness of observation and sharpness of mind—she began to try to talk to the people around her, to ask the names of things, to ask *how* to ask the names of things. The people she talked to, enchanted as people always are by someone who makes a real effort to speak their language—I discovered this on my travels in Italy—talked back, showed her things and told her their names (as they did to me when I visited), gently corrected her mistakes in pronunciation or usage, not so that she would speak "correctly" but only so that she would be better understood, and helped her in every way they could. The result was that very soon she was able to talk easily and fluently with people on a variety of subjects.

At the same time, my father, who thought of himself as trying to "learn Spanish," which meant to learn to speak it correctly, so that *then* he could talk to the people around him, never learned more than twenty or so words in all the years he lived there. Now and then my mother tried to get him to say a few words to the people he met. He couldn't do it, was paralyzed by his school-learned fear of doing it wrong, making a mistake, looking foolish and stupid. He backed away from all these human contacts, all the while telling himself that he really ought to learn Spanish but just couldn't, was too old, did not have the aptitude, and so on.

Since then I have learned something from Ivan Illich, which seemed surprising until I thought about it, when it stopped being surprising at all. He had been traveling a lot in the polyglot, i.e., multi-language, cultures of Southeast Asia and the Indian subcontinent. What he found was that the people who grew up in these cultures before schools were widespread, and therefore, before people began to think that important things, including "foreign languages," had to be learned in school, did in fact learn to speak many languages, just from the experience of daily life. This was true of even very poor, humble, ordinary people. Such people, if they came regularly into contact with people who spoke other languages, and if they had good reason—business, or whatever—to talk with them, learned to talk with them. But among the younger people, who grew up going to school, and so learned—even if they learned nothing else—that important things can only be learned in school, and then only when they are taught, very few learn more than one language.

In short, schools not only make knowledge scarce and expensive, but they make it difficult, by making it abstract, and cutting it off from the powerful motives, incentives, and rewards of daily life. They make the vast majority of people, not more informed or learned, but more ignorant, less eager and less able to learn new things than they would otherwise have been.

ON UNDERSTANDING

The friend I mentioned, in "Life In School" in GWS #6, once wrote to say that many children in her science class had not understood a talk she had given about asteroids, and asked what she might do about it. I wrote back, saying in part:

"... I decided that when we don't understand something, one (or more) of three things are happening. 1) We have heard a word/words or seen a sign, for which we don't know the *referent*—which just means, the object, thing, experience that the word or sign refers to. Thus the referent of the word 'dog' is a four-legged furry animal, usually with tail, etc. If you had never seen a dog, and someone mentioned the name in conversation, you'd be a little puzzled. Or if you were an Eskimo, and someone mentioned a giraffe (I can't imagine why), again, you'd be puzzled. If you had only lived in the far North, it would be very hard to 'explain' to you what a tree was. Or a mountain, if you lived on flat tundra. People who have never seen snow, even though they have heard of it and even seen photos of it, are usually bowled over when they see the real thing.

If you had seen *some* animals, say a horse or a cat, I could explain a dog pretty easily, could say it was smaller than a horse but about the same size or bigger than a cat, with four legs, head, and tail in the same position. If you had never seen a four-legged animal at all, it might be a little bit hard to explain how a four-legged animal is put together. You could perhaps draw a picture. But people who have had no experience of pictures, primitive tribes, cannot connect in their minds pictures of things with the real things, cannot even recognize a picture of themselves or their own house.

Part of your problem in explaining asteroids may have been that many of your classmates didn't have the *feel* for the distances and emptiness of space. They can perhaps imagine what something is like a mile away, but tens or hundreds or thousands of miles don't mean much to them, in which case words won't help.

The second thing that can cause us not to understand is when we hear one thing, and then another, and the two seem to contradict each other. If you had been told that ducks fly in the air, and that snapping turtles live in the water, and later heard someone say that a duck had been caught by a snapping turtle (which happens), you would be confused. How could that be possible? Someone would then have to say that ducks also live some of the time in the water, at which point you would understand.

And the third thing that causes us not to understand is when someone tells us one thing, which seems to make sense, and then some other thing, which also seems to make sense, but we can't see how they are connected, what they have to do with each other. Or someone may tell us something, that we think we understand, but it doesn't seem to connect with anything, we think, 'Why are you telling me that?'

Knowing this about understanding can be useful for people trying to learn things. If you find, reading, or hearing someone talk, that you don't understand something, don't panic. Take a few moments to ask yourself which of those three cases you are in. If you are reading, and are not sure what the referent of a word or phrase is, what thing is being described, you can ask someone, or look it up in a dictionary, or if the book is a textbook, look it up in the index in the back of the book, see on what page the word first appears, and then see what it says about the word on that page. In a math or science textbook, you can usually find the word earlier in the chapter you're reading.

If your problem is that two things seem to contradict each other, it will help to say as accurately as you can what the contradiction is, thus, 'It says that ducks fly in the air, and that snapping turtles live in the water, so how could a snapping turtle catch a duck?' That is an easy question for someone else to answer. When a student says to a teacher, 'I don't get it,' there isn't much the teacher can do about it.

The more precisely we can say what it is that confuses us, the easier it will be for us, or someone, to clear up the confusion."

SEATWORK

A mother—not an unschooler, she was interviewing me for a newspaper—told me the other day about some of the "reading problems" her child is having at school. His problem is that he loves to read and regularly reads books several years ahead of his so-called "grade-level." His teacher complained to his mother that the boy was "falling behind in his reading seatwork." This work consists of copying out vocabulary and spelling lists, reading sample paragraphs and answering questions about them, filling out various workbooks, and doing similar exercises—the kind that people invent who think that the ability to read well consists of hundreds of separate and measurable "skills."

When the children were supposed to be doing this "seatwork," this boy held books in his lap and read them instead. The teacher said that if he did not catch up with his seatwork she was going to give him a C in reading. The mother said, "How can you do that? You know he is a good reader? You know he reads books, for his own pleasure, that are way ahead of his grade level. How can you give such a boy a C in reading?" The teacher admitted that she knew the boy was a good reader, probably the best in the class. But she still insisted that he had to do his seatwork. The mother than said, "But the reason for the seatwork is to get the children to the point where they *can* read and understand the kind of books my son is already reading. Why should he have to get ready to do what he already *knows* how to do?" The teacher would not budge. The children were supposed to be doing seatwork, he had to do seatwork.

GOVERNMENT PROPERTY

From *Manas* (see GWS #3) of 12/20/78, this quote:

"... a month or so ago, a public school official in Los Angeles declared on TV that the child, until he graduates from high school, 'belongs to the state.' "

THE SCHOOLS CONFESS

A recent issue of *Case and Comment,* for which I have no address, reprinted an article on "Teacher Malpractice" which originally appeared in the *American Educator,* journal of the American Federation of Teachers. The article said, in part:

"In 1972, parents of a graduate of the public school system in San Francisco brought a $500,000 suit against the school district charging that after a total of 13 years of regular attendance, their son was not able to read.

During his years in school, according to information compiled on the case, he was in the middle of his classes, maintained average grades and was never involved in anything which resulted in major disciplinary action. His parents claimed that during their son's years in the public school they were rebuffed in their attempts to get information on the progress of their son, but were assured by school officials and teachers he was moving along at grade level.

Shortly after the youth's graduation, he was given a reading test by specialists who concluded the youth was only reading on a fifth grade level...

...the California State Court of Appeals rejected the parents' claim of the school system's failure to educate their son. The court declared it was impossible for any person, most of all the courts, to set guidelines for 'proper' academic procedures which must be followed by all schools and teachers.

'Unlike the activity of the highway, or the marketplace, classroom methodology affords no readily acceptable standards of care, or cause, or injury. The science of pedagogy itself is fraught with different and conflicting theories of how or what a child should be taught, and any layman might, and commonly does, have his own emphatic views of the subject,' read the court's opinion."

The court was, of course, quite right in saying this. But what then becomes of the claim, which the schools make all the time, that they alone know how to teach children? It might not be a bad idea for parents, fighting in court for the right to teach their own children, to quote those words from the California decision.

SMOKING

Every now and then, in the subway or some public place, I see young people, perhaps twelve or thirteen years old, sometimes even as young as ten, smoking cigarettes. It is a comic and pitiful sight. They have obviously practiced (as I once did) all the mechanics of holding the cigarette, taking a puff, inhaling the smoke (if they can), blowing it out casually, flicking the ashes off the end, etc. They want to look as if they had been smoking for years, yet they give themselves away every second. They dart nervous glances in every direction, half wanting to be seen (and admired) by everyone, half fearing that they may be seen by someone who will get them in trouble. Above all, they can't let the cigarette alone for a second. They take puff after puff, one right after another. The smoke they are breathing must be as hot as a burning building.

It is an ordeal. The smoke tastes awful. Children have sensitive taste buds, and that smoke must taste even worse to them than to most nonsmoking adults, which is saying a lot. They have to struggle not to choke, not to cough, maybe even not to get sick. Why do they do it? Because 'all the other kids' are doing it, or soon will be, and they have to stay ahead of them, or at least not fall behind. In short, wanting to smoke, or feeling one has to smoke whether one wants to or not, is one of the many fringe benefits of that great "social life" at school that people talk about.

Some people, when they learn I don't smoke, say, "I wish I had your will power."

I tell them they have it backwards. I *tried* to smoke, but I didn't have enough will power to keep at it. The taste of the smoke itself I could just barely stand, but the taste it left in my mouth—for days—was too much for me. I gave it up.

I was able to give it up only because I was so far on the outside edge of the peer group that being a little farther out made no difference. I had nothing to lose. I longed to be an insider, but smoking, even if I could make myself learn to stand it, was not going to make me one. So why put myself through it. I had already learned, a little bit, and only because I had to, to say, "The heck with them." So I said it. For a few years I smoked only when I got drunk, which meant I had a double penalty to pay the next day. Years later, thinking it might help me fight off drowsiness on a long driving trip, I inhaled a big puff of a cigarette. It almost knocked me down—I thought the top of my head had lifted clean off. Wow, what a drug! Since then, no more.

I feel sorry for all the children who think they have to smoke, and even sorrier for any nonsmoking parents who may desperately wish they could persuade them not to. If the children have lived in the peer group long enough to become enslaved to it, addicted to it—we might call them "peer group junkies"—then they are going to smoke, and do anything and everything else the peer group does. If Mom and Pop make a fuss, then they will lie about it and do it behind their backs. The evidence on this is clear. In some age groups, fewer people are smoking. But more children are smoking every year, especially girls, and they start earlier.

One remedy, of course, is for children to feel themselves full members of a human group or groups whose example and good opinion they value enough so that they don't worry about what the peer group is doing. I don't know any other.

GROWING WITH TREES

A mother writes:

"... I read *How Children Learn* when A was 2 and felt helped by it to see ways of playing and communicating that I'd been missing. I heard part of a lecture you gave on public radio about kids having the right to work and be part of the 'real' world. But I didn't know until GWS #1 came out that you'd gone all the way to *no school*. At that time A was 8 and had never gone to school. It was so exciting to hear that there even *were* any others. GWS has filled a real need, helping us feel less alone and more faith in what we are doing.

T, A, and I ... earn almost all of our money by seasonal orchard work—picking apples. 2 months in the fall and pruning apple trees 2 months in the late winter. We leave home and work in various parts of [apple country].

I've been doing this since I was four months pregnant with A. She is almost 10. The other 8 months we are home, in a neighborhood with 6 or so other couples who also live in the woods, are building their own houses. Most garden, most are self-employed doing crafts or odd jobs. A's best friend—M (8)—is also her cousin and also has never been to school. She's enrolled in the Santa Fe Community School. We are 'keeping a low profile.' Neither of our families have been bothered by the law. A and M play with other kids in the area who do go to school. We don't hide what we're doing but we don't advertise it either. I don't really know how much the local school board knows and whether or not they're purposely looking the other way. (Ed.—this is often the case) Since we three leave home Sept. 1st and March 1st each time for 2 months, it is possible they just assume she goes to school somewhere else.

...A started picking of her own accord one day when she was 5. She put her raincoat on backwards, using the hood as a bucket to hold the fruit until she emptied into the boxes. She was very proud of herself. She worked all day and picked 3 bushels. The next rainy day we made a quarter size bucket out of a plastic waste basket and a pant leg. The cloth bottom opened up for emptying like our buckets. T made her a 10 foot ladder (he makes and sells apple picking ladders). She picked from the bottoms of our trees and we paid her what we earned per bushel before deducting for food and rent.

Now, 5 years later, she has a custom-made 1/2 size bucket and a 14 foot ladder. She works 2 hours or more most days, picking to the same quality standards we use. She keeps her own tally. She pays about 1/2 of her own living expenses from her earnings when we're on the crew. She handles the ladder well, picks as much of the tops as she can.

How much to pay her and how much to expect her to work have been areas of confusion. It didn't seem right to continue to pay her, in effect, more per bushel than anyone else by not deducting any expenses. But if we deducted her full expenses, she wouldn't earn anything (yet). So we compromised. Earning money is not her main motivation but she likes to get paid and it seems good for her to have money to spend.

If she continues to increase her production she'll soon be able to pay her full expenses on the crew and have a good amount left over.

In many poor cultures the kids' earnings help support the whole family. We have to earn enough to live on the rest of the year. So it seems possible that as she gets older she might pay her expenses the rest of the year too, or contribute toward things we'll all use. We are not part of a tradition where the kids work a lot or contribute much to the family's survival. And we are not so close to the line that our survival depends upon her contributions. So when we're in doubt we take the more regular (like our own upbringing) course. I believe she's working a good amount of her own accord when we're on crews. She says she wants to get so she's paying all of her expenses on the crews.

I don't believe in compelling kids to study some subject they don't want to, but I do believe in insisting they do some work, in relation to their abilities and the needs of the family. Since they start with a compelling desire to do what the older family members do, this is no problem. Now sometimes she objects to some chores (It's boring, so-and-so doesn't have to). We insist. If you want to be warm, too, you have to carry firewood, too. She seems to see the justice of it and gives in pretty easily.

She helps with pruning, too. Has her own saw and with direction will sometimes prune a whole tree. But it is a harder skill to learn.

I think living on a work crew has been really good for our family. It helped me set limits and encouraged us to accept time away from each other, but still allowed us to be together when we needed it. Very young, A accepted that I had to work and learned to amuse herself very well. I think that kind of solitude is very important for everyone. She became less clinging and demanding and I learned I could choose which demands I would meet. Before crew life I felt I should give her everything she was asking for. As a result of working with her near I learned that she could accept it and *benefited* when I sometimes let her work it out herself. This led to both of us feeling our own individuality and made our close times closer. And brought my way of being with her into accord with T's way.

Spending a good part of every day outside is another important benefit. There are so many more things to do outside, such good things to choose from. She did not amuse herself outside in the cold part of the pruning season when she was 3 and younger. When it was too cold for her to keep herself warm in deep hard-to-move-in snow, we took turns not working to stay with her. But I remember days when it was snowy but fairly warm and she dug, went sliding, climbed trees, bounced on springy limbs *and found a deer antler.*

Her attitude toward work (and mine) have benefited from the work situation. Most of the crew, most of the time, are working with a willing attitude and there's a lot of enthusiasm that is catching. She works harder and longer with T, who enjoys pushing himself, than with me. She and I talk a lot and concentrate less. Everyone is paid by how much they do and there are a lot of other kinds of companionship fit in around the work. Some people return year after year and some don't, but one season is enough to get very close in a situation like that. Working with someone makes it easy. ...

Even though there's a gap of 7 1/2 years, A and E enjoy each other a lot and play together really well. A is an accomplished baby-sitter, patient, full of good ideas when something goes wrong, a playmate. We make sure they visit during the 8 months we're not on crews because they miss each other. A started baby-sitting on the pruning crew when E was 7 months old. One hour a day in exchange for lessons and a trip to the library

one morning a week with E's mother. That concept of the time with an adult being a privilege put lessons in a wholly different light. They made booklets about aspects of apple trees, like insects that live on them, and pruning. This last picking season it was recorder playing for 1/2 hour or so when she wanted it in exchange for one evening a week baby-sitting.

Another thing that's become a regular tradition is that M and A each spend a week with each family during each work season. She spends a week at home with them and M spends a week on the crew with the 3 of us. M is 2 years younger and the swap was a little hard for her at first but it gets better each time she does it.

How much time we've had for lessons has varied. It's less on crews than the rest of the year but they tend to be more regular since our life is more the same every day. We've done math and word games with me picking and her sitting on the grass under the tree. A favorite pre-reading game went with a book of all the mammals. I would name one. She'd guess what letter it started with and look it up alphabetically, verifying the word with picture, and then write it down. She also wrote lists of things around her. Another favorite was writing a word like *clover* or *dandelion* and then finding the other words inside the big one. I strongly believe in answering a question If I know the answer rather than saying, "You can figure that out," "Sound it out," etc. We were amazed to see that with no "drill" to speak of she got better from lesson to lesson. The lessons were *showing* us that she was learning, rather than *doing* the teaching. I have noticed more and learned a lot about the English language by being involved with her learning to read and write. It's been exciting and interesting, the hardest part learning to shut up, not to push. All along we've read aloud, gone for nature walks and discussed numbers. ...

Since I have been the bookkeeper on the last few crews her interest in math has grown sharply. She helps with the payroll and counts out everyone's final net pay. She seems to have a good solid concept of reading and math. She doesn't gobble them up in quantity but when she's interested in something she follows it through.

Here some of my insecurity about her comes cropping up. How does she compare with other kids her age? I can remember doing more at her age with school stuff (naturally) and being more interested in reading and music and kids' games. But I lived in a city neighborhood, went to school and had 2 sisters, and my parents were more intellectual.

All in all the hardest thing about not sending A to school is the unknown. Since school was such a big part of my life, I can't imagine what it would have been like without it (especially ages 13-18). It's hard to imagine what her life will be without it. Looking back—so far, so good, but looking ahead is one big question mark. Will she be equipped with what she needs to be independent of us? Will she have friends enough during adolescence? She doesn't ask to go to school, will she try it later?

I think we need to do more to help her have access to other parts of the world and help her follow through with more of her interest. Pottery, sewing, cooking, and French are some. These aren't my strong interests or skills and so it will be with friends that she pursues them. We'll continue sending her over to our potter friend's house. We've just found a French woman living not too far away. Maybe she'll tutor A in French.

I'd like for her to try out more extracurricular but school-type things. She was in a swimming class last summer. 4-H?

I sometimes feel unsure in how much to encourage or make things happen for her and how much to wait and let her initiate.

I wonder if we'll get hassled by the law sometime in the future....

A, M, and I went on bike trips last summer. I want to do that more and perhaps include more of the kids in the neighborhood.

We have recently found 2 families, 15 miles away in two different directions, who recently got school board approval for home instruction for their kids. We are meeting one day a week, bringing the kids together and getting to know each other.

REPLY

"...You wonder how A compares with other kids her age? My guess would be that she compares very well, probably smarter, more self-reliant, more serious, more considerate, more self-motivated, more independent, more honest, etc.

I think of the exclusive and expensive school where I first taught fifth grade. My students were the children of many of the leading business, professional, and academic families in this area. I would guess that the average family income must have been at least $40,000 a year, and the average IQ of the children over 120. I worked with three fifth grade classes there, sixty children, grew fond of them, came to know them well. But I felt very strongly that of that group of children not one in four, if even that many, had the kind of health of mind and spirit that I would have wanted for a child of my own. And I suspect they were better than their counterparts at that same school today, for these are harder and more anxious times for children to grow up in.

You say that as a kid her age you were more interested in reading. I was too. But in the school I just mentioned, I can't remember more than a handful of those super-bright children who ever read for fun. At 10 and 11, I read a great deal, on my own. By the time I was 13, away at boarding school, this had stopped. I had plenty of time at school, since I found the work easy, but I can't remember ever, not even once, reading a book that had not been assigned. Many of those that were assigned, I loved—Joseph Conrad, for instance. But I never read any of his other books, just for my own pleasure. Neither did anyone else. We would have been astonished if anyone had suggested it. (No one did.) Reading had become one of those (many) things that you did when, and because, and only because, *They* told you to.

With any luck at all, A should escape that way of looking at reading—and at life.

I suspect A is in any important sense a great deal smarter than most kids, and far more likely to adapt, and adapt well, to any new and difficult environment she might meet. See Jud Jerome's piece in GWS #1 about his daughter who quit school for years, and when she went back found herself way ahead of the kids who had stayed in.

Ever since he wrote, I've been meaning to do a follow-up piece for GWS about How People Get Smart. They get smart by giving constant attention and thought *to the concrete details of daily life,* by having to solve problems which are real and important, where getting a good answer makes a real difference, and where Life or Nature tells them quickly whether their answer is any good or not. The woods are such a place; so is the sea; so is any place where real, skilled work is being done—like the small farm where Jud's daughter worked, like your own orchards.

Like GWS for that matter. In putting out this magazine we do a great deal of what most people would call routine clerical work. But in doing this work we have hundreds of little, immediate problems to solve. Every time we put out a new issue we find ways to do the work a little better and more efficiently. There is nothing like it for sharpening wits.

Two summers ago I spent some time working with a small farmer in Nova Scotia, the neighbor and friend of the friends I was visiting. He had a large garden where he grew almost all his own vegetables, had about 20 acres in hay, raised Christmas trees. He also owned woodlots, from which he cut wood, for his own use and to sell. He was 72 years old, and did all this work himself, with the help of two horses. The skill, precision, judgment, and economy of effort he displayed in his daily work were a marvel to see. The friend I was visiting, a highly intelligent and educated man, no city slicker but a countryman himself, who had long raised much of his own food and killed, butchered, and cured or frozen much of his own meat, said with no false modesty at all that if he farmed for fifteen or twenty years he might—with plenty of luck and good advice—eventually learn to farm as well as this old neighbor.

No use trying to answer all those questions about the future. The future is a mystery and a gamble whether you send her to school or take her out. One thing we are sure of—school is a very destructive experience for most of the children who go through it. Keep her out of it if you can. As for access to the world, as she gets older she will want to see more of it, and will find ways to do it. If she needs your help she will ask for it.

Meanwhile, if your own life and the lives of other adults around you that she knows are rich and satisfying, that will be the best possible example and encouragement for her. And unlike most children, she will not only have seen but shared most of the best parts of your lives."

THE WORK ETHIC

Poster (advertising a savings bank) in the Boston subways:

> WON'T IT BE GREAT WHEN YOU FINALLY QUIT WORKING?

CHILDREN AND PLAY

Candy Mingins (R. D. 1, Albee Hill, Van Etten, NY 14889) wrote us two interesting letters earlier this year, saying in part:

"One of the strongest revelations I have experienced in my life was during the first September out of S-chool since age 5. I was 22, and had plodded along all the proper channels for seventeen years, without questions. I was a 'winner.' But for some reason I dared to *not* take my designated course (to be a social worker, or some such thing) and decided to travel. Life was real! Never had I experienced such exhilaration. And all those compartments—chemistry, math, psychology, philosophy—were real questions and answers about the world. They were living. For the first time for me, the world was whole. And there were so many things to do!

I eventually took a job as a Head Start T-eacher in a rural area where I wanted to live. I wanted to work with young children because it seemed like it would be an enjoyable job. And in many ways it was. ...I left teaching to try my hand at farming, building, and many other interesting activities. I returned four years later to two programs that I was more excited about: one, a cooperative nursery school organized and run by mothers, the other a home-based Head Start program where mother, child and I sit at the kitchen table once a week to engage in an hour's worth of activities. Both, I felt strongly, could work us away from the expert-worshipping that exists in education, because the premise was that parents are teachers and play is learning.

Three major stumbling blocks I have come to in this work are: 1) Most parents' goals are to prepare their children as best they can for S-chool, so that they can be winners. (Ed. note—or at least, not among the worst losers) 2) Although there was progress, most parents see learning as something you *get* in school... *given* by experts who know best. 3) Most parents are not willing to *get on the floor.* I mean this literally and figuratively. That's where these children are most of the time—and that's where you have to be willing to go if you want to really hear what they have to say. Also,

perhaps it is a matter of 'letting go,' or being interested or excited about the world, and getting your hands dirty exploring it. In your words, DOING. To too many people, teaching is lecturing—telling facts to deaf ears. In the realm of Doing, there is something very strange and unnatural about having a place and time solely for the purpose of teaching children.

When parents were active, and creative—DOING— in their own right, that's when things began to flow with the children. During one home-based session we made paper bag puppets. L, her mother, and her grandmother were there. It began with L's mother R instructing her how to make her puppet until I finally convinced R to join us and make one also. This she did, and it met with sarcasm and ridicule from grandma. Finally grandma was convinced to join us too, and when everyone relaxed and let their creativity flow a bit, we created some wonderful characters, and had a nice play.

I'm not going to continue this work after June. There are other things I would like to do, and I'm finding that early childhood education is getting too S-chooled... falling more and more into testing, labeling, ranking, and preparing children for S-chool, and in the process has lost much.

One other thing I'd like to share with you. A four-year-old friend explained to me how she was learning to read. She told me that she has a *Little Red Riding Hood* record and a *Little Red Riding Hood* book. She listens to the record and looks through the book at the same time, and sometimes, when the record goes slow, she can match the words. She was not only learning to read on her own, *but she was perfectly aware of how she was doing it.* (Ed. italics)

C and I are living examples of the effects of Education. I went obediently through 16 years of schooling, doing what I should (never more), and won gold medals for it. C, for the most part, went to school only when he wanted to. (He remembers first skipping school in kindergarten.) His father wasn't at home, and his mother wasn't around very much (going to college and working) and, too, there was an intellectual environment in the family—lots of reading—and plenty of trips and day excursions to botanical gardens, museums, etc.

In ninth grade, C avoided school 90 days out of 180—finding effective ways to beat the system without them realizing. He always did fine on tests and was always in the 'top' classes. Often, in Science, he was way ahead of the class curriculum.

At home, C would pick up his older sisters' Chemistry book and read it cover to cover. Most of his learning was done this way—on his own.

Also he began taking responsibility for maintenance of the house—using tools, puttering around. He put in a new bathroom when he was 13.

C's understanding of things, and how everything relates to everything else, is so much greater than mine.

Another amazing part of his learning (one I'd eventually like to write more about) is the game *Atlas*. The family didn't have much money, and did have plenty of German thriftiness—hence the children were not swamped with plastic toys and gadgets... They had to create their own play, so C and his brother and two sisters (all older) played this on-going game (invented mostly by his brother) for 8 years or more. It was a game of the World. Each child had tribes of people made from: toothpaste caps glued to marbles (the Lilliputians); Hi-Q game pieces (the Microscopians); used magic markers with toothpick swords and aluminum foil shields (the Sudanis); cooking oil bottles decorated with paper (the Criscoeans), etc. The tribes fought battles in the garden, conquered territories, kept maps and records, held art shows, had a newspaper, and had their own languages and money systems.

It was an ingenious invention of play, which the children created entirely by themselves, and which lasted through time, always encompassing new interests and ideas as the children grew."

———————

Tx for fine letters. When I visit (now rarely) classrooms of little children (whom I would rather watch playing in the Public Garden), I always find an out of the way spot and sit down on the floor. Soon children come up and start talking to me, showing me things, asking who I am, etc. Can I be sure that the same children might not have come up to me even if I had remained standing? No. But I think they would probably have waited a lot longer before doing it.

SPORTS

An article by Mark Sarner in the *Winnipeg Tribune*, about the physical unfitness of Canadian children (probably very like U.S. children in that respect), said, "Children are certainly not as active as they used to be. ...Increased organization and supervision of sports such as hockey have resulted in players spending much more time on the sidelines than they did when games were spontaneous and unstructured."

Well, they never were "unstructured." The difference is that they were structured by children, not adults. The further difference is that when children structure a game, they want to get the most activity for everyone, not just imitate an adult game. If some kind of rule in a truly child's game stops the action, someone will say after a while, "Aw, this is no fun," and they will change the rule. The adults who run "children's sports" rarely ever think of this.

I seldom see Little League baseball. When I do, what strikes me most of all is not the famous pressure from parents, *but that so little baseball is being played.* Most of the time, the pitcher is the biggest and strongest kid on the team, and blazes the ball past most of the little kids on the other team. There is very little hitting, base running, or fielding—so kids don't learn how to do

them. If children were running their own sports, those big, strong, precocious kids would be out playing with bigger and older kids, where they could get some good competition, and the little kids would be facing pitchers their own size, and there would be lots of action.

In another Peewee League game, the pitchers were so little that they couldn't get the ball over the plate. Some fool adult was calling balls and strikes, and most batters walked. A pitcher might walk seven, eight, ten batters in a row, while kids slowly walked around the bases and some other solemn adult kept score. Sensible kids running their own game would tell the pitcher to get up close enough to get the ball over, and would tell the batters to stay up there till they struck out or hit something. Bases on balls make sense for adult baseball, but not for little kids—no kids playing ball for fun would ever think up such a rule.

The best remark I ever heard about Little League was made by former Yankee catcher Yogi Berra. He went right to the heart of the matter, said that when he was a kid he used to count a day lost when he didn't get in about 150 at bats, but that he had seen Little League games lasting for hours in which kids only got up to bat three or four times—and then, like as not, walked or struck out.

One year, when I was teaching at the Colorado Rocky Mountain School, still very small and informal, we had about half an hour between lunch and the first afternoon class. In the spring a great game evolved to fill up this half hour. Boys and girls would rush out to a little odd-shaped pasture with a small irrigation ditch running right through it. Not having enough players to make teams, we played four-a-cat. In strict four-a-cat, four people bat in rotation, the other players are in the field. The batters hit and run the bases just as in a regular ball game. A batter stays on the batting team until s/he is put out. If s/he hits a fly ball which is caught, the fielder who caught the fly comes in and takes the batter's place. If the batter strikes out or grounds out, s/he goes out to left field, and the fielding team rotates positions—pitcher goes to the end of the batting rotation, former first base becomes pitcher, second base becomes first base, and so on.

One trouble with this game was that the best batters were almost never put out, so most players didn't get a chance to hit. Also, the teenage pitchers (who had lost a lot of their children's sense about games) were trying to strike out everyone, so the batters had to stand around for a long time waiting for a good pitch to hit. The first problem we solved with a rule—after three hits a batter had to go out into left field, just as if s/he had struck out or grounded out, the fielders rotated their positions, and the former pitcher would join the batters. The fielders naturally kept close track of the batters, and when a batter made a third hit, a great cry of "Rotate!" would go up.

The second problem I solved by making myself the permanent pitcher. What I was able to do, and did, was make every pitch *easy* to hit. One day, which I still fondly and proudly remember, batters hit—hard—fourteen consecutive pitches. Action and excitement for everyone! The sluggers would blast triples and home runs till their three hits were used up. The weak hitters got at least one turn at bat in each full rotation—in a half-hour game everyone would bat at least two or three times. And everyone got to play all the positions. No one kept score—there was no way to—though the sluggers probably remembered their home runs for a day or two. (My friend Hugh McKay hit one off me that *I* still remember.)

Wonderful games! It makes me feel good just to write about them.

A HOMEMADE FABLE

The author of "The World At Two" (GWS #6) told me that she had made up a story for her 2+ year-old boy, in which he was the hero, and all the other characters the animals on their small farm. He loved the story. Later she wrote it down and sent me a copy, saying, "You may find it a bit cute but a 5-year-old boy wondered—in a whisper—all the way through, 'Is it true?'"

When I asked her if I might print it in GWS, she said OK, but that she thought it didn't fit and that people might think I was crazy for putting it in. I think it does fit. Many of our readers have very young children who, like the 5-year-old, might just enjoy hearing the story. But it also makes a larger point, that children, whether in city or country, are more likely to be interested in stories in which they play a part, and which are full of things drawn from their everyday life. Parents, or other people who know the children well, are the ideal people to make up such stories. Even if they are not very polished, such stories are likely to be more interesting than most of the stories in books for little children.

A.S. Neill, at Summerhill, used to make up stories for the children there, in which they were the leading characters, chasing or being chased by various spies, crooks, and villains. And as many know, *Alice in Wonderland* was made up for the real child who was the Alice in the story. So, take a shot at making up stories for your children. As with everything else, as you do it you'll get better at it. Here is my friend's story:

PIG IN THE BED

On Tuesday last week a strange thing went on;
Jack came home early and his parents were gone.
He knew right away that something was up
When he took a look at his friend the pup.
(He was drinking a coke, taking sips as he spoke.)

"Hey Jack! Look out! Better step aside.
The horse and her colt are going for a ride!"

Jack turned around when the pickup truck
Made the sound that it makes when it's just starting up.

The horse put it in gear and sputtered past,
Then before she started going too fast,
She yelled, "Sorry, Jack, to be taking your car,
But it's been a long time since we've gone very far."

Jack stared, then he wondered, then he said, "O.K.,
But will you try to get back by the end of the day?"

He shrugged and went on down to the kitchen,
But when he got there it was full of his chickens!
"Just fixing a little midday treat.
We get awfully tired of old corn to eat,"
Said the hens as they mixed and blended and baked
Until they came up with banana spice cake.

Jack looked at that cake and said, "Best let them be.
I'll go in the living room and watch some T.V."
But there was the billy goat stretched out on the couch,
And when Jack tried to move him he started to grouch.
"I barely sit down for my favorite show
When along you come and tell me to go!"
The nanny and kids were there at his feet
Eating pretzels and popcorn, watching Sesame Street.
Finally Jack said, "O.K., I'll see you around,
But do you think you could please turn the volume down?"

Instead Jack went in to take a quick bath,
But once in the bathroom he started to laugh.
For there quite relaxed in the big bathtub
Was the fat mother cow, having a scrub.

Then Jack got mad. "What do you mean!
Using my tub! You're not very clean!"

"Just the point, Jack. It's been quite a spell
Since I've had a good bath. I was starting to smell."
Jack slammed the door. He was angry and red.
Let me think. I'd better stretch out on my bed.

He went into his bedroom and shut the door,
But stopped when he heard a loud ugly snore.
From his blankets a wiggly tail stuck out,
And on his pillow he saw a big pig snout!"
"A pig in my bed! In between clean sheets!"
The pig rolled over and begged, "Let me sleep.
There's no bed as soft as this in the barn.
I'm sure I'm not doing your bed any harm."

Poor Jack let out a sad long groan.

What can I do? My parents aren't home.
These animals have to go live in the barn.
This isn't a nut house. This is a farm!

Then his dog came along and said, "Listen, Jack,
You get rid of these animals before your parents
come back.
You've got to act tough. Play the part of the boss.
Else this house and your truck will be a big loss."

"I've got it!" said Jack, and he started to scream:
"Up in the barn there's chocolate ice cream!"
The chickens took wing, the pig climbed out of
bed.
The cow left the tub and the goats quickly fled.
Up the road the horse was parking the truck.
Jack ran to the freezer. "Whew! I'm in luck!"

He got out two gallons of chocolate ice.
"Plenty for everyone! As long as you're nice."
He passed it out fairly to all on the farm,
To the pig in the pig pen and the cow in the barn.
"Thank heavens you knew just what to do,"
Said the dog, passing his plate. "May I have some
too?"
"Certainly," said Jack. "But what will mom say
When she sees I ate two gallons of ice cream
today?"

TYPING

When I was in the Navy, I taught myself to touch type. It was one of the best things I ever did.

I had been typing, hunt-and-peck style, since I was 10, when my Grandmother had given me a child's typewriter (only capital letters). At 10, I wrote long stories, or beginnings of stories, on it. In college, I used it to type up class notes. I could type much faster than I could write. But in the Navy much of my typing was copying, where hunt-and-peck doesn't work so well. I had time on my hands (after the war ended), I knew how touch typing worked, and I decided to learn it. I made a diagram of the keyboard, stuck it on the wall over the typewriter, and began to do all my typing looking only at the diagram, not at the keys. I also invented exercises to strengthen the weaker fingers of my left hand, words like "waxed, crazed, sweater," or for the right hand, "monopoly, million," etc. In a few months I could touch type much faster than I could do hunt-and-peck. By the time I left the Navy I was a skilled typist.

No skill I have ever learned (except possibly reading itself) has been more useful to me. I used it all the time in my work with the World Federalists. A few years later, when I came to Boston and began teaching elementary school, I typed all the letters that later made up much of *How Children Fail* and *How Children Learn*. I typed the manuscripts of my first three books, and the rough drafts of all the rest. I usually compose at the typewriter. Except for the first two issues, and a few stories in the third, I have typed everything in GWS. Without this skill, I could not have done, or do, any of the work that has been so important to me.

It is not a hard thing to learn. All you need is a typewriter, a keyboard diagram (which usually comes with the machine, or which you can buy at a stationery store or make yourself), some time, and practice. It is certainly nothing you need go to a school or class to learn. All the young children I have known have been fascinated with typewriters, and Omar Moore found that children five years old or even younger could easily learn touch typing and liked to do it. With electrics, finger strength is no longer a problem.

If I had a child learning at home, I would certainly get a portable electric typewriter. If I could not afford a new one, I would look for a secondhand machine, of which there are many. If that was still too expensive, I would try (using the Directory) to share the cost with one or more unschooling families, with each family having the machine for a certain number of months.

When Omar Moore taught young children to touch type (as a way of teaching reading), he chose a different color for each typing finger. Thus index fingers and all the keys they hit) might be marked blue, second fingers green, ring fingers orange, little fingers red. He marked each child's fingers with a little dab of paint or magic marker on the fingernail. He made colored caps for the typewriter keys, so that the children had to look at the chart to know which key was which (a good trick in teaching yourself). He found they very quickly learned the keyboard, and that their fingers soon became agile.

I would guess that a child who had learned to type rapidly might have a lot of fun writing stories, certainly much more than if he had to go through the slow and painful business of writing them by hand. (Though parents of children learning at home might also do well to look into Italic handwriting, which was for a while at least taught in many British schools—it is easier to learn, quicker, and more stable, handsome, and legible.) Another advantage of being able to type neatly is that a child can write letters (asking questions, etc.) to adults without giving away the fact that he is a child, and so be reasonably sure of getting a courteous and sensible reply. It is, in short, another path into the adult world.

Many years ago I was talking to a 20-yr-old friend, then looking for a job. I asked if she could type. She said No. I said it might be useful to learn. She said, "I don't want to learn it, because if I know how to type then they'll just give me some job where I *have* to type." Well, I suppose that way of looking at things is OK if you are thinking only of "good" jobs and "bad" jobs, or about what "they" are going to make or let you do. But if you are thinking instead of finding meaningful *work*, then it makes sense to think of making yourself as useful as possible to the people who are already doing the work. Being a good typist is one way. Also, if you are a fast and accurate typist, you will almost always and everywhere be able to find some kind of money-making job, if that is what you need in order to do something else that you want.

I would also recommend very strongly to parents who would like to or are trying to take children out of school that if they do not know how to type, at least one of them learn. It will be much better if all letters to school people and/or other officials are typed. For one thing, it is faster, and there may be times when you will want to write very long letters and proposals. For another, it is easier to copy. Most important of all, it is impressive and even a little intimidating to the schools. This is important; it helps to give them the impression, without your actually ever having to say it, that if they get into a battle with you, they are going to lose.

A CASE LOST

GWS #3 reported briefly the case of Tom and Martha Lippitt, who were convicted by a Cleveland Juvenile Court Judge, Angelo Gagliardo, of the charge of civil neglect of their children, because they had taken them out of a church school and were teaching them at home. Recently, a friend has sent us a more complete summary of that case. It says, in part:

"On June 20, 1977, the South Euclid-Lyndhurst Board of Education took the Lippitts to Juvenile Court on a charge of civil neglect. (There is no such charge as civil neglect in Juvenile Court). Judge Angelo J. Gagliardo presided over this court. Mr. Lippitt was not permitted to consult with his attorney under penalty of contempt of court, witnesses were not permitted to testify on Lippitt's behalf, and the Judge continually lost his temper. Therefore, the record does not include the Lippitts' reasons for refusing to send their children to either a public or a private chartered school. These reasons include: Immoral teachers, bad textbooks, the teaching of Secular Humanism... In the chambers the judge also ordered the plaintiff to bring both criminal and civil actions against the Lippitts for the same charge, neglect of their children. The Lippitts lost the civil neglect case and were ordered to enroll their children in either a private or public chartered school.

On November 2, 1977, Tom was brought to trial on criminal neglect charges. Tom demanded a jury trial. By this action the case was taken out of Judge Gagliardo's hands. The evidence proving Alice and Amy Lippitt were receiving a 'proper' and 'necessary' education was so overwhelming that Judge Murray from Madison County ordered a directed verdict of not guilty and said:

> There has been no showing that what was taught, the methods or subjects, was any- thing other than what was proper and necessary... The testing of the children would indicate that they are at grade level and are being taught in accordance with religious

beliefs which their parents are in a position to determine.

On December 7, 1977 Judge Gagliardo stayed the proceedings against Martha Lippitt pending the outcome of the civil neglect appeal. ...The Lippitt case was then placed before a three-judge panel: Judges Stillman, Krenzler, and Wasserman. The judges denied Tom and Martha's appeal. The Lippitts had listed twelve errors in the appeal; however, the judges ad- dressed themselves to only six of the errors...it was not until about two months later that the last six errors of the appeals were ruled on, and then not completely, just as on the first ruling. The judges' opinion was mailed to the Lippitts without being journalized and Judge Gagliardo immediately issued a warrant for Mrs. Lippitt's arrest. The law allows a ten day rest period to present a Motion for Reconsideration.

On March 10, 1978 Martha Lippitt was physically dragged out of her own house and her children were taken... to the Metzenbaum Home for Children and deprived of any visitation rights. Martha was taken to jail and released on a $500 bond. ...The parents had to put up a $1000 guarantee that they would send their children permanently to the Heritage Christian School (a non-chartered school) or another school with an 'approved educational' program. A fine of $100 a day will be levied against the parents for every day they do not send the children to the Christian School. ...The Lippitts appealed their case to the Ohio Supreme Court, but the Court has refused to hear it. Next step? The United States Supreme Court."

WHAT CAN WE LEARN?

I have left out some other horrifying details about the way in which this judge runs his court, which would not have been out of place in Nazi Germany. If this report sent to me is accurate, the judge is an incompe- tent bully and tyrant. There are such judges in many jurisdictions, often appointed in return for political favors and support. The point is that where such judges exist, *lawyers know about them*. They also know whether or not they can be avoided, and how.

Any unschoolers thinking seriously about a court battle with the local schools would do well to find out in what court or courts, and before what judge or judges, they might have to appear. This is the kind of thing lawyers know. GWS has said in earlier issues that about school law itself we may know, and can surely find out, as much as or more than the lawyers. But about judges and courts, a good local lawyer probably knows a great deal more than we could find out. Of course, we should ask some questions, to find out what s/he knows. And it might be a good idea, if it can be done, to make a few visits to the courtrooms of whatever judges we might have to deal with.

One other thing. During the midst of these proceedings, Mrs. Lippitt left town with the children and went into hiding for two months. Understandable enough, but probably not a good idea. I have no objection to people getting their children out of school by whatever tricks they can think up. But if we are going into court, we had probably better do things by the book.

This is by no means the only such mistake the Lippitts made. Indeed, their whole way of bringing this issue before the court can be seen as practically a textbook example of How Not To Do It. Early in the proceedings, Mr. Lippitt said loudly and publicly, perhaps in court, perhaps outside, perhaps both—it makes little difference which, since his remarks (as he surely intended) received wide publicity—that the public schools were "cesspools." In saying this, he needlessly attacked the beliefs and prejudices of a judge who was probably conventional and certainly (as the record shows) highly inflammable. The moral might be, if you are going to have to deal with a judge with a bad temper, find out what things make him angry, and don't say them if you can avoid it. Beyond that, in attacking such a well-established and powerful institution as the public schools, Mr. Lippitt could only have been seen by the judge as inviting him to agree with him. Now there might, somewhere, be a judge or two who might secretly admit to a trusted friend that they thought the public schools were "cesspools." But no judge is going to be willing to make, or even risk appearing to make, such a statement from the bench. There is no use asking judges to agree that the public schools are bad places. They will not, and asking them to do so will only drive them into the position of having to defend the public schools, a position they might not otherwise have chosen to take.

To this mistake the Lippitts, or one of their supporters, added another. At some point in the proceedings she began to picket the courthouse, marching up and down angrily, loudly, and obscenely denouncing the judge. The judge, as might have been expected, overreacted, and (no doubt breaking the law in half a dozen different ways) had her dragged into his courtroom, handcuffed, and forced her to repeat what she had said outside. This bit of 1960's style courthouse drama may well have seriously prejudiced the Lippitts' chances of winning their appeal to a higher court. The courts, rightly enough, think of themselves as not only settling disputes and trying cases, but beyond that, as upholding an entire system of law and justice. They are likely to react very strongly and negatively when they feel that the system as such, the very dignity of the courts and the judges, are being attacked, as they clearly were in this case.

Now there might be times when defendants in court, like the famous Chicago Seven, might choose to use courtroom drama as a way of making certain kinds of political statements to the general public. That is OK if you have already decided that you cannot possibly get a favorable ruling from that court, and therefore, that your purpose in court is not to get a favorable ruling

but to do something else, whatever that might be. But if you want a court to rule in your favor, above all in a matter as radical as unschooling—far more radical than opposition to the Vietnam war—it would be wiser to treat judges and courts with all possible deference and courtesy.

The summary of the Appeals Court ruling says, in part:

"Among a number of assignments of error, Mr. Lippitt, citing *State v. Whisner...* argued that had he been criminally charged... the state would not have prevailed. In *Whisner* the court held that the elementary minimum standards of the state board of education should never be so comprehensive in scope and effect as to abrogate a citizen's fundamental right of religious freedom. In the present case, however, the court of appeals found that the minimum standards concerned do not present the same constitutional problem in that the South Euclid-Lyndhurst Board of Education merely expects the Lippitts to provide their children with an adequate education taught by a properly qualified teacher. Mrs. Lippitt does not possess an elementary teaching certificate, and without it her qualification to teach *was not demonstrated to the Juvenile Court.* (Ed. italics)

The court of appeals, therefore, held that the interest of the state in *insuring* (Ed. italics) that the teachers of its school-aged citizens are reasonably competent and knowledgeable must be protected and enhanced. The court further stated that a certification requirement does not in any way conflict with the Lippitts' stated beliefs, nor does it render instruction at home impossible since Mrs. Lippitt could perform tasks necessary to qualify herself for elementary school teaching. In the present case the Lippitts claimed religious reasons for failing to send their children to both a private and a public school, yet they failed to demonstrate how a public or private education would undermine their religious values. They did not establish that they belonged to an accepted religious group which offered a well-structured alternative to school education.

The court of appeals concluded, therefore, that the Lippitts' First Amendment rights had neither been impaired nor unduly burdened by the provisions of the compulsory education laws of Ohio. The judgment of the juvenile court was affirmed."

Without the full ruling of the appeals court, we cannot tell how fair or unfair that ruling may have been, nor what are the chances that it may be overruled in a higher court. Certainly the Lippitts were able to convince Judge Murray in criminal court that they were qualified to teach and were in fact doing as good a job as the schools. But this was not part of the record of the juvenile court trial, and it was this trial that was being appealed. I don't know whether the findings of Judge Murray were submitted as evidence to the appeals court, or whether they considered it, or if they did not, on what grounds, or whether their failure to consider it may be regarded by a still higher court as possible grounds for reversal. What little I have seen makes me suspect that the appeals court had grounds enough for taking the Lippitts' side, if they wished to do so, but that, perhaps for the reasons I suggested, they did not wish to do so.

It also looks as if Mr. Lippitt and his attorneys relied too heavily on *Whisner*, and did not prepare enough of a case to show that what they were doing at home was at least as good as what the schools were doing. It is not enough, in short, for parents to say what they don't like about the schools; they have to make a strong case that what they are doing will be better or at least no worse.

I underlined the word "insuring" in the summary of the appeals court ruling to make this point, that it may someday be wise or even necessary for an unschooling family to show in court that the requirement that teachers have a certificate does not insure competence at all, and indeed, that there is no evidence whatever to show that people with such certificates are, by whatever measure, more competent than those without them. It could probably also be shown that much of what people have to learn or do in order to get such certificates has only to do with the problems of teaching children in large groups, and is wholly irrelevant to the task of teaching at home.

Beyond that, it might still further be shown that much of what people have to study, and presumably, to appear to agree with, in order to pass education courses and receive a certificate, would and does indeed offend and outrage the religious convictions of a great many people. I have in mind here much of behaviorist psychology, which holds that such ideas as freedom, dignity, choice, and will are illusions and that we are basically like rats, responding automatically to changes in our environment. Many state courts might be ready to rule, if asked, that no one should be required to believe, or pretend to believe, or even to study, such ideas, in order to have the right to teach, whether at school or at home.

And we could add still further that to say to parents who are deeply distressed by things being said or done to their children in school that all they have to do is spend three years of time and $7500+ of money—assuming that there is a school of education near them and that they can get into it—in order to get the teaching certificate that will allow them to teach their own children, is hardly a reasonable remedy for what many people will feel are sharp and immediate wrongs.

A CASE WON

From *The New York Times,* Jan. 26, 1979:

An estimated 5,000 Christian fundamentalist schools that have sprung up in the past few years are claiming the right to keep the state completely out of their affairs... They do not want to be told what textbooks to use, what educational policies to adopt or even that they must be licensed....

Representatives of 20 non-accredited Christian schools in Kentucky fought a 1977 ruling by the State Board of Education that parents who used such schools were liable to prosecution and their children subject to being listed as "habitual truants." They hired William B. Ball of Harrisburg, PA, a lawyer who is a frequent defender of religious freedom.

At least for the moment, they have won. Despite powerful opposition from many political leaders, a Kentucky Circuit Court Judge, Henry Meigs, ruled on Oct. 3 that the state had no right to make its regulations mandatory. Judge Meigs said the board must refrain from limiting the schools' choice of textbooks and from forcing teachers to be certified. The state has appealed...

———

I am trying to get a copy of Judge Meigs' ruling, in which, I have been told, he made a point that as far as I know has not been made in any previous court ruling on compulsory education. He said that no one has been able to show that teachers with certificates are any better at teaching than those without them. This is of course true, and a very good point for unschoolers to make. But this is the first time that a judge has said it. Perhaps we now can get some other judges to say it.

If Judge Meigs' ruling stands, it may be much easier for parents, certainly in Kentucky and probably in many other states, to get their children out of school by calling their own home a Christian school. There is no reason, after all, why the word "Christian" could not just as easily be applied to schools which preach and practice tolerance, brotherhood, kindness, generosity, and love, as to schools which preach and practice (as some at least do) intolerance, racism, cruelty, greed, and hate.

THE RULING

FRANKLIN CIRCUIT COURT
CIVIL ACTION NO. 88314
DIVISION 1

Filed Oct. 4, 1978

Reverend C.C. Hinton, Jr. et al (Plaintiffs) vs. Kentucky State Board of Education, et al (Defendants)

It would not be difficult to find in the record of this case abundant support for a conclusion that the regulatory scheme fashioned by the State Board, and sought by it to be imposed upon these plaintiff schools under the dubious authority of "approval" (KRS 156.160) is far beyond Constitutional limits of legislative delegation. ...

[Plaintiffs'] incontrovertible proof shows—and the demeanor of the witnesses confirms—irreconcilable philosophical differences between their educational concepts, notions of textbook and curriculum content and teacher qualification. These differences are not fanciful or arbitrary, but very real and substantial, having a foundation in firmly held religious belief. ... Expert testimony in this case certainly established that there is not the slightest connection between teacher certification and enhanced educational quality in State schools ...

The State is unable to demonstrate that its regulatory scheme applied to the public schools has any reasonable relationship to the supposed objective of advancing educational quality ... Plaintiffs, on the other hand, have shown that without benefit of the State's ministrations their educational product is at least equal to if not somewhat better than that of the public schools, in pure secular competence.

The rights of the plaintiffs named herein should be declared in accordance with the reasons herein set forth, and upon the Findings of Fact and Conclusions of Law annexed hereto; action and threatened action of the State against these plaintiffs or any of them heretofore enjoined temporarily, is now hereby enjoined (i.e., forbidden—Ed.) permanently, all at defendants' costs.

Given under my hand this 4th day of October 1978.
Henry Meigs
Judge, Franklin Circuit Court.

I hope in the near future to be able to obtain a copy of Judge Meigs' Findings of Fact and Conclusions of Law. I hope also to learn more about the specific kind of expert testimony that established that there is no connection between teacher certification and other state regulations, and educational quality. Meanwhile, I should think that unschoolers, either in their home teaching proposals to schools or, if they are in a legal contest, in their briefs, could make good use of these words of Judge Meigs.

(Note: the Kentucky State Board of Education is appealing this ruling to the State Supreme Court, and has said that if it loses there it will appeal to the U.S. Supreme Court. This will not, of course, be a test of compulsory schooling as such, but only of the right of the State to apply certain standards and requirements to private religious schools.)

LEGAL PROCEDURES

At the risk of explaining the obvious, a word on legal procedure. If someone—a private citizen, a corporation, or a government agency or agent, is doing or trying to do something to you that you think is against the law and violates your legal rights, you can appeal to the courts for what is called "injunctive relief." That is, you can ask the court to "enjoin," i.e., forbid that private citizen, corporation, government agent, or whatever, from doing to you whatever they have been doing. Such a statement from the court, saying in effect, "Stop doing that," is called an injunction.

In two or three places in the country the schools and their attorneys have tried a new, and under the circumstances, perfectly sensible, legal trick. Fearing that if they charge the parents with truancy they, the State, will bear the burden of showing beyond reasonable doubt, as in the Sessions case, that the parents' proposed teaching plan is not adequate or equivalent, they have instead charged the children themselves with truancy, thus putting the matter into Juvenile Court, where the ordinary rules and safeguards of due process do not apply, and where, as in the Lippitt case, the parents may not be allowed to present any evidence to show that their home teaching is in fact adequate.

My guess, which I will check out with those more experienced, is that if and when the schools do this, the best counter move by the parents would be to ask for injunctive relief, i.e. to sue the schools in regular court for attempting to deny them the company and custody of their children without due process. My guess, again, is that many or most courts would enjoin the Juvenile Court from having anything further to do with the matter. The schools could then decide either to charge the parents with truancy in a regular court or to drop the matter and let them teach their children at home.

ASK YOUR LIBRARY

A public library recently subscribed to GWS, saying that they were doing so at the request of one of their (what's the word?) users/subscribers/members.

Quite often libraries will order books and/or publications on request. Readers might ask any libraries near them to subscribe to GWS. More people will learn about unschooling—and the money will help GWS. Thanks.

A TEACHER WRITES

L.M. has written us from N.C., saying, in part:

As a former school teacher, a part-time teacher of my own children, and as a present day violin teacher, I agree with your general ideas. S-chools are inhumane, in their continual testing, ranking, and grading of children and in their rigid rules, and especially in their perpetual, secret, damaging record keeping ...

Reading always seemed easy to teach, a matter of a few months' instruction. My oldest daughter learned to print words and copy letters from her brother's old alphabet blocks. I told her the sounds, got her to practice writing words a bit, maybe a half-hour a day. In a few months she could read her brother's 6th grade books. I did not care about that. What I liked was the wide reading she did by choice at the age of 5, and the imaginative stories she wrote. Nobody told her to write or gave her gold stars. Whatever satisfaction there is about teaching for me is to see a child using reading, writing or violin playing for her own reasons.

The younger daughter also learned to read—supposedly impossible because her IQ was tested at 40 or so! She also learned from those old blocks.

About the peculiar Learning Disability theory that these children see letters upside down, etc. how can this be? The test chart for illiterates looks like this:

and the person tested points out the direction of the figures, thus:

How could such a test mean anything if 1/3 of the population sees letters every which way? This letter is running longer than intended. Please let me know if you find any of it of use. (Ed. note—indeed we do!)

I write a great deal, keep a diary, etc. So much involves the youngest daughter, and I really do not want publicity for her. She is a pleasant young person, spends a lot of time reading, and is not like the people usually described as retarded. ... She is doing about 100 times as well as all the dismal predictions which were made when she was 4 years old. I suppose she is the reason I become so unhappy about all this ranking and classifying of young children, even when it is done by doctors, as in her case. It is even worse when done by S-chools, as you call them."

———————

S-chools refers to a distinction I made, in *Instead of Education*, between S-chools and s-chools. S-chools are places where people have to go, either because the law tells them to, or because they believe (with some reason) that without the tickets they can only get from schools they can't get decent work. What I call s-chools, on the other hand, are places like cooking schools, ski schools, schools of dance or martial arts, craft schools, etc. which, since they are not compulsory, and since they don't give credits, diplomas, etc., people only go to because they want to.

———————

From a later letter:

"In the 1940s I taught in a Nebraska country school. We were required to teach the 'Dick and Jane' reading texts. But actually I used some little old-fashioned primers which were at the back of the school book cupboard. I can no longer recall title, author, or

publisher, but the books appealed to young children. Each page showed a picture illustrating a letter sound, such as a baby reaching for an apple and making the first sound of the word. Also, there were a few other short words containing the sound. I would show and at first read the words to the child, and soon he or she would grasp the two ideas that letters meant sounds and that words are written and sounded from left to right.

In two or three months, without any long drawn out amount of drill, the children were able to read whatever appealed to them. Little children do want to read, and they do not need 500 rules. As you say, 2 principles will suffice.

The old-fashioned school was not so bad. The children had more freedom than they do now. We had fun, did quite a lot of singing, and I used to read aloud to them quite a bit. Perhaps because these farm children were needed at home to do household and farm chores, they were usually responsible youngsters.

Regarding attention span of young children, on Sunday I had a good time watching little J who is 9 months old, cheerful and busy. He crawls about on hands and knees, stands up by chairs. He likes doors, opening and closing them. He pushed a bedroom door almost shut and pulled it open over and over, very carefully so it would not latch. He knew if it did latch, then he could not get it open. He pays attention to his projects for ten minutes or longer. As you have observed, little children are good learners without any teacher at all."

LEARNING EXCHANGES

A friend wrote to say that many of the Learning Exchanges that started in the past few years have closed because of lack of money. I replied in part:

"One reason, maybe the main reason they got in trouble is that they almost instantly got too fancy. They missed Illich's point about being passive networks, and began to think of themselves as active organizations that had to plan and promote something. When Illich spoke of a card file, he meant literally just that, not programs, meetings, newsletters.

Here's a model. To the Learning Exchange in Anytown, Ms Smith sends a letter and a return postcard. In the letter she says, (for example), "I want to learn something about Home Appliance Repair." The Exchange files her card under Home Appliance Repair (or however it wants to index it). One day Ms Brown sends in a card saying that she knows something about repairing appliances that she is willing to share. The Exchange looks under Home Appliance Repair in its files, takes out Ms Smith's card (and any others), puts down Ms Brown's name and address, and mails them back to Ms Smith and others who sent them in. They can then get in touch with Ms Brown and work out some sort of plan. But that isn't the Exchange's business. Its work is done when it sends back those cards.

If Ms Smith is happy with what she can learn from Ms Brown, fine. If not, and she wants to look for more information, she sends a new letter and card and repeats the process. If she also wants to find out about something else, say Chinese Cooking, she sends in another letter and card for that. Ms Brown's card stays in the "Have Information" half of the file. Once every year or two—maybe, if it feels like it—the Exchange prints up, *cheaply*, a list of the people in its "Have Information" file, and maybe gives it away, maybe sells it for $1 or so, more if it is fairly large.

How do people hear of it? Perhaps a few announcements on bulletin boards. People tell other people. A slow process? No doubt. But what's the big hurry? Being in a big hurry is why all those Learning Exchanges have had to fold up.

Hard to see anything here that would cost $10,000+ a year, need government grants, etc. No office, no rent, no phone, nothing but—literally—two card files and a mailing address, which might best be a post office box number. If people write in asking how to use the learning exchange, a form postcard could tell them that."

VOLUNTEERS NEEDED

We need three kinds of volunteer help.

1) People who live in or near Boston who, either during weekdays or on weekends could do some work in the office. Some of this work might involve typing, some not.

2) People who live in or near Boston who could do typing work for us at home.

3) People in other parts of the country who would be willing to help us by writing, or better yet telephoning, some of the 8000 or so people who wrote to us after the Donahue show, or perhaps people whose subscriptions have expired and who have not yet renewed them. People tend to be busy and forgetful, and need to be reminded now and then to do what they really mean to do. We can do some of this reminding from the office, but by no means all.

We are probably going to depend to some extent on such volunteer help for a long time to come. For anything you may be able to do, we will be grateful.

NEW BOOKS ON OUR LIST

We have added three books to the list that we sell here.

The first is my own newest book, *Never Too Late* ($9 + 30¢ post.). This is the story of how, in spite of a non-musical background, I became interested in music, and eventually decided to learn first the flute and later the cello, and the trials, problems, dangers, discoveries, and joys of that experience. It is a book about music, about

finding out what one wants most, about starting something new, about struggling and coping with fear, about learning, about teaching, and probably about some other things as well. It was fun to write, and I think will be fun to read.

The second is *Gnomes* ($13.50 + 60¢ post.). This is a charming, funny beautifully written and illustrated "scientific study" of gnomes, for children of any age, but not just for children. A wonderful book to read aloud. For fuller description, see GWS #3.

The third is a new book by Herbert Kohl, *Growing With Your Child* ($8 + 30¢ post.). The jacket describes it well:

"This is a book on child-raising unlike any other, a book that speaks in direct practical terms of the parents we wish we were and the parents we hope to become. It confronts the basic questions that underlie the daily issues of bedtimes and manners, schoolwork and messy rooms, broken toys and 'talking back,' questions that parents, in one way or another, find themselves asking over and over again: How can I help my child be strong in a world that saps strength? ... How can I pass on values to my children when no one seems to agree on what's right or wrong?"

What is important and different about this book is that it is not simply a book of tricks or techniques, unlike too many others one might name. There are tricks and techniques in it, many of them, things to say, things to do. But these tricks are useful and practical because they arise out of the ways in which Kohl thinks and feels about his children, and himself, and the world around them. He is not *just* a clever trickster, but a humane and intelligent person and parent who thinks about the meanings of things. I know of no book to compare with it. Unlike the trick books, it could make a real difference in the way we see and live with children.

OLD FAVORITE

Most GWS readers have probably seen the *National Geographic Magazine,* or know what it is. For any who may not, it is a monthly magazine, crammed full of beautiful color photographs, about all parts of the earth—land, air, sea, under the sea. The contents of the Sept. 1978 issue give a rough idea: "Solo to the Pole," about the first person to reach the North Pole alone; "Syria Tests a New Stability"; "Undersea Wonders of the Galapagos"; "A Most Uncommon Town," about outstanding modern buildings in Columbus, Indiana; "The Joy of Pigs"; "New Mexico's Mountains of Mystery." Another recent issue had an article about the two men who first crossed the Atlantic in a balloon. And so on.

Over the years I have seen the *National Geographic* often at the homes of friends. This last year I subscribed for the first time, to report on it for GWS. It was always good, but has become much better. There is a wider range of stories, and the photography, which used to tend to look like the kind of photos tourists take, has become very dramatic and beautiful. The writing is clear and easy for children. A wonderful magazine.

You can buy the magazine without joining the National Geographic Society, but since this costs $11 a year, while membership, which includes the magazine, costs only $9.50/yr (U.S.), $12/yr. (Canada), $13.80 elsewhere (U.S.$), it makes more sense to become a member. People with little money can share a subscription with others. This is a magazine all children should have a chance to see. (Write The Sec'y, Nat'l Geographic Society, P.O. Box 2895, Washington DC 20013)

The *National Geographic* also publishes many beautiful and interesting books for children (and others). Also maps, including a map of the oceans showing all the deepest points, which is something that fascinated me as a kid and still does.

Editor—John Holt
Managing Editor—Peg Durkee

GROWING WITHOUT SCHOOLING

Issue #9

May, 1979

Since GWS #8 went to press, many things have happened. Letters keep coming in from the Donahue show, probably by now about 9,000, though we've stopped keeping a daily count.

Newsweek had a full page story about unschooling in their 4/16/79 issue. The monthly magazine *Mother Jones* had a feature article in their 4/79 issue. The Special Education Supplement to *The New York Times* of 4/22 had a full page story about the Sessions family. By the time you read this, many of you will have seen the May 3 CBS-TV show "Magazine," on unschooling. The ABC-TV show "20-20" is doing a program on unschooling, and (as I write) will be taping us here in the office fairly soon. I don't know when that will be aired.

In addition, I was on two TV talk shows here in Boston, one with Peter Perchemlides. I have one scheduled for Washington D.C. (WDVM—Ch. 9, 10–11 AM, May 15). Have also done a number of phone interviews with radio stations. Since the *Newsweek* article came out I don't think there's been a day when some TV or radio station, newspaper, or magazine hasn't called to ask questions.

For this issue we have about 1700 subscribers, almost three times what we had in November (but a long way short of the 7,000 or so we will probably need to be completely self-supporting). And just look at the Directory! (By the way, if you change your address, and are in the Directory, please remind us of that, so we'll change it in both places.)

Ivan Illich writes that in Germany, for the first time (as far as anyone knows) a family has unschooled their children. He sent me a news clip about it (in German, of course—can anyone translate it?)

Still more news in later stories.

COMING LECTURES

I will be speaking at the Alternative Schools Workshop and Conference of the School of Education, Indiana Univ., Bloomington IN 47401, from 3-6 PM, Sat. June 23, and also at another smaller meeting, probably earlier the same day. If any readers are near there, it might be a nice time for us to meet.

Director of the conference is Thomas B. Gregory, Assoc. Prof. at the School of Ed. (Tel 812-337-3015 or 2157). Perhaps I'll see some of you there.

I will also be speaking on Monday Sept. 24 at Western Maryland College in Westminster MD. More details on that in a later GWS.

Theo Giesy has spoken of trying to arrange a meeting for me in the Northern Va. – D.C. area sometime in mid or late May. No definite plan yet, but those interested might get in touch with her.

GOOD NEWS

In the last month four unschooling families have won favorable court rulings, two in Va., one in Mass., one in Iowa—and I have heard a report, not yet confirmed, about still another favorable ruling in Va.

In Norfolk, VA, the Giesy family, who had been teaching their children at home (and other places) for some time while trying to get the approval of the local schools, finally registered their own home as a school. The local Superintendent responded by taking them to court. The judge, in a 25 minute statement, ruled in favor of the Giesys. The Giesys received much local publicity, on the whole favorable. Theo Geisy is sending me a copy of the judge's ruling; I hope to print some of it in the next GWS.

In King George, VA, the O'Toole family (whom I had just met at a conference in MD), not liking what was happening to one of their children in school, had taken the child out. The schools took them to juvenile court (hence Mr. O'Toole's Letter to the Editor, printed elsewhere in this issue), which ruled in favor of the family.

In Somerset, Mass., Frank and Maureen Turano (he a police officer, she a former teacher) took their children out of school. Though Mrs. Turano, having been a teacher, was obviously competent by state standards to teach her children, the schools took them to court. Mr. Turano researched the law very thoroughly, reading state and federal rulings on this matter going all the way back to 1900. Like Joseph Palmer in Minn., he defended himself in court, and so strongly and ably—making at least one Constitutional point that I have not heard before, and about which we will write more—that the juvenile court judge ruled in his favor.

The Omaha World Herald of March 20, 1979, reported:

Bedford, Iowa—A Lenox, Iowa, couple [Robert and Ruth Cochran] can teach their two children in their home, a Taylor County Magistrate Court jury decided Monday...

Richard Jones, Taylor County attorney representing the State of Iowa in the case, said no appeal is planned.

For two years, the Cochran's children—Lillian, 14, and Clifford, 16—have been enrolled in a home teaching program of the Christian Liberty Education System of Prospect Heights, Ill. The Rev. Paul Lindstrom of the Church of Christian Liberty, an independent, nondenominational church that sponsors the correspondence-class program, said he believed the state was violating the couple's right to religious freedom and separation of church and state, guaranteed under the First and 14th Amendments of the U.S.

Constitution. …

The Christian Liberty Academy provided the Cochrans with legal counsel for the trial, [Rev. Lindstrom] said.

———————————

Two Mass. families, one of them writing me for the first time, have told me about the agreements which they have reached with their local schools, allowing them to teach their children at home. In the case of one of these families, the schools have agreed to allow the child to go to school *part time,* to take part in special activities that she likes, including athletics. This is the first such arrangement I have heard of. I hope to be able to publish more, perhaps full details, in the next GWS.

REMINDER

The things that schools and school people say, write, and do (or try to do) to unschoolers often make me so angry that I have to remind myself of a wise old French saying:

Cet animal
     est tres méchant;
Quand on l'attaque,
     il se défend!

Which means (for those who may not know French):

This animal
     is very vicious;
When you attack him,
     he defends himself!

School people feel that they are under attack by unschoolers, and indeed they are. No doubt they greatly overestimate the danger. But the attack is real. The schools have great power over the lives of many people, and most unschoolers would be glad to cut down or take away that power if we could. We mustn't be too surprised if they fight back in whatever ways they can.

A DISCOVERY

…I can't resist the temptation to share some of E's (aged 3) discoveries. She had shown some interest in letters and words about four months ago. She asked me to write the names of some friends, so that she could see the letters. We also wrote the names of objects on masking tape and taped them up around the house, like labels. This game was exciting for her for a short time, but then she lost interest. She said little about words for several months, except for an occasional reading of an alphabet book she had received for Christmas.

About six weeks ago, while we were driving by a Texaco station, she looked up at the big sign and hollered, "Hey! There's an E and an A, just like in my name!" Just how the wheels had been turning inside her head over the months mystifies me. But when she was ready her discovery of letters manifested itself in a really thrilling moment.

Now she spends time almost daily practicing E's and A's, and looks over any printed material she can find for any of the letters she knows. Sometimes she asks me to write things for her. This experience reinforces for me my belief that to put all children of an age together to learn the same thing at the same time in the same way is not only a criminal waste of time and an open door to frustration, but it simply doesn't work.

CHILD ARTIST

A father writes:

"…We have one of the happy stories about un-schooling. Before M was born we had decided not to send her to school. We moved to the country thinking it would be easier there. Now I realize it might sometimes be more difficult.

We were lucky. The teacher and school board of our local school, where I am janitor, have been tolerant and helpful. The teacher is one of the good ones. M goes once a week on a day of her choosing. Any more than once a week, she thinks, would be awful. One defense that we have thought might help if we are given any trouble about not going to school is that she is bilingual and does learning in her other language at home (There are laws protecting bilingualism in CA schools). M's mother is Japanese.

M began to draw when she was 6 months old. Everything she did was treated as important art. By the time she was one year old she could draw better than anyone around her. Knowing that she could do something better than anyone, even better than the ever-competent giants around her, emboldened her strokes. In other areas it gave her the confidence to try something difficult, then to continue until she could do it well.

At one year of age she was given an easel and some tempera paints. On her second birthday she got nontoxic acrylics, the medium she has preferred since. She enjoyed painting so much that she began calling herself an artist.

We became curious about other children artists so we checked out the children's art scene in San Francisco where we were then living. We made the surprising discovery that M is a child artist who does not paint children's art. Her work would look absurdly out of place in a show of children's art. Especially so since she began using acrylics because it is always assumed that children's art should be done with water colors.

For obvious reasons acrylics are easier to use than poster paints or tempera but they cost more. I know people who make 5 or 6 times my subsistence wage who tell me they can't afford acrylics for their children. What this really means is that they think children can't do anything worth that much.

Probing deeper in this direction via an understanding of adultism might begin to explain what I mean when I say that much of what is known as children's art is an adult invention.

In all the contacts we have had with the children's art establishments in San Francisco and Tokyo we have had nothing but unpleasant experiences. They are amazed but they are even more skeptical. I think they are hoping she'll turn out to be the 40-year-old midget in one of your books. (Ed.—this refers to an episode in *Escape From Childhood*) Finally we know they are the enemy. We avoid them, scorn their nonsense books on children's art ("Children will generally not be ready to paint before they are 5 years old"), frown back at the saved missionary smiles they are in the habit of turning on their flock. When they used to say M's work was very good for her age I asked them if they would say Picasso's erotic drawings, done in his latter years, were good for his age.

It is recognized that children have their original imagination destroyed in the socializing process and that as adult artists they must struggle to regain it if they are to create an original vision. There must be some way for people to grow up without losing this although it rarely happens. The most obvious thing to do is to stay out of school and maybe to prevent their exposure to phony children's art. One indication of what might have happened to M if she had been forced to go to school full time is that when she draws at school her drawings are stiff and uninteresting. They are like children's drawings are supposed to be, cute and easy to patronize. She also prints her signature on them like the other children do. She has always signed her name in cursive and has used nothing but cursive at home since she learned it when she was 4 years old. She's 7 now.

M's conversations about what was going on in the paintings while she was doing them were so interesting that I decided when she was 4 years old to get some of her old paintings out to talk about them with her. She enjoyed seeing her treasures again. About the same thing she said originally was repeated but more concisely. She called them poems. During her fifth year she began writing her poems and stories by herself. One of her 4-year-old poems about a painting described what she imagined she did when she was wandering around the world with us five years before she was born: 'When I was in Mama's stomach it was very dark so sometimes I wanted to get out. From a secret door I was looking out of Mama's stomach through her navel. Everywhere Mama went I was watching from my secret door. Each time I looked out she came to a new town. I saw the whole world. That's the place I was born.' "

With his letter the father sent me some reproductions of M's early work, five paintings done between the ages of 26 and 38 months. They were printed in Japan, perhaps by some museum, in connection with a show on children's art. I am guessing, but they look like the postcards of paintings that one can buy in museums. The paintings themselves are stunning. Three of them would stop you dead in your tracks if you saw them in an exhibition of "adult" art. The colors, the shapes, the drawing, the design, the underlaying idea of the paintings, are extraordinary. I wish GWS was rich enough to reproduce them.

I am ready to believe that M is an exceptionally talented child. But that is what I felt when I first heard 4-6-year-old children, students of Suzuki in Japan, playing difficult music of Bach, Vivaldi, etc. in perfect time and tune. Perhaps other children might do work of equal beauty and power if their talents were taken seriously and given scope.

SCIENTISTS

From latest issue of *Outlook* (see GWS # 1—new address, Mountain View Publishing Co., 2929 6th St., Boulder, CO 80302, $8.50/yr.)

"…A three-year-old has moved into a new house and has played in the sunshine on the new roof. He goes downstairs to supper and when he comes back steps into a changed and darkened world. With a wondering glance he says, 'The big shadow is all around.' Another three-year-old sees a thin cloud float across the moon. She watches intently, then says to herself, 'Like ice, like ice.' "

REQUIEM

About eight years ago a mother wrote me some very interesting letters about her daughter (then about 17). She told me about a chant that the girl, when two years and nine months old, had made up one day while swinging on the swing, and seeing something disappear with a crunch into the mouth of her cat. (If either mother or daughter read this, I hope they will write.) The chant went like this:

Oh, we went downtown. . .
Downtown my mother
and Mary Jean went.
We saw some pretty turtles,
some pretty little turtles.
Yes, we did. O yes we did!
Pretty, pretty little turtles. . .
They wiggled and wiggled,
They wiggled their heads,
They wiggled their legs,
And their tails they wiggled, wiggled, wiggled . . O!

My mother buyed me
Two little turtles
Two little turtles and
One little turtle made
The other little turtle
Not lonesome . . O!
He was s'posed to make him
Not lonesome . . O!

Did he make him not lonesome? NO!
He climb out, out. .
He fall on the ground . . O!
Oh, oh, oh, OH!
He climb out
Over and over AGAIN!
I just can hardly believe it!

I look
And I look
On the ground . .
I find that little turtle, O!
I can hardly believe it!

But he wiggle and he climb!
He fall out on the table, O!
That ignorant little turtle, O!
And the Poco-cat
Ate him all UP!

Bad, bad Poco!
That turtle scratch him,
He scratch him, that Poco
In the *stomach*!
I *think!*
I think he scratch Poco
In the stomach!
My *mother* will buy me
Another little turtle. Maybe,
For the GOOD little turtle to
    play with.
Poor, ignorant little turtle!
Oh, Oh, Ohhhhh. . . .

(Turned out later the cat *hadn't* eaten the turtle, who was found under the child's bed.)

SMOKESCREEN

The mother who wrote, "Time of Our Own" (GWS # 5) wrote later that (as so often happens) neighbors reported to school authorities that her children were not in school. I asked how that had all worked out. She replied:

"No excitement, which is good news. After being turned in last winter (we got out of that one because the oldest wasn't yet at the compulsory age in this state) we decided to do a little smokescreening, so enrolled them at a private school, and they started school in September like everyone else, as visibly and audibly as we could manage—new clothes, lunch boxes, much talking about it with neighbors, etc. Then we quietly pulled them out. We don't do anything foolish, like let them wander all over the neighborhood or go to town in the middle of the day, and so far, so good.

I think the private school tactic was good, not only for the obvious reason, but because it offers us a broader margin of safety with the neighbors' suspicions. Holidays, 'early dismissals,' even 'special programs' are all unknown to the neighborhood—much more is 'legitimate' before it becomes reason for suspicion—like being seen not in school at an odd time.

The other day I heard this little tidbit on the radio, one of those 'human interest' news spots:

A mother had parked her car on a steep hill, leaving a baby and a 5-year-old inside while she ran a quick errand. Suddenly she saw the car rolling down the hill. An 11-year-old boy, playing nearby, also saw the car, dashed across the street, ran along side and reached through the window. He managed to turn the wheel enough to get the car off the street, where it rolled a little way and then stopped, occupants unhurt. Had it continued to roll down the street it would have almost certainly have struck another car or crashed into a building at the foot of the hill.

In talking to police officers later the boy's mother explained that her son had been home that day because he had been *suspended from school*, and she hoped the incident would enable him to *start feeling better about himself again.*

And I wonder—how can we as a society allow such hurt and damage to be done to a child that it takes such an exhibit of incredibly quick thinking and selfless courage to even begin to *think* about repairing the hurt?

D, now 6, stood at the edge of the garden the other day, cheeks pink and eyes round, her yellow hair jeweled with mist, and asked, in a voice to match that delicate fragileness, "Mommy, do birds have birthdays?"

With what fragile and tentative fingers of curiosity do children make friends with the world! And with what clumsy thoughtless responses do we punish and inhibit such adventuring imaginations, pushing them back inside the straight-walled edges of our adult perceptions. I try to imagine what response her question would have met in a first grade classroom, and I can only shudder...."

EINSTEIN'S QUESTIONS

Someone (I once read somewhere) asked Einstein how he had got started on the train of thought that led to the Theory of Relativity. He said that it had begun with two questions that he had asked himself, and couldn't stop wondering about. One was, "What does it really mean to say that two things happen at the same time?" The other was, "If I were riding through space on the front of a beam of light, what would I see, how would things look?"

Most people, I would guess, would call the first question obvious and the second one silly. It would be a rare science class indeed in which either question would be taken seriously, or Einstein encouraged in his efforts to answer them. And indeed, his teachers (I have been told) generally reported him as being dull and a dreamer.

"TESTING" ADULTS

In his very good new book, *Growing With Your Children* (see GWS #8), Herb Kohl—like just about everyone who writes about children—says that they have to keep testing adults in order to find limits. I don't agree. They do it all the time, no question about that. But I don't think they have to do it, and I don't think we ought to let them do it. There are other and better ways to find out the rules of family life and human society.

One year, when I was teaching fifth grade, I had a boy in my class who had been kicked out of his local public schools—no small feat. He was a perfectly ordinary looking, middle-sized, middle-class white kid, didn't pull knives or throw furniture, no Blackboard Jungle stuff. It took me a while to understand *why* the public schools had shown him the door. In a word, he was an agitator, always stirring things up. One day, when everyone was trying to do something, I forget what, and he was trying to prevent them, or get them to do something else, I turned on him and shouted in exasperation, "Are you *trying* to make me sore at you?" To my great surprise, and his (judging from his voice), he said, "Yes." It took me a while to understand, or at least to guess, that he had learned from experience that the only way he could be sure of getting the undivided attention of other people, children or adults, was to make them sore at him.

As the year went on, he improved, became only difficult instead of impossible. But he was still a long way from being at peace with himself—the roots of his problem were deeper than I or my class could reach in a year. Our school only went through sixth grade; what became of him later I don't know. Meanwhile, he had taught me something valuable.

At about that time I was beginning to know the interesting but angry and difficult child of a friend. One day I was at their house, talking with his mother about something important to both of us. The boy kept interrupting, more even than usual. I knew by then that children hate to be shut out of adult talk, and tried from time to time to let this boy have a chance to speak. But on this day it was clear that he was trying to keep us

from talking at all. Finally, looking right at him, I said, not angrily but just curiously, "Are you trying to annoy me?" Startled into honesty, like the other boy, by a question he had perhaps never really asked himself, he smiled sheepishly and said, "Yes." I said, still pleasantly, "Well, that's OK. Tell you what let's do. Let's play a game. You do everything you can think of to annoy me, and I'll do everything I can think of to annoy you, and we'll see who wins. OK?" He looked at me for a while— he knew me well enough by this time to know that I would play this "game" in earnest. He considered for a while how it might go. A look at his mother showed that, for the time being at least, he could not expect much help from her if the game went against him. Finally he said, "No, I don't want to play." "Fine," I said. "Then let us have our conversation, and you and I can talk later." Which is what happened.

That was many years ago. From many encounters I have since had with many children, I have come to believe very strongly that children as young as five and perhaps even three are well able to understand the idea of "testing"—doing something to someone else or in front of someone else, *just to see what that other person will do*—and to understand that this is not good. If I thought a child was doing this to me, I would say, "Are you testing me, just doing that to see what I will do?" If the child said "Yes" I would say, "Well, I don't like that, it's not nice and I don't want you to do it. I don't do things to *you*, especially things I know you don't like, just to see what *you* will do. Then it's not fair for you to do that to me." Children like big words; I would introduce them to the word "experiment." I might go on to say that it's OK to do experiments with *things*, trying to stand blocks on top of each other, or mixing paints to see what color you get, and so on. But it isn't nice, it's very bad, to do experiments on people, unless you ask them first and they say it's all right. It's especially bad to do experiments on them that you *know* they don't like.

Where the line is between good experiments and bad—not an easy one for adult scientists to find, even those who look for it—is something that slightly older children might find very interesting to talk about. We would probably agree that hurting animals just to see what will happen—which some people do—is bad. What about trying out medicines on animals to see which ones work, or work best, or maybe hurt the animals in other ways? What about making animals sick so that we can try out medicines on them and see whether any of them make them better? These questions are worth talking about.

Finally, I would say to children, "Do what seems interesting, or exciting, or fun—whatever you want to do. If I think some of those things are unkind, or destructive, or dangerous, I'll tell you, and ask you not to do them. But don't do things *just* to see what I'll say."

As I said, I think children are perfectly able to understand these ideas, to see that they are fair, and to act upon them. When they do, it will make our lives together much easier.

ON AN ISLAND

Gail Myles, 341 Locke Rd., Rye NH 03870, writes:

...In August, 1977, I moved with my three sons to an island we own off the coast of Maine. This decision was the result of my husband's and my opinion that they were not learning in public or private schools. Because we were taking them out of N.H. we had no hassle from the school district. I have worked as a volunteer for several years in the Rye schools and informed the teachers and principals of the plans. Many teachers agreed this was a good idea.

We sent to the Calvert School for their courses and had to have the boys take a placement test. Here was our second confirmation of their not learning in the schools they'd been attending. Bud (13) was to be in 8th grade and was placed by Calvert in the 7th only because I promised I could bring him up to level; Mike (11), a straight A student was placed in 4th, when he should have gone into 6th; and Tim (8), who was the only son who I knew had a love for learning still within him, was placed at grade level—third.

The boys were greatly disturbed at the prospect of this adventure. I found the Count of Monte Cristo's earlier experiences in prison very applicable to their "trauma." They were to live four seasons through experiences only alluded to by Outward Bound programs and alone with only unmechanical Mom. Dad would visit when possible, perhaps once a month for a couple of days.

That was the situation and we stayed till April 1978. But it would take the equivalent of a novel to tell you of the benefits of the total experience and the tremendous heart breaks upon our readjustment to the "hard knocks" of "real" life.

What you have been saying in the books and GWS is true but there is so much more. We now have three boys, 15, 13, & 10, who know there is a better way. Learning can be exciting, in fact one of the most exciting things we ever do. It only takes an interest in a matter and someone who will answer or learn with us the answer. It takes two to ten hours a week to do the busy work for certification. Learning goes on every minute of our lives.

I never expected the boys to express any appreciation for this experience. I figured they might be sitting at a lunch with some business friends when they were thirty and mention the year. What I couldn't have predicted is that they would see the difference so soon. They learned to dig clams with the clammers of Maine, the salt of the earth, in forty degrees below chill factors, they lived through situations where everyone takes responsibility for the lives of each other, they came to like and understand opera because it was available to us through Texaco broadcasts, an interest none of us had prior to this, they learned that out of the eight unexpected puppies born, five had to be destroyed because of the food shortage, and probably the best thing they learned was to get along with themselves and each other. They had to, because there was no one else and if you want something from someone you have to give in return. That should take care of this "social life" garbage. To feel your worth in an adult world side by side with hard working people, is there a better reward? I don't think so. They even had tears at departing from this small coastal community they knew as "in town."

My rewards were beyond measure. No yellow monster took my favorite friends away every morning; when they were exposed to a new vocabulary word I could use it pertinently in everyday happenings, if we wanted to know molecular theory we could work from 9 AM to 4 PM till it clicked, everything they were exposed to in Calvert Curriculum was learned by all, they spent early evenings putting on operas they made up, shows for Dad's pleasure were presented sometimes taking three days just to prepare the staging. We read books, books, and books till 1 AM and no one had to be up at 6:30 for the monster.

An additional reward was the result of the history, literature, mythology, and architecture we were exposed to; we went to Athens, Greece, in April, a trip we would never have been interested enough in taking or felt a need to take if "doors" hadn't been opened to us. Bud came to love the Parthenon and had to see it. Tim was a walking encyclopedia on mythology and gave Jack and me the tour in the Archaeological Museum, and Mike was our history guide—we didn't even need a Greek service. Mike is also a gifted writer, and after reading his final composition for Calvert his teacher said she wished she could fly up to meet him, said he knew what writing was all about—she wanted to fly to Troy and Greece as his subject was the Trojan War. He had made her *feel* something inside.

I enjoyed the Calvert system. Their writers are excellent and really speak to the kids. It was a personal relationship in which they looked forward to hearing from someone who was writing to them. Letters were scarce and they learned the value of the written word. But I must say we *used* the curriculum to our needs and interests and only took the grading so the boys would not be denied the credit upon returning to public school. This was completely their choice—they are encouraged to set policies regarding their futures.

Not knowing the courses well, I went to the island without a large set of reference books and I neglected to bring Shakespeare with us. In one of Mike's history chapters there was a reference to "the noblest Roman of them all." In order to get the point of the title the student was to read the particular scene of *Julius Caesar.* Mike was furious that he couldn't get his hands on that play and I am sure he would have read a great deal of it if I had had it available. Now when we returned to Rye Tim was still finishing up his course and had touches of history offered to him. In each case he would jump to Mike's book, nice paperback, and read more on that event. When he read this particular chapter we had the play available and he and I read it with great interest. That's when you present Shakespeare to a 9-year-old! ...

Bud went on in June to graduate with his 8th grade

but not without hassle, hassle, hassle from the local bureaucrats. Mike was practically a peptic ulcer victim from the intimidations he suffered and Tim stayed home until this fall when he elected to return. In Oct. he was going to quit, and only the concern and interest shown him by his exceptional teacher helped him decide to stay in. He is now thinking of staying out next year. He wants to see who will be his teacher and Jack and I are confident he will make the best decision. ...

We plan in the next year or two, upon the completion of our sailboat we are building, to live abroad and travel with the boys. Their education will be so superior that we have no doubt they will be able to be whatever they choose. If they see people suffering and decide to become a doctor then they will at least know why they are studying medicine....

One closing note—the idea I hate most about public schools is that they should have my children all day when I feed, clothe, doctor, transport, and care most for them, and I am denied those hours with them and the sharing of their learning experiences. I can not reinforce their education if I am denied the subject matter they are exposed to and am only left with tired grumps who eat, do homework, and flop to bed.

READING GAME

A friend (GWS #3, "Capable Children") writes about a good reading game that she plays with her children. She writes a number of sentences, and the children circle those that are true and scratch out those that are not. One day they were going to the grandparents' house for lunch. There was one of those common arguments about which child sits in what seat, which produced this list of sentences (instead of circling or scratching them out, as the children did, I will just mark T or F):

F does not want to read books in the back seat. T
F wants to read books in the front seat. T
We are going to Grandma's house. T
We are going to eat lunch there. T
We are in a green car. T

We are in a green car. T
We are in a yellow car. F
We are in a green airplane. F
We are in a purple rocket. F
We love Grandma. T
Grandma loves us. T
We love liver. F (Ed.—this one scratched out many times. Is there a child in the world who likes liver? Maybe, with enough bacon)
...and so on.

One of the many things I like about this game is that it gives children, and parents, too, a way to get

outside of, to see from a different perspective, what may at the time have been unpleasant events. In this case, what had been a quite fierce quarrel about who sat where was turned, so to speak, into History, something which the children could use. Of course, we have to steer clear of sentences which might just start the quarrel all over again.

We might add a little extra spice to this game by making some surprise sentences, in which we don't know until the last word whether the sentence is true or false. Thus: "Grandma's house is covered with spots," or "Our house is full of elephants," or "We are riding in a green boat," etc. And it might be fun to have the children contribute words to the sentences as we make them up.

MONEY

A mother writes:

"Thought I'd share with you M's 'coming of age' as a consumer. M recently turned three. She received a dollar inside a birthday card sent by one of her friends (a 92-year-old). Last year when he sent a dollar I took it without even showing it to her and bought her some balloons with it. This year she opened all her own mail and instantly recognized that it was money and that it was a present for her. She was quite pleased and put it in her wallet which until now was only for *playing* 'grown-up,' and had held only small change. She discussed the dollar, and that she could buy something—whatever she wanted—for herself.

Next day when she got a five dollar bill in another card we made a fuss again. We discussed the difference in value—on our fingers—of ones and fives, and I thought, 'This is going great!'

Next day, when she got a card with a check for *ten* dollars, I thought, 'Oh, no, this learning experience is getting out of hand.' I hoped she wouldn't realize what a check was so I could spirit it away, but she was too sharp. 'More money!' she exclaimed. So we explained what a check was, and traded it for two fives. M had previously studied the one and the five and pointed out that there were different men on them and asked their names (she's very into everything having a 'name'). So she understood they were different, but we didn't want to introduce a third variable in the form of a ten dollar bill because of the already confusing time we are presently in with counting: she has trouble remembering where to put 3 and is not very consistent with the order of anything over 5. So we felt we were helpful in keeping things more simple, but I wondered later if perhaps it was really just a symptom of a passion to be in some kind of control.

Then M asked me what she could buy with all her 'moneys.' I suggested she look in the toy catalogues. She got very excited over a construction set (tinker toy), and I told her she could look for one like it next time we went to town. So next time Daddy went to town

M grabbed her purse and went along to shop for her present to herself. When she found her 'struction set' and went to the counter to pay for it—her first purchase—Daddy told her to give the woman a Lincoln, expecting her to get back two Washingtons. Drats!—she gave her a Jefferson! M took it right in stride. Perhaps we should have left it alone, but at home Daddy traded it for 2 Washingtons. Controlling it again.

After she played with the Tinker Toy set for a couple of days, she expressed disappointment that she couldn't build a house with it. She checked the catalogues and zeroed in on a Lincoln logs set. The next shopping expedition to town turned one up—for a Lincoln and three Washingtons. We pointed out that she'd spent a lot of money and didn't have that much left. I sense that she has a very balanced feel for money, a good sense of its value, so I'm not worried that she'll either hoard the rest or blow it recklessly.

With all this concern with cash, M didn't lose track of the fact that the money was sent as presents from people who love her. We took pictures of M posed with her presents and a big smile to send along with the thank you notes.

I wonder who found this whole experience more thrilling and instructive, M or us? Liberating, too. M took another step in independence, and we learned—I hope—to give up a little of our desire to control what she experiences. Just flowing with things and being there to answer questions and sort out the confusion if and when it arises—just being a lot less *anxious* about what's going to happen.

Life becomes a lot less tense and more joyful if we can give up our script for how we'd like things to be. How much better and happier and more healthful to not be attached to things being a certain way.

But giving up our script is not just a way to health and happiness. It's also a way to knowledge. We can learn only what we are allowed, or allow ourselves, to be exposed to. M showed us that she was capable of assimilating more than we would have guessed and would have deliberately exposed her to at this time, that the more room we leave for spontaneity the more room we've left for growth. We also need some structure in our lives, but that structure should be as unlimited, as unconfining, as possible—a scaffolding into an uncircumscribed space."

GWS LOCAL CHAPTERS

Nancy Plent writes:

"One mother suggested that we might advertise in local papers that the Monmouth County Chapter of Growing Without Schooling was meeting monthly. I promised I'd check with you on using the name GWS in this way. We don't want to make it a club, cult, movement, or real organization of any kind, but thought the use of the name would attract people who had heard of GWS, and acquaint others with it...."

I said, and say here, that I think it's a fine idea. If any groups of people anywhere else want to try it, by all means go right ahead. Anyone who wants to start a "chapter" of GWS is welcome to do it.

As a matter of fact, if people want to establish some sort of "membership" in the local chapter, charging whatever seems like reasonable dues, that's fine too. They could use the money for various kinds of local promotion or advertising, for holding meetings, for getting extra copies of GWS to distribute, or whatever. Just make sure that people understand that this is the local chapter dues, not some kind of national dues.

I can even see a local chapter charging $5 a year in dues, or even $10, and saying that all members of the chapter would receive GWS. Thus they could use part of the local dues for a group subscription, and have some left over for local expenses.

A word of warning, though. Don't let the local chapter get so busy that it burns out the handful of people who do most of the work. This was a problem we had when I worked with the World Federalists. We tried to find people to organize and run local chapters, but then gave them so many things to do that after a year or two these active people were all worn out. In most membership organizations it works out all too soon that the members exist to serve the organization. I don't want that to happen with us.

Later, Nancy writes:

"A comment on What To Tell Strangers. My neighbor took her son out of school a couple of months ago. She saw that nothing terrible had happened to me, the principal didn't give her a hard time, and she had none of my phobias about not talking too much lest we rock the boat. Once she had decided she was doing the right thing, she told EVERYBODY who would listen. I began to think of tactful ways to shut her up, when she started reporting that this neighbor or that friend had stopped being shocked. They were starting to ask thoughtful, almost approving questions.

Impressed, I tried answering the next few strangers with "He learns at home," or "We have our own school at home." Sometimes people froze up and stopped the conversation. More often, they asked about the legality, recalled their own unhappy school days, and mentioned the Donahue show. I'm convinced. The more people who know, the sooner the surprise wears off and acceptance begins."

As readers know, I have till now been a low profile man. But perhaps the time has come, at least in many places, to take a more vigorous, outspoken, and confident position. We seem to be at the beginning and perhaps even in the middle of one of those big changes in public attitude that happen from time to time. For a great many reasons, most (but not all) of them their own fault, the public schools seem to have lost most of the great amount of public admiration and trust which they enjoyed for so many years. Most of the newspaper stories I have seen recently about unschoolers have put them in a very favorable light.

In Maine a state legislator has introduced a bill to do away with compulsory school attendance. She is in no way an unschooler; her argument is that since truancy laws don't keep kids in school, why not give up the fiction that school is compulsory, and say instead, "Go if you want to, and if you don't, stay out of the way of those who do." No one expects the bill to pass. But it is interesting to see how the newspapers have reacted to it. Ten, maybe five years ago, they would have cried out on their editorial pages that this misguided woman was attacking the very foundations of American democracy. Not now. They are not yet quite ready to support such a bill, but they say that it is an interesting idea that everyone should think about.

Another one of our readers, who lives and works in a fairly conventional part of society, told us recently that within the past few months he has had serious conversations about unschooling—by "serious" he means, at least two hours long—with more than twenty different people.

TRUTH LEAKS OUT

A student in an exclusive private secondary school, mostly for "gifted" students, writes:

"…My——teacher, who is one of our better teachers, very funny and respected and enjoyed by the students, said to us one morning, 'It's a fact, you know, that none of you want to be here.'

Silence. It was true, of course, but no one knew what to do about it. There had to be some catch. Why would he admit this to us? I was glad he had said it, though. I waited. Then it came.

'And it is also a fact that if you were not here you don't know what else you would do.'

Down came my hopes that perhaps he was actually on to something that I had never heard from a teacher before. He continued to talk about how society puts us here because they don't know what else to do with us. Well, that was a surprise. At least there was no pretense—he didn't try to fool us into thinking that we were there to learn.

But then, what he had said was that we are there for only that purpose, yet if we weren't there, there would be nothing for us to do either. That, in other words, we really do not fit in *anywhere*, and so, we might just as well be cooped up as not! This from one of our most open, frank, and honest teachers. I *knew* that they felt this way, but to hear it is something else….

…I was talking to a 5-year-old friend of mine. I asked her, 'What if you didn't have to go to school? Would you still go?' She said, 'But I would have to go.' I said, 'Why?' 'To learn.' I persisted. 'But what if *everyone*, all the parents and teachers decided that no one had to go any more?' She shook her head. It was

an impossibility, such a question could not even be answered. She is already imprisoned. And I am watching another 5-year-old friend resist learning to read when a while ago she wanted to learn so badly…"

HELPERS

A mother writes:

"…My daughter (3) is in the kitchen teaching herself addition and subtraction on the Little Professor Calculator—a machine I don't really approve of—and every time I give her a gentle hint, she flies into a rage, but when I leave her alone and watch her out of the corner of my eye, I see her doing problems like 3 + 5 = 8!

When she was 2, she still hadn't said a word and I could see that our pediatrician was getting worried, but suddenly, a few months later, as I was zipping up her sleeper, she burst out with, 'No! Me do it!' and she's been talking ever since."

Years ago I went to a meeting of Catholic educators, where I heard a talk by a wise, funny old man who had been teaching all his life. One thing he said made us all laugh, and has stuck in my mind ever since: "A word to the wise is *infuriating*!" Yes, it is, because it is insulting, and little children pick up this expression of (often loving and protective) distrust or contempt, even when we're not conscious of sending it.

About talking. Two young people I know, fluent talkers, both of them the youngest child in large families, did not begin to talk until they were three. The parents of one were beginning to worry, but since their child was lively, interested in everything, vigorous, and social, I urged them not to.

The story is told that Thomas Carlyle never spoke a word until he was four, when one day, hearing his baby brother crying, he said to his amazed parents, as if it was the most natural thing in the world, "What ails wee Jock?"

WHY SCHOOLS BEGAN

Many have called me cynical and just plain mistaken for saying what I do about the real purposes of schools (GWS #6). But David Nasaw's new book *Schooled to Order* (Oxford Univ. Press. NY) shows that from the early days of the 19th century the rich and powerful in this country have always seen school, first and foremost, as a way to contain, control, and subdue the children of the unruly poor. This was true—I was surprised to learn this—even when all our poor were native-born Americans, long before the first waves of immigrants came to our shores.

I learned also from this book that when the Irish

first came to this country they made very strenuous efforts, despite their own poverty, to provide education for their children in accordance with their own beliefs. These efforts were in time destroyed by the movement for tax-supported government schools. This had generally been true of American poor and working-class people. They understood all too well that a chief purpose of government schools was to kill the independence and ambition of their children. They wanted their children to believe that they were as good as, and had the same rights as, anyone else, a very subversive and dangerous idea. But they could not long support their own schools and the government schools as well, and these independent ventures died out.

Mr. Nasaw gives us one quote that is almost too good (or bad) to be true. In 1908 James Russell, Dean of Teachers College of Columbia University, said to a symposium of the National Education Association:

"How can a nation endure that deliberately seeks to rouse ambitions and aspirations in the oncoming generations which in the nature of events cannot possibly be filled? If the chief object of government be to promote civil order and social stability (Ed. note—not quite what the Declaration of Independence says), how can we justify our practice in schooling the masses in precisely the same manner as we do those who are to be our leaders? Is human nature so constituted that those who fail will readily acquiesce in the success of their rivals? ...Is it any wonder that we are beset with labor troubles?"

In this same vein James Callaghan, then Prime Minister of Great Britain, said not long ago in a major speech on education that what Britain needed was "round pegs for round holes."

I hope that any people who still think that schools were designed to help the poor to rise will read Mr. Nasaw's book.

A WONDERFUL BOOK

To the list of books we sell here we are now adding Patricia Joudry's *And the Children Played* ($7 + .30 postage). Many people have recommended it to us, and I loved the book myself every time I read it. But I have hesitated to recommend it, lest the book give people an excuse to say or think, "Well, I'd be glad to try to teach my own kids if I lived in a beautiful old English farmhouse and knew people like Rex Harrison and Leonard Bernstein, but I'm just an ordinary person living in an ordinary town, etc. etc."

I still worry a little that some people will react to the book in this way. People wanting reasons to oppose unschooling will find plenty of them in the book. On the other hand, it is such a vivid and affectionate picture of children growing up free and happy, and such a true and funny picture of the generally frank and blunt ways in which such children deal with each other, and such a detailed and convincing description of how these children, though largely free of external "discipline," develop an internal discipline that would put most of today's adults to shame, that in the end I have to hope that as many people as possible will read it.

At a time when Patricia Joudry could not sell any of her plays, and they had almost no money, and feared that at any minute they might be thrown out of their house, the children were busy playing. Mrs. Joudry writes:

"...Play is children's work, and we learned to respect this as we did our own.... They were lucky, for they had space and clumps of materials left around by the builders.... They played with the earnest dedication of artists. Melanie played house; Stephanie played spaceship; together they played safari. They played store, they played charge accounts, they played creditors, they played lawyers, they played landlords, they played magic princes that came on the scene and saved the day.

Did we think they hadn't known what was going on? Our anxieties lingered but theirs they got out of their system with play. Watching this, we came to realize that children's play is more than work, it is therapy. (Ed.—but good work is the best therapy) But it can only be therapy when it is free, wholly created and directed by themselves."

"They also played school ...It was amusing to hear Melanie teaching Stephanie (Ed.—her older sister) math. With the corrections she got from her pupil, she picked up quite a bit.

When they got tired of playing together, they played separately. A favorite was to make up a story, tell it aloud in a low murmur, acting it out as they went. I sometimes walked into a veritable buzz, like a hornet's nest of stories, as each of the three of them walked round in a private world, filled with high drama and every kind of contortion."

"...John and I had been answering the question [how are they going to learn to get along with other people] by saying that you learn to get along with people, or you don't, in your own home. We just couldn't believe, as 'they' did, that the best way to get socialized is to be thrust at a tender age into a class of forty, to fight for your existence."

"...[People] all asked ...'How do you get those children to be so good?'

We really didn't know. We never told them to sit still and keep quiet, but wherever we took them they sat still and kept quiet. We were as surprised as anybody. They developed charming Pleases and Thank Yous, though we never told them to. We hated seeing children badgered to mouth empty phrases. I can't believe John and I were as polite as all that, but they must have picked it up somewhere.

Their voices were modulated; they were well under their own control. Within themselves, they were at peace."

"[Felicity] had not learned a thing by the time she was seven.

She only knew who she was, that she loved life and trusted her parents, her sisters, and God, and knew how the earth yields and how life is made, and why: little things like that. We felt that it would be useful for her in addition if she knew how to read, but that didn't seem to be in the cards. I made a few attempts to teach her, but her brief experience of school had turned her off learning altogether.

We kept quoting the old occult phrase: 'When the pupil is ready, the teacher will arrive.'

…One day Melanie and Figgy (nickname) got into the mother and kid game. It was the old 'Eat your supper, get to bed, you're going to school in the morning' routine. The next morning the game was still on and Felicity went to school. Melanie switched from parent to teacher. She started the Kid on the alphabet.

That evening at supper, Melly announced calmly, 'It doesn't look as though this teacher is going to come along. So I'd better be it.'

Before she went to bed that night, she turned their bedroom into a Bed-Schooler. And the Full Moon School was born. Its founder and teacher was twelve years old.

Every morning from then on Figgy raced through her breakfast with an eye on the clock. 'I have to hurry, I'll be late for school.' Then she'd tear off to their schoolroom, where the teacher and pupils were already at their places.

Melanie was the rest of the pupils, and all the teachers. There were four teachers, two male and two female, for balance, I suppose. Some were lenient and some were strict. The imaginary children possessed their own unique characteristics, and some were well-behaved, while others weren't …

Felicity learned to read, to do sums, and spell long lists of words. They did simple Chemistry experiments, had Botany classes outdoors, cooking classes in the kitchen …and creative projects beyond calculation.

This was all in the mornings. In the afternoons, Melanie attended the Full Moon School—as herself. She settled down alone at the long worktable and went to work on her books. …

She undertook H.G. Wells's *Outline of History* as well as Geography projects like mapmaking; she read poetry and Shakespeare, she wrote compositions, and delved into many books chosen at random from the library."

"Whenever we had an interesting guest—and we had many—the children would gather quietly in the sitting room, and listen through long evenings around the fire, Melanie just sitting and watching the faces, Stephanie knitting (so as not to waste time) and Felicity slowly nodding. Because their ears and their minds were wide open everything they heard went in. And whatever they noticed came out—fortunately after the guests had left.

They learned their manners in the only way that children can learn—by example. Sometimes there were lapses. But they were learning how to behave in the world and wanted to be guided and corrected—though not humiliated in the process."

THOSE VOICES

A memory. When my sister and I were about four and five, perhaps even less, we visited our grandparents. There was a landing on the second floor, with a railing, through which we could just see down the stairs into the room where the adults sat talking after dinner. After we had been tucked into bed and good-nights said, and the grown-ups had gone back downstairs, we would slip out of bed, crouch down by the railing, and listen to the grown-up voices. We couldn't catch more than a few of the words, and in any case couldn't understand what was being talked about. But the pull of those voices was fascinating. Usually after a while we would sneak back into bed. But one night we fell asleep there by the railing, where the grownups found us when they went up to bed. I don't remember what came of this, whether we were scolded or punished, and sternly warned not to get out of bed again, or whether the grownups said nothing about it.

Since then I have seen in many other families that it is very hard to keep young children in bed if a group of adults are having lively conversation not too far away. The children will find a hundred different reasons for coming to checkout what the grownups are doing.

But, some might say, that's all very fine for privileged families that have interesting visitors. But what about most families, average families. The answer is, first of all, that all people are interesting. As Studs Terkel and Robert Coles have shown in their (very different) books, everyone has many good stories to tell. As long as real people are talking, not just people on TV, children will want to hear their voices and see their faces, and will learn much from them.

WORD GAME

When I was little, perhaps six or seven, someone gave me a good book for Christmas. It had perhaps thirty or forty pages. On each page was a word. The rest of the page was blank. The object was to make as many different words as I could out of the letters in the given word. Beneath the given word was printed the total number of words possible, a great challenge and frustration, for I never came close to it. I can only remember two of the given words. One was INGRATE, which held more than 100 words. The other, the last word in the book, was SPECTROHELIOGRAPH, which held more than 200. They left a couple of extra blank pages, to make room for all of them.

For many months I worked in that book, finally did all I could, grew tired of it, set it aside, lost it, forgot all about it. In the late '40's the game turned up again, called The Word Game, in the pages of the World-Telegram, then one of New York's evening papers. Quite often I rode a commuter train out of the city to a suburb where I would be lecturing in the evening. One friend with whom I used to ride was a Word Game fan. Each night the paper would give us a new word, and we would try to reach the listed total before our stop.

In time I left New York, the paper gave up, and I forgot about the game until the other day, when someone wrote about playing it with her children, and having a lot of fun with it. It's a great game; I recommend it.

(By the way, you can't make much out of the word "School.")

GRAMMAR

Talking in *How Children Fail* (av. here) about how our use of words may confuse young children, I wrote the following:

"The conventional teaching of grammar adds to the confusion. We talk about, and use, nouns and adjectives as if they were very different, but in fact they are often very much alike. A green ball, a green top, a green bicycle, and a green stuffed animal are alike in that they are green (adjective) and that they are toys (noun). When we call them green, we mean they are members of a class that have in common the color green. When we call them toys, we mean they are members of a class that have in common the fact that children play with them. Why should a child be expected to feel that there is something very different about these classes? Why is the greenness of a ball different from the ball-ness of a ball? I don't feel the difference. They are both ways of saying something about the object. We tell children that the distinction between one part of speech and another is a matter of meaning, when it really has to do with the way we fit them into sentences."

———————

I later found out that this way of looking at and analyzing language was called Structural Linguistics. For a while this far more sensible way of teaching grammar (if it has to be taught) found its way into a few school textbooks—I once helped edit a series based on this idea. But I suppose the Back to Basics movement has driven even this tiny speck of common sense out of most of our schoolrooms.

WORMS

Why do we ask the questions we ask? How do we get our answers?

A few years ago, when in Canada, I read in *MacLean's* magazine a very short article, about worms. It said that in Western Canada a man who (like many others) had been raising worms for fishermen had found by experiment that these worms would eat—and turn into the richest topsoil—almost any kind of organic wastes, including manures, paper, cardboard, sawdust, wood chips, cotton mill wastes, food scraps, etc. This excited me very much. I wanted to find out all I could about it.

Curiosity is rarely idle. I had strong reasons for mine. Since 1948, when I read William Vogt's *Road to Survival,* I have been interested in what we now call ecology. Even though I then lived in New York City, I subscribed to the magazine *Friends of the Land,* and read many other books about conservation, organic farming, etc. I have known for a long time that all over the country we were exhausting and depleting our soils, that every year we sent billions of tons of topsoil down our rivers and into the Gulf of Mexico, that the six feet or more of black topsoil we found in the great plains when we got here was in most places down to the last six inches—if even that. I knew that someday we were going to have to pay a heavy price for our greed, wastefulness, and stupidity—and the inflation we are groaning about now is only part of that price.

This was not my only concern. I am a city man. I like cities. For twenty-one years I have lived in one of the best of them—Boston—which I love more all the time, and do not plan to leave. A world or a country without cities would not be desirable or even possible. If all cities were destroyed and the survivors in the country had to start from scratch, they would very soon be making new cities again—for reasons Jane Jacobs has made plain in *The Economy of Cities* (av. here).

But our cities right now have many serious problems. One is that they, or the people in them, generate an immense amount of wastes—sewage, garbage, paper, cardboard, etc. Merely getting these out of the city is a problem. Harder yet is finding some place to put them that does not poison our lands, rivers, oceans. Another problem is that cities, all over the world, are filling up with people for whom there are no jobs and no prospects of any. It has seemed clear to me for some time that cities were not going to be able to feed and employ their poor, far less be healthy and prosperous, unless they could learn to do again *what once they all did,* which was to raise much of their own food. But how, and in what soil?

Now it looked as if the worms might be the answer to all these problems. Perhaps they could turn the organic wastes of the cities into rich topsoil, some of which the cities could use to raise their own food, and the rest of which they could send into the country to enrich the land there—which is, after all, what the

Chinese have been doing for thousands of years.

So I needed to find out all I could about these worms. What to do? Sign up for a worm course somewhere? There were none. Anyway, I like to get answers more directly. The *MacLean's* worm article was signed. I wrote the reporter, in care of the magazine, asking if he would send the address of the Canadian worm farmer, and anything else he knew about worms. Back came a nice answer, with the address and several useful clippings. I wrote the worm farmer (enclosing a little money to pay for his time and help the work along— never a bad idea). He wrote back, saying that one very good source of information was North American Bait Farms (1207 So. Palmetto, Ontario CA 91761). I wrote them, got back a list of books they publish, and other information, bought and read some of the books. One of the best was *Earthworms for Fun and Profit,* by Donald Gaddie. It looked more and more as if worms really could do all that people claimed.

It occurred to me that if I was going to talk about raising worms in the city, maybe I ought to *do* it first. It is one thing to say, "These books say you can raise worms in the city." It is quite another to say, "I am doing it." Besides, in doing it I might learn things not in the books.

Late last fall, when the Public Garden was full of piles of leaves, I went out in the early mornings with a plastic garbage can and brought back eight loads (about 250 lbs.), which I piled up in the small sunken court outside my kitchen door. I packed down the leaves with concrete blocks (left from an old bookshelf) and began pouring my gray water (wash water, dishwater, etc.) on them, though without knowing quite what I was going to do with them.

One day I thought, since I have all this good worm food here, I might as well order some worms and get started. Which I did. The worms arrived Dec. 7. I put them in the bottom of a red rubber wastebasket, with the peat moss that came with them. From time to time I added some leaves or food scraps to the wastebasket. As the months went by, the worms multiplied, the wastebasket slowly filled up. Soon I needed more boxes.

The worm book (Gaddie) said that worms didn't like plastic and should be raised in wooden boxes (but not cedar). Having wooden boxes made seemed expensive. Might it not be cheaper to raise them in cardboard boxes (of which the city is full), lined with plastic garbage bags. Since these can double as freezer bags, it seemed unlikely that they would trouble the worms.

I ran a small pilot project, put some worms and dirt in a plastic bread wrapper. After a month the worms seemed to be thriving. So I put three plastic garbage bags into cardboard boxes, and into these put some of the worms and dirt from the original wastebasket. The worms seem to like their new homes. As they continue to multiply, I will use more bags and boxes. Before next summer I should have enough so that they will eat all my food wastes.

I have also been feeding them cardboard (from boxes), cut into narrow strips with a big paper cutter. Recently, hearing that the *Boston Globe* (unlike the *New York Times*) uses ink with very little lead in it, I have given them shredded newspaper. Too soon to tell yet whether, and how fast, they will eat that. Certainly they like the rotted leaves best. They like banana peels better than orange peels—these are acid, and have to sit around for a while before the worms will eat them.

Commercial rabbit farms (one of which I have seen) use worms to eat up rabbit manure. Before next summer I plan to try them on dog wastes, which are plentiful (!) in my neighborhood. Late next spring I will plant some worms in some of the grassy/weedy areas near my apartment where people relieve their dogs, and see what happens. I am hoping they will survive, and thrive, with no more food and attention than this.

In time I want to find out whether, by shaking worm castings up with water and settling or straining out the particles, I can get a liquid that will grow plants hydroponically. I also want to find out whether, using such a liquid, plants will grow in a medium like rough terry cloth. No doubt other questions will come to mind. As they do, I will think of other ways to get answers, and to share them with any others who may be interested.

HOME-BUILDER SCHOOLS

In New England we now have three places where people can go to learn how to build their own homes, for a third or less of what it would cost them to buy them, even from a large-scale builder.

The first of these was the Shelter Institute (Center and Water Streets, Bath ME 04530 207-443-9084), founded and still run by Pat Hennin. After a while Pat's partner, Charlie Wing, split off and started his own house-building "school," Cornerstones (54 Cumberland St., Brunswick ME 04011 207-729-0540). And a third such school has been formed in Mass., Heartwood Owner-Builder School (Johnson Rd., Washington MA 01235 413-623-6677).

Interesting to note that Pat Hennin was a lawyer, his wife Patsy a school teacher, and Charlie Wing a physics professor. I don't know who runs Heartwood.

An article about Shelter Institute, published a little over a year ago, said that it had over 2000 "graduates" from every state, who had built about 250 homes so far. Figures would be higher now. Many, perhaps most of these people came to the courses with no experience in building whatever. Many had not done even simple carpentry or repairing. After a few weeks of class time and hands-on work outside of class, usually helping former graduates to build their houses, these novices are ready to design and build their own. Not that it is easy or quick, no part-time job—figure about an hour and a half for every square foot of house.

The courses at all three places run about three weeks and cost (as of a year ago) about $250 per person

163

or $350 per couple. Write for more up-to-date information.

I see this as being interesting and perhaps useful and important to unschoolers for a number of reasons. In the first place, many unschoolers don't have much money (sometimes by choice), so that building their own house may be the only way in which they (and in these days most people) can have a house. In the second place, because housing is becoming so expensive everywhere, there will surely be a need and a market for home-building schools in many other parts of the country, and this is work that some unschoolers might want to do.

Beyond that, many people write that their teenaged children have nothing interesting or worthwhile to do, and I would guess that many of them might be quite excited about the idea of learning how to build houses—even if they weren't planning to build their own for a while.

By the way, another good source of information about inexpensive and unconventional ways of building houses is *The Mother Earth News* (Box 70, Hendersonville NC 28739), which many GWS readers probably know.

Don't want to give the impression that you have to go to school, even one of these good schools, to build your own house. Last time I saw my friend Karl Hess, he showed me photos of a very nice looking house which he and his wife built for themselves in the hills of West Virginia, working, as he put it, "with the book in one hand and the hammer in the other." But I think any one of these schools might make the job much easier.

COLLEGE AT HOME

Many people ask us about ways to get college degrees without actually having to go to a college, which more and more people can't afford.

The best information I have seen about this was in an article in the Feb. '78 issue of *New Age* (32 Station St., Brookline Village MA 02146, pub. monthly, $12/yr.), by Nancy DuVergne Smith, "Alternatives in Higher Education." It says, in part:

UNDERGRADUATE DEGREES

There are at least three... organizations which provide opportunities to complete undergraduate studies along nontraditional paths—the Regents External-Degree Program of the University of the State of New York, Thomas A. Edison College of the State of New Jersey, and the Board for State Academic Awards of the State of Connecticut.

All three programs accept students from *across the globe* (Ed. italics), demand no specific entrance requirements, and impose no limits on course or exam preparation time, residence, or class attendance. Moreover, the cost incurred in each degree program is a fraction of that levied by standard colleges or universities.

Credit toward either associate or bachelor's degrees is earned in the following ways: transfer of other college credentials, standard proficiency tests, formal course work, or college-level exams administered through the U.S. Armed Services or by government or business employers, or "special assessment" of a student's expertise in areas such as the arts, agriculture, or labor relations. Students complete degree requirements by studying faculty-designed subject outlines, then measure their learning against tests administered periodically around the country by each institution.

All three of the state-accredited schools charge a $50 entrance fee and an average of $20 per examination. Total costs for an associate degree are estimated at $200; for a full bachelor's degree, less than $500.

Contact each program for further information:

1. The Regents External-Degree Prog. of the Univ. of the State of NY (99 Washington Ave., Albany NY 12230) offers Associate of Arts, Science, or Applied Science (nursing) degrees, Bachelor of Arts and of Science.

2. Thos. A. Edison College of State of N. J. (Forrestal Center, Forrestal Rd., Princeton, NJ 08540) grants degrees ranging from Assoc. of Arts, Science in Management, or Assoc. of Applied Science in Radiologic Technology, to Bachelor of Arts and Bachelor of Science in Business Administration.

3. The Board for State Academic Awards of the State of Conn. (340 Capitol Ave., Hartford CT 06115) offers Assoc. of Arts and Sciences degrees; a bachelor's degree program is planned.

University Without Walls

Nonresidential programs in which students earn credits demanded for degrees through highly individualized studies away from the campus center, internships, and other work or experience-related projects are available through over thirty universities and colleges around the nation affiliated with the University Without Walls. The program was initially funded in 1970 by grants from the U.S. Office of Education and the Ford Foundation, through the Union for Experimenting Colleges and Universities, Antioch College, Yellow Springs, OH 45387.

Participating universities and colleges include:

University (hereafter U.) of Alabama, New College, University [sic] AL 35486

Antioch College (hereafter C.)/Philadelphia, 1227 Walnut St., San Francisco CA 94118

Bard C., Annandale-on-Hudson NY 12504

U. Without Walls/Berkeley, 2700 Bancroft Way, Berkeley CA 94704

Chicago State U., 95th & King Dr., Chicago IL 60628

U. Without Walls/Flaming Rainbow, P. O. Box 154, Tahlequah OK 74464

Florida International U./Miami Dade Community

C., 300 NE 2nd Ave., Miami FL 33132

Friends World C., Plover Lane, Huntington NY 11743

Goddard C., Plainfield VT 05677

Hispanic International U., 3602 Navigation, Houston TX 77003

Hofstra U., Hempstead NY 11550

Johnston C., U. of Redlands, Redlands CA 92373

Loretto Heights C., 3001 S. Federal Blvd., Denver CO 80236

U. of Mass., Amherst MA 01022

U. of Minn., Minneapolis MN 55455

Morgan State C., Urban Regional Learning Center, Baltimore MD 21212

Northeastern Illinois U., Bryn Mawr at St. Louis Ave., Chicago IL 60625

U. of Pacific, Stockton CA 95204

Pitzer C., Claremont CA 91711

Roger Williams C., 35 Richmond St., Providence RI 02866

Shaw U., Raleigh NC 27602

Skidmore C., Saratoga Spgs. NY 12866

Stephens C., Columbia MO 65201

Universidad Boricua, 1766 Church St., Washington DC 20036

Universidad de Campesinos Libres, 841 W. Belmont Ave., Fresno CA 93706

Westminster C., Fulton MO 65621

U. of Wisc. at Green Bay, Green Bay WI 54302

Independent Programs

Empire State C. of the State U. of N. Y. has designed an individual study program through which students may earn associate or bachelor's degrees through personal efforts but are only required to meet with guiding professors several hours every few months at one of the twenty learning centers located in New York state.... For more info, write Empire State C., SUNY, Union Ave., Saratoga Spgs. NY 12366.

The Vermont State C. systems offer an external degree program combining independent study, traditional course work, experiential learning, correspondence, or media courses....

Write Vermont State Colleges Office of External Programs, Box 823, Montpelier VT 05602

Students pursuing a degree through the Open U. at the U. of Maryland/University C., College Park MD 20742, complete their studies off-campus, except for an introductory weekend seminar each semester.

The UM bachelor's degree program is patterned after the British adult-oriented Open University system, as are similar programs at University College, Rutgers, the State U. of N.J., New Brunswick NJ 08903, and the U. of Houston TX 77004.

Syracuse U. Independent Study Programs (Rm. 21, 610 E. Fayette St., Syracuse NY 13202) Bachelor of Science in business administration or Bachelor of Arts

in liberal studies, independent work with one eight-day visit to central campus each trimester.

Associate degrees... or college credit... through WTTW programs sponsored by TV college, City Colleges of Chicago Central Office (180 N. Michigan Ave., Chicago IL 60601)

Bachelor of General Studies degree... through non-residence, self-directed study programs involving periodic faculty contacts offered by External Degree Project, Roosevelt U., Chicago IL 60605

Metropolitan State U. of Minn. has no central campus... students... rely on community resources to enrich their individually developed study plans. Write Metropolitan State U., St. Paul, MN 55101

Bachelor of Arts is available through a predominantly off-campus program offered by Upper Iowa U. Students ...must attend four-week seminars on campus periodically. Write: Director, Coordinated Off-Campus Degree Program, Upper Iowa U., Fayette IA 52142

External Degree Programs of California State U. and C. system offer bachelor's degrees in business administration, liberal arts, and the humanities to Cal. residents through 19 centers located across the state. Write: Consortium of the Cal. State Univ. and Colleges, 5670 Wilshire Blvd., Los Angeles CA 90036.

GRADUATE PROGRAMS

The Union for Experimenting Colleges and Universities of Yellow Springs, OH ...can now claim credit for over 200 graduates. Three of the graduate arms of the consortium ...allow students to carry on learning programs in the world through their jobs, at home, on university campuses, or through projects of exploration, service, or research. ...The Doctor of Philosophy degrees offered by the Union schools, as well as degrees sponsored through the consortium's undergraduate wing, the U. Without Walls, are nationally recognized and are the first such programs to win regional approval as candidates for accreditation status by the North Central Association for Colleges and Secondary Schools.

Tuition costs amount to $2800 for each of the maximum four years allowed to complete the Ph.D. program, admission is selective, and candidates able to obtain Ph.D.'s through conventional routes generally are not accepted....

Write: Union Graduate School West, P. O. Box 7999, San Francisco CA 94120; Center for Minority Studies/Union Graduate School, c/o Coppin State College, 2500 West North Ave, Baltimore MD 21216; or the Union Graduate School, 106 Woodrow St., Yellow Springs OH 45387

The Goddard-Cambridge Graduate Program in Social Change is a Massachusetts-based extension of

Vermont's Goddard C. which offers a nontraditional means of earning a master's degree concentrating on either social or cultural issues, Third World studies, feminist studies, or selected independent topics. Write: Goddard/Cambridge Graduate Program, 186 Hampshire St., Cambridge MA 02139

The U. of Oklahoma College of Liberal Studies offers a year-round admission program leading to a master's or bachelor's degree in liberal studies.... Costs and program details available from the university (Norman OK 73069).

Masters of Arts degrees in humanities and in vocational education are open to legal residents of Calif. through a minimum attendance program created by the External Degree Program of Calif. State University and Colleges.

CREDIT BY EXAMS

Credits earned through satisfactory completion of the College-Level Examination Program (CLEP) of the College Entrance Examination Board (CEEB) can validate up to a quarter of the requirements for baccalaureate degrees and are accepted by over 1700 U.S. colleges and universities. CLEP tests... in English composition, humanities, mathematics, natural and social sciences, and history—are administered the third week of every month at over 900 centers in the U.S. ...For complete information on CLEP tests, contact: CEEB, 888 7th Ave., New York NY 10019.

CEEB also conducts Advance Placement (AP) Examinations which evaluate knowledge of specific subjects, often on material covered in customary freshman and sophomore courses. Contact: CEEB, Box 977, Princeton NJ 08540

For further information on all these matters, read:
External Graduate Degree Programs at U.S. Colleges and Universities, Council of Graduate Schools in the U.S., One Dupont Circle, Washington DC 20036. 10pp., free.
On-Campus/Off-Campus Degree Programs for Part-Time Students, by Linda Gordon and Judy Schub, National University Extension Association, One Dupont Circle, DC 20036. 119 pp., $4.
A Guide to Independent Study through Correspondence Instruction, Nat'l University Extension Association, Suite 360, One Dupont Circle etc. 60 pp. $ .50.

SCHOOLS AND JOBS

Joyce Mitchell's *The Work Book—A Guide to Skilled Jobs* (Bantam $ 2.25) might be interesting and useful to unschoolers in a number of ways. One thing it does is show us the world of work as a great many people, including high school students, see it, and are encouraged to see it. Don't misunderstand me—it is (as far as I can judge) a very realistic and truthful book.

Some quotes:

"In the 1980's...skilled jobs will be the bulk (up to 80%) of the work.... Only 20% of all jobs will require a college education. At the same time, fewer than 2% of the labor force in this country will work on the assembly line, and semiskilled operatives and unskilled labor will be a declining 25% of total employment....
The length of in-school preparation is the simplest way to define a skilled job (Ed. italics)..."

The book then gives a long list of jobs, with information about training, salaries, job opportunities and prospects. Most of these jobs were routinely done not very long ago by people many or most of whom had not even finished high school. Why all this need for extra training?

The stock answer is that work has become more complicated. But Ivar Berg, in his book *Education and Jobs: The Great Training Robbery,* pointed out that this is not so, that studies have repeatedly shown, in a wide variety of fields, that there is no connection between the amount of "training" and actual on-the-job performance. So what is the "training" for?

I suggest that it has two real and serious purposes. One is to limit the number of people who can get into any field of work. Make every lawyer (doctor, plumber, etc.) go to some school, cut down the number of schools, and presto! you have held down the supply of lawyers (or doctors, etc.).

The other purpose of training is to serve as a kind of job tax. To get the "best" jobs, you have to go not just to college but to graduate schools, which you can't get into unless you have been to a "good" i.e. exclusive and expensive college. All this may cost you about $50,000. To get somewhat less desirable jobs, you need somewhat less expensive training, i.e., pay a smaller tax, and so on down the line.

Why do employers want their employees to have paid a job tax, and usually the highest job tax they can afford? Joyce Mitchell's book suggests an answer. On page 6 she writes:

"...the truth is that on the average, workers change basic jobs every 5 years ...under the age of 35 most workers look for a job every year and a half, and after 35 they look every 3 years."

These people look for new jobs because they have grown tired of, or can't stand, the ones they had. This is a nuisance for employers, who have to find replacements, and then train them *on the job,* where all real training is done (in law and medicine as well). They think, quite sensibly, that if you have paid a big tax to get the job you have, you are more likely to stay put, and accept whatever comes to you, instead of chasing after a better job.

Why not then require a college degree of every office and factory worker? Because there aren't enough people who have college degrees *and are willing to work more or less indefinitely at those jobs.* It is hard, for example, for a woman with a college degree to get a routine office job, because employers think, "With that degree, she is only going to find something more in line with what she thinks she deserves." What the employer wants is someone who thinks, "This job may not be too good, but it's the best job I am likely to be able to get."

When Joyce Mitchell called her book *The Work Book* I don't think she was making a sly reference to school workbooks. But the connection is there; the school workbook gets you ready for the life work book.

Also from *The Work Book:*

"…As in Japan today, there will be so many benefits which provide workers and their dependents with cheap medical insurance, paid vacations, good recreation, a guaranteed retirement, and all kinds of security that most people will feel that they can't afford to work outside of government, large corporations, or jobs covered by strong unions."

In other words, you can't argue with Big Daddy, can't even talk to him, but as long as you do what he tells you, he will take good care of you.

FRIENDLY PROF.

Prof. David N. Campbell (2828 C. L., School of Education, Univ. of Pittsburgh, Pittsburgh PA 15260) has already helped a number of families (including the Perchemlides) in unschooling efforts—advice on curricula, evaluation, etc.—and has said that if any other families are looking for this kind of help they can get in touch with him directly. (If any others in this field would like to be listed in GWS, please let us know.)

Just to set the record straight, Dr. Campbell is the inventor of the portfolio plan by which the education of the children will be evaluated (see GWS #8).

A USEFUL SCHOOL

Dr. Carl Hedman, Prof. of Philosophy at the Univ. of Wisconsin at Milwaukee, has been working for some time with the Multicultural Community High School there. The *Milwaukee Journal* of 3/20/79 printed this letter from him:

"We at Multicultural Community High School, Inc. were delighted to see *The Journal's* editorial on March 2

challenging the notion that we can solve our school problems by creating 'a batch of new laws …to help schools get the kids in line.'

Our experience with hundreds of young people over the last seven years has shown that 9 times out of 10, the kid who raises a rumpus at the traditional school—and we're not talking about the person who commits an act of violence—does so out of boredom or frustration.

Almost always we've found that the so-called behavior problem disappears when the person no longer has to fend off the cliques that form when large numbers of people are involuntarily herded together.

On our model, we don't *try* to lock up kids all day. Instead, our students voluntarily study hard for a couple of hours in our modest classrooms out in the community and then go off to part-time jobs.

Some people may object that it would be too expensive to provide such individualized learning situations for large numbers of secondary students. Of course, if one assumes that each mini-school must have all the latest equipment and be staffed only by highly paid professional educators, then no society could afford this model.

But if one shares our belief that it doesn't matter what one's physical surroundings are, and that almost any adult can, with support, serve as an educational resource person, then a whole new picture begins to emerge. We don't think, by the way, that such models suit only the so-called slow learner or problem child. We have found that all kinds of young people prosper at our school.

One can begin to imagine a radically different future in secondary education, one where professional educators turn to the community rather than to the courts for help; where they cease to threaten and begin to find ways to use community resources, community centers, parents, older siblings, etc. to create a city full of one room schoolhouses to nurture the intellectual and emotional growth of our adolescents."

As we said in GWS #3, MCHS is part of the Milwaukee Public Schools, which tolerate it and use it as a place to dump troublesome students. People who still feel strongly committed to working with and (if possible) changing public schools might find it interesting and useful to try to get something like MCHS going in their own community—perhaps for primary as well as secondary school students.

A note on facilities. When I was a visiting teacher at Berkeley in 1969, the students waged a huge "strike," actually more a boycott than a strike. As part of this boycott, my students (in four sections of English) asked me to meet the classes in the off-campus apartments where most of the students lived. We did, jamming twenty or twenty-five people into small living rooms and bedrooms. It worked fine, in fact, it worked better—the crowded and natural atmosphere made for much more lively and interesting classes.

The University was very alarmed by all of this, kept urging the faculty to insist on meeting their classes in regular university classrooms. The last thing in the world they wanted people to learn was that most of those fancy and expensive university buildings were not necessary, and that people could share ideas and learn things anywhere.

SUMMER WORK

From July 21–August 11 (3 wks.) the Fellowship of Reconciliation and the Resource Center for Nonviolence will co-sponsor their second work project at Red Wind Native American Community in California.

Red Wind, located 30 miles from San Luis Obispo, is a traditional, self-governing community where about 60 people live and work. (It is not a reservation.) Here Indians and non-Indians share in building an alternative to mainstream culture that includes farming, schooling, and craftswork in a 400 acre site in the high desert.

Workcamp volunteers will participate in the ongoing life of the community contributing to the goal of self-sufficiency. There will be time for recreation and discussions on the spiritual basis of Native American culture, nonviolence, social change, and related issues.

Volunteers are expected to provide their own transportation plus a contribution of $20 for food and expenses. Please return applications by May 15.

Ages 17 and up, Write FOR, Youth Action, Box 271, Nyack NY 10960 212-568-8200, or Resource Center for Nonviolence, Box 2234, Santa Cruz CA 95063 408-423-1626.

THE CROWDED COURT

The March 26, 1979 issue of *U.S. News and World Report* published an article, "Supreme Court—Trials and Tribulations," which included these extraordinary and in some ways alarming figures. In 1930 the Court had 984 cases on its docket—cases waiting to be heard—and issued opinions in 134 cases. In 1940 there were 1078 cases waiting, 137 decided. For 1950 the figures were 1448 and 87; 1960—2178 and 117; 1970—4202 and 108; 1978—4704 and 129! I can well understand that the Justices see and think about this incredible and hopeless backlog of cases with something close to terror.

It's an ill wind that blows no good, as the saying goes. Considering the nature of the present Supreme Court, I think that its overload is probably good news for us. What it means is that the Court will probably not take the time to hear, and so will not overturn, decisions by state and lower Federal courts that are favorable to unschoolers. If we can win in the lower courts, then we are home free; by the same token, if we lose in the lower courts, the Supreme Court won't save us. Since I think this Court would and will be very hostile to unschoolers—they said as much in the *Yoder* case—I will be glad

to see them leave us alone.

I still think that, busy as they are, they will take time to reverse any lower court that rules against compulsory schooling on too broad grounds. But narrow rulings will probably be allowed to stand.

ON EVALUATION

A recent issue of *Manas* quotes from the book *Stage Theories of Cognitive And Moral Development: Criticisms And Applications*, a collection of reprints from the *Harvard Educational Review*. Lawrence Kohlberg and Rochelle Mayer write, in part:

"…After a deluge of studies in the sixties examining the effects of programs on I.Q. and achievement tests, and drawing policy conclusions, researchers *finally* (Ed. italics) began to ask the question, 'What is the justification for using I.Q. tests or achievement tests to evaluate programs in the first place?'

1. The current prevalent definition of the aims of education, in terms of academic achievement supplemented by a concern for mental health, cannot be justified empirically or logically.

2. The overwhelming emphasis of educational psychology on methods of instruction and tests and measurements which presuppose a 'value-neutral' psychology is misplaced.

3. An alternative notion that the aim of schools should be the stimulation of human development is scientifically, ethically, and practically a viable conception which provides the framework for a new kind of educational psychology.

…Advice about means and methods involves value considerations and cannot be made purely on a basis of 'facts.' Concrete, positive reinforcement is not an ethically neutral means. To advise the use of concrete positive reinforcement is to advise that a certain kind of character, motivated by concrete reinforcement, is the end of education."

———

Many present and would-be unschoolers are arguing with school authorities about methods of instruction and evaluation. I think they might find some very useful ammunition in the above quotes. The schools, by their methods, tend to turn out people who will work only for money. People who want their children to grow up into the kind of people who do their work for other and better reasons have strong moral and/or religious grounds for refusing to subject their children to the schools' methods of teaching and evaluation.

We should not fool ourselves, however, that the people at the Harvard School of Education are the friends, or even potential friends, of unschoolers. They are just as interested as any other educators in keeping alive the myth that only people with long and complicated "training" can be trusted and allowed to teach children. What they are trying to do is market and sell a whole new system of training.

Meanwhile, we may be able to make good use of some of their objections to the present system.

A PLACE FOR DOING THINGS

I have been reading school brochures for years. Most of them irritate or infuriate me. Mabel Dennison has just sent me one that I like, from the Sandy River School where she teaches (R.F.D. #3, Farmington ME 04938, Tel. 207-778-2386).

I print it here in GWS for several reasons. Many people, not necessarily unschoolers, write us that they are planning to start a school, and ask for advice. Many unschooling parents are also thinking about starting schools to shelter them from compulsory attendance laws. And in time many parents who are not interested in schools or worried about shelter may begin to think of making some kind of cooperative activity center where their children, if and when they feel like it, can get together and do interesting things. The Sandy River School brochure says, about as well as anything I have seen, what such a school/shelter/camp/activity center might be.

The brochure begins with two photographs, one of a group of children of different ages leaping off a sand dune, the other of two boys holding up a fish which they caught through the ice. Over the first photo is written SCHOOL?; over the second, OR SCHOOL VACATION? The brochure then says, in part:

TEACHERS AND CHILDREN

These photographs are school pictures; they are not vacation pictures. They show some of the kinds of things we expect our children to be doing at the Sandy River School: jumping off a sand dune, ice fishing. We expect children to be on teachers' laps and climbing on their shoulders.

School activities are similar to what children do on weekends and during school vacation. They watch, they listen, they read, they play alone or together, they try out whatever tools and equipment they can get hold of. They bicker, they tease, they pick scapegoats, they practice mock warfare, they gang up girls against boys. And at times they are remarkably generous and caring of each other.

We think that adults who spend time with children should be able to tolerate at least some of the noise and confusion that children create. We feel that adults don't have to deny the desires and choices of children as much as they usually do. We want adults to expand and affirm their own powers of strong feeling and creativity and to become people who can interact with

children as well as order them.

Teachers at the Sandy River School organize regular math, reading, and music practice to add to the normal activities of children. They offer lessons in whatever they know well or can do. They act as companions and guides for the interests of children. They offer suggestions and support. They do what they like doing, whether children are interested or not. They plan, not so much with possible learnings or a curriculum in mind, as simply with the activity itself in mind: making soup, taking a walk, using such and such art materials. Daily life at the Sandy River School is very ordinary and unpretentious.

Teachers supervise children from a distance. They offer more adult supervision, companionship, and guidance than children probably get in vacation, and less adult supervision in the form of direction and teaching than children usually get in school.

We evaluate our children for their overall well-being; their quickness, bright eyes, wit, intelligence, graceful movements, more than for their mastery of subject matter.

LEARNING

We believe that intelligence develops by organization of an ever-increasing amount of skill, memory, knowledge, and experience. Children do this for themselves. It is not necessary for us, and it is probably harmful to children, to parcel knowledge into increments of the next step. Children practice what they need to practice. They absorb what is new, what they are in contact with. They ask what they need to know. Eventually children become aware that they have learned, aware of their initiative and power as learners. Very gradually thinking and learning become more deliberate, and somewhat self-conscious.

…There is nothing wrong with a child's following one bent or interest, or pursuing one or two activities. He/she is just as likely to develop other interests later. A small amount of deeply assimilated learning is worth years of unwanted learning. Wanted learning can be built on, in geometric proportions; unwanted learning is choking, deeply disordering, and destroys integrity.

A PROPOSAL

…If you started with the premise that children's normal activities are valid and that their choices are valid as well, you could set up a school, at which attendance was voluntary, with an indoor and outdoor play area. You would also have classrooms and workshops which would be open and available when there was an adult available to take care of the equipment and act as supervisor, companion, and teacher if requested. There could be a library, a gymnasium, a science lab, a shop full of wires and buzzers and old TV sets, a room where stories were read aloud, movies shown, and assignments given, a storeroom of skis, skates, and sports equipment. You could find out at what age children would make use of what.

Or suppose that the schools, as they are, were open to children and that children were free to make use of the activities and equipment that attracted them. Or suppose places of adult work were open to perusal and limited participation by children. These are the kinds of changes in educational policy and practice we would like to see in this country.

ORDER, ROUTINE, DISCIPLINE, LIMITATION, STRUCTURE

...The usual, and we think unnecessary, routines of school include assignments, curriculums, testing, tracking and administrative procedures.... Regular occurrences, and the rules associated with them, are the routines of a free school: who will feed the cat, who sits in the front seat of a vehicle, trading lunches, daily and weekly scheduled activities, returning library books every two weeks. Fights and disagreements are settled by children alone or by children and adults together. When a child decides deliberately to study recorder playing, the study is as disciplined and structured as anywhere else. When a young person helps an adult build a chimney they build it from the ground up, and find out how well it works. The cheerfulness, happiness, knowledge, and skill of each adult and child are conditions, and ordering forces. Part of the order of math, science, and music, that has been spoiled in schools for many people, is self-evident in daily life...

It is a waste beyond words of the time of life of a child, of the only childhood there is, to divert a child from his or her usual activities of play, talk, movement, invention, and exploration. These are the most intelligent activities he/she could possibly be engaged in. It is a second waste to obscure natural conditions; both the tough hardships of life, and the simple order and beauty of life, by interposing unnecessary limits and controls over children.

We are glad our children are in motion most of the day. We see that they are noticeably strong and healthy. We believe that their fulfillment as adults depends on their lives being built now on experiences that are chosen and self-determined. We want our children to grow against the natural limitations of life, and, we think because of this, to take on with spirit and competence some share of the much needed work of the world.

These are strong and lovely words. Many parents might find it helpful to quote parts of this statement in whatever home teaching plan they might submit to schools.

Two minor disagreements. At one point the brochure speaks of giving out assignments—which it later contradicts. Consider this a slip of the pen. A child working, by choice, on some art, craft, sport, or field of activity or study, might ask a teacher for some special

work to do at home outside of school, but any such "assignment" could be given out anywhere, wherever the two people happened to be. And the brochure speaks of "classrooms." A mistake, I think; a room which is used only for "classes," whatever that word might mean in such a place, would be no good even for that. A room is a room, and people should be able to use it for anything that can be done in it, including hold a "class," if that is what they want to do.

LEARNING DISABILITIES

Still planning a longer article on "Learning Disabilities." For the time being, here is a question that might be interesting and useful to ask school people and other L.D. believers:

"How do you tell the difference between a learning difficulty (which we all experience every time we try to learn anything) and a learning disability? That is to say, how do you tell, or on what basis does someone decide (and who is the someone?) whether the cause of a given learning difficulty lies within the nervous system of the learner, or with things outside of the learner— the learning situation, the teacher's explanations, the teacher him/herself, or the material itself? And if you decide that the cause of the difficulty lies within the learner, who decides, and again on what basis, whether or not that inferred cause is curable, in short, whether anything can be done about it, and if so, what?"

If any readers ask this question of schools, I would like very much to know what answers (if any) they get.

TO AN EDITOR

One of our readers in Virginia, who is trying to take a child out of school, wrote the following letter to a leading Virginia newspaper, I think the *Richmond Virginian-Pilot.* I don't know yet whether the paper printed it, but it seems a good model for other parents to follow.

TO THE EDITOR:

This letter is in reference to the March 15 article on the Giesy family from Norfolk. The Giesys have chosen to educate their own children instead of using any of the traditional school programs.

I cannot help but cry out to my fellow Virginians. I cry out asking that we examine what we meant when we passed a compulsory attendance law. Did we intend that children have educational opportunity or did we mandate that children spend their day, between 9:00 AM. and 3:00 PM., in certain officially designated buildings.

I suggest that the Virginia legislature never meant to enact legislation that would make it a *crime* for parents to educate their own children.

The U.S. Constitution and long tradition of the commonwealth has spelled out the importance of individual rights. These rights of men, women, and families call for restraint by the State in its attempt to prescribe the manner by which a family chooses to educate its children.

I am, as well as many of you may be, a supporter of a healthy public school system. The survival of such a system does not depend on stamping out alternative educational programs. Rather, the healthy growth of our public system depends on the existence of as many alternatives as possible.

I take this opportunity to speak to you of these matters because I, too, find myself and my family at odds with the attitude of the official educators of our society. I, too, am being threatened by the local superintendent of schools to return one of my children to schooling which is acceptable to the superintendent, else my wife and I will have criminal charges brought upon us.

The State Department of Education claims that a teaching credential is required for a parent to teach his own child. An elementary analysis of the education courses required for a teaching credential will readily show that it is designed specifically for those who will teach in classroom settings, not home environments.

The Department of Education gives no credit to parents for the experience gathered over the years. This experience is generally of greater value than courses on classroom management to parents teaching in a home educational setting.

If the Department of Education is fixed upon the concept of credentials for parents who want to teach their own children, then perhaps they should lobby with the State Council of Higher Education to create a "Home Teaching Credential," the characteristics of which might be more suitable to home teaching. Such certificates could be obtained via correspondence courses, tests, classes at community colleges or through continuing education programs of universities. Credit could be given to parents for the experience they already have.

Indeed, the people who should act on this are the people we have elected to represent us in Richmond. It should not be a problem which is dealt with by the vested interest at the Department of Education.

I call on John Chichester and his colleagues from the Senate Education Committee to address the inequity that the Virginia Department of Education has been visiting upon some in our State.

THE LAW SUMMED UP

Let me sum up what the courts have had to say about the right of parents to teach their children at home. The law is an ever-changing body, and this is the law as of today.

1) Parents have a right to educate their children in whatever way they believe in: the state cannot impose on all parents any kind of educational monopoly, of schools, methods, or whatever. *Pierce v. Society of Sisters*, and most recently *Perchemlides*.

2) The state may not deprive parents of this right for arbitrary reasons, but only for serious educational ones, which it must make known to parents, with all the forms of due process. Again, *Perchemlides*.

3) A state that would deny parents these rights by saying that their home education plan is inadequate has a burden of proof to show beyond reasonable doubt that this is so. Parents are assumed to be competent to teach their children until proved otherwise. This Assumption of Competence is kin to and part of the general Assumption of Innocence (of the accused) which holds in all criminal proceedings. *Sessions.*

4) In order to prove that the parents' education plans are inadequate, the state must show that its own requirements, regulations, etc. are educationally necessary and do in fact produce in its own schools better results than the parents get or are likely to get. *Hinton et. al.* (Ky.)

TEXAS LAW

A parent writes from Texas: "I thought you might like to know that it is not against the law to unschool your child in the state of Texas. There is a compulsory attendance law but if a parent signs a waiver, that is all that is necessary to withdraw him from the school system. However in many cases it is not even necessary to sign a waiver. We did not and neither did a friend who withdrew her son and put him in our local university, where he is doing well. The university will not give him his earned credits until he is old enough to take a G.E.D. exam, but they are holding them for him...."

_____

That is certainly interesting news. We need to know a bit more—where does one get the waiver, what does it say, to whom does one give it after signing it, is this true in all school districts or only certain ones? We'll be grateful for any information Texas readers can give us about this.

JUDGE GREANEY'S RULING

In GWS #7 we said that a Massachusetts Superior Court judge had handed down a ruling favorable to the Perchemlides family, and that in a later issue we would print some of the most significant parts of this (very long) ruling. (We will continue to send copies of the entire ruling for $2.)

Judge Greaney's ruling says, in part:

II. CONSTITUTIONAL AND STATUTORY CLAIMS

Central to the Perchemlides' complaint is their assertion that under the United States Constitution, parents derive certain rights and accrue certain protections to choose an alternative to public school education for their children. It is important to note at the outset the exact point of the argument. Plaintiffs do not argue that there exists a federally protected right to *home* instruction, *per se*, but rather that federal protection attaches to a home education alternative which is supplied by state statute and state court decisions. In reply, defendant willingly concedes that parents have a "fundamental right" to send their children to non-public schools as long as those schools meet valid educational standards set by the state…

For reasons discussed below, I conclude that although it is the right and duty of the superintendent or the school committee to inquire into, and either approve or disapprove home education plans, the parents' constitutional rights to decide how their own children shall be educated places reasonable limitations on that inquiry and thus circumscribes the discretion of the local authorities. Due in large part to the novelty of this situation for the Amherst school system, and to a genuine misunderstanding about the scope of parents' rights to home educate their children, the superintendent and the school committee have, in the Court's opinion, applied some standards to the review of the plaintiff's plan which are inappropriate, and the matter must be returned to them for further consideration.

A. *Constitutional and Statutory Protection of the Right to Home Education.*

On a number of occasions, the United States Supreme Court has held that certain personal rights can be deemed "fundamental" or "implicit in the concept of ordered liberty" and are included in a guarantee of "personal privacy" that emanates from the more specific guarantees contained in the Bill of Rights. Because the Constitution does not mention "privacy," courts and commentators have disagreed about the precise constitutional source of the guarantee. Older decisions …looked to the concept of liberty contained in the first section of the Fourteenth Amendment. *Pierce v. Society of Sisters*, 268 U.S. 510 (1925); *Meyer v. Nebraska,* 262 U.S. 390 (1922). More recent cases, while not entirely abandoning this ground, have drawn upon the First, Fourth, Fifth, and Ninth Amendments in various contexts. *Roe v. Wade*, 410 U.S. 113, 152-53 (1973). Whatever the precise constitutional source of the individual right to privacy, the Supreme Court has stated that the right not only protects against the unjustified disclosure of personal matters, but also protects the individual's "interest in independence in making certain kinds of important decisions." *Whalen v. Roe*, 429 U.S. 589 n. 26 (1977).

It has become an axiom of constitutional law that one such kind of decision that individuals may make without unjustified government interference deals with matters relating to "child rearing and education." *Smith*

v. Offer, 431 U.S. 816 (1977); *Carey v. Population Services International*, 431 U.S. 678 (1977); *Whalen v. Roe, supra*; *Paul v. Davis,* 424 U.S. 693 (1976); *Wisconsin v. Yoder,* 406 U.S. 205 (1972); *Griswold v. Connecticut*, 381 U.S. 479 (1965); *Pierce v. Society of Sisters, supra.* The Supreme Court has repeatedly reaffirmed the authority of the *Pierce* holding that "the fundamental theory of liberty upon which all governments in this Union repose excludes any general power of the state to standardize its children by forcing them to accept instruction from public teachers only." *Pierce v. Society of Sisters*, 268 U.S. 510, 535. The nature of the parents' right on a constitutional level, and the fact that it draws support from several branches of the Bill of Rights was concisely expressed in these terms by Justice Douglas concurring in *Roe v. Wade:*

"The Ninth Amendment obviously does not create federally enforceable rights. It merely says, 'the enumeration in the Constitution of certain rights shall not be construed to deny or disparage others retained by the people.' But a catalogue of these rights includes customary, traditional, and time honored rights, amenities and privileges…. Many of them, in my view, come within the meaning of the term 'liberty' as used in the Fourteenth Amendment… [one] is *freedom of choice in the basic decisions of one's life* respecting marriage, divorce, contraception, *and the education and upbringing of children.…*" [Judge Greaney's italics.]

Thus, parents need not demonstrate a formal religious reason for insisting on their right to choose other than public school education since the right of privacy, which protects the right to choose alternative forms of education, grows out of constitutional guarantees in addition to those contained in the First Amendment. Nonreligious as well as religious parents have the right to choose from the full range of educational alternatives for their children. There will remain little privacy in the "right to privacy" if the state is permitted to inquire into the motives behind parents' decisions regarding the education of their children. As plaintiffs here point out, the plaintiffs in *Pierce* included a secular military academy, and the holding in that case did not mention religious beliefs of the Free Exercise clause of the First Amendment. See also, *Farrington v. Tokushige* 273 U.S. 284 (1927); *Meek v. Pittenger,* 374 F. Supp. 639, 653 (E.D. Pa. 1974).

Without doubt, then, the Massachusetts compulsory attendance statute might well be constitutionally infirm if it did not exempt students whose parents prefer alternative forms of education (Ed. note—These are my italics, and these words from Judge Greaney's ruling should certainly be quoted by unschooling parents in any state which does not make something other than school attendance a specifically legal alternative.) …

B. *Scope of the State's Regulatory Powers.*

...Just as the Court in *Roe v. Wade* recognized that the state has important interests in regulating the abortion decision, the state has an important interest in regulating the education of school age children. The defendants accurately point out that attempts by parents to deny that the state has any right to set educational standards for school age children have been consistently rejected by the federal courts...

The Perchemlides do not dispute that under the police power the state is obliged to see that children are educated and to set reasonable standards that define and limit the term "education." Neither do the Perchemlides seek to do that which is proscribed by *Wisconsin v. Yoder*—to "substitute their own idiosyncratic views of what knowledge a child needs to be a productive and happy member of society" for the standards set by duly elected and appointed officials. On the contrary, the plaintiffs appear essentially willing to conform their home education program to the state's bona fide academic and curricular standards. (Ed. note—as to which of these standards are in fact bona fide, see Judge Meigs' ruling in GWS #8, also very much worth quoting in any home education proposal)...

The state may not, however, set standards that are so difficult to satisfy that they effectively eviscerate the home education alternative. (Ed. italics) ...[the state] may not use regulations or standards as a means of discouraging alternatives which are not identical to the public schools. *Farrington v. Tokushige, supra; State v. Whisner*, 351 N. E. 2nd 750 (S. Ct. Ohio 1976)...

It follows from the very nature of the right to home education that the school committee or the superintendent may not reject a proposal submitted by parents on the ground that the home environment is *socially* different from the classroom environment.... Under our system, the parents must be allowed to decide whether public school education, including its socialization aspects, is desirable or undesirable for their children...

III. JUDICIAL REVIEW

...Given the competing interests present in this case... the proper role of the court is as follows: *First*, it must measure the substantive standards used by the superintendent and the school committee against the constitutional limitations already outlined. *Second*, it must analyze the procedural due process aspects of the case to determine how much process is due the parents and whether they obtained the process due. *Third*, once satisfied that constitutional standards have been employed and due process protections accorded, the reviewing court should do no more than examine the school committee's articulated reasons for its decision to see whether it can determine "with some measure of confidence whether or not the discretion... has been exercised in a manner that is neither arbitrary nor capricious" and whether the decision to deny the home education request "was reached for impermissible reasons or for no reason at all." *Dunlop v. Bachowski*, 421 U.S. 560, 571-73 (1975).

IV. FINDINGS AS TO STANDARDS AND PROCEDURAL DUE PROCESS.

...The school committee members and superintendent have stated that "in evaluating plaintiffs' proposed plan, defendants applied the same standards used in approving any other form of alternative education. Such plan had to be equal in thoroughness and efficiency and in the progress made as that of the public schools." That is the statutory standard used in evaluating *private school programs*. Nothing in the statute makes this standard directly applicable to the "otherwise instructed" language in which the Supreme Judicial Court, in the *Roberts* case, found a right to home education. Indeed, the way the statute is written indicates that applying criteria used to evaluate private schools may not be appropriate to a home education request. The statute very carefully delineates the type of schools that form a permissible alternative to public day schools and then reserves alternate education as a separate, distinct classification in this language: "...or of a child who is being otherwise instructed in a manner approved in advance by the superintendent or the school committee."

There are certain ways in which individualized home instruction can never be the "equivalent" of any in-school education, public or private. At home, there are no other students, no classrooms, no pre-existing schedules. The parents stand in a very different relationship to their children than do teachers in a class full of other people's children. In view of these differences, to require congruent "equivalency" is self-defeating because it might foreclose the use of teaching methods less formalized, but in the home setting more effective than those used in the classroom. For example, certain step-by-step programs of graded instruction, involving the use of standardized texts and tests periodically administered, might be unnecessary when the parent-teacher enjoys a constant communication with the child, and so is able to monitor his or her comprehension and progress on an individualized level impossible in a school setting....

In summary, the record shows that school committee members had somewhat contradictory notions about what standards to apply to the Perchemlides application, and that most of the committee members relied upon impermissible standards, to one degree or another. Much of the difficulty encountered by all parties in this situation could be avoided were the school committee and superintendent to draft broad standards setting out their expectations for home education programs. Although I decline to rule that such standards are required in this context, it is significant that federal courts have viewed, in other contexts, "the establishment of written, objective and ascertainable standards" as an "intricate [sic] part of Due Process." *Baker-Chaput v. Cammett* 406 F. Supp. 1134 (D. N.H. 1076), and cases cited....

Some of the reasons cited for the rejection of the Perchemlides' plan, such as lack of group experience, improper motive, and bad precedent, clearly intrude too far on the parents' right to direct their children's education. Other strictly academic standards used may have been perfectly appropriate, but even here it is impossible to know whether the authorities disapproved the plan because Richard could not be expected to learn as much as he would in public school, a permissible reason, or because the actual program of study was not a carbon copy of the public school curriculum, a requirement which is not imposed by statute and intrudes too far on the right to home education.

LET'S USE IT

We print these words from Judge Greaney's ruling so that from now on people will quote freely from them in any home education plan they draw up. These words, in short, are not here just to make people feel better (though we hope and expect that they will do that) but to be used.

We have quoted the parts of the ruling that are most important and helpful to us. But any who think that they may have some sort of conflict with the schools would probably do well to read the entire ruling (av. here for $2). It is an excellent lesson in how thorough and careful judges think—something we cannot know too much about.

No more than lawyers do judges like to lose. For a lawyer, losing is having a court rule against you; for a judge, it is having a higher court reverse you. Judge Greaney has taken great pains to build a ruling that will stand. He has left no weak spots through which a higher court might overturn it. Since his ruling is so strong, there are (so far) no signs that the school district in this case is planning to appeal it.

What has this to do with us? The lawyer, in preparing a legal brief, tries to construct an argument so solid that, in effect, all the judge has to do is sign it. Our job is to put into every home education proposal a legal argument that is so strong that the schools' lawyers will not be able to overturn it in court, or better yet, will not even wish to take it to court. The more we can learn to think like a careful judge, the better our chances of winning in court if we have to go there, or of staying out altogether.

That's why we have had, and will have, all this legal stuff in GWS.

SCHOOL OR CLUB?

Nancy Plent also writes:

"...One more thing I did want to say is about the other mothers I'm meeting. None of us worry about social adjustment stuff, we all know that kids can keep occupied with friends of all ages and with their own interests. But every one of us feels that our kids need more kids. They are feeling 'different' and left out, no matter what their situation. E often greets a sunny day with, 'Boy, it's a great day to ride green machines! I'll call Tommy and .... oh, he's in school today.' No big thing, maybe, but it happens often, to all of our kids, and we worry about it.

For this reason, the talk always comes around to 'maybe if we started some kind of school.' We know it is a problem without an answer right now, but we bat it around wistfully all the time anyway. I can only see an answer when we find more people doing it, convince more people that they should do it. I'm giving it all I've got."

Some thoughts on this. It would be a fine thing if in any community there were more places for children, and indeed people of all ages, to get together and do various kinds of things. I talk about what such places might be like in early chapters of *Instead of Education*, and even more in the appendix of that book, which describes a remarkable place called the Peckham Center, which existed for a while in a part of London in the late 1930's.

But places like the Peckham Center are quite a way down the road. If we had a thousand unschooling families, maybe even five hundred or less, in a not too spread out area, they could probably find the resources to make themselves something like the Peckham Center, a family club. In some ways, the country clubs that rich folks belong to are a much better model of what we want than a school. Take away the eighteen-hole golf courses, the elaborate tennis courts and other facilities, the palatial clubhouse, and what's left is very close in spirit to what we are after. You don't *have* to play golf just because you go to the golf club. You don't have to *do* anything. There are certain kinds of resources there for you to use, if you want, but you can spend the day there sitting in a chair and looking at the sky. Why not an inexpensive version of the same thing? A country club without the country—or perhaps a different kind of country, just a little patch of field or woods or whatever is handy.

If we can keep the idea of a family club in mind, we will probably make fairly sensible choices and decisions. But if we start thinking and talking about "a school," we are very likely to repeat a cycle that by now people have gone through hundreds of times.

It begins with a small group of Founding Families (hereafter FF), who want to start a small cooperative school (maybe day care center). By doing all the work themselves, and keeping everything modest, they hope to be able to pay the expenses out of their own pockets and what little they can raise. They start their school, and the first thing that happens is that they find that most of the new families who bring their children into the school don't want to do much of the work. They want to *use* the school, not build it or keep it going. The FF struggle for a while, trying to get parents to pledge so many hours of work per week, and so on. But the work load grows until finally the FF have to think about hiring some help.

At this point, most of those parents who are doing some work stop doing it. "Why should we have to do this, when we're paying a teacher (or teachers)?" The teachers begin to do the work of the school, and the task of the parents becomes 1) to have meetings to argue about what the teachers should be doing, and 2) to raise money to keep the school going. Many parents are glad to do the first task while the FF find themselves doing most of the second.

After a while one or more of the following things happens: 1) the school can't raise the money it needs, and has to fold 2) the parents are torn apart by arguments about what the school should do, and the school breaks up 3) a group of richer parents who have enough money to keep the school going take control, and make it into a conventional school.

Even if the school avoids all these disasters, the FF eventually become exhausted by their struggles to keep the school alive, and give up. People who started the school because they couldn't stand what conventional schools were doing to their children, say, "I'm exhausted, I can't do any more of this," and send their children right back to those same schools.

Of course, the children are better off for having escaped those schools, even if only for a few years, so perhaps this makes all the struggle worthwhile. But when unschoolers write about starting a school so their children can meet with friends, I don't think this cycle of events is what they have in mind.

By the way, the cycle works about the same when the school is started by teachers. I know one of a small group of teachers, who after years of frustration started their own school so that, at last, they could teach children in a way they believed in. With great effort and sacrifice they kept the school going, and growing. But as it grew it needed more money, and became more and more dependent on a group of rich parents. One day this group said to the teachers and other parents, "We want this school to be more like regular schools. If you want to go along with us in this, fine. If not, and you outvote us, we'll take our money elsewhere." Most parents voted to go along with them. They then said to the teachers, whose work had built the school, "If you want to do things our way, fine; if not, good-bye." Good-bye it was. End of dream.

The money part of this sad scenario may change if things like voucher plans ever go through, which seems more likely now than it did even a year ago. But it will still be true that the more people come into your

school, the greater will be the pressure to turn it into some kind of conventional school—even the kind of pseudo-progressive school I wrote about in *How Children Fail.*

If your school is a true school, it will be used more and more by people who are not unschoolers. The advantage of having a club is that families will have to unschool their children, and take for themselves the responsibility for helping them grow and learn, *before* they can take advantage of your club. So you will be dealing with people who agree with you on basic issues. But, as I say, if you form a regular school, which any people can send their children to, I don't know how you are going to keep it from being taken over sooner or later by people who are not unschoolers.

If readers have ideas about these matters, which I'm sure many will, I hope they will write.

HOME–SCHOOL GUIDES

Richard & Joyce Kinmont, Rt. 2 Box 106-C, Brigham City, UT 84302, have sent me a copy of their book, *American Home Academy: The Journal of a Private Home School* ($4.25, +.50 post., +.20 sales tax in Utah), about how, and why, they unschooled their children and began teaching them at home. Many unschoolers, above all in Utah, will find it very encouraging and helpful. It is partly philosophy; partly a day-to-day account of what they did with their children, the most detailed and useful I have seen; and partly an account, again very detailed, complete with copies of letters from both sides, of their dealings with the school authorities.

On page 59, Mrs. Kinmont writes:

"If you decide not to enroll your children in the public school system, your local district may feel faced with a problem. At best they may be honestly concerned that your children are being well taught. At worst, they may feel threatened by your automatic no-confidence vote and the money their district will lose by not having your children enrolled. In either case, they will probably feel that they hold a stewardship over you. Do they? Should they?

Certainly they shouldn't. If the public schools held stewardship over private education, there really wouldn't be any private education. Who, then, should hold stewardship? Who will check to see that the students are being well taught? The answer is, the private schools should answer to the same people who are now checking on the public schools to see that they are teaching the children well—*the parents.* If the parents don't take the responsibility, no one else can. Both public and private education must answer to the parents! …

… if your school board feels obligated by the compulsory attendance law to know that you are in fact teaching your children, and if they are well motivated, it should be easy to satisfy them. If they are really interested in stopping you and in possessing all power, you will have a more difficult—but not an impossible—time...."

Here is Mr. Kinmont's first letter to school authorities, in this case the State Board of Education:

This letter is to inform you that we have established a private school, known as..., located at the above address.

Our school is in operation at least 180 days per year, at least 5 1/2 hours per day. Our curriculum includes reading, writing, math, social studies, music, art, physical education, science, health, crafts, industrial arts, fine arts, free enterprise, and the Constitution. The student body consists solely of the members of our own family.

To the best of our knowledge, this letter completes our legal obligation. If there are any further requirements *established by law* (Ed. italics—Mr. Kinmont emphasizes this point in all his letters to school people), please let us know and we will promptly comply."

On the facing page, this quote from Justice McReynolds in *Pierce v. Society of Sisters:*

"The child is not the mere creature of the State; those who nurture him and direct his destiny have the right coupled with the high duty, to recognize and prepare him for additional obligations. [The Oregon Compulsory Education Act] interferes with the liberty of parents and guardians to direct the upbringing and education of children under their control."

Later quotes from *People v. Levisen*, 404 Ill. 574, 90 N. E. 2d 213 (1950):

" ...the law is not made to punish those who provide their children with instruction *equal or superior to that* obtainable in the public schools. It is made for the parent who fails or refuses to properly educate his child...."

"...We do not think that the number of persons, whether one or many, make a place where instruction is imparted any less or more a school."

Mrs. Kinmont later writes:

"A few weeks after this visit [from school officials] I received from a friend... a message from an attorney that I should under no circumstances allow any school administrators into my home. I now see that this is very good advice. It would be nice to believe that these men are really only trying to help, as they say they are and as they should be, but we must be prepared for the possibility that they are really looking for ways to intimidate. In every case I know of where they have been allowed in, it has worked out badly for the family involved. Since this advice was unsolicited, and from a good man, we will heed it."

The following letters from Mr. Kinmont to the Director of Pupil Personnel of the local school system seem to me a model of what such letters should be:

"Thank you for your letter of ...We believe it would be most beneficial to be able to insure that our program is giving the equivalent of instruction required in public schools. In order to do this, we will need the following:

1. A copy of that part of the Utah Code which identifies the instruction required in public schools.
2. A copy of the public school curriculum by grades.
3. The minimum learning requirements in each subject.
4. The final examinations which determine that the minimum information has been learned.
5. A description of the action taken when a student does not meet the minimum learning requirements in any subject.

To further insure that we will be in compliance with any possible future court decisions, we would also appreciate receiving the following:

1. The full text of the Attorney General's opinion.
2. The qualifications you would require of a private school teacher if that responsibility were ever legally granted to the District.
3. Copies of the laws you mention relating to health of children, construction of buildings, course of study, etc..."

"We appreciate the kind tone of your letter. As my wife informed you on the telephone, however, we no longer feel a personal visit to our home would be necessary or appropriate.

We would be happy to inform you about our courses of study. We cover a great many subjects; and you are, of course, only concerned with those courses which are required by law. So if you will please provide us with a copy of the law which identifies the required courses, we will be happy to provide you with the information you requested.

To insure that we have met the minimum standards of the public schools, we do want to set up some minimum learning requirements and testing procedures for those courses prescribed by law. Again, we are awaiting information from you as to what these classes and the minimum standards are...."

Some final remarks by Mrs. Kinmont::

"If we should ever be required by a court of law to enroll our children in the public schools, we would do so. But I would continue to teach them during non-school hours, *and I would spend a great deal of time in their school classrooms* (Ed. italics—and I would sure like to be a fly on the wall during some of those school visits!)... .

This little book is not meant to be a tirade against the public school system. No matter how great their schools were, we would still want to teach our own children. Ours is much less a step away from the public schools and much more a step toward family education. ...

Help your children develop their creativity. As they do, you will find them more and more going off and learning things on their own. Then they will begin bringing exciting new creations and ideas to you. (Andrea wrote about a new idea yesterday: when a pencil is used up it is not really gone, but is spread all over dozens of pieces of paper.) Sometimes you will feel like you have pushed a small snowball over the side of a tall mountain and you are standing in amazement watching it gather speed and grow to giant proportions..."

———————

I do strongly recommend this book—the Kinmonts wrote me that they were preparing a newer and more up-to-date version—above all for parents who would like to teach their children at home but don't know how to begin.

Joyce Kinmont said to me in a letter that if she were starting all over again, knowing what she does now, she would do much less teaching, less planning of the children's learning. But that is all right. Parents who start to do this have to do it in a way that makes them comfortable, otherwise their worries will worry the children and the whole thing won't work. If it gives parents a little needed security at first to say that we will have Reading at 9 AM and Arithmetic at 10, that's OK.

Just a few days ago I received from Phil Donahue's office another booklet on home schooling, along with a letter from the author, Mary Bergman, who had asked that these materials be sent on to me. The booklet is called "Legal Papers and Letters Used for Establishing PIONEER TRAILS ACADEMY." I can't find anything in it which says how much it costs, but you can find out from the author, at Pioneer Trails Academy, PO Box 265, Morgan UT 84050. It is from this book that Richard Kinmont got the text of the letter that he first wrote to the State Board of Education; I gather that the Bergmans have been schooling their children at home for longer than the Kinmonts—their first pupil is about to graduate from college. I hope to be able to quote some material from the booklet in the next GWS.

Meanwhile, here are some encouraging words from Mary Bergman's letter:

"...We use these books with seminars for setting up families into schools. *This summer we established over three hundred home schools* (Ed. italics).

I would like to answer several of the questions which were asked on this program. First, and most important to the average inquirer is the social adjustment of a home taught student. They are more outgoing, friendlier, more self-confident, better conversationalists, and stronger leaders than the public school variety.... Our children graduate from our home academy and are admitted directly into college with no difficulty. At present 19-year-old Cathy is a graduating senior (Ed. note—she entered at 15) at Weber State College; Mark, our 17-year-old, is an advanced freshman at Southern Utah State; and Kevin, our 13-year-old, is being considered for early admission to a prestigious technical institute."

MATH BY DISCOVERY

Joyce Kinmont wrote to me late in Jan., saying, in part:

" ...I have finally been able, this year, to drop the public-school-at-home routine. I see my friends struggling with that problem, and I realize that it does take time.

I spend only 2 1/2 hours a day with my children now. The first hour we study religion together, the next 1 1/2 hrs. I help them read something, write something, and do a page in their math books. The reading and writing they enjoy, but math is boring. I am still looking for a 'John Holt' math program—something that asks questions and calls for experimentation, etc. Is there such a program?"

I wrote back, in part::

"Yes, there is such a program (or programs). (Yes, Virginia, there is a Santa Claus.) It is in my book, *What Do I Do Monday?*, which you can get from us here. I enclose a copy of a few pages, to give the general drift of it. I think it may be exactly what you are looking for...."

A few quotes from those pages:

"...we learn best ...when we feel the wholeness and openness (to us) of the world around us, and our own freedom and power and competence in it....

...My friend and I did some [beginning work in calculus]—all stuff he had had in the course. But now he said, 'So that's it. Why didn't anybody tell me that? It's so simple *when you see what it's about.'*

Exactly. What I had done, clumsily enough, was not to try to hand him a lump of knowledge, which people had already handed him and which he could not take hold of (Ed. note—he was a brilliant student at Harvard at the time), but to take him on a kind of human journey with the people who had first thought about and discovered these things.

...Instead of wasting endless time trying to get children to memorize meaningless and disconnected 'facts' and recipes, we should use numbers inside the classroom to do what people use numbers to do outside the classroom—to measure, compare, analyze, predict.

[Doing these experiments] we can see what an extraordinary amount of work with numbers—observing, recording, adding, subtracting, plotting—would be involved in all this. I hope that teachers will not think that the *point* of all this activity, all this investigation of skill growth and skill loss (Ed. note—what the experiments were about), is just to do some disguised arithmetic. Whoever thinks this way will completely miss the point, and will, in addition, spoil all this activity for the children. The *point* of all this investigating is to find answers to questions; the only use of the arithmetic is to help us find them. People did not think of measuring things so that they would get good at arithmetic; they measured things because they wanted or needed to find out or remember certain things about them, and they became better at arithmetic because they used it to do their measuring, and found that it helped. But it was the measuring, not the arithmetic, that was of chief importance. The need, the act that requires the skills, *creates* the skills."

(For more discovery math, see GWS #4 and #6.)

TIDBIT FROM MANAS

...in France, Fontanelle, although a popularizer of Cartesian cosmology, saw where this excess of simplicity might lead. In *Plurality of Worlds* (1686) he wrote:

"I perceive," said the Countess, "Philosophy is now become very Mechanical." "So mechanical," said I, "that I fear we shall quickly be ashamed of it; they will have the World to be in great, what a watch is in little; which is very regular & depends only upon the just disposing of the several parts of the movement. But pray tell me, Madam, had you not formerly a more sublime Idea of the Universe?"

A PRIVATE READER

"The best thing I wanted to share with you is that E is reading. I was prepared to see him a nonreader still at the age of 10, 12—who could tell? He was fascinated with the shapes of letters on his father's truck when he was two, picked out letter shapes in sidewalk cracks, read short words on signs, played games with beginning sounds (his idea, not mine) and generally always liked words.

Getting from that stage to actually reading books left a blank in my mind. If he didn't want me to help him, didn't sit down and work at it, how was he going to read beyond the shopping center signs stage? It must

be at this stage that school people nervously rush in with methods and phonics rules, and at times I had to stop myself from doing the same. Teaching habits die hard. He knew so much! But he wasn't pulling it all together, wasn't even interested in opening a book to see if he could read the whole thing. I was dying of curiosity to see if he could, but I kept on biting my lip every time a "lesson" threatened to come out.

He started about three months ago curling up with a comic book in the mag. section of the supermarket every week. Sometimes he'd buy one, and after we read it to him once, he'd take it off to a corner and study it for a while. He began "reading" them in bed. I knew something was happening because he got very quiet at these times, never asked me what a word was, and never made comments on the pictures. It became clear to me that reading was a private thing to him. After a while, he picked out easy books for bedtime reading and offered to read them to me. There were very few words he didn't know, and I'll never know how he learned the others. But it doesn't matter. He did it because he wanted to. I just hope I can keep on resisting all the pressures to do otherwise and let him set his own priorities.

Even the newest books on child raising are full of timetables for kids. *The Mother's Almanac* (Doubleday) advises to ignore 'bad words' in the very young, but swearers after the age of four should have their mouths washed out with soap and be given a hug after they stop crying.

It also included this gem:

'Almost every child will point to what he wants, instead of trying to name it, which will annoy you more and more. (Ed. note—why?) When he points to his juice next time, pick up the salt cellar, the pot holder, the tea strainer, saying. "Is this it? You mean this?" And finally, when he is almost furious, "Oh, the bottle. Say BOT TUL," and say the word face to face, several times, after you give it to him. He'll be too angry to say it then, but he'll try the next time or the next.'

(Ed. note—On the whole, I am against book-burning, but I think a good case could be made for burning that one, as cruel in spirit as it is stupid. When little children of that age point to things, they are asking us to name them, without teasing, insult, or sarcasm. They probably have a hunch what the things are called, but they want to test the hunch a few times to be sure of it before committing themselves—above all in families where they run some risk of being scolded or laughed at or otherwise humiliated if they make a mistake.

As for the soap, I'd like to make the author of that book *eat* a whole bar of soap—and no hug afterwards! There is a sensible and courteous, and therefore *effective* way of dealing with the whole question of forbidden words, about which I'll write a separate short piece. But it shows how much cruelty toward children is in our very national bloodstream that a publishing house as established as Doubleday would publish such a book.)

The mother continues:

"Not long ago we took E bowling. He's been crazy about the idea since he was tiny, and always got a turn with grandpop's bowling ball. As in a lot of things, we had better sense than to show him how or mark his score when he was tiny. For some reason, his new height led us to assume he wanted to play like adults. We bowled by frames, marked the scores, coached his throw when it began to go off, and watched unhappily as he got worse and worse and enjoyed it less and less.

Finally it dawned on us. He just liked the feeling of throwing the darned thing, and didn't really care about score. In fact, every number we wrote made his actions stiffer and his face more anxious. We told him the game was over and we would just roll a few with him. Immediately his pleasure in the game returned and he rolled a couple of strikes.

We play golf and tennis the same way. Bat the ball around, sometimes make up our own rules and contests, and quit whenever it bores us. Like the mother in GWS who learned she didn't have to be all that aggressive in Monopoly, I'm seeing that I have to question a lot of things we all grew up thinking of as the 'right' way to do things. GWS serves to 'remind' me of something new with each issue."

S. R. C. IN PAPERBACK

The American paperback edition of Alison Stallibrass's delightful and important book *The Self-Respecting Child* (GWS #1) is now out (Warner Books), and we are selling it for $5.35 + .30 postage. I can't recommend it too strongly.

MANY THANKS

Many people have very kindly responded to our request for volunteer help. We are gradually beginning to organize our work to make more and more use of it. If you volunteered, and we don't get something to you quickly, please be patient—we will have something for you sooner or later.

Editor—John Holt
Managing Editor—Peg Durkee

GROWING WITHOUT SCHOOLING

Issue #10

July, 1979

Unschooling is still much in the news. Iowa has ended its prosecution of the Sessions family, and New Hampshire (according to a news report) has dropped its case against Betsy Tompkins, largely because the local school district has (wisely) decided it is costing too much money.

In Minnesota a small town jury found Mrs. Wunsch guilty of violating compulsory attendance laws, but the verdict was so obviously prejudiced, and against the whole weight of the evidence, that the judge (rightly and legally) overturned the verdict.

Rev. Paul Lindstrom of the Christian Liberty Academy writes that in the nine unschooling cases with which his organization has been involved, the parents have won seven and lost two.

Two families, one in Indiana (a first for that state, as far as I know) and one in New Hampshire, have persuaded their local schools to cooperate with their home schooling plans.

A mother on Cape Cod tells me that she has been teaching her children at home with the *enthusiastic* cooperation of the local schools, who welcome the children any time they want to go to school for special projects, field trips, etc. More on this in the next issue.

The ABC "20-20" show taped us here in the office, and also taped much of the Ohio meeting of the National Coalition of Alternative Community Schools. They tell us they plan to air this show in early September, but probably won't be able to give us a definite date until just a few days before the show. This is too bad, as it won't give us time to send out a notice to GWS readers. Needless to say, we will do so if we can.

So many readers and supporters called up radio station WRNG in Atlanta, GA, asking them to talk about unschooling, that the station is going to do a phone interview with me at 7 PM, Tues. July 9. Readers in other places may be able to get radio stations to do the same.

I may also appear on the Joel Stevak TV show in Philadelphia, 9 AM on Mon. July 16, but that is not yet definite.

Donna Richoux has moved from St. Louis to Boston to work with us at the office—and her help is very valuable, too.

The group of people who took out a 74X sub to GWS have since bumped it to 86X!

Someone wrote that, not knowing how to get in touch with us, she asked all the libraries in her area about GWS, and none had even heard of it. If libraries in your area don't know about us, please tell them.

COMING LECTURES

I will be speaking during the day on Wed. Sept. 5 at the Devereux School in Berwyn PA (near Philadelphia). Also on Fri. Sept. 14 at an in-service meeting of New Mexico schools, at the Holiday Inn De Las Cruces, in Las Cruces, NM. I have one meeting from 1–3:15 PM, and will talk again, on more or less the same subject, at the Las Cruces Teacher Center from about 6 to 8:30 PM. My contact for this meeting is Kathy Easterling, Title I In-service Coordinator, who can be reached c/o Hatch Valley Municipal Schools, Hatch NM 87937. Also Mon. Sept. 24, at Western Maryland College, Westminster MD (about an hour from Baltimore), afternoon workshops and an 8 PM meeting.

Next is Thurs. Nov. 29, an 8:15 PM meeting at Texas Tech Univ. in Lubbock, TX. Contact Robert DiPietro, Lecture/Fine Arts Dept.

Later meetings are 4/14/80, 8 PM at Huntington College, Huntington IN (25 mi. from Ft. Wayne): 4/17/80, Univ. of Wisconsin at Lake Geneva, WI; 4/19/80, Rutgers Univ., Newark, NJ. (That schedule is rather tight, in the middle at least.)

Since one of the chief ways we get the money we need to produce GWS is from my lecture fees, one of the ways in which some GWS readers might help the work along is by helping me get fee-paying lectures. If any of you have any connection with the kinds of groups and institutions that hire speakers (colleges, conferences, etc.), and that might be interested in hearing about unschooling, you might raise this possibility with them.

When I am already scheduled to speak at a meeting, any other group in the same area (or on the way to or from it) that wants me to speak either just before or just after that meeting can have my service without having to pay all those travel expenses. The lecture fee itself may also be smaller, since it may be based on how long the new meeting delays my return to Boston.

Anything any of you may be able to do about this will be a great help. And, of course, it will be nice to see any of you at the above meetings.

CHANGE IN GROUP SUBS

Please note under SUBSCRIPTIONS that in one small respect we have had to raise our prices. Until now, the cost of a group subscription (for any given number of issues) was equal to the cost of a single subscription for that same number of issues, plus $2 per person per year (1 yr. = 6 issues), up to a 20X sub, after which the cost of additional subscriptions became $1 per person per year. That $1 part is now no longer in effect—the cost of extra subs will remain $2 per person per year, no matter how big the group sub gets. The reasons is that it costs us more than $1 just to print 6 issues.

Perhaps someday, if and when we get so big that we can print 6 issues of GWS for well under $1, we will bring back that old $1 offer. But that probably won't be for a while.

NEWS FROM N.H.

Last month we successfully got our son J, who is seven and in second grade, excused from school until June. We will have to reapply for each successive school year, but presumably the process will become easier as time goes on.

According to a recent policy set out by the N.H. State Board of Education, a local school board can give parents permission to teach their children at home if the parents can prove that their children are suffering a "manifest educational hardship" by remaining in the public school.

We proved "manifest educational hardship" in J's case by showing that, basically, he had learned everything he knows *at home*, not at school, and that because we have the time and dedication etc. to teach him, it was a hardship to keep him in school, where he spent the day doing mimeographed papers, and had no individual time with the teacher.

Since then the changes that have occurred in J have been unbelievable. Gone are the fits of temper that erupted every day around 4 PM, gone are the headaches, the lines of tension around his mouth, and gone is his depression. He used to complain bitterly that he had no time to read (schools don't let you read these days until you've mastered the 1,000 "skills" deemed necessary to learn this "most difficult subject"!), and consequently he read every free second he had outside of school and rarely played. He didn't eat his lunch because it got stale at school, he came home with wet, cold feet acquired at recess and he barely spoke to us. We had thought, "J is going through a stage. All kids are like this etc.", but boy were we wrong! These days J sleeps well, eats well, *laughs, plays, and learns.* He gets his (apparently psychologically necessary) reading done in the morning, does his "school work" happily because we learn about the things he wants to learn about— Indians, dinosaurs, binary numbers—and then he has time to do woodworking, skiing, art, and playing. The school board was worried that J would become a social misfit, but just the opposite has happened.

AND PROVIDENCE, R.I.

Peter Van Daam writes:

"There was a radio poll a few weeks ago... More called in saying that they could teach children better at home—739 Yes, 664 No.

That same radio interviewed the R.I. Commissioner of Education who admitted that the State does not know how many children are learning at home, but that they have legitimate reasons for doing so (which he listed).

Last Friday local public television featured Brigitta and me on a panel about home-based education.

The lawyer representing the R.I. Dept. of Education made a strong observation that everyone seems to be getting 'hung up' on due process. (Ed. note—an odd way, to say the least, for a lawyer to talk about a Constitutional right.)

The state's largest community action group has invited us to their congress in two weeks where they will help me introduce a resolution affirming the parent's right and responsibility to control the education of his child and the state's obligation to assist the parents to fulfill that obligation.

The state-wide Coalition for Consumer Justice had a special 'new issues' committee meeting where I presented the concept of children as unwilling consumers of unwanted (and harmful) services in unresponsive schooling structures that refuse to acknowledge any accountability. They are following that up.

A major radio station taped a 1/2 hour session for its 'community access' program which apparently has a broad audience. And one of the major TV stations is coming to our home this Sunday to focus in on the perplexities faced by two parents sincerely concerned about their parental responsibilities.

So... I think home-based education is much more a community issue. People recognize and greet us. Three families nearby have taken their children out of school after counseling with us. A fourth wrote two days ago seeking encouragement and information.

I find that people respond most profoundly when I bring up the issue of love and individualism. They seem to identify with my desire that my children learn to be vulnerable, open, giving, kind, patient, long suffering and tolerant rather than another organization person who has found his own edge over his fellow man."

Peter also sent me a copy of a letter from the Principal of the school where his daughter was enrolled. It says, in full:

"Because Julia has not attended school at all this year, in what was to be her third grade experience, and state law requires children to attend school between the ages of seven and sixteen, I am compelled to retain Julia in the third grade. She will be carried on a third grade register here at King for the 1979-80 school year until that time [sic] she appears in school or the matter is adjudicated."

An interesting example of petty and vindictive school harassment. The principal is not "compelled" by state law to do any such thing. If the Van Daams had been out of the country for a year or more, the local school would have tested her to see where she should be placed in school.

The Principal's letter notes that copies were sent to two other school officials, one a "Student Relations Coordinator," the other a "Segment Administrator." What do these people do, I wonder, and how much do they get paid for doing it? Taxpayers might like to know the answers to these questions. They might find in them some of the reasons why schooling has become so expensive.

Paul Goodman wrote, many years ago, I think in his book *Compulsory Mis-education* (well worth reading), that there were more public school administrators in the state of New York, with a population of 17 million, than in all of Western Europe, with a population of 200 million. And I would guess that there are more administrators per pupil now than there were then.

Unschoolers facing a possible conflict with their school district might find this matter worth looking into. How many non-teachers are on their school district's payroll, what do they get paid, what do they do?

The *Providence Journal-Bulletin* of 4/29/79 carried a news story, saying, in part:

"...This was the first organizational meeting of a still-unnamed group of Rhode Island and Massachusetts parents who believe in educating their children at home—a volatile constitutional and educational issue that has abruptly burst onto the local scene.

Thirty adults and a dozen or so children showed up for the session that had been called by Peter and Brigitta Van Daam, the East Side couple who were arrested April 11 for keeping their eight-year-old daughter, Julia, out of school. Their Family Court case has been continued to May 15....

The group included an auto mechanic, a Newport policeman, the chairman-elect of the Libertarian Party of Rhode Island, and a commercial artist.

Some came only to observe, but at least six of the families who participated are educating their children at home.

Most are doing so without the approval of school authorities—like the Van Daams and another Providence couple who didn't want their names used for fear it would speed the truant officer to their door.

Others reported that they have won School Committee permission for their home programs.

David Kendrick of Rehoboth, Mass., for example, said he has been given the okay to educate his nine-year-old daughter at home this year, using a correspondence course supplemented by a tutor who visits once a week.

...Virtually all asserted that home education is a constitutional right that supersedes state laws requiring school attendance for children between the ages of 7 and 16.

Most indicated that their interest in home education was rooted in their dissatisfaction with formal education, particularly public education....

The group represented a wide range of philosophic and religious points of view....

At least one parent came with questions and left convinced. [She] said that she intends to take her two children out of the Providence elementary schools tomorrow."

IN THE WOODS

...I moved to Canada, to the country, without electricity or running water, with firewood to cut and food to grow, and eventually children to care for and learn with. Somewhere along the line I decided that my children would never go to any school unless they wanted to go. And that if they wanted to go to school we would find a school we were all happy with. I have given this more importance than most other things.

I like spending a day as often as possible (usually about once a week) when I have no other responsibilities than to be with children, follow their interests, show them things I think they might like, talk, read, explore. Most of the time I am very busy, and of course that's great learning time for us all. But so much of the time I'm either too busy or tired to really respond to some questions or help a child with an intricate problem or project or to just fall into their play and antics.

In GWS I've been reading about unschooling and learning not being separated from life and that we all are teachers and learners. At the same time I think a healthy community can include the adults (especially those who want to) spending part of their time giving undivided attention to children rather than always relating with children while in the midst of other responsibilities.

When I devote a day to the children, I let a few other children in the area know they are welcome to come over for the day. This gives the children here a chance to spend the day with their friends—a big thrill. We usually have a wonderful time together. We all enjoy a great deal of creative activities—painting, dancing, using clay, drama, costuming, singing. We also really enjoy going for walks or doing something in the garden or orchard. Or talking. Something they always want me to do is to read to them (none of them read really fluently yet). I let everyone choose a book or story. Those who can, do part of the reading. We read all kinds of books—simple and complex, with and without pictures.

I often write on a scrap of paper a few ideas of things to do together before the day starts. Sometimes we do those things, sometimes we don't. I am very willing to follow the lead of the children. I find these days very fulfilling and worthwhile. Whether or not we call it school is irrelevant to me.

Last fall we had a school group meeting twice a week. Mostly 2–4 year olds and mostly girls with one 5 year old girl and a 6 year old boy. Altogether there were about 12 children. It was quite a delightful group.

This is the day I remember best from that time: We began painting, and working with clay, and playing in the yard in front of the house. As lunch time neared we decided to have a picnic in the little pine tree forest. (This was one of the favorite nice weather activities.) The little pine trees are about 12 years old and a wonderful size for little people to climb and create fantasy worlds within.

As we were eating, I noticed some tiny green plants growing within the browns, reds, oranges of the fall leaves. I looked closer at the little plants and suggested that the children near me help me look for the various tiny plants growing around us. We found my favorite spring greens—sorrel and peppergrass—and some clover and a couple of plants none of us were familiar with. We nibbled the greens and were pleased with our discovery.

Soon the wonderful game of "roaring lions in the forest" began. The other mother and I sat to rest for a while. One child (3 years) stayed with us looking at the plants. She was a very quiet child and often stayed by herself very absorbed for long times with her interests while all the others very easily related and played and talked with each other. Sometimes I wondered if she wanted help getting to know others, if she was lonely and frightened in her solitude. But from observing her I'd decided she was actually quite happy on her own a lot. She almost never talked at school, but I knew she could talk because I'd heard her talk to her older sister quite freely. So when she began talking to me about the plants I was delighted. We looked very closely at many little plants and she pulled some out to look at the roots. Then she looked at the different levels of dead leaves—the brand new, bright crunchy ones were pushed away by her delicate finger, next there were softer brown ones, then black matted ones, then dirt, We talked throughout this examining of the magic of plants and earth.

When that was complete we moved off to join the others who led us through the pines to the edge of the swamp—cedars and black gooshy mud and water. Someone took shoes and socks off and within a very short time all shoes and socks came off. There was a great deal of splashing and stamping and singing and joy. Someone fell down and got his pants mucky. (I thought—what are his parents going to think?—they were obviously having way too much fun to stop them.) Soon all clothes were being taken off and put on the moss under the cedars. And the jolly dance continued. The little girl I described earlier was joining right in with all the others looking quite radiant. One child stayed back from the muck and the wet. He didn't seem disturbed by the others dancing in the muck, but

obviously it didn't appeal to him. Exploring the swamp went on until it was time to dry off, get dressed and go home.

I thought about that day and wondered how most of the parents would have responded. Some, I don't think would have allowed the naked water play—others probably would have. Some probably would have felt there wasn't much happening that day as much of it was spent on a long walk. But I was glad that the other mother who was there was as willing as I to follow the littler people on their adventure and I loved that day!

CALVERT NEWS

A mother writes:

...I had no problem enrolling Sean in Calvert—we move a lot—and all they require is—for legality's sake— a change in address every four months. If we didn't move every four months then I was required to go to the school and get an approving letter from them, which I've never had to do!

I've been very pleased with the Home Course—it is variable and easy to work with and learn from. Sean finished a 9 month course in 6 months and is looking forward to his 4th grade course. He got "messed up" (to put it mildly) his 3rd year in public schools and cured me of that.

GROWING IN DENMARK

From a Danish government pamphlet, by Frede Petersen, about Carl Nielsen (one of my favorite composers):

"It was in Hans Andersen's island of Funen... that Carl Nielsen, Denmark's greatest composer of recent times, was born on June 9, 1865. His parents were simple, indeed poor, people; the father was a housepainter but would do odd jobs on farms in order to augment the income of an ever-growing family. Carl was the seventh of... twelve children...

...The craft of music came to play no small part in the life of this large family: Painter Niels, as he was invariably called in the neighborhood, was also a village musician. Music was his chief interest and he was a valued player at feasts and dances in the island, where he also taught music and dancing....

...Scarcely anyone has described this island... more lovingly than Carl Nielsen...

'If, from a lofty mountain in the middle of Funen, we could look down over the whole island, tracing its outline against the blue sea, we would make the delightful discovery that, viewed this way too, Funen is one of the fairest of lands. We would reflect on all the island's beauties for the hundredth time and never weary—the breadth in proportion to the circumference, the blue inlets in relation to the sky, the little plains and the plump hills in contrast to the woods and hedges—oh, there is so much! Nowhere else in the world have I seen lanes and footpaths wind so snugly sweet, making you want to lie down on the ground and kiss it. We have all read in books of men kneeling and kissing their native soil. But that would be in the *great* moments, perhaps after long absence, and the grand manner comes easily then. Here it is quite different; not solemnly, but spontaneously, sincerely, suddenly; as if one's heart wanted to pop out and play with little red and blue balls in the spring air, hopping and skipping for joy like lambs that do not bleat but cluck.'

...His boyhood in Funen tending geese and cows, in close contact with Nature, developed his sense of all that showed growth and energy. He would lie for hours in the field watching for drifting clouds, the rhythmical waving of the corn, or a little feather floating over the rippling surface of the pond. This awareness of the exuberant life around him is reflected later in his art.

His first steps in music were taken when he was a small boy. One day, when he was ill with measles, his mother gave him one of his father's violins which hung on the wall, and on it he tried to find the tunes she sang to him. His father's only comment on this early start was to take the violin from him and tune it. Later, his father gave him regular guidance and soon Carl was able to go with him to play for dances, weddings, and other feasts. To this primitive form of music Carl Nielsen ascribes no little importance in the development of his compositional talent. In the long run, however, the routine playing, as second violin, of three- and four-part dance rhythms failed to satisfy him. Like his companions he soon began to improvise counter melodies and rhythms to the simple harmonies which governed this dance music. He also composed tunes, and in his reminiscences he quotes one which provoked his father's distaste on account of its liberal syncopation, which 'nobody could dance to.'

Besides this utilitarian music, Nielsen in his boyhood made some acquaintance with the classics, which were played *under simple forms* (Ed. Italics) in local music societies, and together all this helped to refine his sense of music. ...At the age of fifteen, after an interrupted period of apprenticeship to a local grocer, he was encouraged by his father to practice for a month on a new instrument, the bugle, and apply for a vacant post as bugler in the regimental band at Odense, which he obtained in competition with other applicants. His career as a musician was thus marked out. He continued to study the violin, mastered the elementary secrets of piano-playing, and soon began to compose..."

How different it was to be poor, in that place and that time. Today we think of music, especially classical music, violins, pianos, etc. as being for the middle and even upper middle class, wholly out of the reach of the poor, most of whom, though poor by today's standards, would not have looked poor to the Nielsen family, who in ten years could not have saved up the price of a TV set (if there had been such a thing).

A Danish friend of mine told me a little about his boyhood in the Danish countryside in the 1920's. His family raised (among other things) strawberries; but except perhaps once a year, for a very special treat, the children could not eat them—they needed every penny they could get by selling them. One of the minor tragedies of his young life came one day when, as he was about to eat the dozen or so berries that were to be his treat for the summer, he mistakenly put salt on them instead of sugar.

J. B. Priestley, in one of his books, describes the lives of working-class poor people in the wool district in Yorkshire in which he grew up. It was not at all uncommon for these families, living on the edge of bitter poverty, to have a piano in the house, on which at least one member of the family could and regularly did play some of the great classics, Miners, factory workers, mill workers, sang in great choruses of hundreds of voices, which every year sang "The Messiah" and other great works. (Many of these choruses still exist, though whether many working class people still sing in them I do not know.)

And though Carl Nielsen had to start doing real work very early in his life, at the same time how much space and leisure there was in that life, time for his interests and talents to show, and grow.

Like the gypsy children of whom we wrote in an earlier GWS, who learned to play by playing in a working gypsy band, Carl Nielsen was from very early in his life a working musician. He was not studying music so that someday he might make music. He was making music as he went along.

AND IN CANADA

A mother writes:

"I made up my mind two days ago not to force Michael (8) to read. I had pretty well decided I'd better and had even gotten together all the necessary stuff, but then I finished a book, *Better Late Than Early,* by Raymond Moore. Do read it....

Anyway, that same afternoon I happened to watch Michael out the window—he was hanging around the yard waiting for his father to come home (so he could grab a ride on the back of the truck—the excitement in that being in jumping *onto* a moving vehicle.) So I just stood there watching him a bit—and I became quite overwhelmed by a feeling of the universe unfolding as it should. He was puttering around like he usually does—not doing anything in particular, just 'bonding to the earth' as Pearce says in *Magical Child.*

Then, all of a sudden, he must have heard or seen a bird. (He's been quite deeply interested in birds lately.) And I watched in awe as he stalked it with all the grace, agility, and instinct of a long-ago Indian who was native to this prairie bushland. The bird must have flown away, because just as suddenly he turned back into an 8-year-old sauntering down the road, quite at peace with the world out there because it made no demands on him.

I can't quite find the words for how I felt—a just-rightness—seeing my son growing up so at home with himself and the earth. And knowing that this is what made the exhausting battle with the School Authorities all worthwhile, and that this in essence is what we are fighting for: our children's right to grow as their individual natures move them.

I resolved then and there not to make him read. And if it comes down to a real crunch—make him read, or go to jail—we will move. However, there are so many avenues of delay available in our case that by the time we come to the end of them, he may have already started reading and writing. He's almost 9 now."

———————————

P.S. The mother has just written me that he *has* started reading—without saying a word about it.

FROM A MOTHER

We read to our 4-year-old, J, every night and try to pick up things we've read in *National Geographic* or GWS that he would be interested in as well as children's books. J particularly enjoyed the poem in #8. I wonder if a mimeographed collection of such child-centered stories would be enjoyed. [Ed.—Yes.] We've made a story up for J too, probably most everyone has. No great literary merit, but the intention in the making shines through them. Also compared with vast amounts of what passes for literature for children, they are quite good, I'm sure.

He also enjoyed most of the story about A and her apple picking. It has provided him with much fantasy material about how he can make money when he gets a bit older, how he wants to pick fast and well and help pay his own way, what he'll spend the money on (a telescope and "gas balloon"—this last from the *NG* story of the first men to ride a balloon across the Atlantic).

Want to substantiate what was mentioned in #8 about the rapid growth of children's attention spans when they are regularly read to. J would listen until our tongues were numb if we would read that long. We've read all the Little House (Laura Ingalls Wilder) books, *The Wizard of Oz, Charlotte's Web, Heidi, Swiss Family Robinson, Alice in Wonderland, Through the Looking Glass,* to mention many but not all of the lengthy books, in the past two years (J aged 3 to 4). Now H, age 2, when tired will also climb up to hear stories such as these. From *Swiss Family Robinson,* J developed some funny locutions as crying "Seize her" of his sister who interfered with his play or "I gave chase" in his hunting games. This is the first place, I know, where they learn to relate what they don't understand to the context of what they do, to pick out the key words or phrases which once understood, open up the meaning of the rest. The first and primary place is probably that intense attention they give to adult conversation, not only but especially when it deals with love/hate, sex, death/birth, people they know, and all that good stuff we all pay attention to. They usually know to keep quiet at the time. Then weeks or months later, you'll get a question like, "Why did Uncle John not want to marry Sarah and whose baby was it anyhow?" (We try to answer as fully as we can and honestly.)

Some books, though, e.g. *Wind in the Willows,* have proven for us too wordy. We realize we're out of step, but neither W nor I enjoyed it and after a few chapters, we set it aside explaining that J could read it himself when he was able to if he chose. Another thing we've done is to pick out interesting parts of books, the whole of which was too advanced to be appreciated, like the chapters about the wolves in *Never Cry Wolf* (Farley Mowat) or the story line in *Hans Brinker* (which has a long section about a skate trip the rich boys take, intended to educate about Holland, which we skipped.)

...On learning to read. I've noticed as two of my own children and several others have passed through this stage, they've been able to recognize and form the letters, put them into words, copy them, and thus write quite legibly and competently before they read more than a few words. They can write many things, real things, letters to one another (with no phone we send many notes), letters to Grandma, make lists (things to buy a favorite), write stories. These need not be perfect or even be sent. That can be left up to the child. Attention span here again incredible. The diligence. All this writing and being read of notes, lists, leads obviously and simply to that flash of recognition that is being able to read.

...Learning to type. I too taught myself to type at about age 12 when at loose ends one summer. I had a teach-yourself-to-type book which was quite sufficient, cost maybe 75 cents at that time. I wouldn't have the abstracting job I have now if I weren't a typist, and, since it's piece work, the pay rate would be much lower if I weren't a fairly skilled typist. I've never had any sort of instruction, but have had plenty of practice, mainly all the times when I've been doing schoolwork or making money with it. A good practice gimmick would be to borrow foreign books or journals from the library. I often have foreign journals to abstract and they have very different letter combinations from English: central Europe strengthens those zxcvb, little finger, left hand letters; Japanese many vowels, and so on.

I also taught myself to knit from a book and have some of my most creative pleasure from it. I learned and knit and that's how I got to be good at it. Just as with typing or any other skill. In the middle class milieu where I grew up everyone made a great fuss about talent. This person was artistically talented or that one academically talented. I have learned, at some cost, since then that although some people may do some tasks with greater initial ease, anything that you do over and over again you will get to be good at. My mother, who considered herself to have a rather good voice, could not stand to hear me sing because I "had no talent." Of course, since I never sang, except secretly to myself, when no one including myself could hardly hear me, I still can hardly sing. We all do this so often to children. I see people constantly instructing 3- and 4-year-olds in the *proper* way to draw a house or face, what color valentines must be, which clothes go together. We refuse to let them practice, play, do, try for themselves. Perhaps we have been raised so terrified of error that we are terrified of what might strike our children. They might fail first grade.

Anne Herbert writes in the winter '78 *CoEvolution Quarterly* about how our whole culture deceives us into thinking a thing must be done perfectly or not at all. No amateurs in life. Perhaps the root of this is things no longer made by hand. I remember growing up being mystified as to how things as perfect, gleaming and sleek as cars were made, being told they were made in factories, and deciding factories must be where machines lived as obviously only a sleek and gleaming machine could produce another. Such a Black Box theory of artificery was only natural, I think, in a home where nothing was made, grown, or even devised. The middle class suburbs in the 50s and 60s. Everything, food, clothes, furniture was bought and every job was done by a hired expert: the cleaning lady, even; the garage man; the plumber. What was done was done by the rules. There was a certain form for writing a letter, decorating the house (it's hard to think of examples, so little was done). School was a place where you went to learn the rules, to become an expert, and then if you did everything just as you were told, you'd get an A in life.

This belief in error is, anyhow, just the flip side of a belief that there is a Correct color for objects, anyhow. The elementary teacher's idiocy of white rabbits, orange pumpkins, the Pilgrims were the first to set foot in the new world, and all the other little knowledges that mask unadmittable and vast ignorances—the human lot.

When I mention not sending my children to public school to my family, I get two standard reactions (and occasional violent, disturbing, personal outbursts—this fear of violating the norm is so deep. I'd be interested in hearing how others deal with tantrums, threats, and such, if they see them also). The two standard reactions are: But you loved school, and But you did so well. First on loving it. I wouldn't go so far as to call it love, myself. It was all that I knew. I went. We all went. Everyone went and always had and always would as far as I knew. Insofar as I was emotionally involved in it, as implied, it was because I did well and therefore, people gave me attention. The main reward was that I felt good about myself because I did well in school, was smart. I only hoped to do even better and discover, thus, that I was brilliant, equivalent to me at that time to being one of the chosen few.

I almost fainted on the school bus on the way home from the final day of first grade when my seatmate, a mature second grader, told me that I could fail, be kept back. That my report card, which I could not read, might say that I had failed. Of course, I had done well all year, but it never occurred to me that this was a summation; the whole thing had seemed arbitrary all year. With a child's clarity I saw that it was unfair. R, my neighbor, who sat next to me and couldn't read and still wet his pants in class was failed; he just wasn't ready to read and for that they failed him. So who knew what they might have gotten me on. And What Would My Family Do To Me?

… J, 4, took another quantum leap. We're market gardeners. He asked for and has his own plot, marked off with string (to his specs) for which he raised plants in the greenhouse and in which he's raising radishes for money. This is all on his own, but we try to help carry out his suggestions and ideas. Including when he's asked me to thin his radishes as he was "too tired." However, yesterday while I was working steadily transplanting, he took up a hoe and hoed every part of the garden that needed it *because he saw it needed to be done.* It took about an hour of hard work in which he did as good a job as I. Usually when he does something well I find myself commenting with some praise, but this time such was obviously, even ridiculously, superfluous. As if I would tell my husband he was a good boy for working so hard. J was at that time in that enterprise my equal. I was thrilled.

A BOOK OF FREE THINGS

A reader recommend to me a book called *The Rainbow Book* (a book of items children can send for free), by Pat Blakey, Barbara Haislet, and Judith Hentges (Parkway Press, Inc., 3347 East Calhoun Parkway, Minneapolis, MN 55408—$3.50). I sent for one, and like it very much. It tells children, in lively clear language, and shows with good illustrations, how to send away for things, how to write addresses, send self-addressed stamped envelope, etc. and then lists a big variety of very interesting-sounding pamphlets, folders, maps, buttons, etc. that they can send away for. (One of these is a free copy of *Cricket* magazine, recommended in GWS.) Many children like writing letters, and most love getting things in the mail. I would think they would have a lot of fun with this. Reading and writing for an immediate, real and serious purpose.

BOOKS—AND GUNS

A mother writes from Ontario:

About helping children make books: I really enjoy getting together with a young friend or friends, folding several pieces of paper into the size and number of pages that we want, cutting edges where necessary. Next we either staple or sew a binding. If we want to we add a cover (not always needed). Covers are easily made from pieces of wallpaper books. (Wallpaper books are a great free source of beautiful paper for all kinds of projects!) Or a cover can be a piece of cardboard folded and covered with cloth—glued, stapled, or sewed together with the pages.

So now we have a book or books. We work on them together or individually—what we feel at the time. Often the children draw pictures in their books, that go with a story they are making in their minds. After they have drawn the pictures they tell me what words they want written on each page, and I write the words. Some children of course can write their own words. Some of the children like me to write out the words on a separate paper for them to copy. Some books just have drawings. Some even remain empty. Some get swept up and thrown in the fire by someone who doesn't realize it's a book. Sometimes several of us work on one together. Anyway, they're usually a lot of fun to make and read or look at.

One of C's books had a beautiful white satin cover. He made himself a quill pen from a chicken feather. This book had to be drawn and written with a quill as it's a story set in the Middle Ages. It's a story of two mice princes who are cousins and have adventures with a blimp, a rat, and a lovely kangaroo. I've decided to make marionettes of the characters in this story which I'm in the process of doing. C has helped with some of the sewing and shaping and drilling of the wooden controls for one of the mice. A. plans to help make the kangaroo.

Writing about this story brings to my mind a topic which concerns me at times: violent play and play with toy weapons. The story of C's I was just describing has quite a bit of sword brandishing and arrow shooting, being about two princes of the Middle Ages named Swift Sword and Fast Lance. No one is injured in it, there are no gory scenes. I don't feel it's harmful for him to fantasize about mice, rats and kangaroos running around with swords. But sometimes I wonder about violent play in general—whether or not it can lead to a realer violence and where limits should or shouldn't be drawn. I guess I'd like some feedback on what other people observe and think about this.

Here are some of my observations and thoughts: I was raised in a pacifistic family where peace is truly attempted. I never wanted to play with guns or watch violence on t.v. or in movies. My younger brother occasionally wanted to play with guns. I probably tried it a few times myself. Our parents let my brother have a few toy guns when he really wanted them. I don't remember ever wanting one. I do remember that my mother had a rule that if we played with guns we were not to point them at people or animals and pretend to kill them. We both accepted the rule.

Now as a mother, toy guns again have entered my life. When C first wanted a toy gun I balked. I tried to talk him out of it explaining that to me it's not a good idea to pretend to hurt or kill even with toys. But he *really* wanted a gun. I never did, so how can I totally understand? I finally got him a cap gun for his 4th birthday. He was thrilled, but lost it almost immediately.

Since then (he's 8 now) he has had a few other guns, some he bought with his money. Once he won a prize in a Halloween party contest with his dinosaur costume—the prize was a gun. I think he was happy, but a little worried as to whether or not I'd approve.

In general he's gone along with my mother's rule of not aiming at any one and pretending to kill. He's had a few experiences with men friends with real guns—gone hunting with one and was offered the chance to shoot at a target with another. He chose not to try it and said he felt he wasn't ready. Gun play isn't such a passion for him now as it was when he was 4. He has other more intense interests. Basically I have felt that I didn't want to say "No this is something you can't do." I thought that by doing that I would possibly just push him into being almost obsessed with a desire for the forbidden. But I do want him to understand that guns are dangerous and if he later wants to use real ones I will find someone I trust or more likely he'll find someone he trusts to help him learn to use them safely. I don't want to dictate to my children what to do or be. I want to help them develop their potentials and interests even if I don't always understand or approve. But sometimes this is difficult or confusing.

I recently saw a mother and son of about 4 years. He was running around shooting a stick. In a gentle voice she told him not to play shooting and gave some good reasons. 15 minutes later I was in a different room away from them. The son ran in happily shooting the stick. So telling them not to do it doesn't necessarily stop it.

CHILD PUBLISHERS

Ed Nagel has sent us this announcement:

HOME STUDY EXCHANGE Newsletter
The HOSTEX News

This is a newsletter of children learning at home, published by children and for children like themselves. The first issue is composed of material by/from/for children who are enrolled at the Santa Fe Community School but who do most of their real learning at home, by themselves, with their parents, friends or neighbors in their local community. In future issues, other children who are learning at home may find this idea a useful tool for them in expanding their reach among peers outside the home without actually "attending" a school in the traditional sense of that word. Children will be "attending" each other, and the ideas exchanged thereby will become an organic "curriculum" of common experience upon/with/through which HOSTEX will "run".

The editorial staff of the HOSTEX News is composed entirely of students under the age of 18, who hold full and unabridged decision-making power to print or not to print any material which they may consider important/useful/entertaining in the market place of *their* readership. The children who collect, edit, type and layout articles for the publication and distribution of the HOSTEX news do have access to adults with the expertise for helping them do all these things (Ed.—I hope that as soon as possible the children learn to do without this help), but the choices will always belong to the children; the work will be that of the children; the credit or blame will belong to them; so will the money.

To do the first issue, students at the Santa Fe Community School have negotiated a loan which they hope to pay back with the money they get from subscriptions (mostly) and advertisements. With such a limited budget, the content and format of the newsletter likewise has been limited at the outset and the first mailing has been distributed on a rather small scale. How the newsletter looks and works and how often it appears in the future will depend upon reader interest and support....

...Only paid subscriptions can receive copies of the HOSTEX news. Upon payment, subscribers receive all copies published during that year (including any back issues) regardless of the date payment is made, so that all subscriptions will expire together. For the rest of 1979 and up through June 30, 1980, the subscription price for HOSTEX News (bimonthly, more or less) is $10.00. (Individual sample copies can be ordered for $2 each, which payment can later be applied toward a subscription for that same year.)

The children at SFCS do appreciate that some who want HOSTEX News cannot afford it, so requests for a "free" subscription (or "sample" copy) may be made at any time. Based on postmark dates, a waiting lists of such requests will be maintained at HOSTEX, but copies will be sent only if/when funds become available to cover the cost. (Tax deductible contributions to SFCS for this purpose are therefore invited.)

No policy has been set yet on advertisements, so describe or send what you want advertised, and make an offer or include payment. Send checks or money orders to: Treasurer, HOSTEX News, c/o SFCS, PO Box 2241, Santa Fe, NM 87501.

Good luck to this new publication. As I say, the sooner the children can make this publication 100% their own, i.e. run it without any assistance from adults whatever, the better. As long as they have to depend on adults to help them, the magazine will not be truly theirs.

AND VOLUNTEERS

A twelve-year-old writes about being an office volunteer:

In July 1978 my mother was asked to work at the C.E.A. office. At that time we had a three-month-old baby named C. So my mother asked me if I would like to go to the office to mind C while she did her work. But when I went in, it seemed that C slept most of the time except when she was hungry. So I started to do a little work. Mrs. L gave me some little jobs to do. Her daughter R (who is now a very good friend of mine) helped me to get into bigger things. She taught me to make registration packets. Even now I do about 100 a week at home. She taught me to run the folding machine so that we were able to fold the papers for the registration packets and also for the Memo. We enjoyed that a lot. I can even do it better than my mom because she gets the papers stuck sometimes. I also learned what to say when I answered the phone, even though I had a hard time getting "Childbirth Education Association" out in one breath and I sometimes disconnected people instead of putting them on hold.

I can't forget the literature orders. That was the best. We really had fun doing those. Finding the right papers and counting them out. Writing out bills and addressing the envelopes was lots of fun. R and I both knew what literature was there and what wasn't, so we could answer questions about what was in stock better than our Moms.

I also had to do the postage meter at the end of the day. I always tried to use Mrs. L's adding machine to figure out the totals, but sometimes I would have to use my brain; then I didn't like it so much.

But it wasn't all work; sometimes R, her brother and I would play game or go to the library. I really looked forward to coming in to the office. But soon the bad part came. I had to go back to school. So as soon as I got my school calendar I sent in a paper with all the days I had off from school so I could come into the office.

Now I am waiting for the summer to come so I can go into the office and help out. I enjoy being a C.E.A. volunteer.

PHOTOS

Alma Marks writes from Nova Scotia:

"Enclosed are three (Ed.—delightful) photos we'd like to share with you. Perhaps other families would enjoy sharing pictures of their children's unschooling experiences. After a fair number of photos were collected and mounted, the book could be used as a pictorial essay. Like the film, it could be rented to make money for GWS. (Ed.—the film makes some money, but very little.)

The kinds of things the children do here but that we haven't captured yet on film are: yoga, carpentry, gardening, cooking, exploring magnifying glasses, binoculars & microscopes, discovering math with concrete materials, dreaming, pondering, older children reading to and otherwise assisting younger children, etc. The list for every family will be different and of course growing with the children and their interests. It's another way we could learn from each other. It could even be published!

I like this idea. Some questions: 1) How many people would be interested in renting such a book, if it existed? What seems like a reasonable rental fee? 2) How many people would like to contribute photos of their own children to such a book? 3) Would one of our volunteers be willing to take full responsibility for getting such a book together, renting it, etc. We are swamped at the office and for the time being could not take this project on, but I'd like to see it happen if others want it to happen. Tell us what you think.

THEY DON'T KNOW

Since schools have been losing so many unschooling cases, and getting so much bad publicity, one might well wonder why they keep taking parents to court.

There are probably a number of reasons, which vary from school to school. Many of them are terrified (and say so) that if they let one student go, next day they will all go. Some of them, at least, really believe in their quack pseudo-science of "education," and think that only they can teach. But perhaps the most important reason is that the schools, and in most cases their lawyers, *don't know the law.* They may be able to quote a few sentences of the compulsory school attendance laws in their state, but they know nothing about what the courts have ruled about the meaning of these laws.

Not long ago I was speaking to a large meeting of educators from Southeastern Massachusetts. This is mostly affluent country, so we can assume that school people here are about as well informed as anywhere. At one point I asked people to raise their hands if they had even a rough idea of what was meant or referred to in the phrase *Pierce v. Society of Sisters.* I had expected to see perhaps a dozen hands. Not one was raised.

As a matter of fact, it is safe to assume that most judges in Family or Juvenile Courts, where most unschooling cases will first be heard, don't know the law either. This is not a part of the law with which they have had much to do.

What this means is that when we write up home schooling plans, we are going to have to cite and quote from these cases. The more of this legal material we can quote, the less likely that schools will want to take us to court, and the better the chances that, if they do, we will win. We have to remember that under our adversary legal system the task of judges is not to decide what "justice" is, but to decide which of the parties before them, in terms of existing laws, court decisions, etc. has the strongest argument. Judges are not going to do our legal work for us. If we don't cite favorable court cases in our plans, or briefs, judges (who may very well not even have heard of them) are not going to put them in their rulings.

"GOOD TEACHING"

Old Bad Joke #1: "The operation was successful but the patient died."

Old Bad Joke #2: "I taught my dog to whistle." "That's funny, I never heard him whistle." "I said I taught him, I didn't say he learned."

No Joke At All: The May 1979 issue of *McCall's*, in the article "Are Teachers Failing Our Children?", reports that at a recent conference of the New Jersey Educational Association teachers were saying, "I *want* to be evaluated, but by how well I teach—not by how my students do."

Since teachers in New Jersey are probably about like teachers everywhere, we can assume that most educators in this country believe that being a good teacher has nothing whatever to do with whether your students are learning anything.

The *McCall's* article doesn't say what these teachers thought "good" teaching means, but it isn't hard to guess. It means, first and foremost, keeping the students still, silent, and busy. It means planning everything in advance, leaving nothing to chance, or inspiration, or, needless to say, the interests of the learners. As the chairman of one education department wrote recently, "The teacher has to know what he will be teaching tomorrow, next week, next spring." It means having for every one of these daily, weekly, monthly etc. lesson plans a precisely stated behavioral objective, saying that the student will be able to do this or that, and a test to show whether the student can do it. Finally, it means laying out all these lesson plans and tests, like the 283 skills of reading invented by the experts of the Chicago schools (GWS #2), in some exact order, which someone, somewhere—a professor of education, perhaps a textbook publisher, but in any case not a classroom teacher—has decided is the best order for learning.

If you do all these things, everything that experts somewhere have decided you should do, then, so the theory goes, you are a "good" teacher. If your students aren't learning, it means there's something wrong with them. It's not your fault and you can't and shouldn't be expected to do anything about it. It's up to the school to label these children defective and turn them over to some kind of specialists who will in turn try out some other learning plan on them.

This is what most teachers are taught, or anyway learn, to believe.

As I have said, the schools run on a (for them) great rule, that when learning happens, schools and teachers take the credit, and when it doesn't happen, the students get the blame. The same people who say that good teaching has nothing to do with whether people learn anything are now putting out bumper stickers saying, "If you can read, thank a teacher." In GWS #5 I said that the main reason why schools are incompetent is that they will not take the responsibility for the results of their own work. The *McCall's* piece is just one more proof of it. Because the schools refuse to judge their methods by how much learning they produce, they never learn anything, neither from their failures nor their successes. They are immune to experience.

It is hard to think of any other human work, certainly not one that (in the U.S.) spends close to a hundred and fifty billion dollars a year, in which the workers all say that how well they work has nothing to do with what kinds of results they get. What would the auto industry be like if from the start it had run on the rule that any time a car didn't work right, wouldn't start, wouldn't run, went out of control, it was the driver's fault, never the fault of the people who designed and built it. Suppose this industry had a monopoly on making cars, and that all citizens had to buy a new car every year whether they wanted one or not. What kind of cars would we have? What kind of people would work in that industry? What would happen to those few who kept saying, "Wait a minute, if none of these cars we build will run, maybe there's something wrong with them, not the drivers?" How long would such people last?

We have to remember that when (say) the Chicago schools tell all their teachers to teach children to read by teaching them 283 separate skills in a rigidly prescribed order, in doesn't mean that somewhere *in* Chicago there were some teachers who had actually done that and had turned out many great readers. The people who made up that list of 283 skills (which started out as 500) were almost certainly not teachers, and the chances are good that many of them had never been teachers. Where did they get such an idea? Out of their heads, or perhaps out of a book, or perhaps out of someone's study of laboratory rats. But

not out of anyone's experience of actually teaching children.

Every so often, probably several times every year, a brave, observant, thoughtful, skeptical, imaginative, inventive teacher finds out how to make learning happen, or rather, and this is the real discovery, how to allow and help it to happen. What happens to these teachers? Sometimes (as Herndon describes in *The Way It Spozed to Be*) they are fired. Other times (as he describes in *How to Survive in Your Native Land*) they are simply ignored. In his first school, a black inner city junior high school, he had students reading, writing, and talking about what they had read, most of whom had never read, written, or done any schoolwork since they had entered the school. His students were learning while all the other students in the school were rioting, locking teachers out of their rooms, throwing materials and furniture out the window, etc. As he writes:

"...I met with [the principal} for his official evaluation of my year's work. ...he found [it] unsatisfactory on every count; he could not recommend me for rehire in the district. Furthermore he had to say he considered me unfit for the position of junior high school teacher in any school, anywhere, now or in the future, and would so state on my evaluation paper.

...the children were not in their seats on time, they did not begin lessons promptly, many of them sat around doing nothing, there was not an atmosphere conducive to study, no effort was made to inculcate good study habits, there was no evidence of thorough preparation of lessons or goals. I appeared to encourage activities that were opposed to efforts of the faculty in general, I appeared eager to discuss with the students matters irrelevant or unfit for the classroom, I had no control over their actions, and I steadfastly rejected advice and aid from more experienced people.

I had to talk about results. What about the riots, I wanted to know... What was the good of the order of these experienced teachers if it ended up in chaos? No one in my class had rioted, I pointed out; no one locked me out, or threw my hat out the window. None of this happened in my classes. So who had the better control, I argued.

He wasn't impressed. He knew there had been riots, he knew that I'd had none. ... A riot meant that some order had been imposed, some control established, since it was against that control that the children were rebelling...."

In the last year or two I have been corresponding with a teacher in a Southern state. He teaches in a rural elementary school in a poor county. Like Herndon, he came to teaching after having done a number of other kinds of work (always a good idea). Like Herndon, he is resourceful, inventive, and unorthodox. (After all, in schools where nobody learns anything, good teachers have to be unorthodox.) For about seven years now, the students in his classes have been learning, according to the tests the school believes in, about twice as much as they learn in any other single year in the school. During that time the school principal has not given him one satisfactory evaluation, and has indeed threatened to fire him more than once—and probably would have, except for the trouble this teacher might make. The other teachers all know every class' test scores, and so know how well this man's students learn. But none have ever visited his class, or even talked to him about his methods or asked for any advice. None are his friends. He is a shunned outsider.

This happens to many innovative and successful teachers. Not long ago a mother talked to me about her child, at school in a Boston suburb. She had just had the best year in school she ever had, or that any of this mother's children had ever had. But, the mother said, the child's marvelous teacher was not coming back. "Why not?" I asked. "Because none of the other teachers would speak to him."

There may be more good teachers who are frozen out this way than are actually fired. They are not as tough as Herndon; to have few or no friends, and maybe a lot of enemies, among the people they work with, is too hard for them. Most of them don't stay long. Hundreds of them write me, saying that they couldn't stand doing what they were made to do, or not being allowed to do what clearly needed to be done, or what they saw being done all around them.

It is like the natural selection we hear about in biology, only in reverse—the most capable (all but a few) leave, the less capable remain. Fifty or a hundred years of this process have given us—what we have.

I see nothing within the schools that is likely to reverse this process. But if—in time—enough people could and did take their children out of bad schools, if good teachers had more and more students coming to their classes by choice, while bad teachers had less students of any kind, the schools might begin to have serious reasons (including financial) for learning to do their job well. But that day is still probably quite a long way off.

HELPING LEARNERS

From a father's letter:

...It seems to me that the educational establishment, including all of the reformers who have surfaced over the years, have committed what I call "the Greek mistake": The ancient Greeks, who did such excellent work in pure mathematics and philosophy, for example, were duds at and probably retarded the growth of experimental science, because of their scorn for observation and deduction. There is the tale, perhaps apocryphal, that the great Aristotle, based on some obscure philosophical induction, claimed that men had more teeth than women. We moderns laugh at this, recognizing that all Aristotle had to do was ask Mrs. Aristotle to open her mouth and take a careful look. But this "Greek mistake" is in principle precisely the

one made by the educational establishment: Instead of observing, checking, framing testable hypotheses, listening, and in general drawing the principles of education out of the perceived nature of the subject matter—the kids—we conjure up notions of how we imagine kids *ought* to learn, out of thin air as it were and having no foundation in observable reality. Then we try to make the subject matter conform to the theory, and are puzzled that it doesn't. In short, what the Greeks and the educational establishment never understood is, that if you want to find out if a horse will eat apples, you don't philosophize about it—you offer the horse an apple and see what happens.

My wife and I have employed this approach in helping our own two boys (6 and 4 1/2 years old) to learn. It is difficult to express verbally—indeed, *that's* the point!—the continual revelations we have had. In the first place, we have found that the boys, unlike those who attend schools, are incapable of distinguishing between any "special time for learning" and the rest of life. Have you ever reflected upon the intellectual harm we do children by the fact that we herd them into special places at special times for what we call education?: "O.K. kids, it's 8:45 in the morning, you *will* start learning...O.K. kids, it's 3:15, you can knock off with the learning stuff." Like some maniac theologians preaching that we can be religious only while attending church, we actually *teach* the kids that "real" learning is what happens only at special times in special buildings under the supervision of special people. Alas, they eventually believe us.

Sometimes, I'm asked whether our unschooling approach is "successful." I can only reply, "Successful by whose standards?" The boys have little notion, for example, of when George Washington lived and what he did—and their interest in the matter is even less than their knowledge—but they know more about dinosaurs than I ever imagined there was to be known. Yet where is it carved in stone that a knowledge of dead politicians is more important than a knowledge of dead reptiles? By *my* standards, I might prefer that the boys be more interested in, say, history, for which—now—they care very little, than in, say, astronomy, which they devour, and I must constantly be on guard to resist the temptation to subtly impose upon them my standards of what is "important." So, have we been "successful"—you'll have to ask the boys!

Yet many who are too timid, or prejudiced, or arrogant, to trust kids to learn without being taught, ask, "What about the basics? Suppose a child wants to learn *only* about dinosaurs or planets, and shows no interest in more fundamental matters?" Such a question reveals at least two absurdities in the mind of the questioner: First, what makes him think (1650) that, say, a knowledge of astrology is more foundational than a knowledge of agronomy, or (1980) that a knowledge of economics is more fundamental than a knowledge of poetry? Secondly, they are concerned with a problem that, for kids who do not have educationist theory shoved down their throats, simply does not exist: it is not possible for an inquisitive child to delve deeply into dinosaurs without wondering about, and learning, how big they were (measurements), how many roamed a certain area (arithmetic), where they lived (geography), what happened to them (history), etc., etc. And, after exhausting daddy's knowledge of dinosaurs—which happened pretty quickly—a lot of reading was necessary. In short, it simply isn't possible to learn a lot about dinosaurs or anything else without along the way learning and using knowledge and skills that are intellectually prerequisite. After all, the reason that we call "the basics" by that phrase is that they *are* basic, and to worry that a kid will learn just about anything without learning and using the basics is like being worried that he might decide to build a house starting with the roof first.

It's hard work, of course, for us to adjust ourselves to the kids' interests. They wake up every morning curious but, alas, rarely curious about the particular topics that we might be prepared to talk about or might by our standards prefer they be curious about—that's when temptation rears its head and must be ruthlessly suppressed. It's a waste of time and quickly degenerates into intellectual bullying to try to side-track a kid onto topics you think he should be learning. Of course, going along with the kids' interests may, as it recently did in our family, find you subjected to six straight days of inquiry into space exploration. But, if you will just be patient and observant, the time comes when the kid, because *he* realizes that it's pertinent to learning about his primary interest, will, almost offhandedly (but it sticks), add rocket thrusts, multiply fuel loads, distinguish ellipses from circles, etc. Keep your mouth shut when you are not needed, and be ready to help when you are. The kid will learn.

Perhaps the reason that so many adults—including, I confess, myself—find it hard to refrain from "helping" kids, is that it wounds our egos to see how well they get along without us! How can that dumb kid of mine learn so much without a smart fellow like me to teach him? We try in effect to horn in on the kids' sense of pride of accomplishment and, all too often, particularly in schools, we succeed. The results are psychologically and intellectually catastrophic for the victims...

FROM THE NORTHWEST

...Just wanted to let you know that a week ago I and some others were guests on a teenage talk show (radio) concerned with the topic of un- (and de-) schooling.

My brother (seven years younger, plagued all through school by having to follow in my footsteps) listened to the show, and afterwards had *much* to say (that was a surprise—he usually says very little), mostly about the terrible destruction to his own (already shy and fragile) self-esteem by "teachers" who are "not to be questioned," who do not share the opinions nor possess the knowledge of some children and so discredit them (rather than learning *from* them); and the crippling effect of spending so much of one's young life in an *unreal place*, so that at age 18 the temptation (among those who have at least learned to survive within the system) is to *stay in school* rather than risk the "real world." He points out that most "teachers," themselves, have never been out of school for any appreciable length of time.

One question asked on the show was the common one—"In our ever-more-technologized society can we *afford* to let education be non-compulsory?" It is a silly question, of course, but for those who take it seriously, here is one more point to ponder:

My brother is an electronics technician, by trade, and an electronics whiz by vocation. While still a teenager he *taught himself* all the mathematics, language, etc. necessary and built many complicated things—an oscilloscope, a computer, etc. He is now making a lot of money (I am not!) as a skilled technician (I am not!) while continuing to develop his own very creative ideas in electronics in his free time, with his own equipment, at home. The point here is this: he excelled in electronics because it wasn't taught in school. He wasn't competing with anyone, he wasn't being mystified by teachers, he wasn't wasting his time doing a lot of meaningless busywork that bore no relevance to "real life." It was not an area that was "touchable" by teachers, or school—it was his and it was real. The profound sadness is that for him (and for so many other kids) school was so overpowering that he emerged from it thinking that his "C" average, his mediocre ratings were his "real" self; his success in electronics didn't count for much...

The current issue (July '79—Ted Kennedy on cover) of the magazine *Quest* has a story about a young man who designed and built his own airplane. He has no training in aeronautics, engineering, physics, etc., does not even know calculus, and his plane violates a number of supposed "laws" of aircraft design. But it is substantially cheaper than, and out-performs in every way, the best commercially designed and built planes of comparable size. Worth reading.

A BOOK ON TESTS

We are adding to our list of books a very interesting, important, and useful new book, *The Complete Guide to Taking Tests,* by Bernard Feder, (Prentice Hall, $9 + post.) Dr. Feder has a Ph.D. in Education (which may make his arguments even more convincing to some people), and has been a teacher and administrator in the New York City public schools, and an Associate Professor of Education at Hofstra University.

The book itself is at one and the same time the best book I have seen about what is wrong both with testing in general and the tests most widely used in schools, and also, about how to beat those tests. Unschoolers who don't want their children tested, and least of all by standard school tests, will find much in it that may help them avoid this. But it is also the best possible way to prepare children for tests if they can't be avoided. I can't recommend it too highly.

It is also very clearly and often amusingly written. I think that many children from ten on up would enjoy it. I would suggest recommending it to the attention of your legislators—you might send them a few pertinent quotes. And it would be helpful, of course, if as many school people as possible would also read it. A very fine book.

WHY SHE LEFT

...I have delayed getting G's 2nd and 3rd grade experiences on paper, because I had hoped she would write you herself. She asked if it would be printed in the newsletter. I told her you might use an excerpt with her permission for GWS. She considered and then said that perhaps someone besides ourselves receives GWS in this area. She is afraid the teachers will see what she thinks of them.

The second grade changed classes! Our 7-year-old was not ready for that. There was the home room teacher plus 3 other teachers. None of these teachers had time nor the desire to talk to parents. I was told by other parents that the best thing I could do for G was not to interfere with the second grade teachers.

The writing and spelling teacher felt G's printing was not what it should be and she should have learned to write in the first grade. In fact the first 12 weeks of school the children who had been in Ms. M's first grade room were told what a poor teacher they had had last year. (Pure unadulterated jealousy.) G received F's on her spelling papers. She did not tell us nor did she mention anything about the spankings that she received from this woman or the breaks she was forced to miss to study the words.

I first became aware of the situation when my aunt with whom G was staying during the week told me that I should help G with spelling. That weekend, bit by bit, G told me the ugly story. She had not told her father or myself, because she had been shamed into believing that her parents would be disappointed or ridicule her, or worse yet punish her. It seems to be common practice in this area for parents to punish kids if the kids receive punishment in school. Anyway, I asked to see the spelling book. G said that they did not have enough books to go around and she did not have a book! After several phone calls I obtained Ms. L's (her teacher) unlisted number. Much to G's apprehension, and amid pleas for me not to talk to Ms. L, I did call her. I talked to her for some time about my concern for G in regards to no book, being punished for something she had little control over, etc. (The four 2nd grade slave drivers felt G was not trying.)

After I hung up, my husband remarked, "You had

to stroke her." Ms. L had brought up the subject of us (she & I) playing together while growing up. Ms. L is a few years younger than I. I had not recognized her or her married name. She was supposedly surprised to learn of G's fears of her and the child's hatred of spelling. Ms. L had a copy of the textbook that G could borrow. Why she had not lent G the book before I phoned her, I don't know. The conversation was quite amiable. G was loaned the spelling book for one weekend and then a couple of weeks later issued one to keep for the school year.

Later G came home upset because Ms. M, the science teacher, had told G in front of the class that if her mother (me) should call her, Ms. M, in regards to G getting a D on a busywork class assignment, she—Ms. M, would hang up on G's mother. Ms. M then explained how she did not have time to talk to anyone's parents on the phone because she had her baby and house to care for. After that I heard from other sources how I had "Bawled Out" Ms. L.

The reading teacher decided G could not comprehend what she read. The math teacher was not getting good results from G in math. There was the constant threat of being retained in the 2nd grade. All this time G was in their top group, making A's, B's and C's on her report card. Her father and I never stressed high grades. The thing that puzzled me was: is the child in the 2nd/3rd group making A's equal to the first group's B or what??? At the end of the year the school gave an achievement test and apparently the teachers had decided to keep G in 2nd grade another year. Her testing scores caused them to reconsider. G's total battery score was 4.5, which supposedly means equal to a kid that has been in the fourth grade 5 months. A breakdown of her score went: Reading 4.2, Language 5.2, Mathematics 3.7, Science 4.2, and Social Studies 3.8. However, the damage that was done to that child is beyond belief. She went from an outgoing, eager-to-learn child to one that's shy and reluctant to find out about new things. She is slowly coming out more this spring. Our home school has been in operation since December.

G did have to attend the third grade for three months. She did not go back Aug. 10, 1978 when school first started, but she was forced to return Sept. 10, 1978. She did not get the third grade teacher that she had been assigned the first of the year. This was because too many other parents with political pull had felt Mrs. L was superior to Ms. S. Ms. S would have made a fine commandant for a concentration camp. She spanked G for various things; e.g., the bus that made the run by our farm broke down, hence another driver had to make the run before she could make her regular run. The kids living on our road were dismissed one hour early in order that transportation could be arranged for them. The next morning Ms. S asked G where her English homework was. The assignment had been made after G's bus ran and she did not know anything about the assignment. Ms. S paddled G and then G told her that she had had to leave before

English class. Ms. S said she was sorry, but G should have answered her quicker.

When I talked with Ms. S about this she said that G had a habit of not answering whenever she was asked a question. This is true, and I remarked that a mule had nothing on G, and she might think how one got the best work out of a stubborn plow mule. Ms. S only stared at me and said that she had too many children in her class to give individual attention to each one. This was one of her favorite remarks or excuses. [Ed. note— many parents tell me this.]

One of G's science test papers from Ms. S has this question, "_____ live on Earth." G had filled in the blank with We. This was marked wrong. "People live on Earth." G told me how a boy answered a question orally, by saying, "moonshine" meaning the light reflected from the moon instead of "moonlight." Ms. S went into a lecture on moonshine being whiskey. This is amusing, but it was not funny to that 8-year-old boy who has listened to his grandfather or some other relative talk about moonshine lighting up the path around the ridge while out with the fox hounds.

Enclosed is a story that I wrote for G when she was 4 or 5. She drew pictures for the story while in the first grade and we submitted the story with the drawings to a local newspaper. The story was published along with the art work on Sept. 13, 1978 (two years after submission). G's first grade teacher was very happy because G had done the drawings for her.

G does a lot of reading now. She averages 4 to 7 library books per week (e.g. Nancy Drew, Hardy Boys, Charlie Brown's Questions and Answers books—tons of info in them—and biographies).

G'S STORY

In a stall in a big log barn on a warm Sunday morning in June, Broomhilda, the goose, heard her eggs breaking. Cheep, peck, cheep. For twenty-eight long days and nights Broomhilda has been sitting on twelve eggs.

She had sat on her eggs while her gander, sister and brothers went off to pick grass and hang round the back door of the farm house in hopes of a handout. Broomhilda sat on the nest while the other geese, Bertha, Samuel, Homer Cecil, and Harvery, Broomhilda's gander, went swimming in the branch that ran past the barn. Broomhilda even sat on her nest the day that a big wind and rain storm came.

The wind swirled the rain around the barn and rattled the tin on the roof. Hail pounded the roof, lightning flashed, thunder boomed, and the wind raced through tree tops. The branch overflowed, and the stream that trickled off the hill back of the barn raged to the branch. The tiny stream came out of its rocky bed and ran though the barn hall. The water ran into the stall where Broomhilda sat on her eggs. The nest became wet and soggy, but still Broomhilda stayed with her eggs.

At night the people would put in corn and fresh water for Broomhilda. Harvery would come to sleep in the stall with her. Harvery discouraged small predators from coming around the nest. He did this by pinching with his beak and hitting with his wide strong wings any rat, coon, or skunk that was brave or foolish enough to come shopping for eggs.

Bertha and the two remaining ganders would be locked up in the goose house to prevent them from appearing as the main attraction for supper in a fox's den.

Now the long days of sitting were over. The goslings were pecking their way out of the egg shells.

When G and her Daddy looked in on Broomhilda that Sunday morning they could see bits of yellow fluff peeping out from under Broomhilda's gray feathers. Upon returning from church that afternoon the whole people family paid a visit to the stall to see the new arrivals. Baby D became very excited when she saw the eight fluffy balls. Each ball had a neck and two legs! She wanted to get down from the backpack on her Mother's back. This was not allowed; Aunt Bertha, Uncle Homer Cecil, and Uncle Samuel were in the stall to assist the parents, Broomhilda and Harvery, in guarding the goslings.

People, dogs, cats, goats, and pony were permitted to look only. Anyone getting too near the goslings were warned by loud hissings. If the warnings went unheeded the guilty party would receive some hard pinching from the beaks of the ganders.

On that quiet June Sunday the farm began the perilous adventures of raising goslings to goosehood.

A FATHER WRITES

...I have read the books you have written, and between them and Bob (4), I've found, for me, the best way to teach is by example, and the best way to learn is by doing. (Bob continually tells us "I don't want to know that" when we try to teach him something he doesn't want to learn.) Linda and I are impressed by how quickly he picks things up, but what impresses me the most is his ability to just sit and think. I never knew young children did that until Bob showed me. He also repeats and repeats things until he has them. We put him to bed at 9 PM, and often at 11 we can hear him talking to himself as he goes over things he wants to get straight. This is how he learned the alphabet and how to count to 129. That's his favorite number and he counts to it over and over and over. Somehow he has picked up the idea that number means a quantity of objects, and I am amazed he has learned that level of abstraction so quickly and completely.

...I've tried to let Bob and David learn what they want to at the rate they set, but sometimes it is hard not to teach. There is one story I enjoy, simply because it was the only time I've been successful at teaching when Bob wasn't interested. When Bob was learning to count, he asked me what comes after 113. I didn't answer his question, but instead I asked him what comes after 13.

Well, he got mad because that's not what he wanted. I remained stubborn and he finally said "14 comes after 13, what comes after 113," very indignantly. I immediately said "114." At first he was still disgusted because I didn't answer his question the first time, but then he understood what I had just done. He broke out in a big grin and covered his face. We like to trick each other, and I had just gotten him.

...While I was typing this letter, Bob was playing with a meter stick. It is interesting because it has all the centimeters numbered from 1 to 99. Bob has used it quite a lot, and I think it has helped him get the concept of numbers. Especially things like 1 to 10 is the same as 81 to 90 (you wrote about this and how you used rolls of cash register tape to work with this concept in one of your books). I thought other children might enjoy playing with a meter stick, besides they can measure things with it. (Bob loves to measure anything that stands still.)

LOOKING AT BABIES

Caleb Gattegno, who is perhaps best known for his work in math teaching with the Cuisenaire Rods, has written a number of books about education, teaching, children, etc. (Available from Educational Solutions, Inc., 80 Fifth Ave., New York NY 10011.) One of these, *In the Beginning There Were No Words—The Universe of Babies*, I have just ordered. Skimming through it just after it arrived, I found these lovely quotes:

"A few observers have told us that the world of childhood has to be entered on tiptoe and not with the heavy tread of laboratory technicians seeking only the confirmation of their visions; has to be entered with every tentacle and sensor alerted and not with a ready-made theory that filters out what cannot be reconciled to it; with love and respect for the person, who is as complete at every age and stage of childhood as he will be at any adult age and stage."

"A principle that can serve us well, when we are looking at young children investigating their world, is *the need to know*. Much of what looks like idle play is the methodical examination of the unformulated question. The question becomes clearer to the observer if he stops sticking to a hypothesis of idle play and tries to ask: 'What does the child need to know that he can get from this?'"

"In homes where no spanking exists, or any other abuse by parents of their physical power or their economic and social know-hows, it is clear to children that some things must be done, and they obey as easily as those who are threatened. This perception of one's interest as a member of a group, and the acceptance of the fact that to stop a game to eat or go out is part of the order of things, is a gift children make in the cause of family peace. To understand it as the outcome of the working of fear and a sense within the child of his own inferiority, is not to do justice to fact."

ON N.H. GUIDELINES

Comments by David Armington on the proposed *Home Study Guidelines* (For presentation at a public hearing held by the N.H. State Board of Education, June 19, 1979):

… As I read the proposed guidelines I am struck by the phrase "manifest educational hardship." As a parent I must prove my child is suffering "manifest educational hardship" at the hands of the school before I can even ask for a school board's permission to educate my child at home. Why should I have to prove that the school is *injuring* my child? I don't have to prove any such thing if I have the money to send him or her to a private school. I simply do it. If education is the process through which we try to discover our maximums, why should I have to prove that the school is failing to look after my child's minimums? Surely, the least I can expect from the school is that there will be no hardship inflicted. If I want to educate my child at home, shouldn't it be enough that I state my own educational values, aims and objectives, with evidence that I know how to help my child grow in these directions?

… I have a good friend, a teacher in Massachusetts, whose first grade child has been judged (by the school) to be a "special needs child" and she's to be put in a "special needs class," but the parent completely disagrees with the assessment and is frantically trying to avoid the special treatment. It is fashionable nowadays to talk about "special needs," and loads of people are making their living by researching them, writing about them, designing programs for children having them or thought to have them, teaching such programs, teaching the teachers of such programs, etc.

… If the proposed guidelines seem pertinent and useful in situations where the child is afflicted with an obvious handicap, and dubiously useful in situations of dubious handicap (as with my Massachusetts friend), I find the guidelines quite irrelevant to situations in which parents or guardians want to take over the educational function because the program of the school clearly violates, or is incompatible with, their deeply held beliefs and values.

… It is simply not true that the schools are society's great equalizer of opportunity in the race of life, for we're not all trying to run the same race, and some of us don't even believe in running. It is simply not true that the schools are, or ever could be, value-free or value-neutral, for even a stance of steadfast neutrality or objectivity communicates a value. It is simply not true that we keep religion out of the schools. Identifiable creeds and churches, yes. Religion, no, for education is essentially religious, because at its center is the individual human soul.

A lot is said and written about Quality Education, and one gets the impression that if our words were only clear enough to express our thoughts, we would all agree on what Quality Education means. But we do *not* agree, nor will we ever agree so long as our society remains as free and pluralistic as it is today. I have often thought that if you closed your eyes and dropped your finger on a map of the United States, it would hit a community where the differences on questions of education are as great as, or greater than, the differences on questions of religion. Yet in that community, if it's a smallish one, you would find several churches but only one school!

One might be inclined to say that such differences are really only differences of detail, of method, of technique; different routes to objectives we all share. This is not true. I am not talking about alternative methods for teaching reading, or whether to teach old math or new math, or whether to offer sex education, environmental studies, and four years of French. I am talking about different educational objectives, different values and priorities, which can reflect different views about the nature of learning and human potential, and different views about the role of the school and of education in our society.

—A classroom in which children are expected to compete with each other is very different from one in which competitions arise naturally and spontaneously from the cooperative life of the group.

—A classroom which measures children against each other or against outside standards is very different from one in which each child is encouraged to assess himself.

—A classroom in which children learn by doing is very different from one in which they learn by being told.

—A classroom in which the work is fed to children in tiny sequential bites is very different from one in which children tackle problems in full and lifelike complexity.

—A classroom in which the children share significantly in planning what happens to them is very different from one in which things are planned for them, and both are very different from a classroom where children run the show.

—A classroom that encourages self-discipline is very different from one in which the teacher disciplines. Both are very different from a classroom artfully regulated by rewards. All three are very different from a classroom with no discipline at all.

—A classroom in which the rigors of learning are teacher-imposed is very different from one in which rigor arises from personal identification with what is to be learned. Both are very different from a classroom that is limp and without rigor.

...What should the guidelines expect of parents who wish to educate their children at home? I think parents should be expected to specify their educational objectives and the values and priorities undergirding them. They should be expected to describe adequately the manner in which the objectives are to be achieved and the kinds of evaluation they consider appropriate. From such descriptions it should be clear that the parents not only envision but can provide an educational environment offering adequate scope for meeting a child's needs—physical, intellectual, social, and emotional. Such descriptions must not be limited by institutional standards and procedures, however, for it is precisely these from which many parents are seeking escape. In this connection I note that the preliminary draft of the guidelines stated that "the application of institutional standards in a non-institutional setting cannot be literally insisted upon," a statement that does *not* appear in the latest draft. It deserves to reappear, and in more positive form, so that it embraces a broader range of educational aims and approaches ...

BAD SCENE

A mother writes from Illinois:

I found that I needed to be very well informed as I dealt with the principal and the Assistant County Superintendent. As I told you on the phone, the first meeting with the principal and N's "teacher" was not good. The principal refused to transfer N because S.F.C.S. [Santa Fe Community School] was not on the list of approved schools in Illinois. I was lectured on the inadvisability of home study, including all the classic statements such as "we have certified teachers to do that, what makes you think you can teach him? What are your qualifications? Do you know how much money we've lost due to N's absences already?" (They knew down to the penny.) "Well, it's different and I guess that's the way you like it." "You certainly are sure of yourself; if we were all so sure of ourselves the world would be in sad shape. I guess we don't do well by either of your children." (A snide remark referring to our foster child in third grade who has "problems" resulting in many a conference with her teacher, the social worker, the psychologist, the remedial reading teacher, etc.)

Asked what I would do about teaching N reading I replied that he already reads and now needs the space to do so on his own. I was nearly laughed out of the room and told that I obviously didn't know the fundamentals of reading and could not teach it to N. N's teacher told me with great concern that there is no way that N could pass a test to get into third grade if he did not remain in school (her school of course) for the last few months of this year. (Strangely, there is no such test for children passing from one grade to the next.)

Anyway, I won't carry on about this meeting further except to say that I did expect to meet with resistance but was still amazed to be treated with total lack of respect. The "meeting" ended with the principal backing out of the room and popping back in a time or two to toss an additional insult while the teacher slid quietly into an adjoining room without a word busying herself at some task. I was left in the room to exit through another door by myself but didn't make it out the front door before the principal came around and met me in the hall, lecturing me on the way out.

If I needed more proof that I was doing the right thing to take N out of such a place (which I didn't) I certainly got it that day.

Onward and *upward?* My next meeting was with the Assistant County Superintendent [hereafter ACS]. The ACS was more calculated in his response. He informed me right away that it was impossible to teach N at home, that it was against the law, and that we were violating the truancy law by his absences and would be prosecuted for it. He quoted the statute which says, "Whoever has custody or control of any child between the ages of seven and sixteen years shall cause such child to attend some public school in the district wherein the child resides." I informed him that the statute goes on to exempt "any child attending a private or parochial school where children are taught the branches of education taught to children of corresponding age and grade in the public schools." He then immediately contended that we were not providing N with an equivalent education.

The issue shifted quickly here. I was prepared to explain our program for N but he was not interested in hearing about it. Instead he simply declared that our program was not equivalent because we did not use the text books N was using in public school (I answered that I had tried to get the names of the textbooks from the school but they had not cooperated. His comment: "the school doesn't have to cooperate") and told me that I would be subjected to an (oral) masters degree level exam before he would be convinced that I was qualified to teach N. He referred to all these mystical things that only teachers know, about the components of learning and how the branches interrelate. He stated that the school would have to meet the provisions in the School Board Document #1. (Later we find this is totally untrue, that it is a completely different and more lenient set of rules than Document #1, which is for public schools.) The proper document being "Policies and Guidelines for Registration and Recognition of Nonpublic Elementary and Secondary Schools."

Dr. H., the ACS, did not use my name when talking to me but continually referred to me with a sarcastic "friend."

He stated that I did not have a sufficient program and *must* send N to school the next day or be in violation of truancy. I had indicated several times earlier in the conversation that I would not send N to school but because I found it senseless to respond to his final decree as I left, he seized upon my silence to quote me as admitting to having no program and agreeing to send N to school. He stated this to my husband on the phone. My husband had called him to further explain the law, being a lawyer, as I had promised to Dr. H that he would. By the end of the conversation my husband felt manipulated into the same type of situation and so ended by stating that he agreed to nothing except to call Dr. H again tomorrow.

In this phone conversation my husband was told that a "bank of six lawyers" in Springfield (the capital) had told Dr. H. that homeschooling was clearly illegal.

Meanwhile my husband had stopped at the public school to get N's workbooks (which already had been refused to me: "why would I give you his work books; I consider N to be truant"). We also requested to see N's records and to make a copy of them. We were refused. My husband then requested that a record of this refusal be put into N's record at this time. The principal refused to make this a matter of record. My husband wrote out a note himself and asked the principal to include it in N's file. The principal refused. My husband said he would leave it on the principal's desk. The principal replied that he had never seen the note and it did not exist. My husband then went to the front desk and asked the person there to be aware that the note was left in the principal's office. The principal ran out of his office to say that this person could not come into his office and the note did not exist. Ho Hum.

This all led to an argument in the hall that I'm sure was heard throughout the school. After this incident and the conversations with Dr. H, we decided that we would be wise to involve a third party. From then on we dealt with the officials through another attorney with valuable experience with school boards as their attorney. Thus we proceeded to prepare for the meeting where we were to present our program.

Fortunately, with your good advice, and the help of a friend who is an ex-teacher, now chicken farmer, still certified in Illinois as a second and third grade teacher, we put together a convincing package to present to the officials. It helped that our attorney had paved the way with some blunt statements to them. By this time *someone* had given them the word to change their attitude and approach and they did their best to cooperate. Dr. H told us as we were leaving that he was sure N would get an excellent education from us but he had trouble getting this out audibly. When my husband did not quite hear all of it and asked him what he had said, he almost died and simply could not repeat it.

We found your advice to keep a telephone log of conversations and to ask many questions and get it clear what each person's interest is to be very valuable and in keeping with my husband's approach from the legal sense. It is exactly the way we proceeded, after bungling the beginnings, that is.

Your experience with those school people certainly confirms what a number of people have said, and what we have by now printed in GWS, which is that all dealings with school people should be in writing. If you can't avoid a personal or telephone conversation, it is important to take detailed notes of it as you go along, saying if necessary, "Wait just a second while I write that down," and going to some pains to get the words straight. Then as soon as possible after these conversations you should write a confirming letter, saying more or less, "This is my understanding of the essence of our conversation of today (date given). If this does not agree with your understanding of our conversation please let me know in writing as soon as possible wherein it differs. If I do not hear from you, I will assume that your understanding of this conversation is substantially the same as my own." This puts the ball in their court; if they say nothing, your version goes down on the record as the official one. In other words, you put something down on the record and require them to put something else on the record if they want to change it.

THE MAGIC GUN

A reader has sent us a clip from *Advocate,* published by the Illinois Education Association. The story reads, in full:

"*The Ragan Report,* a communications newsletter, recently carried an item which may give some insights to [sic] the burgeoning school discipline problem— which has topped the Gallup Poll's list of the public's top concern [sic] in the schools for nine of the last ten years. This is how a young teacher in a one-room school house handled this issue at the turn of the century: 'I stood on top of my desk and commanded three young men to sit. They cursed me and laughed. I pulled a revolver which was concealed under my coat, cocked the hammer, and stated with some authority for them to sit down or we would bury them in the school yard. They sat down. The school has settled down to business.'"

Frankly, I doubt very much that any such thing happened. But how strange it is, and how sad, and how scary, that so many of our fellow-countrymen just *love* to hear stories like that. The Magic Gun—just point it, and all your problems are solved.

BOOK BARGAINS

The latest catalog of Publishers Central Bureau (1 Champion Ave., Avenel NJ 07131) lists some outstanding book bargains, including:

#274817—*The New Columbia Encyclopedia,* 3052 pg., 1 vol. $29.50 (orig, price $79.50). a beautifully bound and printed, fascinating book, perfect for browsing.

Five books by the great archaeologist Heinrich Schliemann, discoverer of the buried cities of Troy. Would probably be ideal for older children interested in ancient history and archaeology—as quite a few are.

A whole set of children's classics illustrated by

Arthur Rackham. These were important books for me (as I suspect for many others) when I was little, full of magic.

#266555—*Just So Stories,* by Kipling. Facsimile of first edition. Good read aloud stories. $2.98.

#231697—*Larousse Encyclopedia of the Animal World.* Over 1000 full color illus. $19.95 (orig. $50.00). Well worth having (bet you won't find it in most schools).

#290405—*Guinness Book of World Records.* Latest Edition, $3.98. Sure-fire for just about all children.

As I wrote in an earlier GWS, it is well worth while getting on this company's mailing list.

The New Columbia Enyclopedia can also be bought at that same price from Barnes & Noble, for those of you who may live near one of their stores.

The best dictionary for children I have seen (many others agree) is *The American Heritage School Dictionary,* pub. By Houghton Mifflin (our copy says $7.95, a very reasonable price). It is very well laid out and printed, with many interesting illustrations. The definitions are clear and useful, unlike those in some dictionaries I have seen, which are more complicated than the words they are defining, or which lead the reader around in circles. A pleasure to use, or (perhaps better yet) just to browse through.

If enough readers were interested, we might even someday carry it here.

A very good section at the beginning tells how the dictionary was made (something I never knew until long after I was grown up). Unfortunately, this is written in a style much too hard for most children. Too bad—it would be easy to write it in words that most children could understand. If the children were interested in this, as I think many would be, parents might read this part, explaining it as they went along.

An amusing footnote. Since the book is designed for schools, the publishers have printed on the inside of the jacket the kind of sheet that school libraries usually glue into their books—spaces for the name of the school, names of pupils signing it out, warning to the students not to write in it, and at the very end, these words, directed at the teachers:

"The following terms should be used in recording the condition of the book: NEW, GOOD, FAIR, POOR, BAD."

From the Smithsonian in D.C. I ordered a set of the *McGuffey Eclectic Readers*—the Primer, and Vols. 1-6. I like the Primer and the first two volumes very much, certainly much more than any basal readers I ever saw in a school. The stories are good, or as good as stories written with very few words can be, and the woodcut engravings are charming and beautiful. (What an amazing art that was, now almost lost.) There is more sense of the color, light, and shade of the real world in these black-and-white engravings than in the color illustrations in most modern children's books.

However, I don't like and can't recommend the

later books. The moralizing of the earlier volumes, which seems perfectly right and natural for little children, becomes ponderous and preachy. I could read the earlier volumes aloud with pleasure, and without feeling that I was reading anything I would not want to say—many of the stories urge children to be kind (to each other and to animals), generous, helpful. But the later stories talk too much about being obedient, going to school, working hard, earning money, being a success. I know too much about what those schools were really for to be able to read those stories with pleasure or comfort.

Perhaps more important, the clear, direct, interesting style of the earlier volumes turns more and more into the elaborate, pompous style that many people then liked. Most of it sounds like bad political oratory. The poetry is no better. Very little truly great or even good American poetry or prose got into those later readers. Too bad.

NEW BOOKS HERE

To the books *about* children we have been selling, we are going to add more and more books *for* children. Here are some of our first titles:

The Animal Family, by Randall Jarrell (Dell, $1.10 + post.) Years ago someone (I forget who) sent me this book. I had known Jarrell only through some of his poetry, most of all his famous (and grim) "Death of a Ball-Turret Gunner." I started *The Animal Family,* not knowing what to expect—the person who sent it wisely did not say that it was a children's book. Within a few pages, I disappeared into another world. The story begins with a hunter, living by himself in a forest at the edge of the ocean. One evening, while on the beach, he sees a mermaid in the water, watching him. She is a very different kind of creature—Jarrell makes us understand how different—and it takes a long time for the hunter to overcome her shyness. In time she decides to come live with him in his little cabin. There, one by one, the other members of the family join them—a bear, a lynx, and finally, a small boy, washed ashore in a lifeboat after a shipwreck. The bear is a real bear, the lynx a real lynx, not people disguised as animals. Yet they are a real family. It is part of the magic of Jarrell's tale that he persuades you that five such creatures might someday, somewhere, be able to and want to live together.

I hated to come to the end of the book, which I have read many times since, and always with as deep pleasure. Later I sent it to a niece, about nine, next to youngest in a large family. She read it and loved it—but not till after all the older members of the family had read it first. I hadn't said anything about it to them. Obviously they hadn't been able to keep from taking a look at it, just to see what it was about, and once they started, they had to finish.

The Bat Poet, also by Jarrell (Collier Books, MacMillan; $1.85 + post.) a very different, but also unique and charming story. A young bat, sleeping on a porch with all the other bats, decides one day to stay awake when daylight comes. He discovers a whole new world, including many other animals. He is so excited by what he sees that he begins to make up poems about it, which he recites to the other animals. Sometimes they like them, sometimes not. The bat is fascinated, as Jarrell surely was and many readers surely will be, by the ways in which poems are different from other kinds of talk, and by the process by which he makes up his poems, or by which they come to him. He has interesting things to say about this to the other animals, some of whom like to hear it. And the poems themselves (and illustrations by Sendak) are lovely. A nice story, the only one I can think of among all the children's stories I know in which the leading character is himself an artist.

The Education of Little Tree by Forrest Carter (Delacorte press, $7.00 + post.) This is the story, true or at any rate based on truth, of a five-year-old boy (the author) growing up with Cherokee Indian grandparents high in the Tennessee mountains on a tiny farm where they grow corn, which they use to make whisky, their only cash crop. The child quickly becomes a serious, responsible, and useful member of the hardworking family, and we feel how important this sense of being useful is to his growth and happiness. Their life together is an idyll, except for the white people in the valley below, who earlier drove the Indians off their land, and at one point in the story take the child (for a while) away from his grandparent.

The book makes a number of points, without being too preachy: how courteously and respectfully his grandparents treat the little boy, as a worthy and responsible equal, and how much this kind of treatment makes him want to be worthy of it; how much wiser, less gullible, less easily fooled and misled, these illiterate Indians are than most of the richer and literate whites of the valley; how superior their Indian civilization, philosophy, morality, and way of life was to the white, Christian, commercial world which drove them out.

The book is not unbiased about this. It is very heavily (though believably) slanted on the Indian side. The few Indians we meet are very good people; of the whites we meet, *only* a few are good people, the rest foolish, dishonest, bigoted, and cruel. Those who may be strongly offended by this way of looking at things might do better to avoid the book. All others should enjoy it—a very moving and instructive story.

Rootabaga Stories, by Carl Sandburg (Harcourt Brace Jovanovich, 2 vols., $1.75/$1.50 + post.) I had seen this title for years, in lists of Sandburg's works, but had never seen them, assumed they were long out of print. A couple of summers ago, I was visiting a friend in Santa Fe and his seven year old son. Came bedtime and the father pulled out an old worn copy of

Rootabaga Stories and read a couple of them aloud. The boy was entranced and so was I. After he went to bed I read all the rest of the stories, thinking, "Isn't it a shame such a fine book is out of print." Found out later to my great pleasure that they were still in print, and in paperback, and decided to sell them from here.

Hard to say what they are about—they are not *about* much of anything. They are short fantasy tales, set right in the middle of the American Great Plains. Certain people and places appear now and then in the stories, but there are no plots to speak of, and not much happens. The stories are mostly a kind of word-magic, very hypnotic for sleepy children about to go to bed. Here is a little sample, from the story, "How Six Umbrellas Took Off Their Hats to Show Respect to the One Big Umbrella."

"Then [the umbrellas] all got up, took off their straw hats, walked up to the stranger and laid those straw hats at his feet. They wanted to show him they had respect for him. Then they all walked out, first the umbrella that feeds the fishes fresh buns every morning, then the umbrella that fixes the clocks free of charge, then the umbrella that peels the potatoes with a pencil and makes pink ink with the peelings, then the umbrella that eats the rats with pepper and salt and a clean napkin, then the umbrella that washes the dishes with a washer, then the umbrella that covers the chimney with a dishpan before it rains, then the umbrella that runs to the corner to get corners for the. handkerchiefs. They all laid their straw hats at the feet of the stranger because he came without knocking or telling anybody beforehand and because he said he is the umbrella that holds up the sky, that big umbrella the rain goes through first of all, the first and the last umbrella."

Very soothing, charming, nonsensical, lovely stories. Fun to read aloud. (But then, come to think of it, I can't imagine my recommending a book that I wouldn't want to read aloud.) Wonderful illustrations, too.

Also, *Gnomes* (see GWS #3) is now available here in paperback—$8.95 + post.

MAPS

One year when I was teaching fifth grade I saw for the first time a relief map of the United States, molded out of plastic so that the mountains were actually raised up off the surface. It was so much more exciting to look at, and said so much more about the country, that I bought one for my class (out of my own pocket, though the school later repaid me).

The children liked it, called it "the bumpity map," would go over from time to time and stare at it, feel mountains with their fingers, run their fingers down valleys. It told me, in a vivid and immediate way, why New York became a great seaport. The whole Eastern Seaboard is cut off from the interior by the Appalachian Mountains, except at the gap where the Hudson River comes down, and New York stands at the ocean end of that gap. If it had not had a great natural harbor people would in time have built one, because that is the right spot for it.

Also realized why the New York Central Railroad used to advertise itself as The Water Level Route, and what a great advantage that was. While the Pennsy huffed its way up the hills, the NYC sailed along the edge of the Hudson.

You can get one of these maps of the U.S., 22" x 35", from Hubbard, PO Box 104, Northbrook, IL 60062, for $12.95. They also make much more detailed raised maps of smaller areas, also for $12.95. There are 300 of these. Each map (about 22" x 34") covers an area of about 110 x 70 miles. The series covers the entire Western third of the U.S., the Appalachian country in the Eastern states, and also Hawaii. If you live in any part of this area, you and your children may find it fascinating to look at the raised map of your area, particularly if you are in very mountainous country. If you ski, or hike in high country in the summer, you can see and feel on the map the actual slopes you ski or walk on. Very exciting. Send for their brochure.

OUR PENTAGON PAPER

We have received in the mail a copy of a memorandum, dated Mar. 12, 1979, sent to Davis Campbell, Deputy Superintendent for Programs in the California State Department of Education. It says, in part:

Subject: PRIVATE SCHOOLS: A BRIEF SUMMARY OF CONDITIONS, CURRENT LEGISLATION, AND OPERATIONS.

There are approximately 3040 private schools for kindergarten through twelfth grade with an approximate number of enrollees equaling 451,320. ...

Any person, regardless of health history, criminal background, or educational attainment can have his or her own private school merely by filing a two-page form, the Private School Affidavit ...

This form, when submitted to 5th California State Department of Education, "authorizes" the exemption of students from compulsory attendance in a public school, the conferring of diplomas, and the hiring of administrators and teachers for whom there are no minimum qualifications. ...

However, private school students, because of existing legislation do not enjoy protection equal to that of students in public schools. There are no checks and balances built into the system to provide recourse on complaints through the offices of a principal, superintendent, and an elected board. ...

These limited examples of "regulations" show that they are dysfunctional on many levels: 1) they fail to accomplish what must have been originally intended, 2) they falsely imply to the general public that state oversight and remedies are available as needed, 3) they deny child welfare, consumer protection, and right of franchise to parents and private school children, 4) they lend themselves to unscrupulous advertisements such as "fully approved or accredited by the Department of Education" without consequences to the school. ...

I recommend that legislation be proposed which comprehensively parallels the consumer protection afforded in private preschools and in private post-secondary schools. ...

As an alternative to this, I would recommend that legislation be developed which would strike from the California Education Code all the existing private school "regulations" in that they are totally dysfunctional, and maintain a private-school-serving facade for the State of California oversight [sic] while in reality they serve to disenfranchise the 450,000 California children in these schools.

When we consider that the parents of a boy who was graduated from the schools of San Francisco with the reading scores of a fifth-grader were denied recourse or damages of any kind, and that these same schools defended themselves by saying that since no one agreed on what was the best or proper way to teach, they could not be judged negligent for not having taught that way (GWS #8—"The Schools Confess"), and when I think of what people have written me just in the past few months about educational malpractice in California public schools, this State Education Department memo is as outrageous as it is grotesque.

One might think that as the number of problems which the schools cannot solve continues to rise, they might grow a bit more modest. Not a bit of it. The more they fail, the more grandiose and sweeping become their claims.

The time to nip this proposed legislation in the bud is now, before it even gets into the legislature. I hope that GWS readers in California will bring this memo to the attention of the governor, legislators, newspaper editors, and any others who might have an interest in it. I would suggest that along with it they quote what we had to say about that San Francisco case, and also what Judge Meigs in Kentucky had to say about the educational "regulatory scheme" of that state.

In addition, some of the parents who have tried long and hard, and with no success whatever, to use some of that "consumer protection" and "recourse" to prevent their children from being mentally and physically abused by local schools might tell some of their personal experiences to a larger public.

Given public feeling against taxes, government expense, etc. we should be able to stop this latest effort by educational bureaucrats to expand their turf.

Editor—John Holt
Managing Editor—Peg Durkee
Associate Editor—Donna Richoux

GROWING WITHOUT SCHOOLING

Issue #11

October, 1979

As you can see, as far as type goes, this issue is a bit of a hybrid. Since GWS #3, we have been using an IBM Memory Typewriter to type up the magazine. Recently we bought a new machine, an Olivetti, which does all the things the IBM did, plus a few others, does them faster, and lets us store as much material as we want, which is very important for the unschooling book I am working on. Since some of the material in this issue was stored in the IBM, we have used it for those stories, rather then retype them. All the material in the new typefaces has been done on the Olivetti.

Until now, GWS has been typed in a typeface called Letter Gothic, Elite in size, which means there are 12 characters per inch. Since none of the available Olivetti Elite-sized typefaces seemed to me as legible (don't laugh!) as the Letter Gothic, we are doing the main body of the text in a Pica-sized typeface—10 characters per inch. This loses us a few words per page, which I regret. If you find the new type easier to read, it's worth it.

For the Directory, we are still using an Elite-sized typeface, since people won't really be reading the entire Directory, just looking up a few names in it. Also, by the time GWS #12 comes out, the complete Directory will take up quite a lot of room.

There are now seven communities in Massachusetts in which parents are teaching their children at home, with the knowledge and support of the schools. In two of these the parents needed a court decision to do this. In the other five, the schools took a more helpful position from the start. In two of these, one of which we write more about later, the unschooled children are able to use the schools for special activities. Let's hope that many more schools follow these good examples.

No further news in the Van Daam case in Providence, RI. The whole matter was more or less set aside during the summer.

We have now made a new version of the basic GWS flyer. If weight permits, we will enclose it with this issue; if not, with #12.

COMING LECTURES

Sept 24, 1979: Western Maryland College, Westminster MD; afternoon workshop, 8 PM lecture; contact Joan Nixon, (301) 848-7000 ext. 265.

Oct 17: Ithaca College, Ithaca NY; 7:30 PM lecture in Ford Hall; contact Jeff Bradley, Speakers Chairperson.

Oct 22: Lake Park High School Conference, District 108, 600 South Medinah Rd, Roselle IL; 9 AM Opening addresses, interaction sessions; contact David

D. Victor, conf. dir.

Oct 25: Vermont Conf. of Social Concerns, at Lake Morey Inn; contact Veronica Celani, Dept of Social Welfare, State Ofc. Bldg, Montpelier 05602, (802) 241-2800.

Nov 14: Eastern Montana College, Billings; aft workshop, 8 PM lecture.

Nov 29: Texas Tech Univ, Lubbock; 8:15 PM at U.C. Theater.

Apr 14, 1980: Huntingdon College, Huntingdon IN; 8 PM

Apr 17: University of Wisconsin at Whitewater; 8 PM lecture at Lake Geneva WI.

Apr 19: Conference on Literature and the Urban Experience, Rutgers U, Newark NJ; contact Michael C. Jaye, conf. dir.

Apr 26: Children Studies Symposium, Hobart & William Smith Colleges, Geneva NY; contact Marilyn Kallet

Since one of the chief ways we get the money we need to produce GWS is from my lecture fees, one of the ways in which some GWS readers might help the work along is by helping me get fee-paying lectures. If any of you are connected with groups and institutions that hire speakers (colleges, conferences, etc.) and that might be interested in hearing about unschooling, you might raise this possibility with them.

When I am already scheduled to speak at a meeting, any other group in the same area (or on the way to or from it) that wants me to speak either just before or just after that meeting can have my service without having to pay all those travel expenses. The lecture fee itself may also be smaller, since it may be based on how long the new meeting delays my return to Boston.

Anything any of you may be able to do about this will be a great help.

Some of the above lectures may not be open to the public: check with the contact listed. Of course, if you come, it will be nice to see any of you at the above meetings.

FROM A WORKING MOTHER

A mother writes from Canada:

J stayed home from school the next day—he didn't need any coaxing. He has been out of school ever since and I have felt better and better about the move as time goes on. It seemed he had been asking forever to be able to stay home. After a few days he missed some of his friends but still didn't want to go back. We managed to see some of them on weekends, and that seemed to satisfy him.

I go to work on weekdays and he is left home in the apartment (reminds me of Ann McConnell in GWS). This worried me at first, but he said it was fine, and he has become quite self-reliant. A great weight has lifted from our relationship. I was no longer pushing him to school against his will, and he started to trust me again as he did in his preschool days—I had almost forgotten. I had more time for him too, now that I no longer was spending time at the school. One day he talked of his mom "rescuing" him from school. I felt like a heroine.

…One of the best times we had in the euphoric first two months out of school, was a marathon session in the biochemistry lab where I work. I had a 48-hour experiment going which had to be checked in the middle of the night. J went in with me the first night and we had trouble with one of the machines, a fraction collector which moves test tubes along under the end of a length of fine tubing which slowly spits out the stuff to be collected. We stayed there until 5 AM and J occupied himself almost the whole time with a stopwatch checking the rate of drips from the tubing, the rate of movement of the tubes, and the rate of a monitoring pen on another machine—all work that was necessary for getting the job done—and he revelled in it.

We left the building just as the last stars were leaving the sky. Sheep and cattle were grazing quietly on nearby university pastures. Only the birds provided sound. J was amazed that he had really passed through all the dark hours without sleeping. I thought of all the kids who could not have the kind of exhilaration he had just had because of their confinement to hours dictated to them by schools.

We slept all that morning and went back to the lab for checks during the afternoon and again at night and the following day. J wanted to stay with it right to the end and did. He learned all sorts of things in that short span of time about units of volume and time, about multiplying and dividing, about fractions, about light absorption, magnets, solutions and probably other things. The same boy had been completely turned off by school math and was regarded by some as "slow" and "lazy."…

SUCCESS STORY—CAPE COD

From the *Cape Cod Times*, June 22, 1979:

An aquarium sits on the kitchen counter and colored squares of construction paper line the refrigerator door. A bowl of turtles is on a coffee table in the living room, and a quail cage sits on the fireplace. This is the Mahoney home in Centerville—and it is also the schoolhouse for Elaine Mahoney's daughters, Kendra, 11, and Kimberlee, 9, who are being taught by their mother at home instead of attending school.

The experiment was initiated by Mrs. Mahoney, 31, last September after months of research and study.

"I think, so far, that this is the best way for my children," Mrs. Mahoney says. "There are so many different ways of learning, and it doesn't have to be confined to the four walls of a school, five days a week for nine months. Education is not something that should be done to you, but something that you do."

Mrs. Mahoney's …criticisms of the Barnstable schools, however, are not an attack on the administration or teaching staff. Instead, she is more concerned with the structure of public education itself.

"The Barnstable system is the closest to the kind of schools I'd like my children to attend," she says. "The school committee and staff have been very receptive to my children's needs and to my ideas. But, I'm looking for a special way of educating my children, by assuring their independence, fulfilling their individual needs, teaching them through experience and pacing their work accordingly. The school tries to match learning and individual development but this is impossible in a classroom of 20 students who all make demands on one teacher."…

Consequently Mrs. Mahoney, who is divorced, approached William Geick, Assistant Superintendent of the Barnstable Schools last spring with her proposal.

"Mrs. Mahoney came to me not as a parent angry at the school system, but as a parent with a different philosophical approach, based not only on her opinion but on sound recommendation," Geick says. To his knowledge, Mrs. Mahoney is the only parent on the Cape who has suggested and carried through with a plan for home education…

"The duty of the school is to act in the best interest of the child," Geick says, "In that respect, Mrs. Mahoney's program seemed sound, and her criticisms of her children's previous educational experience were valid ones."

Although the children were never individually consulted by school officials, before approval of the plan Geick said that they felt confident that Mrs. Mahoney knew her children's needs better than anyone.

"All we can do is guide their education, and act on good faith. In Mrs. Mahoney's case, this has had a very positive result."

Geick and Mrs. Mahoney then presented her proposal to the five-member school committee, whose reactions were mixed in the beginning.

"I wasn't very receptive to the plan until I met Elaine," said the head of the committee. "She impressed me as a serious, conscientious woman who was able to give this time to her children. It's quite a responsibility and we felt she could handle it."

A major concern of the committee was not only the quality of education the children would be receiving at home, but also the social disadvantage of their not attending school with their peers.

"Children must learn to live in large groups and interact. In that sense, we didn't want to see the children hurt by a home education plan," [the chairperson] said.

However, through a written contract between the Barnstable schools and Mrs. Mahoney, a flexible plan for home education was agreed upon and is reviewed annually for renewal. For academic guidelines, Mrs. Mahoney is required to rely on a certified teacher... Mrs. Mahoney is also relying upon the Calvert School instruction booklets, a prescribed home teaching program as a backbone for teaching the basics. She says the children are drilled at least three hours a day in reading, writing, and arithmetic,.

"Since I only have a high school education, I'm learning with my daughters," she says. "If I feel inadequate in a subject matter, I go to outside resources, particularly in the community." When her daughters expressed an interest in electronics, Mrs. Mahoney took them to a sound studio.

The school committee has made it possible for the Mahoney children to attend special programs offered in Cape schools in order to round out their education and provide opportunities for them to socialize with their peers. In the past year Kendra and Kim have attended school workshops in solar energy, wood carving, beekeeping, jazz, and arts and crafts. Both are members of the 4H Club and the YWCA and Kim is currently the only girl on a little league baseball team.

"I think the girls are interacting as much as ever with kids their own ages," their mother says. "In fact, even more, because they have met many new people, from classmates to community members who have opened their doors to us."

"Elaine has sought out more resources to teach her daughters in nine months than most teachers do in four years," [a special education teacher] says. "I'm amazed at the number of things she's thought of. When the children express an interest in an area, she picks right up on it, whether it be marine life at a beach, or physical fitness. They go, and do, and see, something that public schools just can't do when on a strict class schedule." ...

When the school committee reviewed the Mahoney's progress this past month, they were unanimously pleased with their achievements. They were particularly impressed with a scrap book the girls had made illustrating a year of activities. Although the girls were not graded, they will be required to take the Iowa Basic Skills Tests.

"Learning goes on every hour of the day," Mrs. Mahoney says, "so how can you grade or test that accumulated knowledge?"

She indicates the reactions of parents in the community were mixed. "Some were very supportive and others angry or fearful because my way of education is threatening an established institution."

Kim's notes that her friends called her "a lucky duck" when they learned she's been staying home all year to learn.

"When they find out the things we do and places we go, they want to go too."

And the future? Mrs. Mahoney plans to continue teaching again next year. In fact, the girls will still be "in school" this summer on a lighter schedule so they don't have to review in the fall.

"I'd like to go on doing this for as long as we can." But after next year, Kendra will be of junior high age, so an entirely different set of circumstances may enter into their decision.

"I might want to go back to school then," Kendra says, although she adds she sees her friends all the time. "It'll be my choice."...

So far, no other parent in the Barnstable school system has approached the administration with an alternative education plan. "We regard it as a valid premise, although what follows is no snap decision," Geick says. "But, we are pleased with the Mahoney family."

Mrs. Mahoney only has words of praise for the school committee. "I respect them because they care. Because of that, anything is possible. I'd like to see more parents and children attempt this system and I encourage other parents to come to me for suggestions."...

UNSCHOOLING SURVEY

I'd like to ask readers to help us make an informal (and confidential) survey of unschoolers. Please let me know if you are teaching one or more of your children at home, and if so, which of the following statements describe your situation. (Feel free to answer simply with numbers and letters, though if you want to add more details, that will be fine. Don't feel you have to answer all questions—if you're not sure of an answer, just skip it.)

1. Our local school system (please name) knows about, and a) supports, or b) at least tolerates and allows, our home teaching plan.

2. Our local schools would be willing to be listed in GWS as allowing or supporting our home teaching.

3. Our local schools, as far as we know, do not know that we are teaching children at home.

4. Our local schools support or tolerate our home teaching plan, but only after a court decision in our favor. (Please give the name of court and judge, the title of the case, i.e. *People v. Jones*, and date of ruling.)

5. We are able to teach our children at home because we have registered our own home as a private school. (Please give name.)

6. We are able to teach our children at home because we have registered them with a school a) in our town b) in our state c) out of state, which supports our home teaching program. (Please name school.)

7. This school would be willing to be listed in GWS as supporting our home teaching.

8. We have some arrangement not listed above (please specify).

9. Our local schools are supporting and assisting our home teaching program a) by helping us get needed materials b) by giving us assistance which we

find helpful (please specify) c) by allowing our child(ren) to go to the school to use special facilities or to take part in special activities.

10. Our local schools are impeding our home teaching program by a) making us conform to their curriculum b) making us prepare an elaborate curriculum for their approval c) making us teach subjects we would prefer not to teach d) making us give the children tests we would prefer not to give them (please specify).

11. Our local schools send people to our home to inspect/oversee our program (please say about how often).

12. On the whole, these inspectors seem to be a) friendly, helpful, etc. b) the opposite c) indifferent.

13. In order to get the local schools to approve our program, we submitted a formal proposal to them (please indicate roughly how long).

14. In our home teaching proposal we included some references to court rulings in this field.

15. In preparing our plan, we had the aid of a lawyer. (Please give name and address.)

16. Our lawyer would be willing to be a) referred to other unschoolers looking for legal help b) listed in GWS as being willing to do this.

17. The decision to allow us to carry out our program was, as far as we know, made by a) the superintendent of schools b) the school board c) other (please specify, if you know).

18. In getting approval for our plan, we had to, or chose to deal with authorities at the state level. (Please specify.)

19. In getting approval, we used the assistance, advice, support, etc. of one or more outside organizations. (Please specify).

20. In teaching our children at home, we make some use of formal curriculum materials, such as Calvert, Home Study Institute, etc. (Please specify.)

21. In order to get these materials, we had to send a letter of approval from some school (please name).

22. In using such materials, we feel a) they are really helpful b) we would rather not use them, but are using them as part of our arrangement with the local schools, or for some other similar reason, i.e. to protect ourselves in case of trouble.

23. Our home schooling has received some mention in the local media. (Please specify.)

24. On the whole, we feel that the local media have been a) favorable b) unfavorable.

25. As far as we know a) quite a number of people in our community know about our home schooling b) few if any people know about it.

26. As far as we know, the people who know about our home schooling seem to be a) favorable, supportive, etc.. b) indifferent c) unfavorable, hostile, etc.

27. As a result of media attention to our program, or for whatever reason, other people in our community have asked us how they might unschool their children. (About how many?)

This is probably enough questions for now. If you think of an important question that we did not ask, please suggest it.

Thanks very much for whatever information you can send. As I said, anything you say will be confidential, unless you tell us otherwise. But this information will help us to have a slightly better idea of how many people are teaching children at home. And it will be a great help to future unschoolers.

AN UNSCHOOLED SPECIAL CHILD

A mother who has unschooled her teenaged daughter (born with Downs Syndrome) writes about this experience:

… As for unschooling L, I had long wanted to do this with my older children, and everything I read in GWS and have experienced with her makes me quite sad to have missed the opportunity to have allowed them the same thing. Of course the time was not right—in the world or in me—so it probably would not have worked anyway. But I saw in them all the things GWS describes, and did try to help them along in an extracurricular way. They had some tutoring, took time off on occasion on regular school days (as when one went to Stevens Inst. to fool around with computers), and I had the strength of mind to tell the school secretary, who asked "And is this going to be a regular thing?" that it just might be. I was always strong-minded but not often enough strong-spoken, unfortunately, when it came to dealing with these insufferable school systems. Only when it was as obviously desperate as it clearly was to save L from their awful effects was I able to do what I knew was the only way to proceed.

Anyway, L only once had any special ed. involvement, at a nursery school run by the local association for retarded children, and it was bad to useless. From there on she went to regular schools—private nursery schools, private kindergarten, a public school which was running an experimental open primary, and a Catholic private academy. All this was expensive and time-consuming. Six of those years I drove her back and forth—16 miles each way (x 4 trips a day). The local public school system only once honored my demands for reimbursement of tuition, after the county special ed. people managed to point out that one of L's teachers had a learning disabilities certification and therefore the class could be defined as a special program. They did say they'd provide transportation to the public school, but I preferred to drive her myself, since I wanted to keep her out of special ed. situations, which I feel *increase* the degree of handicap by providing handicapped models of behavior. And the transportation, of course, was in the special ed. vans. Besides, I wanted hot-off-the-classroom readings of her moods and responses, not her reactions 45 minutes after leaving school.

In planning to unschool, I went through the usual mental discussions about how much time I should allocate, how to re-create a parallel school system for one child, and so forth. Of course I quickly realized the futility of that idea just on the basis of money. To provide even one week of tutoring according to the time allotments of schools (4-6 hours a day) rapidly used up all the money I was paying for a year of private schools. No wonder people feel the schools are a good buy just in terms of the *cheapness* of the baby-sitting.

From the beginning, L and I have planned what she'd do. I collected clippings from all over for a year, then sorted out the ones I could afford, and presented those to her for her consideration. Choices like cooking, horseback, trips to New York and elsewhere, tutoring. We did have to keep changing things when, for instance, a teacher who was going to give her cooking lessons (an overnight deal) got divorced and went to work in New York.

But we kept consulting and revising, and ended up with the present schedule of swimming, ballet, drawing and painting, and needlepoint. There were other considerations besides the learning ones involved too. I felt it was not safe for her not to swim well, and her ear operations had made her fearful of going whole hog on her own. So she has private lessons in that. And I read about a ballet dancer who had taken ballet initially to overcome flat feet, so we began this mainly for that reason. Too, the more I went into it, the more I decided that what L needed was a reprieve from the morass of schoolwork that, in spite of the good-as-possible situations I'd been able to find, was not at all as helpful or satisfying as I felt might be possible—somewhere, somehow. So I decided not to do anything at all academic for awhile. Just say the heck with it.

So we went to the beach in the lovely October and even November weather that had been denied us as prisoners of school, played kickball in the back field, and proceeded with the courses.

On one trip to the shore, paying tolls, it was again clear that L still didn't know one coin from another, so that became the first academic venture. And it provided one of my first principles: though the general ideas are the same for L as with regular kids out of school, certain things have to be done differently. While other kids probably need only a bit of assistance and guidance in following what they learn and are interested in, L really has to have regular exposure. Not lengthy but regular—daily, if possible, including weekends.

Every day I put prices on four things and she worked them out with a plastic measuring cup full of change—a permanent collection of coins. I remember trying to get the school people to have her use real money but they seemed to think that was quaint. They just loved their big cardboard coins. Within a month she had it cold. I switched to numbers on paper, and she could do it that way too. (Ed.—and in the schools we have all those "normal" children who after years of school arithmetic still supposedly can't make change.)

However, a second principle of unschooling with L is this: Like freelance writing, unschooling is subject to cancellation at any time, whenever somebody comes to visit, or the neighbor's car breaks down and she calls you to go pick her up, etc. Now this is probably one of the advantages of unschooling with other kids—that you can live your regular life and still keep learning. But with L, Christmas, and long visits from my mother, who had not been well, meant a far less-than-hoped-for routine. I had a hard time concentrating on what I was working on, and L would get tense. Early in our unschooling one of the first things I saw was an increased sense of success—a euphoric "I can do it" feeling, in contrast to the tight lips, lowered head, long hair hiding eyes that had been typical of the earlier work with school stuff. Yet when life got hectic that same posture quickly returned. (Ed.—this is an example of the kind of important sign that parents can learn to notice, but that classroom teachers are usually too busy to notice.)

I worried about the possibility that it was only the one-to-one situation that was doing the job—and then answered myself that this was what all kids could use. Yet it did seem somewhat unrealistic to try to manage it when life was so uncooperative. I still haven't solved this problem. I suspect it's a problem with others to some degree too, but it's more difficult when the youngster has some learning barriers.

In fact, it seems to me that this question of scheduling is central. I suspect that it's only the school requirements that keep some families at it all, and that in doing so, they *undo* some of the benefits of trying unschooling in the first place. That is, feeling under pressure to produce for the satisfactions of the schools and their requirements, they may lay a lot of pressure and guilt on the kids.

In our case, though, it just seems as though things don't stick in her head unless we keep to some kind of regular routine. But though we require something regular, it doesn't need to be lengthy, and the generally free feeling I have about the whole thing is one of the best things about it. We've been able, at times, to really be flexible about things like going outside on a nice day when the forecast calls for rain later. Or grocery shopping early when the stores aren't busy instead of later when the lines get long. Nevertheless, the problem of interruptions persist. And I'm not sure I can do much about it. Any suggestions?

There are some problems, of course, beside this. One I would really appreciate your thoughts about. After the money, I began fooling around with sentences, which have been a problem for a long time. I keep wondering how important it is at all to have her learn about sentences, *except* that she is a wild and wonderful letter writer. She's been sending out two or three letters a day, to friends and relatives, and would send them to strangers too if allowed. She has her own address book, and usually includes several riddles that she copies out of one of her books. But the structure, though eminently clear in content, is pretty frustrating in design. The letters are really remarkable in what they say—she's tremendously articulate—but the sentences all run together, and she leaves out "a," "an," and other small items.

I've tried to get straight in her mind the difference between a sentence and a question, and found a curious thing. It turns out—and this is something I'm sure a school would never have found out—that to L a sentence and a question are essentially the same thing, you just say them differently. For instance, you could say, "The mail will come today." Or you could ask, "The mail will come today?" She does this with everything. I think the problem might be solved in some other language. But it makes letter writing a problem even if it works out in conversation. The usual way of distinguishing sentences from questions, by raising your voice at the end, doesn't work in writing. She does that when speaking, but in writing uses exactly the same form. As I say, who cares, as long as she communicates. But I would like to make it easier on her letter-readers, and make it more likely that they would reply.

I feel I have done nowhere near enough in this letter to indicate how enthusiastic I am about the whole unschooling enterprise, in spite of the difficulties I've indicated. L's typing goes well, her needlepoint is terrific (and her instructor is out of her mind with joy and amazement), in ballet she is just barely less competent than the older girls in the class (20–40), and in art, according to her teacher, she is really gifted. As for the calligraphy (Ed.—Italic writing), she really likes it when she does it, but doesn't often choose to do it. The early stages can be quite frustrating, and L has very high expectations for herself.

I do want to write a chronicle of L's experiences and mine—both the vitamin developments and the unschooling. But it really overwhelms me when I think of all the small threads that I've watched along the way, and when I read my scribbled notes. Incidentally, I keep forgetting to include one of the first courses. This was a gardening course, run by Morristown's Frelinghuysen Arboretum. The kids each had a 10 x 15 plot, seeds and plants, and help in planting and cultivating. It started on Saturdays from 9 – 12 in April '78 then switched in June to 9–1:30 two mornings a week, through Aug., with evenings open for harvesting crops as required through Sept. Besides the gardening, they made candles, dried herbs and flowers, cooked zucchini bread and squash fritters, collected bugs, and other stuff—all very skillfully, not just cutely. The teachers were great. It's running again this year, but with slightly shorter hours and lower fees, in order to try to reach more kids. So L will take it again—she generally profits more from a twice-around plan, to give her a chance to really get into things that she got introduced to the first time.

For the past year she's been taking a variety of vitamins, thyroid, etc. She has lost 15 pounds. Weight is often a problem with children with mongolism, but in her case this turned out to be largely a result of a gluten allergy, hitherto unsuspected. She has also grown 5/8", her general appearance has improved greatly, and her intellectual functioning is enhanced. Her art teacher says of her, "This is not the same child I met last fall."

Earlier this year we had so many letters from people asking about *Growing Without Schooling*, and about teaching children at home, that we could not answer them all. In the magazine I asked readers if some of them, who could type and also had a cassette tape recorder, would help with this. Many offered to do so, among them L's mother. She asked if it would be OK, for the letters she was doing, if L addressed (in handwriting) the envelopes. I said fine. I sent them a tape of letters, which came back soon afterwards, the letters typed, the envelopes neatly addressed. Then I sent them a big stack of letters from all over the country, that we had already answered, but that now needed to be broken down by states so that we could send them to people in the various states for a closer follow-up. Along with these I sent a tape of instructions. About this, L's mother wrote:

...L was thrilled with the whole project, and most impressed with being addressed by name on the tape. She took to the sorting and filing with gusto. I hadn't mentioned that this was another part of our "program," again one where I had tried to convince the schools to do something "real." They kept trying to get her to alphabetize on paper, and I wanted them to give her index cards, recipes, etc. or folders. No use. So when we started our planning this year, I had her make up a bunch of file folders, for each course or planned activity, and she puts receipts, brochures and stuff in them. Also we keep her papers for figuring out money, arithmetic problems, sentences, etc. Also, since I need some shape for my days and am a chronic list-maker, we'd make up daily schedules (especially so she could go about her work without having to check with me every minute, something she really enjoys—the independence, I mean). These schedules, if more than routine, also go into the folders.

So she was already used to that. She made up the folders (with my help in listing the states and assorted abbreviations). The first round, I went through the letters and underlined the state. The second time around I just screened them to be sure there *was* an address and that it was legible, but didn't note them— she figured them out herself. Anyway, L loves the job, and can't wait to get started, at night even, after supper. All this seems ideal for L's purposes—some work experience, plus the exposure to the filing, alphabetizing, state names and abbreviations, etc. all without any formal "instruction," just doing it—the perfect way, but hard to find, especially for her.

(Ed.—In a later letter, she reports that L now has a paying part-time job.)

TYPING HELP AVAILABLE

The experience of many people who have tried, some successfully, some unsuccessfully, to take their children out of school and teach them at home, has shown very clearly that your chances of being able to do this are much better if you prepare for the school a very detailed statement about why you want to do it, how you plan to go about doing it, and what the various court decisions are that uphold your right to do it.

Three things to say about this document. First, it cannot be too long. The more you can put in about why and how you want to teach your own children, the more educational authorities you can quote, the more court decisions you can cite, the better. Your plan is a thinly disguised legal brief. In it you are speaking, not just to the school superintendent and school board, but beyond them to an invisible judge, should the schools be unwise enough to try to take you to court. You may not say anything about going to court in your plan—indeed it is wiser not to, but instead to talk as if you assumed that the schools were going to be reasonable and cooperative (as indeed some have been). But if your plan is complete enough, and shows enough knowledge of the law, the school people, if tempted to oppose you, are going to ask themselves, "What's going to happen if we have to argue against this in front of a judge?" You want them to feel that if they push matters that far, they are going to lose.

Secondly, you should send copies of your plan to as many school people as possible, certainly to all members of the school board, to the superintendent and leading members of his administrative staff, and perhaps other as well. On every copy you send put a list of all the people who will receive it. Most of them will feel that they have to read it, and then discuss it with all the others. Your task is to make them feel, not only that you are serious, responsible, and knowing, but also that it is going to cost them much time and trouble if they try to oppose you. These people are busy, they already have to go to many more meetings than they like, and you want their hearts to sink a little bit at the prospect of still more meetings.

Thirdly, your plan should be typed, neatly and accurately, in good business form, on good 8 1/2 x 11 paper, preferably a business letterhead if you have one. This will impress the school people, and beyond them, that invisible and (you hope) avoidable judge. Appearances may not be everything, but in this world they count. Make (on paper) the best appearance you can.

The problem is, of course, that many people who may want to take their children out of school can't type, or type well, or quickly, or may not have access to a good typewriter (and it should be reasonably good). That is what this memo is about. Many people, all over the country, have very kindly offered to help, and have already helped GWS with some of its typing work. They will surely be glad to help you. So if you need people to help type up your home education plan, and any other letters you may have to write, let us know, and we will put you in touch with skilled and willing typists.

WRITING A "CURRICULUM"

From a letter to a parent:

... As far as curriculum goes, I think the most important thing is to put something down on paper that the schools will accept, without being so specific that it ties your own hands. It's not necessary to tell the school people what you will be doing, far less to convince them that it is right. Since practically everything in the school curriculum falls within the boundaries of ordinary daily life, things which young people are interested in simply because these things are part of the world, I think you could very well fill out some kind of paper saying you'll be studying English, mathematics, history, science, etc. After all, nobody can look at a magazine or a daily paper without running into these things. I wouldn't say that you will be teaching a particular subject between 9 and 10 AM every Thursday, or anything as specific as that. But I wouldn't hesitate to say that any one of these subject will be "covered" for as many hours a week as happens in school.

THE "SOCIAL LIFE"

I find more and more, and others do too, that when we talk to people about unschooling one of the first responses we get is the question, "What about the social life?"

As GWS readers know, I reply to this by saying that the social life of most of the schools and classrooms I have ever seen or heard about is so mean-spirited, status-oriented, competitive, and snobbish, that I would be glad to keep a child out of it in any way I could.

What I find more and more remarkable is how people—by now they must number into the hundreds—respond to this reply of mine. I cannot remember even *one* person who has said to me "You're wrong about the social life at school, it is kindly, generous, supporting, democratic, friendly, loving, etc., and the children love it and benefit from it, etc." No, without exception, when I condemn the social life of school, people then say, "But that's what the world is like. That's what the children are going to meet in Real Life."

A news story on my desk quotes one superintendent as saying, "I would be particularly worried about the social adjustment of the child. He just wouldn't know what it's like to be working in groups." (As if there were no groups anywhere in the world except in schools.)

Another said, "We can't keep our kids in the closet all their lives. Sure, there are some things in the schools that are not perfect—but that's what life is about. What we have to teach children at home is how to cope with the bad things, not lock the kid up to protect him."

A recent issue of *EVAN-G* (End Violence Against the Next Generation—see GWS #1) reports that a school in Fort Lauderdale FL recently paddled 100 children for running in the playground during recess. About this, the vice-principal (and paddler), William Smith, said, "We cannot guarantee their safety if they continue to run." He later announced that the paddling had had "a positive effect" because there were few violations of the no-run rule and no accidents.

But it couldn't have worked too well, for a few weeks later the school removed all basketballs, jump ropes, and tetherballs from the playground as well.

A parent in a fairly rich Boston suburb called me only a few days ago to report that her children had recently told her that they were forbidden to run or play games during recess—probably for the same reason.

So much for keeping kids "locked in closets," etc. As a matter of fact, this may not be a bad time to report what one other parent wrote me a few months ago. Her child, a third or fourth grader, who lives quite close to the school, had been late coming home. The mother started to walk to school to see if she could find her. On the way she met the child's teacher. When the teacher saw the mother, a startled expression came over her face, and she quickly turned and went back to the school—to let the child out of the closet into which she had locked her some time before, which she had completely forgotten.

Naturally, the mother made quite a fuss about this, and naturally, nothing was done about it.

To return to my main point, a very large number of people, including many or most school people, seem to accept and support the idea that school is a place where children have a lot of bad experiences to get them ready for the bad experiences they will later have in Real Life.

Well, if people who feel that way about life want to have that kind of training for their children, I suppose it is their right. But people who don't feel that life is basically boring, meaningless, and cruel should not be compelled to watch their children being brainwashed, programmed, and bullied into that belief.

One other point. I suspect that most of the people who worry about their children "fitting in" are people who have never felt that they themselves really "fitted in," but felt instead more like the losers and outcasts of whom our schools are so full.

SUCCESS STORY—INDIANA

...Let me tell you what happened to our son after we removed him from a local public school's first grade last November. He stopped wetting his bed, he stopped suffering from daily stomach upsets and headaches and he has not had a cold for six months although he averaged one cold a month, while attending school. He has gained five pounds and has grown almost two inches. And he is *happy!* ...

My husband and I had become increasingly concerned about the lowered academic standards in the public schools and the increasing availability of drugs—even in the primary grades. We had also watched our older children lose their innate intellectual curiosity by fourth grade, sometimes never regaining this priceless enthusiasm. ...

We moved to Evansville three years ago. P attended kindergarten '77–78, in a class of 42 youngsters. He stuck it out because every morning he and five other kindergartners attended a reading class for half an hour. During this time he was absent from the noise and general chaos of a large class which he so disliked. I began to look into other schools at this time. ...

[Reading GWS], added to our 25-year interest in *Summerhill*, convinced us that not only was it possible to raise a child without formal schooling, but it is the most probable way to insure that child's lasting interest in all that surrounds him. I decided not to register P for first grade, reasoning that the public school would probably assume that we had put him in private school and vice versa! My husband, however, was uneasy... he did not relish the idea of being hauled into court. (His attitude changed during the following weeks.) We decided to let P attend first grade. Maybe he would like it, etc.

After the second week of school we knew that we would have to take him out. There were thirty children in his class. Each Monday morning the paddle, used freely in this southern Indiana city (Ed.—and all over the state) was removed from the teacher's desk drawer and prominently displayed. In some of the other classrooms in this school the paddle was hung on a nail next to the blackboard. P was so terrified of the possibility of his being paddled and humiliated in front of his friends that he could think of little else. He never would have been paddled, of course, being as frightened as he was of doing something to initiate the wrath of his teachers. (Ed.—in such schools a small child does not necessarily have to "do something" in order to be paddled.) Nevertheless, he refused to be convinced that he had nothing to worry about and in four weeks he had dropped from the top reading group to the lowest.

Some other incidents: 1) he was backed up against the wall of the bathroom by a larger first grader who asked yet another first grade boy, "Want to see me beat up this kid?" P kicked him and escaped. 2) On the playground at lunch time P threw his arms around a boy from the other first grade class whom he had known the year before in kindergarten and whom he had not seen all summer. Two fourth grade boys saw this display of affection and called P "gay" thereafter, taunting him at school and on the school bus. 3) P fell on the playground, hit his head and wandered back into the classroom to tell his teacher—who told him *never* to come back into the building until the bell rang. When P told her about his head she told him to report it to the playground supervisor. P did not know there was such a person on that crowded macadam square!

The children were not allowed to converse in the lunchroom and the 'hostess' wielding the inevitable paddle reminded them what would happen to them if they did. P would come home from school exhausted, irritable, often crying and carrying his lunch—untouched. (This lunchroom situation has been going on for four years despite formal protests from various parents.)

We contacted a young, interested and sympathetic lawyer who after some research found out that Indiana requires school attendance except in cases where the child is so physically or mentally handicapped that he/she cannot attend. Then, the child must be taught in English by a certified teacher and receive an education equivalent to what he/she would be getting in the public schools. Our attorney also discovered that 'equivalency' has not yet been established in Indiana.

On his advice we had P tested by a child psychologist to assure "the authorities" that he had no emotional or mental disorders. Next we secured a first grade curriculum from a correspondence school and had it evaluated by the Dept. of Education at a local university.

Four weeks after we began our campaign we flew with our lawyer to Indianapolis to meet with the superintendent of Indiana public schools. He was stone-faced and unsympathetic and told us that if we took our son out of school we would be prosecuted. Later on during the interview he did tell us of a couple of Indiana families who had removed their children from schools (for religious reasons) and, after a court hearing and some investigation into their home schooling, had been permitted to teach them at home. My husband told them that we had hired an attorney and had gone to great lengths and considerable expense to remove our son from school as discreetly as possible. He felt that if this whole thing hit the newspapers the Evansville-Vanderburgh School Corp. would be the ones to suffer—not us. I guess that the superintendent must have agreed, inwardly, for he directed us to the state Attendance Officer. She was sympathetic but not hopeful. She suggested that we meet with the local Attendance Officer and tell him of our plans, hoping that he would wait a couple of weeks before handing us a citation.

Two weeks later we had interviews with the attendance officer and the superintendent of the elementary schools. We found out later from our lawyer that the officials in Indianapolis had called the local officials advising them to let us take P out of school. An emergency meeting was called and it was decided to let us go ahead with our plans without prosecuting. This did not mean that they were happy about it! The school superintendent was alternately distraught and angry. He wound up, however, begging me to let P try any school in the city—they would forego the usual zoning restrictions for him. But it was too late for that. P *hated* any mention of school. The fact that neither my husband or I are teachers and have never even taken an education course was never mentioned. (We do both have master's degrees.) So, we were free to take him out of school provided I sent a monthly attendance report to the local officer . . .

The first couple of months of home schooling were rocky. P, relieved to be out of the formal school situation, went along with a fairly rigid home schedule for two weeks. Then it was nothing but rebellion. I think the only thing that made him go along with any reading, math, science, etc. was the fear that he might have to return to school. I over-organized his days and weekends with activities including children his own age, so afraid was I that he would end up some sort of weird recluse.

Along about mid-Feb. I reread *Summerhill, And the Children Played*, and your book *How Children Learn*. I reread some of the GWS issues and gradually have come to my senses. Some mornings we have "school," some mornings we don't. We visit museums, libraries, farms, and parks. We go to the movies. We meet my husband for lunch and go horseback riding. At home P builds villages with his Lincoln Logs, plays in his treehouse, skateboards, rides his bike, plays with his dogs, jumps on the trampoline, paints pictures and (sometimes) practices his violin. Last winter we sledded every day. Late in the afternoon our backyard is the gathering place for youngster of all ages. During a recent trip to Florida, P was as much at ease with adults as with the vacationing youngsters in the hotel. So, I let up on the forced sociability along with the unreasonable academic demands. The books are there when he wants to look at them and now that I am no longer pressuring him, he wants to learn.

…I just wanted to tell you about our own very special experience with unschooling. And we want to thank you for publishing GWS. Without it we would probably not have had the courage to do what we did.

(From a later letter:)

Many people have asked me if I used a curriculum with P and I did—this past year, from the Home Study Institute in Washington, D.C.… I was not planning to use a definite curriculum this year but I have changed my mind, simply because I think it is a good idea to have some text books around in case the school authorities start snooping!

I wanted to tell you of our experience with P and a compass. A few weeks ago he bought a small camper's compass with money he had earned doing chores. We took a walk around the neighborhood with the compass noting how our direction changed although the needle always pointed North. But this was not enough. P wanted me to explain the numbers along the edges of the compass and wanted to know exactly how they were used. I referred him to his father and they spent hours working out hypothetical 'problems' on paper. During this time P asked me to read to him from our encyclopedia about compasses. There *we* learned that the first compass (1000 A.D.) was merely a magnetic piece of iron stuck into a cork floating in water. P proceeded to unearth two nails from our basement both of which had some magnetic qualities. He stuck one of them in a cork so that it was evenly balanced, filled a bowl with water and lo and behold!—a homemade compass that actually works!

Later my husband drew an intricate compass course which P followed with very little help, at the end of which he found a dollar bill 'prize' in our mailbox. My husband tells me that he didn't know that much about reading a compass until he was in the Army. (He never was a Boy Scout) …I am hoping that eventually we will have several unschoolers in our area. It will then be easier to exchange ideas and, perhaps, to organize a day each week when the children can be together…

THE VIOLIN AT TWO

As some my know, in the Suzuki method of violin instruction, at least as first conceived and practiced, the parents of a child, while it is still a baby, begin to play for it, and many times, recordings of the easy violin pieces which it will itself learn to play at the age of three. Kathy Johnson and I have (in letters) talked often about Suzuki. Recently she wrote:

…You asked me last December to let you know how my home adaptation of Suzuki violin with my two-year-old daughter is working. I hadn't actually brought home the 1/16 size violin then, but in self-defense had to get her one to keep her from having tantrums (Ed.—i.e., feeling angry about being left out) when my Dad and I played. Her being well into the "No" stage now is living proof of why they don't organize a class of young Suzuki violinists until age three.

But I feel you *can* do more at an early age than merely playing the record. With no big fanfare, one day when a tantrum started during our duet, I simply suggested that she play her own violin—that little one over there in the corner. She gave me a look as if to say, "Oh yes, but of course!" And before the duet was over, had figured out how to open the case, get the violin out, and saw the bow upside down over the strings a few times. She was delighted.

In the past four months, whenever we saw such a gross mistake on her part, either my dad or I (whoever was closer) would *very briefly* reach down and show her a better way to play as we went along. Of course, she had to learn some rules: not to carry her instrument around

the house, especially on non-carpeted surfaces, not to handle the bow hair (or it won't make any sound on the strings), etc. We were amazed how fast she learned to respect her instrument. She even keeps the bow rosined!

She hasn't mastered the technique of playing just one string at a time yet, but she has darn good position, and a wonderful time developing those long full bows.

We were amazed when out-of-town relatives came to visit and our *shy* little daughter brought out her violin to squawk on the strings in front of a roomful of adults. We were all proud—but not as proud as she was! I think the important thing my dad and I learned very quickly was to recognize that moment when she needed help, capitalize on it briefly, then leave her alone to experiment. Praise is used, but in not much greater amounts than Dad and I praise each other. We play for enjoyment. I think she does, too.

She won't stand for a "lesson." Help that is a few seconds too long or in the wrong tone of voice brings loud "No-No's" followed by her putting her violin away and being angry. At this age, there's a fine line between happiness and tears. When she wants, if she wants, we'll see an expert.

AUTO EXPERT AT SEVEN

John McPhee, in his book about Alaska, *Coming into the Country,* tells a number of stories about people teaching their children at home, or learning things outside of school. One story is about Stanley Gelvin, who at age seven bought for ten dollars an old broken down Chevy that had not run for years, sent away for parts, and, reading out of a book on auto mechanics, rebuilt the engine and made it run. His parents ran a truck stop, and Stanley would regularly advise the drivers about the state of their machines. He warned one driver that his differential was in bad shape. The driver told him not to worry, it always sounded funny. Twenty miles up the road, the differential completely broke down.

…AND A COMPUTER EXPERT

From a teacher in Vancouver:

…I saw an interesting thing this past week. I was down at a little storefront place called the Community Computer Institute (a small business which rents time on computers—the little personal ones—for very good rates; they also have self-teaching programs which you can use to have the computer teach you how to use the computer). While I was there an older man and a young boy, about 11, came in and were looking around. The kid was fascinated and the man was a little perplexed and amazed, … "they're finally here… my, my…". However, the kid began to show the man some games on one of the simpler computers and within a few minutes both were engrossed in a major "star trek" like game. After the game the kid explained some rudimentary principles of programming to the man, who by this time was very interested.

So was I, because here was a classic example of a teaching/learning situation between two people without regard for age, roles or formal structure. I felt very good watching this whole episode and wondered what kind of things we could invent to facilitate this kind of thing happening throughout the city. I tried to explain this to some of the teachers I work with and they just ignored me... "that's not real learning and it just gets in the way of teaching them math skills." Here was an 11-year-old kid who had taught himself more about computers than I know by hanging around this place before it officially opened (so they let him use the computers for free) and by reading simple articles about programming. And they tell me that it's not real learning!...

CALVERT AD

A reader sent us a copy of an ad in a recent issue of the *Western Airlines* magazine:

CALVERT SCHOOL

Kindergarten through 8th grade. Educate your child at home with approved home study courses, or use as enrichment. Home is the classroom, you are the teacher with the help of step-by-step instructions. Start anytime, transfer to other schools. Used by over 300,000 students. Nonprofit. Write for catalogue. Admits students of any race, color, national or ethnic origin. Box WW5-9, Tuscany Rd,. Baltimore, MD 21210

This is very interesting. I have done a great deal of flying in the last ten or fifteen years, and (being a print-o-holic, read anything within reach) I always read the airline magazine in the seat pocket. But I have never yet seen a Calvert ad.

If you know these magazines, you know they are aimed at rich, successful, prominent, etc. people. Ads for expensive resorts, expensive products, and the like. Obviously, Calvert thinks that these folks may now be open to the idea of teaching their children at home.

Another interesting point. The "Box WW5-9" business has nothing to do with a real box. It is a code, so that when someone writes in reply to the ad, Calvert will know which ad s/he saw, and so, know which ads are the most effective. Standard practice in the advertising business. What it tells us in this case is that Calvert has placed, or is getting ready to place, ads in a number of publications.

This can only be good news for unschoolers, for many reasons. With these ads, Calvert is spreading the idea, and to many people who may not for a long time hear of GWS. As Calvert gets bigger, they may grow less nervous about not sending their materials except to people who have the approval of the local schools. Finally, the bigger Calvert gets, the more interested they will be in having legislatures make home schooling explicitly legal, or at least, in preventing legislatures from making it specifically illegal, which in time the school lobbies may try to get them to do.

In short, whether they know (or like) it or not—but I think they must know it—Calvert is an ally of unschoolers. The stronger they get, the better off we are.

And note that figure of 300,000 students. I would surely like to know how many of these are in the U.S., and of these how many are full-time home schoolers. I have been saying, and have been widely quoted as saying, that the number of families teaching their children at home was somewhere between 1000 and 10,000, probably closer to the latter. But perhaps my guess is far too low. Next time I am asked, I will quote the Calvert figure, and let people interpret it how they will.

Meanwhile, if any readers find these or similar ads, for Calvert or anyone else, please let us know.

A GOOD IDEA

A reader writes:

...I am working at a Family Health Center, where many families and their children come for medical help. I put a note on the bulletin board about "Growing Without Schooling," and am receiving a lot of requests for more subscriptions. . .

RULING IN VA.

The following excerpts from a recent Virginia court may be useful to unschooling parents in a number of states.

VIRGINIA: IN THE JUVENILE AND DOMESTIC RELATIONS DISTRICT COURT OF THE CITY OF NORFOLK
COMMONWEALTH OF VIRGINIA V. THEO GIESY No. A08202-A COMMONWEALTH OF VIRGINIA V. DANIEL GIESY No. A 08202-1
April 4, 1979
Johnny E. Morrison, Assistant Commonwealth Attorney, for plaintiff. Thomas B. Shuttleworth for defendants.

...The statute at bar is a part of the Compulsory Attendance Law (Sections 22-275.1–22-275.23). It is not a part of the Juvenile and Domestic Relations District Relations District Court Law (Sections 16.1-226–16.1-330).

Confrontation with it reveals that, under the present circumstances of Virginia Law, it is a fragile statute, vulnerable to assault on its integrity. Its infirmity is occasioned by legislative changes in the Juvenile Law.

The Virginia Juvenile Law has been modified to accord with concepts imposed by Congress in the Juvenile Justice and Delinquency Prevention Act of 1974 (Ti 42, USCA Sect. 5602). Although Congress is without jurisdiction generally in the field of juvenile law it imposes its will upon states by withholding federal funds from states which do not conform their law to the provisions of such Act. Virginia, in its revised Juvenile Law, effective 1 July 1977 has conformed.

The changes effected by the 1977 revision which bear on the case at bar relate to status offenses.

A status offense is an offense which would not be an offense if committed by an adult. The essential status offenses relate to incorrigibles (children beyond parental control), runaways and truants.

It is with truancy that we deal. Truancy is failure to participate in schooling.

Incident to the revision of the law truancy has been "decriminalized" (as have other status offenses).

A cogent factor in the philosophical rationale which impelled the forces which influenced the General Assembly to "decriminalize" status offenses was the concept that to punish juveniles for offenses for which adults could not be punished deprived juveniles of due process guarantees in the sense of obvious, fundamental fairness—of due process of law and of the equal protection of the law, both rights being guaranteed by Section 1 of the Fourteenth Amendment of the Constitution of the United States.

It appears that the Court must now recognize such rationale to be implicit in the present Virginia law affecting truancy.

The former Virginia law recognized juveniles and adults as constituting two separate classes of citizens. As to status offenses, including truancy, the differentiation between such classes no longer exists. Children and adults are of the same class. The distinction between them has been wiped out.

Constructions of the Fourteenth Amendment make much of distinctions between classes. The law is tolerant toward permitting different penalties for the same offense if the perpetrators are of different classes. But it forbids different penalties for the same offense by perpetrators of the same class. They are entitled to equal protection of the law.

In Juvenile Law a *delinquent offense* is defined as one which could be punished as a crime if committed by an adult. Truancy was formerly identified as a delinquent offense and was punishable like other delinquent offenses. But, according to the new rationale, since an adult cannot commit truancy, and so cannot be punished for it, neither can a child. They are now of the same class and enjoy identical rights.

...Coexistent with such law at that time (and still extant) was the law—the statute at bar—making it a criminal offense for parents not to require their children to attend school.

...With the major reenactment of the Juvenile Law in 1977 the Court .. .can no longer make a child attend school in a truancy case. But the criminal statute affecting parents not being a part of the Juvenile Law, was left unchanged.

...Synchrony no longer subsists between the Juvenile Law and the Compulsory Attendance Law.

The theory of the statute affecting parents is that parents who refrain from exercising their authority to make their children attend school are contributing to the delinquency of their children; that they are, in effect, conniving with their children in the commission of a delinquent and criminal offense.

...The salient issue is whether one who aids or abets another of the same class in the commission of an act which is not in itself either criminal or delinquent is guilty of a crime.

Otherwise stated, if a child's constitutional rights be deemed violated if he can be punished for an offense for which an adult cannot be punished, are an adult's constitutional rights equally violated if he can be punished for aiding and abetting the same offense for which the child, now a member of the same class, cannot be punished.

Due process and equal protection of the law work both ways.

However, the Court refrains from declaring this statute unconstitutional.

...The statute involved in the case (Sect. 22-275.6) directs the defendants, as parents, as to each child, to "cause the child to attend school or receive instruction as required by this article."

...Section 22-275.1 of the same Article spells out the options available to the parents .. (1) to send their children "to a public school," or (2) "to a private, denominational or parochial school," or (3) to have such children "taught by a tutor or teacher of qualifications prescribed by the State Board of Education and approved by the division superintendent in a home."

The parents in this case ... have elected course (2), a private school, and maintain that they are in *bona fide* compliance therewith.

The defendant parents, in compliance with course of action (2) have established their own private school. It is denominated "the Brook School," after Mrs. Giesy's maiden name. It has a faculty of essentially one teacher, Mrs. Giesy. It has a student body of four, the four children of the family.

The Commonwealth maintains that this is no true school, but a mere subterfuge of a school, in violation of the Compulsory School Attendance Law and is established as a device to circumvent that law; and that the defendants are, by virtue thereof, criminally responsible.

With respect for the Commonwealth's position, examination of the Commonwealth's own laws on the subject is in order. They are embraced within Title 22, entitled Education, of the Virginia Code.

...As to course of action (2), private schools, those for primary and secondary education contemplated by the case at bar, the statutory law of Virginia provides only a wall of silence.

...The legislative wall of silence is not deemed to be accident or oversight, but rather an eloquent expression of formal state policy.

As in the case of the silence of Congress, failure of the General Assembly to exercise the power of regulation is deemed to be an expression of its will that the subject should remain free from restrictions. See 16 Am. Jur. 2d, Const. Law Sect. 209.

...As to private schools, the law provides no guidance—no definition, no delineation of institutional parameters, no prescription as to faculty, students, curriculum or accreditation—nothing whatsoever.

What constitutes a private school may be determined by academicians or citizens, but the state refrains from participating in such determination.

The mission of the Court is to construe the will of the legislature. Where the legislature provides no law to construe, the Court refrains from construction. The Court does not make law.

...So the Court is without legal ability and is without legal authority to say that the Brook School constitutes a private school or to say that it does not constitute a private school.

It may or may not, and reasonable minds may differ.

The issue before the Court is narrow—whether by placing their children in the Brook School the defendants are in violation of Section 22-275.6 and guilty of a crime.

There is no proof that they are guilty beyond a reasonable doubt, and we therefore dismiss the case.

James G. Martin, IV
Judge

PARENTS' SCHOOL

Barney McCaffrey, who was the music teacher in the First Street School (see *The Lives of Children*), writes from Ontario:

...Thought I might tell you something of our school, the Community School of Killaloe. It's a cooperative, alternative school that combines the legal (and social) authority of "school" with being taught at home.

We've been going since 1970. Ontario law states that with 5 school age children (minimum), you can have a school as long as you run it on some school day during the year during school hours. If you don't ask for any money from the government you don't need any qualified teachers and you don't have to follow the state curriculum—you can choose to be an uninspected, nonaccredited school. This is the route

we have chosen. On one of the three forms you must fill out every year the province asks if you have been inspected by local fire, health and municipal authorities. As we use our homes and are located in a rural area, we see very little if any of these people as authorities, but know most of them personally.

At present, we are 5 families and 11 children, ages 4 to 13, with several more families on a waiting list. The parents are the teachers and we go 3 days a week all year round, using a different home each of the 3 days. Parents whose homes are not used teach at one of the other homes. In some families both parents teach at the same time, in others one parent at a time. Homes and parents vary according to seasons and conditions (which parent is working, etc.). Children stay at each others homes, one night at various homes but not ours.

On the second night my wife and I have all the children stay at our place as we find certain subjects (music, Spanish, photographic development, astronomy, etc.) can best be taught at night. The social instruction that they give each other before, during and after bedding down and waking up—especially with the wide range in ages—is probably worth more than all our adult instruction. As much as possible we try to let them do much of this by themselves in our summer kitchen—a separate building—and we're now constructing, mostly with the help of the kids, a larger solar heated building out of old barn logs, which can be used year round. 2 of our families live on the edge of town and 3 on farms, and the exchange of knowledge between the two lifestyles is another big plus of the kids staying over, not to mention that the parents get one free night a week and transportation costs are cut down (at present there are 20 miles between our farthest away families.)

Getting to and from school is and has often been quite an adventurous, educational experience, involving pushing out snow and mud stuck cars, caravans of ponies and buggies, and/or bicycles and walkers, keeping in touch by CB radio from stretches of 3 to 6 miles (without an adult at times), strong winds blowing small children over the snow, etc. At one time we tried renting a central farmhouse and hiring one of our parents as a regular teacher—at the grand salary of $25 per week. The kids used to carry a log of wood each, up and down at least 3/4 a mile of unploughed driveway to heat "their" school building. (With our present system, school costs—excluding transportation and food—run about $100 a year.)

Each day goes differently—depending on location and personalities of parents involved. One couple is responsible for reading and science, one mother for history, another for arithmetic. When the mom who teaches history got a job, her husband took over and taught journalism—his specialty—and the kids put out 4 issues of a newspaper.

Generally each family or group of parents is responsible for their day—subjects, routine, etc., and we avoid hassles by sticking to that pretty much. There is, of course, communication between all as to what is happening. Last year we realized that once a week with arithmetic just wasn't enough, so now it is taught almost every day. Quite often, after the regular subjects (or sometimes in place of them), special subjects are carried out—a Tai Chi demonstration from a visitor, or a series of lessons in French, or archery, or meditation, or eurythmics, or pony vaulting, or wood working from a visiting volunteer. Or we may have a day of maple sugaring, or swimming, or fixing a vehicle, or splitting and stacking wood, or a group music session, or preparing a float for a community parade—we've won a few prizes with the latter. One of our most ambitious and successful ventures along this line was a 20 mile round trip with 10 children, 5 ponies and a horse, with a buggy and a sulky (and 1 adult), to a horseshow. We camped over 2 nights, drove and rode in the parade, entered gymkhana events—a great relaxed learning experience. We've found ponies to be great confidence builders. Several times a year we also have school trips—our biggest last year—5 days 600 mile round trip, financed largely by a carnival run mostly by the kids.

Our farm, and one other of our families, has no electricity. Our particular day begins around 5 in the afternoon, when the children are brought to us—in winter this involves a 1/2 mile walk. In summer the kids eat and play outdoors until 7 or 8, then an hour or so of lessons and practice, and off to bed. In winter, there is less outdoor play and more individualized lessons—usually music. In the morning there's breakfast—sometimes prepared by the children themselves, then all help with the chores, washing dishes, feeding animals, etc. Around 10—earlier in summer and later in winter—we begin our "academics." Right now this includes calligraphy (italic writing which sometimes includes making your own quill pen or ink—most of the kids write 3 handwriting styles), arithmetic, touch typing, music (individualized lessons on keyboard, guitar, violin, trumpet, etc.), meditation, (vipisana or insight meditation) and Swedish massage. Of course not everyone covers all these in one day but we keep track so that over a month everyone covers everything at least once. Massage depends very much on temperature considerations, so it is not practiced as regularly as the other subjects.

Before lunch we have a half hour of organized physical activity. In very cold weather, because of lack of space we have to forego it—in spring and fall we use our summer kitchen, and in summer we go out into the fields. When possible, all exercises are carried out in the nude. A 1/4 mile run is followed by the sun salute and other yoga exercises. Then comes acrobatics, including backbends, headstands, handsprings, cartwheels, etc. In the summer kitchen a trapeze provides hours of fun and limbering exercise. When there is time and desire, we end with an Aikido session (a completely self defensive, mindpower martial art). On hot days a dip in the beaver pond before lunch, and/or an ESP session (reading cards or symbols). The afternoons are for what the kids want to do. Sometimes it's to play, or make a raft, or do arts and crafts, or walk through the fields (sometimes studying beavers or wild plants along the way). Last year a lot of time was spent riding horses and ponies to practice for the horseshow. Right now it's building that new school house, which sometimes takes a bit of animation and organization, and sometimes doesn't happen. School day ends around 4 or 5, when parents come for the kids, or they are driven home.

We've had an interchange of about a dozen children over the years with the public school. Some of the kids coming from it were better than ours of equal age in reading and arithmetic. Some were worse. All but one were comparatively stiff or weaker in body. In other areas—except television programming—the general knowledge of our kids seemed greater, especially, of course, in music, but that may be our prejudice. Again it may be our prejudice, but our children seem to have a natural confidence about them—not overconfidence or brashness, but a good estimation of their own abilities. In part this probably comes from not having marks—the children compete only with themselves—can you do it?—can you do it better? It is well understood that each one has certain abilities and talents—everybody has something unique and "best", and they are encouraged to communicate this to the others. One day we had a 5-year-old, good at music, giving a piano lesson to a 12-year-old. My older boy, who because of minimal brain damage, has some learning problems, has a tremendous natural self-confidence for a boy of 13—it's amazing how he shines in some of the straightest situations. A lot of it comes from a good ability to work with his hands and body—to carry a job through completely—developed in his farm work, and from not being put down in school or distracted with the general "let's play hate school" games of the so-called "slow learners." This fall, at 14 (legal age for early school leave) he's off to try other schools, to work and apprentice himself with selected friends. I don't think we'll worry about him too much. (Incidentally it's amusing to see that the occupations kids [Ed. note—I guess this means the same as "vocational"] I taught at the local high school years ago are now the ones with the new houses and cars, living in the area. Only a few of the very sharpest academic contemporaries have managed to set up a local profession—many of them have had to take jobs in the city or the far north). A girl who had been in our school 2 years, went to first grade at public school, was given 3rd year work, and at the start of her 2nd year, asked to come back to our school ("I learned all that stuff last year"). She's been with us since—a 10-year-old now with few signs of boredom…

GROWING IN CANADA

Our Canadian friend (GWS #6, 7) writes:

"... When Lisey was 2–3 she liked to carry a purse with money in it, though she never spent a cent. (That was before she found out about the candy bar rack at the store. Rats.)

A few months ago that purse turned up again and she found a $1 bill in it. The next day we were writing to her Great Gramma, sending a card of some sort (birthday perhaps) and Lisey ran to get the $1 and insisted on enclosing it—since she knew full well that was one thing important that people do with paper money—enclose it in cards as a present. Lisey's comment was, 'I need to owe Great Gramma it.' (I think this means, 'I *ought* to give it to her because she always sends *me* money in cards.')

I know she has picked up the phrase from our constantly 'owing' each other money. I borrow from the kids, they borrow from each other. I owe the cleaning lady. We owe such and such a company, etc. ...the adults acting according to prior agreements amongst themselves—that she of course wants to be part of (since she still has little desire to have money to spend on herself).

About adults and their mysterious (to kids) world. When I drove to the city to see the CBS show, it was the first time for 1 1/2 years that I had taken the car to the city. I was surprised to find that almost all the gas stations were now self-serve. I don't like pumping gas and decided to teach Heidi & Michael (11 and 8). To their utter delight. They of course fought over it—despite it being a freezing cold windy day. Driving home, Michael said, 'You know, you have to be 16 to drive a car. Well, I thought you had to be 16 to fill it up with gas, too.'

But then, how would he ever have thought otherwise, never having seen a kid pumping gas. (I haven't, have you?) (Ed.—No.)

A boring, time-consuming chore to me. But to them, a handle on the Big, Mysterious Adult World. For the time being, anyway."

TRYING OUT SCHOOL

A mother writes from Canada:

...Once L turned five last summer, most adults she encountered in the community seemed to say to her a variation of this: "Oh, you're five now. Aren't you lucky? You can go to school in the fall!"

We (her parents) didn't want her to go and said so. But we told her that it was her decision. We also advised her that we would never force her to go to school. Enchanted with the idea of riding the school bus, L happily decided to go.

She quit, the first time, the second day of school because the teacher (one to 32 children) took a book from her, presumably to do a mimeographed pre-reading exercise or other activity the teacher had chosen. (I found out later that L disliked pre-reading work. After leaving school permanently, she still went to visit her class, teacher and principal from time to time. On one visit, a gift of some mimeographed pre-reading material was given to her by the teacher. On examining it at home, L asked me what she was supposed to do with it. I explained and she immediately asked, "Do I have to do it!?" I answered, trying to restrain my glee, "You never have to do these again," I suspect she understands all too well the ludicrousness of pre-reading when you've been reading for a year.)

We gently convinced L to return since she had only a glimpse of what she was quitting. Quite frankly, we wanted her to know her enemy well. This may have been taking a chance with some children, as many "adjust" and end up staying. I suspect it's because they realize that they have no choice. We knew because of her independent nature that she'd soon be home. A few days later, she quit for the second time. We asked for a conference with the teacher and principal. The teacher had by that time a chance to observe L read. Despite her experience in a long career, where surely she had met up with five-year-olds who could read, she blurted out, "What am I going to do with you? You'll have to go to the first grade!" L bounced back, "Don't forget, I'm only five years old." We were horrified as first grade was described as even more restrictive than this "primary" (kindergarten elsewhere) grade which had no pretensions of even the open classroom approach. We were against first grade, and the reading teacher and others observed correctly that temperamentally she would have a difficult time "adjusting."

Since L's main complaint was the lack of reading opportunity for her and not enough by the teacher, the school offered her the option to attend a reading class of "slow" first graders to give her more reading and them "inspiration." She bit the bait and returned to school.

This is the point where L's story becomes most interesting. After a time at school (late November or early December) I noticed that she was reading less at home and not only that, she exhibited nervous behavior and other signs of anxiety when she was reading. Could this be the same child who the previous summer had sat reading for long stretches of time, totally absorbed and happy?

One day L came home from school with a book from the library. She was thrilled. I was never advised that Thursday was "library" day and the book must be returned the following Thursday. The day came and the book remained at home. L and several other children were punished by not being allowed to go to the library. They also were told to write a page of fives. The children did not write the page of work and for that were kept inside during recess. Those children never escaped the fluorescent lights all day. We were beside ourselves and advised the teacher and principal that L was never to be treated in that manner again.

Shortly before the Christmas holidays L left school for good. Three months later she did some sight reading which we recorded just for the fun of it. As we listened to it replay, I observed with surprise that she was actually enjoying herself again and showed no sign of anxiety. We're so very happy that she had the sense to get out when she did. Also, since we had just moved to the area, she had no close friends in the class who she would miss dreadfully if she quit. I really fear that had she stayed, say a year, permanent damage might have occurred.

Now L often has read several books before the rest of us wake in the morning. She also reads off and on throughout the day—everything from Spiderman and Tintin to the wonderful picture books we get from the library.

On the last visit to school, the teacher asked if L was reading at home. I answered, "Yes," and she seemed surprised and explained that L had refused to read any words off the board to her!

I should say that the entire time L attended school, we attempted to support the school and refrained from bad-mouthing it in front of her. We wanted to support her and the environment she had chosen. The choice of attending or not attending then, was hers.

Once L was home, we were able to spend more time together. I found her asking me what certain words or phrases meant. She would glean them from stories on tapes or records or from family conversation. If I knew a half-decent definition I would tell her; if not, we would both look it up in the dictionary. I didn't think much about the process happening in her mind until one day she asked me what "entire village" meant. I knew she had listened to the story, "Martze" (delightfully read by Mitch Miller of all people) on record three hours before. I told her it meant "all the people in the village" and she said her usual thank you and went about her business. Three hours before, she had heard that phrase! She had spent those three hours in a manner which, on the surface, wouldn't have appeared particularly "productive" to a great many teachers. (She had been painting, playing with sand and other relaxed activities.) A coincidence happened that day which tickled L's father and myself. I asked him a question to which he answered by using the simple word, "partially." L immediately asked for a definition of *that* word.

Since we're able to have a one-to-one relationship often enough when she asks me to define something, I'm able to spend the time asking quite natural questions if I need a clue, such as "In what context is that word?" She picked up on the word "context" right away because *it* was in context and so L learns even more words through relaxed conversation which is not available to children in a 32 to 1 ratio. [Ed. note—it could be. See comment at end.]

L is now asking where words come from. For instance, why is "tree" called "tree." Aside from tracing its language base in the dictionary, I'm at a loss! Is there a book, I wonder, which could shed more light on this?

A neighbor child who is several years older than L comes to play after school sometimes. She's pleasant and cooperative but when she plays "school" with our children, she is "teacher" and changes into a nagging, demanding tyrant. It got so bad that L was refusing to play the game. I finally had to point out to this child that she was reflecting her teacher's behavior and that L left school to avoid that kind of human contact. This same child could read when she entered school two years ago. She is now having "problems" in reading. One day, this same child started lecturing L about school. Wasn't she coming back? And if she didn't, she wouldn't learn anything. L flashed back with, "That's why I left school. I wasn't learning anything." She still maintains that is her primary reason for leaving. The other thing she couldn't tolerate was the violence among the children…

———————

But I have to say something about the business of relaxed conversation not being available in classes of 32 children. It isn't true. Or rather, probably it is true, in almost all classes, but it doesn't have to be true. Once teachers learn that they don't have to spend all their time deciding what the children are to do, and then telling them to do it, and then explaining to them how to do it, and then making or trying to make them do it, and then testing them (one way or another) to make sure they have done it—once they give all that nonsense up, as I, and Jim Herndon (and probably some others) learned to give it up, they find they have plenty of time for as much relaxed conversation as the children need or want. As Jim Herndon writes in *How to Survive in Your Native Land* (avail. here):

"And while teachers are complaining they haven't any *time* you see that you have all the time in the world, time to spend with Lucy and Sally telling them they got glue on their heads and threatening them about what you're going to do if they get on the hood of your car again until they are satisfied, time with Eileen and Rosa, who have discovered that if they get caught a couple times smoking in the bathroom their mothers will react most satisfactorily, time to talk with Howard, who has discovered simultaneously a real woods out in back of the drive-in and The Byrds and is trying to make sense out of both (the woods have foxes and a skunk and a red-tailed hawk flying overhead and some kind of marvelous purple moss which the Museum of Science don't know about and who would have thought that right here in this prototype [his word] of suburban developments there would be a real woods, and here too that is just what The Byrds are singing about)— every day there are going to be kids who want to spend some time talking to you, as adult, as teacher, as whatever you are, wanting to relate their adventures and troubles and excitements and miseries and aspirations and confusion or hoping perhaps to get some clear idea of the world they live in through you . . .You have time to protect some kids and get mad at others, you have time to answer over and over again questions about what kind of cigarettes you smoke and when did you start to smoke, are you married, how many kids do you have, would you let your kids smoke, let them grow long hair, do you think Robert is really smart? What would you do if your kids cut school, got an F, smoked in the bathroom, what kind of car, what was the war like, did you get in any fights, can you dance, did you like girls when you were thirteen, don't you think the PE teacher is unfair about giving out checks. Mrs. so-and-so said this yesterday, do you agree with that? . . Time to live there in your classroom like a human being instead of playing some idiot role which every-one knows is an idiot role, time to see that teaching (if that is your job in America) is connected with your life and with you as a human being, citizen, person, that you don't have to become something different like a Martian or an idiot for eight hours a day."

GAMES

Susan Price, mother in "Capable Children" (GWS #3), writes:

"Here is how we play SORRY now. Whoever sets up the game makes it so that each person gets out [onto the board] the first time around. (You need a 2 or a 1 to get out.) A 4 card used to mean you had to go backwards; now we say you can go either frontwards or backwards. They have had the idea about winning more. I guess you were right about school knocking the [everybody wins] spirit out of them.

We sometimes say, if we feel like it, that you don't have to have the exact number to get your man in home but can use a larger card and let someone else use the remaining numbers. The other night we were playing and F was going to get her last one in a little bit ahead of me. She needed only 2 spaces to get home with. She drew 11 and I suggested that she let me use it so that we could get home at the same time. So she agreed, and as she kept not getting 2's, kept giving them to me until I came close to home, and then she got a 7 and used it to get home with (7's are the only card you can legally split up). She gave me the remaining 5, and on my next card I was able to get home. She thought it was neat that we had both won at the same time."

I sent away for some games the other day, to see if I could find some to recommend in GWS. Didn't find any I was wild about. Some were ingenious, but all were competitive, I-win-you-lose, and if you want that kind of game, chess is hard to beat. But I thought, and thought again reading this mother's letter, isn't it too bad there aren't some games in which the players can cooperate to reach a real goal.

Then I suddenly remembered something that I had completely forgotten. When my sister and I were little, we used to visit my mother's mother in Maine in the summer, very happy times for us. She loved crossword puzzles, and it was part of the ritual of Sunday that she would do the big crossword in the *Sunday Herald Tribune*. She was good at them, and almost always finished the puzzle, or came very close.

Somehow, beginning when my sister and I were about 10, and without anyone ever doing much thinking about it, it became a part of our family custom that when Granny was doing the puzzle my sister and I would sit beside her, one on each side, and help. Of course, at first we weren't much help, but as we learned the rules of the game, and grew used to the kinds of clues the paper gave and the kinds of words it liked to use, we became really helpful, and doing the puzzle became a very exciting kind of cooperation. What a triumph it was for all of us when one of us could find one of those huge words, sometimes two words joined together, that went the whole length or width of the puzzle.

There was no feeling at all of who was finding the most words. We were all interested in finishing the puzzle, and as quickly as possible. It was a true team effort, and all the more exciting because doing the puzzle was not something Granny had cooked up to amuse and/or educate us.

There are books of easier puzzles for children, and it might be fun for a family to work together on them. But I think it might be a good idea for the adults to start this by themselves, and let the children join in if and when they want. And of course it wouldn't work for people who really didn't like doing such puzzles.

Funny, I haven't thought about doing those puzzles with Granny since the time we did them, perhaps because it was such a natural and organic part of our life together.

It now occurs to me that another good cooperative game might be the Word Game I wrote about in GWS #9. And still another would be doing jigsaw puzzles, which many children like.

Granny and Jane and I did use to play some competitive games. Our favorite was Mah Jongg, a game something like Gin Rummy, but played with (instead of cards) beautiful little rectangular pieces of bamboo, with faces of ivory carved into lovely figures. These figures were like the four suits of cards. As I remember, they were Dragons, Bamboos, Characters, and Circles. Players drew from a pool of pieces, face down in the middle of the table, and tried to get three or four consecutive pieces (2, 3, 4, 5 etc.) of the same kind.

Granny had an old and authentic Chinese set, and the feel and sound of the pieces, and the smell of the box, were lovely. She was fun to play with, serious without being mean. She liked to win, but enjoyed the game much more than winning. (Strange for me to think that this very regal woman was younger than I am now.)

Talked about these games with Peg Durkee. She said that a noncompetitive game that she and her family always loved to play was *Clue*. Do any readers know it?

PROBLEM SOLVED

Last night, as I write this, I solved a mathematical problem that I have been working on, off and on (more off than on), for about twenty-five years.

In the 50's, when I was teaching at the Colorado Rocky Mountain School, I read a paperback book called, I think, *The World of Number*. At one point, the author was talking about factorial numbers. (I will say what these are a bit later.) He gave two theorems about factorials, saying that although the proof of these theorems did not involve anything more than simple algebra, probably only people with quite a bit of mathematical talent would be able to work them out. Thus challenged, I began to work on the first theorem (I have long forgotten the second). I spent hours on it, and got nowhere. I decided that I was going to work it out, no matter how long it took.

I never read any further in the book, because I feared that I might see the proof somewhere, and so would never be able to find it for myself. I worked on the problem again a few days later. Again, nothing. And I have continued to work on it since. Sometimes I have forgotten it for a year or more; then something has reminded me of it and I have tried again, always without success.

Once, a few years ago, I thought I had a proof—but realized after a while that I had done some circular reasoning, and that my proof was no good.

About two days ago something put it in my mind, and I began to work on it again. I tried a new, or almost new, approach. It looked interesting, but after a while it had not led me anywhere. The work had made me sleepy, so I lay down for a short nap. I woke thinking of the problem, seeing some of the symbols in my mind. Still half asleep, I tried a couple of steps. They led to something I couldn't remember having done before. I considered it for a second, then sat up, wide awake, saying, "It can't be that easy." I grabbed some paper, wrote out the steps I had done in my half-awake mind. They were OK. I hadn't made any mistakes. Would my proof work for all cases? Yes, it would. I could hardly believe it—it was so easy, only five steps. I realized that I had been close to it all those years. How could I have missed it? Anyway, now I had it.

A fine feeling.

Factorials. Quite a long time ago, mathematicians become interested in this family of numbers:

1
1 x 2
1 x 2 x 3
1 x 2 x 3 x 4
1 x 2 x 3 x 4 x 5, etc.

Someone invented a name and a symbol for them, called 1 x 2 "2 factorial," 1 x 2 x 3 "three factorial," etc. and wrote them like this 2!, 3!, etc.

When people think about numbers and their properties, the kinds of things we can or can't do with them, one of the elementary properties they look into is what can these numbers be divided by.

One of the things they soon saw about factorials was that

4! could *not* be divided by 5
5! *could* be divided by 6
6! could *not* be divided by 7
7! *could* be divided by 8
8! *could* be divided by 9
9! *could* be divided by 10
10! could *not* be divided by 11
11! div. by 12 Yes
12! div. by 13 No
13! div. by 14 Yes

It became obvious that a factorial could not be divided by the next higher number if that next number was what they call "prime," which means that it can only be divided evenly by itself and 1. (The prime numbers are 2, 3, 5, 7, 11, 13, 17, 19, 23, 29, 31, 37, 41, 43, 47, 53, 59, ...etc. Some mathematicians are very interested in prime numbers, and are still trying to find a formula for *all* the prime numbers.)

With a little more looking around they saw this pattern:

4! + 1 is div. by 5
6! + 1 is div. by 7
10! + 1 is div. by 11
12! + 1 is div. by 13
and so on.

When mathematicians find something like this, that seems to be true for many numbers, they begin to ask themselves whether it is true for all numbers, and whether they can prove that it is. If and when they can, they have what they call a Theorem. This particular theorem about factorials, the one I saw in the book, was written like this:

Where N is any prime number,
(N–1)! + 1 is div. by N

By modern standards, this is very primitive math. I don't know when this particular theorem was proved, or by whom—it may go back to the classical Greeks, who were fascinated with numbers. In any case, finding the proof was an exciting adventure for me.

NEW AGE ARTICLES

The current (Sept. '79) issue of *New Age* (32 Station St., Brookline Village MA 02146—monthly, $12/yr.) contains a number of articles that GWS readers may find very interesting.

First is "Deschooling: The Legal and Emotional Challenges," by Michael Harris, a very well-informed and sympathetic article, perhaps the best unschooling article I have seen in print. We will probably add it to our list of reprints.

There is also an article on "Superlearning," a kind of semi-hypnotic approach to memorizing which makes use of music and other stress-relaxing methods. This is hard to describe in a few words, and it may or may not work as well as the article claims. But it is something I think we all ought to know more about.

Also a very interesting and promising article about learning to draw; a good article about the Heartwood home-building school, one of three such schools we wrote about in GWS #9; and other good things. Worth looking up.

CALVERT BOOKS WANTED

…I am wondering if "D" doesn't want to sell me any of his Calvert books, if you could connect me somehow to some people who would—or Home Study Institute books. I don't have to say in a letter to the school board that they are doing a home correspondence course—just say that they are using *materials* from The Calvert Institute (established 18—, used by many children of missionaries, etc, etc.) Maybe I would buy the whole 1st and 2nd grade year of books from someone—just to have around for my kids to see what kinds of stuff other kids are doing in school and to show my mother…

NEW BOOKS AVAILABLE HERE

We are adding two more books to the list we sell here. The first is *Good Work* ($9 + post.), the latest and last book of E. F. Schumacher, who died two years ago. It is largely made up of lectures that he gave while on tour of the U.S. not long before his death. Like *Small is Beautiful*, it is not primarily about children or education, but like that earlier book, it puts schooling into the context of the kind of world many of us would like to see, and so doing helps us to answer the argument (or our own fears) that unschooling is unrealistic, has no connection with the world as it is, and cannot help children learn to live and work in that world. Beyond that, it is a wonderful book for people of any age who have not yet found work that seems really worth doing and don't know how to look for it. In that sense it seems ideal for any young people in their teens who are not sure what they want to do next, or even that there is anything really worth doing.

The book is full of wonderful quotes, of which these two may have special meaning for GWS readers:

"Recently I was seated in a restaurant, next to a family of three, a father and mother and a very bright little boy, I would think between eight and ten years of age. They studied the menu and the boy said, 'Oh, I want liver and bacon.' The waitress was there; the father studied the menu, the mother studied the menu, and then the father ordered three steaks. The waitress said, 'Two steaks, one liver and bacon,' and went off. The boy looked at his mother and said, 'Mummy, she thinks I'm real!'"

"…I then also found that in all human traditions there has been a very great antagonism against all this counting business. I don't know how many of you still know your Bible, but you can find it in two places, in Chronicles and Kings. The first chap who arranged the census was King David, and when he arranged the census the Lord was utterly furious. He gave him a choice of three penance punishments. And David said, Yes, yes, I know I have sinned …He immediately understood that there was something wrong in having a census which treats people as if they were units, whereas they are not. Each is a universe."

The other book we will be selling here is *Kids: Day In and Day Out*, subtitled *"A Parents' Manual—A compendium of ideas, recommendations, insights, inspirations, facts and suggestions, problems and solutions for living with kids every single day."* The editor, and contributor of many of the nicest bits, is Elisabeth Scharlatt. (Price $7.25 + post.)

The book is almost entirely made up of short excerpts, sometimes from books, mostly from letters written to the editor. The tone is informal, conversational, down-to-earth. Most of the writers, like the people who write to GWS, are writing about their own children or children they know, and who they like and enjoy. Most of the time they are writing about things that they have really done and that have worked.

The book is huge—500 big pages—and a good buy. Sections include: Child-Rearing, or, some thoughts about living with children rather more calmly; The Body; Children and Sex (Ed.—the approach of these two chapters is that there is nothing inherently wrong, immoral, disgusting, dirty, etc. about the body or any of its natural functions, so any who might find this offensive could skip these chapters, cut them out, etc.); Fears Kids Have; Handicapped Kids; Schools and Learning; Babysitting and Day Care; Food and Nutrition; Kids' Rooms and Environments; Clothing; Money; Science; Pets and Other Animals; Plants; Books and Reading; Music; Television; Making Things; Going Places With Your Kids; Sports; Outdoor Play; Games, Puzzles and Magic; Toys and Dolls; Gifts; Parties and Special Occasions.

The people who contribute ideas do not always agree with each other, and I don't always agree with them. But there are very few things in the book I strongly dislike, one of them an article about teaching kids to swim by throwing them in the water, etc. One article says that weightlifting does not improve coordination. From my own experience, both with myself and with students I have coached, I know that this is totally untrue; weight training, properly done, can enormously improve coordination.

Only one of the contributions to the Schools and Learning section is about unschooling, a good letter from Art Harris, but many of the contributors sound like potential unschoolers.

Scattered here and there are some lovely photos of kids. All in all, a very entertaining and useful book.

Editor—John Holt
Managing Editor—Peg Durkee
Associate Editor—Donna Richoux

GROWING WITHOUT SCHOOLING

Issue #12

December, 1979

Sorry #11 was so late in getting out. We sent it to our printer on Sept. 21. About mid-October we called to find out what had happened to it. They told us we would have it in a couple days. Nothing came. Next time we called we were told they had lost not only the photos of our copy, but the original copy as well. So Donna and Peggy had to spend three hectic days laying out the whole issue again.

Thanks to Louise Andrieshyn and other unschoolers there, I spent three very busy days in Winnipeg, Manitoba, in early November lecturing and doing TV interviews, one for a CBC program on home schooling. Meetings were packed, audiences friendly, interviewers perceptive. By the way, an Ontario court has just ruled in favor of an unschooling family, one of the first Canadian rulings I have heard of. Details in the next issue.

Some readers may wonder what happened to that program on unschooling that ABC's *20/20* filmed late in the spring. The answer is that they decided not to show it. Some higher-up decided that it would be more sensational and exciting to do an entire program on the Singer family instead. (Whether they have done it, I don't know.)

More articles about home schooling: *McCall's* (Sept. '79), *Wall Street Journal* (Sept. 13), *Boston Magazine* (Oct.), *Chicago Tribune* (Nov. 7). The last two, in particular, were long, thorough, and friendly. The list of magazines newspapers, radio and TV stations that have interviewed us, in person or on the phone, now runs to three pages.

Mother Earth News (Hendersonville-NC) which now reaches more than 3 million people, wants me to write an article on home schooling, which I will do as soon as I finish my book (same subject) for Delacorte. We may want some photos of home schooling children to go with it. More about this in later issues.

John Merrow interviewed me here in the office for his National Public Radio program *Options in Education.* When I hear the cassette of it, I will report; others might want to order the cassette.

The subscription count for #11 was over 2600. A group in New Zealand has taken out a 40X subscription. And a group in Maine has bumped their sub to 48X.

Good news, of different kinds, from California, Wisconsin, Kentucky, and North Carolina (details in this issue).

A HOLIDAY GREETING

To all our readers, we send with our very best wishes this poem by William Blake:

THE DIVINE IMAGE

To Mercy, Pity, Peace, and Love
All pray in their distress;
And to these virtues of delight
Return their thankfulness.

For Mercy, Pity, Peace, and Love
Is God, our father dear,
And Mercy, Pity, Peace, and Love
Is Man, his child and care.

For Mercy has a human heart,
Pity a human face,
And Love, the human form divine,
And Peace, the human dress.

Then every man, of every clime,
That prays in his distress,
Prays to the human form divine,
Love, Mercy, Pity, Peace

And all must love the human form,
In heathen, turk or jew;
Where Mercy, Love & Pity dwell
There God is dwelling too.

COMING LECTURES

Jan 28, 1980: Phi Delta Kappa, Central Mass. Chapter; 7:30 PM, Assumption College, Worcester MA. Free, open to public. Contact Manuel Zax, (617) 755-3960.

Feb 13: Unity Church—Unitarian, 732 Holly Av, St. Paul MN 55104; aft. meetings, 7:30 pm lecture. Contact Margaret Hasse, Wider Ministry Program.

Mar 29: NCTE Conference on English Education 12:30 pm luncheon, Omaha, Neb. Contact Robert Harvey, NCTE 1111 Kenyon Rd, Urbana IL 61801— (217) 328-3870.

Apr 14: Huntingdon College, Huntingdon IN; 8 pm. Contact Dal Hammel, Artist-Lecture Committee.

Apr 17: Dept of Special Ed, U of Wisc at Whitewater; 8 pm at Playboy Resort, Lake Geneva WI. Open to public. Contact Garry Libster (414) 472-1660.

Apr 19: Confer. on Literature and the Urban Experience, Rutgers U, Newark NJ; contact Michael C. Jaye, conf. dir.

Apr 26: Children Studies Symposium, Hobart & William Smith Colleges, Geneva NY; contact Marilyn Kallet.

Some of the above lectures may not be open to the public; check with the contact listed. Of course, if you can come, it will be nice to see you.

LOCAL GROUPS

Organization of unschoolers at the local level continues to grow. In two states and Canada, small groups of unschoolers have started their own newsletters.

In Ohio, the group *Ocean* (Ohio Coalition for Educational Alternatives Now), 66 Jefferson Ave, Columbus 43215, has started publishing the newsletter *Children at Home*. Cost of the newsletter is $5/yr.

The West Virginia newsletter is *Alternatives in Education*, Rt 3, Box 171A, Spencer 27276. Cost is $2/yr.

Both newsletters are about five pages long. They contain announcements, news on legal developments, letters from parents sharing ideas and experiences, children's art and writing, etc. The Ohio group organized a state-wide meeting; the WV paper lists a whole page of names and addresses of members.

Wendy Priesnitz of *The Canadian Alliance of Home-schoolers,* Box 640, Jarvis, Ont. N0A lJ0, writes: "Already we have helped a number of families with advice and received much media attention for the side of loving nurturing of children as opposed to the processing procedure of many school systems... Membership costs $3 per family and includes a small periodical newsletter, as well as access to the resources that we have compiled. Specific requests for information from non-members must be accompanied by a self-addressed, stamped envelope..."

And, families in Manitoba can join the *Manitoba Association for Schooling at Home*. Write Mary Catherine Figuel, 824 Barry Ave, Winnipeg R2C lMl.

We are delighted to hear about these groups, and would like our readers to let us know of any other local or regional groups forming.

GOOD NEWS FROM WISC.

From Michael Ketterhagen, administrator of the *New Learning Network*, 3569 W. 34th St, Greenfield WI 53221:

...We have started a school specifically to allow parents to educate their children at home. Initially, it was for our son Joshua, who would have been in first grade. Brigid and Larry Horbinski encouraged us to go through the necessary Wisconsin state law procedures

to become a bona fide private school. We are now listed in the 1979–80 Directory of private schools in the state of Wisconsin.

Presently, we have 10 families involved in the "school," the New Learning Network, and 12 little people enrolled. They range in age from 6 to 12. Recently, because of the growing unrest in the Milwaukee Public High Schools, I have had a number of requests from high school age people. It's really exciting and we're learning so much.

...Our students are from six different school districts in Wisconsin and the parents meet regularly, on the last Tuesday of the month. At our parent meetings we give each other the support and encouragement that we need...

––––––––––

These folks also recommend a helpful public official: Mildred Anderson, Private School Liaison, Wisconsin Dept. of Public Instruction, 1425 E. Washington, Madison.

WRITING FIRST

Ann Kauble, 1706 W. Huntsville, Springdale, AR 72764, writes:

...I would like to tell GWS my story: it might help others who, for one reason or another cannot or do not wish to take their kids out of school. Our girls, ages 11 and 7, are "working independently above grade level" and have "very poor attendance records." In other words school is a place where the body has to be sometimes but you learn what you are interested in learning and not necessarily when the school says it's time to learn it. This has worked for us because our girls have wanted to learn the basics before the school has been ready to teach them, and I discovered that any one, even me, can "teach," i.e. simply tell my kids what they want to know, or if I don't know the answer I can learn along with them.

I will explain our 7-year-old's experience so far. When she was 3, she wanted to learn her letters, so I taught her how to write her upper case manuscript letters properly (I like Zaner Bloser method of penmanship instruction.) I taught upper case only, because it is so easy to learn with all letters touching headline and base line, and no worry about when to capitalize. Then *we* started learning phonics. Eventually she learned all the phonemes and sound-symbols as they are taught in the Kottmeyer *Basic Goals in Spelling* series, only she did them in upper case. We sounded out and she wrote short words like KAT.

Then on one historic day when she was five and a half, she discovered on her own that she could sound and write any word she could think of. This came about when she was SO MAD at me she left the dinner table and was gone to her room with door closed for about an hour. Then she silently presented me with a paper that said, "I HAT U MOM. I AM GOOIN TO ET MI VENCHTUBULZ BUT I AM NOT GUIN TU ET MI FICH. IF YU DONT FED ME I AM GOEN TO ET ALSO (all the) CUCEZ." [Ed. note—there are appropriate marks over the long vowels that we cannot reproduce here.] It wasn't even perfect sound-spelling, but it communicated! (She ate her fish next day in a sandwich and liked it, and no cookies.) My older girl made the same spontaneous discovery that she could write her thoughts when she was 5 and a half.

Anyway, Gena, my youngest, was now free to express herself in writing. She was SOUND-SPELLING, and she knew this was sound spelling, and that later she would spend years learning how to REAL-SPELL. Much of her early writing was practical: IOU's, lists, maps, instructions for us to follow, reminders for herself or us, mad notes to people she wasn't speaking to, money accounts, etc. Some was poetry. My favorite was: "A SONG UV LOVE. AZ TH MIWZIK PAST BI A HIWMIN SED U R TU BE A SLAV." I saved a lot of it.

I never really taught her to read, but my older girl and I took turns reading to the three of us at night. At this time Gena was learning to recognize lower case letters because I had started teaching her lower case manuscript. Also, I had ordered all the *Basic Goals* workbooks and teacher's manuals from McGraw-Hill, and Gena first joined in on our nightly reading by reading the Read and Spell boxes in the 2nd grade level *Basic Goals* speller. She was very happy to read just individual words, and these were groups of words with one spelling option (or two spelling options) for one particular sound. Following this same principle, we did lots of "WORD FAMILIES": example—the ALL family—ball tall hall, etc.

When she was six, she announced one night that she was going to read us a book—a 37 page Disney edition of Peter Pan. I know that what made her long to read that book was that the illustrations were so exciting and mystifying, and nobody seemed to get around to reading it to her. It took her a week to read it out loud to us, and from then on she was reading on her own. She continued reading the Read and Spell boxes and doing word families, but she was doing this for the purpose of word recognition more than for learning real-spelling. At this point she had two different skills going on at the same time: writing her thoughts in upper-case sound-spelling, and learning to recognize printed words in lower case while she also learned to write her lower case manuscript.

I asked her not to use lower case when she wrote her own thoughts until she had more skill in lower case penmanship, in order to avoid tHis SOrt oF tHing. I think many kids may be afraid to write because real-spelling and lower case penmanship are so formidable. But Gena was able to keep up her confidence by relying on sound spelling when she wrote her thoughts. She would copy perfectly spelled words in lower case for penmanship practice, but when she had something to say in writing—back to sound spelling. This seemed

perfectly natural to me. When she had mastered using upper and lower case letters together, she started formally learning real-spelling by working in the 2nd grade level of the *Basic Goals* workbook. It was easy because she already knew the sound-symbols and phonemes used in this series. If she has formally learned how to real spell a word, I mention that she got it wrong here and help her get correct spelling, but she is still free to sound-spell any other word she wishes to use...

UNSCHOOLED CHILDREN

From a letter by a mother of four:

...Another myth brought up on the show is the "kids drive me crazy having them around all day" retort. It just ain't necessarily so! I have four, ages three to ten, and most of the time we enjoy each other and get along very well. We have our off days but that in no way overshadows the good times. In my "experiment" of never sending any of mine to school, I have had the opportunity to compare my experiences with women sharing my philosophy of childrearing who send theirs to school. I notice a syndrome which causes them to feel sorry for me for being stuck all year with FOUR. It comes from having three or four at home all day during three months' summer vacation with "nothing to do" (that is, nothing scheduled by some authority) and bickering constantly (because they don't know one another as well as they know their cronies at school). These mothers think that is what I put up with daily, but mine who have had the responsibility for most of their own time, who interact constantly with family with little interruption, I find behave quite differently.

Another myth is that socialization is retarded with children at home. I have not found that true, but quite the opposite. They may be somewhat shyer and naive about cruelty but they seem to be extremely sensitive to the needs of others and possess advanced conversational skills. Interaction with peers is limited but when it happens they handle it beautifully. My mother (who was a supervisor with the state board of education) used this argument exclusively as the reason I should send mine to school. As you said, the social life kids get in schools is, to me, a good reason to keep them *out* of the schools, not the other way around.

Still another myth is the time it takes to teach a child some skill. Observing how my babies learn motor skills taught me a valuable lesson and gave me my favorite education concept... READINESS. In a nutshell, when they're ready, they'll do it with minimum effort. Sounds too simple but it works every time from toilet training to riding a bike, mathematics, reading, etc.... The time spent in teaching a child who is ready is minimal—no rote, no busywork. Just minutes for most things...

People tell me that I am protecting my children

from the cold, cruel world, and think children should have to take bad treatment in schools in order to cope with the real world. By that logic we should be putting the child's head in a vise every day to prepare them for the headaches they will suffer as adults. ...

Each child of mine is unique. Nighttime is often the only quiet, uninterrupted time for us, so lots of "learning" and interacting go on in the middle of the night. Our "school" is open twenty-four hours a day (even on snow days), seven days a week. The teachers love the students and often the roles of teachers and students are exchanged—I am the children's best student as I have probably learned the most from them about love, psychology, and subjects they show an interest in and share with me. ...Another difference in the way we feel about our home-educated children from parents who struggle with theirs in traditional ways is that we *like* our kids—as well as love them. I find in my dealing with families that there is, just as Ashley Montagu said, "a disdain for the state of childhood" in America. Children are tolerated, but rarely liked for just what they are. The rewards of my motherhood I am getting *now*, not looking forward to the future when they are grown...

NJ CENTER

Ann Bodine sent us a notice she is putting the *N.J. Unschoolers:*

I am organizing an Activity Center—School Without Walls to provide companionship for unschooled children and some free time for their parents. Although the Activity Center will not be in full, twice-weekly operation until the next school year (1980-81), the Center will offer four Gym Days (active free play in a gymnasium) during Feb. 1980 and two Nature Education Days at the Great Swamp Outdoor Education Center in spring 1980. Participants' evaluation of these activities will determine the 1980-81 program.

The Activity Center will employ no teaching staff and parents will participate on a rotational basis. Attending children will share the cost of insurance, gym rental, snacks and supplies. Costs will be kept as low as possible.

In addition to its primary function of providing companionship for unschooled children and free time for their parents, the Center will enable our children to participate in some activities which are only open to school groups and to receive certain services which are only offered to schools.

For further information contact me at 201-464-0149. Address: 83 Knollwood Dr., New Providence, NJ, 07974.

RESEARCH

Stephen Arons, a professor of legal studies, is doing research on conflict between parents and school authorities over value socialization in schooling. Examples might include struggles over home education, selection or censorship of books, secularism and religion in schooling, etc. Arons is trying to discover the strains which such conflicts place on the family, and the political and institutional interests which the school authorities are seeking to protect during such conflicts. Means of resolving these disputes without resort to the courts are of special interest. Professor Arons will protect the anonymity of any willing to meet with him to describe their own struggle. Please contact him at 20 Madison St., Cambridge, MA 02138.

HOME STUDY SCHOOL

Pat Montgomery, director of Clonlara, 1289 Jewett St, Ann Arbor, Michigan 48104, wrote us this summer:

...Clonlara does have home-study students. I have received four calls since last spring and out of the four, three have enrolled as home-study students. Please continue to keep our name as one of the schools offering home-study and keep publicizing it. We currently have eight bona fide home-studiers...

HELPFUL

From a father in a town near Boston:

...We spoke on the phone nearly a year ago about a home-grown education for our then 4-year-old daughter. Now 5, she is enjoying her "kindergarten" year more at home than her friends seem to be at school.

We are in a very amiable process with the superintendent of schools to secure authorization to continue the home-learning up through the grades.

We hoped it would be amiable, and came on that way, not criticizing the schools, just earnest about the obvious student-teacher ratio advantage any interested parents can offer at home ... he had received from the Massachusetts Association of Secondary Superintendents *a copy and summary of Judge Greaney's decision on the Perchemlides case.* It has been sent out to all Mass. Superintendents. And it made him amiable.

He proceeded to use that document as the guidelines for our arrangements with the school district. What an enormous service the Perchemlides have done for us! And probably for all would-be Mass. homeschoolers...

NEWS FROM ILL.

From Cinny Poppen, *Valley Cooperative School*, RR 2, Box 518, Dundee IL 60118:

...Last spring we had an adventure with the local authorities that you might be interested in. After almost ten years of a fairly placid existence as a free school we were written up by a reporter for one of those newspapers people use to line their garbage pails with, investigated by the truant officer, and called in for a hearing with the county superintendent of schools. We got legal advice from the Alternative Schools Network in Chicago and the Northwestern University Legal Clinic and asked to postpone the hearing until we felt ready. We prepared a set of documents including our philosophy, history, curriculum, credentials, and current schedule, and went into the hearing five strong, two women and three men. The officials were expecting two mothers and were impressed with our organization and the way we talked about education. (I'm guessing that; they didn't exactly say they were impressed.) They told the newspaper reporter, for his follow-up article, that we were doing a good job of educating our children. If you think anything in that experience would be helpful to other readers of the newsletter, let me know. We have copies of the newspaper articles and our documents which we'd be glad to share...

LETTER TO SCHOOLS

Shawn and David Kendrick, of Rehoboth, Mass., recently wrote a letter to their local Superintendent of Schools saying why they were teaching their children at home. It seems a model of what letters should be. We are quoting large parts of it here. If you would like a copy of the complete letter, please send us $1.

...The purpose of this letter is to respond to the issues you raised at our meeting on August 23, 1979, and to inform you of changes in the learning plan which our daughters will follow and the reasons for those changes.

We have always felt and continue to feel that, as the people closest to our children, with the greatest opportunity to know and observe them, and with the most compelling motivations of love and concern for their mental health and emotional well-being, we have the ultimate duty and responsibility to provide them with the best possible environment in which they are free to learn and live as God and nature intended them to. We firmly believe that environment is a loving home in which the natural authority of the parents does not exclude the child's rights as a person. Through close, meaningful interaction we are able to observe and know our children well, and to supply them with the emotional support necessary to the development of a positive self-image. In such a setting we can best present our own spiritual and moral beliefs while simulta-neously satisfying the State's interest in an educated citizenry.

An additional advantage of the home environment is the small child-to-adult ratio which allows the individual differences and needs of our children to be recognized and provided for with greater proficiency. Our study plan is based on each child's interests and abilities because we feel that true learning, the kind which lasts a lifetime, is self-discovered and cannot be communicated directly to another. Such learning is frequently inhibited by the fear of failure, by ridicule and humiliation, by overstimulation, by the tension which accompanies competition, and by pressures to achieve beyond one's present ability. In order to encourage true learning, therefore, we have provided a calm, positive atmosphere, learning materials, and access to friends, mentors and community resources. We have chosen to avoid the above-mentioned pressures which often prevent learning or make it a negative experience.

As a result, we have modified our use of the Calvert School correspondence course. Although we will continue to include the Calvert instruction in our plan, we will no longer adhere rigidly to the time frame of the lessons. We have found from last year's experience that such adherence interferes with an individualized program which allows the child "saturation learning," i.e., to study a subject thoroughly before going on to another area of interest. Our daughter Anna, for example, will often complete several days' reading or math assignments in one sitting because we allow her enthusiasm for the subject to take precedence over notions that one must study only what is allotted for in that period. Similarly, because of a high interest, she read the first-grade health book over the past summer and is now reading the second-grade book. The idea that one learns more over the nine-month school year than at any other time is foreign to our children, since their school year is year-round. Not having been encouraged to believe that one must go for certain months of the year to a place called school in order to learn things, they view the world around them and every day of their lives as the place and time in which they are free to learn. To respond to their broad interests, we have arranged for our children to meet regularly with Mr. Jack Friedel, a certified teacher and natural scientist, and are including other subjects, such as photography, film animation, and zoology, in our study plan. Whereas our daily activities will not follow a set pattern, over a period of days or weeks all of the various subjects will be studied and discussed.

We have found that our children learn most readily and with retention when they have a need to know something and an opportunity to assimilate in experience what they have learned through their own initiative. One example was our daughter Celia's difficulty learning to write cursively. Despite daily attempts, little progress was made. We discontinued the writing lessons for a period of time until Celia asked us to help her learn cursive writing again. This time, with her own initiative as the key factor, her progress was rapid. As another example Celia did not seem to recall the various ways of telling time when working in her arithmetic workbook. Her interest in the exercises was minimal. On her birthday, however, she received a watch as a present, and the next day was able to recite the time accurately and with no difficulty at all. Similarly a page of arithmetic problems holds little appeal to Celia, yet when working out a purchase, budgeting her allowance, keeping track of a game score, or measuring an object to construct, her interest is high. Celia especially looks forward to selling berries next summer that she is helping to grow in our garden and handling the cash flow herself. The practical application of arithmetic in her life stimulates her toward achievement.

It is the close and continuing relationship we have with our children which enables us to observe their growth in skills and comprehension without the use of standardized, routine testing... Although quantitative testing may be the most practical method of charting students' progress in school where a high teacher-student ratio exists, it is not necessary in our own situation.

A tremendous amount of confusion shadows the issues of competency and accountability, all pointing to the difficulties of measuring a child's needs and development in a system of mass education. New standardized tests are being devised to determine at a late stage in a child's school years what his classroom teachers would be able to ascertain at every grade level if more individualized attention were possible. Testing itself is not necessarily an accurate indicator of a person's knowledge or capabilities. The tensions and pressure of the testing process itself are enough to obscure facts from memory. The language of tests is often ambiguous, so that more than one answer would seem logical to someone who has not acquired "test consciousness" or does not have the cultural bias which would point out the best answer. Tests are designed to cover a certain area of knowledge, but one is not given credit for knowledge outside of that area. Even the state of one's health and mental outlook on the days of testing can make test scores vary widely.

It is the objectives of testing, however, with which we primarily disagree. Because of the administrative difficulties of mass education and its underlying assumption that children must be taught something in order to learn it, it is deemed necessary that by a certain age a certain body of knowledge must have been accumulated. This premise denies the individual differences between people, the fact that many children are not ready to learn certain things by a certain age, and that children have the capacity to learn independently. The fact that a child does not know a particular math skill or history date by age 7 or 8 does not mean that he or she will never know it. Conversely, that a child does know that skill or date at age 7 or 8 does not mean that he or she will retain that knowledge into

adulthood. Indeed, when a child is especially motivated to learn something, the material that would normally take years to cover repetitiously in public or private schools call be assimilated in a matter of days or hours.

A natural approach to children's learning does not force facts and skills on them before they are ready, but allows their own interests and talents to lead them into areas of knowledge and provides them with assistance and resources when they are asked for. Having been read to frequently, our daughter Celia began to recognize words when she was three years old. I decided to enlarge this ability and sat down with her intending to teach her how to recognize other similar words. This first and only "reading lesson" lasted five minutes; Celia closed the book and said that was enough. She simply was not ready to be taught, and yet, before she was five, she learned to read on her own. The first book she read unassisted at age four was *Curious George* by H. A. Rey, a book on the first or second grade level. At that young age she was able to read as fluently as most adults. Still there are words to figure out and questions to ask which we are more than willing to answer. We provided her with reading materials, the time to read aloud to us, verbal language games, and the answers to her questions. By not compelling her to read, but rather supplying the opportunity to do so, her ability grew at a tremendous rate. Given this approach to learning and instruction, we feel that the only legitimate form of evaluation is qualitative and descriptive rather than quantitative.

Our concern to lead as natural a life as possible is a factor in our decisions regarding our children's education. Our lifestyle is based on a vegetarian diet, and a philosophic outlook and spiritual beliefs which rely on faith, intuition, common sense and traditional ways of life, such as natural childbirth, more than on analytical science and technology. The idea of grouping large numbers of children all the same age with one adult figure in a room for six hours a day, nine months a year, is certainly not based on any natural or traditional way of learning or living. Schooling as we know it today is a social experiment founded not on proven psychological, sociological, or scientific grounds, but rather on politics and economic need. When the Massachusetts Compulsory Attendance Act was first passed in 1852, attendance was required for a minimum of 12 weeks per year, only 6 of which had to be consecutive, and for a duration of just 6 years. Attendance was not required of a child being "otherwise furnished with the means of education for a like period of time," or a child who had "already acquired those branches of learning which are taught in common schools." What the legislators first intended by compulsory education is completely different than what is intended now. Even Thomas Jefferson, who emphasized that education was essential to the welfare and liberty of the people, was reluctant to directly force instruction of children "in opposition to the will of the parent."

...We have not felt right about sending our children

out of our home to be influenced in their formative years by people whom we do not know personally and whose morals, values, and political and religious beliefs may differ from ours. Once a child starts school, the home becomes school centered, not family centered. The hour before school getting ready, the six hours of school, the hour or two of unwinding afterwards and the hour or more of homework later in the evening leave little time for parents and children to communicate and involve themselves jointly in activities not directly related to school. We do not feel that this amount of routine and regulation is essential to education *per se*, but rather is the outcome of attempting to teach large numbers of people with few teachers. The necessity for control and discipline outweighs the energy devoted to discovering and meeting each child's needs.

...In our own county just recently, a Somerset couple appeared in the Bristol County Juvenile Court to answer to charges of failure to comply with the compulsory attendance law after they had withdrawn their two children from the Somerset schools. The attending judge agreed with the couple's claim to a Constitutional right to educate their children at home. On the grounds of the Fourth and Fifth Amendments, the couple asserted that the results of the evaluation which they were best qualified to make on their children's progress could not be made available to the School Committee without their permission. The judge again agreed with the couple's position, and the issue was settled with the understanding that the couple would evaluate their children's performance, but that the results would not be sent to the School Committee.

Interested by their arguments, we began to read material relating to our situation and have found reassurance in both Federal and State court rulings that our decision to educate our children at home is a Constitutionally protected right and that our actions are within the law. In a 1923 decision the United States Supreme Court stated:

> Corresponding to the right of control, it is the natural duty of the parent to give his children education suitable to their station in life...

In 1925, the Supreme courts held:

> ...The fundamental theory of liberty upon which all governments in this Union repose excludes any general power of the State to standardize its children by forcing them to accept instruction from public teachers only. The child is not the creature of the State; those that nurture him and direct his destiny, have the right, coupled with the high duty, to recognize and prepare him for added obligations.

In 1944, the Supreme Court said:

> It is cardinal with us that the custody, care and nurture of the child reside first in the parents...

This decision also recognized "... the private realm of family life which the state cannot enter." In 1965, the Supreme Court stated that "...the right to educate one's children as one chooses is made applicable to the states by the First and Fourteenth Amendments." In 1972, the Supreme Court noted

> ...The history and culture of Western civilization reflect a strong tradition of parental concern for the nurture and upbringing of their children. This primary role of the parents in the upbringing of their children is now established beyond debate as an enduring American tradition.

The State courts, relying on the position of the Federal Supreme Court, have reaffirmed the rights of parents. An 1893 Massachusetts Supreme Court ruling provides for "...instruction ... by the parents themselves, provided it is given in good faith, and is sufficient in extent." In 1904, an Indiana court stated:

> One of the most important natural duties of the parent is his obligation to educate his child, and this duty he owes not to the child, only, but to the commonwealth.

In 1976, the Ohio Supreme Court wrote:

> It has long been recognized that the right of a parent to guide the education, including the religious education, of his or her children is indeed a 'fundamental right' guaranteed by the due process clause of the Fourteenth Amendment.

And in a recent Massachusetts Superior Court case it was written:

> Without doubt, then, the Massachusetts compulsory attendance statute might well be constitutionally infirm, if it did not exempt students whose parents prefer alternative forms of education.

This same decision held:

> Under our system the parents must be allowed to decide whether public school education, including its socialization aspects, is desirable or undesirable for their children.

Whereas the United States courts recognize that the State has a "wide range of power for limiting parental freedom and authority in things affecting the child's welfare," they also caution against unrestrained police power in matters pertaining to constitutionally guaranteed rights. In 1923, the United States Supreme Court stated:

> Determination by the legislature of what constitutes proper exercise of police power is not final or conclusive, but is subject to supervision by the courts.

This same ruling said:

> That the state may do much, go very far, indeed, in order to improve the quality of its citizens, physically, mentally, and morally, is clear; but the individual has certain fundamental rights which must be respected.

In 1948, a New York court found that:

> freedom of choice as to the education of children, and the teaching of subjects not immoral or clearly inimical to the existence of society may not be denied under the police power.

A U.S. Supreme Court decision of 1972 reads:

> ...a State's interest in universal education, however highly we rank it, is not totally free from a balancing process when it impinges on fundamental rights and interests...

This decision also says:

> ...however strong the State's interest in universal compulsory education, it is by no means absolute to the exclusion or subordination of all other interests.

Many other courts have ruled that it is the goal of education, not the means of obtaining it, that is the crucial factor. In 1893, a Massachusetts court ruled regarding the compulsory attendance law:

> The great object of these provisions of the statutes has been that all the children shall be educated, not that they shall be educated in any particular way.

In 1904, the Indiana court stated:

> The result to be obtained, and not the means or manner of attaining it, was the goal which the lawmakers were attempting to reach.

This was reaffirmed by the Illinois Supreme Court in 1950:

> The object is that all children shall be educated, not that they shall be educated in any particular manner or place.

The recent Massachusetts Superior Court ruling held that the State:

> may not use regulations or standards as a means of discouraging alternatives which are not identical to the public schools.

This decision also said:

> There are certain ways in which individualized home instruction can never be the 'equivalent' of any in-school education, public or private. At home, there are no other students, no classrooms, no pre-existing schedules. The parents stand in a very different relationship to their children than do teachers to a class full of other people's children. In view of these differences, to require congruent 'equivalency' is self-defeating because it might foreclose the use of teaching methods less formalized, but in the home setting more effective than those used in the classroom. For example, certain step by-step programs of graded instruction, involving the use of standardized texts and tests periodically administered, might be unnecessary when the parent-teacher enjoys a constant communication with the child, and so is able to monitor his or her comprehension and progress on an individualized level impossible in a school setting. In any event, whatever the merits of any particular program, institutional standards in a non-institutional setting cannot be literally insisted upon. That is, one may assume, why the legislature chose to impose the equivalency standard only on other than public *schools*.

The situation as the courts see it, then, is that both parents and the State have an interest in the education of children, that the State must be cautious in its use of the police power, and that it is the goal of education more than the means of obtaining it which is crucial. It is not only our own rights as parents, but also those of our children which we feel obligated to uphold...

In this matter, you as the Superintendent of Schools, the School Committee, and we as the parents of our children all have the same goal in mind, that is, that our children be educated. We hope that we have made it clear to you in this letter that our children are being educated, that the manner in which they are being educated is of their own choice as well as ours, that the Massachusetts Supreme Court respects that children need not be educated "in any particular way," and that the U.S. Supreme Court recognizes that parents have "the right to educate one's children as one chooses."

We have made a detailed presentation of the facts

and our beliefs to assure you that our actions are sincere and within the law, and that in cooperating with our plans to educate our children, you are satisfying the State's objectives and interests. We do not wish to go to court; the courts are overburdened already. Yet we do believe that our position would be upheld.

In view of this statement, we do not feel that it is necessary for you to meet with our children. We thank you for your concern and again assure you that our deepest commitment is to our children's welfare.

[Ed.—there follows a complete list of the cases cited.]

KY. RULING

News story from Frankfort, Kentucky:

The Kentucky Supreme Court ruled Tuesday [10/9/79] that the state cannot force private schools to meet the accreditation standards regarding courses, teachers and textbooks that it sets for public schools.

...But the high court left open the possibility that the state can monitor the schools' performance through a standardized achievement testing program.

In effect, the ruling shifts the burden of proof from the schools, which previously had been required to show they were worthy of accreditation, to the state, which now can take action against the schools only if it demonstrates they are inadequate.

The decision, written by Justice Robert Lukowsky, hardly touched the federal constitution around which many of the oral arguments centered.

It *focused on the state constitution* [Ed. italics], specifically Section 5 which never has been tested in Kentucky courts and which says in part:

"...Nor shall any man be compelled to send his child to any school to which he may be conscientiously opposed."

...The justices said the question was to what extent the state can control a school outside the free public system.

They concluded that the state constitution does not permit the state to prescribe standards for teachers and textbooks in private and parochial schools.

They said the state must approve operation of such schools unless it shows they really are not schools as contemplated by the authors of the state constitution...

...Former Gov. Bert T. Combs, who defended the state board during the lengthy court proceedings, said he'll recommend the state board seek a rehearing in the case. But Combs said he doesn't know whether the board has the right to appeal to federal courts because *yesterday's decision was based on the Kentucky Constitution, not federal law* .

...Yesterday's opinion delved into the debates of the 1899 constitutional convention. It relied on the "Beckner Amendment," which the court said represents

the position "that while the state has an interest in the education of its citizens which could be furthered through compulsory education, the rights of conscience of those who desired education of their children in private and parochial schools should be protected."

Hence, the court said, that does not "hamper future legislatures in constructing a system of free public schools and requiring attendance at them by all save those who hold conscientious objection to them.

"It is beyond quibble that the delegates (to the constitutional convention) meant to leave to the legislature the question of compulsory education.

"...it becomes necessary to identify the limits of this state power where the boundary between the state's interest in quality education and the individual's conscientious objection to public education is indistinct." the opinion said...

———————————

The moral of this story is that home-schoolers and would-be home-schoolers should read not only the compulsory school statutes in their states, but also their State Constitutions, to see what these may have to say about rights of parents, religious freedoms, etc. There is at least some possibility that the clauses governing these matters in the State Constitution may be more explicit and more favorable than anything in the Federal Constitution. In any case, we should as far as possible try to get decisions based upon such clauses, for the state will probably not appeal these decisions in the federal courts, where I believe our chances are much worse.

NEWS FROM NC

Recently the North Carolina State Supreme Court ruled that the state had no power to regulate private schools. I have not seen details of the case, and do not know whether this was the case under present legislation, or whether they were taking the rather broader position that any legislation on private schools was in violation of the state constitution. This decision is, naturally, of great interest to unschoolers in NC.

Someone on the State Board of Education, perhaps the Chairman, perhaps the Attorney, at the same time said that this did not cover people teaching their own children at home. But, as the courts already ruled in Virginia in the Giesy case (GWS #11), if the law says the state cannot regulate private schools, by the same token the state cannot say that a school registered in the home is not a private school.

Here is another unschooling news story, from the *Charlottesville (NC) Observer*, Oct. 25, 1979:

STATESVILLE—Joe Clendenin, charged with violating the state's compulsory school attendance law, will not be tried in criminal court.

..."The whole question is whether Clendenin is operating a legal school or not," [the Assistant District Attorney] said, "and that's not a question to be decided in criminal court."

...Clendenin, who lives near Statesville, has refused to send his three children to Iredell County public schools. He has told state officials he is opening a private religious school.

During its last session, the General Assembly amended the private education law and relaxed state control over private school textbooks, teacher certification and curricula.

The amendment also cleared the way for parents to operate schools at home under religious charters.

...Calvin Criner, coordinator of the state's Office of Nonpublic Instruction, said Clendenin said in an Oct. 11 letter he was setting up the "Maranatha School" and would use the Iowa State Achievement Test to chart students' progress.

... "That's all that's required (under the new law) in setting up a private religious school," Criner said. "Nobody has to ask permission, they just tell us they intend to do it."...

A TROUBLED UNSCHOOLER

The following excerpts are from letters written by one GWS reader to another:

May 23 ...I am sending for GWS now because I am trying to change the schooling for my eldest, Phoebe, who is in first grade ... Reading through GWS 1–8 I am reassured by much that I read, but there are still several issues to settle. The biggest is whether I want to take care of my own children full time; whether it will be mutually beneficial. I would like to think yes, but there are times when a week of vacation seems too long. Perhaps that's because we aren't used to always being together. My preferred course of action would be to send her for the music-art part of the day and keep her home the rest of the time. A half day away would be fine: she still would have the energy when home to direct her own activities.

...We have two other children. Jennie is 3 1/2 and so has one year before she would enroll in kindergarten. Nathaniel is 8 months, and it was because he was born that I was glad to send Phoebe off last fall. He is older now, my perspective seems different... I am slowly thinking of withdrawing Phoebe next year and trying a year at home. If it doesn't work out, I'll let her go back the next year when she and Jennie would go off together. With no alternative school close, this is a very hard decision for me to make.

...I should add that I took Phoebe out of public kindergarten last year in Pennsylvania when the teacher wouldn't let her read, and put her into an alternative that was *very* exciting growth for mother and daughter. I guess I hesitate now because I have no such "school" to offer.

...School vs. no school seems to come down to the issue of having faith in the inherent nature of growing... My faith grows; our family nurtures and helps strong people start.

July 11 ...We went to the principal and second grade teacher and asked to be able to do home-study with Phoebe in the morning and have her attend school in the afternoon when they do a lot of nonacademic stuff—gym and art and music. Today the principal finally returned our call and said that we could do this. We will be meeting with the superintendent of schools, etc. setting up a Calvert program and having a certified teacher check her every two weeks or so and review what she's doing. We're free! I am really hopeful that this will meet our needs—to be more in touch with her growth, make sure she is getting the emotional as well as the academic, and free her to read to her interests and do piano and bake with me (this is how we work on fractions). And half a day is something I can easily live with...

Sept. 14—We have begun our fall schedule of keeping Phoebe at home half the day. I am very happy to have her here but I struggle with record-keeping to help us justify what we're doing, and confrontations with the principal over testing and so forth. I am somewhat timid by nature and all of this is difficult for me. We are operating on guidelines from the state office of education which allow homestudy with a correspondence course with "progress" monitored by a certified teacher each month, with written reports to a superintendent each quarter. Our superintendent is most cooperative; Phoebe's principal is still trying to control what is no longer hers to control... She wants to test Phoebe three times a year for reading level and has said she expects to see "more than a year's growth" from Phoebe because she is bright... We have been told that we are a test case in Maine in that we want half-and-half split time, and hence are being "watched closely." What a nuisance!

The time we have Phoebe now is great—she has time to read and breathe and do her own things. I find I struggle with allowing her mistakes in her work—I know that to deal with her long term I must relax—but I still wonder if she will learn to spell without spelling tests, although she does most other things well. How lovely it is to have her again, even though school has started.

...I feel our adventure is well begun. Phoebe is happy and relaxed. And learning. All else is superfluous...

Oct. 16 ...The reason we sought half-time was because I felt Phoebe was expending too much energy in school and needed more freedom each day; I missed her presence five days a week and she wasn't being challenged or stimulated enough academically. But, I felt there was some benefit to her being there. I needed a break from all three kids all day, and I think there are many benefits from regular contact with the kids and feeling part of the group. As we get into this plan I have misgivings about trying to mix home and school and wonder whether we will end up pulling her completely out...

Since September I have had both happiness and sadness over this whole thing. The sadness reflects my uncertainty over what to do (the correspondence course is woefully inadequate) and difficulty standing up to the principal. The happiness is that the routine of Phoebe working with me is getting established and she plods through a little piece of language arts daily and has lots of free time which she occupies very productively. I love watching her creative juices flow. I didn't see enough of that last year: I got only a crab home in the afternoon from school and to bed early in preparation for the next day. (I was amazed that the whole summer passed this year and Phoebe never said she was bored, or asked me what she could do.)

I feel that what we are doing is right. Whether it wouldn't be much better to have her completely free, I can't tell yet. I will hopefully let that be her choice by next year. As it is, she hates school right now. Sheds a few tears some mornings before she goes in. I feel that this may reflect her picking up things from me that she may have overheard in a phone conversation or some such. I used to be very discreet, and not speak of my philosophical differences in front of her at all. At any rate, I am going to bat for the teacher a little, and selling Phoebe on it. I encourage her to talk to her teacher about what goes wrong for her and I think the teacher listens. I'll need more time about that to be sure. Ultimately, if Phoebe still wants out, OK.

Doing half time in school is almost untenable in a lot of ways. Who would believe in freedom and only half-carry it out? I feel guilty making Phoebe go. (If she resists too much longer I'll have to opt for total home study.)...

...In ways I don't really want to unschool at all, I just wish there was a freer school available to us. I would like to participate and be respected for my abilities there and have Phoebe and the other kids pace *themselves*. A community. Growth for kids and parents both.

So. A complex picture. Phoebe does "reading" and language arts and art with me and goes to school at 10:45 to join in lunch and recess before the afternoon classes begin. Afternoons feature math, gym, music, and odds and ends. Phoebe is telling the teacher the math is boring and the teacher promises more stuff.

We are under a spotlight to a certain extent. We have been told how people are watching to see how this turns out—new in the state o'Maine, etc. That probably makes me a little reluctant to let her out of her half day right now, without a good trial.

...The correspondence course doesn't measure what she does and how she is growing, but neither do those tests the principal so loves. But then again, the school is hard put to prove that she benefits from the repetition she gets in school (they claim that they individualize within the classroom and they do only some) or that our way of dealing with her has in any way failed to help her develop her potential.

...I am rereading *The Lives of Children* and enjoying it. I think I never read it through before. There is much food for thought and much stimulus for me. I am just beginning to be comfortable in a formal teaching relationship though the same rules apply as in the informal one we've been doing for years—I try to quit when I meet resistance. Often it is me not Phoebe, who flies off the handle. I am learning to expect less. This little 7-year-old body doesn't know punctuation because she's never been told about it or given it much thought. Much, much joy in dealing with her. Jennie, who is 4, *demands a place at the study table* [Ed. italics] and struggles to read. How nice it is to see the girls together learning...

MORE ON 'EQUIVALENT'

A mother from Georgia told me that when she asked her local school district what they did about children who were too sick to go to school, they said that they would send tutors to the child's home—two days a week, an hour and a half a day.

The disciplinary vice principal of a high school in a Chicago suburb told me that his district had a very strict policy on drugs—students using drugs in school were without exception expelled for the rest of the term. When I asked if they could keep up with their schoolwork, he said, "Oh, yes, they can attend evening classes." I asked how many classes they had to attend. His answer—two nights a week, two hours each night. That has proved to be enough.

I urge as many readers as possible to find out what schools do about sick children, etc, in their districts and/or states. When you find out, please let us know. This information can be very useful, either in actual court cases or for people trying to persuade their local schools to support home schooling.

MINIMIZING SCHOOL

More from Ann Kauble:

...Gena was six years old and still not in school, because Arkansas law says children must begin compulsory school attendance on their 7th birthday. I researched state law and local school policies to find out how I could MINIMIZE SCHOOL ATTENDANCE. I did several things before Gena's 7th birthday:

(1) I taught her study methods that would enable her to work in workbooks without much instruction or supervision. Examples: circling important clue words in instructions; crossing off answers already used when all answers are provided in mixed-up fashion; doing what she KNOWS first so she can find right answers to what she doesn't know through a simple process of elimination, etc.

(2) I went to the school and discussed the whole situation with the person I thought would be most

helpful and understanding; in this case, the instructional supervisor, who is still the person who makes it all possible for me.

(3) I had the instructional supervisor inventory Gena's reading ability, and I saved the inventory results for future documentation.

(4) I decided which teacher would be right and saw to it that Gena got that teacher. Schools will generally [Ed.—well, sometimes] let the parent choose if they do so before school actually starts.

I picked a teacher who isn't like the usual "model good teacher." She's my idea of the perfect teacher. She's disorganized, which means she isn't hung up on her own structure or routine—the kids can move around a little more in her class. She does not demand "high levels of achievement," which means the kids in her class don't get so nervous and aren't as likely to compete viciously with each other. She doesn't usually get "the smart kids" put in her class. She could talk really gruff, which bothered some parents who were used to sticky-sweet-voiced teachers, but it never bothered the kids, because they knew she was all bark and no bite (she almost never spanked), and she just plain loves kids and treated them like real people. Her class had a calm spirit, and Gena loved her!

Gena started out in an advanced reading group, but before long I asked that she be allowed to work independently in reading because, since I taught her to read by Kottmeyer encoding methods, the decoding methods taught in the reading series couldn't help her learn what she already knew, and could only confuse, at best. (I think it helps to know some education-related terms.) (I did not formally teach her to read, but I think the school is more receptive if I say "I'm teaching," because they are *trusting in my competence,* even though I have absolutely no "academic qualifications.") Gena says, "The *speller* teaches you how to read!"

Permission granted to work independently; and good-bye reading groups—hopefully forever. She just does the workbooks with my assistance and the instructional supervisor tests her out of that level when I say she's ready. I asked for a copy of the reader, but she is not required to read from it or answer any "comprehension" questions. She reads what she wants to read, in or out of school, and we usually discuss her current book.

As for spelling, she just took HER OWN WORK-BOOK to school and continued on in it. As for math, she has casually learned much math and is far beyond grade level (Dataman helped) [Ed.—a small calculator], so the instructional supervisor will test her out of any level when I say she's ready. It should be the same for language. She will probably do science and social studies projects in her class, working on grade level. I save all work she does. Gena got tired of watching Electric Co. at school, so she asked her teacher if she could go someplace quiet and read a book while the class watched TV. Permission granted. She was engrossed in the "Little House" series by Laura Ingalls Wilder—a wonderfully easy-to-read series [Ed.—we'll be adding it to our list].

As I mentioned earlier, I researched state attendance laws and local attendance policy. Any school district should have a book of school board policies: parents should know this! Gena was absent a lot last year, and will probably be absent more in the future. Her birthday is in January, so she started in the second semester. (Too bad her birthday isn't in June!) State law allows 25 days' absences, and local policy says a student who leaves school after 10:30 will be counted 1/2 day absent, so theoretically that's 50 days she's allowed to leave at 10:30, although I didn't use that many.

State law only considered two types of absences: parentally caused absence and truancy, which is when the parent thinks the child is in school and he is not. State law gives the parent complete control over deciding whether the child is truant or not, inasmuch as they require a written statement from the parent saying that the absence is the fault of the child before they will prosecute for truancy. This is important to know because the local school district has lots of policy concerning "acceptable reasons for being absent" and "counseling for more judicious use of absences" and giving the impression that the school can declare the child truant, but it is all a lot of baloney for psychological effect. When I write a note to the school, I just say "Gena was absent on (date)," which shows it is a parentally caused absence and not a truancy. Actually I communicate a lot more than that with the teacher, but that's all I say in the note. This has been a long digression, but it may help others understand about absence.

Once Gena had established that she was working above grade level in all subjects, I started taking her out every day at 1:30, because students who leave after 1:30 aren't counted absent at all. Even if she ever became in violation of the 150 days compulsory attendance requirement, and was referred to the Prosecuting Attorney's office (truants—so declared by the parents—would be prosecuted in juvenile court and parents causing more than 25 days' absences would be prosecuted in probate court), there is some question in my mind as to whether or not the prosecuting attorney would *choose* to prosecute under the circumstances. Prosecuting attorneys like to win cases, and the fact that I can so well *document* the fact that Gena is working above level, and she is, after all, enrolled in the school and continuing to attend, *might* make the case seem a little pointless and ridiculous.

Anyway, now it is time for Gena to start second grade. My conversation with the instructional supervisor went like this:

Me: Could you test Gena out of the (3rd grade) level workbook in reading, spelling or math groups? Also Gena wants to learn cursive now, so I will be teaching her that for the next couple months. She won't start working in *her* third grade spelling workbook until she has learned cursive, because she wants to do it in cursive.

Her: Fine!

Me: I think she is ready to test out of the second grade math book, but she has gotten to the point where she will not do all the problems and assignments, because once she knows how to do the work she rebels against having to do tedious and repetitious work, and I want her to stay interested and not get turned off!

Her: Yes. Once she knows it, it's just busywork. I'll talk to the teacher. Will you be sending things for Gena to do to school each day?

Me: Yes, but she'll be doing music, science and social studies with the class.

Her: Okay. I'll talk to you about testing next week.

This is NOT a liberal school district; the superintendent has extremely tight control. This school district has one of the toughest attendance policies in the state, and they expel and suspend more students for poor attendance in secondary (secondary is not compulsory by law) than any other district of comparable size. They even have a policy, which I believe is illegal, which says they will *expel* K–8th graders for truancy. So we are getting by in spite of a very tough attendance policy here. I go to school board meetings so I can get a *real* education regarding what I would be up against if it ever comes to a confrontation.

I'm afraid I've given the impression that Gena spends most of her time drudging in workbooks. Actually, she does a week's worth of work in the time the teacher allots for a day's worth, so many days she doesn't work in the workbooks at all. She might read a book, or just play or be absent. She really likes and needs the spelling and penmanship workbooks *I have provided* and she takes to school (they will provide *consistent* lessons through the eighth grade, whereas the school may adopt a different series in a few years). She completed one reading workbook in a week this summer. We don't take the reading workbook skills seriously—just "do the page." In reading and math, she is just doing enough to learn the skills taught in the book, to be tested, so she will spend a lot less time doing assignments than most kids.

The important thing to the school is that her progress is tested and documented, and the important thing to me is that she still wants to learn. So that is our story. It is not an unschooling story. But I wonder what would happen if the schools had to deal with a lot of students who were "working independently above grade level and had very poor attendance records"?

Years ago I did take one of my boys out of school for the last part of his third grade year. He was in a bad situation and developing signs of severe nervous tension. The doctor said there was nothing physically wrong with him. I asked him if he thought I should try to get permission to take him out. He said, "The trouble is, we ask permission too much these days. If you are convinced it is the right thing to do, then just do it." I did. The principal called after a while, and I told him Steve wouldn't be back. His teacher wrote a nasty evaluation of his "immaturity and irresponsibil-

ity," which is still in his school file. This happened in another state, and the next year he changed schools and repeated third grade and did better. I know that both my boys were harmed by public school, but I have now learned not to expect the schools to teach my children, and to be sure they are happy in class.

I took my older girl out of school for a couple of weeks when a substitute had them doing things like writing "I will obey" 400 times a day! I finally managed to get rid of the substitute and get Linda back in school. (I pointed out to the administration that this lady was not a *certified* teacher, and they are supposed to hire only certified teachers for *extended periods*.) I don't think they are being harmed now. I would get them out somehow if I ever think they are being harmed.

There is one more thing I would like to share regarding school and home study. Gena knows that she will always wind up getting 100% on the work she does, but not always on the first try. The first try tells you what you know and what you need to study. It does NOT EVER tell you how smart or dumb you are, and it does NOT EVER have anything to do with anybody else, even though the school makes you think you should compare how you did with how someone else did. There is no point at all in grading a paper if you don't correct the mistakes afterward and wind up with 100%! This year I am putting a note in my kid's file that says I do not want them to ever be punished for academic failure, as I do not think the state corporal punishment law (alas! there is one) allows it…

WORLD OF 'WEEPULS'

A mother writes:

… But at the same time we are, deep inside, ready to "unschool." I am absolutely convinced of its rightness. My problem is my children, especially the older one (10). After five years of schooling he has made it palatable and even enjoyable by creating a world within a world there with a couple of his friends. The school work is no problem; he goes so that he can get together easily with 2 or 3 other boys for playing baseball or whatever. Also, their world contains its own society of "weepuls"—scores of ping-pong ball sized fuzzy creatures of different colors with big feet and tiny antennas. For almost a year they had their city covering our 20x12' sun porch (forced to be dismantled because we are remodeling). I haven't read *Gnomes*, but doubt if it could be a more complete study than these kids have with weepuls: the cast of characters, layers of their society, their soccer and football fields, space ports and ships, disco, museum, school, movie theater, transportation system all made in detailed miniature with great care and skill; their diet of only bananas and banana juice, their death by contact with water, and so on. When J went on a scout trip to the snow, the weepul King Eeker went with him on skis made out of tongue depressors. The weepuls go to school and hide in the desks until break time when they come out and make school their place and the boys can do what they want with and through them. Homework and boredom are put up with for the chance to meet A and K and play with the weepuls. One wonders about our art forms and rituals helping us accept and overcome boredom and mediocrity without getting at their sources. I wish my son would actively dislike, fight school, and refuse to do the work. That would make it easier. But he has created a strong and attractive world within the world of school from which I cannot pull him.

He wants letter grades now because he was the only one who didn't get them last report, and since his are high, why should he let the others think they are no good and he has to have them covered up with checks instead. He will take the standardized (but not even required this year) tests that I have been fighting about all year because he doesn't mind. I cannot fight this amorphous enemy. As you said in the last chapter of *Instead of Education*, I try to provide as much life outside of school, but *school takes so much time from kids*. We had to return *Huckleberry Finn* to the library because we didn't have time to finish it because of school...

COPS 'N ROBBERS

This letter was written to the mother in "Books and Guns," GWS #10:

The thoughts you shared concerning "playing guns" brought to mind some old memories.

Nobody ever told me not to play guns. But, when I was a kid, and the gang played cops 'n robbers, I had a problem because I couldn't "die." Some kid would shoot me, and I would want to fall down and die but somehow I couldn't, and I would just stand there and look dazed. And if I shot somebody, he would just ignore me because he knew I hadn't really killed him.

After I grew up and had kids of my own, and they had taught me *how* to play cops 'n robbers, I realized that I had been a very schizoid child, very uptight, totally lacking in spontaneity, frozen out of the NOW— and playing guns is a kid's way of getting really "with" other kids and into a very fast-moving, action-packed *present*.

My observation (of about 15 years watching such games) is that only very free-spirited kids can play a really good game of cops 'n robbers, and that many games of cops 'n robbers are ended by a child who *does* have feelings of violence and cruelty and causes an "accident" to happen in which someone is hurt. Usually that child wants to put an end to the game because of jealousy—he *can't* share in the fun not because he has been excluded by the others, but because he isn't capable of playing.

I don't think "playing guns" usually has anything to do with guns, violence, hostility, or cruelty; it is a game of awareness. Feelings, other than joy, get in the way of

awareness, and you can explode your feelings by experiencing the sound of the cap exploding in a cap pistol, for instance.

In playing guns, I believe it goes like this: If I am *aware* of you first, I can shoot you, and you have to die! If I get surprised by you, then I KNOW you are more aware than I am because *you* surprised *me*, so I've got to die. I just give up all awareness (falling in the process) until I feel a surge inside me that says I'm ready to be born again—MORE alive than before! Sometimes you and I catch each other at exactly the same time, and then we have to battle it out Bang! Bang! Pow! Pow! I got YOU! NO you didn't, I got you FIRST!—until we both know that one of us has bested the other. One of us must die and be born again!

If, instead, one of us gets MAD—then the game quickly ends.

Oh, I love a good noisy game of cops 'n robbers!

I am an old fossil of almost forty who couldn't play guns now to save my soul, but at least I still remember that I learned something from some kids a long time ago.

I'm trying to tell you something that can only be experienced, which tells me that I'm a fool. So, my suggestion is that you find a free-spirited kid (maybe you have one in your home?) and see what you can learn from him.

I believe that it's best to learn to look at the spirit— the feelings expressed—in what your child does, and see through the material object. After all, a child can express his feelings of cruelty and hostility when he pets the dog, and he can express his joy and delight when he shoots his gun. If your child is a joyful child and he WANTS a gun, I think you can trust in his joy, because the Bible says the things of this world are perishable, but the things of the spirit are everlasting, and I, personally, think kids are born knowing this.

Even if a child uses his toy gunplay to drain off his anger and hostility, without hurting anything or anyone in the process, what's the harm in it? My husband says he can remember having those feelings when he played guns as a kid (whereas I never saw such feelings expressed when our kids played guns). He said he thought it was a good thing that he had that outlet, as he had a very unhappy home...

READING POETRY

...I am reminded of my six-year-old daughter, who is so intent on expanding her reading ability that she has recently taken to memorizing Emily Dickinson's poems in order to successfully read them. She struggles for sometimes an hour at a time, totally absorbed in "solving" her own "mystery." No longer content to have me read these very challenging poems to her, she allows me to read a poem aloud only after she has mastered it. I suspect this labor of love has little to do with the classroom ritual of reading groups...

LEARNING TO TYPE

Donna Richoux writes:

The remarks in GWS #8 about typing reminded me of how I taught myself to type when I was around 13. I got a manual from the library that showed which fingers to use and provided step-by step drill. The manual (and my mother) emphasized the importance of not looking at the keyboard. Once I had the basics down, I took my favorite book, *The Lord of the Rings,* which I was deeply immersed in at the time, and just started copying from it, page after page after page. Sometimes I worked on speed, sometimes accuracy.

Also, when I was on the schoolbus, or sitting in class, or otherwise in need of passing the time, I would type *mentally,* thinking of sentences and lightly tapping my fingers...

The *Boston WANT ADvertiser*, a weekly booklet of classified ads, offers many typewriters (both manual and electric) for $50 or less. Surely in other parts of the country they are available for similar prices. Definitely worth the investment.

GAME IDEAS

Ann Kauble writes:

...We all study lots of things at home. We play a lot of games. Here's a list of games that are good learning experiences. They are more or less listed in order of difficulty, easy to hard.

Chutes and Ladders—for counting 1-100.
Alphabet blocks—for learning the alphabet.
Peanut Butter and Jelly—for fractions 1/4, 1/2, two 1/4's make 1/2.
Avalanche—how can you get the most marbles to fall?
Chinese checkers and checkers—sequencing
Obsession—for adding 1-12 on the dice
Hangman—I use words from her speller that she knows.
Monopoly—decision-making and handling "money"
Clue—logic and deduction
Anagrams and Scrabble—we use the tiles to make up simple word games for beginners.
Uncle Wiggly—for reading the instruction cards, which rhyme.
Dataman—I can program it, putting in ten math problems of my choice.
Mastermind—we have all learned so much from this game. When we play (Gena plays the simple form well), we think out loud, so the kids can learn how we figure it out. Example: "if I have only two right colors,

that's lucky, because now I KNOW the two colors I didn't use are right colors for sure!" A marvelous game for thinking.
Chess—young kids can learn.
The wonderful world of computer games has not yet reached our neck of the woods, I'm sorry to say.

There are so many more. I hope GWS readers share things like this about books and games and things kids like...

TEACHING CHEMISTRY

To a parent, I wrote:

...With respect to your question, about how a parent could teach something like chemistry, there seem to be a number of possibilities, all of which people have actually done in one place or another. 1) The parent finds a textbook(s), materials, etc., and parent and child learn the stuff together. 2) The parent gets the above for the child, and the child learns it alone. 3) The parent finds, or the child finds, someone else, perhaps an individual, perhaps a teacher in some kind of school, or even college, who knows this material and learns from them.

As for equipment, you say that your high school had a very extensive chem lab, but I'll bet that very few of the students ever used more than a small part of the materials in the lab. I have known kids who were interested in chemistry and did it in their own base-ments, who were able to do a great deal of work with, at today's prices, less than $200 or maybe $100 worth of equipment. The catalog of the Edmund Scientific Corp. is full of such equipment. Same thing is true of physics. As for biology, except perhaps in the heart of the city, it is not difficult to find animals for examination, dissec-tion, etc, if that is what children want to do.

I won't say these are not problems, but people who want to solve them can solve them.

You ask "Would you expect a parent to purchase test tubes, chemicals, instruments, etc., that would perhaps only be used for one or two years, only to have the child become an artist or musician?" Well, why not? People purchase bicycles, sports equipment, musical instruments, without knowing that their children will ever become professional athletes, musicians, etc. None of this equipment (unless broken) loses any of its value—it could probably be sold later for at least a significant part of the purchase price. And, as time goes on, and more people are teaching their children at home, it will be easier to get these materials from other parents who have used them, or to arrange for swaps, etc.

I see no real need for "institutional" education at *any* age. There is a man named Ovshinsky, in Michigan, who stood physics on its ear by inventing a theory by which non-crystalline substances could be used to do things which, according to orthodox theory, only crystalline materials could do. For a number of years orthodox physicists dismissed Ovshinsky's ideas. But he was able to demonstrate them so clearly in laboratory experiments that they were finally obliged to admit that he was right. *But he never finished high school.* There are probably more cases like this than we know, and there would be a great many more except for compulsory schooling laws. It is a kind of Catch 22 situation to say, first, that all children have to spend all that time in schools, and then to say that all kinds of things can *only* be learned in school. How do we know? Where have we given people a chance to learn them somewhere else?

A very important function of institutions of so-called higher learning is not so much to teach people things as to *limit* access to certain kinds of learning and work. The function of law schools is much less to train lawyers than to keep down the supply of lawyers. Practically everything that is now only done by people with Ph.D's was, not so very long ago, done by people with no graduate training or in some cases even under-graduate training. Schools do not create much learning. What they mostly do is collect it, hoard it, and sell it at the highest possible prices. Thank you for writing. I hope you will not doubt your competence to help your child/children learn anything they want to learn, or indeed their competence to learn many things without your help.

SCIENCE RESOURCES

National Geographic puts out a children's monthly magazine called *National Geographic World*. We sent for a copy, and I think it is delightful. The photographs are colorful, interesting, and exciting. What is important for children, a great many of the photos show children *doing* things—feeding or petting an animal, working a piece of scientific apparatus, etc. The text is clear and easy to read, but not a bit cute or written-down. I would guess that most children from ages 5-12 (and perhaps even older) would love it. Subs are $5.85/yr. (for Canada, $8.06 in Canadian funds). Can't recommend it too highly. Write Nat'l. Geog. Society, P.O. Box 2330, Washington DC 20013.

A magazine I very strongly recommend for older children is *Natural History*. From the few issues I have seen, I judge that it is mostly about the sciences that deal with living creatures (including human), as op-posed to sciences like physics, chemistry, etc. It has more text and fewer photos than the *National Geo-graphic*. But there are still many color photos, all beautiful and some astonishing. A recent issue carried an article about wasps, with some close-up photos of queen wasps fighting. How those photos were taken I can't imagine. The current issue has, among other things, a fascinating article about butterflies and how they get their needed body heat from the sun, and another about a culture in Africa in which people learn (starting when they are very young) to tell very compli-

cated stories on drums. *Natural History* is not a children's magazine, and the text, though clearly written, would probably be too hard for most children under the seventh grade. But for children who are interested in nature and science, and who read well, I would think that it would be fascinating. Subs are $10/yr (12 issues) in the US, $12/yr elsewhere. Write: *Natural History*, Box 6000, Des Moines IA 50340.

Another useful resource is the catalog of the Edmund Scientific Co., 101 E. Gloucester Pike, Barrington NJ 08007; $1.00. The company sells many kinds of scientific equipment, much or most of it more cheaply than you could get it anywhere else. There is a big section on astronomy—telescopes, lenses, etc; a large collection of magnets; also microscopes; magnifi-ers; biofeedback; all kinds of science construction kits; kites; 8 ft. and 16 ft. diameter weather balloons; hot air balloons; lenses; motors; lasers; holography; a machine for making badges and buttons; weather instruments; and more.

Some of this material is too expensive for most families. But there are many good bargains here, and the catalog is fun to read, just for what it says about what is out there in the world. Well worth the $1.

A valuable resource for many unschooling families might be the quarterly *Medical Self-Care*—$10/yr, $25/3 yr. ($11 or $28, Canada), PO Box 717, Inverness CA 94937. The magazine's sub-title is "*Access to Medical Tools,*" which includes books, information, etc. One chapter in a recent issue reviews and rates various medical reference books. Some of the books listed and recommended in the magazine are for children. But many children would find the magazine itself very interesting and instructive.

We have a few single copies of *Medical Self-Care, National Geographic, Smithsonian Magazine,* and *Natural History* which we will send free to people who want to see them. Send large S.A.S.E. First come, first served.

SKI ADVENTURE

From a father:

This is a copy of the letter I sent to all the ski resorts in the West. I guess I did just the right amount of work in publicity.

Dear People,

You would be doing the undersigned and his son a great service if you would put the accompanying notice on your bulletin board and make its contents known to anyone of your acquaintance who might be interested. It would benefit you directly in the amount of lift tickets sold and ultimately perhaps in acquiring the services of a teaching professional and member of the ski patrol, as S earnestly desires a career in that field.

To Whom It May Concern:

My son, S, is a 14-year-old who wants to be where the snow is more often than the weekends which the Ski Club grants him. He is a responsible independent person, who wishes to demonstrate to himself and to the world that he can assume the responsibilities of his impending manhood. He is already a skillful skier who can manage himself and assist those around him. He would like the opportunity to do more. To be specific: I would like to place him with one or more adults in a responsible environment during the coming ski season of 1978-79. He can live in our camper, thus taking care of his food and shelter. I will pay you $100 monthly for any inconvenience and out-of-hand expenses. He is capable of taking care of himself but the state requires nominal supervision by an adult. Anyone interested please contact the undersigned.

Only one ski area answered. S spent an interesting, difficult, exciting, productive winter there.

CAPABLE

From the "Kids Did It" section of *National Geographic World.*

DANCE, DANCE, DANCE

Austin Grunde, 15, manages a teenage disco, called The Zodiac, in Albuquerque, New Mexico. Most of the work in running The Zodiac is done by Austin and his friends, who range in age from 14 to 18. Austin has managed The Zodiac *for the past 2 1/2 years* [Ed. italics]. The disco is open on Friday, Saturday, and Sunday nights. On Saturday nights, as many as a hundred teenagers crowd inside to dance to recorded sounds.

EXPLORING WORK

From a letter I wrote to a high-school student who had said that she wanted to work in Interior Design:

May I ask you a few questions about Interior Design. How much do you know about it—*as work?* That is, how much do you know about what interior designers *do* on an average working day? Do you know any interior designers? Have you ever worked for one? Have you ever designed any interiors yourself? Do you like to draw pictures of rooms, furniture, floor plans? Do you read magazines about architecture art, painting, design?

These are not questions for you to answer to me, but to yourself. If you have answers to those questions, then maybe your decision to choose interior design,

not as "a career" but *as work,* may be a sound one. If you don't have answers, there is a danger that you may have picked interior design because it sounded good. "What would you like to be?" "Oh, I'd like to be an interior designer." "Gee, that sounds exciting." And so on. That isn't a bad reason for *first* getting interested in a certain kind of work, but you should know a lot more before you commit yourself to it.

I would strongly urge that *before* you spend money on some kind of school of interior design (how could you tell whether one was any good?), and before you even leave high school, you begin to find out all you can about that subject. There is a magazine called *Interiors.* Have you seen it? Ask at the library about it—if they don't have it, and they probably won't, they have an index of periodicals from which you can get the address. Another good one is *Architectural Digest.* Find the names of some interior designers near you, tell them of your interest, see if you can visit their stores or shops or studios, see if you can find out what people do there, and what you would have to know in order to do it. One thing you would probably have to know is mechanical drawing.

What I'm saying is, *learn all you can on your own* before you spend any money on a school. Don't spend money on a school until you have found that there are some things you have to know in order to work as an interior designer that you can learn only (or most easily) in schools. The people to ask about that are interior designers. Find out where they learned what they now know.

Another skill to learn, and to learn right away, is typing. It is easy to learn and you don't have to go to school. I taught myself when I was in the Navy and I never learned anything more valuable. One reason for learning it is that you will need it in business, and indeed, when you are looking for any kind of work you will be much more valuable if you are a skilled typist. (All it takes is practice.) Another reason is that if you write someone a neatly typed, error-free letter in good standard business form—like this letter—you are much more likely to get an answer than if you do it in handwriting. Many adults, I'm sorry to say, don't take young people very seriously. But if you type neatly, and don't say how old you are, they will assume you are an adult and treat you accordingly.

Now mechanical drawing, or engineering drawing, or drafting (not sure which they call it) may be something they teach at your local school, in which case try to take it. If they don't teach it, or won't let you take it, find out what kind of equipment they use and what books, if any, then get some of the equipment and start teaching yourself. I don't know how big a town yours is but there is probably someone somewhere near there who will help you get started on this.

Go to an art supply store and see what sort of books and materials they have about colors, for you will need to know a lot about that.

Write a letter to the Dept. of Architecture at the

State University asking for whatever information they can give you about the study of interior design.

As you read about this subject, every time you see something that interests you, write a letter to the author saying so and asking for more information. Some people won't answer your letter, but many will. Much of what I know I learned by writing letters.

Start doing some of these things right away, and let me know what happens. I hope to hear from you again before long. Good luck.

PS—If none of this sounds very interesting or exciting, that's OK, but it is probably a pretty good sign that you don't really want to be an interior designer.

NEWS ABOUT TESTS

From *Newsweek*, Oct. 29, 1979:

A COURT BAN ON IQ TESTS

For a decade, the State of California placed pupils in classes for the mentally retarded on the basis of intelligence-test scores, and a disproportionate number of black children were falling into these classes. Contending that the tests were "culturally biased" against blacks, the NAACP filed suit to stop the practice. After a five month trial, U.S. Judge Robert F. Peckham last week declared the IQ tests unconstitutional as used and ordered them halted.

Peckham found that educators were using "an assumed intellectual inferiority" among black youngsters to avoid solving their educational problems. "We cannot truly define, much less measure, intelligence," he said. The ruling, which California officials expect to appeal, applies so far only in the state. But Peckham's decision, based in part on violation of the Fourteenth Amendment's equal-protection clause, is likely to encourage similar lawsuits against intelligence tests in other states.

The Summer '79 issue of *The Testing Digest* reports that in July, 1978 the National Educational Association, to which most American teachers belong, endorsed the following resolution:

The National Education Association recognizes that testing of students may be appropriate for such purposes as a) Diagnosing learning needs. b) Prescribing instructional activities. c) Measuring student progress *in the curriculum content utilizing tests prepared or selected by the classroom teacher.* (Ed. italics)

The Association opposes the use of tests that deny students full access to equal educational opportunities.

The Association opposes the use and will continue to seek the elimination of standardized tests, which are:

a. Damaging to a student's self-concept and contribute to the self-fulfilling prophecy whereby a student's achievement tends to fulfill the negative expectations of others.

b. Biased against those who are economically disadvantaged or who are culturally and linguistically different.

c. Used for tracking students.

d. Invalid, unreliable, out-of-date, and restricted to the measurement of cognitive skills.

e. Used as a basis for the allocation of federal, state, or local funds.

f. Used by book publishers and testing companies to promote their financial interests rather than to improve measurement and instruction.

g. Used by the media as a basis for invidious public comparisons of student achievement test scores.

h. Used to test performance levels as a criterion for high school graduation.

From the *New York Times* Oct. 28, 1979:

Consideration of a Federal truth-in-testing law was put off this week because of opposition by the companies that administer the examinations taken by most students in the country planning to go to college.

The measure's sponsor Representative Ted Weiss, Democrat-Liberal of Manhattan, said that action by the subcommittee on postsecondary education was delayed, probably until next spring, but he remained confident that it would finally be approved.

...The bill's opponents, which include the Education Testing Service, the company that develops the Scholastic Aptitude Test, have argued that the measure would substantially increase the costs to students because it would require making the test public after their administration, therefore making it impossible to reuse them.

...AND TEST INFO

McGraw-Hill Publishing Co., 1221 Avenue of the Americas, New York NY, lists a number of books designed to help students prepare to take certain standardized examinations. Among their titles are *How To Prepare For the Scholastic Aptitude Test (SAT); How To Prepare For the American College Test (ACT); How To Prepare For the Miller Analogies Test* (used by most graduate schools); and others. Worth reading, for any who may be getting ready to take such tests. And younger children might find them interesting to browse through—another slice of the Big World. Some of them might be interested in making up some test questions of their own.

Parents who are trying to avoid having their unschooled children tested by standardized tests, or who hope to avoid this in the future, will be interested in two new anti-testing organizations and their publications. One is PROJECT DE-TEST, 1129 21st St N.W.,

Washington DC 20036. They publish a quarterly called *The Testing Digest* ($6/yr, $2/copy). The Summer '79 issue has some extraordinarily important material on the history of standardized testing, the assumptions of the people who first thought of the idea, and the ways in which the tests are designed to support these assumptions. There is far more good material than we have room to quote here, except for (elsewhere in this issue) the NEA statement on standardized testing. Much of it would be very valuable ammunition in home schooling plans and/or legal briefs.

The other magazine is *The Measuring Cup* ($15/yr. Box 22723, Savannah GA 31403). Perhaps slightly more than PROJECT DE-TEST, they are concerned about, and opposed to, standardized testing and minimum competency exams as they relate to low-income groups and racial minorities. This difference in point of view of the two papers is slight, and both are very much worth having.

HER OWN DECISION

...While we sensed from the beginning that school was an evil, we also thought that forcing our child to stay out of school would be almost as bad as forcing her into school.

Our daughter is almost six, so she (and we) are approaching the dreaded time when she is supposed to start school. The approaching deadline has up until very recently brought a lot of apprehension.

Peer pressure was mounting on our little girl; all her friends, of course, are in school or getting ready to start. Until recently C thought school would simply be another adventure and a chance to meet new friends.

A blessing in disguise appeared: A prestigious private school offered a four week summer camp. Approximately half the time would be spent in "academic learning" and the other half in activities such as swimming, bowling, skating, hiking, etc.

We decided to let her go, risking the possibility that she might equate this "fun time" with school. We felt that if it were truly a good experience, then she should have it anyway.

The first week was great. She met new friends, the activities she loved, and the "academic learning" was all right (even though sitting in class seemed to be something of a bore).

The second week the pressure began and all of a sudden C couldn't seem to do the academic work even though she had done more advanced things at home. C was visibly upset and all her behavior showed it.

Our role at this point was to talk and listen as openly and honestly as we knew how.

We talked to the teacher and told her that "academic learning" was not important to us and we told C that she could just go later in the morning and skip the lessons. She skipped a couple of days that week.

She continued to go during the time for "academic learning" with mounting frustration; apparently she didn't want to be different. She wanted to be involved in the activities but even these seemed to change for her. Too, it seemed as though her new-found friends, who were so much fun the first week, weren't so great in the third.

In order to avoid confrontation she began to play games with the teacher. Instead of giving her teacher the opportunity to chastise her about her work, she simply didn't turn it in (papers were graded and turned back, but not recorded). We were uneasy about this game-playing as we were afraid it was building bad habits. But we were delighted that she confided in us almost every detail about how she "tricked" the teacher. After talking with her we realized that she didn't think trickery was good, but under the circumstances it was all she could do.

At the end of the third week there was a whole day of activities and we expected her to be excited. Instead, she announced rather matter-of-factly she could do those things anytime with Mommy—she didn't return to school after that.

Little or nothing was said about the subject of school for several weeks. (We also decided early that we would not preach or bludgeon our child with the moral evils of school.)

One day a neighbor of ours, a large, loud, threatening woman demanded of C, "Are you ready to start school?" C very frankly stated, "I'm not going to school. They never do anything there."

We find now that our apprehension was for naught. We merely had to support and nurture our child—she seems to have ferreted out very well what was good for her. She wanted new friends and exciting activity. We suspect that in school she found something wrong with the children and, therefore, she found the activities there to be lifeless.

Now that she has made HER OWN DECISION to stay out of school, we feel she will have no trouble being "different." We notice that if her friends pressure her on the subject of school, if a simple explanation will not do, she simply changes friends.

We think children do want the companionship of peers, but that children get nothing from friends who are under pressure to perform like circus animals. We think that children, if allowed, will naturally choose loving support at home...

BOOT CAMP

Ann Kauble writes:

...Here's another item—a quote from a local Head Start worker, on a tape recording I made of a recent school board meeting. The Head Start people were asking to continue to use a school building for their program, and they justified their importance to the school board as follows:

"I think we should be considered part of the

Springdale school system because we are teachers. As a Head Start teacher, I'm not in there running the schools, but when our kids get read for the first grade they are TOTALLY READY FOR THE FIRST GRADE. They have been through the school "system": I mean THEY KNOW ABOUT SETTIN' STILL, ABOUT RECESS, ABOUT LUNCH TIME, BECAUSE THEY ARE TAUGHT THIS from the time they get into Head Start until they get into public school."

Board member asks: "What ages attend Head Start?"

She answers: "Three through six."

They got continued use of public school property (an old house).

THEY HAVE A CHOICE

Many people write to say that when they take their children out of school and the local school superintendent begins to take legal action against them, he says that he "has no choice." Most of the people who say this are probably sincere. Because they don't know the law about home-schooling, they really think it is illegal, and so believe that if they allow it to happen, they will be aiding and abetting a crime, which is itself against the law. This may well be why so many of them move so quickly—though there are surely other reasons.

The fact is, however, that in thinking that they "have no choice," they are mistaken. This is true not only because of what the courts have said about the rights of parents to teach their own children, but even more, because the compulsory education statutes in all states—certainly all those I have heard about—say that for one reason or another, children may be excused from regular school attendance provided that the local school authorities approve this. In other words, the law in most, and I suspect all, states very specifically gives the superintendent the right to approve home schooling if he wishes to do so. There is no legal burden of proof on him to show to some other authority that his reasons for doing so are justified. If he say it's OK, it's OK, and that is an end of the matter. So if and when a superintendent says to you that he has no choice but to take you to court, or that it is his legal duty to do so, be sure to correct him on this matter. If he takes you to court, it is only because he *wants* to, not because he has to. And it would probably be a good idea to make this point clear early in the discussions, even before the question of court comes up.

TENN. REPORT

A teacher writes:

...I work for the public schools as a sort of reformer. I started out as a homebound teacher, teaching kids who can't come to school for one reason or another. I started getting students who got physically sick from *school* itself—it made some kids so nervous and upset that they would get headaches, throw up, run away, cry, just at the mention of school. These kids were great students at home with the pressure off, but compulsory attendance laws have compelled the superintendent and director of special ed to try to figure out what to do with these kids. They *have* to be served *somehow*, but homebound was not considered the way to do it. Teachers complain that homebound is being abused by these kids who have no physical reasons for not going to school. (Their problems are emotional and therefore not "real.")

After checking into the situation in more depth, I found an incredible number of kids not going to school *at all*, first graders through 12th graders. (Kids cannot quit until age 17 legally, lower limit is age 7.) I started some digging, going through old attendance records, talking with kids and teachers, and came up with a list of 300 kids not going to school in our county, out of about 3000 students total. I figure this a conservative estimate because a lot of kids probably never start school here and therefore we don't know about them. Also, the attendance records were mostly garbage—obviously falsified for the purpose of getting state money. Some teachers had no absences marked for the *entire year*.

With so many kids not going to school, it seems like a physical impossibility to do much of anything about it. In the past, nothing ever was done about it. The "attendance teacher" (our version of the truant officer) has *never* taken any kids to court for truancy, and doesn't want to start. No truancy cases have ever been brought to court in the history of the county. If someone reports a child to the attendance teacher, he will go and check it out, talk to the people, and that's all.

I've been working on setting up alternative classes next year as a sort of "haven" where some kids can go to school and not be pressured by grades and expectations, and where hopefully they can feel comfortable and at home. Of course these classes could not even begin to touch the *numbers* of kids unwilling to go to school.

It really makes sense to me for the school to officially approve home education, because that is what is happening here on a fairly large scale. Our superintendent is open-minded enough to realize that the schools are inappropriate for large numbers of kids, and he's not willing to *force* the kids to go to school, at least not until there is something better to offer.

I have no intention of sending my own 4-year-old son to school when he is school age. I anticipate no problems either. About 15 other like-minded families are getting together to start our own private school—which I anticipate will be our legal structure for getting around the laws, while most of the teaching will go on at home. In Tenn., only a charter is needed for starting a private school. It is not necessary to be approved; there are hundreds of private schools in the state now that are not approved. We have requested a charter application but have not received it as yet—so I don't know yet what that will involve.

Some families say they are willing to move to escape legal battles. We would welcome them here and offer our support....

UNSCHOOLING IN HOLLAND

Brigitta Van Daam sent us this translation of a Dutch news story:

1 May 1979—NRC Handelsblad, Rotterdam

PARENTS AGREED WITH BY JUDGES OF DISTRICT COURT, CHILD ALLOWED TO STAY HOME

Groningen, 21 April—Parents who object to whatever education is available may keep their children home. This is the most important conclusion from the verdict given by two judges from Groningen, M. H. de Wildt and F. V. Gimbrere, to two fathers who had refused to enroll their little sons of six and seven years of age in an elementary school. The two fathers, Mark Dunning Lester, 32, and Simon Chajes, 31, are members of the alternative living community "Impuls" in the village of Pieterburen.

Simon Chajes was exempted from sending his son to school for one year last year, by the municipality of Eenrum. Prior to this, a lengthy correspondence and countless meetings with the municipality of Eenrum, the superintendent and the department of education were necessary.

The city refused to renew the exemption for this year, also to Mark Dunning, whose son became of school age. Both parents were summoned for breaking the compulsory education law.

Two weeks ago, the public prosecutor requested acquittal based on Article 5b of the compulsory education law. It states that parents, if they have considerable objections against the education of the schools in the neighborhood, are exempted from the duty to have their children schooled.

The Groninger district court judges accepted the conclusion of the public prosecutor. They did state though, that the consequences of the verdict could be less happy. Parents could also object to a school with a democratic and antiauthoritarian direction or object to a school admitting Jewish or black children. "A lawful exemption in that case goes against the grain," said the judges in their accounts.

They did find the considerations of the two "Impuls" fathers respectable.

SUCCESS STORY—ARK.

...With the start of the new year we took our three children out of public school. We followed the procedure suggested by Hal Bennett in *No More Public School*, sending a letter to both principal and home room teachers, explaining that the children would no longer attend that school and had been enrolled in a private school. Everything went very smoothly, with which we are very pleased. This is a small community pop. 5,000, and the news about our kids out of school spread from people just being curious to people wanting to do the same thing. Some people wondered which private school they were attending as there are only two small parochial schools in the area. We explained to them that we had enrolled them in the Calvert School which is a correspondence school that offers a home study program and that teaching my own children was something I had been wanting to do for many years and felt the time was right for us to take this step.

The law on school attendance in Arkansas says that children need to be enrolled in a public, private or parochial school. On further checking with the State Department of Education, I found out that a private school need not be state approved and there are no rules governing unapproved private schools, except that it would be expected that the private school work toward state approval.

...There are several other unschoolers in the area. One family who took their child out of a neighboring school several years ago had a lot of trouble including having to go to court. Eventually the case was dropped. This year two other families took their children out without any resistance. We are very pleased to see this cooperative attitude...

LEGISLATIVE APPROACH

People in a number of states and provinces of the U.S. and Canada (notably N.H. and Manitoba) have told me that some of their state/provincial legislators are interested in passing some kind of resolution or law favorable to home schooling. And even where legislators have not yet expressed any such interest, we should be thinking about ways to get them to do so.

The question is, what kind of resolution or legislation do we want? Some unschoolers have suggested some kind of special state board or commission to review all proposals for home schooling. Others have suggested that the legislature draw up a set of guidelines for home schooling proposals.

I have been thinking hard about this, and my strong feeling right now is that both of these proposals would work against us sooner or later, and probably sooner. The idea of the impartial board mediating between unschoolers on the one hand and the schools on the other, is appealing. But what has happened to the regulatory commissions of the U.S. government would almost certainly happen to this board—it would soon be taken over by the organization it was trying to regulate. It seems almost certain that any unschooling board of review or whatever it was called would very quickly be dominated by professional educators, whose real interest would be in protecting the interests, not of home schoolers, but of the schools.

In the same way, if legislatures were to set up guidelines governing home schooling, the chances are first, that professional educators would have a lot to say about these guidelines and secondly, that the guidelines would be so strict and narrow that many well qualified unschoolers would not be able to pass them, and if they did, would find that they did not have much real choice about how to teach their children. In short, under such guidelines many people now teaching their own children would not be allowed to teach them as they chose, or even to teach them at all. These regulations would surely be biased in favor of affluent people with much schooling.

What I think we want from the legislatures—and this might be much easier to get—is a statement of general principles which will make it much easier for unschoolers to bargain with their local schools on a case by case basis. Something like the following might do the job:

The compulsory school attendance laws of this state/province shall not be construed as authorizing any educational authorities to impose on students under their jurisdiction a uniform curriculum, or uniform methods of instruction or evaluation. There are and will continue to be large and legitimate differences of opinion, among experts and laypersons alike, on the subjects that should be taught to children, on the order and ways in which these are to be taught, on the materials which are to be used, and on the ways in which this teaching and learning are to be evaluated. Only by allowing and supporting a wide range of education practices can we have the diversity of experience from which we can learn to educate our children more effectively, and it is the intent of this legislature to allow and encourage such variety.

I think we may be able to get statements of this kind passed in a number of places—though we can expect the professional educators to oppose even this much with all their strength—and I think that any such statements of legislative intent will make things much easier for unschoolers.

In talking to legislators about this, we should point out that what we are asking the legislators to say is only what the U.S. Supreme Court has already said, first in *Pierce*, then again in *Farrington v. Tokushige* 273 U.S. 284 (1927). In the latter, speaking of legislation passed by the legislature of the territory of Hawaii to regulate Japanese language private schools, the Court said:

"Enforcement of the Act probably would destroy most, if not all, of [the Japanese-language private schools]; and, certainly, it would deprive parents of fair opportunity to procure for their children instruction which they think important and we cannot say is harmful. The Japanese parent has the right to direct the education of his own child without unreasonable restrictions ... Apparently all [the provisions of the Hawaii Act] are parts of a deliberate plan to bring foreign language schools under a strict governmental control for which the record discloses no adequate reason..."

In short, the courts have always held that while the states have a right to regulate private schools, they do not have a right to say that private schools must all do exactly what the public schools are doing. Parents are entitled under the Constitution to choose not just which school building they will send their children to, but *what kind of schooling* they want for them. They are entitled to a real educational choice, which means, the right to an education which may be in many ways significantly *different* from that given by the public schools (which, by the ways differ widely among themselves).

NEW BOOKS AVAILABLE HERE

We are adding *Understood Betsy* by Dorothy Canfield Fisher to our list of children's books ($1.35 + post.) Donna Richoux writes: "This was one of my absolutely favorite books when I was younger, and I was delighted to find, upon rereading it recently, that it had lost none of its appeal. Elizabeth Ann is a shy nine-year-old who lives with aunts who constantly fuss over her, until she is sent (because of an aunt's illness) to live with her strange, forbidding Vermont cousins. We see almost every moment of those first few days through the eyes of Elizabeth Ann—now 'Betsy'—and with her, we find that her cousins' silence and 'queerness' is actually acceptance, warmth, and humor. Bit by bit, her awkwardness and fear drop away, as she starts to learn how to help on the farm, to understand the jokes and to look after herself. GWS readers will appreciate the contrast between the big, brick, modern school she went to in the city, and the tiny friendly one-room schoolhouse in Vermont. The book is funny, touching, and very perceptive—I wholeheartedly recommend it."

Man's Domain: A Thematic Atlas of the World (McGraw Hill, pub; $5.35 + post.)

Is a fascinating book to browse through. The back cover tells a lot about how maps are made. Inside are lists of the most populous countries, the largest countries, the most densely populated countries, the largest cities, the largest islands, the largest mountains (by continents), the oceans, the longest rivers, the largest lakes, the highest waterfalls—just the kind of world-book-of-records information that children (and many adults) like.

Did you know that not counting the Great Lakes themselves, there are seven lakes bigger than Lake Erie?

On pages 2–27 there are maps of the world, showing Glaciation; Continental Drift; Volcanic and Earthquake Zones; Ocean Currents; Time Zones; Religions; Races; Languages; Population; Income; Population Growth; Climate; Agriculture; Rainfall; Precipitation; Winds; etc, etc. Later, more of the same kinds of maps, but in more detail, for the continents and regions of the world.

In short, the kind of book that makes you turn the pages thinking, "Well, I never knew that."

Possum Living, by Dolly Freed ($3.50 + post.) is a delightful book, direct, candid, unsentimental, and very funny, about how two people, the author (an 18-year-old girl) and her father, live very comfortably and happily about 40 miles from Philadelphia on a cash income of about $1200 per year. They raise, make, or else do without most of the things that most people have to buy (or think they have to). They are not mystics or fanatics, or even ascetics—they enjoy the pleasures of good food and drink, among many others. What they have done is solve a problem that most people would like to solve but don't know how—how to live a life they enjoy without having to pay for it by spending a lot of time doing work they hate.

The schools like to say—sincerely—that they are teaching children survival skills. What they in fact teach children is to be totally dependent on economic institutions over which they have no control and which often break down unpredictably (as now). This book does teach survival skills, and as such will be very valuable to unschoolers and their children.

Steady State Economics, by Herman Daly ($5.85 + post.) This (as far as I know) is the first serious economics textbook for the general reader about how a stable and nondestructive economy would work, and why the conventional arguments against it are based on false assumptions and bad reasoning. I emphasize "for the general reader." Though it is a textbook, a carefully and closely reasoned piece of scientific writing, it is not at all obscure, nor does it depend on a lot of mathematics that only specialized experts can understand. With a little effort, the ordinary reader can grasp most, if not all, of what Daly is saying, and it is well worth the effort, for it will convince us that our hopes for a different world are practical, even as the world understands the term. A book to feed the mind and stiffen the spine.

We are planning to add many new titles to our book list during the next year, particularly books for children. If there are any books (still in print, preferably paperback) that you loved reading as a child, or that your children love, please tell us about them.

Editor—John Holt
Managing Editor—Peg Durkee
Associate Editor—Donna Richoux

Index

The following pages are copies of original front pages of GWS.

GROWING WITHOUT SCHOOLING

Issue No. 1

This is the first issue of a newsletter, about ways in which people, young or old, can learn and do things, acquire skills, and find interesting and useful work, without having to go through the process of schooling. In part, it will be about people who, during some of their own growing up, did not go to school, what they did instead, and how they made a place for themselves in the world. Mostly, it will be about people who want to take or keep their children out of school, and about what they might do instead, what problems come up, and how they cope with these. We hope, also, that children who are, right now, growing without schooling will let us know how they feel about this. If they do, we will not identify them as children, except as they do in their own writing.

GROWING WITHOUT SCHOOLING, or GWS as we will call it from now on, will be in part an exchange. Much of what is in it, we hope, will come from its readers. In its pages people can talk about certain common ideas, needs, concerns, plans, and experiences. In time it may lead to many informal and personal networks of mutual help and support.

GWS will come out whenever we have enough material to make an interesting issue. This may at first be only three or four times a year. Later, as more people read it and send in material, it may come out as often as six times a year.

GWS will not be much concerned with schools, even alternative or free schools, except as they may enable people to keep their children out of school by 1) Calling their own home a school, or 2) enrolling their children, as some have already, in schools near or far which then approve a home study program. We will, however, be looking for ways in which people who want or need them can get school tickets - credits, certificates, degrees, diplomas, etc. - without having to spend time in school. And we will be very interested, as the schools and schools of education do not seem to be, in the act and art of teaching, that is, all the ways in which people, of all ages, in or out of school, can more effectively share information, ideas, and skills.

SUBSCRIPTIONS

GWS will be supported entirely by subscriptions, not by advertising, foundations, universities, or government grants, all of which are unreliable. We will do our best to print as much useful ma-

terial as possible at the lowest possible cost. But we think it best that those who use a service should pay the cost of it. We also want those who work on GWS to be paid a decent wage, if only for the sake of staying power. People who work for nothing or for token wages soon grow tired of this and quit. We want this newsletter to come out as long as people feel a need for it. This can only happen if those who put it out do not have to do so at great personal sacrifice.

This first issue is four pages. All following issues will be eight pages, perhaps in time more than that. Subscriptions are $10 for six issues. A Times Two or 2X subscription (we mail two copies of each issue) will be $12 for six issues; a 3X subscription will be $14 for six issues, and so on, $2 more for each additional copy per issue. Thus, two or more people or families can take out multiple subscriptions and split the cost. In this way, two people can get GWS for $6 a year each; four for $4 a year each; eight, for $3 a year each, and so on. Or, people, or bookstores, can take out multiple subscriptions and resell individual subscriptions or copies. Also, people may buy in quantity copies of any issue.

All subscriptions to GWS will begin with Issue #1 unless you tell us otherwise, i.e., please begin my subscription with Issue #2, or #3, or whatever.

Someday, if we get enough subscribers, we may be able to lower the subscription price. This will not be for a while; even at its present price, GWS will probably not be self-supporting until we have around 2,000 subscribers. And as we said, we think GWS must be self-supporting. Charity is fickle, and we mean to be around for a while.

ON SOCIAL CHANGE

In starting this newsletter, we are putting into practice a nickel and dime theory about social change, which is, that important and lasting social change always comes slowly, and only when people change their lives, not just their political beliefs or parties. It is a process, that takes place over a period of time. At one moment in history, with respect to a certain matter, 99% of a society think and act one way; 1% think and act very differently. Some time later, that 1% minority becomes 2%, then 5%, then 10, 20, 30, until someday it becomes the dominant majority, and the social change has taken place. Some may ask, "When did this social change take place?" or "When did it begin?" There is no answer to these questions, except perhaps to say that any given social change begins the first time one person thinks of it.

I have come to understand, finally, and even to accept, that in almost everything I believe and care about I am a member of a minority in my own country, in most cases a very small minority. This is certainly true of all my ideas about children and education. We who do not believe in compulsory schooling, who believe that child-

ren want to learn about the world, are good at it, and can be trusted to do it, without much adult coercion or interference, are surely not more than 1% of the population and perhaps much less than that. And we are not likely to become the effective majority for many years, probably not in my lifetime, perhaps not in the lifetime of any readers of GWS.

This doesn't trouble me any more, as long as those minorities of which I am a member go on growing. My work is to help them grow. If we can describe the effective majority of our society, with respect to children or schools or any other question, as moving in direction X, and ourselves, the small minority, as moving in direction Y, what I want to do is to find ways to help people, who want to move in direction Y, to move in that direction, rather than run after the great X-bound army shouting at them, "Hey you guys, stop, turn around, you ought to be heading in direction Y!" In areas they feel are important, people don't change their ideas, much less their lives, because someone comes along with a bunch of arguments to show that they are mistaken, and even wicked, to think or do as they do. Once in a while, we may have to argue with the X-bound majority, to try to stop them from doing a great and immediate wrong. But most of the time, as a way of making real and deep changes in society, this kind of shouting and arguing seems to me a waste of time.

WHY KEEP THEM OUT?

Jud Jerome (Downhill Farm, Hancock, MD 21750) has written us a long letter, which we will print in this and the next issue. (I hope many other readers will follow his good example.) His youngest child, Topher, after a year of kindergarten, did not go to school again until he was 10. Then he went for a few months to a small "free School" on another commune. After a while, his parents took him out. Of this, Jud writes:

...In regard to Topher, though, I should add that though we were glad he was happy and enjoying himself [in school], we were also sad as we watched him deteriorate from a person into a kid under peer influence in school. It was much like what we saw happening when he was in kindergarten. There are certain kinds of childishness which it seems most people accept as being natural, something children have to go through, something which it is, indeed, a shame to deny them. Silliness, self-indulgence, random rebelliousness, secretiveness, cruelty to other children, clubbishness, addiction to toys, possessions, junk, spending money, purchased entertainment, exploitation of adults to pay attention, take them places, amuse them, do things with them -- all these things seem to be quite unnecessary, not "normal" at all [note: except in the sense of being common], and just as disgusting in children as they are in adults. And while they develop as a result of peer influence, I believe this is only and specifically because children are

thrown together in schools and develop these means, as prisoners develop means of passing dull time and tormenting authorities to cope with an oppressive situation. The richer the families children come from, the worse these traits seem to be. Two years of school and Topher would probably have regressed two years in emotional development. I am not sure of that, of course, and it was not because of that fear that we pulled him out, but we saw enough of what happened to him in a school situation not to regret pulling him out.

I have snatched this paragraph out of the middle of Jud's letter because it seems to me to answer so perfectly a question many ask me when they first think of taking their kids out of school: "But won't they miss the social life?" To this I say that if I had no other reason for wanting to keep kids out of school (and I have many), the social life would be reason enough. In all the schools I have taught in, visited, or know anything about, the social-life of the children is mean-spirited, competitive, exclusive, status-seeking, full of talk about who went to who's birthday party and who got what Christmas presents and who got how many Valentine cards and who is talking to so-and-so and who is not. Even in the first grade, classes soon divide up into leaders, energetic, and (often deservedly) popular kids, their bands of followers, and other outsiders who are pointedly excluded from these groups.

And I remember my sister saying of one of her children, then five, that she never knew her to do anything really mean or silly until she went away to school - a nice school, by the way, in a nice small town.

USEFUL RESOURCES

N.A.L.S.A.S. (National Association for the Legal Support of Alternative Schools, P.O. Box 2823, Santa Fe, NM 87501). This small organization, under the leadership of Ed Nagel, has done much important research into compulsory attendance laws, the right of people to start and run their own school, and the right of people to enroll their children in distant alternative schools which then approve and supervise a home study program. People from at least two other states have enrolled their children in the Santa Fe Community School (where Ed Nagel teaches) in this way, and in at least one case, and I think more, local courts have upheld their right to do this. N.A.L.S.A.S. needs and deserves support.

THE LAST ? RESORT, newsletter of the Committee to End Violence Against the Next Generation (or EVAN-G), 977 Keeler Ave., Berkeley, CA 94708. Members of the Committee ($10/yr) receive the newsletter, a very complete survey of court cases, newspaper stories and editorials, and other events in this field. Newsletter is scary reading; large numbers of children are still being brutally beaten, often for the most trivial offen-

GROWING WITHOUT SCHOOLING

6

The label or address on your GWS (or envelope) will have on it a symbol like 1 06, 3 12, etc.. The second numeral is the number of the last issue of your subscription. If you like GWS, as we hope you do, please renew. You may renew for one year, two, or three. The latter will save you money and help us. Many thanks.

A reader from Florida, who is teaching her two children at home, writes, "As far as neighbors or strangers are concerned - everyone has thought it great that K and L are home and that we're working and learning together."

A new subscriber writes that she saw GWS (or something about GWS) on the bulletin board of the children's section of her public library. Other readers might see whether their library would post GWS on one or more of their bulletin boards. Or, subscribers might take out an extra sub for their library - though it might be a good idea to show GWS to the librarian first, and ask if they would like to have a sub.

The group subscription record has moved to Temple, ME, where readers have taken out a 16X sub.

Donnelly/Colt, Box 271, New Vernon, NJ 07976, sells a number of bumper stickers and buttons, mostly on anti-nuclear themes. But the button I like best (50¢ ea. for 20 or more) just says "QUESTION AUTHORITY."

When ordering books from us, please make checks out to Holt Associates, Inc. This will save us the work of transferring the money from the GWS account. Postage on all orders, 30¢ for first book, 15¢ each additional book.

NEWS ITEM

A friend sent a clipping from the New York Daily News, May 28, 1978. It may be worth noting that the NEWS is a popular tabloid, generally more Right than Left in politics and aimed at the "man in the street." The story reads, in full:

SCHOOL'S OUT FOR FAMILY

Grand Rapids, Minn. (AP) - An Itasca County jury has found a Deer River couple innocent of violating the state's mandatory school attendance law in refusing to send their two children to public schools.

The jury agreed Friday with Joseph Palmer's argument that his wife, Ann, was capable of teach-

ing the children, aged 8 and 10, at home.

In their two-day trial, the couple maintained that public schools were a corrupting influence on children and said the education provided by Mrs. Palmer, who has had one year of college, was adequate. Palmer is a custodian in the Deer River school system. (Ed. note - italics mine)

EQUIVALENT

Friends of ours live in a rich suburb with "good" public school system. Last winter one of their boys broke his leg and had to wear a huge cast, which made it impractical to send him to school. The family (not unschoolers) told the school they wanted to be sure the boy kept up with his class. The school said, no problem, we'll send around a tutor, which they did, every week - for an hour and a half. It was enough.

EINSTEIN SAID

"It is, in fact, nothing short of a miracle that the modern methods of instruction have not yet entirely strangled the holy curiosity of inquiry; for this delicate little plant, aside from stimulation, stands mainly in need of freedom; without this it goes to wrack and ruin without fail. It is a very grave mistake to think that the enjoyment of seeing and searching can be promoted by means of coercion and a sense of duty. To the contrary, I believe that it would be possible to rob even a healthy beast of prey of its voraciousness, if it were possible, with the aid of a whip, to force the beast to devour continuously, even when not hungry, especially if the food, handed out under such coercion, were to be selected accordingly."

FROM A PARENT

A parent (from MO) writes, in part:

"... I have found your newsletter increasingly interesting and valuable. As I wrote to you about a year ago, I will not be sending my children to school (the oldest, now five, would normally be entering Kindergarten this September). He has been reading now for about a year. I would not have believed anyone who told me a child could make the kind of progress D has made. He is interested in Space Travel and Astronomy and we have made available to him all literature on the subject we could find. (Ed. italics) He gobbles it up at incredible speed and begs for more. He reads books about the planets and can discuss intelligently the effects of gravity on the various planets and moons (e.g. that the moon has no air because it has insufficient gravity to hold the air, and that on Jupiter he would be squashed flat). Needless to say we are delighted, and more convinced than ever that this is the way to go."

Tx for good letter. D and others who share these interests might want to read (if they are still in print) a number of science fiction novels by Hal Clement (one title I remember is A MISSION OF GRAVITY), all of them about what happens when living creatures from one kind of planet try to explore a very different kind of planet. In one, a group of aliens from a planet much hotter than Earth land here, and the story is about how they try to deal with our (to them) incredible cold. Worth looking up.

Before long, of course, it will be possible to show D (and other children like him) how they can look up and find for themselves literature on whatever interests them, and ask others the questions their parents can't answer.

THE CHILD TAKERS

From the Juvenile Rights section of the 1977 report of the ACLU:

"In the past year, the ACLU's Juvenile Rights Project secured a major victory in its struggle to prevent the state from arbitrarily and unnecessarily separating children from their parents. The U.S. Court of Appeals for the Eighth Circuit upheld a lower court decision forbidding the state of Iowa from using its parental termination statute to sever the relationship between Charles and Darlene Alsager and four of their children.

The appeals court ruled that the state cannot 'terminate' parents without proving that they are harming their children in substantial and serious ways. For the first time a court recognized that there must be a more compelling reason for separating families than the state's assertion that it is 'in the best interests of the child.'

Relying on the Alsager decision, the ACLU then challenged a Virginia statute which authorized the temporary separation of children from their families in 'emergency' situations. The case, Ives v Jones, was successfully settled, and as a consequence the Virginia law was changed. No longer may children be withheld even temporarily from their parents unless clear and substantial danger to the child is shown. Moreover, parents whose children have been taken under a so-called emergency are entitled to an immediate hearing at which they may have counsel and other due process rights.

The Alsager decision also prompted a federal court in Alabama to rule that the state's neglect statute was unconstitutional because of vagueness and amorphous definitions of 'child neglect.'..."

Of all the threats that schools make to unschoolers, the most terrifying is the threat to take their children away. The decisions cited in the ACLU report suggest that, in some states at least, the courts may not allow the schools to carry out that threat. But of course this de-

pends on whether these courts would rule that unschooling children was harming them "in substantial and serious ways," or constituting a "clear and substantial danger" to them. In the politically so-called "conservative" states cited, the courts might so decide; what they are refusing to allow is the state taking children away from parents on what might be called psychological grounds i.e. because (as in the Alsager case) the parents had low I.Q.s.

I suspect that for some time to come we will not be able to get the ACLU or other civil liberties organizations to oppose compulsory schooling on Constitutional grounds. But we might be able to get these organizations and/or their state and local branches to say that unschooling children ought not to be grounds for the state to take them away from their parents. This in itself would be an important step. Let's look further into this. Do tell us what you find out.

GOOD NEWS FROM VT.

Catherine Lowther, R.D.2, Hardwick, Vt. 05843, wrote us, in part:

"I am sorry to hear that so many people are having such a hard time taking their kids out of school. I thought you might like to balance the scales a little with a positive story.

I never sent my kids to school. They are 9 and 7 and I have always taught them at home. I have been approved by the State every year, the local authorities have been friendly, supportive, and even enthusiastic. The local school board has bought all our books and materials, to be returned to them when we are finished with them.

I noticed in GWS#4 you said that the burden to prove that a program is not equivalent to public school should rest with the state. In Vt. it does. [State Supreme Court decision.]

I also know three other families in Vt. who have taken their kids out of school without harassment."

Along with the letter, C.L. sent a copy of Vermont state law. Title 16, V.S.A., Section 1121(b) as amended Mar. 30, 1967, reads as follows:

"Attendance by children of school age required
a) A person having the control of a child between the ages of seven and sixteen years shall cause such child to attend a public school continually for the full number of days for which such school is held, unless such child is mentally or physically unable to attend; or is otherwise being furnished with equivalent education ...

b) The determination of equivalency referred to in subsection (a) of this section shall be made by the State Department of Education and certified to the school directors." (Ed. note - I take it that school directors are

GROWING WITHOUT SCHOOLING

12

Sorry #11 was so late in getting out. We sent it to our printer on Sept. 21. About mid-October we called to find out what had happened to it. When they told us we would have it in a couple days. Nothing came. Next time we called, we were told they had lost not only the photos of our copy, but the original copy as well. So Donna and Peggy had to spend three hectic days laying out the whole issue again.

Thanks to Louise Andrieshyn and other unschoolers there, I spent three very busy days in Winnipeg, Manitoba, in early November lecturing and doing TV interviews, one for a CBC program on home schooling. Meetings were packed, audiences friendly, interviewers perceptive. By the way, an Ontario court has just ruled in favor of an unschooling family, one of the first Canadian rulings I have heard of. Details in the next issue.

Some readers may wonder what happened to that program on unschooling that ABC's 20/20 filmed late in the spring. The answer is that they decided not to show it. Some higher-up decided that it would be more sensational and exciting to do an entire program on the Singer family instead. (Whether they have done it, I don't know.)

More articles about home schooling: McCall's (Sept. '79), Wall Street Journal (Sept. 13), Boston Magazine (Oct.), Chicago Tribune (Nov. 7). The last two, in particular, were long, thorough, and friendly. The list of magazines, newspapers, radio and TV stations that have interviewed us, in person or on the phone, now runs to three pages.

Mother Earth News (Hendersonville NC) which now reaches more than 3 million people, wants me to write an article on home schooling, which I will do as soon as I finish my book (same subject) for Delacorte. We may want some photos of home schooling children to go with it. More about this in later issues.

John Merrow interviewed me here in the office for his National Public Radio program Options in Education. When I hear the cassette of it, I will report; others might want to order the cassette.

The subscription count for #11 was over 2600. A group in New Zealand has taken out a 40X subscription. And a group in Maine has bumped their sub to 48X.

Good news, of different kinds, from California, Wisconsin, Kentucky, and North Carolina (details in this issue).

A HOLIDAY GREETING

To all our readers, we send with our very best wishes this poem by William Blake:

THE DIVINE IMAGE

To Mercy, Pity, Peace, and Love
All pray in their distress;
And to these virtues of delight
Return their thankfulness.

For Mercy, Pity, Peace, and Love
Is God, our father dear,
And Mercy, Pity, Peace, and Love
Is Man, his child and care.

For Mercy has a human heart,
Pity a human face.
And Love, the human form divine,
And Peace, the human dress.

Then every man, of every clime,
That prays in his distress,
Prays to the human form divine,
Love, Mercy, Pity, Peace.

And all must love the human form,
In heathen, turk or jew;
Where Mercy, Love & Pity dwell
There God is dwelling too.

COMING LECTURES

Jan 28, 1980: Phi Delta Kappa, Central Mass. Chapter; 7:30 pm, Assumption College, Worcester MA. Free, open to public. Contact Manuel Zax, (617) 755-3960.

Feb 13: Unity Church - Unitarian, 732 Holly Av, St. Paul MN 55104; aft. meetings, 7:30 pm lecture. Contact Margaret Hasse, Wider Ministry Program.

Mar 29: NCTE Conference on English Education, 12:30 pm luncheon, Omaha, Neb. Contact Robert Harvey, NCTE, 1111 Kenyon Rd, Urbana IL 61801; (217)328-3870.

Apr 14: Huntington College, Huntingdon IN; 8 pm. Contact Dal Hammel, Artist-Lecture Committee.

Apr 17: Dept of Special Ed, U of Wisc at Whitewater; 8 pm at Playboy Resort, Lake Geneva WI. Open to public. Contact Garry Libster (414)472-1660.

Apr 19: Confer. on Literature and the Urban Experience, Rutgers U, Newark NJ; contact Michael C. Jaye, conf. dir.

Apr 26: Children Studies Symposium, Hobart & William Smith Colleges, Geneva NY; contact Marilyn Kallet.

Some of the above lectures may not be open to the public; check with the contact listed. Of course, if you can come, it will be nice to see you.

LOCAL GROUPS

Organization of unschoolers at the local level continues to grow. In two states and Canada, small groups of unschoolers have started their own newsletters.

In Ohio, the group OCEAN (Ohio Coalition for Educational Alternatives Now), 66 Jefferson Ave, Columbus 43215, has started publishing the newsletter Children at Home. Cost of the newsletter is $5/yr.

The West Virginia newsletter is Alternatives in Education, Rt 3, Box 171A, Spencer 27276. Cost is $2/yr.

Both newsletters are about five pages long. They contain announcements, news on legal developments, letters from parents sharing ideas and experiences, children's art and writing, etc. The Ohio group organized a state-wide meeting; the WV paper lists a whole page of names and addresses of members.

Wendy Priesnitz of THE CANADIAN ALLIANCE OF HOME SCHOOLERS, Box 640, Jarvis, Ont. NOA 1J0, writes: "Already we have helped a number of families with advice and received much media attention for the side of loving nurturing of children as opposed to the processing procedure of many school systems... Membership costs $3 per family and includes a small periodical newsletter, as well as access to the resources that we have compiled. Specific requests for information from non-members must be accompanied by a self-addressed, stamped envelope..."

And, families in Manitoba can join the MANITOBA ASSOCIATION FOR SCHOOLING AT HOME. Write Mary Catherine Figuel, 824 Barry Ave, Winnipeg R2C 1M1.

We are delighted to hear about these groups, and would like our readers to let us know of any other local or regional groups forming.

GOOD NEWS FROM WISC.

From Michael Ketterhagen, adminstrator of the New Learning Network, 3569 W. 34th St, Greenfield WI 53221:

...We have started a school specifically to allow parents to educate their children at home. Initially, it was for our son, Joshua, who would have been in first grade. Brigid and Larry Horbinski encouraged us to go through the necessary Wisconsin state law procedures to become a bona fide private school. We are now listed in the 1979-80 Directory of private schools in the state of Wisconsin.

Presently, we have 10 families involved in the "school," the New Learning Network, and 12 little people enrolled. They range in age from 6 to 12. Recently, because of the growing unrest in the Milwaukee Public High Schools, I have had a number of requests from high school age people. It's really exciting and we're learning so much.

...Our students are from six different school districts in Wisconsin and the parents meet regularly, on the last Tuesday of the month. At our parent meetings we give each other the support and encouragement that we need...

These folks also recommend a helpful public official: Mildred Anderson, Private School Liaison, Wisconsin Dept. of Public Instruction, 1425 E. Washington, Madison.

WRITING FIRST

Ann Kauble, 1706 W. Huntsville, Springdale, AR 72764, writes:

...I would like to tell GWS my story: it might help others who, for one reason or another cannot or do not wish to take their kids out of school. Our girls, ages 11 and 7, are "working independently above grade level" and have "very poor attendance records." In other words, school is a place where the body has to be sometimes, but you learn what you are interested in learning and not necessarily when the school says it's time to learn it. This has worked for us because our girls have wanted to learn the basics before the school has been ready to teach them, and I discovered that anyone, even me, can "teach," i.e. simply tell my kids what they want to know, or, if I don't know the answer I can learn along with them.

I will explain our 7-year-old's experience so far. When she was 3, she wanted to learn her letters, so I taught her how to write her upper case manuscript letters properly (I like Zaner Bloser method of penmanship instruction.) I taught upper case only, because it is so easy to learn with all letters touching headline and baseline, and no worry about when to capitalize. Then we

For more information about GWS, homeschooling, and learning outside of school for adults and children, request our free catalog of materials:

John Holt's Bookstore
2380 Massachusetts Ave. Suite 104
Cambridge, MA 02140
(617) 864 - 3100

www.holtgws.com